Cleopatra

Titles in the
People Who Made History Series

Cleopatra

Don Nardo, *Book Editor*

David L. Bender, *Publisher*
Bruno Leone, *Executive Editor*
Bonnie Szumski, *Editorial Director*
Stuart B. Miller, *Managing Editor*
David M. Haugen, *Series Editor*

Greenhaven Press, Inc., San Diego, CA

Every effort has been made to trace the owners of copyrighted material. The articles in this volume may have been edited for content, length, and/or reading level. The titles have been changed to enhance the editorial purpose. Those interested in locating the original source will find the complete citation on the first page of each article.

Library of Congress Cataloging-in-Publication Data

Cleopatra / Don Nardo, book editor.
    p.   cm. — (People who made history)
    Includes bibliographical references and index.
    ISBN 0-7377-0321-0 (pbk. : alk. paper) —
ISBN 0-7377-0322-9 (lib. : alk. paper)
    Cleopatra, Queen of Egypt, d. 30 B.C. 2. Cleopatra, Queen of Egypt, d. 30 B.C.—In literature. 3. Queens—Egypt—Biography. I. Nardo, Don, 1947– . II. Series.
DT92.7.C53   2001
932'.021'092—dc21   99-085743
[B]   CIP

Cover photo: Christie's Images/SuperStock
"The Meeting of Anthony and Cleopatra"
by Lawrence Alma-Tadema, 1836–1912
Library of Congress, 16, 85
North Wind Picture Archives, 21, 51, 66

Copyright ©2001 by Greenhaven Press, Inc.
PO Box 289009
San Diego, CA 92198-9009
Printed in the U.S.A.

CONTENTS

provinces and small kingdoms of the East into what came increasingly to resemble their own private empire.

tra's story, she meets a strange man one moonlit night. She tells him she is hiding from a terrifying monster named Caesar, not realizing that the man before her is Caesar himself.

Foreword

In the vast and colorful pageant of human history, a handful of individuals stand out. They are the men and women who have come variously to be called "great," "leading," "brilliant," "pivotal," or "infamous" because they and their deeds forever changed their own society or the world as a whole. Some were political or military leaders—kings, queens, presidents, generals, and the like—whose policies, conquests, or innovations reshaped the maps and futures of countries and entire continents. Among those falling into this category were the formidable Roman statesman/general Julius Caesar, who extended Rome's power into Gaul (what is now France); Caesar's lover and ally, the notorious Egyptian queen Cleopatra, who challenged the strongest male rulers of her day; and England's stalwart Queen Elizabeth I, whose defeat of the mighty Spanish Armada saved England from subjugation.

Some of history's other movers and shakers were scientists or other thinkers whose ideas and discoveries altered the way people conduct their everyday lives or view themselves and their place in nature. The electric light and other remarkable inventions of Thomas Edison, for example, revolutionized almost every aspect of home-life and the workplace; and the theories of naturalist Charles Darwin lit the way for biologists and other scientists in their ongoing efforts to understand the origins of living things, including human beings.

Still other people who made history were religious leaders and social reformers. The struggles of the Arabic prophet Muhammad more than a thousand years ago led to the establishment of one of the world's great religions—Islam; and the efforts and personal sacrifices of an American reverend named Martin Luther King Jr. brought about major improvements in race relations and the justice system in the United States.

Each anthology in the People Who Made History series begins with an introductory essay that provides a general overview of the individual's life, times, and contributions. The group of essays that follow are chosen for their accessibility to a young adult audience and carefully edited in consideration of the reading and comprehension levels of that audience. Some of the essays are by noted historians, professors, and other experts. Others are excerpts from contemporary writings by or about the pivotal individual in question. To aid the reader in choosing the material of immediate interest or need, an annotated table of contents summarizes the article's main themes and insights.

Each volume also contains extensive research tools, including a collection of excerpts from primary source documents pertaining to the individual under discussion. The volumes are rounded out with an extensive bibliography and a comprehensive index.

Plutarch, the renowned first-century Greek biographer and moralist, crystallized the idea behind Greenhaven's People Who Made History when he said, "To be ignorant of the lives of the most celebrated men of past ages is to continue in a state of childhood all our days." Indeed, since it is people who make history, every modern nation, organization, institution, invention, artifact, and idea is the result of the diligent efforts of one or more individuals, living or dead; and it is therefore impossible to understand how the world we live in came to be without examining the contributions of these individuals.

INTRODUCTION: THE MOST QUEENLY QUEEN

On a cloudless day in early September in 31 B.C., the most famous woman of her day, and indeed probably of all times, stood resolutely on the deck of her warship in the waters off Actium, in western Greece. Cleopatra VII, of Greek descent yet ruler of Egypt, had assembled her fleet for the fight of her life. Along with her lover and ally, Rome's Marcus Antonius (Mark Antony), she was prepared to come to death grips with another powerful Roman, Octavian, adopted son of the recently assassinated dictator, Julius Caesar. It would be truly a battle for the world; for if they won, Cleopatra and Antony would rule over Rome's vast realm, which then encompassed almost all the lands ringing the Mediterranean Sea, the heart of the known world at the time.

This was not what fate had in store for the lovers, however. They ended up losing the battle and escaping to Egypt, where Octavian eventually came after them. When Cleopatra died soon afterward, she was already a legendary figure; for she had proven herself an intelligent and capable national leader in what a noted historian calls "essentially man's world."[1] In one of his propaganda speeches against her, Octavian summed up how the Romans viewed any woman who had the gall to think she could assume the "manly" role of ruling a country:

> We Romans are the rulers of the greatest and best parts of the world, and yet we find ourselves spurned [rejected] and trampled upon by a woman of Egypt. This disgraces our fathers . . . [who] would be cut to the heart if ever they knew that we have been overcome by the pestilence of a woman.[2]

Fortunately for Cleopatra, the verdict of posterity has been considerably kinder. Later folklore emphasized how she had lived and died for love, and over the centuries her highly romantic legend continued to grow. Her deeds became the subject of numerous poems, plays, novels, and motion pictures, and millions of people around the world came to see her as a colorful, powerful, and accomplished woman. Ably summing up her compelling image, the nineteenth-century French writer, Théophile Gautier, called her

> the most complete woman ever to have existed, the most womanly woman and the most queenly queen, a person to be wondered at, to whom the poets have been able to add nothing, and whom dreamers find always at the end of their dreams.[5]

Such modern romanticized visions of Cleopatra do not always square with the small surviving body of factual information about her. Indeed, it is often difficult nowadays to separate fact from fiction regarding her physical attributes, talents, and deeds. Inevitably, then, she will remain for future ages what she has been for most of the past two thousand years—a supremely romantic, mysterious, and larger-than-life figure.

This volume for Greenhaven Press's *People Who Made History* series examines both the factual and fictitious aspects of Cleopatra's life and legend, pointing out the differences wherever possible. Some of the authors of the essays presented herein are ancient historians and writers, most of whom lived in the few generations following the famous queen's demise. These tracts contain a good deal of important factual information about her. Yet they are also biased by the same sort of male disdain for independent, powerful women that Octavian expressed in his propaganda speeches; so they must be examined with caution. The more contemporary writers excerpted in this anthology are or were (until their deaths) noted historians or professors at leading colleges and universities.

Among this volume's several special features, each of the essays explains or discusses in detail a specific, narrowly focused topic; the introduction to each essay previews the main points; and inserts interspersed within the essays serve as examples of ideas expressed by the authors, offer supplementary information, and/or add authenticity and color. The list of study questions aids the reader in picking out and evaluating the most important and thought-provoking themes and ideas in each chapter. And the bibliography is conveniently divided into subsections for easy access and reference.

Though seemingly large, this list of sources contains only

a small portion of the huge body of literature generated about Cleopatra through the ages. That so much has been and will no doubt continue to be written about her is a testament not only to the major impact she made in her own male-dominated world. It also demonstrates the natural tendency of ordinary people in all places and ages to choose, admire, and perpetuate the memories of a few extraordinary heroes and heroines.

NOTES

1. Colin Wells, *The Roman Empire*. London: Fontana, 1992, p. 271.

2. Quoted in Dio Cassius, *Roman History*, excerpted in *The Roman History: The Reign of Augustus*. Trans. Ian Scott-Kilvert. New York: Penguin Books, 1987, pp. 52–53.

3. Théophile Gautier, *One of Cleopatra's Nights*, quoted in Lucy Hughes-Hallett, *Cleopatra: Histories, Dreams and Distortions*. New York: HarperCollins, 1991, p.1.

CLEOPATRA: A LEGEND FOR ALL TIMES

Cleopatra VII, the woman who would one day boldly challenge the Roman colossus and in so doing become a legend for all times, was born in Egypt in 69 B.C. Her father, then the ruler of that ancient land, was Ptolemy XII, popularly known as Auletes, "the Piper," because of his skill as a flute player. Her mother's identity is somewhat uncertain, but she was probably Auletes' sister, Cleopatra V Tryphaina.

The name Ptolemy is Greek and betrays the fact that the Ptolemaic dynasty, the royal family line that produced these rulers, was of Greek rather than Egyptian ancestry. Established in the late fourth and early third centuries B.C. by Ptolemy I, one of the leading generals of the Greek conqueror Alexander the Great (who died in 323 B.C.), the Ptolemaic Kingdom was one of three major monarchies that emerged from the wars fought by Alexander's successors.[1] In the centuries that followed, the Ptolemies ruled Egypt as it had always been ruled, as an absolute monarchy. For the average Egyptian, apart from the fact that the royal family was now Greek, nothing had really changed. Most of the Ptolemies, including Cleopatra's father, were mediocre and unsympathetic leaders who refused even to bother learning the local language. The result was a cultural barrier between the Egyptian masses and the unpopular royal court, where Greek language and ways remained supreme.

Egypt had long been rich in gold, grain, and ships. But by the time Cleopatra was born, it had become a third-rate power. Though still an independent nation, it, like others before it, had come to be dominated in the international scene by Rome, the most powerful nation-state in the known world. Indeed, the Egypt of Cleopatra's childhood was little more than a client (a state economically and militarily dependent to another) of Rome. Given that Roman leaders generally looked on both Egyptians and Greeks as inferiors, it might seem odd that the two men with whom Cleopatra eventually fell in love and had children—Julius Caesar and Mark Antony—were both powerful Romans. "To ask what Cleopatra thought of the Romans," noted historian Michael Grant points out,

> is a question without a simple answer. She devoted a great part of her life to striving for the cause of her fellow Greeks; and they had absolutely no cause to love Romans. Obviously, she must have agreed with most other Greeks in believing certain of Rome's imperialistic [aggressive, expansionist] attitudes to be wholly deplorable and all too likely to lead her own country into the subjection into which others had already been plunged. Nevertheless, she took individual Romans as she found them, liking some and disliking others.[2]

Moreover, the politically astute Cleopatra knew that, to get ahead and make her mark in what was clearly a Roman world, she needed to befriend rather than alienate Roman leaders. In fact, it was her rivalry with a third powerful Roman, Caesar's adopted son Octavian, that eventually brought about her downfall. Concisely summarizing her life, the second-century A.D. Greek historian Dio Cassius wrote: "Through her own unaided genius she captivated the two greatest Romans of her time, and because of the third, she destroyed herself."[3]

A YOUNG QUEEN INHERITS A TROUBLED THRONE

Cleopatra's initial rise to power in Egypt followed a series of mistakes made by her father. Largely an incompetent ruler, Auletes regularly mismanaged government money, causing the country's economic conditions to worsen. He also debased the coinage, reducing the silver content of coins to one-third, which caused the cost of living to rise. Worse still, in an effort to make up for these blunders he imposed heavy, unfair new taxes on his people, who by 59 B.C., when his daughter Cleopatra was ten, were on the brink of rebellion.

Attempting to strengthen his position, both at home and abroad, Auletes asked a few of the richest and most influential Romans of the day, including Julius Caesar, to declare him "friend and ally" of Rome. This lofty title, the Egyptian king hoped, would make him more feared in Egypt. Caesar and the others agreed, but they demanded large bribes in return, which further drained Auletes' already dwindling treasury.

After that, conditions in Egypt continued to worsen, making Auletes' more unpopular than ever with his people. Desperate, in 57 B.C. he traveled to Rome in an attempt to gather more support, but this turned out to be a mistake, for in his absence his daughter Cleopatra Tryphaina (sister of Cleopatra VII and namesake of their mother) seized the Egyptian throne. Not long afterward, Auletes' few remaining supporters murdered the young usurper. But then another daughter, Berenice, grabbed power for herself. For a hefty price, a Roman nobleman helped Auletes regain his throne. But all of the Egyptian king's efforts eventually came to nothing, for he died, miserable and hated by nearly everyone, in 51 B.C. In his will, he stipulated that Cleopatra VII, now aged eighteen, and her ten-year-old brother, Ptolemy XIII, were to rule the country jointly.

As one might expect, the life young Queen Cleopatra led in the Egyptian royal palace (in Egypt's capital, Alexandria, on the Nile Delta) was luxurious, sheltered, and largely carefree. There were hundreds of royal attendants and servants, including scribes, doctors, maids, valets, cooks, bakers, weavers, tailors, sculptors and artists, chariot drivers, palace guards, and so forth, all at her beck and call, day or night. And at the royal court, dozens of courtiers regularly paid their respects to her, bowing low when they approached. These were the fortunate few, with titles like First Friends, Kinsmen, and Successors (groups possessing varying degrees of prestige), who made up the kingdom's small elite of nobles. They and their elegant way of life comprised a tiny, separate, and guarded island of wealth and privilege in a vast sea of ordinary farmers, laborers, and tradesmen, most of them poor. And while the sea was Egyptian, the island was Greek. Describing the atmosphere and trappings of Cleopatra's private, privileged world, scholar Jack Lindsay writes:

> We must imagine her court as composed not of men and women in the sort of Egyptian costumes that we see in the paintings, reliefs, and statuary of the Pharaonic periods [i.e., earlier ages in which Egyptian pharaohs ruled the land], but of courtiers in Greek robes and wreaths and officers in Macedonian mantles and high boots. Egyptian priests might be present for some particular reason, in their linen robes and with their shaven heads; but they were the exceptions and did not in any way set the style of the court.[4]

If the youthful Cleopatra thought that she could simply settle into this splendid life style and enjoy an easy-going, trouble-free reign, she was sorely mistaken. Indeed, from

Cleopatra, pictured here with a servant, was arguably the most famous woman of ancient times. Of Greek descent, she ruled Egypt during one of the most pivotal eras in history—as the Roman Republic was disintegrating and giving way to the more autocratic Roman Empire.

the moment she ascended the throne, she was beset by tensions, petty rivalries, and veiled threats to her royal status. Her brother's regent (adult adviser and protector) and the most powerful figure in the Egyptian court, a disagreeable man named Pothinus, resented her and wanted to see the boy become sole ruler. Taking every opportunity to discredit her, Pothinus blamed her for the country's continuing economic problems. Thanks to him and those courtiers who intrigued with him, she became increasingly unpopular at court. And finally, in September 49 B.C., she was forced to flee the capital and go (accompanied by some still loyal servants and guards) into hiding. Soon afterward, she took refuge in the neighboring land of Syria.

CLEOPATRA CAPTIVATES THE MIGHTY CAESAR

But Cleopatra's exile was short-lived. Fortunately for her, the Roman state was undergoing major power realignments, which came to a head in a bloody civil war. Two formidable generals, Julius Caesar and Pompey the Great, faced off in this conflict, and she correctly reasoned that one or both of these men would need and seek Egyptian grain and money to support his troops. Unlike Ptolemy, Pothinus, and her other adversaries at the court, who hated and staunchly resisted Roman influence, she recognized the political reality of the day. This was that making and exploiting alliances with strong Roman men was the logical way for any minor ruler, but especially a female one, to get ahead.

As it turned out, Cleopatra's chance to form such an alliance came sooner than even she expected. In 48 B.C. Caesar decisively defeated Pompey at Pharsalus, in Greece, and Pompey turned to Egypt's leaders for protection and support. In his *Commentary on the Civil Wars,* Caesar recorded:

> It happened that the boy-king Ptolemy was at Pelusium [in northern Egypt] with a large army. He was at [odds] with his sister Cleopatra, whom he had driven from the throne a few months earlier. . . . Pompey sent [messengers] to Ptolemy asking him . . . to receive him into Alexandria and to use his power to protect him in his misfortune.[5]

When Caesar, in pursuit of Pompey, arrived in Egypt, he was surprised to find that Ptolemy and Pothinus had ordered Pompey's murder. "It may be," Caesar later wrote,

> that they were really afraid that Pompey might tamper with the loyalty of the royal army and occupy Alexandria. . . . Or it may be that they regarded his prospects [in the civil war] as hopeless and acted according to the common rule by which a man's friends become his enemies in adversity.[6]

Whatever their motives, Ptolemy and Pothinus expected Caesar to be pleased when they presented him with Pompey's severed head. Far from pleased, however, he was actually outraged to see such savage treatment of a great Roman leader. Moreover, he suddenly and firmly demanded that the Egyptians pay him a large sum, supposedly some of Auletes' still outstanding debts.

Meanwhile, seeing her chance to take Caesar's side against her enemies, Cleopatra acted swiftly and boldly. She returned to Egypt and, according to Caesar's first-century A.D. Greek biographer, Plutarch:

> Taking only one of her friends with her, (Apollodorus the Sicilian), [she] embarked in a small boat and landed at the palace when it was already getting dark. Since there seemed to be no other way of getting in, she stretched herself out at full length inside a sleeping bag, and Apollodorus, after tying up the bag, carried it indoors to Caesar. This little trick of Cleopatra's, which showed her provocative impudence, is said to have been the first thing about her which captivated Caesar.[7]

Caesar was so taken with the Egyptian queen, in fact, that he, fifty-two, and she, twenty-one, quickly became lovers. Proceeding to back her in the local power struggle, he demanded that she and Ptolemy marry and rule jointly as Auletes had intended. Ptolemy and Pothinus unwisely chose to defy and fight Caesar and both soon paid for the mistake with their lives. (Caesar had Pothinus executed and Ptolemy's corpse was later found floating in the Nile.)

An eminently practical man, Caesar realized that Cleopatra, as his lover and confidant, would make him and Rome a valuable ally. So he reinstalled her on the Egyptian throne with great pomp and ceremony. He also tried to please the Egyptians by having her, according to local custom, marry her surviving brother, twelve-year-old Ptolemy XIV. Since this young man had no powerful regent like Pothinus, Cleopatra was now, in effect, sole ruler of Egypt.

CAESAR MEETS AN UNTIMELY END

Caesar lingered for some months in Egypt, during which time Cleopatra took him on a pleasure cruise up the Nile.[8] According to the second-century Greek historian Appian, "He made a voyage on the Nile to look at the country with a flotilla [fleet] of 400 ships in the company of Cleopatra, and enjoyed himself with her in other ways as well."[9] The number of ships Appian cites is almost certainly a wild exaggeration. But there can be little doubt that the two were accompanied on their ship or ships by a retinue of servants and splendid creature comforts befitting their lofty station.

Eventually, Caesar had to cut short his lavish holiday to return to the pressing duties of fighting a civil war and becoming master of the Roman world. He departed Alexandria early in 47 B.C. to quell an uprising in Asia Minor (what is now Turkey), leaving Cleopatra in complete control of her country. What they told each other prior to his leaving will never be known. But both were shrewd political realists more than they were romantics and she likely took his departure in her stride. In any case, they parted with the thankful knowledge that they were sure to meet again, for when his ship's sails disappeared over the horizon, she was carrying his child.

Sure enough, about a year later, after defeating the last of his rivals, Caesar summoned Cleopatra and the new baby, a boy, to Rome, there to witness the triumphs (victory parades) celebrating his long string of military successes. According to the second-century Roman historian Suetonius, Caesar heaped "high titles and rich presents" on her. "He even allowed her to call the son whom she had borne him by his own name." Thus, the child became widely known as Caesarion, although his Egyptian title was Ptolemy XV. "The boy closely resembled Caesar," Suetonius added, "in features as well as in gait [the way he carried himself]."[10]

Unfortunately for father, mother, and son alike, Caesar did not live long enough to get to know Caesarion. On March 15, 44 B.C., a group of Roman senators, angry that he had recently declared himself dictator for life, stabbed Caesar to death in the Senate House. Soon afterward, his close friend and supporter, the powerful general Mark Antony, managed to discredit the conspirators, most of whom then fled Italy for Greece. Meanwhile, with her famous benefactor and protector dead, Cleopatra thought it prudent to take Caesarion back to Egypt and they reached Alexandria in July.

ANTONY SUMMONS CLEOPATRA TO TARSUS

During the two years following Caesar's assassination, three ambitious men stepped into the power vacuum he had left. Antony, Octavian (then only eighteen, younger even than Cleopatra), and Lepidus (a popular general) formed a political alliance known as the Second Triumvirate, aiming to "restore order" by establishing a three-man dictatorship. They proceeded to kill many of their political opponents, including the great Roman orator and statesman Cicero, in a reign of terror; simultaneously they prepared to fight Brutus and Cassius, the leaders of the conspiracy against Caesar, who were raising their own troops in Greece.

Cleopatra knew that the best course for her was to back the party most likely to win the ensuing conflict. But at the time it was impossible to know who the victor would be. So she took the safe course and claimed she was unable to help either side, citing as an excuse ongoing bouts of pestilence and famine in her land. She watched with interest as the triumvirs defeated the conspirators in Greece in 42 B.C. and then greedily divided up the Roman world among themselves. Antony got the wealthiest and most populous part—the "East," giving him control of the Roman provinces in Greece and the Near East and influence over weak independent eastern kingdoms like Egypt.

This turn of events inevitably brought Antony and Cleopatra into close contact, although they had met briefly twice before. (The first time was in 57 B.C., when she was twelve and he was a young officer in the Roman force that rescued her father's throne; the second was the short interval when she was in Rome just prior to Caesar's murder in 44.) In need of Egyptian money and grain, in the late summer of 41 B.C. Antony summoned Cleopatra to his headquarters at Tarsus, in southern Asia Minor, and there she made one of history's most memorable entrances. "She came sailing up the river Cydnus," Plutarch wrote,

> in a barge with a stern of gold, its purple sails billowing in the wind, while her rowers caressed the water with oars of silver which dipped in time to the music of the flute, accompanied by pipes and lutes. Cleopatra herself reclined beneath a canopy of gold cloth, dressed as Venus [goddess of love] ... while on either side ... stood boys costumed as Cupids, who cooled her with fans. Instead of a crew, her barge was lined with the most beautiful of her waiting-women attired as [minor goddesses], some at the rudders, other at the ... sails, and all the while an indescribably rich perfume ... was wafted from the vessel to the river-banks. Great multitudes [of local people] accompanied this royal progress, some of them following the queen on both sides of the river from its very mouth, while others hurried down from the city of Tarsus to gaze at the sight.... The word spread on every side that Venus had come to revel with Bacchus [or Dionysus, a reference to Antony's identification of himself with this popular fertility god] for the happiness of Asia.[11]

Antony was apparently even more captivated by Cleopa-

Cleopatra's magnificent pleasure barge leisurely makes it way through Mediterranean waters. The Greek writer Plutarch described its gold and silver decorations and billowing sails of royal purple. He also told how the spectacle duly impressed Rome's Mark Antony.

tra than Caesar had been. Ancient historians made much of the ensuing love affair between this rough-mannered soldier and the Egyptian queen and blamed her for his subsequent turn against his own country and steady slide into political and moral oblivion. These accounts usually pictured her as a "wicked creature" who had "bewitched" him, made him her "sexual captive," and "deprived him of his wits." In retrospect, it is clear that such distortions, which sullied Cleopatra's name for centuries to come, were tainted by strong Roman biases against both foreigners and any women who dared to intrude in the "manly" game of politics. The truth was that on the one hand Antony was an alcoholic, an inept administrator, and a headstrong adventurer given to making bad decisions (although he was still a capable battlefield general). On the other hand, he and Cleopatra were mature and ambitious adults who saw the chance to use each other to their own ends and enjoy themselves at the same time. In short, the blame for Antony's mistakes lies ultimately with Antony, not Cleopatra.

AN EFFICIENT AND CARING RULER

Perhaps what drew Antony to Cleopatra was the fact that she, a foreign woman, had so many of the personal leadership qualities that he, a Roman man, sorely lacked. During much of the time that they were allied, she administered Egypt alone, and evidence suggests that she was a caring, capable, and efficient ruler who managed the economy well and treated her people justly. During her reign, in glaring contrast to those of her predecessors, there were no rebellions and tax collection proceeded normally. She improved and expanded agriculture, producing large surpluses of grain and other foodstuffs, thus eliminating food shortages and lowering food prices. Proof of her wise administrative policies and concern for her people's welfare takes the form of a surviving decree, issued in her name, and also in Caesarion's, on April 13, 41 B.C.:

> Nobody should demand of them [the farmers] anything above the essential Royal Dues [basic taxes], [or] attempt to act wrongfully and to include them among those of whom rural and provincial dues, which are not their concern, are exacted [collected]. We, being extremely indignant [about over-taxation] and considering it well to issue a General and Universal Ordinance [regulation] regarding the whole matter, have decreed that all those from the City, who carry on agricultural work in the country, shall not be subjected, as others are, to demands for *stephanoi* and *epigraphai* [gifts and special taxes people were forced to give the government] such as may be made from time to time. . . . Nor shall any new tax be required of them. But when they have once paid the essential Dues, in kind [in the form of goods and services] or in cash, for cornland and for vineland . . . they shall not be molested for anything further, on any pretext whatever. Let it be done accordingly, and this [decree] put up in public, according to Law.[12]

Cleopatra showed her diligence and thoughtfulness as a ruler in other ways. First, she took the time to become fluent in Demotic Egyptian, the local language, and used it, along with Greek, at court. (Some ancient sources claim she spoke eight languages in all.) Even more impressive, she went to great lengths to observe Egyptian religious rites, portraying herself as the earthly representative of Isis. An important Egyptian mother and fertility goddess, Isis was thought to oversee the growth and harvesting of wheat and barley (crops essential to Egypt's well-being); she was also associated with forgiveness of sins and other kinds of religious purification. At certain times, most Egyptians believed, the goddess communicated to humans and accomplished various tasks through the queen's person. So Cleopatra began to take on the traditionally accepted appearance of Isis (as portrayed in Egyptian art) whenever she was in public. On such occasions, Plutarch tells us, she "wore the robe which is sacred to Isis, and she was addressed [by her subjects] as the New Isis."[13] Cleopatra's earnest effort to assume her responsibility as the goddess's earthly counterpart won her the support of many Egyptians who had long distrusted the foreign dynasty.

FINAL DEFEAT AND HUMILIATION

Unfortunately for Cleopatra and Egypt, her talents as a ruler could not keep her and her country from being engulfed in the dangerous currents of Rome's latest power struggle. The Second Triumvirate fell to pieces as Antony, commanding the eastern Roman sphere, and Octavian, in charge of the western one, squared off in a new civil war.[14] Cleopatra backed Antony, partly out of loyalty (by this time they had children together) and also in Egypt's national interest, for if Antony won, the country might regain much of its former greatness.

In the months leading up to the outbreak of fighting, Cleopatra and Antony were at first very confident of victory. This was partly because they had much larger reserves of ships and manpower to draw on than Octavian had. The lovers had over 500 ships, many of them large with deadly catapults mounted on the decks, and at least 140,000 land troops (counting horsemen); by contrast, Octavian could count on only 400 smaller ships and perhaps 80,000 land troops.

However, what Octavian lacked in numbers he more than made up for in other ways. First and foremost, he had at his disposal a talented, shrewd, and experienced military commander—Marcus Agrippa. Second, Octavian seized the strategic advantage by advancing his forces into Greece before Cleopatra and Antony had time to organize their own forces effectively. In a series of swift and skillful moves, Agrippa trapped his opponents near Actium, in western Greece, leaving Cleopatra and Antony no choice but to fight a sea battle to break free. No doubt to the surprise of most of those involved, that single battle, fought on September 2, 31 B.C., ended up deciding the outcome of the whole war. Cleopatra and Antony suffered a major defeat, although they managed to escape the fray with some of their ships and sail back to Egypt. There, they evidently planned to use the considerable contents of her royal treasury to build a new fleet and launch a fresh offensive.

But the lovers soon discovered that their cause was lost. Most of Antony's troops deserted him and none of Cleopatra's neighbors were willing to risk incurring Octavian's wrath by sending troops, supplies, and other support. When Antony sent messengers to ask for aid from the neighboring kingdom of Cyrene, for example, the local ruler immediately had them killed. Alone in Alexandria, their dreams of a new Mediterranean world order dashed, Cleopatra and Antony waited for the inevitable showdown with Octavian.

Realizing that his opponents' powers had been effectively neutralized, Octavian took his time in finishing them off. Only after he had tended to some pressing affairs in Italy for several months did he finally advance on Egypt, landing several miles east of Alexandria in July 30 B.C. Antony, still the hardened soldier, shook off the depression that had lately overcome him and rode out with his few remaining troops to meet the enemy. But the end result of the skirmishes that followed was the same as that at Actium—defeat for Antony. And the next day brought him and Cleopatra still closer to the brink of ruin. First, her ship captains, whom Antony hoped to assemble for an attack on Octavian's vessels, saw the futility of fighting against impossible odds and surrendered to the Romans. Then Antony's handful of surviving land troops deserted him and surrendered, too.

THE LAST DAYS OF A PROUD QUEEN

At this point, Alexandria was in chaos. With the fleet in enemy hands and the city virtually unguarded, the streets were filled with people, some running for the imagined safety of their homes, others fleeing toward the countryside. In the midst of all this confusion someone mistakenly informed Antony that Cleopatra was dead. This news, combined with his humiliation over his losses, drove Antony to commit suicide by falling on his sword; however, he did not die right away. Learning of his condition, Cleopatra ordered some of her servants to bring him to her in the still unfinished tomb she had been building for herself. She feared that if she unlocked the doors the Romans might gain access to the structure, so she and her maids threw down ropes, which the servants on the ground tied around Antony. Plutarch later recorded the heartbreaking scene that followed:

> Those who were present say that there was never a more pitiable sight than the spectacle of Antony, covered with blood, struggling in his death agonies and stretching out his hands toward Cleopatra as he swung helplessly in the air.

The task was almost beyond a woman's strength, and it was only with great difficulty that Cleopatra, clinging with both hands to the rope and with the muscles of her face distorted by the strain, was able to haul him up, while those on the ground encouraged her and shared her agony. When she had got him up and laid him upon a bed, she tore her dress and spread it over him, beat and lacerated her breasts, and smeared her face with the blood from his wounds. She called him her lord and husband and emperor.[15]

Soon after Antony died in Cleopatra's arms, Octavian sent soldiers to take her into custody. Octavian's plans for the "treacherous creature" who had caused Rome so much trouble included marching her in chains through the streets of Rome to show what would happen to women who did not know their place in the Roman world. But she decided to rob him of that satisfaction by taking her own life. (Legend has it that she allowed herself to be bitten by an asp, a poisonous snake, but this remains unconfirmed.) Learning of the proud Egyptian queen's intention to do away with herself, Octavian ordered some men to stop her. But they were too late. "When they opened the doors," Plutarch writes,

they found Cleopatra lying dead upon a golden couch dressed in her royal robes. Of her two women [maid-servants], Iras lay dying at her feet, while Charmian, already tottering and scarcely able to hold up her head, was arranging the crown which encircled her mistress's brow. Then one of the guards cried out angrily, "Charmian, is this well done?" And she answered, "It is well done, and fitting for a princess descended of so many royal kings," and, as she uttered the words, she fell dead by the side of the couch.[16]

THE STUFF OF LEGEND

In her thirty-nine years, twenty-one of them as Egypt's queen, Cleopatra had demonstrated no less intelligence, political skills, and sheer courage and audacity than the powerful male leaders with whom she had dealt. In the end, they and their totally male-dominated system devoured her. But they could not erase the memory of her extraordinary personality and deeds, nor destroy the future vision she stood for and dreamed of—a world in which men and women might meet on an even playing field. In a sense, then, as noted historian Peter Green says, "Cleopatra achieved her dying wish." Only Alexander the Great, her renowned Greek predecessor, Green suggests,

eclipsed the mesmeric [hypnotic] fascination that she exercised down the centuries, and still exercises, upon the European imagination: the perennial symbol of what, had Actium gone the other way, might have been a profoundly different world.[17]

Thus is the end of her story, like its beginning, wrapped in the stuff of legend.

NOTES

1. The other two were the Seleucid Kingdom, encompassing large parts of what are now Iraq, Iran, and Turkey; and the Macedonian Kingdom, made up mainly of mainland Greece.

2. Michael Grant, *Cleopatra.* New York: Simon and Schuster, 1972, pp. xiii–xiv.

3. Dio Cassius, *Roman History,* excerpted in *The Roman History: The Reign of Augustus.* Trans. Ian Scott-Kilvert. New York: Penguin Books, 1987, p. 76.

4. Jack Lindsay, *Cleopatra.* London: Constable and Company, 1970, p. 23.

5. Julius Caesar, *Commentary on the Civil Wars,* in *War Commentaries of Caesar.* Trans. Rex Warner. New York: New American Library, 1960, p. 328.

6. Caesar, *Commentary on the Civil Wars,* p. 328.

7. Plutarch, *Life of Caesar,* in *Fall of the Roman Republic: Six Lives by Plutarch.* Trans. Rex Warner. New York: Penguin Books, 1972, p. 290.

8. "Up" because, although they traveled away from the Mediterranean port of Alexandria and southward geographically speaking, the Egyptians referred to the portion of their land lying toward the Nile's source (south on a modern map) as "Upper Egypt" and the portion nearer the Mediterranean (north on a modern map) as "Lower Egypt."

9. Appian, *The Civil Wars.* Trans. John Carter. New York: Penguin Books, 1996, p. 117.

10. Suetonius, *Julius Caesar,* in *Lives of the Twelve Caesars,* published as *The Twelve Caesars.* Trans. Robert Graves, rev. Michael Grant. New York: Penguin Books, 1979, p. 36.

11. Plutarch, *Life of Antony,* in *Makers of Rome: Nine Lives By Plutarch.* Trans. Ian Scott-Kilvert. New York: Penguin Books, 1965, p. 293.

12. Quoted in Lindsay, *Cleopatra,* pp. 127–28.

13. Plutarch, *Antony,* in *Makers of Rome,* p. 322.

14. They had earlier pushed the weaker Lepidus aside, placing him under permanent house arrest.

15. Plutarch, *Antony,* in *Makers of Rome,* pp. 341–42.

16. Plutarch, *Antony,* in *Makers of Rome,* p. 347.

17. Peter Green, *Alexander to Actium: The Historical Evolution of the Hellenistic Age.* Berkeley: University of California Press, 1990, p. 682.

CHAPTER 1

Cleopatra and Caesar: The Making of a Queen

The Young Cleopatra Is Forced into Exile

Ernle Bradford

This well-written narrative by noted classical historian Ernle Bradford chronicles the events in Egypt before the arrival of Cleopatra's eventual mentor, the great Roman general Julius Caesar. Bradford begins with the death of Ptolemy XII, Auletes, and the ascension of Cleopatra and Ptolemy XIII to the throne. Then he introduces the court intriguers—Pothinus, Achillas, and Theodotus—and tells how they forced Cleopatra to flee into exile. Finally, Bradford covers the rivalry between Caesar and his political-military opponent, Pompey, which forced the latter to travel to Egypt, where he was murdered.

Ptolemy XII, having done all he could to ensure the succession, was now able to appreciate his palace and gardens for his few remaining years, his music and . . . the enjoyment of wine and revelry. What he had done by having himself restored and maintained on his throne by the might of the Roman legions, was to make his country a client state of Rome. And client states had a habit of ending up as part of the steadily expanding Roman Empire. This was what Cleopatra was to spend all her years as Queen trying to prevent.

In the spring of 51 B.C. Ptolemy the Flute-Player died. He was succeeded by Cleopatra, who was then eighteen, and her brother Ptolemy XIII, who was ten. There can be little doubt that they were now formally married, as was the custom. Since Ptolemy was a minor, a board of guardians was appointed to look after his interests and, in the corrupt and scheming court of Alexandria, these guardians were inevitably looking after their own. One of them was Achillas, commander of the army; another a Greek rhetorician Theodotus who was to supervise the young King's education; and the third a eunuch, Pothinus, a typically devious palace intriguer, who was minister of finance. These three quickly saw that it would be to their advantage to attach the boy-King to their interests, and if possible get rid of Cleopatra.

It seems that from the very first she displayed the strength of character and political intelligence which were to be so evident throughout her life. A clear instance of this occurred in 55 B.C., when the Roman Governor of Syria sent his two sons to Alexandria requesting that the legions stationed in the city should be released, to aid him in a campaign against the ever troublesome Parthians [the inhabitants of Parthia, a kingdom occupying much of what are now Iran and Iraq]. . . . However, the troops . . . had settled down happily among the comforts of the city. They had taken wives and mistresses, and they had no wish to march north and fight against the toughest enemies of the Roman people. They not only mutinied, but proceeded to murder the Syrian Governor's sons. Cleopatra immediately ordered the arrest of the mutineers, and had the ringleaders dispatched to Syria. She knew from the beginning that her position depended upon her friendship with Rome.

But the fact that the young Queen showed an independence of action was not at all to the liking of the triumvirate [group of three] surrounding her brother. They wanted an amenable monarch, and it was clear that Cleopatra had her own thoughts and judgments. Better, Pothinus and the other two must have thought, that they continue to mould Ptolemy to their ways, and marry him off to his sister Berenice. A typical court intrigue now developed. Cleopatra (warned by her advisers as well as her own instincts) managed to avoid the fate that befell unsuccessful Ptolemies, and fled the country. The year was 48 B.C., and she was twenty-one; her whole life had been lived in a spider's web of intrigue, corruption, bribery and murder.

Cleopatra made her way to Syria where her political act in sending the mutineers back no doubt secured her a favourable reception. Pothinus and his friends, for their part, must have been delighted, since they now seemed to have the whole situation under control. Achillas, the army commander, became in effect governor of Egypt, and the others must have felt secure in the knowledge that they had got rid of the young woman who had seemed the only potential threat to their dominance of the country. They had reckoned without Cleopatra's resource and determination.

CAESAR VERSUS POMPEY

While Cleopatra was busy rallying her supporters, and gathering together an army in Syria, momentous events had been taking place on the far side of the Mediterranean. The coalition between the three predominant Romans of the era, Caesar, Pompey and Crassus, had already broken up, largely because their individual ambitions were too great to tolerate any rival. Crassus was removed from the scene when in 53 B.C. he decided to take Roman arms into Parthia. He was jealous of both Pompey's and Caesar's military renown, and wished to achieve a military victory on his own account—as well, perhaps, as laying his hands on the wealth of the East. His army was completely destroyed at the battle of Carrhae, and Crassus was killed. It was one of the most disastrous defeats in Roman history, and was never to be forgotten. But the major effect of Carrhae was to leave only Caesar and Pompey in the dispute for power. It was inevitable that the great struggle for supreme authority should now take place.

Julius Caesar, most of whose great achievements had been in Gaul and the far north-west, meant relatively little or nothing to the Alexandrians. Pompey the Great, on the other hand, had been their patron, the friend of Egypt, and its protector. It was natural that they should favour his cause. Indeed before her flight to Syria Cleopatra had received Pompey's son in the city and, in response to an appeal from his father, had dispatched a number of merchant ships laden with corn to help to feed his troops in the civil war raging between him and Caesar. When, only a year later, the news reached Egypt of Pompey's utter defeat on the battlefield of Pharsalia in Thessaly, there must have been consternation. They had backed the wrong horse. What would now be the attitude of the all-powerful Julius Caesar to Egypt and Egyptian affairs? Would he descend with his triumphant legions and seize the country—just as Alexander, nearly three centuries before, had seized it from the Persians?

After fleeing from the scene of his defeat, Pompey made his way to Cyprus. He still had hopes that there might be a second round in this battle for the world. He learned that . . . his fleet, one of the mainstays of his strength, was still loyal and willing to fight for his cause. What he really needed was money, grain for his troops, and further military support. It was natural that immediately he should think of Egypt. After all, it was through his influence that Ptolemy Auletes had been restored, and it was the Flute-Player's son who now sat upon the throne. He would go to Alexandria, and claim some visible return for his earlier help and patronage. Pompey and his wife Cornelia accordingly embarked in a large galley, and prepared to make the easy down-wind crossing to Egypt.

Cleopatra in the meantime, showing so early the courageous and indeed pugnacious side of her nature, had raised an army in Syria and was preparing to invade her kingdom. Her troops stood on the borders of Syria and Egypt, while moving up to oppose her came the Egyptian army commanded by Achillas. It was at this juncture, when civil war between brother and sister was just about to break out, that Pompey arrived near Pelusium where the Egyptian army was encamped. He dropped anchor off the small harbour and waited to see what emissaries would come out to him. As soon as the presence of the great Pompey became known there was an immediate and agitated discussion. In this, one may presume, the young Ptolemy can have had little share. Between the three councillors, Achillas, Theodotus and the eunuch Pothinus, the debate raged as to what kind of reception they should accord this defeated Roman, who had once seemed to them the future master of the world. As Plutarch remarks: 'It was a tragic situation that the fate of Pompey the Great should have been determined by three such men; and that he, riding at anchor off the shore, should have been forced to wait on the decision of such a tribunal.'

The argument went roughly as follows. Since he had been Egypt's patron in his days of power it was only right to accord him asylum. Besides, was there not always the chance that he might prove the ultimate victor? Set against this went their recently acquired knowledge that Caesar was undoubtedly the greatest soldier of his time. Perhaps, they reasoned, they might suggest that he took asylum in another country. But then, the thought must certainly have crossed their minds, suppose that country was Syria? With Pompey's formidable military abilities behind her, Cleopatra might drive Ptolemy from the throne. It was Theodotus who, with a lawyer's guile, proposed the ultimate solution. They should lure Pompey ashore—and then make away with him. In this way they would not only prevent any possibility of his talents going to assist Cleopatra, but they would also find favour with Caesar. They would put an end to this contest in the Roman world, and lay the victorious Caesar under an obligation. Once they had defeated Cleopatra they would ensure that Egypt—theoretically ruled by the young Ptolemy—would remain in their hands. 'And besides,' concluded Theodotus, 'dead men don't bite.'

POMPEY TREACHEROUSLY SLAIN

It was natural that Achillas, as commander of the army, should be the one selected to meet this Roman who had been one of the greatest generals and admirals of his time. He took with him, to give further authenticity to the military nature of the reception, Septimius, a Roman officer who had once held command under Pompey, together with a Roman centurion. The three of them were rowed out in a small boat to bring the great Pompey ashore. Arriving at the galley, Achillas invited Pompey to step aboard, saying that it was the only way, since his galley had too deep a draught to enter the harbour. Pompey's wife, Cornelia, was immediately suspicious, and cautioned her husband not to go. But Pompey, who had already noticed that a number of Egyptian warships were active off the shore, realized that, as Caesar had remarked when he crossed the Rubicon to begin the Civil War, 'the die was cast.' As he went down to the boat, in company with a freedman called Philip, he quoted in farewell to Cornelia the lines of [the fifth-century B.C. Greek playwright] Sophocles:

> He that once enters at a tyrant's door
> Becomes a slave, even if free before. . . .

There was a curious silence in the boat, and Pompey, prompted to break it, looked at Septimius the Roman officer, and said: 'Surely I recognize you? Did you not at one time serve under me?' The latter nodded, but made no reply. Disconcerted, Pompey took out a small book and continued to read until they reached the beach. Then, as the boat grounded, he got to his feet and made ready to step ashore. At this moment Septimius drew his sword and stabbed him in the back. His action was immediately followed by Achillas and the centurion. Pompey drew his robe over his head (as his enemy Caesar was one day to do) and fell dying in the bottom of the vessel. Cornelia, watching from the galley, witnessed the whole scene and raised a great cry that was heard by all those on shore. The galley's crew and Pompey's supporters immediately urged the captain to up-anchor, or they would all be killed. Before the Egyptian warships could get under way, the galley bearing the widowed Cornelia was headed out for the open sea.

The murderers cut Pompey's head from his body and held it aloft in triumph. They intended to have tangible proof for Caesar, when he arrived, that his great rival was dead. They left the body itself lying on the foreshore, and Pompey's loyal freedman, whom they had not molested, was allowed to make a funeral pyre and reduce his remains to ashes. (These were later sent by Caesar to Pompey's widow, who had buried them in the grounds of his Alban villa—the very villa where Pompey had once given sanctuary and hospitality to Auletes.) The life of Pompey the Great, the man who had cleared the Mediterranean of pirates, one of the outstanding generals of his time, was over. The whole Mediterranean was Caesar's.

CAESAR MOVED TO TEARS

While Cleopatra's and Ptolemy's armies still lay confronting one another Caesar and some four thousand men were crossing the Mediterranean in thirty-five galleys, headed for Alexandria. Caesar knew that Pompey had fled to Egypt, and he wanted to secure his victory of Pharsalia before Pompey could once again rally his forces. Upon his arrival on 2 October 48 B.C. . . . he disembarked his legionaries and cavalry in 'The City.' It was a small enough force with which to meet a potential enemy and possibly subdue a country. But Caesar, like his great predecessor Alexander, was a man with an instinct for the moment, and had no hesitation in acting when he felt that his star directed him. He was, after all, from a family who believed themselves to be descendants of the goddess Venus—and to the gods, or demi-gods, all things are possible.

Caesar's object at this moment was most probably to effect a reconciliation between the warring brother and sister—as well as to track down Pompey and his supporters. It can only have been a matter of moments after his landing in Alexandria that he heard of his enemy's death. His troubles were at an end. But when, a few days later, the instigator of the whole plot, the cynical Theodotus, came back from Pelusium bearing the head and signet ring of Pompey, and proudly showed them to Caesar, the latter is said to have burst into tears. To have killed Pompey on the battlefield would have been one thing; or to have had him make an end of his life in the old Roman way [i.e., suicide]; but to know that he had been treacherously murdered by degenerate Egyptians and Greeks was another thing altogether. To the amazement of Theodotus, who was undoubtedly expecting some reward, Caesar dismissed him from his presence with the contempt that would normally have been reserved for a slave.

To the Alexandrian, used to all the deviousness and cruelty of local politics, the whole incident must have seemed incomprehensible. These 'barbarian' Romans seemed to have an extraordinary set of standards! Pompey had been Caesar's enemy; the latter, had he met Pompey on the battlefield, would undoubtedly have killed him; and in that case what more could he desire than the head of his enemy? Shortly afterwards Theodotus, realizing that he had incurred the hatred and scorn of Caesar, fled from the city and became a wandering refugee in Syria and Asia Minor. . . .

To the consternation of the Alexandrians, Caesar had all of Pompey's followers (whom the 'loyal' citizens had had imprisoned) released from jail and pardoned. Caesar was a hard and ruthlessly ambitious man, but he had always known that the best policy towards the defeated—provided that they were 'little men' and not leaders—was magnanimity [generosity]. By being magnanimous he intended to attach to his own cause men who had formerly been his enemies. It was a policy that would one day rebound on his own head, for there are some men who can never forgive the favours that are done to them.

Caesar Restores Cleopatra to Power

A.J. Langguth

In this spirited excerpt from his popular book, *A Noise of War*, about the power struggles that brought down the Roman Republic, scholar A.J. Langguth begins with the famous first meeting between Cleopatra and Caesar, in which she had herself smuggled, hidden inside a bedroll, into his quarters. Langguth then describes the uneasy weeks in which the opposing parties in the local power struggle—Caesar and Cleopatra on one side and Ptolemy XIII and his advisers on the other—coexisted in the palace. Finally, Langguth relates how Caesar won the so-called Alexandrian War and installed Cleopatra firmly on the throne, getting her pregnant in the process.

Caesar arrived in Alexandria as a Roman consul, behind 12 attendants carrying his *fasces* of power. The Roman soldiers who were serving as Ptolemy's guard rushed to greet him, and the Alexandrians took that show of respect as a slight to their king. They roamed the streets in mobs, killing soldiers. But the murder of Pompey had convinced Caesar that Ptolemy's advisers would accept him. Moving into the royal palace, Caesar sent Pompey's ring back to Rome as proof he was dead and ordered that Pompey's head be buried decently.

Egypt had initially supported Pompey, and Caesar intended to tax the nation harshly for its bad judgment. He set a figure that included the 17.5-million-denarii debt that Auletes had incurred 11 years earlier. Pothinus balked at the payment and fanned the city's resentment against Caesar.

Caesar continued to stay at the palace but sat up all night to avoid the kind of sneak attack from Pothinus that had killed Pompey. Perhaps the Egyptian queen, still exiled outside Alexandria, would be more pliant than her brother and

Reprinted with the permission of Simon & Schuster from *A Noise of War*, by A.J. Langguth. Copyright ©1994 by A.J. Langguth.

his eunuch. He sent an invitation for Cleopatra to join him.

The queen chose a Sicilian named Apollodorus to help her, and together they sailed at dusk from Pelusium in a small skiff. They reached the palace to find her brother's troops standing guard. Slipping past cordons of enemy soldiers might have daunted another woman. But Cleopatra was a queen, with a lineage that made the Romans look only slightly more civilized than the woad-painted Britons.

She instructed Apollodorus to lay out a sack of bedding. She stretched out full length as he tied up its ends with cord. Hoisting the bedroll to his shoulder, he carried his queen inside the palace and untied the sack at Caesar's feet. Out sprang a 21-year-old creature unlike any woman Caesar had ever known.

THE OPPOSING PARTIES COEXIST IN THE PALACE

The next morning, Caesar invited Ptolemy to call on him. The young king arrived to find that his half sister had not only slipped into the palace but in a single night had converted Caesar to her cause. Tearing the crown from his head, Ptolemy ran outside to a crowd of protesters, wailing that he had been betrayed. Caesar's men seized the king and returned him to the palace, but they lacked the numbers to put down the insurrection that was spreading among the city's half-million people. Caesar turned instead to diplomacy. Displaying a copy of the Flute Player's [Auletes'] will, Caesar promised that Ptolemy and Cleopatra would rule together as Auletes had intended. He gave the two younger royal children the sop of a joint command in Cyprus, which Rome had annexed . . . a decade earlier.

To celebrate the royal reconciliation, Cleopatra ordered a feast. . . . In a paneled hall, its beams covered with gold, its walls and floor laid with agate, onyx and marble, the queen reclined between Caesar and her brother, eating from gold dishes on ivory tables. Their slaves had been imported from across the world. Most were dark, but Caesar also saw servants blonder than the Germans of the Rhine.

Caesar flattered his hosts by asking about the origins of their sacred river. He said that in his language, "to seek the source of the Nile" meant to search for the impossible. Cleopatra's priest answered that the source remained hidden from foreigners, but that he could assure Caesar the river was older than the oldest race of men.

Caesar's tact had for the time stilled the unrest, but then Pothinus ordered the Egyptian army back to Alexandria from Pelusium. Caesar knew those 20,000 men could swamp the Romans, so he had Pothinus executed as a traitor. The royal army, caught up in nationalistic fury, ignored Ptolemy's call to lay down its weapons. To control the crowds, Caesar's men had to set fires around the city, and one blaze destroyed Alexandria's library, the greatest of its time. No one could say how many scrolls were lost—at least 400,000, possibly twice that number.

The ships that had gone out in support of Pompey were burned as they returned to Alexandria's harbor. At great cost in lives, Caesar seized the island of Pharos in the harbor to give his reinforcements a place to dock.

Cleopatra's younger sister [Arsinöe], dissatisfied with the bribe of Cyprus, escaped to join the Egyptian army. But the street fighting had begun to subside. Caesar drew a cordon around the city's center and settled down to wait for his relief forces. He had Cleopatra with him to pass the time.

PLAYING AT LOVE

Cleopatra's first plan had been to arouse Caesar's pity. The night they met, she had wept and raged at the indignity of a queen of heaven being humiliated by a boy and a eunuch. But she soon saw that she could draw on emotions more powerful than Caesar's sympathy, even though hers was no ordinary beauty. Her nose was long and thin, her mouth fleshy, her hair coarse. But Egyptian women knew arts of makeup that aristocratic Roman women shunned—ways of enhancing the eyes, causing the hair to shine, beguiling the senses with subtle perfumes. Lampblack could make the eyelids dramatic and darken the eyebrows to contrast with the pallor of powdered skin. Mulberry juice served as rouge and lipstick. Should Caesar request it, Cleopatra even knew a treatment for baldness—burnt mouse and horse's teeth, bear grease and deer marrow, mixed with honey and rubbed into the scalp until hair sprouted again.

Caesar was 52. Whatever the depth of his romances at home, they had almost always involved women who could advance him politically. But Caesar was not in Rome. And Cleopatra, who had been surrounded by brothers and eunuchs, may have come to Caesar a virgin but wise in the arts of seduction. She had already proved her daring and verve on the throne, and those qualities appealed to a gambler like Caesar. Her voice was thrilling as she fixed her bright eyes on him. For more than a decade in Gaul, Caesar had been living a rough soldier's life. His youth was gone, middle age was riding him hard, and now he had found an incomparable woman who could make the liaison between Rome and

WAS CAESARION CAESAR'S CHILD?

Noted classical historian Sarah B. Pomeroy here offers some of the arguments, for and against, relating to the ancient controversy over Caesarion's paternity (i.e., who his father really was).

Ancient sources hostile to Cleopatra—emanating from Octavian, whom Caesar designated in his will as heir—as well as modern scholars have argued that Caesarion was not, despite the assertions of Cleopatra and Antony, Caesar's son. The date of Caesarion's birth has been disputed. Plutarch gives conflicting testimony. From his *Life of Caesar* we learn that Caesarion was Caesar's son and that he was born in 47 B.C. A Demotic text confirms this date. Yet, in his *Life of Antony,* Plutarch writes that Caesarion appeared to be Caesar's son and was born after Caesar's assassination. Some scholars admit that, if Caesarion was born in 47 B.C., Caesar could have been the father, but, calculating from Caesar's movements, he could not have fathered a child born in 44 B.C. This argument makes the Romans appear extremely credulous. If the dates when Caesar could have had intercourse with Cleopatra were not appropriate to the birthday of the baby, surely the Romans and Egyptians would have figured it out—even if they did believe babies were born only in the eighth or tenth, rather than the ninth, month after insemination. An argument that Caesar's history proves that he was sterile after the birth of [his only daughter] Julia (ca. 54 B.C.) is also questionable. . . . Cleopatra was unlikely to be having intercourse with a younger brother in the course of her affair with Caesar. Ptolemy XIII was barely old enough to have fathered Caesarion; and he was dead, at any rate, in 47 B.C. Ptolemy XIV was assassinated in 44 B.C. at about the age of fifteen. Yet no one has proposed a candidate other than Caesar for the father, and rumor would have named one if he existed. Rumors about sexual liaisons were rife in Rome in the first century B.C., and the hated Cleopatra would not have been immune from gossip.

Sarah B. Pomeroy, *Women in Hellenistic Egypt: From Alexander to Cleopatra.* New York: Schocken Books, 1989, pp. 25–26.

Egypt something more than a crass political deal. Caesar may not have loved a woman since his daughter Julia died, and he may have been too worldly to succumb to Cleopatra now. But he couldn't resist playing at love with this spirited young queen.

CAESAR AND CLEOPATRA VICTORIOUS

The siege of Alexandria dragged on. Caesar went out to his troops each day and returned at night to the palace and Cleopatra. But by December two very different events were giving Caesar great satisfaction: a legion from Asia arrived by sea, and Cleopatra was pregnant. The queen had every incentive to have a child by the most powerful man in the world. And if for any reason he hadn't been able to oblige her, she would have been clever enough to find a substitute. Actual paternity mattered less than whom her nation believed the father to be.

The Alexandrians told Caesar that if Ptolemy was allowed to leave the palace, he could negotiate peace. Under Caesar's eye, the boy had been docile, and Caesar let him leave to join his younger sister with the Egyptian army. But as soon as he was on his own, Ptolemy swore he would drive Caesar from Egypt. Cleopatra divorced him; in time, she would marry a younger half brother.

By March, Caesar's reinforcements had reached Egypt's eastern border. Among the Syrian and Arab troops were Jews led by Antipater, who had been placed in power by Pompey and had taken his side. He was making amends now, leading troops to relieve Caesar in Alexandria.

Caesar stationed enough guards at the palace to protect Cleopatra, then slipped past the Egyptian lookouts and joined the reinforcements. On March 27, he routed the Egyptian army. That night, he came back to Cleopatra as the master of her capital.

Ptolemy XIII had drowned during an attempt to escape. Caesar ordered the Nile dredged until his body in its gold armor was recovered. He did not want Egyptians believing stories that the river had made the boy-king immortal.

Cleopatra's younger sister had been captured in the battle and shipped to Rome to await Caesar's triumph [victory parade, in which she would march in chains]. Cleopatra's latest consort, the 12-year-old Ptolemy XIV, would be less troublesome in Cyprus, and Caesar sent him there. To reward the Jews, Caesar returned the territories that Rome had stripped away, including the port of Joppa. He also had the senate remove synagogues in Rome from the restrictions that outlawed the city's other guilds and congregations.

Caesar controlled the capital, but in the rest of the country Cleopatra's subjects distrusted the city and felt estranged from it. Caesar assembled an armada of . . . ships to sail down the Nile to demonstrate that the queen could depend on Caesar to protect her. It was . . . a belated honeymoon of sorts. Caesar put aside his laurel wreath for a headdress made of flowers, and the couple sailed on a pleasure barge decorated as an arbor.

Caesar's troops, now many months in Egypt, were growing restless and were pressuring him to take up his duties in Rome. By summer, Caesar had returned to Alexandria, and arranged to station three legions of troops there to protect Cleopatra. In gratitude, the queen began building a vast monument in the harbor; it would be called the Caesareum.

And when she gave birth soon after Caesar left Egypt, her subjects accepted her son as another prize from Caesar's stay among them. She called the infant Caesarion.

Why Caesar Found Cleopatra So Fascinating and Attractive

Christian Meier

This brief but very informative excerpt from University of Munich scholar Christian Meier's critically acclaimed biography of Caesar examines Cleopatra's character and speculates as to why and how she was able to captivate the most powerful man in the known world. Drawing on the descriptions of ancient writers, including the Greek Plutarch and Roman Suetonius (both of the late first and early second centuries A.D.), Meier points out that she was politically wise, talented, and extremely charming, if not all that physically beautiful. These and other attractive and compelling personal traits, he says, somehow penetrated the hardened soldier's tough exterior and won his heart and his allegiance.

One evening at dusk a small ship entered the harbour of Alexandria and moored close to the palace. A Greek from Sicily disembarked with a long bag, tied about with straps, which he carried into the palace, in order to deliver it to the Roman consul. From this bag at Caesar's feet the young queen emerged, attractively attired, as may be imagined; one source describes her appearance as both majestic and pitiful. She apologized charmingly for choosing this unusual way of coming to visit Caesar. But how else could she have come? And had not Caesar summoned her? Plutarch reports that the ruse won Caesar's heart and that he was utterly captivated by her grace and charm.

A WOMAN WHO KNEW WHAT SHE WANTED

Cleopatra has since captivated the imagination of humanity—
the sensation-seekers during her lifetime, and later the
poets. It is hard to form a precise picture of her. But of some
features we can be reasonably sure. To judge by extant portraits she was not really beautiful. . . . Yet she must have enthralled Caesar, as she later enthralled Mark Antony. Suetonius tells us that among foreign women she was to
Caesar what Servilla [mother of the Roman senator Brutus]
was among Roman women: the one he loved most. Indeed,
he loved her so much that for her sake he not only involved
himself in a highly dangerous war—he may not have foreseen this—but stayed with her for weeks afterwards, when
there was a pressing need for him to depart. During this
time he sailed up the Nile with her in her large and superbly appointed barge, which was decorated with fine
frescoes; they would have sailed as far as Ethiopia, had not
Caesar's soldiers refused to go on. And it was certainly not
merely for political reasons that Caesar summoned her to
Rome in 46 B.C. and kept her there for nearly two years.
Suetonius tells us that 'he also allowed a son born of their
union to bear his name.'

Cleopatra was a highly educated woman and spoke
many languages as well as her own. Politically she was un-
commonly gifted, cunning and capable of any intrigue. As
a child she had witnessed the difficulties and indignities
suffered by her father, and his desperate, often unscrupu-
lous efforts to assert his rule: she was up to every trick. At
eighteen she assumed the reins of government. She knew
what she wanted, but she was not popular with her people
and had difficulty in outwitting her brother's experienced
courtiers. She seems to have possessed the imperious pride
of the Ptolemies and was at home—and not just superficially—in the sophisticated Egyptian culture they had
adopted. She was versed in every fashionable refinement,
and a work on cosmetics was even named after her. Yet this
daughter of the New Dionysos, as her father had styled
himself, was celebrated as the goddess Isis, and she must
have had about her something of the mystique of an age-
old culture. Even when—indeed precisely when—she was
clearly acting the part.

Our sources would have us believe that she was not only
beautiful, but had a charming voice. 'It was a delight to hear

its tone; her tongue was like a many-stringed lyre.' She is said to have had a bewitching manner and radiated an irresistible fascination that had everyone spellbound.

She exploited her physical charms in the service of her political interests. And in her relations with Caesar politics and love seem to have been interfused.

This is probably what enthralled him—the politics of charm, which became the charm of politics. Here they could meet, recognize and understand each other. It may be that the twenty-two-year-old queen was the first and only person, since the death of his daughter Julia, who had understood Caesar, that she not only amused him and allowed him to conquer her, but knew how to pierce the shell of isolation that increasingly surrounded this man of fifty-two, to tempt him out of it and release him from it—with such insight and affection, such subtlety and grace, that he could perhaps even learn from her and allow himself, in some measure, to be conquered by her, as by no other. He was superior, and she was calculating. Both had to work hard to assert themselves; both were ruthless, proud and self-sufficient. They clearly discovered a mutual affinity and continued to take the same delight in it as they had in its discovery. After the first divine honours conferred on him, Caesar must have been intrigued to meet a member of a dynasty that had been accustomed for generations to such honours. The notion of divinity must have amused him, but also given him pause for thought. This was a further stage in his quest for self-understanding.

CHAPTER 2

Cleopatra and Antony: Battle for the World

Cleopatra and Antony Become Lovers and Allies

Michael Grant

In this well-informed essay, distinguished Edinburgh University scholar Michael Grant chronicles the initial meeting in Tarsus and subsequent alliance between Cleopatra and Antony. Grant provides considerable detail about Antony's image in the eastern sector of the Roman Empire and his ambitions to make war on Parthia (a Near Eastern realm occupying much of what are now Iran and Iraq). It was Antony's need for supplies for that upcoming war that prompted his invitation to Cleopatra, although he undoubtedly also wanted to determine why she had not taken sides in the recent conflict between himself and Caesar's assassins. Grant also explains the lovers' religious identifications—Antony's with the fertility god Dionysus and Cleopatra's with the goddesses Aphrodite and Isis. In the narrative, Grant liberally draws on and quotes from Plutarch's *Life of Antony*, the major ancient source for this and certain other parts of Cleopatra's story.

When Antony and Octavian were dividing up the Roman world, all Octavian's prestige as the adoptive heir of Caesar could not compensate for Antony's superior advantages. For one thing, Antony was a highly experienced man of forty or forty-one, whereas Octavian was twenty years younger. Although he had made remarkable progress since Caesar's death, there was a measure of truth in Antony's sneer that he was a boy who owed everything to a name. Besides, Octavian had not distinguished himself in the Philippi campaign [in which Antony defeated Caesar's assassins, Brutus and Cassius], partly because of ill health. Indeed, although he lived on for another fifty-seven years, it was believed at the time that his illness, whatever it was, would prove fatal.

ANTONY REIGNS SUPREME IN THE EAST

Those of the Republicans who surrendered after the catastrophe preferred to surrender to Antony, and some of them took the opportunity to insult Octavian at the same time. . . . After the battle, he [Antony] could probably have taken any region of the empire that he liked. One reason why he selected the east was because of its immense wealth. This had tempted Pompey and numerous others, and Antony urgently needed money for all his troops who were demanding demobilization. Moreover, in Roman eyes, one of the most pressing tasks of the future was to renew the war against the Parthians: it seemed scandalous that their defeat of Crassus in 53 B.C. had not yet been avenged. Caesar had intended to avenge it by one of the greatest expeditions the world had ever known, and he had been on the very point of undertaking this enterprise when he was murdered. Although disappointed of Caesar's formal heirship, Antony still remained his obvious military heir since he had held large commands and had further enhanced his military prestige at Philippi. To lead the Parthian war which Caesar had planned was a patriotic duty, and it could bring him unprecedented glory. Moreover, Antony's previous experience had given him a wide knowledge of the area.

The eastern provinces he was now called upon to govern were five in number: Macedonia, which included Achaea (Greece); Asia, the extremely rich western region of Asia Minor, including the former kingdom of Pergamum; Bithynia-Pontus to its north and east . . . ; Syria, the heavily populated nucleus of the former Seleucid state, and key to the Parthian frontier; and Cilicia, a command area in south-eastern Asia Minor which within the next few years was abolished and, for the most part, merged with Syria. Beyond the provinces, too, Antony possessed many valuable contacts in the dependent or semi-dependent kingdoms which fringed the frontier and played an essential role in its defence. The most important of these states was Cleopatra's Egypt.

After establishing a settlement for ex-soldiers at Philippi itself . . . Antony spent the winter of 42–41 B.C. in Greece. There he attended literary discussions and religious festivals and ceremonies. In fact, he adopted an amiable phil-

Hellenic [pro-Greek] attitude, which was politically desirable, so as not to invite unfavourable comparison with Brutus, who had behaved in the same way. But it also came much more easily to Antony than to most Romans, since his attachment to the Greek way of life was genuine.

Then, early in 41 B.C., he crossed the Aegean and visited the ancient city of Ephesus. Echoing Roman coinages which stressed the alleged Concord between the Triumvirs, the civic mint of Ephesus issued pieces displaying the heads of all three men side by side—a courtesy which no western mint of Octavian's reciprocated. Nevertheless, it was only a courtesy, for Antony was the hero of the day, and in these eastern provinces he reigned supreme. . . .

Antony enacted certain beneficial measures and extended the rights of asylum of the city's Temple of Artemis—without, so far, laying hands on Cleopatra's hostile half-sister, Arsinoe, who had been given sanctuary there. While extorting huge sums of money from the Asian cities, he pointed out to them that his method of extraction, based on a sliding system of tithes on their produce, was more humane than the fixed taxes of the Hellenistic kings. He then left Ephesus and moved eastwards, raising more money all the time, but also rewarding any communities which had helped him and his fellow-Triumvirs and incurred punitive measures from Brutus and Cassius.

Along the frontiers many client-kingdoms needed reform, because their rulers had compromised themselves with the Republicans, or because they were not strong or loyal enough to play an effective part in the forthcoming war against Parthia. These, however, were problems with which for the time being Antony seemed hardly concerned. . . .

CLEOPATRA SUMMONED TO TARSUS

Antony's dealings with another monarch, however, could not be postponed, and that was Cleopatra. The position of Egypt in any forthcoming hostilities against the Parthians was vital, since he would need Egyptian money and other material support. Moreover, the role the queen had played in the recent Philippi campaign against the assassins of Caesar seemed ambiguous and obscure—or at least that was what her enemies informed him. Antony therefore decided that, before extending his travels any further, he must see Cleopatra. As their meeting-place he selected Tarsus in Cilicia, one of the cities which had been oppressed by Brutus and Cassius. His intermediary, ordered to fetch her to Tarsus from Alexandria, was a certain Quintus Dellius, a man who, although a scholarly historian, attracted in the course of his varied life a bad reputation as a homosexual friend of Antony and then his pimp, and a writer of improper letters to Cleopatra. In pursuit of this mission, Dellius now proceeded to Egypt—with letters going before him—and requested the queen to report to Antony. After a suitable delay, designed to show, perhaps, that a divine monarch was not at everyone's beck and call, she obeyed and set out for Tarsus.

Antony, whom she already knew . . . , was a nobleman of a famous but impoverished family, the grandson of a great orator and the son of a well-known but easy-going and unsuccessful commander. Antony's own military talents were considerable, though they were displayed to better advantage in the tactical than in the strategic field, and most of all in his capacity to get the very best out of his soldiers, who admired his generosity and endurance. . . .

Antony's very considerable intelligence sometimes failed to produce the best results owing to a certain laziness and lack of psychological insight which made him a poor judge of character. It was easy to ignore his failings, however, when confronted with his imposing and somewhat pugilistic looks, bluff natural charm, and strong sense of humour, including a splendidly un-Roman capacity to laugh at himself. [According to] Plutarch . . .

> He was completely ignorant of much that was done in his name, not merely because he was of an easygoing disposition, but because he was simple enough to trust his subordinates. His character was, in fact, essentially simple and he was slow to perceive the truth. Once he recognized that he was at fault, he was full of repentance and ready to admit his errors to those he had wronged. Whenever he had to punish an offence or right an injustice, he acted on the grand scale, and it was generally considered that he overstepped the bounds far more often in the rewards he bestowed than in the punishments he inflicted. As for the kind of coarse and insolent banter which he liked to exchange, this carried its own remedy with it, for anyone could return his ribaldry with interest and he enjoyed being laughed at quite as much as laughing at others. And in fact it was this quality which often did him harm, for he found it impossible to believe that the real purpose of those who took liberties and cracked jokes with him was to flatter him. He never understood that some men go out of their way to adopt a frank and outspoken man-

ner and use it like a piquant sauce to disguise the cloying taste of flattery. Such men deliberately indulge in bold repartee and an aggressive flow of talk when they are in their cups, so that the obsequious compliance which they show in matters of business does not suggest that they associate with a man merely to please him, but seems to spring from a genuine conviction of his superior wisdom. . . . His weakness for the opposite sex showed an attractive side of his character, and even won him the sympathy of many people, for he often helped others in their love-affairs and always accepted with good humour the jokes they made about his own. . . . Well versed in the art of putting the best possible face on disreputable actions, he never feared the audit of his copulations, but let nature have her way, and left behind him the foundations of many families.

Nevertheless Antony was married, heavily married. His wife, the beautiful Fulvia, played a very large part in his public life, just as she had already figured prominently in the careers of two remarkable previous husbands. . . .

Like Fulvia, Antony had been married twice already, but neither of his previous wives had exercised anything like as much influence in public affairs as she did. . . . Cleopatra, then, was well aware that the Mark Antony she was about to meet at Tarsus, although very susceptible to women, possessed a Roman wife whose forcefulness and power were strongly reminiscent of the royal Hellenistic women of her own line. However, being determined, for the sake of her future and Egypt's, to convince him of her own desirability as a queen, Cleopatra appreciated that this probably meant convincing him of her desirability as a woman as well—a campaign she may have begun already during her encounters with Antony at Alexandria or Rome.

APHRODITE MEETS DIONYSUS

And so Cleopatra came from Alexandria to Cilicia, and sailed up a lagoon of the river Cydnus to the ancient city of Tarsus. In Plutarch's description of the scene, in his *Life of Antony,* one cannot suppose that every detail is authentic or unexaggerated, since the dramatic tale had already passed into legend. But his evocation of the event is one of the masterpieces of his vivid biographical method:

> She relied above all upon her physical presence and the spell and enchantment which it could create. . . . She came sailing up the river Cydnus in a barge with a poop of gold, its purple sails billowing in the wind, while her rowers caressed the water with oars of silver which dipped in time to the music of

the flute, accompanied by pipes and lutes. Cleopatra herself reclined beneath a canopy of cloth of gold, dressed in the character of Aphrodite (Venus), as we see her in paintings, while on either side to complete the picture stood boys costumed as Cupids who cooled her with their fans. . . .

Antony then sent a message inviting Cleopatra to dine with him. But she thought it more appropriate that he should come to her, and so, as he wished to show his courtesy and goodwill, he accepted and went. He found the preparations made to receive him magnificent beyond words, but what astonished him most of all was the extraordinary number of lights. So many of these, it is said, were let down from the roof and displayed on all sides at once, and they were arranged and grouped in such ingenious patterns in relation to each other, some in squares and some in circles, that they created as brilliant a spectacle as can ever have been devised to delight the eye.

On the following day Antony returned her hospitality with another banquet. But although he had hoped to surpass her in splendour and elegance he was hopelessly outdone in both, and was the first to make fun of the crude and meagre quality of his entertainment. Cleopatra saw that Antony's humour was broad and gross and belonged to the soldier rather than the courtier, and she quickly adopted the same manner towards him and treated him without the least reserve. . . .

And so Cleopatra, captivating Antony by her personal attractions and royal glamour, became his mistress.

Yet her arrangement of the whole scene, the banqueting and the seduction, was not intended purely for Antony's pleasure, or hers. Plutarch knows what she had in mind when he assures us that '. . . *the word spread on every side that Aphrodite had come to revel with Dionysus for the happiness of Asia.*' Keenly alive to the feelings of the near eastern peoples, Cleopatra raised the whole occasion far above the level of mere entertainment, and endowed it with the religious significance that would exert the maximum appeal. Antony had entered Asia as the New Dionysus, the conquering, immortalizing god who meant so much to the peoples of these lands. And now Cleopatra, making her entrance at Tarsus, assumed the pose of Aphrodite, surrounded by her train. Aphrodite, too, was a goddess of these times, the mistress of nature, the mother of the Universe, who, in her Roman guise of Venus, had recently inspired the Roman poet Lucretius to utter his heartfelt tribute: 'it is you, who fill rich earth and buoyant sea with your presence! It is through you that every living thing achieves its life.'

Cleopatra's encounter with Antony at Tarsus, stage-managed with her incomparable resourcefulness, did not, of course, comprise a marriage on an earthly plane. But it was an earthly reflection of the Sacred Marriage between two great gods, which seemed profoundly appropriate to all Egyptians, and indeed all inhabitants of the east. For Dionysus was the Egyptian Osiris, and Aphrodite was Osiris' sisterwife, the divine Isis—the true and natural partner of the occupant of the throne. The incarnation of Isis upon earth was Cleopatra herself, and her consequent identification with Aphrodite seemed abundantly right and clear. . . .

The goddess Isis made herself manifest upon earth in the person of the queen of Egypt. And so Cleopatra VII, too, was declared the New Isis. When Caesar died, she had to search for a new partner, a new incarnation of Osiris. And now she had found him. For Antony, being Dionysus, was Osiris too. The people of Tarsus understood this clearly enough, for the religion of Osiris and Isis was well known to them. . . .

By the time Cleopatra and Antony became lovers, she had already adopted the habit of appearing in public in the trappings of the Egyptian goddess Isis, thereby ensuring her people's continued respect and devotion. Here, priests and others take part in a religious ceremony honoring that deity.

ANTONY GOES TO ALEXANDRIA

There must have been not only all the legendary feasting and love-making at Tarsus, but also a good deal of unromantic negotiation. There must have been hard bargaining, up to the limits which a Ptolemaic monarch could hazard when dealing with the Romans. And Antony, before moving onwards into Syria, was anxious to know how he stood with Egypt. At the moment the country was freer, in practice, than it had been for some time, since the Roman garrison which had departed two years earlier for Syria never returned. It had left in somewhat equivocal circumstances during the civil wars between the Caesarians and Caesar's assassins, and Cleopatra had been summoned to Tarsus partly in order to answer charges that she had assisted the anti-Caesarian side. She was able, however, to explain that she had done nothing of the kind, in spite of severe and repeated pressures from Cassius; and if her Egyptian political enemies cherished any hopes that her civil war record might undermine her position, they miscalculated.

More important were the assurances Antony needed about the material help she could provide for his forthcoming Parthian war. Her agreement was only obtained on certain conditions. First and foremost, she demanded the execution of her half-sister Arsinoe IV, never forgiven for establishing a rival régime in Alexandria in 48 B.C. Cleopatra was glad to be able to point out to Antony that, although she herself had not helped Cassius and Brutus, there might well be strong reason to suspect Arsinoe of having done so. On Antony's orders, Arsinoe was torn from her Ephesian sanctuary and executed.

All the other five of the offspring of Cleopatra's father had now perished by violent deaths—three as her enemies, and two of the three through her own personal initiative. The death of Arsinoe, like the death of Ptolemy XIV, must have seemed to Cleopatra an act of self-preservation, since many of the Egyptian ruling class who disliked Cleopatra might have supported her half-sister. Cleopatra also requested Antony to execute the high priest of Artemis at Ephesus, since it was he who had saluted Arsinoe as queen. But an Ephesian deputation came to see Cleopatra, and the priest was spared. . . . Yet another enemy was also killed at Cleopatra's request. This was a youth at the Phoenician town of Aradus (Arvad) who claimed to be Cleopatra's older half-brother and husband Ptolemy XIII. After the young king's drowning in the Nile, in mysterious circumstances, Caesar had been afraid that false reports of his survival would get about, and now this person at Aradus had justified these fears by declaring that he himself was the king. So he, too, was executed on Antony's instructions. . . .

With the exception of Judaea, however, Antony still did not tackle the problem of the eastern client kings, many of whose loyalties had been so dubious in the civil war. For his omission, he was retrospectively blamed. His critics declared that he showed an indecent impatience to be with Cleopatra again—and it is true that he now went on to Egypt, to spend the winter of 41–40 B.C. in her company. But in any case it must have seemed to him that the eve of a major Parthian war was the wrong time for far-reaching revisions in the dependent states. If some of the princes had bad consciences, so much the better; they would be more likely to watch their behaviour now. Besides, Alexandria was not only where Cleopatra lived; it was also, although outside the empire, a reasonable place for his own provisional headquarters, owing to the important part that Egypt was expected to play in the forthcoming campaign.

However, remembering the bad reception Caesar had got in 48 B.C. when he disembarked with the insignia of a Roman consul and a contingent of troops, Antony was careful to enter the city as a private citizen, unaccompanied by soldiers. He was already popular in Alexandria because fourteen years earlier, when serving with Gabinius, he had prevented a slaughter of Egyptian prisoners. Now he once again created a favourable impression, not only because of his known phil-Hellenic tastes, but also because of his obvious desire to show he was coming as the guest of an independent queen. Roman policy to Egypt had always veered between covetousness and friendship, and although Antony wanted Egyptian aid, he made it clear that he was seeking it as a friend.

The only shadow on the horizon must have been Antony's loyal wife Fulvia, at present representing his interests in Octavian's Italy. . . . Cleopatra may very well have indicated to Antony that she considered him a better man than Octavian, and she may also have criticized his wife. More probably, however, she concentrated on making his life so pleasant that he would find it better to live with her than with Fulvia. The numerous parties she arranged for him, for example, now and later, are described with imaginative gusto by Plutarch. Then, during the winter, she became pregnant, and there was no doubt that Antony was the father.

ANTONY AND CLEOPATRA PART COMPANY

It was presumably Antony's intention to leave Egypt in the spring of 40 B.C. and visit his other eastern territories as a prelude to the invasion of Parthia. As it happened, however, his departure was accelerated owing to the receipt, in February or early March, of the gravest possible news. For the Parthians, he now learnt, instead of waiting passively for Rome's expected attack, had themselves launched an ambitious two-pronged invasion of the Roman empire. Their king's son Pacorus descended upon Syria, while a Roman renegade in their service, the ex-Republican Quintus Labienus, advanced rapidly into Asia Minor, accompanied by other Roman Republican refugees like himself. Both columns attracted wide support among Rome's Greek and native subjects.

Antony left Egypt and sailed rapidly north to Tyre, where he heard not only that a number of client-kings had defected, but that his own troops in Syria (many of them former opponents of Caesar) had also gone over to the Parthians; and the governor of the province was reported killed. Antony moved on to Asia Minor. There he received further information, this time from Italy: for news reached him that Fulvia and his brother Lucius Antonius, consul in 41 B.C., without receiving any instruction from himself, had launched a rising against Octavian. After a savage campaign, they had been utterly defeated, and Fulvia had fled from Italy towards the east.

Caught between these two disasters, Antony was unable to devote any further time to Cleopatra. The ancient writers' romantic . . . emphasis upon the Tarsus meeting, followed by the winter they spent together at Alexandria, tends to divert attention from what happened now. For from this time onwards, they were parted for no less than three and a half years: from the early months of 40 B.C. until the autumn of 37. Even if, as the writers assure us, he had fallen in love with her at Tarsus, any degree of ascendancy she had established over him was now to be interrupted by a prolonged and continuous separation. Obviously, this separation weakened her influence over his actions. Whether she could ever regain what she had lost, time alone would show.

The Lovers Begin to Remold the Eastern Mediterranean

Edith Flamarion

After leaving Cleopatra in 40 B.C., Antony traveled to Syria and eventually back to Rome, where, following the death of his wife, Fulvia, he married Octavian's sister, Octavia. Antony was not only a member of the Second Triumvirate (the political alliance forged among himself, Octavian, and Lepidus), he was ostensibly its strongest partner. This was because he had charge of the East, the richest and most populous sector of the Roman Empire. Edith Flamarion, a researcher at Paris's Centre National de la Recherche Scientifique, here tells how the overconfident Antony eventually returned to Cleopatra (in 37 B.C.) and attempted to exploit his strengths. Although he suffered some defeats in his ill-fated expedition against Parthia (a Near Eastern kingdom occupying much of what are now Iraq and Iran), he and Cleopatra managed to consolidate many of the Roman provinces and small kingdoms of the eastern Mediterranean. (They disagreed on how to treat Herod, king of the small kingdom of Judaea, in Palestine; she disliked him, while Antony sought his support.) Eventually, in a grand ceremony that came to be called the "Donations of Alexandria," the lovers announced their dominance over most of the East. To many at the time it looked as though they were trying to resurrect the long-defunct Egyptian empire. Because much of this territory was still part of the Roman realm, their audacious acts were sure to bring them into conflict with Octavian.

Antony left Cleopatra at the end of winter 40 B.C., called away by the alarming situation abroad: Parthian armies were oc-

Excerpted from *Cleopatra: The Life and Death of a Pharaoh*, by Edith Flamarion. Translated by Alexandra Bonfante-Warren. Copyright ©1997 by Harry N. Abrams, Inc. Reprinted by permission of Harry N. Abrams, Inc.

cupying southern Asia Minor, Syria, and Judaea, and increasingly becoming a threat to Rome. Herod was forced to take refuge in Rome. Six months after Antony left, the queen gave birth to twins: Cleopatra Selene ("Moon") and Alexander Helios ("Sun").

ANTONY, TRIUMVIR IN THE EAST

Antony did not stop in Syria, but steered a course for Athens, where his wife, Fulvia, had provoked an uprising against Octavian, which had gone awry. The encounter between husband and wife was stormy and Antony, in a fury, sailed to Brundisium (modern Brindisi, in southern Italy). He never saw his wife again, for she died some months later. After thorny preliminaries, Antony achieved an agreement with Octavian and Lepidus in October 40 B.C.: the East would be his, the West Octavian's, and Africa would go to Lepidus.

Cleopatra had reason to be pleased with this division of the world, yet she was anxious, for not only did Antony remain in Rome, he remarried there. To seal their agreement, Octavian had given Antony his sister Octavia in marriage and their first child, a girl, Antonia Major, was born in the summer of 39 B.C. Despite the warnings of an Egyptian astrologer, Antony confirmed his alliance with his brother-in-law by inaugurating the new cult of the Divine Julius (Octavian's deified adoptive father), with himself as *flamen*, or priest. Italy seemed to be at peace at last, for in the same year the Triumvirs reached an accord with their last great opponent, Pompey's son Sextus, who was occupying Sicily.

But Rome also reinforced its position at the Egyptian border: a few months earlier, the Senate had named Herod— Cleopatra's enemy, but Antony's longtime ally—king of Judaea, Edom, and Samaria. The queen of Egypt had reason to be concerned.

A FRAGILE ACCORD

In the fall of 39 B.C., Antony and Octavian sailed to Athens, where they remained until the spring of 37. There, too, Antony lived the sybaritic [pleasure-seeking] life he loved: he was the patron of the gymnastic games; as the New Dionysus, he was joined in a mystical ceremony with the goddess of the city, Athena Polias, in the winter of 39. He gave the Athenians festivals and banquets—usually paid from the tribute he extorted from them.

Meanwhile, his army had won two battles against the Parthians: his leadership in the East was beginning auspiciously indeed, but his relations with Octavian, who married Livia in 38 B.C., were once more becoming tense. War between them was narrowly averted, thanks to Octavia's pacifying intervention. In the summer of 37 B.C., Antony, Octavian, and Lepidus met in Tarentum, in southern Italy, and renewed the Triumvirate for five more years.

That fall Antony abruptly left Italy and Octavia, who was expecting their second child, and went east to the Syrian city of Antioch. Was love drawing him to Cleopatra, or did he need to renew his alliance with the queen, in view of the massive expedition he was planning against the Parthians? Cleopatra and the twins, his children, met Antony in Antioch, and there she married him according to the Egyptian rite, which unlike Roman law permitted polygamy.

Egypt's queen decreed that the years of her reign be renumbered from that moment. She led a life of luxury with Antony in the Daphne quarter of the city famous for its laurel trees and cypresses, but did not neglect her ambitions. In exchange for financial support of his war she asked him to give her the territories of Coele-Syria and Judaea, which bordered Egypt. He granted her less than she asked for: the kingdom of Chalcis, the Syrian coast, Cyprus, and a few scattered areas in Cilicia, Crete, and Judaea, where King Herod functioned as a tax collector in the city of Jericho. Antony meant to keep this vassal and ally of Rome close to Egypt, despite—or perhaps because of—Cleopatra's enmity toward him.

A DISASTROUS WAR AGAINST THE PARTHIANS

In the spring of 36 B.C., Antony, well-supplied with Cleopatra's money and troops, moved to engage the Parthians. The queen, pregnant again, accompanied him as far as the Euphrates River, then, in royal panoply [queenly attire], returned to Egypt, passing through Damascus and her new territories in Judaea. (It is said that Herod attempted to assassinate her; failing, he escorted her to Pelusium, on the Egyptian border.) From Jericho Cleopatra brought back cuttings of balsam trees (called balm of Gilead in the Bible), which she planted in Egypt.

In Alexandria once more, Cleopatra ordered coins struck commemorating her enlarged empire. She and Antony were portrayed as paired Hellenistic rulers, new figures of Dionysus and Aphrodite, Osiris and Isis. But the child she bore to him that year was clearly identified with his Egyptian heritage: Cleopatra named Antony's last child Ptolemy Philadelphus, making him a true member of her dynasty.

In the meantime, in Parthia Antony suffered defeat upon defeat. He was forced to a dangerous retreat in the heart of an icy winter, his army decimated by dysentery, hunger, and the onslaughts of the redoubtable Parthian archers. In all, Antony lost twenty thousand infantry and forty thousand cavalry. The pitiable march ended in Syria, where the conquered general awaited aid from Cleopatra; though his soldiers were in rags, their misfortunes had in no way diminished their affection for him. Plutarch reported: "The obedience and affectionate respect they bore their general and the unanimous feeling amongst small and great alike, officers and common soldiers, [was such that they preferred] his good opinion of them to their very lives and being. For this devotion, . . . there were many reasons, as the nobility of his family, his eloquence, his frank and open manners, his liberal and magnificent manners, his familiarity in talking with everybody, and, at this time particularly, his kindness in visiting and pitying the sick, joining in all their pains, and furnishing them with all things necessary, so that the sick and wounded were even more eager to serve than those that were whole and strong." The queen of Egypt arrived with provisions, clothing, and money, and took the survivors back to Alexandria.

CLEOPATRA'S INTERNATIONAL POLICY

During the winter of 35 B.C. Cleopatra engaged in intense diplomatic activity with neighboring states. She began by forging an alliance with the king of Armenia, sealed by the betrothal of her son Alexander Helios to the king's daughter. In Judaea Herod's mother-in-law, Alexandra, had begun an insurrection against him; when it failed Cleopatra offered her asylum. Finally, she negotiated a treaty with the king of Media against Parthia; war there was once more a possibility. Despite the Armenian king's refusal to aid them, Cleopatra and Antony went on a brief campaign and reconquered the lost parts of Syria.

Cleopatra was apprehensive. Trouble was clouding the western horizon, as Octavian, burning with seemingly limitless ambition, took Sicily from Pompey's son Sextus and

Africa from Lepidus. As sole master of the entire region, he posed a powerful danger to Antony. More alarming still, Octavia, sent by her brother, had just set sail with provisions and ships to reinforce her husband's army.

Cleopatra moved heaven and earth to keep Antony in Egypt, out of the distant campaign—and away from his Roman wife. She lamented, wept, refused to eat: "When he entered the room, she fixed her eyes upon him in a rapture, and when he left seemed to languish and half faint away" (Plutarch). Whether or not she was dramatizing, she succeeded, and Antony broke with Octavian. He sent word to Octavia that he would not meet her, and sent her back to Rome, while he returned to Alexandria with Cleopatra.

A ROMAN-STYLE TRIUMPH?

The disastrous Parthian campaign was in some measure erased by a swift expedition against Artavasdes, king of Armenia, who had betrayed Antony more than once. In the spring of 34 B.C., Antony, now settled in Syria, reached a new agreement with Herod, despite Cleopatra's hostility. He then occupied Armenia, imprisoned Artavasdes, took his treasury, and declared the country a Roman province. When he returned to Syria, he formed an alliance with the Median king.

The pharaoh's palace in Alexandria was considerably embellished as well as enriched by the Armenian booty, and in the fall of 34 B.C. the Egyptian capital witnessed a sumptuous ceremony in honor of Antony's victory. An immense procession crossed the city to the square in front of the Serapeion [a temple with a golden roof].

Cleopatra, dressed as Isis, sat on a golden throne. Before her was set the chariot in which stood the victorious Antony, dressed as Dionysus, preceded by the king of Armenia and his family, wearing chains of silver in recognition of their royal rank; the trophies and spoils of war came behind. The reference to Cleopatra and Antony as heirs of divine blood was clear. At the end of the day, a gigantic feast was provided to the soldiers and people of the city.

THE "DONATIONS OF ALEXANDRIA"

A few days later, in the immense Gymnasium, a sort of stadium, the Alexandrians attended an extension of the ceremonial triumph. Antony and Cleopatra, seated on high thrones of gold on a silver dais, presided over the assembly.

On thrones lower down were seated King Ptolemy, called Caesarion, thirteen years old, and the couple's three children: the twins—almost seven years old—Cleopatra Selene and Alexander Helios, the latter dressed as a Median king in an embroidered gown and high tiara [crown] adorned with peacock feathers; and Ptolemy Philadelphus, two years old, garbed as a Macedonian king in purple *chlamys* [robe], royal cap, and little boots.

Antony gave a speech, reportedly in Greek, distributing the territories that were recent Egyptian acquisitions and those he had conquered. The pharaonic couple—Cleopatra, titled Queen of Queens, and Caesarion, King of Kings—received Egypt, Coele-Syria, and Cyprus. Alexander's share was Armenia and Media . . . and Parthia, yet to be conquered; Cleopatra Selene received Libya and Cyrenaica; and Ptolemy Philadelphus, northern Syria, Phoenicia, and Cilicia. All this, for the moment, was Cleopatra's to administer as regent.

It was the return of the great Egypt of the early Ptolemies—except that Cleopatra's realm was under Roman domination, clearly a vassal state. In Rome Octavian had a field day exploiting negative interpretations of the ceremony for propaganda purposes, claiming that Antony had placed a vast kingdom, as large as Italy, in the hands of his dangerous Oriental mistress.

The Road to War Between East and West

Jack Lindsay

War between the East, controlled by Cleopatra and Antony, and the West, in Octavian's grip, seemed inevitable. This information-packed essay by noted Cleopatra biographer Jack Lindsay covers the fierce and often mean-spirited propaganda war that preceded the actual outbreak of hostilities. As he shows, each side tried its best to discredit the other in the eyes of the Senate, the military, and the Roman people, as well as the rulers and peoples of other Mediterranean lands.

When news of the Alexandrian Triumph reached Rome, Octavian wrote an angry letter reproaching Antony for his conduct. Antony's reply seems the letter that mockingly details Octavian's own amorous failings . . . but he also raised serious issues. He claimed his rights according to the Treaty of Brundisium to half the recruits levied in Italy and to allotments for his veterans. Where were his promised legions? He declared that only Octavian stood in the way of the republic's restoration. (This point, with Antony's name in place of Octavian's, was a stock argument on the other side.) Octavian did not answer the genuine charges, but jeeringly suggested that Antony should find his veterans lands in conquered Parthia, and renewed the attacks on his enslavement by Cleopatra.

This reply reached Antony in Armenia in autumn 33 B.C. . . . He felt that he should try to regularize things by a formal approach to the Senate at Rome. In a dispatch he asked for his Acts, which included the Donations, to be ratified, and expressed his readiness to lay down his powers if Octavian did likewise. From now on the war of vituperation [abusive attacks] was open and continuous. . . . With the last day of December the period of the Second Triumvirate expired.

Now was the crucial constitutional moment; and our sources are not helpful. Mainly pro-Octavian, they dodge the issue, since their favourite had a weak legal position. There were few precedents for the situation. The holders of such offices as the triumvirate could argue that the law had merely fixed a day up to which they could hold their powers, but it needed a formal act of abdication or a vote of termination by the granting body (the Roman People) to end their tenure. Antony kept the title; Octavian with his superior tactical position at Rome dropped it—though whether he gave up its powers is another matter. He . . . knew that any illegalities would be given restrospective legalisation as long as he won: as indeed happened in 29 and 28. If he lost, what did illegalities matter? So he writes in his *Res Gestae* simply that he held the triumvirate for 'ten consecutive years'.

Meanwhile Antony and Cleopatra had met at Ephesos, where the contingents of the client-kings were gathering from Syria, Asia Minor, Thrace. Of Roman troops in the east, there were nineteen legions (some 70,000 men) as his main force, with four as reserve and defence in Cyrene, and seven more in Egypt and Syria. Warships were being busily built, though Cleopatra had 200 ships and a war chest said to hold 2,000 talants. Timber was scarce and on Kos Antony's men felled even the sacred forest of Asklepios. Cleopatra took charge of the docks at Berytos near the Lebanon cedars. In the end some 800 ships were perhaps available for various purposes. . . . Cleopatra supplied the provisions. Everywhere she went at Antony's side, on horse or in litter, at banquets and at councils; and already her intrusive presence in a war situation was offending and irritating Antony's Roman supporters.

THE PROPAGANDA WAR BEGINS

Cassius of Parma [a spokesman for Antony] in his satirical verses was making much of Octavian's mean descent. From the abuse of this period no doubt came many of the traditions of his family's disgraceful past: that his father was a moneychanger and usurer, even one of 'those who distributed bribes and performed other tasks in the Campus'. Antony jeered at his maternal stock, saying his great-grandfather 'had been of African birth and had conducted now a perfumery shop and now a bakery at Aricia'. . . .

In deriding Antony, Octavian [tried] . . . to show that Antony had an alien quality, inflated and Asiatic, with bom-

bastic jingles; he himself prided himself on a sober style like
Julius Caesar. One of Messala's polemics seems to deal with
accusations that Antony let Cleopatra carry off works of art
from many places to Alexandria. She may have done so, but
a Roman leader was the last person to make such charges,
in view of the vast lootings by Roman generals and others
for a century and more. . . .

ANTONY SCOLDS OCTAVIAN

*After Antony designated various eastern lands to Cleopa-
tra and their children in the ceremony known as the Donations of Alexandria, Octavian sent a letter severely criticiz-
ing the lovers' relationship. Antony's reply, which follows, was
luckily preserved by the Roman historian Suetonius in his biography of Octavian/Augustus.*

What has come over you? Do you object to my sleeping with
Cleopatra? But we are married; and it is not even as though
this were anything new—the affair started nine years ago.
And what about you? Are you faithful to Livia Drusilla? My
congratulations if, when this letter arrives, you have not been
in bed with Tertullia, or Terentilla, or Rufilla, or Salvia Titise-
nia—or all of them. Does it really matter so much where, or
with whom, you perform the sexual act?

Suetonius, *Lives of the Twelve Caesars*, published as *The Twelve Caesars*. Trans.
Robert Graves. Rev. Michael Grant. New York: Penguin Books, 1979, pp. 92–93.

Octavian had taken care to withdraw from Rome before
the new year began; and at last Antony had a chance to
make men in Rome listen to his case. Speeches in the Senate were one of the best ways of getting arguments through
to the Italian *municipia* [towns], to Antony's settled veterans,
and others. Sosius [one of Antony's supporters], entering office [as consul] on 1 January 32 B.C., . . . praised Antony and
attacked Octavian for his bad faith, but did not ask for confirmation of Antony's Acts, knowing well what antagonisms
that would raise. He failed to put a motion against Octavian,
as one of the latter's partisans, Nonius Balbus, a tribune of
the *plebs,* vetoed any resolution. Octavian now decided that
he had given the consuls enough time to show their hand. At
the next session he appeared with an armed bodyguard of
friends and soldiers. Launching a violent diatribe against
Antony and his Donations, he complained of his and Sosius'
behaviour, and offered to produce documentary proof of his

charges at the next meeting. His show of force made any reply impossible; and he knew quite well that after it there
would be no 'next meeting' of the Senate. The two consuls,
considering that he had destroyed the constitution, fled with
three to four hundred senators to Antony. That so many
leading men, at this juncture, threw in their lot with Antony
is remarkable; they made up about a third of the Senate. The
fugitives joined Antony at Ephesos.

He was now able to make a good display of legality, with
the two consuls and a large body of senators driven to appeal
for his aid against an armed attempt to overawe the officers
of the Republic. He had every right to declare war on Octavian as a usurper, on the lines of Pompey's declaration
against Caesar after the latter had seized Rome: the legitimate government was wherever the consuls and the Senate
were. He at once set about mobilizing for war on sea and
land. Octavian's act had removed his qualms about fighting
the Roman in command of Italy. And now at last Cleopatra
was ready to contribute all she could, in men, ships, supplies, money. Antony called up all his client-kings. . . .

RESENTMENT FOR A FOREIGN QUEEN

From now on the contradictions in Antony's position became
ever more evident and disastrous. As a Roman challenging
Octavian he had some reason to think victory possible; as a
Hellenistic ruler wedded to Cleopatra, he stirred up a maximum of resistance in the west. In the confused situation he
might have made out a good juristic case against Octavian,
which would have appealed to large numbers in the *municipia*, at Rome, and among the veterans—but only as long
as he spoke securely as a Roman. By his continued association with Cleopatra he made all Octavian's accusations seem
true, and put an intolerable burden on his own supporters.
Some [of Antony's officers] indeed like Canidius or Turullius
were so closely connected with his career that they had little
choice but to follow him, whatever they thought; but many
others, like Ahenobarbus, were ready to stay at his side only
as long as they felt him a fellow-Roman with understandable
motives and aims that they could in some degree share. Others again, like Titius or Dellius, merely wanted to be on the
winning side; and the more they saw of Cleopatra's dominance in the war councils, the more they felt that the time for
desertion was at hand. Many men were painfully swayed be-

tween a genuine admiration for Antony and a conviction that by supporting him they were betraying Roman ideals in unforgivable ways. The more ardent adherents of Cleopatra and her opponents were in continual clash. At one moment Antony did tell her to go back to Egypt and let him fight out the war on his own. She refused. Canidius backed her, arguing that she paid and fed the army, manned the fleet, and had a better head than most men. His opponents said that she had bribed him. Ahenobarbus, who liked Antony and whose son was betrothed to Antony's elder daughter by Octavia, opposed Cleopatra's queenly arrogance with the haughty manners of a Roman noble and refused to address her except by name. Antony tried to make the best of both worlds by announcing that six months after victory he would lay down his powers. But who could credit any such statements while he could not send Cleopatra home? . . .

ANTONY CHOOSES CLEOPATRA OVER HIS WIFE

Cleopatra was to some extent using festivals to take Antony's mind off the problems she created for him. When they moved their H.Q. [headquarters] to [the Greek island of] Samos, the whole body of Dionysiac Artists gathered on the island. 'While almost all the world around was filled with groans and lamentations, a single island for many days resounded with flutes and stringed instruments. Theatres were filled and choral bands competed. Every city also sent an ox for the general sacrifice and kings vied in entertainments and gifts. Everywhere men began asking: How will the winners celebrate their victories if the war-preparations are marked by such costly festivals? When the events were over, Antony gave the Dramatic Artists Priene as a place to live in, and sailed for Athens, where sports and theatres again took up his time. Cleopatra too, jealous of Octavia's honours there (for Octavia was a special favourite of the Athenians), sought by many splendid gifts to win the people's favour. So they voted her honours and sent a deputation to her house with the vote, among them Antony: for was he not a citizen of Athens?' Antony delivered the speech for the city. But to Rome, we are told by Plutarch, he sent men with orders to eject Octavia from his house. 'And she left it, taking with her all his children except the eldest son by Fulvia, who was with him; she was in tears of distress that she too would be regarded as one of the causes of the

A carving, done on a precious stone long after Cleopatra's death, depicts her likeness. Despite her legendary love affairs and lavish life-style, she was apparently a capable and effective ruler.

war. But the Romans pitied Antony, not her, and most of all those who had seen Cleopatra and knew she was not Octavia's superior in youth or beauty'. But can we imagine Octavian, in the midst of a war, allowing agents of Antony access to Rome and standing idle while they turned his sister out? Even if Antony had succumbed to pressure from Cleopatra and attempted such a stupid act, we cannot believe he would have succeeded in carrying it out. The plainest interpretation is that Antony did accept Cleopatra's argument that it was impossible for him to remain married to Octavia in the circumstances and that he sent her letters of divorce. Octavia then had no legal right to his house and would have accepted her brother's insistence that she should move out. The story of her ejection by agents of Antony would be a spontaneous response to the news of her removal or a version put about by Octavian's agents.

Antony's adherents in Italy kept sending messages about the bad effects of his union with Cleopatra, but she was now in a strong enough position to turn the messengers out. Octavian, despite the flight of the consuls, had all the advantages that came from holding Rome. He summoned the remaining senators, read them a detailed defence of his own acts and position, and attacked those of Antony, especially the Donations. . . . But he was badly in need of money. The west was generally poorer than the east. . . . A general tax was imposed: all freeborn landholders had to pay a quarter of their income, freedmen an eighth of their property if it was worth over 200,000 sesterces. The result was riots, arson, uprisings. Propaganda had no effect and Antony's partisans had an easy time in stirring up discontent. There were street fights at Rome of boys on opposite sides. Soldiers had to be used to restore order. But as Plutarch remarks, 'As long as the people were being plagued by the tax collectors, they were furious; after they'd paid, they quieted down'. If Antony had got rid of Cleopatra and invaded Italy in the summer of 32, he would have struck against an unprepared enemy. But he did nothing and Octavian was able to control the situation. . . .

MORE CHARGES LEVELED AGAINST ANTONY AND CLEOPATRA

Desertions began from Antony's camp. Plancus and Titius went over to Octavian with useful information about his plans. . . . Plancus told Octavian that Antony's will had been deposited [in Rome] a short while before . . . and described its contents. Octavian realised, the tale goes, that here was the document he needed. . . . He . . . seized it by force and read it out to the Senate. We are told that the clauses included a declaration that Ptolemy Caesar was the true son of Caesar and Cleopatra; legacies to his children by Cleopatra; directions that he should be buried at her side in Alexandria. In the heated atmosphere the clause about his burial was taken to give further proof of his intention to remove the world-capital from Rome to Alexandria. The other clauses served perfectly to authenticate all that Octavian had been saying of Antony's views and aims. . . .

Everything we know of the will shows it to have been exactly the sort of document that Octavian wanted at this juncture to complete his propaganda against Antony. That Antony should so opportunely have provided his enemy with all the proofs of his derelictions (from a Roman viewpoint), is something a little too good to be true. He was capable indeed, under pressure, of stupid actions that played into Octavian's hand, actions like the divorce of Octavia; but what argues against authenticity of his will is the pointless nature of the cited clauses. Quite possibly there was a will, and the clause about being buried in Alexandria may well have been in it; for that can be taken as a plea to Octavian, in the event of his triumph, to treat his body at least with mercy. But the other clauses do not carry conviction. [In other words, much of it was likely forged.] . . .

The abuse of Cleopatra grew yet stronger, together with the usual condemnation of Egyptians in general as beast-worshippers. Calvisius (whom Plutarch calls an *hetairos* or close personal friend or companion of Octavian) made a set of detailed charges against Antony: that he'd given Cleopatra the Pergamon libraries, that at banquet with many guests he'd stood up and rubbed her feet 'in compliance with some agreement and compact', that he'd let the Ephesians in his presence salute her as Lady [*kyria*], that often, seated on the tribunal and dispensing justice. . . . Further charges declared that he used a golden chamberpot. . . .

A WORLD IN DISORDER?

Octavian could now take the final steps. He got the Senate to vote for war against Cleopatra and the cancellation of the authority which 'Antony had surrendered to a woman'. He declared that Antony had been drugged and was no longer master of himself, and that the Romans were in fact at war with Mardion the eunuch and Potheinos, with Eiras, the tire-woman of Cleopatra, and Charmion, who were in charge of the main matters of government. Thus, cleverly, Antony was ignored as no longer a responsible agent, and the war became a war against a foreign country, Egypt, with its allies.

Octavian now had a strong legal position. Antony was deprived of his triumviral powers and of the right to be consul in 31. Octavian, as Ferial Priest, in front of the temple of Bellona [goddess of war], went through the formal proclamation of *bellum justum* [showing why war was justified]. Marching into the Field of Mars, he hurled a spear dipped in fresh blood from the temple towards the east, the direction of the enemy. In 36 he had announced the end of the Civil Wars; by naming Cleopatra as the enemy, he saved himself from having to admit that those wars had not really been ended, as well as rallying all waverers in a sacred war, a national war, against a degenerate queen who wanted to destroy the whole Roman tradition. Between him and Antony there was merely *inimicitia*, a feud. . . .

During the turn of 32–1 Antony with his fleet and army wintered in Greece. Octavian gathered his forces at Brundisium and Tarentum. All the while the propaganda war grew fiercer. Much of what was then alleged has affected historians up to the present day, especially the picture of Antony as a drunken sot unable to leave Cleopatra's arms. Certainly she had established something of an ascendancy over him, in which sexual aspects played their part; but at no point could the situation be reduced to simple terms of drink, sex, and the rest of it. Antony had slowly got himself into an untenable position. Now he relied so much on Cleopatra for material aid that he could not turn her out without wrecking his war preparations and laying himself open to attacks from both Octavian and the Parthians. He could only struggle ahead on the unstable basis he had created for himself, hoping somehow or other to light on a way of reconciling his role as Roman general with that of Cleopatra's ally and lover. She, clear-sighted as she was in many ways, seems blind to the insoluble nature of the problem she had brought upon him. All she could see was that the world was in hopeless disorder and confusion, and that a strong ruler was needed– –a man with the qualities which Antony, mated with her, was excellently suited to provide.

Octavian Prepares His Troops for Battle

Dio Cassius

In the summer of 31 B.C., Octavian and his chief commander, Marcus Agrippa, trapped Antony's and Cleopatra's forces near Actium, in western Greece. It soon became clear that the lovers would attempt to break out by sea; and on September 2, both sides prepared to come to death grips. As was customary in ancient times, the commanders delivered morale-boosting speeches to their troops just prior to battle. Following is an excerpt from the paraphrase of Octavian's battle speech recorded later by the second-century Greek historian Dio Cassius. (The exact wording of the speech was not preserved, so Dio's version is based in large degree on secondhand reports and hearsay.) Note that Octavian hammers home two main themes. First, he ridicules Antony and defames Cleopatra, stressing that she is an impudent, dangerous woman who has bewitched a once-noble Roman. Second, Octavian assures his men that the enemy's ships, though many are larger than those commanded by Agrippa, will be a disadvantage rather than an advantage to Cleopatra and Antony.

'Soldiers, there is one conclusion that I have reached, both from the experience of others and at first hand: it is a truth I have taken to heart above all else, and I urge you too to keep it before you. This is that in all the greatest enterprises of war, or indeed in human affairs of any kind, victory comes to those whose thoughts and deeds follow the path of justice and of reverence for the gods. No matter how great the size and strength of our force might be—great enough perhaps to make the man who had chosen the less just course of action expect to win with its help—still I base my confidence far

Excerpted from *The Roman History: The Reign of Augustus*, by Dio Cassius, translated by Ian Scott-Kilvert. Copyright ©1987 by Ian Scott-Kilvert. Reprinted by permission of Penguin Books Ltd.

more upon the principles which are at stake in this war than upon the advantage of numbers. We Romans are the rulers of the greatest and best parts of the world, and yet we find ourselves spurned and trampled upon by a woman of Egypt.

'This disgraces our fathers, who defeated [the Greek leaders] Pyrrhus, Philip of Macedon, Perseus and Antiochus; who uprooted the Numantines and the Carthaginians from their homes; whose swords slew the Cimbri and the Ambrones. It disgraces our own generation, who have conquered the Gauls, subdued the Pannonians, marched as far as the Danube and beyond the Rhine, and crossed the sea to Britain. The men who achieved these feats of arms I have named would be cut to the heart if ever they knew that we have been overcome by this pestilence of a woman. Would we not utterly dishonour ourselves if, after surpassing all other nations in valour, we then meekly endured the insults of this rabble, the natives of Alexandria and of Egypt, for what more ignoble or more exact name could one give them? They worship reptiles and beasts as gods, they embalm their bodies to make them appear immortal, they are most forward in effrontery, but most backward in courage. Worst of all, they are not ruled by a man, but are the slaves of a woman, and yet they have dared to claim our possessions, and to employ our fellow-countrymen to lay hands on them, as if we would ever consent to surrender the prosperity which belongs to us.

ANTONY BEWITCHED?

'Who would not tear his hair at the sight of Roman soldiers serving as bodyguards of this queen? Who would not groan at hearing that Roman knights and senators grovel before her like eunuchs [castrated men]? Who would not weep when he sees and hears what Antony has become? This man has twice been consul and many times Imperator [supreme commander of armies]. He was appointed with me to take charge of the affairs of state and entrusted with the government of many cities and the command of many legions. Now he has abandoned his whole ancestral way of life, has embraced alien and barbaric customs, has ceased to honour us, his fellow-countrymen, or our laws, or his fathers' gods. Instead, he makes obeisance to that creature as if she were an Isis or a Selene, names her children Sun and Moon, and finally adopts for himself the title of Osiris or Dionysus. And to crown it all, he bestows gifts of whole islands and parts of continents as though he were master of the entire earth and sea. These things must seem to you amazing and hardly to be believed, but that should only make you the more angry. For if an event which defies belief turns out to be true, if Antony's self-indulgence leads him into actions of which even the bare mention is painful to hear, it is only reasonable that your anger should exceed all bounds.

'And yet, I myself was at first so attached to him that I granted him a share in our command, gave to him my sister in marriage, and transferred legions to his army. After that, I was so kindly and warmly disposed to him that I shrank from waging war merely because he insulted my sister, neglected the children she had borne him, preferred the Egyptian to her, and presented that woman's children with almost all your possessions—or indeed because of any other of his provocations. I acted so, first, because I did not think it right to treat Antony in the same way as Cleopatra. I considered her, on account both of her foreign birth and of her actions, to be an enemy of Rome, but Antony to be a citizen of Rome, who could still, I believed, be brought to reason.

'Later still I hoped that he might, if not voluntarily, at least under pressure, decide to change his course in consequence of the decrees that were passed against her. It was for these reasons that I did not declare war upon him at all. But he has treated all my efforts with contempt and disdain, and refuses to be pardoned, although we offer him our pardon, or pitied, although we offer him our pity. He is either blind to reason or mad, for I have heard and can believe that he is bewitched by that accursed woman, and therefore disregards all our efforts to show him goodwill and humanity. And so, being enslaved by her, he plunges into war with all its attendant dangers which he has accepted for her sake, against ourselves and against his country. What choice, then, remains to us, save our duty to oppose him together with Cleopatra and fight him off? . . .

THE ENEMY FORCES ARE INFERIOR

'You must not imagine that the size of their ships or the stoutness of their timbers is any match for our courage. What ship has ever killed or wounded any by its own efforts? I believe that their height and their solid construction will make them more difficult for their rowers to keep under way, and less responsive for their helmsmen to steer. What use can ships like these be to the fighting-men aboard when they can attack neither head-on nor abeam, the two manoeuvres which you know are essential in naval warfare? I do not suppose that they intend to use infantry tactics against us at sea, nor are thcy thinking of shutting themselves up behind wooden walls and inviting a siege, so to speak, since it could only be to our advantage if we were faced with an immobile wooden barrier. If their ships remain motionless, as if they were moored there, we can rip them open with our rams, or else bombard them from a distance with our siege engines, or burn them to the water's edge with our incendiary missiles. On the other hand, if they do venture to move, they will be too slow either to overtake or to escape our vessels: their weight makes them too cumbersome to cause damage to us, and their size makes them most liable to suffer it themselves.

'I need not waste any more words on their fleet, since we have already had many encounters with it, both off Leucas and lately in these waters. So far from finding ourselves inferior to them, we have every time gained the upper hand. You can take heart now not so much from my words as from your own actions, and resolve to put an end to the whole war without further delay. And you can rest assured that, if we conquer today, we shall have no more to do. It is a general rule of human nature that when a man fails at his first trial of strength, he becomes discouraged for any others. In our case, we are so indisputably superior to our enemies on land that we could beat them even if they were coming fresh to the contest.

'They themselves know this so well—and here let me give you the intelligence I have received—that they have lost their nerve at what has already happened, and despair of saving their lives if they remain in their positions. So they are trying now to flee to some destination or other, and are making this sortie not to offer battle but to find a way of escape. They have loaded into their ships the best and most valuable of their possessions in the hope of breaking out with them if they can. And so, since they have clearly admitted that they are weaker than us, and since they carry the prizes of victory in their ships, let us not allow them to slip away anywhere else, but defeat them here on the spot and make all these treasures our own.'

Cleopatra and Antony Suffer Defeat at Actium

William L. Rodgers

With their forces blockaded at Actium, Antony and Cleopatra faced a crucial choice. Should their attempt to break out be by land or sea? This is the starting point taken in this essay by noted military historian William L. Rodgers. Drawing on the ancient accounts of Dio Cassius and Plutarch, Rodgers goes on to describe the great naval battle of Actium (fought on September 2, 31 B.C.), which more or less sealed Cleopatra's and Antony's fates. Rodgers also speculates about the reasons for the Egyptian queen's notorious sudden departure at the height of the battle. His narrative follows the defeated lovers back to Egypt and ends with Octavian's arrival there a few months later.

In making his choice Antony was no doubt influenced by the entire change in the political outlook both of the Romans with him and of Cleopatra, which had come about owing to the misfortunes of the summer. Antony's movement on Italy was originally supported by the Roman party, because its members wanted to go back to Rome and resume their life as Roman aristocrats with Rome as the center of the Mediterranean world. They were never warmly in favor of a desperate battle and now negotiation was their best hope. Cleopatra's original desire for overcoming Octavian was because victory would make her dynasty secure in Egypt through Antony's gratitude for her assistance with the wealth and the fleet of Egypt. She wished no negotiation in which she felt her own position at home might be a principal point at issue. But the gradual impairment of the situation of the eastern army by hunger entailed changes in the political objectives which it was possible to reach by its military efforts. As the Romans became doubtful of the outcome of battle, they began to go over to the opposite camp and make their personal terms with Octavian while it was yet time. It must be remembered that by the Roman practice the great military commands were occupied by holders of the principal civil offices, and the seceders probably felt that leaving Antony was a political act, and not so much a military desertion as it would now be.

To the last Cleopatra continued to hold her original objective, but she now realized that it was no longer probable that it could be reached through defeating Octavian. She felt that she could make herself and her family secure in Egypt only by persuading Antony to renounce his designs upon Italy and against Octavian and retire to the provinces he had ruled since the battle of Philippi, continuing to govern them by her help and riches as Queen of Egypt. Antony's soldiers still retained their confidence in the great leader they had followed so long and the generals and officers who remained faithful no doubt thought that it was better to hold the greatest positions in the East rather than secondary ones at Rome. Should Antony effect a retirement, it appeared unlikely that Octavian would follow him to the East to restore the unity of the Roman state, for Octavian was not liked in Italy and had difficulty in maintaining his authority there.

PREPARATIONS FOR BATTLE

Accordingly, about the end of August 31 B.C., Antony resolved to retire from Actium and hold only Asia, Syria, and Egypt, and possibly Greece. It was not advisable to make the primary move by the army, for on its leaving the gulf the fleet would be unprotected and lost. . . .

So Antony resolved to take his fleet to sea. If, contrary to his expectation, he should defeat Agrippa, he might hope to gain Italy, but if otherwise he would withdraw into Syria and Egypt with his fleet and all the soldiers on board and have the army follow as it could.

It was the best that could be done short of surrender, but the discussion and decision caused great controversy in the camp. The Romans accused Cleopatra of every villainy and even of attempting to poison her husband. Antony began to suspect her and insisted on her tasting the dishes served to him. To show the futility of such precautions, at the next banquet she put a chaplet on his head and later invited him to cast the flowers in his goblet and drink her health. As he was about to raise his glass, she stopped him and, calling a condemned slave, she told him to drink the cup. As he did so he fell dead. The Queen turned to Antony and said "you see how easy it would be for me to poison you, but I cannot do without you," and so she persuaded him that his suspicions were false and that she was loyal. Under such circumstances did Antony make up his mind to retreat and make a new start, determined to rule in the East at least, if not in Rome. The date of departure was set for August 29.

In preparation for battle, Antony's advanced camp on the north shore was abandoned. The ships lacked rowers and Antony is alleged to have destroyed many so that the rest might have less inadequate complements, and among these he retained 60 Egyptian ships upon which he placed his treasure, i.e., the army funds, of which most must have been Cleopatra's gift. Contrary to custom before battle, Antony placed the ships' sails on board for use on the long voyage to Egypt, but under the pretext that they would serve to pursue the enemy. As for the total number of ships which went out to battle, we have varying accounts. We may believe that Antony had under 200 vessels, among which the 60 Egyptians made a single squadron under Cleopatra. Antony embarked 20,000 legionaries and 2,000 archers. The number of men embarked corresponds well to about 170 to 180 large ships. The seamen and rowers may have numbered 40,000 to 45,000 men (very few).

The vessels were high and large compared to their adversaries. . . . The others were intermediate in size. They carried high towers of several stories bearing heavy mechanical artillery and the archers. They relied on grappling irons and a boarders' fight.

The knowledge that Antony had little hope of seizing Italy encouraged desertions of noble Romans and others. Amyntas, King of Galatia, and Dellius, a typical Roman turncoat, now went over to Octavian and brought positive news of Antony's change of policy and his intention of fighting at sea. On hearing of it Octavian was at first inclined to let him go and then chase him, but Agrippa convinced him this should not happen. Dio says Agrippa used the tactical argument that the enemy was taking his sails and could not be overtaken, but the political argument is far stronger that the long civil war called for immediate settlement and that Octavian could not seem to wish to postpone it. So both sides prepared for a naval battle.

Many of Agrippa's smaller ships had probably fought at [the prior naval battle of] Naulochus, where they had won against still smaller ships. Now they had to win against ships bigger than themselves and Agrippa prepared to turn the scale by the provision of new devices for throwing fire. I do not mean to say that fire-throwing was previously unknown . . . but Romans had been accustomed to win at sea against inferior soldiers by the exertions of hard-fighting legionaries on the ships' decks. Here would be legionaries on both sides and Agrippa was preparing a tactical surprise. Contrary to Roman practice, he was going to make a principal effort against ship structure instead of relying chiefly on infantry.

On his fleet of 260 or more ships Agrippa embarked, according to Orosius, 8.5 legions, probably about 30,000 men. . . . In addition there were probably a few archers and slingers, perhaps as many as 2,000 or 3,000. Roughly, we may believe that Agrippa had about one-half more soldiers on shipboard than Antony and perhaps over a half more ships, with 50,000 to 55,000 rowers and seamen. The big ships of Antony were handicapped not only by a shortage of rowers, but also by their heavy loading, for they were equipped for a cruise while those of Agrippa were stripped light for battle. On the other hand, the greater height of Antony's ships and heavy structure was an advantage should Agrippa's ships close with them. . . .

Previous to battle the usual allocutions [battle speeches] were made on both sides, on this occasion with many political appeals. Antony praised his men and himself and abused Octavian, who had, he said, behaved badly towards him and would ill-treat the soldiers after victory. He admitted the superiority of the western army (his own had deteriorated during the summer), but magnified the strength of his ships and dwelt on their great size and the thickness of their sides to resist ramming by their light opponents. He showed that victory at sea would turn the tables and ruin the enemy through loss of his line of supply. Octavian also talked politics and made the point of Antony's subjection to the Egyptian siren who hoped to rule Romans. He went on to say that no ship ever hurt anybody by itself and that the size and thick timbers of the enemy would not avail against his soldiers' valor. The hostile ships, he said, could neither attack frontally nor by envelopment. If they were to remain motionless they would be subject to the ram and the fire-throwing engines and, if they moved, they were slow, either for attack or pursuit.

THE FINAL SHOWDOWN

Antony was ready to go out on the appointed day, August 29, but the weather was unfavorable until the morning of September 2, when it was calm and both fleets embarked their crews and shoved off from the shore.

As Octavian with his staff was going down to the beach before dawn he met an ass-driver who saluted him. Octavian fell into conversation and asked his name. He answered "my name is Eutychus (Good Fortune) and that of my ass is Nicon (Victory)." Whereupon all went on their way rejoicing at the omen, which was doubtless communicated to the whole fleet. After the battle, Octavian put up a bronze statue of the ass and his driver on the spot where he had met them. The story is illustrative of the thought of the time, but more-over it is militarily important if we take the meeting as pre-arranged and as an effective bit of propaganda by an efficient staff to increase the battle ardor of the combatants.

Although Antony contemplated a withdrawal under sail from Actium, if unsuccessful, the customary sea breeze was not due until the afternoon and it was preferable to issue from the narrow strait under oars. Probably both sides moved about dawn. The western fleet would easily be the first in position. It drew up opposite the entrance where it waited, divided into three squadrons. Although Agrippa was in command, Octavian put himself in the place of honor with the right squadron under M. Lurius. Arruntius took the center and Agrippa chose the left squadron in which he might expect to face Antony, the hostile commander in chief. The leading friends of Octavian took station in dispatch boats to move along the line carrying orders and information and encouraging the fight. After issuing from the strait, the eastern fleet formed in four squadrons parallel to the shore and rather close to it. Antony went with the right which was under Publicola. Sosius had the left, and M. Insteius and M. Octavius . . . were in the center, all three making the front line. The fourth squadron was the Egyptian of 60 ships under Cleopatra which took position in the rear as reserve, and to hold position without effort, it seems to have dropped anchors under foot. Antony moved about in a dispatch boat and ordered his vessels to hold their stations and receive the attack. Agrippa formed line opposite and remained inactive at a distance of about 1,600 yards. We may suppose the average interval from ship to ship to have been from 40 to 45 yards. Antony's line of about 110 to 120 larger ships would then have been about 5,000 yards long. Agrippa, with not less than 260 smaller ships would have had a longer line even if each division kept some vessels in a rear line as a reserve. His front must have been at least 8,000 yards long. The fleets remained motionless for a time after they had faced each other.

About noon Antony's left wing opened the battle by advancing, as Agrippa's inaction required him to do. . . . The battle was now on, and Antony's ships had increased their intervals from one another to avoid envelopment, but in so doing they fell into another difficulty. Owing to their superior mobility, the western ships were now able to combine three or four at once against single adversaries. Owing to the sluggishness of Antony's vessels and the comparatively short range of missile weapons, many of them lacked enemies within effective range.

Soon after the fight opened, say at one o'clock, the usual fresh afternoon sea breeze sprang up and a little later, while the outcome was not yet decided, Cleopatra's squadron in the rear made sail, charged through the center of both lines and made off. Antony put himself in a light craft and followed her while the action still continued. His departure had no immediate effect; a few ships only were able to follow him as they should have done. These threw overboard towers and equipments to lighten ship and made sail.

For the remainder, the battle increased in intensity. Antony's ships were higher and used their artillery and hand missiles. By a quick advance, the ships of Agrippa attacked with the ram and swept away oars and rudders. If a vessel sank an opponent, good. But if not, she backed off. Agrippa's ships avoided delay at long range, nor did they remain in contact for a boarders' fight after they had made their ram stroke. The efforts of the eastern ships to grapple seem to have met little success.

At first, Agrippa was anxious to make prizes to secure any money on board, but in the end, to decide the event, he brought into use the incendiary weapons which he had previously held in reserve. Many of Agrippa's ships must by now have worked in rear of the hostile line. As Dio Cassius says,

> the assailants coming from many sides shot blazing missiles and with engines threw pots of flaming charcoal and pitch. The defendants tried to ward off these fiery projectiles and when one lodged it was quenched with drinking water. When that was gone, they dipped up sea water, but as their buckets were small and few and half-filled they were not always successful. Then they smothered the fires with their mantles and even with corpses. They hacked off burning parts of the ships and tried to grapple hostile ships to escape into them. Many were burned alive or jumped overboard or killed each other to avoid the flames.

With soldiers of the same nation, accustomed to the same method of fighting and with the same fleet organization, it was the unexpected weapon, the flames, which decided the victory in Agrippa's favor. By four in the afternoon the battle was finished and the remains of Antony's fleet escaped and entered the harbor before a fresh breeze.

Plutarch alleges that Agrippa captured 300 ships, but it may be this number refers to the losses of the entire campaign. . . . That many ships re-entered port is shown by the fact that Agrippa and his fleet anchored for the night on the scene of the battle to close the exit.

CLEOPATRA'S PART IN THE BATTLE

The world has always been attracted by the romance of the two lovers as it affected world history in this memorable battle which secured the unity of the Roman state for over three centuries. We need not believe contemporary gossip nor the assertion of the ancient historian (Dio Cassius) as to Cleopatra that "true to her nature as a woman and an Egyptian, tortured by suspense and fearful of either outcome, she turned to flight herself and raised the signal for others." The same authorities who condemn her conduct in the battle tell us that as a sovereign she was as capable as a man. It is certain that it was politically important to Octavian both before and after the battle to vilify her as the wicked foreigner who had misled and betrayed the noble Antony. After the war the abuse of Cleopatra was something in which the survivors on both sides could cheerfully agree. . . .

Let us believe then that she and her chief pilot used her squadron as Antony planned to use it . . . [as] a last bid for victory. Under oars, her heavy ships could not move fast enough to ram their lively opponents, but charging under sail with a free wind every Egyptian had one chance to sink an enemy. The charge did not turn the scale of battle and once down to leeward the squadron could not re-engage. For it, the battle was over and Cleopatra went on to Egypt according to plan. Unfortunately, for her and Antony, it did not prove possible for the ships in the main line of battle, violently attacked by fire and missiles, to break off the action and follow Antony as they should have done.

I cannot believe . . . that the battle was purely a measure for escape. Like every good commander, Antony was ready for the worst while hoping for the best. If, contrary to his expectations, his fleet should get the better of the enemy, the relative position of the two opponents as it had existed all summer would be reversed, and he would enter Rome, as he told his soldiers. But to provide for failure, he gave orders that in that case ships were not to return to port where starvation awaited them. He preferred to escape with as many soldiers as he could and make a new stand in Egypt with the eleven legions he had there and in Africa and Syria, for the political indications in Rome were such it was very possible that Octavian would not dare to attempt to disturb him in the East.

THE PURSUIT AND SUBSEQUENT OUTCOME

The pursuit of the escaping Egyptians was slight and short, for Agrippa's ships were without sails. After leaving the battle in his light craft, Antony was taken up in Cleopatra's ship, but he did not meet her. Instead, he went to the bow of the ship where he sat in despair for three days (for his fleet had not followed him), until they reached Taenarum (200 miles), in spite of the messages Cleopatra sent him by her women. There some ships and friends joined him from Actium and he resumed relations with his wife. He learned there, also, that his fleet was lost, but that [his officer] Canidius still held the army intact. He sent orders to lead it through Macedonia into Asia.

In the meantime, the day after the battle, Octavian summoned Canidius to surrender. The latter refused, but when it became apparent that Antony had gone off, desertions of Roman leaders and eastern princes began again. Canidius himself slipped away by night to join Antony in Egypt, and a week after the battle the army broke up. A part surrendered to Octavian and some escaped to their homes.

The news of the battle at sea and of Antony's flight with the Egyptian woman and the surrender of the army completely destroyed Antony's prestige both in Rome and elsewhere, turning public opinion strongly and seemingly most unexpectedly in Octavian's favor, so making it possible for him to pursue the fugitives to the center of their power in Egypt. Octavian easily occupied Greece and found Asia Minor free of troops. These provinces fell to him without difficulty, and after returning to Italy to settle some disturbances during the winter of 31–30, his departure for Asia in the spring of 30 met with general approval, since the financial basis of eastern opposition to the rule of Rome lay in Egypt and its conquest would end the civil war.

As for Antony and Cleopatra, they landed in Egypt and the Queen made the most gallant efforts to meet the coming attack. As Octavian drew near from Syria, she opened negotiations with him, apparently in the hope that before hostilities were renewed she might be able to arrange terms permitting her to hold her throne as a client of Rome, but she met with no success. At last Octavian arrived before Alexandria.

Cleopatra and Antony Take Their Own Lives

Plutarch

Plutarch was a Romanized first-century Greek who wrote a now famous and widely read series of biographies of noted Greeks and Romans. The following excerpt from his *Life of Antony* covers events in Egypt shortly after Octavian arrived in 30 B.C. to finish off his rivals, whom he had defeated at Actium the year before. First, Antony's troops deserted him. Then he committed suicide, after which Octavian's men captured Cleopatra. Plutarch provides much illuminating information about the talks and dealings between Octavian and Cleopatra and then proceeds to describe how she deceived him into thinking she wanted to live but instead took her own life. Also included in the narration are details about Antony's and Cleopatra's burials.

As soon as it was light, Antony posted his infantry on the hills in front of the city and watched his ships as they put out and advanced against the enemy. Then, as he still believed that his fleet might carry the day, he stood and waited for the issue of the battle at sea. But his crews, as soon as they drew near the enemy, raised their oars in salute, and, when their greeting was returned, they went over to Octavius [Octavian] as one man, and so the two fleets, now combined into one, changed their course and headed straight for the city. No sooner had Antony witnessed this than he found himself abandoned by the cavalry, which likewise deserted to the enemy, and finally when his infantry was routed he retreated into the city, crying out in his rage that Cleopatra had betrayed him to the very men he was fighting for her sake. Then the queen, in terror at his fury and despair, fled to her mon-

Excerpted from *Makers of Rome: Nine Lives by Plutarch*, translated by Ian Scott-Kilvert. Copyright ©1965 by Ian Scott-Kilvert. Reprinted by permission of Penguin Books Ltd.

ument, let down the hanging doors which were strengthened with bars and bolts, and sent messengers to tell Antony that she was dead. Never doubting the message, he said to himself, 'Why delay any longer, Antony? Fate has taken away the one excuse which could still make you desire to live,' and went into his room. There, as he unbuckled his armour and laid the pieces aside, he exclaimed, 'O, Cleopatra, it does not hurt me to lose you, for I shall soon be with you, but I am ashamed that an Imperator [high-ranking military commander] such as I have been should prove in the end to have less courage than a woman.'

ANTONY'S LAST MOMENTS

Now Antony had a faithful servant, whose name was Eros. He had long ago made this man swear to kill him if the need arose, and he now ordered him to carry out his promise. Eros drew his sword and raised it as if he were about to strike his master, but suddenly turned away and killed himself. As he fell at his master's feet, Antony cried out, 'That was well done, Eros. You have shown me what I must do, even if you had not the heart to strike the blow yourself.' Then he stabbed himself with his own sword through the belly and fell upon the bed. But the wound did not kill him quickly. Presently, as he lay prostrate, the bleeding stopped and he came to himself and implored the bystanders to put him out of his pain. But they ran out of the room and left him writhing in agony and crying for help, until Cleopatra's secretary, Diomedes, arrived with orders from the queen to bring him to the monument.

When he understood that Cleopatra was still alive, Antony eagerly ordered his slaves to lift him up, and they carried him in their arms to the doors of the tomb. Even then Cleopatra would not allow the doors to be opened, but she showed herself at a window and let down cords and ropes to the ground. The slaves fastened Antony to these and the queen pulled him up with the help of her two waiting women, who were the only companions she had allowed to enter the monument with her. Those who were present say that there was never a more pitiable sight than the spectacle of Antony, covered with blood, struggling in his death agonies and stretching out his hands towards Cleopatra as he swung helplessly in the air. The task was almost beyond a woman's strength, and it was only with great difficulty that

Cleopatra, clinging with both hands to the rope and with the muscles of her face distorted by the strain, was able to haul him up, while those on the ground encouraged her with their cries and shared her agony. When she had got him up and laid him upon a bed, she tore her dress and spread it over him, beat and lacerated her breasts, and smeared her face with the blood from his wounds. She called him her lord and husband and emperor, and almost forgot her own misfortunes in her pity for his. Antony calmed her lamentations and called for a cup of wine, either because he was thirsty or because he hoped it might hasten his death. When he had drunk it, he urged her to think of her own safety, if she could do this without dishonour, and told her that of all Caesar's [Octavian's] associates she would do best to put her trust in Proculeius. Last of all, he begged her not to grieve over this wretched change in his fortunes, but to count him happy for the glories he had won and to remember that he had attained the greatest fame and power of any man in the world, so that now it was no dishonour to die a Roman, conquered only by a Roman.

Cleopatra clings to Antony, who lies dying, in this modern rendering of the famous lovers. Following his suicide, she, too, took her own life, bringing a crucial chapter of Mediterranean history to a dramatic close.

CLEOPATRA'S CAPTURE

The breath was scarcely out of his body when Proculeius arrived from Octavius Caesar. After Antony had stabbed himself and while he was being carried to Cleopatra, one of his bodyguards named Dercetaeus snatched up Antony's sword, hid it, and slipped out of the palace. Then he ran to Octavius and was the first to bring him the news of Antony's death, while at the same time he showed him the sword covered with blood. When Octavius heard what had happened, he retired into his tent and wept, for Antony was not only related to him by marriage, but had been his colleague in office and his partner in many great enterprises and battles. Then he brought out the letters they had exchanged, and calling in his friends, he read them aloud to let them hear in what moderate and conciliatory terms he had written, and how contemptuously Antony had always replied. After this he dispatched Proculeius with orders to make every possible effort to capture Cleopatra alive, for he was afraid, as I have already mentioned, that the queen would set fire to her treasure, and he also felt that her presence would greatly enhance the splendour of his triumphal procession in Rome. Cleopatra refused to surrender herself into Proculeius's hands, but she consented to talk to him when he came to the monument and stood outside one of the doors at the ground level. This door was strongly secured with bolts and bars, but it was possible to speak through it. There they held a parley in which Cleopatra asked that her children should be allowed to succeed to her kingdom, while Proculeius urged her to take courage and trust Octavius Caesar in everything.

Meanwhile, Proculeius took careful note of the monument, and, when he had made his report to Octavius Caesar, [a Roman officer named] Gallus was sent to hold a further interview with the queen. Gallus walked up to the door and engaged Cleopatra in conversation, while Proculeius fixed a scaling ladder against the monument and entered by the window through which the women had lifted Antony. Then he ran down with two servants to the door where Cleopatra was standing with her attention fixed on Gallus. One of the waiting women caught sight of him and screamed aloud, 'Unhappy Cleopatra, you are caught!' In the same instant the queen turned, saw Proculeius, and tried to stab herself, for she carried in her girdle a dagger of the kind which robbers wear. But Proculeius rushed up, flung both his arms around her, and said, 'Cleopatra, you do yourself and Caesar a great injustice. Do not refuse him this opportunity to show his generosity towards you. He is the gentlest of commanders, but you are acting as if he were a treacherous and implacable enemy.' At the same time he snatched away the weapon and shook out her dress to see whether she had hidden any poison. Octavius Caesar also sent one of his freedmen named Epaphroditus, whose orders were to allow her every concession which might comfort or give her pleasure, but to take the strictest precautions to keep her alive.

OCTAVIAN ARRIVES IN ALEXANDRIA

Meanwhile, Octavius Caesar made his entry into Alexandria with Areius the philosopher at his side. He gave him his right hand and kept up a conversation with him, so as to increase Areius's importance in the eyes of the Alexandrians and make him respected on account of this signal honour which he was being shown by Caesar. When he entered the public gymnasium and mounted a tribunal which had been erected there, the people were beside themselves with fear and fell on their faces before him. But Octavius told them to rise and assured them that he had no intention of holding their city to blame, first because it had been founded by Alexander, secondly because he himself admired its beauty and spaciousness, and lastly because of his regard for Areius. This was a special mark of honour which he conferred upon Areius, and at his request Octavius also granted a number of individual pardons. . . .

As for Antony's children, Antyllus, his son by Fulvia, was betrayed by his tutor Theodorus and executed. When the soldiers beheaded him, the tutor contrived to steal a precious stone which the boy wore around his neck, and sewed it into his belt, but although he denied the theft, he was found guilty and crucified. Cleopatra's children and their servants were kept under guard, but otherwise they were generously treated. However, Caesarion, who was supposed to be Cleopatra's son by Julius Caesar, was sent away by his mother with a large sum of money to travel to India by way of Ethiopia. Before long his tutor Rhodon, a man of the same type as Theodorus, talked him into believing that Octavius would make him king of Egypt and persuaded him to return. It is said that while Octavius was making up his mind how to treat him, Areius . . . remarked to him,

It is bad to have too many Caesars. . . .

After Cleopatra's death Octavius acted on his advice and had Caesarion executed. But as for Antony, although a number of kings and generals petitioned Octavius to allow them to perform the last rites for him, he would not take the body away from Cleopatra, and she buried it with her own hands and gave it a funeral of royal splendour and magnificence, for which she was granted all the resources she needed. Because of the grief and pain she had suffered—for her breasts were inflamed and lacerated from the blows she had given them—she gladly seized upon her illness as a pretext to refuse food and so release herself without further interference from the burden of living. One of her trusted attendants was a physician named Olympus to whom she confided her true intentions: it was on his advice and help that she relied to bring about her death, and he confirms the fact in a history of these events which he has published. Meanwhile, Octavius Caesar had become suspicious and began to frighten her by uttering threats about the fate of her children. By applying these pressures in much the same way as a general uses siege-engines, he quickly undermined her resistance, so that she gave up her body to be treated and nourished as he desired.

THE QUEEN DECEIVES OCTAVIUS

A few days later Octavius paid a visit to talk to Cleopatra and try to reassure her. She had abandoned her luxurious style of living, and was lying on a pallet bed dressed only in a tunic, but, as he entered, she sprang up and threw herself at his feet. Her hair was unkempt and her expression wild, while her eyes were sunken and her voice trembled uncontrollably: her breasts bore the marks of the cruel blows she had inflicted on herself, and in a word her body seemed to have suffered no less anguish than her spirit. And yet her charm and a certain reckless confidence in her beauty were still by no means extinguished, and despite her sorry appearance they shone forth from within and revealed themselves in the play of her features. At any rate after Octavius had urged her to lie down and seated himself close to her, she tried at first to justify her part in the war, making out that her actions had been forced upon her by necessity and through her fear of Antony. But as Octavius contradicted her on every point and demolished her excuses, she quickly changed her manner and began to appeal to his pity with prayers and entreaties, as if she still clung above all else to the hope of saving her life. Finally, she handed to him a paper, which was supposed to be a complete inventory of her treasures, but when Seleucus, one of her stewards, made it clear that she was concealing and making away with a number of her possessions, she leaped to her feet, seized him by the hair, and pummelled his face. Octavius smiled at this episode and at last restrained her, whereupon she said, 'But is it not outrageous, Caesar, when you do me the honour to come and speak to me in my wretched condition, that I should be accused by my own servants of putting aside a few women's trinkets like these? They were not meant for my poor self, you may be sure, but simply to have some little present by me for Octavia and your wife, Livia, so that I could appeal to them to make you kinder and more merciful.' Octavius was pleased at this speech, because it convinced him that Cleopatra still wished to live. He told her that she could settle any details of this kind as she pleased, but that in most important matters he would treat her more generously than she could possibly expect. Then he took his leave, feeling confident that he had deceived the queen, but the truth was that she had deceived him.

One of the members of Octavius's staff was a young aristocrat named Cornelius Dolabella. He was by no means insensible to Cleopatra's charms, and now when she pressed him, he contrived to warn her secretly that Octavius was planning to march through Syria with his army, and had decided that she and her children were to be sent away within three days. When the queen heard this, her first action was to beg Octavius to allow her to pour her last libations [liquid sacrifices] for Antony, and when this request was granted, she had herself carried to the tomb. She was accompanied by the women who usually attended her, and there at the tomb she clasped the urn which contained his ashes and said, 'My beloved Antony, it is only a little while ago that I buried you with these hands. Then they were free, but now, when I come to pour libations for you, I am a prisoner, guarded so that I shall not disfigure this body of mine by beating it or even by weeping. It has become a slave's body, and they watch over it only to make me adorn their triumph over you. But after this you must expect no more honours or libations; these are the last that Cleopatra the captive can bring you. For, although in our lives nothing could part us, it seems that death will force us to change places. You, the Roman, have found a grave in Egypt, and I, unhappy woman, will receive just enough of your country to give me room to lie in Italy. But if there is any help or power in the gods of Rome, for mine have betrayed us, do not abandon your wife while she lives, and do not let me be led in triumph to your shame. Hide me and let me be buried here with you, for I know now that the thousand griefs I have suffered are as nothing beside the few days that I have lived without you.'

HER NOBLE SPIRIT

So Cleopatra mourned Antony, and she crowned his urn with a garland and kissed it. Then she ordered a bath to be made ready, and, when she had come from the bath, she lay down and was served with an exquisite meal. Presently, there arrived an Egyptian peasant carrying a basket, and when the guards asked him what was in it, he stripped away the leaves at the top and showed them that it was full of figs. The guards were astonished at the size and beauty of the figs, whereupon the man smiled and invited them to take some, and in this way their suspicions were lulled and they allowed him to bring in his fruit to the queen. When Cleopatra had dined, she took a tablet on which she had already written and put her seal, and sent this to Octavius Caesar. Soon afterwards she dismissed all her attendants except for two faithful waiting women, and closed the doors of the monument.

Octavius Caesar opened the tablet, and as soon as he read Cleopatra's prayers and entreaties that she should be buried with Antony, he immediately guessed her intention. His first thought was to go himself to save her life, but he restrained this impulse and sent messengers to hurry to the queen and discover what had happened. But the tragedy had moved too swiftly for them. The messengers rushed to the monument and found the guards still unaware that anything was amiss, but when they opened the doors, they found Cleopatra lying dead upon a golden couch dressed in her royal robes. Of her two women, Iras lay dying at her feet, while Charmian, already tottering and scarcely able to hold up her head, was arranging the crown which encircled her mistress's brow. Then one of the guards cried out angrily, 'Charmian, is this well done?' and she answered, 'It is well done, and fitting for a princess descended of so many royal kings,' and, as she uttered the words, she fell dead by the side of the couch.

According to one account, the asp [the poisonous snake she supposedly allowed to bite her] was carried in to her with the figs and lay hidden under the leaves in the basket, for Cleopatra had given orders that the snake should settle on her without her being aware of it. But when she picked up some of the figs, she caught sight of it, so the story goes, and said, 'So here it is,' and, baring her arm, she held it out to be bitten. Others say that it was carefully shut up in a pitcher and that Cleopatra provoked it by pricking it with a golden spindle, until it sprang out and fastened itself upon her arm. But the real truth nobody knows, for there is another story that she carried poison about with her in a hollow comb, which she kept hidden in her hair, and yet no inflammation nor any other symptom of poison broke out upon her body. And indeed the asp was never discovered inside the monument, although some marks which might have been its trail are said to have been noticed on the beach on that side where the windows of the chamber looked out towards the sea. Some people also say that two faint, barely visible punctures were found on Cleopatra's arm, and Octavius Caesar himself seems to have believed this, for when he celebrated his triumph he had a figure of Cleopatra with the asp clinging to her carried in the procession. These are the various accounts of what took place.

Octavius Caesar was vexed at Cleopatra's death, and yet he could not but admire the nobility of her spirit, and he gave orders that she should be buried with royal splendour and magnificence, and her body laid beside Antony's, while her waiting women also received an honourable funeral. When Cleopatra died she was thirty-nine years of age, she had reigned as queen for twenty-two of these, and been Antony's partner in his empire for more than fourteen. [Plutarch is in error here. Cleopatra and Antony were allies for only ten years, about three of which they spent apart.] Antony was fifty-six according to some accounts, fifty-three according to others. All his statues were torn down, but those of Cleopatra were allowed to stand, because Archibius, one of her friends, gave Octavius Caesar two thousand talents to save them from the fate of Antony's.

CHAPTER 3

Depictions of Cleopatra in Plays, Novels, and Movies

People Who Made History
Cleopatra

Shakespeare Dramatizes Plutarch's Narrative of Cleopatra

William Shakespeare

About the year 1607, the great English playwright William Shakespeare first presented his tragedy *Antony and Cleopatra*. Later viewed as one of his finest works, the play relies heavily on Plutarch's *Life of Antony* for the basic characters and plot. However, Shakespeare managed to infuse an old story with a new life and spirit better suited to the dramatic stage. Plutarch had attempted to tell, in a fairly straightforward manner, the tragic story of two famous people who were unable to realize their lofty ambitions; whereas Shakespeare elevated Antony and Cleopatra to larger-than-life status. His Cleopatra, for example, is on the one hand selfish, greedy, and devious. Yet she is also able to rise to the occasion and display courage, loyalty, and even nobility. The following excerpt from Shakespeare's version is her death scene and its follow-up, including several elements from Plutarch's version, among them the poisonous snake, Octavian's order to bury her with Antony, and even the exchange between the guard and Charmian.

[Enter Iras with a robe, crown, etc.]

Cleopatra. Give me my robe, put on my crown, I have
    Immortal longings in me. Now no more
    The juice of Egypt's grape shall moist this lip.
    Yare [nimbly], yare, good Iras; quick. Methinks I hear
    Antony call: I see him rouse himself
    To praise my noble act. I hear him mock
    The luck of Caesar, which the gods give men

Excerpted from *Antony and Cleopatra*, by William Shakespeare, act V, scene ii, 1623.

To excuse their after wrath. Husband, I come:
Now to that name my courage prove my title!
I am fire, and air [the lighter of the four elements, associated
with immortality]; my other elements [water and earth]
I give to baser life. So, have you done?
Come then, and take the last warmth of my lips.
Farewell, kind Charmian, Iras, long farewell.
                    [Kisses them. Iras falls and dies.]
Have I the aspic [asp, a poisonous snake] in my lips? Dost
fall?
If thou and nature can so gently part,
The stroke of death is as a lover's pinch,
Which hurts, and is desired. Dost thou lie still?
If thus thou vanishest, thou tell'st the world
It is not worth leave-taking.
Charmian. Dissolve, thick cloud, and rain, that I may say
The gods themselves do weep.
Cleopatra. This proves me base:
If she first meet the curlèd Antony,
He'll make demand of her, and spend that kiss
Which is my heaven to have. Come, thou mortal wretch,
            [To an asp, which she applies to her breast.]
With thy sharp teeth this knot intrinsicate [intricate]
Of life at once untie. Poor venomous fool,
Be angry, and dispatch [be quick]. O, couldst thou speak,
That I might hear thee call great Caesar ass
Unpolicied! [Outwitted!]
Charmian. O Eastern star!
Cleopatra. Peace, peace!
Dost thou not see my baby at my breast,
That sucks the nurse asleep?
Charmian. O, break! O, break!
Cleopatra. As sweet as balm, as soft as air, as gentle—
O Antony! Nay, I will take thee too:
                    [Applies another asp to her arm.]
What should I stay—

                                                    Dies.

Charmian. In this wild world? So, fare thee well.
Now boast thee, death, in thy possession lies
A lass unparalleled. Downy windows, close;
And golden Phoebus never be beheld
Of eyes again so royal! Your crown's awry;
I'll mend it, and then play—

Enter the Guard, rustling in.

1. Guardsman. Where's the Queen?

Charmian. Speak softly, wake her not.

1. [Guardsman]. Caesar hath sent—

Charmian. Too slow a messenger.

[Applies an asp.]

O, come apace, dispatch, I partly feel thee.

1. [Guardsman]. Approach, ho! All's not well: Caesar's beguiled [tricked].

2. [Guardsman]. There's Dolabella sent from Caesar. Call him.

1. [Guardsman]. What work is here! Charmian, is this well done?

Charmian. It is well done, and fitting for a princess
   Descended of so many royal kings.
   Ah, soldier!   *Charmian dies.*

Enter Dolabella.

Dolabella. How goes it here?

2. Guardsman. All dead.

Dolabella. Caesar, thy thoughts
   Touch their effects [become fulfilled] in this; thyself art coming
   To see performed the dreaded act which thou
   So sought'st to hinder.

Enter Caesar [Octavian] *and all his Train, marching.*

All. A way there, a way for Caesar!

Dolabella. O sir, you are too sure an augurer:
   [The deed] that you did fear is done.

Caesar. Bravest at the last,
   She levelled at [guessed] our purposes, and being royal,
   Took her own way. The manner of their deaths?
   I do not see them bleed.

Dolabella. Who was last with them?

1. Guardsman. A simple countryman, that brought her figs.
   This was his basket.

Caesar. Poisoned, then.

1. Guardsman. O Caesar,
   This Charmian lived but now, she stood and spake;
   I found her trimming up the diadem
   On her dead mistress; tremblingly she stood,

And on the sudden dropped.

Caesar. O noble weakness!
    If they had swallowed poison, 'twould appear
    By external swelling; but she looks like sleep,
    As she would catch another Antony
    In her strong toil [net] of grace.

Dolabella. Here on her breast
    There is a vent [discharge] of blood, and something blown [swollen];
    The like is on her arm.

1. Guardsman. This is an aspic's trail, and these fig leaves
    Have slime upon them, such as th' aspic leaves
    Upon the caves of Nile.

Caesar. Most probable
    That so she died: for her physician tells me
    She hath pursued conclusions [experiments] infinite
    Of easy ways to die. Take up her bed,
    And bear her women from the monument.
    She shall be buried by her Antony.
    No grave upon the earth shall clip [clasp] in it
    A pair so famous. High events as these
    Strike [touch] those that make them; and their story is
    No less in pity than his glory which
    Brought them to be lamented. Our army shall
    In solemn show attend this funeral,
    And then to Rome. Come, Dolabella, see
    High order in this great solemnity.

                                    Exeunt omnes [everyone exits].

Cleopatra and Antony Sacrifice Everything for Their Love

John Dryden

The great English writer John Dryden (1631–1700) wrote his acknowledged masterpiece, *All for Love*, in 1677. Like Shakespeare's *Antony and Cleopatra*, Dryden's play deals with the relationship between the legendary Egyptian queen and her headstrong Roman lover/ally, Antony. But Dryden's version differs significantly from Shakespeare's. First, Shakespeare covered a period of some eleven years and set his scenes all over the Roman world, from Italy to Egypt. By contrast, the whole of Dryden's play takes place in the Egyptian capital on a single day—the last day of Antony's life. Also, Dryden's Cleopatra and Antony are less grand in stature than Shakespeare's and speak more like ordinary people who have become hopelessly entangled in dire circumstances. In the following excerpt from *All for Love,* the lovers confront each other, while Antony's friend and military officer, Ventidius, and Cleopatra's attendant, Alexas, stand by. At first, encouraged by Ventidius, who feels Cleopatra has ruined his friend's life, Antony expresses his anger, bitterness, and regret that she has led him into such a fallen state. But Cleopatra soon brings Antony around, reminding him that the one constant throughout her relationship had been their deep love for each other; and for her, that love has not wavered. In the end, the lovers exit arm-in-arm, to face their fate; and later, Dryden has them die together (rather than separately, as in Plutarch's and Shakespeare's versions).

Excerpted from *All for Love; or, The World Well Lost*, by John Dryden, 1677.

(*Enter Cleopatra, Charmion, and Iras. The queen looks at Antony coyly.*)

ANTONY: (*without feeling*) Well, madam, we are met.

CLEOPATRA: Is this a meeting?
Then, we must part?

ANTONY: We must.

CLEOPATRA: Who says we must?

ANTONY: Our own hard fates.

CLEOPATRA: We make those fates ourselves.

ANTONY: Yes, we have made them; we have loved each other,
Into our mutual ruin.

CLEOPATRA: (*with the suppressed fury of a woman scorned*)
The gods have seen my joys with envious eyes;
I have no friends in heaven; and all the world,
As 'twere the business of mankind to part us,
Is armed against my love: even you yourself
Join with the rest; you, you are armed against me.

ANTONY: (*coldly*) I will be justified in all I do
To late posterity, and therefore hear me.
If I mix a lie
With any truth, reproach me freely with it;
Else, favour me with silence.

CLEOPATRA: You command me,
And I am dumb.

VENTIDIUS: I like this well; he shows authority.

ANTONY: That I derive my ruin
From you alone—

CLEOPATRA: O heavens! I ruin you!

ANTONY: You promised me your silence, and you break it
Ere I have scarce begun.

CLEOPATRA: Well, I obey you.

(*He folds his arms and turns away from Cleopatra.*)

ANTONY: When I beheld you first, it was in Egypt.
Ere Cæsar saw your eyes, you gave me love,
And were too young to know it; that I settled
Your father in his throne, was for your sake;
I left the acknowledgment for time to ripen.
Cæsar stept in, and, with a greedy hand,
Plucked the green fruit, ere the first blush of red,
Yet cleaving to the bough. He was my lord,
And was, beside, too great for me to rival;
But, I deserved you first, though he enjoyed you.
When, after, I beheld you in Cilicia [at their meeting at Tarsus

in 41 B.C.],
An enemy to Rome, I pardoned you.
    CLEOPATRA: I cleared myself—
    ANTONY: (*turning to look at her*)
Again you break your promise.
I loved you still, and took your weak excuses,
Took you into my bosom, stained by Cæsar,
And not half mine: I went to Egypt with you,
And hid me from the business of the world,
Shut out inquiring nations from my sight,
To give whole years to you.
    VENTIDIUS: (*aside*)
Yes, to your shame be't spoken.
    ANTONY: (*berating himself and her*)
How I loved.
Witness, ye days and nights, and all ye hours,
That danced away with down upon your feet,
As all your business were to count my passion!
One day passed by, and nothing saw but love;
Another came, and still 'twas only love:
The suns were wearied out with looking on,
And I untired with loving.
I saw you every day, and all the day;
And every day was still but as the first,
So eager was I still to see you more.
    VENTIDIUS: 'Tis all too true.
    ANTONY: Fulvia, my wife, grew jealous
(As she indeed had reason), raised a war
In Italy, to call me back.
    VENTIDIUS: But yet
You went not.
    ANTONY: While within your arms I lay,
The world fell mouldering from my hands each hour,
And left me scarce a grasp—I thank your love for't.
    VENTIDIUS: Well pushed: that last was home [i.e., made a
direct and strong impression on her].
    CLEOPATRA: Yet may I speak?
    ANTONY: (*browbeating her*)
If I have urged a falsehood, yes; else, not.
Your silence says, I have not. Fulvia died
(Pardon, you gods, with my unkindness died);
To set the world at peace, I took Octavia,
This Cæsar's sister; in her pride of youth,

And flower of beauty, did I wed that lady,
Whom blushing I must praise, because I left her.
You called; my love obeyed the fatal summons:
This raised the Roman arms; the cause was yours.
I would have fought by land, where I was stronger;
You hindered it: yet, when I fought at sea,
Forsook me fighting; and (O stain to honour!
O lasting shame!) I knew not that I fled;
But fled to follow you.

    VENTIDIUS: What haste she made to hoist her purple sails!
And, to appear magnificent in flight,
Drew half our strength away.

    ANTONY: (*waxing more wrathful*)
All this you caused.
And, would you multiply more ruins on me?
This honest man, my best, my only friend,
Has gathered up the shipwreck of my fortunes;
Twelve legions I have left, my last recruits.
And you have watched the news, and bring your eyes
To seize them too. If you have aught to answer,
Now speak, you have free leave.

    ALEXAS: (*aside*) She stands confounded:
Despair is in her eyes.

    VENTIDIUS: Now lay a sigh in the way to stop his passage:
Prepare a tear, and bid it for his legions;
'Tis like they shall be sold.

    CLEOPATRA: (*gathering all her femininity about herself*)
How shall I plead my cause, when you, my judge,
Already have condemned me? Shall I bring
The love you bore me for my advocate?
That now is turned against me, that destroys me;
For love, once past, is, at the best, forgotten;
But oftener sours to hate: 'twill please my lord
To ruin me, and therefore I'll be guilty.
But, could I once have thought it would have pleased you,
That you would pry, with narrow searching eyes,
Into my faults, severe to my destruction,
And watching all advantages with care,
That serve to make me wretched? Speak, my lord,
For I end here. Though I deserved this usage,
Was it like you to give it?

    ANTONY: (*warming to her words*)
Oh, you wrong me,

To think I sought this parting, or desired
To accuse you more than what will clear myself,
And justify this breach.
    CLEOPATRA: Thus low I thank you;
And, since my innocence will not offend,
I shall not blush to own it.
    VENTIDIUS: After this,
I think she'll blush at nothing.
    CLEOPATRA: (*placing her hand on Antony's cheek*)
You seemed grieved
(And therein you are kind), that Cæsar first
Enjoyed my love, though you deserved it better:
I grieve for that, my lord, much more than you;
For, had I first been yours, it would have saved
My second choice: I never had been his,
And ne'er had been but yours. But Cæsar first,
You say, possessed my love. Not so, my lord:
He first possessed my person; you, my love:
Cæsar loved me; but I loved Antony.
If I endured him after, 'twas because
I judged it due to the first name of men;
And, half constrained, I gave, as to a tyrant,
What he would take by force.
    VENTIDIUS: O Syren! Syren!
Yet grant that all the love she boasts were true,
Has she not ruined you? I still urge that,
The fatal consequence.
    CLEOPATRA: The consequence indeed,
For I dare challenge him, my greatest foe,
(*pointing to Ventidius*)
To say it was designed: 'tis true, I loved you,
And kept you far from an uneasy wife,—
Such Fulvia was.
Yes, but he'll say, you left Octavia for me;—
And, can you blame me to receive that love,
Which quitted such desert, for worthless me?
How often have I wished some other Cæsar,
Great as the first, and as the second young,
Would court my love, to be refused for you!
    VENTIDIUS: Words, words; but Actium, sir; remember
Actium.
    CLEOPATRA: (*undaunted*)
Even there, I dare his malice. True, I counselled

To fight at sea; but I betrayed you not.
I fled, but not to the enemy. 'Twas fear;
Would I had been a man, not to have feared!
For none would then have envied me your friendship,
Who envy me your love.

ANTONY: We are both unhappy:
If nothing else, yet our ill fortune parts us.
Speak: would you have me perish by my stay?

CLEOPATRA: If, as a friend, you ask my judgment, go;
If, as a lover, stay. If you must perish—
'Tis a hard word—but stay.

VENTIDIUS: (*desperately attempting to win Antony back*)
See now the effects of her so boasted love!
She strives to drag you down to ruin with her;
But, could she 'scape without you, oh, how soon
Would she let go her hold, and haste to shore,
And never look behind!

CLEOPATRA: (*giving Antony a letter*)
Then judge my love by this.
Could I have borne
A life or death, a happiness or woe,
From yours divided, this had given me means.

ANTONY: (*excitedly*) By Hercules, the writing of Octavius!
I know it well: 'tis that proscribing hand [i.e., the hand
that proscribed (listed) their mutual enemies when they
were triumvirs together],
Young as it was, that led the way to mine,
And left me but the second place in murder.—
See, see, Ventidius! here he offers Egypt,
And joins all Syria to it, as a present;
So, in requital, she forsake my fortunes,
And join her arms with his.

CLEOPATRA: (*triumphantly*) And yet you leave me!
You leave me, Antony; and yet I love you,
Indeed I do: I have refused a kingdom;
That is a trifle;
For I could part with life, with anything,
But only you. Oh, let me die but with you!
Is that a hard request?

ANTONY: Next living with you,
'Tis all that Heaven can give.

ALEXAS: (*aside*) He melts; we conquer.

CLEOPATRA: (*mockingly insistent*)

No; you shall go: your interest calls you hence;
(*she takes his hand*)
Yes; your dear interest pulls too strong, for these
Weak arms to hold you here.
Go; leave me, soldier
(For you're no more a lover): leave me dying:
Push me, all pale and panting, from your bosom,
And, when your march begins, let one run after,
Breathless almost for joy, and cry—She's dead.
The soldiers shout; you then, perhaps, may sigh,
And muster all your Roman gravity:
Ventidius chides; and straight your brow clears up,
As I had never been.
    ANTONY: (*raising his arms heavenward*)
Gods, 'tis too much; too much for man to bear.
    CLEOPATRA: (*softly*) What is't for me then,
A weak, forsaken woman, and a lover?—
Here let me breathe my last: envy me not
This minute in your arms: I'll die apace,
As fast as e'er I can, and end your trouble.
    ANTONY: (*passionately*)
Die! rather let me perish; loosened nature
Leap from its hinges, sink the props of heaven,
And fall the skies, to crush the nether world!
My eyes, my soul, my all!
(*He embraces her.*)
    VENTIDIUS: And what's this toy,
In balance with your fortune, honour, fame?
    ANTONY: (*sanguinely*)
What is't, Ventidius?—it outweighs them all;
Why, we have more than conquered Cæsar [Octavian] now:
My queen's not only innocent, but loves me.
This, this is she, who drags me down to ruin!
(*mocking Ventidius with his own words*)
"But, could she 'scape without me, with what haste
Would she let slip her hold, and make to shore,
And never look behind!"
(*turning on Ventidius angrily*)
Down on thy knees, blasphemer as thou art,
And ask forgiveness of wronged innocence.
    VENTIDIUS: I'll rather die, than take it. Will you go?
    ANTONY: (*in a near trance-like state*)
Go! whither? Go from all that's excellent?

Faith, honour, virtue, all good things forbid,
That I should go from her, who sets my love
Above the price of kingdoms! Give, you gods,
Give to your boy, your Cæsar,
This rattle of a globe to play withal,
This gewgaw world, and put him cheaply off:
I'll not be pleased with less than Cleopatra.

  CLEOPATRA: (*exuberantly*)
She's wholly yours. My heart's so full of joy,
That I shall do some wild extravagance
Of love, in public; and the foolish world,
Which knows not tenderness, will think me mad.

  VENTIDIUS: (*in anguish*)
O women! women! women! all the gods
Have not such power of doing good to man,
As you of doing harm.
(*He goes out, shaking his head in disbelief.*)

  ANTONY: (*exultant, his arm around Cleopatra*)
Our men are armed:—
Unbar the gate that looks to Cæsar's camp:
I would revenge the treachery he meant me;
And long security makes conquest easy.
I'm eager to return before I go;
For, all the pleasures I have known beat thick
On my remembrance.—How I long for night!
 That both the sweets of mutual love may try,
 And triumph once o'er Cæsar ere we die.
(*They go out arm in arm.*)

Cleopatra Depicted as an Innocent Young Girl

George Bernard Shaw

Following in Shakespeare's and Dryden's footsteps, in 1899 the incomparable modern English playwright, George Bernard Shaw (1856–1950), wrote his own theatrical interpretation of Cleopatra's exploits, *Caesar and Cleopatra*. Just as Dryden had departed from Shakespeare in style and setting, Shaw drastically departed from them both. First, as the title reveals, Shaw's version depicts the famous queen's relationship with Caesar, rather than with Antony. Second, Shaw abandoned Plutarch's renowned historical account of their first meeting (with her stealing into his chamber hidden in a bed roll); instead, the two meet on a moonlit night in front of a stone Sphinx near the palace. Third, Shaw's Cleopatra is not the politically savvy, designing woman so often pictured, but a young, innocent girl who is herself easily deceived. Fourth, the Shaw version is much lighter in tone than Shakespeare's or Dryden's, with a good deal of witty, sparkling, and humorous dialogue. Excerpted here is the play's opening scene, one of the greatest ever written for the theater, in which the unwitting young queen meets a strange older man, completely unaware that he is the great Julius Caesar. (Note Shaw's extensive use of stage directions to describe the settings and the characters' gestures and reactions.)

[The moon] *rises full over the desert; and a vast horizon comes into relief, broken by a huge shape which soon reveals itself in the spreading radiance as a Sphinx pedestalled on the sands. The light still clears, until the upraised eyes of the image are distinguished looking straight forward and upward in infinite fearless vigil, and a mass of color between its great paws defines itself as a heap of red poppies on which a girl lies motionless, her silken vest heaving gently and regularly with the breathing of a dreamless sleeper, and her braided hair glittering in a shaft of moonlight like a bird's wing.*

Suddenly there comes from afar a vaguely fearful sound. . . . Silence: then a few faint high-ringing trumpet notes. Then silence again. Then a man comes from the south with stealing steps, ravished by the mystery of the night, all wonder, and halts, lost in contemplation, opposite the left flank of the Sphinx, whose bosom, with its burden, is hidden from him by its massive shoulder.

THE MAN. Hail, Sphinx: salutation from Julius Cæsar! I have wandered in many lands, seeking the lost regions from which my birth into this world exiled me, and the company of creatures such as I myself. I have found flocks and pastures, men and cities, but no other Cæsar, no air native to me, no man kindred to me, none who can do my day's deed, and think my night's thought. In the little world yonder, Sphinx, my place is as high as yours in this great desert; only I wander, and you sit still; I conquer, and you endure; I work and wonder, you watch and wait; I look up and am dazzled, look down and am darkened, look round and am puzzled, whilst your eyes never turn from looking out—out of the world—to the lost region—the home from which we have strayed. Sphinx, you and I, strangers to the race of men, are no strangers to one another: have I not been conscious of you and of this place since I was born? Rome is a madman's dream: this is my Reality. These starry lamps of yours I have seen from afar in Gaul, in Britain, in Spain, in Thessaly, signalling great secrets to some eternal sentinel below, whose post I never could find. And here at last is their sentinel—an image of the constant and immortal part of my life, silent, full of thoughts, alone in the silver desert. Sphinx, Sphinx: I have climbed mountains at night to hear in the distance the stealthy footfall of the winds that chase your sands in forbidden play—our invisible children, O Sphinx, laughing in whispers. My way hither was the way of destiny; for I am he of whose genius you are the symbol: part brute, part woman, and part god—nothing of man in me at all. Have I read your riddle, Sphinx?

THE GIRL [*who has wakened, and peeped cautiously from her nest to see who is speaking*] Old gentleman.

CÆSAR [*starting violently, and clutching his sword*] Immortal gods!

THE GIRL. Old gentleman: dont run away.

CÆSAR [*stupefied*] "Old gentleman: dont run away"!!! This! to Julius Cæsar!

THE GIRL [*urgently*] Old gentleman.

CÆSAR. Sphinx: you presume on your centuries. I am younger than you, though your voice is but a girl's voice as yet.

THE GIRL. Climb up here, quickly; or the Romans will come and eat you.

CÆSAR [*running forward past the Sphinx's shoulder, and seeing her*] A child at its breast! a divine child!

THE GIRL. Come up quickly. You must get up at its side and creep round.

CÆSAR [*amazed*] Who are you?

THE GIRL. Cleopatra, Queen of Egypt.

CÆSAR. Queen of the Gypsies, you mean.

CLEOPATRA. You must not be disrespectful to me, or the Sphinx will let the Romans eat you. Come up. It is quite cosy here.

CÆSAR [*to himself*] What a dream! What a magnificent dream! Only let me not wake, and I will conquer ten continents to pay for dreaming it out to the end. [*He climbs to the Sphinx's flank, and presently reappears to her on the pedestal, stepping round to its right shoulder*].

CLEOPATRA. Take care. Thats right. Now sit down: you may have its other paw. [*She seats herself comfortably on its left paw*]. It is very powerful and will protect us; but [*shivering, and with plaintive loneliness*] it would not take any notice of me or keep me company. I am glad you have come: I was very lonely. Did you happen to see a white cat anywhere?

CÆSAR [*sitting slowly down on the right paw in extreme wonderment*] Have you lost one?

CLEOPATRA. Yes: the sacred white cat: is it not dreadful? I brought him here to sacrifice him to the Sphinx; but when we got a little way from the city a black cat called him, and he jumped out of my arms and ran away to it. Do you think that the black cat can have been my great-great-great-grandmother?

CÆSAR [*staring at her*] Your great-great-great-grandmother! Well, why not? Nothing would surprise me on this night of nights.

CLEOPATRA. I think it must have been. My great-grandmother's great-grandmother was a black kitten of the sacred white cat; and the river Nile made her his seventh wife. That is why my hair is so wavy. And I always want to be let do as I like, no matter whether it is the will of the gods or not: that is because my blood is made with Nile water.

CÆSAR. What are you doing here at this time of night? Do you live here?

CLEOPATRA. Of course not: I am the Queen; and I shall live in the palace at Alexandria when I have killed my brother, who drove me out of it. When I am old enough I shall do just what I like. I shall be able to poison the slaves and see them wriggle, and pretend to Ftatateeta that she is going to be put into the fiery furnace.

CÆSAR. Hm! Meanwhile why are you not at home and in bed?

CLEOPATRA. Because the Romans are coming to eat us all. You are not at home and in bed either.

CÆSAR [*with conviction*] Yes I am. I live in a tent; and I am now in that tent, fast asleep and dreaming. Do you suppose that I believe you are real, you impossible little dream witch?

CLEOPATRA [*giggling and leaning trustfully towards him*] You are a funny old gentleman. I like you.

CÆSAR. Ah, that spoils the dream. Why dont you dream that I am young?

CLEOPATRA. I wish you were; only I think I should be more afraid of you. I like men, especially young men with round strong arms; but I am afraid of them. You are old and rather thin and stringy; but you have a nice voice; and I like to have somebody to talk to, though I think you are a little mad. It is the moon that makes you talk to yourself in that silly way.

CÆSAR. What! you heard that, did you? I was saying my prayers to the great Sphinx.

CLEOPATRA. But this isnt the great Sphinx.

CÆSAR [*much disappointed, looking up at the statue*] What!

CLEOPATRA. This is only a dear little kitten of a Sphinx. Why, the great Sphinx is so big that it has a temple between its paws. This is my pet Sphinx. Tell me: do you think the Romans have any sorcerers who could take us away from the Sphinx by magic?

CÆSAR. Why? Are you afraid of the Romans?

CLEOPATRA [*very seriously*] Oh, they would eat us if they caught us. They are barbarians. Their chief is called Julius Cæsar. His father was a tiger and his mother a burning mountain; and his nose is like an elephant's trunk. [*Cæsar involuntarily rubs his nose*]. They all have long noses, and ivory tusks, and little tails, and seven arms with a hundred arrows in each; and they live on human flesh.

CÆSAR. Would you like me to shew you a real Roman?

CLEOPATRA [*terrified*] No. You are frightening me.

CÆSAR. No matter: this is only a dream—

CLEOPATRA [*excitedly*] It is not a dream: it is not a dream. See, see. [*She plucks a pin from her hair and jabs it repeatedly into his arm*].

CÆSAR. Ffff—Stop. [*Wrathfully*] How dare you?

CLEOPATRA [*abashed*] You said you were dreaming. [*Whimpering*] I only wanted to shew you—

CÆSAR [*gently*] Come, come: dont cry. A queen mustnt cry. [*He rubs his arm, wondering at the reality of the smart*]. Am

---

 SHAW EXPLAINS HIS DEPICTION OF CLEOPATRA

In his notes accompanying Caesar and Cleopatra, *Shaw included this rationale for his choice of making the Egyptian queen young and somewhat childish.*

Cleopatra was only sixteen when Cæsar went to Egypt; but in Egypt sixteen is a riper age than it is in England. The childishness I have ascribed to her, as far as it is childishness of character and not lack of experience, is not a matter of years. It may be observed in our own climate at the present day in many women of fifty. It is a mistake to suppose that the difference between wisdom and folly has anything to do with the difference between physical age and physical youth. Some women are younger at seventy than most women at seventeen.

It must be borne in mind, too, that Cleopatra was a queen, and was therefore not the typical Greek-cultured, educated Egyptian lady of her time. To represent her by any such type would be as absurd as to represent [England's] George IV by a type founded on the attainments of Sir Isaac Newton. It is true that an ordinarily well educated Alexandrian girl of her time would no more have believed bogey stories about the Romans than the daughter of a modern Oxford professor would believe them about the Germans. . . . But I do not feel bound to believe that Cleopatra was well educated. Her father, the illustrious Flute Blower [Ptolemy XII, Auletes], was not at all a parent of the Oxford professor type. And Cleopatra was a chip off the old block.

George Bernard Shaw, "Notes to *Caesar and Cleopatra*," in Shaw, *Caesar and Cleopatra.* Baltimore: Penguin Books, 1966, p. 131.

I awake? [*He strikes his hand against the Sphinx to test its solidity. It feels so real that he begins to be alarmed, and says perplexedly*] Yes, I—[*quite panicstricken*] no: impossible: madness, madness! [*Desperately*] Back to camp—to camp. [*He rises to spring down from the pedestal*].

CLEOPATRA [*flinging her arms in terror round him*] No: you shant leave me. No, no, no: dont go. I'm afraid—afraid of the Romans.

CÆSAR [*as the conviction that he is really awake forces itself on him*] Cleopatra: can you see my face well?

CLEOPATRA. Yes. It is so white in the moonlight.

CÆSAR. Are you sure it is the moonlight that makes me look whiter than an Egyptian? [*Grimly*] Do you notice that I have a rather long nose?

CLEOPATRA [*recoiling, paralysed by a terrible suspicion*] Oh!

CÆSAR. It is a Roman nose, Cleopatra.

CLEOPATRA. Ah! [*With a piercing scream she springs up; darts round the left shoulder of the Sphinx; scrambles down to the sand; and falls on her knees in frantic supplication, shrieking*] Bite him in two, Sphinx: bite him in two. I meant to sacrifice the white cat—I did indeed—I [*Cæsar, who has slipped down from the pedestal, touches her on the shoulder*]—Ah! [*She buries her head in her arms*].

CÆSAR. Cleopatra: shall I teach you a way to prevent Cæsar from eating you?

CLEOPATRA [*clinging to him piteously*] Oh do, do, do. I will steal Ftatateeta's jewels and give them to you. I will make the river Nile water your lands twice a year.

CÆSAR. Peace, peace, my child. Your gods are afraid of the Romans: you see the Sphinx dare not bite me, nor prevent me carrying you off to Julius Cæsar.

CLEOPATRA [*in pleading murmurings*] You wont, you wont. You said you wouldnt.

CÆSAR. Cæsar never eats women.

CLEOPATRA [*springing up full of hope*] What!

CÆSAR [*impressively*] But he eats girls [*she relapses*] and cats. Now you are a silly little girl; and you are descended from the black kitten. You are both a girl and a cat.

CLEOPATRA [*trembling*] And will he eat me?

CÆSAR. Yes; unless you make him believe that you are a woman.

CLEOPATRA. Oh, you must get a sorcerer to make a woman of me. Are you a sorcerer?

CÆSAR. Perhaps. But it will take a long time; and this very night you must stand face to face with Cæsar in the palace of your fathers.

CLEOPATRA. No, no. I darent.

CÆSAR. Whatever dread may be in your soul—however terrible Cæsar may be to you—you must confront him as a brave woman and a great queen; and you must feel no fear. If your hand shakes: if your voice quavers; then—night and death! [*She moans*]. But if he thinks you worthy to rule, he will set you on the throne by his side and make you the real ruler of Egypt.

CLEOPATRA [*despairingly*] No: he will find me out: he will find me out.

CÆSAR [*rather mournfully*] He is easily deceived by women. Their eyes dazzle him; and he sees them not as they are, but as he wishes them to appear to him.

CLEOPATRA [*hopefully*] Then we will cheat him. I will put on Ftatateeta's head-dress; and he will think me quite an old woman.

CÆSAR. If you do that he will eat you at one mouthful.

CLEOPATRA. But I will give him a cake with my magic opal and seven hairs of the white cat baked in it; and—

CÆSAR [*abruptly*] Pah! you are a little fool. He will eat your cake and you too. [*He turns contemptuously from her*].

CLEOPATRA [*running after him and clinging to him*] Oh please, please! I will do whatever you tell me. I will be good. I will be your slave. [*Again the terrible bellowing note sounds across the desert, now closer at hand. It is the bucina, the Roman war trumpet*].

CÆSAR. Hark!

CLEOPATRA [*trembling*] What was that?

CÆSAR. Cæsar's voice.

CLEOPATRA [*pulling at his hand*] Let us run away. Come. Oh, come.

CÆSAR. You are safe with me until you stand on your throne to receive Cæsar. Now lead me thither.

CLEOPATRA [*only too glad to get away*] I will, I will. [*Again the bucina*]. Oh come, come, come: the gods are angry. Do you feel the earth shaking?

CÆSAR. It is the tread of Cæsar's legions.

CLEOPATRA [*drawing him away*] This way, quickly. And let us look for the white cat as we go. It is he that has turned you into a Roman.

CÆSAR. Incorrigible, oh, incorrigible! Away! [*He follows her, the bucina sounding louder as they steal across the desert. The moonlight wanes: the horizon again shews black against the sky, broken only by the fantastic silhouette of the Sphinx*].

[*Cleopatra leads him to her throne room, which is empty. There, a few moments later, Roman soldiers enter and shout "Hail Cæsar!", saluting him with their swords. Suddenly realizing who he is, she falls, greatly relieved, into his outstretched arms.*]

A Novelist Portrays the Famous Lovers' Last Moments Together

Martha Rofheart

In addition to the many plays that have been written about Cleopatra and her Roman lovers, a number of novels have tackled the Egyptian queen's timeless tale. Among the best and most critically acclaimed is *The Alexandrian*, published in 1976 by Martha Rofheart, author of *Fortune Made His Sword* and *My Name Is Sappho*. Rofheart's Cleopatra is a capable, caring queen, wife, and mother who stands by her man in the end. Also, the author's choice of telling the story in the first person lends it a fresh, immediate, believable, and appealing edge not found in many other versions. This excerpt includes Antony's suicide, which the reader hears about rather than witnesses first hand, and, in a truly moving passage, the lovers' parting words. (Note that, to add a realistic and personal touch, Rofheart's Cleopatra refers to Antony by his praenomen, or given name—Marcus— rather than as Antony.)

The ships of Egypt moved out slowly, under sail; they were a remnant only, but still it was a proud sight, brilliant against the pale dawn. The land breeze ruffled my hair, blowing it into my eyes; I pushed it away impatiently. I stood on the royal stairs, where so often I had watched ships come and go, where I had watched my Neo sail away, so long ago, where I had flown to meet Marcus, wild with a goddess passion; the wind freshened, and I held my cloak together at my throat; it was late summer, and would be a hot day; still I shivered.

113

ANTONY'S FORCES DESERT TO THE ENEMY

Far away, lining the horizon, and almost fading into the colorless sky, were the sails of Octavian's fleet, blockading the harbor; white mist hung over all.

To the north, Marcus' legions were drawn up for the attack, the golden eagles blinding bright, the banners brave. Marcus, with his officers, stood on a little hillock, commanding a view of land and sea; I could just make out the purple of his horse's trappings. In the stillness, a horse neighed loudly, then another; the sound was like the tearing of cloth. I saw Iras, beside me, put her hands over her ears.

The ships moved slowly, so slowly, though we saw from the silver wake that they were using oars as well; it was an unbearable thing to watch.

"Why don't they attack?" It was Antyllus [Antony's son by Fulvia], sounding fretful, like a small child.

"Well," I said, my voice sounding thin and strange in my ears, "they are not close enough yet—and they must take down their sails, too—"

"No, no, Lady . . . I mean the legions!" And he pointed toward the ranks of them. "Octavian's troops are on the move already!" He was right; the huge dust cloud was coming closer.

"Your father will know when . . . never fear." So often had I heard Marcus say that there is a time, not too soon or too late, that is perfect, and one must trust to instinct; I prayed it would not fail him now, that instinct. "Watch the ships, Antyllus . . . soon we will see them loose the fire baskets, for at last they are getting near enough. . . ."

We looked, straining our eyes, but they were like pictures still, or toys. "What are they doing, Lady?" Panic rose in Antyllus' voice. "Look, they are shipping their oars!" His eyes were younger; the rest of us saw it a moment later, the bright wakes gone that had streamed behind, the sea unbroken, and there, as we watched, incredibly, our ships lining up with the enemy in an ordered pattern.

"Oh, Gods, we are lost!" cried Charmion [Cleopatra's maid-servant] softly. "They have joined forces—they will not do battle!" I held my breath till I thought my chest would burst; when I let it out, it was on a long whistling sigh. We stood helpless as the two fleets moved slowly together towards the eastern harbor.

From the north there came a far-off iron sound, a clang, a ring; I thought the troops were closing in at last, in the first charge, and turned to look. But, clear in the morning light, we saw that the sound was the sound of weapons dashed to earth, and the iron-shod horses galloping in even lines to meet the advancing Octavians.

"Lady, they have deserted! They are marching back together . . . Romans all!" It was Antyllus again; poor lad. . . .

It was true, though—only the legions, with Marcus at their head, held firm. But not for long. A spear went high, pointing towards the harbor, where the ships moved serenely eastward, nearly gone from sight. Even above the war clamor, coming close, I heard the high, keening cries, the harsh jangle of arms, the hoofs striking; suddenly the whole line of the legions broke and ran, scattering, into the city. I could not find Marcus among them; I supposed he had no choice, borne with them as he was; he would make for his quarters. On that entire hill where once stood a thousand men and horse, there was nothing now but some few flung standards, and here and there the gleam of a dropped spear; the ground, though, was as it is always under an army, trampled and torn, with deep ruts and the chaotic pattern of hoof marks upon it. The dust cloud that was the enemy was a cloud no longer, but banners and shields, plumed helmets and faces beneath; the first line had even now reached the barren hill; panic sang in my veins. I snatched at Antyllus' arm, gripping it. "Get to your father! He will be in his quarters I think . . . but find him! Tell him I shall bolt myself into the mausoleum [her half-finished tomb] and open to none but him . . . tell him I await him. Go!" And I pushed him forward.

"Charmion . . . Iras [another serving woman] . . . the children! Find the children! Come!"

CLEOPATRA AVOIDS OCTAVIAN'S SOLDIERS

And we three women, like creatures driven by the Furies, ran into the Palace, throwing open every door, wild with terror. As, at the end of the corridor, the nursery door yielded under our hands, little Ptolemy looked up, surprised, from where he rode a wooden painted steed. "Come, my darling," I cried, and snatched him up, clutching him close. "Mama, you hurt!" he protested, and squirmed in my arms.

"Hush, baby . . . hush, mama's darling! Where is your nurse? Where is your sister?" I frightened him; I could not help it. I made an effort and loosened my grip on him, though still I held him close. "Selene?"

He pointed to the window; she was leaning far out, her feet in their small flat slippers off the ground. "Selene!" I called.

She turned her head. "Mama! So many soldiers—and horses! Where are they going?" Her eyes were round with excitement and her cheeks flushed. "Never mind, sweetheart . . . go with Charmion!" The nurse was nowhere to be found; we could spare no time to search, but ran, each with a child, and Iras, with an armful of snatched-up toys and clothes, back down the hall.

The part of the palace above the mausoleum stood apart from the rest, reached by a covered walkway. Between the columns that lined the passage we could see, to our right, the sea, empty. We rushed through the great door, panting, and flung it closed. I put little Ptolemy down; he began to cry. "Selene . . . comfort your brother," I said, as I turned to tug at the heavy bolt that barred the door. As we three women shot the bolt home, gratingly, I heard Selene. "Cry-baby!" I could not worry about her manners now, but beckoned to the others. We tried all the locks on doors and windows; they were secure. "We had best go upstairs," I said, "for double safety . . . at least there we can have a window open. . . ."

The first of the Octavian soldiers had reached the palace walkways; as we watched from the upper window, we saw two officers, faceless behind their cruel helmets, come out onto the steps where moments ago we had stood. They were looking out to sea, empty sea now, as we had; one of them dragged off his helmet to see better. Then he gave a short harsh laugh and said something we could not hear, flinging an arm across his companion's shoulder. They strolled away then, past us to the east, as if they took their ease in a park; an insult. At the same time we heard hammering below, and the great doors ringing hollow under the spear-butt blows. Then creaking as it gave, and footsteps, steel-shod in the hallways. Fast on this sound came a pounding at the door below, where we were refuging. Iras' hand went to her mouth. "Oh, sister, they have found us!"

"Hush . . . do not answer!" I listened, my heart knocking hard.

"Lady . . . oh, Lady . . . !" It was Antyllus' voice; it broke, as it often did now, on the last word.

"Come—" I said to Charmion, taking her by the hand. "Watch the children, Iras!" And we crept down the stairs and close to the door, waiting. Antyllus' voice came again. "Lady?

Are you there?"

"I dare not open," I said. "There are Octavians all through the Palace—and this bolt is rusty as well. . . ."

"Oh, Lady. . . ." And I thought he could not speak, a sob was there, under. "Lady, it is my father. He is wounded—I think he may be dying . . . His sword—" And he choked on the words, and then went on. "It is still in him, his sword. I think he fell upon it, to take his own life . . . his man Eros is already dead."

"Oh, Gods," I cried, and tugged at the bolt, uncaring. Even as he slipped through, we saw soldiers in pairs, starting toward us from either end of the walkway. Antyllus was alone, his face all smeared with fears and dirt.

Marcus—where is Marcus?" I wailed, shaking him. "Oh, Charmion—shut the door!"

"I could not lift him, Lady . . . and should I pull the sword out . . . ?"

"He is still in his rooms?" I asked. He nodded, and I shook him again. "You must not give way, now—you are his son. Listen . . . go and find Olympos the doctor . . . if you cannot, get help and make a litter . . . bring your father here. Where we stood this morning—if it is clear of Romans—the upstairs window gives onto that place. Bring him there . . . get ropes— we will haul him up. I cannot open the doors again . . . hurry!"

ANTONY'S PARTING WORDS

I thought that he would never come. I thought I must rush after him, and twice started to, and was stopped by Charmion. I paced the upstairs chamber, wringing my hands; the children, terrified by my behavior, sobbed softly in a corner; Iras watched by the window. I heard, through my own soft sobs, noises on the stairs below and ran to the window to look. Antyllus was beneath, with a secretary, Diomedes, and Olympos; between them they bore a litter, such as is used to bring wounded off the field. The form stretched on it looked so long, so flat; a sheet covered it, already bloodsoaked, and a red trail marked the path they had come. I could not see his face, but he did not move where he lay; the way down seemed very far. Charmion, she was ever a useful woman, had found some rope somewhere and was letting it down, snaking past the walls.

Olympos looked up. "Is he . . . ?" I could not finish. He nodded.

"He is dying, Lady . . . but there is still a little time left to him."

I cannot think how it was accomplished, for Marcus was a big man, and heavy with his death upon him, and we were three slight women, but we pulled him up somehow, and into the chamber. It is said that the gods send strength when it is sorely needed.

Dimly I recall that Antyllus had got a ladder from somewhere, and the men climbed up afterward. There was blood all over Marcus, even on his face; he must have tried to stem the flow with his hands and then wiped his face, my poor love. The color was gone from him; he was like a waxen candle, his face scored with deep lines beside the mouth and black marks below the eyes. Olympos had wound many thicknesses of cloth about his body, but the blood still welled from the place; already a pool was forming on the floor. I wondered dimly how so much blood could be in one man, and that surely he was a god.

They had laid him on a long table; I bent over him, and put my hand to his face; I did not dare take him in my arms, for fear I might hasten his end. His eyes opened; around his mouth there was a little tremor, the ghost of a smile. "I made a bad job of it, darling . . . wouldn't you know I'd miss the heart? The gut, that's where I got it, sweet . . . but at least— this way—we can say farewell. . . ." He held so tight to my hand that its bones scraped together; I knew he suffered dreadfully.

"Oh, my darling," I whispered. "Why . . . ?"

One eyebrow raised, a parody of the old gay Marcus. "It was the only way," he said. "The August One [Octavian] would have made it harder—think you he would not? Crucifixion, maybe. . . ." He closed his eyes; I knew it was a great effort for him to talk at all. He was trying to wet his lips with his tongue, over and over. I turned and asked for water.

He opened his eyes. "Not water—wine. . . ." And he nearly managed a true smile. "Not what you think, poor girl . . . but it will help, truly. . . ."

I looked at Olympos. He nodded and said, softly. "It will finish him. . . ." I put my hand to my mouth, but still a cry escaped.

"Let him have it, Lady . . . he is in great pain." And he took the cup that Charmion had brought.

Marcus shook his head, a small and weary movement. "You—sweet—I want you to give it to me. . . ."

I took the cup, willing my hand not to shake, and with the other hand raised his head gently to meet the cup; he tried to sip it, but the wine all ran down his chin. He raised his eyes to mine. "Weak I am . . . so weak. Well, we die as we are born. . . . I could not drink from a cup then either." And I thought I saw a fleeting slyness in those eyes, the beginning of a jest, incredibly. Oh, my Marcus—there is no other like you. . . . I held the cup again; this time he drained it, and fell back against the litter. "There was salt in it, my dear . . . no good for a queen . . . no good." He shook his head from side to side. "Do not weep, my own. . . . I die a Roman death . . . be happy for our happiness, for it was great. . . ." And then his eyes glazed over, staring past me; Antyllus came forward, but he was already gone.

"He did not say good-bye. . . ."

I looked at him; what did he have left, poor boy? I took his hand and drew him close, for I was still calm, as though frozen. "Listen, Antyllus . . . he said good-bye—and that you must be brave, and a good Roman. It is that he could not speak loud enough. . . ."

"Oh, Lady!" And he put his head down upon my shoulder and wept.

I held him till he had finished, and turned away. I kneeled still where he had left me, beside my husband. A little breeze blew upon me from the open window; it would be a hot wind, this time of year, but I shivered. I looked down, seeing that the whole front of my robe was soaked with blood, and my hands looked as though they had been dipped in it; my face, too, was wet with tears I did not know I had shed. From the far corner came a whimpering, like puppies hurt; oh, gods—it was my babies, poor innocents. And at the thought, the ice broke in me somewhere, and I wept aloud, and could not stop.

Cleopatra on Film: From the Silent Screen to Elizabeth Taylor

Jon Solomon

This highly informative and entertaining piece is from classical historian Jon Solomon's impressively researched and thoroughly fascinating book, *The Ancient World in the Cinema.* He begins with the several silent film versions of Cleopatra's story and then proceeds to the sound versions, quite appropriately devoting the lion's share of space to the 1963 version starring Elizabeth Taylor. As Solomon tells in excruciating, eye-opening detail, the making of this truly spectacular film was in many ways as colorful and gossip-ridden as the real Cleopatra's life and exploits.

While an infamous number of jealous senators were attacking Julius Caesar by Pompey's statue on March 15, 44 B.C.—plunging deadly daggers into the aging dictator's bowels—two . . . acquaintances of his dwelled in other parts of the eternal city; one was his general and the other his mistress—Antony and Cleopatra. This most famous couple came together in the wake of mighty Caesar's death, and before they were to part, they themselves would be involved in the ultimate struggle for control of the massive Roman domain. Their lives centered around love, politics, and power, and for those glamorous few years they spent together, they have become a legend.

THE SILENT CLEOPATRAS

On film they have appeared at least ten times. After George Méliès's 1899 version, the earliest feature film called *Cleopatra* was produced by the Helen Gardner Players in upstate New York in 1912. One of the very first "full length" American feature films, this primitive, one-hour movie seems very

Excerpted from *The Ancient World in the Cinema,* by Jon Solomon (New York: A.S. Barnes, 1978). Reprinted by permission of the author.

crude to our modern eyes. A still camera views a cardboard barge "sailing" across a stage before a painted matte of the sea; a hefty Cleopatra, (Helen Gardner) steps out and waves, gestures, pleads, embraces, faints, supplicates, and strokes a cumbersomely uniformed Antony. The spherical Miss Gardner's acting is emotive and varied, but all else in this early American film lacks conviction. The sea battle of Actium shows Cleopatra and Antony ridiculously rocking back and forth while buckets of water are tossed at them.

[The Italian film studio] Cines produced *Marcantonio e Cleopatra* in 1913 starring Antony Novelli (Antony) and Giovanna Terribili Gonzales (Cleopatra). Displaying the same fine photography used in *Julius Caesar* the following year, the Cines company hit their creative peak with this totally spectacular and fascinating silent. Superbly acted dual scenes (Cleo and Antony, Antony and Octavia), quick-paced action, and large crowds were essential to other Cines films of the era, and they are here as well; but small touches such as Charmian's bizarre death amid alligators, the Roman Senate's declaring Antony a traitor, a lovely shot of Octavian's troops reflected in a pool of marshy water, and the battle at Alexandria, give this film its particular quality. Of special interest is the scene after Antony's death. In all the other film versions of the story, Cleopatra commits suicide immediately after Antony does so. Here, however, Cleopatra lives on for a little while. She stares longingly at her lover's throne; she even fondles his armor, and then she dreams of herself in Octavian's triumphal procession amidst festooned ballustrades and the people-filled porches of Rome (like the triumph in *Julius Caesar*). Rather than have this nightmare come true, she gives a poisonous asp a taste of her breast.

DEMILLE'S CUTE BUT SPECTACULAR VERSION

In 1917 [American actress] Theda Bara vamped a version of *Cleopatra* that was quite dazzling and impressive for its day, but its limited scope was to be drowned out by the roar of Cecil B. DeMille's *Cleopatra* (1934). A Cleopatra who can speak can become a more complex character than a silent Cleopatra, and the charming, calculating, yet vulnerable chatter of Claudette Colbert's Cleopatra is as complex as the layered gauze wrapped around a mummy. She is matched with an unmovably haughty, coming, seeing, and conquering Caesar (Warren William) and a hotheaded, wildly fascinating and debauched Antony (Henry Wilcoxon). All the witty dialogue is spouted before delightfully lavish sets and very able character actors. . . . The movie has the inimitable DeMillish combination of grand magnificence, cute dialogue, and forcefully climactic action.

An exciting chariot run with rousing music sees Cleopatra deposited in the desert by her political enemies. Left alone to die with her aide Apollodorus, she hears Apollodorus' sage suggestion to ally herself with Rome. She regally replies with a childish pout, "Why do you talk about Rome and politics? I'm hungry!" Soon we see Julius Caesar in Alexandria testing a new siege engine. Enter a merchant with a rolled-up Persian carpet; impatient Caesar is not amused when Cleopatra is unrolled from the tapestry. "I'm too busy." But wily Colbert, fresh after her Oscar for *It Happened One Night*, comments in a low, tempting voice, "It's strange to see you working. I've always pictured you either fighting . . . or loving." Caesar: "I've had experience with fighting." Cleopatra: "But not with loving, I suppose?" Caesar: "Not with pretty little queens."

This coy, cute dialogue is only a small part of DeMille's attack on the legendary and historical story. Antony's visit to Cleopatra's wonderful, swan-necked barge displays DeMille at his most lavish. After Cleopatra wheedles Antony into drinking and having an enjoyable evening despite himself, she then gives the signal; two flowing curtains are crisscrossed before our eyes, rose petals fall gently from the ceiling, and long festoons are raised. The camera fades away taking in the lightly clad dancers, graceful women, and large Nubian slaves. The compelling music builds and builds while stylized animal-headed oars move into motion at the crash of a huge drum. A muscular conductor (*hortator*) pounds out a throbbing beat in his angular attack on the drum as the music climaxes and the scene disappears. The barge scene is without parallel in grandeur, grace, and romantic power.

DeMille can also be humorously cynical. Cleopatra is convinced by a very sinister Herod that she must poison Antony. We then see a condemned slave tell Cleopatra she is "merciful" for letting him test her new poison; he will be happy to die a quick death without pain. Antony sees the slave's body carried out and hears in wonder that, "The queen is testing poisons." And despite his unique ability at portraying both the graces and the intrigues of court life, DeMille also excelled in portraying war. The whole naval battle of Actium and land battle of Alexandria consume less than two minutes, yet this brilliantly edited sequence strikes us with an incredible impact. Borrowing several shots from *The Ten Commandments* (1923) a smoke-filled screen of Stygian gloom moves in rapid succession from Nubian to Roman tubae, marching spearmen and standards, deafening chariots, a gigantic battering ram, falling and grimacing faces, a huge rolling . . . spike, catapults of fire, underwater shots of dead, all ending in a large fireball shot right at the camera.

SHAW'S *CAESAR AND CLEOPATRA* REACHES THE SCREEN

Twelve years later Gabriel Pascal followed up his screen versions of George Bernard Shaw's *Pygmalion* and *Major Barbara* with another Shavian [having to do with Shaw] masterpiece, *Caesar and Cleopatra* (1946). Spending just under three million dollars to create lavish sets and regally splendid costumes, Pascal captured the essentially witty, yet semiserious atmosphere that characterizes most of Shaw's work. Shaw himself wrote the dialogue for the film. His genius combined well with the elegant continental music of Georges Auric and the fascinating sets by Oliver Messel and John Bryan. Claude Rains plays Caesar, the father-figure, who tries to teach young, giggly Cleopatra (Vivien Leigh) how to be a queen. Their relationship is a playful one amid the soft bluish tint of the Egyptian sky (cyclorama) and before a large, imposing sphinx. In her childish simplicity, Cleopatra rues that "Julius Caesar's father was a tiger, his mother was a burning mountain, and his nose is like an elephant's trunk." She has heard that Caesar will gobble her up in one bite. But the charming and kind, "old" Caesar encourages her to act like a queen. Cleopatra asserts her newfound royalty by beating a helpless slave; "I'm a real queen, ooo!" The other two main characters are played by Flora Robson and Stewart Granger. Flora Robson plays Cleopatra's humorless nurse, Ftatateeta. Caesar constantly refers to her as "Teeta Tota" or "Tota Teeta," and eventually with an exasperated "Tota." He does this to such an extent that one laughs at the mere thought of her name. Granger plays the reckless Oriental swashbuckler from Sicily with much conviction.

Some epic sweep appears in the battle at the film's end, but for the most part *Caesar and Cleopatra* concentrates on intellectual wit and mundane play. For instance, Cleopatra and her effeminate teenage brother and husband, Ptolemy, dispute their right to the throne of Egypt. Cleopatra (whose sweet smile, batting eyelashes, and wily plans suggest the plausible image of a Miss Scarlett vying for an Egyptian Tara and a Roman Rhett [a reference to the 1939 film *Gone With the Wind*, in which Vivian Leigh played Scarlett O'hara]) runs into the room and rather ignobly pulls her brother from the throne onto the floor. After some silly verbal squabbling, Roman troops enter under Rufio's generalship. All of a sudden the young Egyptian king and queen are "Roman guests." Ptolemy sticks his tongue out at his "mean" sister while his older regent, Pothinus, demands to know from Caesar "Where is your right to do this?" Caesar replies in a superior tone, "In Rufio's scabbard, for the moment."

Shaw's wonderful ability to mix learned humor with the most mundane actions and words finds its perfect home in the film when Caesar hears from a frantic Egyptian that the famous Library of Alexandria is burning. Caesar replies, "Is that all? I'm an author myself." And all the while, Caesar keeps teasing Cleopatra by promising to introduce her to a handsome young general of his named Antony.

A Cast, Crew, and Set Plagued by Problems

The next two versions of Cleopatra were cheap and disappointing. Columbia produced *Serpent of the Nile* in 1953, which drastically changes the story of the two lovers; here Cleopatra (Rhonda Fleming) actually loves Antony's best friend! The film serves only as an item of curiosity since Antony is played by Raymond Burr (shortly before he passed the bar exam [a reference to his famous TV role as the brilliant lawyer Perry Mason]). In 1961 Vittorio Cottavafi directed *Legions of the Nile*, also entitled *Legions of Cleopatra*. This cinematic comic book contains a huge amount of brutal ruffians, sleazy or sassy girls, and overbold heroes. Each character is cut from the thinnest cardboard. Thanks to some spirited action scenes and some amusing romantic play, the film becomes almost tolerable.

And then came THE version of *Cleopatra*. What is there to write about a film that caused an international scandal and the firing of its company president, its producer, its two directors, and a clutch of scriptwriters? What can be justified about a film that cost over sixty million dollars to put on the screen and opened in six hundred theatres? What can be described about a movie that has over ninety-six hours (120 miles!) of film in the cans yet is shown in slightly over three hours? And what words can be used to analyze a film so well-known that its advertisements did not even need to include the name *Cleopatra*?

Plenty. Filmmakers and critics alike still shudder when they think of the most expensive, the longest, the most publicized, and the most controversial picture ever made. Opinions range widely, but few could deny that in one way or another, for better or for worse, the 1963 version of *Cleopatra* is the most spectacular movie that will ever be made.

It all started with Theda Bara in 1917. Fox had produced her version, and it had been quite successful. Since that time a remake had been planned by Fox and producer William Wanger (whose credits include such a variety of films as *Stagecoach, Joan of Arc,* and *The Invasion of the Body Snatchers*). But earthquakes start as small tremors, so Wanger and Fox's president, Spiros Skouras, planned a two million dollar quickie with Joan Collins playing the title role. Soon Audrey Hepburn and Susan Hayward were being considered, but Elizabeth Taylor, fresh from her contract's termination at MGM, agreed to do the part for a few hundred thousand dollars. Skouras and Wanger knew that the big name in the title role would make the picture successful, and Liz had just won her Oscar for *Butterfield 8*. Rouben Mamoulian was hired as director, and location shooting was planned for Egypt and Italy, then changed to Turkey, then to London, yes, definitely London. This was 1959.

By September 30, 1960, eight and one-half acres of ancient Alexandria had been built at Pinewood Studios outside of London. The first day of shooting was buried in fog, and the fog lasted all week. Liz contracted a fever. The delays continued. By November 1, the two million dollars was already spent. The cold and damp weather remained. Whenever someone spoke, frosty vapors came from their mouth. This was Egypt? In mid-November, Liz's illness continued, so production was closed down until January 3, 1961. Soon a new scriptwriter was hired (Nunnally Johnson), but Mamoulian quit on January 18. So far, the film had cost only seven million dollars, taken sixteen months, and had produced twelve minutes of footage. [The famous insurance company] Lloyds of London paid part of the losses back, so

Skouras went ahead and hired Joseph L. Mankiewicz (*Julius Caesar*—1953) as new director. His salary was large, to say the least.

A fresh start? Within a week Elizabeth Taylor was in the hospital near death with pneumonia and anemia; she underwent a life-saving tracheotomy. The director decided to shoot the rest of the picture in Hollywood, no, Rome. Meanwhile, Peter Finch had been replaced as Caesar by Rex Harrison. . . . Richard Burton then replaced the contract-obligated Stephen Boyd to play Antony. He willingly left his Broadway *Camelot* role. Once Liz was healthy, they could shoot this picture.

In September of 1961, one interior set of forty-seven was ready; the costumes had been ripped somehow. In November a windstorm suddenly arose and caused production cancellation for the day—cost: $75,000. In the winter of 1962 began the world famous "Le Scandale." Richard Burton's first words to Miss Taylor were, "Has anybody ever told you that you're a very pretty girl?" Corny, but it worked. By the spring Liz and Richard were oppressed by the *paparazzi*—the Italian gossip hounds. Photographers came to the door of their three thousand dollars per month house dressed as carpenters, servants, and priests. In April, a cat and her kittens were heard meowing underneath *Cleopatra*'s bedroom set. Production was held while the set was dismantled, the cats were freed, and the set was reassembled—cost: $17,000. Production costs, including overtime for the stars, was now costing $500,000 per week.

On March 2, 1963, came the last day of shooting. By this time, Wanger had been fired; Skouras had been ousted and Daryl Zanuck had taken over Fox. Zanuck sent Mankiewicz to the employment bureau with this announcement: "In exchange for top compensation and a considerable expense account, Mr. Joseph Mankiewicz had for two years spent his time, talent, and $35,000,000 of Twentieth-Century Fox's shareholders' money to direct and complete the first cut of the film *Cleopatra*. He has earned a well-deserved rest."

WHY THE HUGE EXPENSE?

Finally ready for release, the film was advertised on the world's largest billboard in New York. Newspaper ads showed a reclining Cleopatra with Antony standing above her. There was no title in the ad; the whole universe had been hearing about the film and its personalities for three years, so who needed a title?

It was June 12, 1963. *Cleopatra* opened at the Rivoli theatre at one hundred dollars a ticket amid a Manhattan street crowd of ten thousand. Postcards with "Cleopatra-scented" perfume were for sale in the lobby. Before the première, *Cleopatra* was already the eighth biggest box-office hit of all time with fifteen million dollars paid in advance rental. On opening night, the film was four hours, twenty-four minutes long. Within two weeks it was mysteriously four hours, three minutes. In a few months, it was being shown in just over three hours. *Newsweek* called the film "The Amputee."

What happened? Skouras admitted that the film should have cost half as much as it eventually did ($62,000,000 including printing and distribution costs). Mankiewicz bemoaned that "this was a chance to flirt with disaster." "This picture was conceived in a state of emergency, shot in confusion, and wound up in blind panic." The star reluctantly viewed a print of the finished (and cut) movie, described it as "vulgar," and promptly ran to the powder room to throw up. She called Zanuck and offered to redub some of her weaker voice parts. He would not spend a cent more on the monstrous enterprise.

Cleopatra suffered from poor planning and ill fortune. Gossip and adverse publicity blamed Liz's romance, overeating, and high living for the delay and expense of the film. This was cruel and untrue. Her illness was not her fault, and Mankiewicz once had strep throat, Roddy McDowall (Octavian) had a skin ailment, Harrison had food poisoning, and Burton missed shooting one day thanks to an Antony-esque drinking bout the night before. He nobly offered to pay for the lost day. Any self-respecting Roman general would have done the same.

Bad weather in London and Rome, excessive prices charged by the Italians, and other delays and costs added daily figures onto the growing budget. At one point, elephants were hired for the famous scene in which Cleopatra enters Rome in a magnificent show. The elephants ran loose and disrupted the shooting. Mankiewicz ordered the beasts off the set and called them "wild." Fox was then sued for $100,000 for "slandering" the elephants! To build the Alexandria exteriors, a beach at Anzio was rented. Rental alone cost $150,000. By the end of shooting, the weary production manager became a laughing stock; he turned frugal at the wrong time in the wrong way. He told the cast, "Save on the paper cups." Miss Taylor's hairdresser was earning eight hundred dollars per week. Her chauffeur was also making extraordinary amounts of money. Rex Harrison became insulted since his chauffeur was making less; "Why the hell should Elizabeth Taylor's chauffeur get more than mine just because she has a bigger chest!"

Another big reason for the great expense was the panic caused by the upper echelon [corporate managers] of Twentieth-Century Fox. "Hurry up," they insisted. Mankiewicz was forced to rewrite the script over the weekends and to shoot the film in historical sequence in the following week. No film is ever shot in this way. Unused actors cost the same amount of money as used ones, and 250 days of shooting add up; Taylor was receiving $50,000 per week, Harrison $10,000. Then one day, 1500 spears were "lost" somehow. Once, the Italian locals delivered an $80,000 bottled-water bill to Fox. Liz calculated that to average two and one-half gallons of water per person per day! Someone was outfoxing Fox.

But these are the extraordinary expenses that were not visibly part of the film itself. The luxury that pervades the screen reveals the vast expenditures for sets and costumes. Cleopatra's costumes and wigs (thirty) and jewelry (125 pieces) cost over $130,000. Her twenty-four-carat gold-thread dress for the entry into Rome alone cost $6,500. A huge cast of extras for the battles of Pharsalia, Actium, Philippi, and Alexandria (including the awesome "turtle") needed twenty-six thousand costumes; that cost half a million. The beautiful, beautiful barge that carried Cleopatra to meet Antony at Tarsus cost $250,000 and the entry into Rome another half million. In the early sixties such gory details of scandals and expenses went on and on until Mankiewicz wisely commented, "Every aspect of Cleopatra has been written, gossiped, lectured, and talked about—except the film."

THE MAJOR PERFORMERS

The film, ah yes, the film, *Cleopatra* has three serious faults that no one tries to deny: Taylor's voice, the length, and the editing. Elizabeth Taylor herself bemoaned her occasionally shrill voice, and Mankiewicz knew that audiences would think four hours was too long; he originally wanted two films of two hours, twenty minutes each, entitled *Caesar and*

Cleopatra and *Antony and Cleopatra.* Fox nixed Liz's offer to redub and Mankiewicz's plan. And even magazine critics who declared that the film "bumps from scene to ponderous scene on the square wheels of exposition" realized that this rough-flowing lethargy was largely a result of the extensive cutting." In fact, even without the additional cutting the film underwent after its initial release, Antony's character portrayal was already demolished by the first bit of surgery. In the released version, Burton plays a dissolute, weak, passionately amorous pawn who expectedly loses a battle to the severe Octavian and his most able admiral, Agrippa. What we do not see is that Antony was at one time Caesar's most trusted general, a fully competent strategist who had Octavian equally matched until Octavian's cheap, slanderous propaganda campaign turned all of Rome against him and his "Nilotic serpent." The Antony of history and the Antony of the unused portions of the film began as the competent military and political successor to the mighty Caesar; his fall could only be a tragic one. The Marcus Antonius of the released *Cleopatra* cannot be the tragic hero that Antony really was; a tragic hero has to be an epic personage who is felled from the zenith of his pride by the cruel and inexplicable force of destiny. This cinematic Antony starts at the bottom and falls sideways.

Another example of the poor cutting is the scene in which Caesar is assassinated. All of a sudden Cleopatra is seen gazing into an oracular fire, and through the flames she sees the assassination pantomimed to the tense succession of buzzing viola chords. Cut from the film was the whole explanatory scene in which Cleopatra's dependence on fire-worship and oracles was made clear. We can look at the amputated oracular scene as it stands only in total bewilderment. Then there is the scene in which Octavian reads Antony's "will" to the Senate. Cut from the film is the necessary scene that explains how the shrewd Octavian obtained this fictitious piece of paper.

But enough of flaws. Rex Harrison well deserved his Best Actor Award from the National Board of Review; he also earned nominations from the Academy and the New York Film Critics. He displays a smiling confidence in his worldly knowledge, practical wisdom, and aristocratic air, yet he allows himself to have a human love for his son and for the young Cleopatra. Like Warren William's Caesar in DeMille's

version, Harrison's Caesar is not impressed with the lovely
young queen at first. "Have you broken out of your nursery,
young lady, to annoy us adults? . . . You are what I say you
are, and nothing more," he snaps angrily. His sense of humor is splendidly controlled. When he sees Apollodorus
carry in the famous Oriental carpet all tied up with the
queen concealed inside, he knowledgeably quips, "This rug
may require some cutting." When planning his battle at Alexandria, he omits some details from his explanation to
Agrippa. When Agrippa asks what will happen at dawn,
Caesar condescendingly answers, "I thought you knew. The
sun comes up."

Cleopatra is hardly a match for such a magnificent figure
as Julius Caesar, yet she holds her own when they quarrel.
Cleopatra, kindred of Horus and Ra, beloved of the moon
and sun, daughter to Isis, and of upper and lower Egypt,
queen, reminds the haughty Caesar that "you Roman generals take on divinity so quickly—a few victories, a few mas-
sacres. Remember, yesterday Pompey was a god!" Earlier,
Caesar had been offered Pompey's head in a jar.

The love scenes between Antony and Cleopatra do drag a
bit, but their acting is most competent and the script is at
least literate, if not particularly fluid. Taylor acts very impressively at her suicide, and she becomes matronly when
she tells Caesar, "I am the Nile; I will bear many sons." Her
passionate side is revealed when she hears that Antony has
left her and married Octavia, Octavian's sister. She grabs a
sword and hacks apart his clothes and their bed with the
greatest of furor. Like Richard Burton in *Alexander the
Great,* Taylor has a particularly difficult part to play. She
must be a beautiful queen, an ambitious politician, a soft
woman, a determined mother, and a desperate snake. It is
perhaps too much to ask of an actor or actress that he or she
completely find the character of one of the most complicated
people in history. Legendary historical figures have been
some of the greatest and most involved humans ever to be
born. That a "mere actor" be expected to re-create perfectly
such a unique person is asking for the impossible.

Antony is played spritely by Burton. He characteristically
fires off lines and lines of passionate bursts in an intense
flurry, and his humor drips with sarcasm as he is about to
stab himself with his sword, "I always envied Rufio his long
arms." There can be no doubt, however, that the editor at

Twentieth-Century Fox made the unkindest cut of all to Burton's role as Marcus Antonius.

The supporting cast adds to the color and complication of the plot. Martin Landau plays the faithful aide to Antony, Rufio; Gregoire Aslan (Pothinus) and Herbert Bergof (Theodotus) act to perfection the effeminate eunuch regents of young Ptolemy. . . . Roddy McDowall capsulizes one of the most shrewd politicians in the history of mankind, Octavian, in a few brief scenes. Most effective for this characterization is Octavian's decisive victory over Antony's fleet at the battle of Actium. Agrippa planned, directed, and fought the entire battle while Octavian laid ill below deck. Agrippa runs in to tell the man who would soon be named "Imperator Augustus" that he has won a tremendous victory. Octavian weakly raises himself on his sickly arms, looks briefly at the spirited, bearded admiral, and collapses in nauseated apathy. This is right from the pages of history (though Octavian's sickness actually came at Philippi); the scene characterizes Octavian perfectly, even if he does not say one single word. . . .

THE MOST SPECTACULAR SCENES

The great hullabaloo about Elizabeth Taylor's elegant costumes, wigs, and splendid jewelry was certainly not exaggerated; it set fashion trends for months. The costly sets of Alexandria's harbor, of the Queen's palace, and of Rome, were equally well worth the price. But two scenes, in terms of lavishness and cinematic spectacle, are triumphant over all others—the barge and the entry into Rome.

The arrival of Cleopatra's barge at Tarsus (in Turkey) was designed, politically speaking, to make a gigantic impression on Antony. DeMille's splendid scene in the interior of the barge had to be equalled, if not bettered. Mankiewicz decided to build a full-scale, working barge since DeMille's exterior shots had been of a mechanical model. Then he planned to shoot the scene in the bay of Naples. One quarter of a million dollars later, the 250-foot barge with its 100-foot masts was ready for filming. It had a gracefully curved hull with two linen sails rising from it. An exotic palm tree stood in its middle. Cleopatra stood underneath light curtains at the back of the barge, resembling Plutarch's description in the *Life of Antony*, "dressed as a painted Venus." Thirty-five handmaidens throw coins over the steep sides of the boat as young men swim alongside to recover the discarded gold, and forty more lovely Egyptian maidens strew flowers into the bay. Antony must have been impressed if the real thing was as elegant and luxurious as this. In fact, Twentieth-Century Fox was so pleased with the appearance of the barge that they almost decided to pay to have the vessel brought to the New York World's Fair.

The entry of Cleopatra into Rome might be the most spectacular pageant sequence ever filmed. Seriously cut in its present form, the procession still includes seven minutes of constant entertainment, dance, spectacle, color, crowds, excitement, and grandeur. In a large square in Rome, from beneath a well-reconstructed Arch of Constantine enter white horses bearing *tubae*-players in two rows. Rows of racing chariots crisscross, and they are followed by slaves tossing red ribbons through the excited air. Fifty archers shoot colors into the sky, and a yellow caped and feathered, African dance troop perform an undulating act intriguingly blurred by thick yellow smoke. Oxen, zebra, and the (slandered) elephants follow, and huge fifteen-foot sistra are carried and shaken. Then enter men carrying long, white, ostrich-feather fans, winged and gilded women with a pyramid float that releases fluttering white doves, and soon the crowd of senators, wives, and Roman rabble step back in awe-inspired unison. Alex North's rhythmic and penetrating score leads in three hundred dark slaves in six rows. They slowly sway from side to side as they pull the two-ton float behind them. The camera views the crowded spectacle from all angles as the porphyry float enters the square. At the top . . . sit the incarnations of Isis and Horus—golden-robed Cleopatra and the young son of Julius Caesar, Caesarion. The crowd runs to her and cheers loudly. Antony looks on with great interest, not yet capable of imagining how this spectacle will influence his future. Caesar, the man of reality and vision combined, ignores the entire impressive procession except for what concerns him most. "See how unafraid he is!" he says referring to his son. Antony is not listening; he has his eyes on a different Egyptian. The Senate of Rome rises and a red carpet is rolled out. Stairs are miraculously unfolded from the float, and nine Nubians bear Cleopatra's litter. Cleopatra winks at Caesar; she and he know that Rome has been conquered. No greater single scene of pomp, color, and display was ever filmed. . . .

When the scene was being filmed, four thousand five hundred Italian extras filled the set. There had been a bomb scare the night before, and Liz feared that the reaction of the crowd would be an angry one on account of her affair with Burton. As the mob of people closed in on her float at the climax of the scene, they ignored their prescribed shouting of "Cleopatra, Cleopatra," and replaced it with a heart-warming "Leez, Leez." Amazingly, Leez, er, Liz, had survived some of the most vicious publicity any movie star had ever faced.

One more scene deserves some comment, the naval battle at Actium. This massive sea battle of September 2, 31 B.C. was, according to most historians, unequalled in ancient history. Octavian, Antony, and Cleopatra each sent in a few hundred ships to decide who would rule Rome, but for some unknown reason, Cleopatra all of a sudden pulled out of the battle; Antony followed her in ignominious defeat. The battle sequence in *Cleopatra* is frighteningly realistic. Cleopatra's flagship carries on its deck a memorable relief map with which we can follow the maneuvers of the conflict. Antony's men clash their spears against their shields in a deafening roar; urgent signals are flashed with mirrors in the sunlight; and heavy war ships are equipped with massive ramming spikes. Ballistas send roaring, smoking, firebombs of pitch into the quickly obscured sky. Trails of smoke and thunder lead to ships blazing on contact. Helpless men are soon seen swimming for their lives amidst the flotsam and fiery waters. . . . The battle of Actium in *Cleopatra* brings the bitter struggle between Octavian and Antony to an appropriately horrifying conclusion. . . .

In the final analysis, *Cleopatra* is a mighty and mighty choppy spectacle with some serious flaws and some magnificent moments. The first half is generally superior to the second, and Fox might have been wise, ironically, to have spent a little more money to put a corrective finish onto the second half. In any event, the leading characters are well-developed people for the most part. A living, breathing Caesar, Antony, Octavian, and Cleopatra seem to be inextricably involved in a most excitingly desperate era of politics, war and destiny; we could probably say the same about the making of the movie itself.

DISCUSSION QUESTIONS AND RESEARCH PROJECTS

CHAPTER 1

1. How did Egypt come to have a Greek ruling dynasty?

2. What was the political situation in Egypt when Caesar arrived there in 48 B.C.? Why had Cleopatra been forced to flee from Alexandria?

3. Describe the famous first meeting between Cleopatra and Caesar. What are some of the personal qualities that the two shared as leaders?

4. Describe the circumstances of Caesar's assassination. Where was Cleopatra at the time of the murder? Why did Caesar's death put Cleopatra in a potentially precarious or even dangerous situation?

CHAPTER 2

1. Why did Antony summon Cleopatra to Tarsus in 47 B.C.? Describe her famous entrance and the banquet that followed.

2. What advantages did Antony and Cleopatra hope to exploit in controlling the lands of the eastern Mediterranean?

3. What happened at the event known as the "Donations of Alexandria"? Why did this event upset Octavian and most other Romans?

4. How did Octavian portray Cleopatra and Antony in the propaganda war between East and West, and how was this strategy calculated to affect the attitudes of the Roman people?

5. Describe the battle of Actium, fought in 31 B.C. Who were the opposing commanders? What were the sizes of the opposing forces? What were the overall opposing battle strategies and tactics? What was the outcome of the battle? Where did Antony and Cleopatra go afterward?

6. Why did Antony attempt to take his own life? How did Cleopatra die, according to Plutarch's account?

CHAPTER 3

1. What are some of the similarities between Cleopatra's death scene as recorded by Plutarch and as dramatized by Shakespeare?

2. Compare Cleopatra's character in Shakespeare's version to that in John Dryden's *All for Love*. Which is more realistic and why?

3. In the scene excerpted from Dryden's play, why is Antony at first upset with Cleopatra?

4. How is the way George Bernard Shaw portrayed Cleopatra's character different from that in earlier versions?

5. How does the death scene in Martha Rofheart's *The Alexandrian* differ from that in Plutarch's and Shakespeare's versions?

6. What were some of the difficulties the filmmakers encountered while attempting to shoot the 1963 movie version of Cleopatra's story?

RESEARCH PROJECTS

1. Using Dio Cassius's depiction of the battle of Actium (see Document number 6) as a guide, construct a four- or five-part series of diagrams showing the various stages of the battle. Include a key indicating the symbols representing the opposing ships.

2. Rent and watch the videotape of the 1963 film "Cleopatra," starring Elizabeth Taylor in the title role, Rex Harrison as Caesar, Richard Burton as Antony, and Roddy McDowell as Octavian. Afterward, compile a detailed list of the historical events and facts the filmmakers got right and another list of those they got wrong. In the case of the inaccuracies, tell what the actual events or facts were, citing the historical accounts of Plutarch, Dio Cassius, and others to back up your statements.

Appendix of Documents

Excerpts from Original Documents Pertaining to Ancient and Medieval Accounts of Cleopatra

Editor's Note: Cleopatra was such a colorful, controversial, and larger-than-life figure, it was inevitable that she would become a favorite subject of poets and other kinds of writers. The original ancient and medieval documents that follow represent but a small sampling of the hundreds of tracts written about the notorious queen. For the most part, Roman writers vilified her, which is not surprising considering that she had challenged Rome and supposedly seduced two of its leading figures. Even her fellow Greek, Plutarch, perpetuated the fable that she "bewitched" the gullible Antony. By medieval times, she had taken on legendary proportions and was still portrayed by some, including the Italian Boccaccio, as a disreputable person. However, other writers, among them England's Chaucer, came to treat her more sympathetically, stressing the romantic notion that she had died for love. These competing negative and positive impressions of Cleopatra have persisted to the present.

Document 1: One of Cleopatra's Contemporaries Describes Her Capital

The Greek geographer Strabo (ca. 64 B.C.–ca. A.D. 23), who was only a few years younger than Cleopatra, resided for a while in her capital, Alexandria. Much of his description of the city, excerpted here, has been confirmed by archaeology.

The advantages of the city's site are various; for, first, the place is washed by two seas, on the north by the Aegyptian Sea, as it is called, and on the south by Lake Mareia, also called Mareotis. This is filled by many canals from the Nile, both from above and on the sides, and through these canals the imports are much larger than those from the sea, so that the harbour on the lake was in fact richer than that on the sea; and here the exports from Alexandria also are larger than the imports; and anyone might judge, if he were at either Alexandria or Dicaearchia and saw the merchant vessels both at their arrival and at their departure, how much heavier or lighter they sailed thither or therefrom. And in addition to the great value of the things brought down from both directions, both into the harbour on the sea and into that on the lake, the salubrity of the air is also worthy of remark. And this likewise results from the fact that the land is washed by water on both sides and because of the timeliness of the Nile's risings; for the other cities that are situated on lakes have heavy and stifling air in the heats of summer, because the lakes then become marshy along their edges because of the evaporation caused by the sun's rays, and, accordingly, when so much filth-laden moisture rises, the air inhaled is noisome and starts pestilential diseases, whereas at Alexandria, at the beginning of summer, the Nile, being full, fills the lake also, and leaves no marshy matter to corrupt the rising vapours. At that time, also, the Etesian winds blow from the north and from a vast sea, so that the Alexandrians pass their time most pleasantly in summer.

The shape of the area of the city is like a *chlamys* [a cloak]; the long sides of it are those that are washed by the two waters, having a diameter of about thirty *stadia* [about 3½ miles], and the short sides are the isthmuses, each being seven or eight stadia wide and pinched in on one side by the sea and on the other by the lake. The city as a whole is intersected by streets practicable for horse-riding and chariot-driving, and by two that are very broad, extending to more than a *plethrum* [about 100 feet] in breadth, which cut one another into two sections and at right angles. And the city contains most beautiful public precincts and also the royal palaces, which constitute one-fourth or even one-third of the whole circuit of the city; for just as each of the kings, from love of splendour, was wont to add some adornment to the public monuments, so also he would invest himself at his own expense with a residence, in addition to those already built, so that now, to quote the words of the poet, "there is building upon building." All, however, are connected with one another and the harbour, even those that lie outside the harbour. The Museum [university and research center] is also a part of the royal palaces; it has a public walk, an Exedra with seats, and a large house, in which is the common mess-hall of the men of learning who share the Museum. This group of men not only hold property in common, but also have a priest in charge of the Museum, who formerly was appointed by the kings, but is now appointed by Caesar. The Soma also, as it is called, is a part of the royal palaces. This was the enclosure which contained the burial-places of the kings and that of Alexander [the Great, the Greek king who founded the city in the fourth century B.C.]. . . .

Strabo, *Geography.* Trans. Horace L. Jones. Cambridge, MA: Harvard University Press, 1967, pp. 69–71.

DOCUMENT 2: CLEOPATRA'S LAVISH BANQUET

Plutarch was not the only ancient writer who described the sumptuous banquet the Egyptian queen threw for Antony when they met in

Tarsus in 41 B.C. This version is by the second-century Greek historian Socrates of Rhodes.

Meeting Antony in Cilicia, Cleopatra arranged in his honour a royal symposium [dinner party], in which the service was wholly of gold and jewelled vessels made with exquisite art; even the walls were hung with tapestries woven of gold and silver threads. And having spread twelve tables, she invited him and his chosen friends. He was overwhelmed with the richness of the display; but she quietly smiled and said the things he saw were a gift to him. She invited him to come and dine with her again on the morrow, with his friends and his officers. On this occasion she provided an even more sumptuous symposium by far; the vessels used the previous time appeared paltry things; and once again she presented Antony with everything. As for the officers, each was allowed to take away the couch on which he had lain. Even the sideboards, as well as the couch-spreads, were divided among them; and when they went off, she supplied litters for guests of high rank, with bearers, while for the larger number she provided horses with silver-plated harness. For everyone she sent Ethiopian slaves to carry the torches. On the fourth day she distributed fees amounting to a talent [6,000 drachmas, a very large sum at the time] for the purchase of roses; the floors of the dining-rooms were strewn with them a cubit deep, in net-like festoons spread over everything.

Quoted in Michael Grant, *Cleopatra.* New York: Simon and Schuster, 1972, p. 117.

DOCUMENT 5: CLEOPATRA'S FAMOUS PEARL TRICK

One of the most famous stories about Cleopatra concerns some fabulous pearls that she supposedly dissolved by dropping them into a container of vinegar. The source is the large work on natural history written by the Roman encyclopedist Pliny the Elder (A.D. 23–79). In reality, vinegar does not dissolve pearls; so either Pliny's own source was mistaken, or Cleopatra tricked Antony by swallowing the pearl whole and retrieving it later by "natural" means.

Two specimen pearls were the largest of all time. Cleopatra, the last queen of Egypt, owned both, which she had inherited from the kings of the East. When Antony was taking his fill every day at choice banquets, Cleopatra, headstrong woman as she was, with a haughty contempt, poured scorn on all his elegance and splendour. When Antony asked how it could be more magnificent, Cleopatra replied that she would spend 10 million sesterces on one banquet.

Antony wanted to know how this could be achieved, although he did not believe it possible. So bets were laid and next day, when the dispute was to be settled, Cleopatra put before Antony a banquet sufficiently splendid for the day not to be wasted, but one such as was served every day; he laughed and complained at its limited budget. She explained that this was just the starter and that the banquet proper would complete the account—her dinner alone would cost 10 million sesterces. Cleopatra ordered the main course. Following her instructions, the servants set before her only a single vessel of vinegar, the acidity of which can dissolve pearls.

On her ears she was wearing that remarkable and truly unique work of Nature. Antony waited breathlessly to see what on earth she was going to do. Cleopatra took off one ear-ring, dropped the pearl in the vinegar and, when it had dissolved, swallowed it. Lucius Plancus, who was umpire for the wager, put his hand on the other pearl when she prepared to destroy it in a similar way and declared that Antony had been defeated—an omen that was to be fulfilled. The story is told that when Cleopatra, who had won this substantial wager, was captured, the second pearl was cut in two so that half a dinner might adorn each ear of the statue of Venus in the Pantheon at Rome.

Pliny the Elder, *Natural History*, excerpted in *Natural History: A Selection*. Trans. John F. Healy. New York: Penguin Books, 1991, pp. 136–37.

DOCUMENT 4: CLEOPATRA'S CURE FOR BALDNESS

A number of ancient sources credit Cleopatra with authoring a popular treatise on cosmetics. If she did in fact produce such a work, it has not survived. However, this supposed excerpt from it, purporting to be a cure for baldness, was preserved in the works of other writers.

For bald patches, powder red sulphuret or arsenic and take it up with oak gum, as much as it will bear. Put on a rag and apply, having soaped the place well first. I have mixed the above with foam of nitre and it worked well. . . .

The following is the best of all, acting for fallen hairs, when applied with oil or pomatum; acts also for falling-off eyelashes or for people going bald all over. It is wonderful. Of domestic mice burnt, 1 part; of vine-rag burnt, 1 part; of horse's teeth burnt, 1 part; of bear's grease, 1; of deer's marrow, 1; of reedbark, 1. To be pounded when dry, and mixed with lots of honey till it gets the consistency of honey; then the bear's-grease and marrow to be mixed (when melted), the medicine to be put in a brass flask, and the bald part rubbed till it sprouts.

Quoted in George Bernard Shaw, *Caesar and Cleopatra*. Baltimore: Penguin Books, 1966, p. 126.

DOCUMENT 5: THE ONGOING ANIMOSITY BETWEEN CLEOPATRA AND HEROD

The Jewish historian Josephus (born ca. A.D. 37) mentioned Cleopatra a number of times in his works, usually in unflattering terms. In this excerpt from The Jewish War, *he describes the hatred and rivalry between the ambitious Egyptian queen and her neighbor, Herod, king of Judaea (the area roughly occupied by modern Israel). Herod (the same one in the Bible who orders all the male children in Bethlehem killed in an effort to kill the newborn Christ) was one of the eastern rulers subordinate to Antony; so the Judaean king was forced on occasion to tolerate Cleopatra, despite his dislike for her.*

King Herod did not make the mistake of treating all the citizens alike: by bestowing honours on those who had taken his side he increased their devotion; the supporters of [his old enemy] Antigonus he liquidated. As money was now tight, he turned all his personal treasures into cash and sent it to Antony and his staff. Even so he could not buy freedom from all trouble: Antony, ruined by his passion for Cleopatra, had become the complete slave of his desire, while Cleopatra had gone right through her own family till not a single relation was left alive, and thirsting now for the blood of strangers, was slandering the authorities in Syria and urging Antony to have them executed, thinking that in this way she would easily become mistress of all their possessions. She even extended her acquisitiveness to Jews and Arabs and worked in secret to get their kings, Herod and Malchus, put to death.

Antony was sober enough to realize that one part of her demands—the killing of honest men and famous kings—was utterly immoral; but he cut them to the heart by withdrawing his friendship. He sliced off large parts of their territory, including the palm-grove at Jericho in which the balsam is produced, and gave them to Cleopatra along with all the cities except Tyre and Sidon south of the river Eleutherus [in Palestine]. Mistress now of this domain she escorted Antony as far as the Euphrates on his way to fight the Parthians, and then came via Apamea and Damascus into Judaea. Herod placated her hostility with costly gifts, and leased back from her the lands broken off from his kingdom, at two hundred talents a year! Finally he escorted her all the way to Pelusium, showing her every attention. It was not long before Antony reappeared from Parthia, bringing a prisoner—Artabazes the son of Tigranes—as a present for Cleopatra, to whom, along with the money and all the booty, the unfortunate Parthian was immediately handed over.

When the war that ended at Actium broke out, Herod prepared to take the field with Antony, having settled all disturbances in Judaea and captured Hyrcania, a fortress till then in the hands of Antigonus' sister. But he was prevented by Cleopatra's cunning from sharing Antony's dangers; as mentioned already, she was scheming against the kings, and now she persuaded Antony to entrust Herod with the war against the Arabs—if he won she would become mistress of Arabia, if he lost, of Judaea, and she would be using one ruler to get rid of the other.

It was Herod, however, who benefited by her scheme. He began by plundering enemy country, then he got together a large force of cavalry and sent them into battle near the city of Dium, emerging victorious despite determined resistance. This defeat led to feverish activity among the Arabs, who gathered at Canatha in Coele Syria in enormous strength and awaited the Jews. There Herod arrived with his army, and endeavouring to conduct his campaign with great circumspection ordered a camp to be fortified. His soldiers, however, disregarded his commands, and elated by their earlier success attacked the Arabs, routed them at the first charge and followed in pursuit. But in the pursuit Herod was the victim of treachery, the inhabitants of Canatha being sent against him by Athenio, one of Cleopatra's generals who was permanently hostile. Their onslaught restored the morale of the Arabs, who turned about, and joining forces on rocky, difficult ground routed Herod's men, slaughtering them wholesale.

Josephus, *The Jewish War.* Trans. G.A. Williamson. Rev. E. Mary Smallwood. New York: Penguin Books, 1981, pp. 75–76.

DOCUMENT 6: THE BATTLE OF ACTIUM

This is the complete description given by Dio Cassius (ca. 163–ca. 235) of the naval encounter at Actium in 31 B.C., the battle that effectively ended Cleopatra's and Antony's dreams of a new world order and decided the fate of the Roman world for many years to come.

[Octavian] drew up a plan to allow Antony's ships to sail through, and then to attack from the rear as they fled. For his part, he hoped that his vessels could muster enough speed to capture Antony and Cleopatra quickly, and he calculated that once it became clear that they were trying to escape, he could, through their action, persuade the rest to surrender without fighting. But this scheme was opposed by Agrippa, who feared that their ships, which were using oars, would be too slow to catch the fugitives, who intended to hoist sails. Also a violent rainstorm accompanied by a tremendous wind had in the meanwhile struck Antony's fleet, leaving it in total confusion, though it had not touched his own, and this gave him some confidence that he would win easily enough. So he abandoned his plan, and, like Antony, posted large numbers of infantry on his ships. He also embarked his subordinates in auxiliary craft: they were to move rapidly between the ships, giving the necessary instructions to the men in action, and reporting back all that he needed to know. Then he waited for the enemy to sail out.

At the sound of the trumpet Antony's fleet began to move, and, keeping close together, formed their line a little way outside the strait, but then advanced no further. Octavian put out, as if to engage should the enemy stand their ground, or else to make them retire. But when they neither came out against him, nor turned away, but stayed in position and even increased the density of their closely packed formation, Octavian halted his advance, being in doubt as to what to do. He ordered his rowers to let their oars rest in the water, and waited for a while; after this he suddenly made a signal and, advancing both his wings, rounded his line in the form of an enveloping crescent. His object was to encircle the enemy if possible, or, if not, at least to break up their formation. Antony was alarmed by this outflanking and encircling manoeuvre, moved forward to meet it as best he could, and so unwillingly joined battle with Octavian.

So the fleets came to grips and the battle began. Each side uttered loud shouts to the men aboard, urging the troops to summon up their prowess and their fighting spirit, and the men could also hear a babel of orders being shouted at them from those on shore.

The two sides used different tactics. Octavian's fleet, having smaller and faster ships, could advance at speed and ram the enemy, since their armour gave them protection on all sides. If they sank a vessel, they had achieved their object; if not, they would back water before they could be engaged at close quarters, and either ram the same ship suddenly a second time, or let it go and turn against others. When they had damaged these as much as they could in a short time, they would seek out fresh opponents over and over again, constantly switching their attack, so that their onslaught always came where it was least expected. They feared their adversaries' long-range missiles no less than their superior strength in fighting at close quarters, and so they wasted no time either in the approach or the clash. They would sail up suddenly so as to close with their target before the enemy's archers could hit them, inflict damage or cause enough confusion to escape being grappled, and then quickly back away out of range.

Antony's tactics, on the other hand, were to pour heavy volleys of stones and arrows upon the enemy ships as they approached, and then try to entrap them with iron grapnels. When they could reach their targets, Antony's ships got the upper hand, but if they missed, their own hulls would be pierced by the rams and they would sink, or else, in the attempt to avoid collision, they would lose time and expose themselves to attack by other ships. Two or three of Octavian's vessels would fall upon one of Antony's, with some inflicting all the damage they could, while the others bore the brunt of the counter-attack.

On the one side the helmsmen and rowers suffered the heaviest casualties, on the other the marines. Octavian's ships resembled cavalry, now launching a charge, and now retreating, since they could attack or draw off as they chose, while Antony's were like heavy infantry, warding off the enemy's efforts to ram them, but also striving to hold them with their grappling-hooks. Each fleet in turn gained the advantage over the other: the one would dart in against the rows of oars which projected from the ships' sides and break the blades, while the other fighting from its higher decks would sink its adversaries with stones and ballistic missiles. At the same time each side had its weaknesses. Antony's ships could do no damage to the enemy as they approached: Octavian's, if they failed to sink a vessel when they had rammed it, would find the odds turned against them once they were grappled.

For a long while the struggle was evenly poised and neither side could gain the upper hand anywhere, but the end came in the following way. Cleopatra, whose ship was riding at anchor behind the battle lines, could not endure the long hours of uncertainty while the issue hung in the balance: both as a woman and as an Egyptian she found herself stretched to breaking-point by the agony of the suspense, and the constant and unnerving effort of picturing victory or defeat. Suddenly she made her choice—to flee—and made the signal for the others, her own subjects. So when her ships immediately hoisted their sails and stood out to sea, a favourable wind having luckily got up, Antony supposed that they were turning tail, not on Cleopatra's orders, but out of fear because they felt themselves to have been defeated, and so he followed them.

At this, dismay and confusion spread to the rest of Antony's men, and they resolved likewise to take whatever means of escape lay open. Some raised their sails, while others threw the turrets and heavy equipment overboard to lighten the vessels and help them to get away. While they were thus engaged, their opponents again attacked: they had not pursued Cleopatra's fleeing squadron, because they themselves had not taken sails aboard and had put out prepared only for a naval battle. This meant that there were many ships to attack each one of Antony's, both at long range and alongside. The result was that the struggle took many forms on both sides and was carried on with the greatest ferocity. Octavian's soldiers battered the lower parts of the ships from stem to stern, smashed the oars, broke off the rudders, and, climbing on to the decks, grappled with their enemies. They dragged down some, thrust others overboard, and fought hand to hand with others, since they now equalled them in numbers. Antony's men forced their attackers back with boat-hooks, cut them down with axes, hurled down stones and other missiles which had been prepared for this purpose, forced down those who tried to scale the ships' sides, and engaged all who came within reach. A witness of the battle might have compared it, if one can reduce the scale, to the spectacle of a number of walled towns or islands set close together being besieged from the sea. Thus one side strove to clamber up the sides of the ships, as it might be up a cliff or fortress, and brought to bear all the equipment which is needed for such an assault, while the others struggled to repel them, using all the weapons and tactics which are known to defenders.

As the fighting remained evenly balanced, Octavian, who found himself in doubt what to do next, sent for fire from his camp. Until then he had been unwilling to use it, since he was anxious to capture Antony's treasure intact. He now resorted to it because he saw that it was impossible to win in any other way and believed that this was the only weapon which would help him. The battle then changed its character. The attackers would approach their targets from many different points at once, bombarding them with blazing missiles and hurling by hand javelins with torches attached to them; from a longer range they would also catapult jars filled with charcoal or pitch. The defenders tried to ward off these missiles one by one, but when some got through, they ignited the timbers and immediately started a blaze, as is bound to happen on a ship. The crews first put out the flames with the drinking water which they carried on board, and when that ran out, they used sea water. If they managed to throw this on the fire in great quantities at once, they could sometimes quench it by the sheer volume of the water. But this was not always possible, since their buckets were few and of no great size. In their confusion they sometimes only half filled them, and in that case instead of reducing the blaze they only increased it, since small quantities of salt water poured on a fire make it burn all the more strongly. So when they found that they were failing to check the flames, they threw on their heavy cloaks and even dead bodies, and for a time these stifled the conflagration, which seemed to die down. But later, and especially when the wind blew strongly, the flames leaped up more violently than ever, fed by their own efforts.

So long as only a section of the ship was on fire, the men would stand close by and jump into it, cutting away some of the planks and scattering others; in some instances the men threw the timbers into the sea, and in others against their adversaries, in the hope that they might cause them some hurt. Others would take up position in the part of the ship that was undamaged, and would ply their long spears and grappling-hooks more desperately than ever, in the hope of making some enemy ship fast to theirs and boarding her, or, if not, setting her alight as well. But when none of the enemy came near enough, since they were guarding against this very possibility, and when the fire spread to the encircling sides of the ship and descended into the hold, they found themselves in the most terrible plight of all. Some, especially the sailors, were overcome by the smoke before the flames ever came near them, while others were roasted in the midst of the holocaust as if they were in ovens. Others were incinerated in their armour as it grew red-hot. Others, again, to avoid such a fate, or when they were half burned, threw off their armour and were wounded by the missiles shot at them from long range, or jumped into the sea and were drowned, or were clubbed by their enemies and sank, or were devoured by sea-monsters. The only men to find a death which was endurable in the midst of such sufferings were those who either killed one another in return for the service, or took their own lives before such a fate could befall them. These were spared the torments I have described, and their corpses were burned on board the ships, as though they were on a funeral pyre.

When Octavian's men saw that the battle had taken this turn, they at first held off from the enemy, since some of the latter could still defend themselves. But when the fire had taken hold of the ships, and the men aboard them, so far from being able to injure an opponent, could no longer even defend themselves, they eagerly sailed up to Antony's vessels in the hope of seizing their treasure, and tried to put out the fires which they themselves had started. The result was that many of them perished, both from the flames and from their own greed.

Dio Cassius, *Roman History,* excerpted in *The Roman History: The Reign of Augustus.* Trans. Ian Scott-Kilvert. New York: Penguin Books, 1987, pp. 57–61.

DOCUMENT 7: VIRTUOUS AUGUSTUS TRIUMPHS OVER A SHAMEFUL QUEEN

In his magnificent Aeneid, *the first-century B.C. Roman poet Virgil sang the praises of Rome and its "glorious" champion, his friend Augustus, who was of course the former Octavian. In contrast to Dio Cassius's straightforward historical account of the battle of Actium, Virgil's is stylistic, set in poetic verse, and heavily biased in favor of the victor, Augustus. The poet makes it appear as though Augustus orchestrated the battle plan, mentioning the real master strategist, Agrippa, only in passing. And Virgil disdains even to mention the "shameful" Cleopatra's name, calling her Antony's "Egyptian spouse" and "the Queen."*

Between these scenes on a broad swathe there swept
A golden semblance of the swelling sea,
Its blue billows flecked with whitening wave-crests,
And all about it dolphins silver-bright
Threaded, and thrashed the surface with their tails.
Then you could see as centerpiece the battle
Of Actium and the brazen-armored fleets,
All Leucate was clear as it throbbed with warwork,
And the waves gleamed with gold. There was Augustus
Leading the Italians into baffle, the whole Senate
And people behind him, and the small household Gods,
And the Great of Heaven—he stood on the high stern:
Twin flames played round his joyous brow, the Star
Of his Fathers dawned above his head. Elsewhere
Agrippa, with the aid of winds and gods,
Towering led his line and on his brows,
A proud war-emblem, gleamed the naval crown
Embellished with its replicas of ships' rams.
Opposing them was Antony backed by the riches
Of all the East and various nations' arms,

A conqueror from the far East and the shores
Of the Red Sea, enlisting with him Egypt
And the strength of the Orient and the farthest limits
Of Bactria and—shame!—his Egyptian spouse.
The navies closed at speed and the whole sea
Boiled with the oar-strokes and the three-pronged rams.
They sought the open sea and you would think
The Cyclades uprooted were afloat,
Or that high mountains crashed against high mountains
So bulked the embattled poops on which the warriors
      mustered;
Wads of blazing tow and a whirl of steel
From every hand came hurling and Neptune's fields
Were newly incarnadined. In the midst the Queen
Rallied her forces with her native timbrel
Nor did she give us yet a glance at the pair
Of asps in wait for her. Here were her gods,
Monsters of every kind, to the baying dogheaded Anubis [an
      Egyptian god],
With weapons poised against Neptune, against Venus,
Against Minerva [Roman deities]. In the thick of the fray
Raged Mars [god of war], picked out in iron, and from the sky
Loomed the grim Furies; Discord swept along
Rejoicing, her mantle rent, and Bellona [goddess of war]
      followed her
With a bloody knout. Apollo of Actium
Seeing all this from above, was drawing his bow
In dread of which every Egyptian, Indian, and Arab, every
      Sabean there
Was turning his back for flight. The Queen herself
Was shown as she whistled for the wind of flight
And setting sail she was shaking loose the sheets.
The Master of Fire had printed upon her the pallor
Of her approaching death, as she forged ahead
Cleaving the slaughter, with following wind and tide.

Virgil, *Aeneid*. Trans. Patric Dickinson. New York: New American Library, 1961, pp. 189–90.

DOCUMENT 8: CLEOPATRA'S LAST DAYS ON EARTH

In this excerpt from his massive history of Rome, Dio Cassius describes the last few days of Cleopatra's life. Although similar in many ways to Plutarch's account of the same events, it makes a stronger point about the uncertainty of the means of her death.

[After Antony's death,] she now believed that she could place some degree of trust in Octavian and at once sent word to him of what had happened, and yet she could not feel completely confident that no harm would befall her. She therefore remained in seclusion within the building, so that even if there were no other reason for keeping her alive, she could at least trade upon Octavian's fear concerning her treasure to obtain a pardon and keep her throne. Even when she had sunk to such depths of misfortune, she remembered that she was queen and preferred to die bearing the title and majesty of a sovereign rather than live in a private station. At any rate she kept ready fire to destroy her treasure, and asps and other reptiles to end her life; she had experimented before on human beings to discover how these creatures caused death in each case.

Now Octavian was much concerned not only to make himself master of her wealth, but also to capture her alive and lead her in his triumph at Rome. However, as he had given her a pledge of a kind, he did not wish to be seen as having tricked her; rather he wanted to make her appear as his captive, who had been to some extent subdued against her will. He therefore sent Gaius Proculeius, a knight, and Epaphroditus, a freedman, to visit her, and instructed them carefully as to what they should say and do. The two accordingly obtained an audience with Cleopatra, began by discussing a number of reasonable proposals, and then, before anything had been agreed, suddenly laid hands on her. After this they removed from her any means of ending her life, and allowed her to spend some days in the monument where she was engaged in embalming Antony's body. They moved her to the palace, but did not dismiss any of her accustomed retinue or attendants: their object was that she should continue to cherish the hope of obtaining her wishes, and so do nothing to harm herself. At any rate, when she sought an audience with Octavian, her request was granted, and to further the deception he promised that he would visit her himself.

So she prepared a superbly decorated apartment and a richly ornamented couch, dressed herself with studied negligence—indeed her appearance in mourning wonderfully enhanced her beauty—and seated herself on the couch. Beside her she arranged many different portraits and busts of Julius Caesar, and in her bosom she carried all the letters Caesar had sent her. Then as Octavian entered, she sprang to her feet, blushed, and cried, 'Greetings, my lord, for now the gods have given supremacy to you and taken it from me. But now you can see with your own eyes how Caesar looked when he visited me so many times, and you have heard tell of how he honoured me and made me queen of Egypt. You should learn something of me from his own words; these are the letters which he wrote with his own hand: take them and read them.'

So saying, she went on to read many of Caesar's passionate expressions of his feelings for her. At one moment she would weep and kiss the letters, and then she would kneel and bow her head before Caesar's portraits. She kept turning her eyes towards Octavian and lamenting her fate in a plaintive musical tone. Her voice melted as she murmured, 'How can thy letters, Caesar, help me now?' and 'And yet in this man thou livest for me again,' then, 'Would that I had died before thee,' and still again, 'But if I have him, I have thee.'

Such were the subtle tones of speech and changes of expression with which she addressed Octavian, casting sweet looks towards him and murmuring tender words. Octavian understood the passion with which she was speaking and the seductive power of her gestures; however, he acted as if he were unaware of these, looked towards the ground and merely replied, 'Do not distress yourself, lady, take heart, no harm shall come to you.' But her spirits were utterly cast down, because he neither looked at her, nor made any mention of her kingdom, nor uttered so much as a word of love. She threw herself on her knees, burst out weeping, and said, 'I have no desire to live, nor can I live. But this favour I beg of you, in memory of your father, that since the gods gave me to Antony after him, I too may die with Antony. I wish that I had perished at the very instant after Caesar's death. But seeing that it was my fate to suffer that parting from him, send me to Antony. Do not grudge that I should be buried with him: as I die because of him, so may I live with him, even in Hades.'

So she spoke, in the hope of arousing his pity, but Octavian made no reply. As he was afraid that she might still end her own life, he urged her yet again to take heart. After this he did not dismiss any of her attendants, but treated her with especial care in his desire that she should make a brilliant spectacle at his triumph. She guessed that this was his plan, and since she felt such a fate to be worse than any number of deaths, she now truly longed to die. She begged Octavian time and again that her life should be ended by one means or another, and of her own accord she thought of many ways to bring this about. Finally, when she could put none of these into effect, she professed to have undergone a change of heart and to place great hopes for the future both in Octavian and in Livia [Octavian's wife]. She said that she would sail to Rome of her own free will, and prepared a number of specially treasured chosen ornaments to take as gifts. In this way she hoped to convince them that she did not intend to die, and hence that she would be less closely guarded and thus enabled to kill herself

So it came about. As soon as the others, and in particular Epaphroditus, who had been charged with her safe keeping, had become convinced that her state of mind was as she described it and so relaxed their strict surveillance, she prepared to die as painlessly as possible. First she gave a sealed paper to Epaphroditus himself to deliver, in which she begged Octavian to give orders for her to be buried beside Antony. She pretended that the letter concerned some other matter, and using this pretext to get the freedman out of the way, she set about her task. She put on her finest robes, seated herself with majestic grace, took in her hands all the emblems of royalty, and so died.

No one knows for certain by what means she perished, for the only marks that were found on her body were tiny pricks on the arm. Some say that she applied to herself an asp [poisonous snake], which had been brought to her in a water jar, or perhaps covered beneath some flowers. According to others she had smeared a pin with some poison whose composition rendered it harmless if the contact were external, but which, if even the smallest quantity entered the bloodstream, would quickly prove fatal, although also painless; according to this theory, she had previously worn the pin in her hair as usual, but now made a small scratch in her arm and caused the poison to enter the blood. In this or some similar way she had died, and her two waiting women with her. . . .

When Octavian heard of Cleopatra's death, he was astounded and not only came to see her body, but called in the aid of drugs. . . .

As for Octavian, when he found that it was impossible to revive Cleopatra, he felt both admiration and pity for her, but he was bitterly chagrined on his own account, as if all the glory of his victory had been taken away from him.

Antony and Cleopatra were the cause of many misfortunes to the Egyptians and many to the Romans. These were the circumstances in which they fought the war and met their deaths. They were both embalmed in the same manner and buried in the same tomb. The qualities of character which they possessed, and the fortunes which they experienced, may be described as follows. Antony had no superior in recognizing where his duty lay, and yet he committed many senseless acts. There were times when he excelled in courage, and yet he often failed through cowardice: he was capable equally of true greatness of spirit and of extreme baseness. He would plunder the property of others and squander his own. He showed compassion to many without cause, and punished even more without justice. Thus although he rose from most weak beginnings to a position of great power, and from the depths of poverty to the possession of great riches, yet he gained no profit from either situation. Instead, after hoping that he alone would rule the empire of the Romans, he took his own life.

Cleopatra was a woman of insatiable sexuality and insatiable avarice. She often displayed an estimable ambition, but equally often an overweening arrogance. It was by means of the power of love that she acquired the sovereignty of the Egyptians, and when she aspired to obtain dominion over the Romans in the same fashion, she failed in the attempt and lost her kingdom besides. Through her own unaided genius she captivated the two greatest Romans of her time, and because of the third, she destroyed herself.

Dio Cassius, *Roman History,* excerpted in *The Roman History: The Reign of Augustus.* Trans. Ian Scott-Kilvert. New York: Penguin Books, 1987, pp. 72–76.

DOCUMENT 9: A ROMAN SENATOR'S DISDAIN FOR CLEOPATRA

The great first-century B.C. Roman senator, orator, and writer, Marcus Tullius Cicero, who had been one of Caesar's longtime political opponents, mentioned Cleopatra in some of the many letters he wrote to his friend Atticus. In this excerpt from the letter of June 13, 44 B.C., a few months after Caesar's murder, Cicero candidly expresses his feelings about the Egyptian queen, who by that time had returned to Alexandria with her son.

I hate the queen! And the man who vouches for her promises, Ammonius, knows I have good reason to do so; although the gifts she promised me were of a literary nature and not beneath my dignity— the sort I should not have minded proclaiming in public. Her man Sara too, beside being a rogue, I have found impertinent towards myself. Once, and once only, have I seen him in my house; and then, when I asked him politely what he wanted, he said he was looking for Atticus. And the Queen's insolence, when she was living in Caesar's house in the gardens beyond the Tiber, I cannot recall without indignation. So no dealings with that lot. They seem to think I have not only no spirit, but no feelings at all.

Quoted in Michael Grant, *Cleopatra.* New York: Simon and Schuster, 1972, p. 96.

DOCUMENT 10: LAMENT FOR A "MONSTROUS QUEEN"

Cicero was not the only one of Cleopatra's Roman contemporaries who disliked her and everything she stood for. After her death, the poet Horace (65–8 B.C.), part of the circle of writers and artists that included Octavian/Augustus's friend, Virgil, composed this poem about her. Note that, although Horace is highly critical of her through most of the piece, at the end he cannot help but admire her pride and courage.

Cleopatra

DRINK, my companions, drink!
Shake the ground with your dancing,
Deck the couch of the gods,
And eat as you would eat
At an old-time Saliar feast!

Ere now it would not have been fitting
To take the Caecuban wine
Out from the cellars ancestral,
While that queen was preparing
The ruin of our city,
And the funeral of our empire,
For which she had hoped in her madness—
She, and her loathsome herd
Of creatures vile with disease,

So ungoverned,
So drunk with success,
That they could hope for anything!

But when the battle had ended,
When the sound and the fury was done,
She found herself
With scarce one ship
Saved from the flames;
And the captives,
Whom the Marean battle
Had made mad with fright,
Knew true terror now.

Caesar [Octavian] pressed on from Italy
Against the fugitives,
Like a hawk after doves,
Or a hunter in the snowy
Haemonian fields
Against a swift hare,
So that he might give
This monstrous queen to chains.

Seeking a more noble end,
She shuddered not
With a woman's fear of the sword;
She sought not to escape
With her swift fleet to sonic distant realm,
To supplant her lost Egypt.
With eyes serene, she dared
To look upon her fallen palace
Dared to take in her hands
The maddened vipers [poisonous snakes],
That her body might deeply drink
Of their deadly venom.
And once resolved to die,
She was more fiercely proud.—
—How she hated our cruel Liburnian sailors!—
She was a woman,
Yet her spirit fell never so low
That she could let herself,
Yesterday a queen,
Become tomorrow
A captive in a Roman triumph.

Horace, "Cleopatra," trans. Barklie Henry, in Francis R.B. Godolphin, ed., *The Latin Poets*. New York: Random House, 1949, pp. 243–44.

DOCUMENT 11: NEVER FEAR, FOR AUGUSTUS IS HERE

The Roman poet Propertius (48–16 B.C.) was another contemporary of Octavian, Cleopatra, and Antony who derided the notorious queen in the years immediately following her death. The "Caesar" of the title of the following poem is not the one assassinated in the Senate, but rather Octavian, who by the time the poem was written had already been granted the title of Augustus, the "exalted one." Propertius (who incidentally used rhyme more often than any other Latin poet) here expresses thankfulness for both Cleopatra's demise and Augustus's leadership.

Cleopatra and Caesar

WHY WONDER that the other sex
The tenor of my life should vex
And make a man a woman's thrall,
A bondsman [slave or servant] at her beck and call?
My courage you should not arraign
Because I cannot break my chain:
The sailor has a right to fear,
None better knows when death is near;
The soldier who has fought and bled
Has cause the battle-field to dread.
I also in my earlier days
Boasted the principles you praise;
But now from my example learn
To fear that next will come your turn. . . .
What of that
Woman, she whose charms
Brought scandal on the Roman arms,
And, strumpet [whore] to her very thralls,
Aspired to pass the Roman walls
And rule our Senate, as the fee
Due from her lover's lechery?
Cursed Alexandria, Memphis curst,
Thou land in cunning deeply versed,
How often on thy noisome silt
Has Roman blood been freely spilt! . . .
How could that Rome at whose command
The fasces [symbols of Roman power] broke in [the last Roman
     king] Tarquin's hand,
Alike by name and nature proud,
Before a woman now have bowed?
Then triumph, Rome, and, safe again
Pray that Augustus long may reign.
The city on the Seven Hills
That rules the nations as it wills,
She caused, by war's alarms beset,
To tremble at a woman's threat.

Yet did she flee, and haunt awhile
The marshes of the affrighted Nile,
Until, submitting in despair
Her wrists the Roman fetters wear.
I've seen the sacred adder's [poisonous snake's] fang
Upon her bosom close and hang,
And her whole body slowly creep
On the dark road to endless sleep.
'Why, Rome, should I have caused you dread,'
Her own besotted voice had said,
'While you among your men of state
Could count a citizen so great?'. . .
Although so long as Caesar's [i.e., Octavian/Augustus's] here
Scarce Jove [Jupiter] himself need Romans fear!
Apollo on the Leucadian coast
Shall call to mind that routed host:
So grand a militant array
Was shattered in a single day! [a reference to Cleopatra's defeat
    at Actium]
You sailors, whether starting out
Or for your home ports put about,
Thank Caesar that you're roaming free
From end to end the Ionian Sea.

Propertius, "Cleopatra and Caesar," trans. Seymour G. Tremenheere, in Francis R.B. Godolphin, ed., *The Latin Poets*. New York: Random House, 1949, pp. 368–71.

DOCUMENT 12: CAESAR JUST AS DISGRACEFUL AS CLEOPATRA

In his epic poem, The Civil War *(also known as* Pharsalia*), excerpted here, the Roman writer Lucan (Marcus Annaeus Lucanus, A.D. 39–65) recalled the bloody conflict between Julius Caesar and Pompey that culminated in Pompey's defeat at Pharsalus (in Greece) in 48 B.C. Lucan cast Caesar as the villain and Pompey as the hero, supposedly because Pompey sought to uphold republican traditions and Caesar to destroy them (a somewhat distorted view of the actual events). Part of what made Caesar corrupt, the poet holds, was his seduction by and relationship with the "evil" Cleopatra.*

Cleopatra, the shame of Egypt, the lascivious fury who was to become the bane of Rome, . . . resembled Helen of Sparta, whose dangerous beauty ruined Mycenae and laid Troy in ashes; at all events the passions she aroused did no less damage to our country. You may say, incredible though it sounds, that the noise of her brazen rattle maddened the Capitol of Rome; that she used the spells of cowardly Egypt to destroy Roman armies, that she nearly headed an Egyptian triumph and led Augustus Caesar a chained captive behind her. Until Actium had been fought it seemed possible that the world would be ruled by a woman, and not a Roman woman, either. Her insolence began on the night when she first gave herself to Caesar; it is easy to pardon Mark Antony's later infatuation when one remembers that she fired a heart so flinty as Caesar's. Despite his rage and madness, despite his bloody memories of Pharsalus, he consented in that palace haunted by Pompey's ghost to let an adulterous love affair complicate his military anxieties; and even begot a bastard son on the girl. What a disgrace to forget his daughter Julia, the dead man's wife, and posthumously present her with a half-brother, child of that abominable Ptolemaic princess! He even allowed his defeated enemies to rally in far-off Libya, while he wasted time on a sordid intrigue; and quietly deeded Egypt to Cleopatra instead of conquering it for himself.

She approached him in the manner of a suppliant, with a sorrowful face, but no resort to weeping, confident in her beauty. Though she had pretended to tear her hair in grief, it was not sufficiently disarranged to lose its attraction. "Great Caesar," she said, "birth may count for little, yet I am still the Princess Cleopatra, a lineal descendant of King Lagus of Egypt. I have been driven from the throne, and shall never regain it without your help; which is why I, a queen, herewith stoop to kiss your feet. Oh, please, become the bright star that blesses Egypt! If you grant my request, I shall not be the first woman to rule the Nile valley; we have no law against female sovereignty—as is proved by my father's testament, in which I am married to Ptolemy and appointed co-heir to the throne. Were Ptolemy only his own master, he would show that he loves me; but Pothinus dominates him. I am not pleading to inherit my father's monarchy; I simply want you to rescue our royal house from a shameful tutelage and let Ptolemy be a real king by breaking Pothinus's ruthless hold on him. That presumptuous menial, who boasts of having beheaded Pompey, is now threatening your life as well—I pray the Gods that he will fail! It is pretty disgraceful for you, Caesar, and for all mankind too, when a fellow like Pothinus gains the credit of having killed Pompey the Great!"

Cleopatra would have stood no chance at all with stern-hearted Caesar, but for the evil beauty of her face and person; she bribed her judge and wickedly spent the whole night with him. . . .

Lucan, *The Civil War*, quoted in Edith Flamarion, *Cleopatra: The Life and Death of a Pharaoh*. New York: Harry N. Abrams, 1997, pp. 115–16.

DOCUMENT 13: CLEOPATRA KNEW A THOUSAND KINDS OF FLATTERY

Plutarch (ca. A.D. 46–ca. 126), of course, composed one of the main surviving sources about Cleopatra's life and deeds, the Life of Antony. *In this excerpt, the author, like other writers in the generations immediately following her demise, perpetuates the myth that she somehow bewitched the gullible Antony. Yet in the long description of the lovers playing and fishing together, the two emerge as happy, fully consenting adults, each of whom truly loves and enjoys the other's company.*

Such being Antony's nature, the love for Cleopatra which now entered his life came as the final and crowning mischief which could befall him. It excited to the point of madness many passions which had hitherto lain concealed, or at least dormant, and it stifled or corrupted all those redeeming qualities in him which were still capable of resisting temptation. The occasion on which he lost his heart came about as follows. While he was preparing for the campaign against the Parthians, he sent word to Cleopatra, ordering her to meet him in Cilicia to answer the charge that she had raised money for Cassius and sent him help in his war against the triumvirs. Dellius, who carried out this mission, was struck by the charm and subtlety of Cleopatra's conversation as soon as he set eyes on her, and he saw at once that such a woman, so far from having anything to fear from Antony, would probably gain the strongest influence over him. He decided to pay his court to the Egyptian queen and urged her to go to Cilicia dressed in 'all the splendour her art could command', as Homer puts it [a reference to the scene in Homer's *Iliad* in which the goddess Hera dresses up to seduce her husband, Zeus], and to have no fear of Antony, who was the gentlest and most chivalrous of generals. Cleopatra was impressed by what Dellius told her. She had already seen for herself the power of her beauty to enchant Julius Caesar . . . and she expected to conquer Antony even more easily. For Caesar . . . had known her when she was still a young girl with no experience of the world, but she was to meet Antony at the age when a woman's beauty is at its most superb and her mind at its most mature. She therefore provided herself with as lavish a supply of gifts, money, and ornaments as her exalted position and the prosperity of her kingdom made it appropriate to take, but she relied above all upon her physical presence and the spell and enchantment which it could create. . . .

Plato speaks of four kinds of flattery, but Cleopatra knew a thousand. Whether Antony's mood were serious or gay, she could always invent some fresh device to delight or charm him. She engrossed his attention utterly and never released him for an instant by day or by night. She played dice with him, drank with him, and hunted with him, and when he exercised with his weapons, she watched him. At night, when he liked to wander about the city, stand by the doors or windows of ordinary citizens' houses, and make fun of the people inside, she would dress up as a maidservant and play her part in any mad prank that came into Antony's head, for it was his custom to go out disguised as a slave. On these occasions he was always received with torrents of abuse, and sometimes even found himself beaten up before he returned to the palace, although most people guessed who he was. The fact was that the Alexandrians had a weakness for his buffoonery and enjoyed taking part in these amusements in their elegant and cultivated way. They liked him personally, and used to say that Antony put on his tragic mask for the Romans, but kept the comic one for them.

Now it would be a great waste of time for me to describe all the details of Antony's childish amusements, but a single instance may serve as an illustration. One day he went out fishing, had no luck with his line, and was all the more enraged because Cleopatra happened to be present. So he ordered some fishermen to dive down and secretly to fasten on to his hook a number of fish they had already caught. Then he proceeded to pull up his line two or three times, but the queen discovered the trick. She pretended to admire his success, but then told her friends what had happened and invited them to come and watch on the next day. A large party got into the fishing boats, and when Antony had let down his line, Cleopatra ordered one of her own servants to swim immediately to his hook and fix on to it a salted fish from the Black Sea. Antony, believing that he had made a catch, pulled up his line, whereupon the whole company burst out laughing, as was natural, and Cleopatra told him: 'Emperor, you had better give up your rod to us poor rulers of Pharos and Canopus. Your sport is to hunt cities and kingdoms and continents.'

Plutarch, *Life of Antony*, in *Makers of Rome: Nine Lives By Plutarch.* Trans. Ian Scott-Kilvert. New York: Penguin Books, 1965, pp. 292–97.

DOCUMENT 14: AFTER TWELVE HUNDRED YEARS, STILL A "WRETCHED WOMAN"

Unfortunately, the damage done to Cleopatra's reputation by Roman writers endured into the late Middle Ages and Renaissance, an era in which European intellectuals rediscovered and came to revere many of the ancient Latin texts. Here, the great Italian poet Giovanni Boccaccio (1313–1375) regurgitates the standard biased version of the Egyptian queen's deeds, calling her lewd, insatiable (incapable of being satisfied), covetous, greedy, audacious, and wretched.

Antony had treacherously seized the king of Armenia, . . . had taken vast treasures from him and was bringing him along shackled with silver chains. To bring covetous Cleopatra to his embraces, effeminate Antony gave her, as she approached, the captive king in all his regalia, as well as the booty. The greedy woman, happy at the gifts, embraced the ardent man so seductively that he made her his wife with great love, after repudiating [his wife] Octavia, the sister of Octavian Caesar. I shall not discuss the Arabian ointments, the perfumes of Saba, and the drunken revels. As Antony gluttonously stuffed himself continuously with delicacies, he asked what magnificent thing could be added to the daily banquets, as if he wanted to make his dinners for Cleopatra more splendid. The lewd woman answered that if he wanted she could have a dinner costing more than one hundred thousand sesterces. . . .

As the insatiable woman's craving for kingdoms grew day by

day, to grasp everything at once she asked Antony for the Roman empire. Perhaps drunk or rising from such a noble supper, Antony, who was not in full possession of his mental faculties, without properly considering his own strength or the power of the Romans, promised to give it to her, as if it were his to give. Good Lord, how great was the audacity of the woman who requested this! And the madness of the man who promised it was no less! How generous was this man who so rashly gave away to an entreating woman an empire which had just been gained after so many centuries, with such difficulty and bloodshed, through the death of so many great men and even peoples, and with so many noble deeds and battles, as if he wanted to give it away at once like the ownership of a single house! . . . For this reason war broke out after both sides had gathered their forces. Antony and Cleopatra proceeded to Epirus with their fleet adorned with gold and purple sails. . . . [At Actium Octavian] attacked them with a great fleet and marvelous daring. When battle had been joined, Mars kept the result in doubt for a long time. Finally, when Antony's forces seemed to be succumbing, proud Cleopatra was the first to flee on her golden ship with sixty other vessels. Antony lowered the ensign of his praetorian ship and immediately followed her.

 . . . The conqueror Octavian followed them and destroyed their power in several victorious battles. They asked for last minute peace terms. Unable to obtain them, Antony despaired, and, according to some, entered the royal mausoleum, where he killed himself with his sword. When Alexandria had been captured, Cleopatra tried in vain with her old wiles to make young Octavian desire her, as she had done with Caesar and Antony. Angry at hearing that she was being reserved for the conqueror's triumph, and without hope of safety, Cleopatra, dressed in royal garments, followed her Antony. Lying down next to him, she opened the veins of her arms and put two asps in the openings in order to die. Some say that they cause death in sleep. In this sleep the wretched woman put an end to her greed, her concupiscence [lust], and her life. . . .

Giovanni Boccaccio, *Concerning Famous Women.* Trans. Guido A. Guarino. London: Allen and Unwin, 1964, pp. 83–84.

DOCUMENT 15: NEVER LIVED A TRUER QUEEN!

The English poet Geoffrey Chaucer (ca. 1342–1400) penned a short piece on Cleopatra (excerpted here) in his Legend of Good Women, *written in 1386, shortly before he began work on his famous* Canterbury Tales. *Indeed, unlike the devious, self-centered despot pictured by Roman writers and his contemporary, Boccaccio, Chaucer's Cleopatra is a "good woman" who braved a hideous death to be reunited beyond the grave in perfect love with her husband.*

After the death of Ptolemy the king,
Who had all Egypt in his governing,

Queen Cleopatra governed in that land,
Until it happened that, by Rome's command,
A senator was sent throughout the earth
To conquer kingdoms and increase the worth
Of Rome, as was the custom of that nation,
And so to have the world in subjugation.

This senator, Antonius by name
(Whom Fortune as it happened owed a shame),
Had reached the summit of prosperity
When he grew tired of Rome's authority.
And Caesar's sister, to whom he was wed,
He left—and not a word to her was said—
To take another woman as his wife.
Thus with both Rome and Caesar he had strife.

Nevertheless, authorities agree,
He was a man of great nobility,
And a great loss was suffered when he died.
But passion's ropes had him so tightly tied,
And love had brought him to so sad a state—
His love for Cleopatra was so great—
That the whole world he valued not at all.
All other joy in life began to pall.
To love and serve her was so gratifying,
He had no fear of fighting or of dying
To keep her safe and to maintain her right.

And she, the queen, in turn adored this knight
For his great worth and for his chivalry.
And if books do not lie, then, certainly,
His body and his breeding were so good—
Also his wisdom and his hardihood—
That he ranked with the best in every way.
And she was lovely as a rose in May.
And (since to brevity this work aspires)
She married him, and had all her desires. . . .

This Cleopatra suffered for his sake
With sorrows such that no tongue could narrate.
But at the dawn [of her last day on earth, shortly after
Antony's death] she could no longer wait,
And had her skillful craftsmen make a shrine
Of all the rubies and the jewels fine
Of Egypt, that she could find anywhere,
And put in spices to perfume the air,
And had the corpse embalmed; then, at the last,

She had the dead corpse in the shrine sealed fast.
Next to the shrine she had men dig a pit
And drop as many serpents into it
As they could find about them; then she prayed,
"Beloved, whom my heart always obeyed
So fervently from that first blissful hour
When I first swore to put it in your power—
Antonius, my knight, it's you I mean—
That not one waking moment have I seen
When you were absent from my memory
For dance or song, for woe or jollity;
And to myself I made a promise there
That all your feelings, good or bad, I'd share,
As far as it lay in my might to do
(If it were fitting to my wifehood, too);
What you felt, I'd feel also, life or death;
And this same covenant, while I have breath,
I will fulfill; and then this shall be seen:
There never lived and loved a truer queen."

And with that word, naked, this woman brave
Leaped down among the serpents in the grave,
Choosing to make that adders' pit her tomb,
And take their bites upon her as her doom.
This agony and death she meets with cheer
For Antony, who was to her so dear.
This is historical, this is no fable.
Until I find a man so true and stable,
Who will for love his death so freely take,
I pray to God our heads may never ache!

Geoffrey Chaucer, "The Legend of Cleopatra," in Geoffrey Chaucer, *The Legend of Good Women*. Trans. Ann McMillan. Houston: Rice University Press, 1987, pp. 82–86.

CHRONOLOGY

B.C.

332

Greek conqueror Alexander the Great liberates Egypt from Persian control and soon afterward establishes the city of Alexandria in the Nile Delta.

323

Alexander dies, leaving his leading generals to fight over his empire.

305

Alexander's former general, Ptolemy, declares himself King of Egypt, initiating Egypt's royal Ptolemaic dynasty.

100

Birth of Julius Caesar, the Roman aristocrat who will one day conquer the Mediterranean world and have a son with Cleopatra.

CA. 83

Birth of Marcus Antonius (Mark Antony), the Roman army officer who will later become Caesar's supporter and Cleopatra's lover and ally.

80

Ptolemy XII, Auletes, ascends Egypt's throne.

69

Cleopatra VII, daughter of Auletes, is born.

63

Birth of Octavius Caesar (Octavian), later Caesar's adopted son and later still, Augustus, the first Roman emperor.

60

Caesar, the noted general Pompey, and the wealthy businessman Crassus form a ruling coalition that later becomes known as the First Triumvirate.

57

Auletes travels to Rome to gain the support of Roman notables.

51

Auletes dies, leaving his throne to Cleopatra, now eighteen, and her younger brother, Ptolemy XIII, and intending for them to rule jointly.

49

At the urgings of his regent and other ambitious courtiers, Ptolemy drives Cleopatra away and she takes refuge in Syria; with Crassus dead and the Triumvirate in shambles, a Roman civil war erupts, pitting Caesar against Pompey.

48

Caesar defeats Pompey at Pharsalus (in Greece); Pompey flees to Egypt, where Ptolemy has him murdered; Caesar arrives, forms an alliance with Cleopatra, and backs her in a local civil war against her brother.

47

Caesar defeats Ptolemy and his advisers and reinstalls Cleopatra on the Egyptian throne; Caesar returns to Rome; later that year, his and Cleopatra's son, Caesarion (Ptolemy XV), is born.

44

Cleopatra, accompanied by Caesarion, visits Caesar in Rome; on March 15, Caesar is stabbed to death in the Senate House by a group of disgruntled legislators who hope to restore the power and dignity of the disintegrating Roman Republic; Caesar's leading assassins flee to Greece as his friend and supporter, Mark Antony, emerges as his possible successor.

43

Antony, Octavian, and a powerful general named Lepidus form the Second Triumvirate and murder many of their political opponents.

42

Antony and Octavian defeat Caesar's assassins at Philippi (in Greece).

41

Antony, now the leading triumvir, summons Cleopatra to his headquarters at Tarsus (in Asia Minor); the two become lovers and allies.

40

Antony and Octavian sign a treaty of mutual support; Antony marries Octavian's sister, Octavia; Cleopatra gives birth to twins, Alexander Helios and Cleopatra Selene, both by Antony.

37

Antony sends Octavia back to Italy and rejoins Cleopatra.

36

Antony's military expedition against the Near Eastern realm of Parthia is unsuccessful; he and Cleopatra have another child—Ptolemy Philadephus; Octavian removes Lepidus from the Triumvirate and puts him under permanent house arrest.

34

In a lavish ceremony known as the "Donations of Alexandria," Antony grants several eastern lands and royal titles to Cleopatra and their children, raising the ire of Octavian and most Romans.

33–32

Octavian engages in a heated propaganda war with Antony and Cleopatra, suggesting that Antony has lost his wits and Cleopatra wants to become queen of Rome; Antony divorces Octavia; Octavian declares war on Cleopatra.

31

Octavian and his talented commander, Marcus Agrippa, defeat Antony and Cleopatra at Actium (in western Greece); the lovers flee to Alexandria.

30

Octavian pursues his adversaries to Egypt; Antony and Cleopatra commit suicide; Octavian has Caesarion killed; Octavian annexes Egypt as a Roman province.

27

The now powerless Roman Senate confers on Octavian, who has emerged as the most powerful man in the known world, the title of Augustus, the "exalted one." Modern historians mark this event as the beginning of the Roman Empire.

FOR FURTHER RESEARCH

ANCIENT AND MEDIEVAL SOURCES DEALING WITH CLEOPATRA AND HER LEGEND

Appian, *The Civil Wars.* Trans. John Carter. New York: Penguin Books, 1996.

Giovanni Boccaccio, *Concerning Famous Women.* Trans. Guido A. Guarino. London: Allen and Unwin, 1964.

Julius Caesar, *Commentaries on the Civil Wars,* in *War Commentaries of Caesar.* Trans. Rex Warner. New York: New American Library, 1960.

Geoffrey Chaucer, *The Legend of Good Women.* Trans. Ann McMillan. Houston: Rice University Press, 1987.

Cicero, *Letters to Atticus.* 3 vols. Trans. E.O. Winstedt. Cambridge, MA: Harvard University Press, 1961.

Dio Cassius, *Roman History,* excerpted in *The Roman History: The Reign of Augustus.* Trans. Ian Scott-Kilvert. New York: Penguin Books, 1987.

Francis R.B. Godolphin, ed., *The Latin Poets.* New York: Random House, 1949.

Josephus, *The Jewish War.* Trans. G.A. Williamson. Rev. E. Mary Smallwood. New York: Penguin Books, 1981.

Naphtali Lewis and Meyer Reinhold, eds., *Roman Civilization, Sourcebook I: The Republic;* and *Sourcebook II: The Empire.* New York: Harper and Row, 1966.

Pliny the Elder, *Natural History,* excerpted in *Natural History: A Selection.* Trans. John F. Healy. New York: Penguin Books, 1991.

Plutarch, *Parallel Lives,* excerpted in *Fall of the Roman Republic: Six Lives By Plutarch.* Trans. Rex Warner. New York: Penguin Books, 1972; also excerpted in *Makers of Rome: Nine Lives By Plutarch.* Trans. Ian Scott-Kilvert. New York: Penguin Books, 1965.

William G. Sinnegin, ed., *Sources in Western Civilization: Rome.* New York: Free Press, 1965.

Strabo, *Geography.* Trans. Horace L. Jones. Cambridge, MA: Harvard University Press, 1967.

Suetonius, *Lives of the Twelve Caesars,* published as *The Twelve Caesars.* Trans. Robert Graves. Rev. Michael Grant. New York: Penguin Books, 1979.

Tacitus, *The Annals,* published as *The Annals of Imperial Rome.* Trans. Michael Grant. New York: Penguin Books, 1989.

Virgil, *Aeneid.* Trans. Patric Dickinson. New York: New American Library, 1961.

BIOGRAPHIES AND OTHER STUDIES OF CLEOPATRA

Ernle Bradford, *Cleopatra.* New York: Harcourt, Brace, Jovanovich, 1972.

Edith Flamarion, *Cleopatra: The Life and Death of a Pharaoh.* New York: Harry N. Abrams, 1997.

Laura Foreman, *Cleopatra's Palace: In Search of a Legend.* New York: Discovery Communications, 1999.

Michael Foss, *The Search for Cleopatra.* London: Michael O'Mara Books, 1997.

Lucy Hughes-Hallett, *Cleopatra: Histories, Dreams, and Distortions.* New York: HarperCollins, 1991.

Michael Grant, *Cleopatra.* New York: Simon and Schuster, 1972.

Mary Hamer, *Signs of Cleopatra: History, Politics, Representation.* London: Routledge, 1993.

Jack Lindsay, *Cleopatra.* London: Constable, 1970.

Emil Ludwig, *Cleopatra: The Story of a Queen.* Trans. Bernard Miall. New York: Garden City Publishing, 1937.

Don Nardo, *Cleopatra.* San Diego: Lucent Books, 1994.

Hams Volkmann, *Cleopatra: A Study in Politics and Propaganda.* London: Elek Books, 1958.

PLAYS, NOVELS, AND MOVIES ABOUT CLEOPATRA

Alice C. Desmond, *Cleopatra's Children.* New York: Dodd, Mead, 1971.

John Dryden, *All for Love, or The World Well Lost*. Ed. Benjamin W. Griffith Jr. Great Neck, NY: Barron's, 1961.

Margaret George, *Memoirs of Cleopatra*. New York: St. Martin's Press, 1997.

Martha Rofheart, *The Alexandrian*. New York: Thomas Y. Crowell, 1976.

William Shakespeare, *Antony and Cleopatra*. Ed. Maynard Mack. Baltimore: Penguin Books, 1960.

George Bernard Shaw, *Caesar and Cleopatra*. Baltimore: Penguin Books, 1966.

Jon Solomon, *The Ancient World in the Cinema*. New York: A.S. Barnes, 1978.

Marilyn L. Williamson, *Infinite Variety: Antony and Cleopatra in Renaissance Drama and Earlier Tradition*. New Haven: Mystic, 1974.

BIOGRAPHIES OF CAESAR, ANTONY, AND OCTAVIAN (AUGUSTUS)

Ernle Bradford, *Julius Caesar: The Pursuit of Power*. New York: Morrow, 1984.

John Buchan, *Augustus*. London: Hodder and Stoughton, 1937.

John B. Firth, *Augustus Caesar and the Organization of the Empire of Rome*. Freeport, NY: Books for the Libraries Press, 1972.

J.F.C. Fuller, *Julius Caesar: Man, Soldier, and Tyrant*. New Brunswick, NJ: Rutgers University Press, 1965.

Michael Grant, *Caesar*. London: Weidenfeld and Nicolson, 1974.

Elenor G. Huzar, *Mark Antony: A Biography*. Minneapolis: University of Minnesota Press, 1978.

A.H.M. Jones, *Augustus*. New York: W.W. Norton, 1970.

Christian Meier, *Caesar*. Trans. David McLintock. New York: HarperCollins, 1982.

Don Nardo, *Julius Caesar*. San Diego: Lucent Books, 1997.

THE LIVES AND ACHIEVEMENTS OF WOMEN IN ANCIENT TIMES

Sue Blundell, *Women in Ancient Greece*. Cambridge, MA: Harvard University Press, 1995.

Eva Cantarella, *Pandora's Daughters: The Role and Status of Women in Greek and Roman Antiquity.* Trans. Maureen B. Fant. Baltimore: Johns Hopkins University Press, 1987.

Mary R. Lefkowitz and Maureen B. Fant, eds., *Women's Life in Greece and Rome: A Source Book in Translation.* Baltimore: Johns Hopkins University Press, 1992.

Vicki Leon, *Uppity Women of Ancient Times.* Berkeley: Conari Press, 1995.

Don Nardo, *Women in Ancient Greece.* San Diego: Lucent Books, 2000.

Sarah B. Pomeroy, *Women in Hellenistic Egypt: From Alexander to Cleopatra.* New York: Schocken Books, 1989.

———, *Goddesses, Whores, Wives, and Slaves: Women in Classical Antiquity.* New York: Shocken Books, 1995.

ROME, GREECE, AND EGYPT IN CLEOPATRA'S TIME

Lesley Adkins and Roy A. Adkins, *Handbook to Life in Ancient Rome.* New York: Facts On File, 1994.

E. Badian, *Roman Imperialism in the Late Republic.* Ithaca, NY: Cornell University Press, 1968.

Mary Beard and Michael Crawford, *Rome in the Late Republic: Problems and Interpretations.* London: Duckworth, 1985.

J.M. Carter, *The Battle of Actium.* London: Hamish Hamilton, 1970.

Tim Cornell and John Matthews, *Atlas of the Roman World.* New York: Facts On File, 1982.

F.R. Cowell, *Cicero and the Roman Republic.* Baltimore: Penguin Books, 1967.

Michael Crawford, *The Roman Republic.* Cambridge, MA: Harvard University Press, 1992.

Charles Freeman, *Egypt, Greece, and Rome: Civilizations of the Ancient Mediterranean.* New York: Oxford University Press, 1996.

Michael Grant, *History of Rome.* New York: Scribner's, 1978.

———, *From Alexander to Cleopatra: The Hellenistic World.* New York: Charles Scribner's Sons, 1982.

Peter Green, *Alexander to Actium: The Historical Evolution of the Hellenistic Age.* Berkeley: University of California Press, 1990.

———, ed., *Hellenistic History and Culture.* Berkeley: University of California Press, 1993.

Erich Gruen, *The Hellenistic World and the Coming of Rome.* Berkeley: University of California Press, 1984.

Lawrence Keppie, *The Making of the Roman Army: From Republic to Empire.* New York: Barnes and Noble, 1984.

A.J. Langguth, *A Noise of War: Caesar, Pompey, Octavian and the Struggle for Rome.* New York: Simon and Schuster, 1994.

Peter Levi, *Atlas of the Greek World.* New York: Facts On File, 1984.

Naphtali Lewis, *Life in Egypt Under Roman Rule.* Oxford: Clarendon Press, 1983.

———, *Greeks in Ptolemaic Egypt.* Oxford: Clarendon Press, 1986.

Don Nardo, *The Age of Augustus.* San Diego: Lucent Books, 1997.

———, *The Collapse of the Roman Republic.* San Diego: Lucent Books, 1998.

———, *The Decline and Fall of Ancient Greece.* San Diego: Greenhaven Press, 2000.

William L. Rodgers, *Greek and Roman Naval Warfare.* Annapolis: Naval Institute Press, 1964.

Henry T. Rowell, *Rome in the Augustan Age.* Norman: University of Oklahoma Press, 1962.

Chris Scarre, *Historical Atlas of Ancient Rome.* New York: Penguin Books, 1995.

Lily Ross Taylor, *Party Politics in the Age of Caesar.* Berkeley: University of California Press, 1968.

F.W. Walbank, *The Hellenistic World.* Cambridge, MA: Harvard University Press, 1993.

Colin Wells, *The Roman Empire.* Palo Alto, CA: Stanford University Press, 1984.

INDEX

ABOUT THE EDITOR

Historian Don Nardo has written or edited numerous volumes about the history, culture, and leaders of ancient Greece and Rome, including *The Age of Pericles, The Decline and Fall of Ancient Greece, Life of a Roman Slave, Rulers of Ancient Rome,* and biographies of Julius Caesar and Cleopatra, as well as Greenhaven Press's *The Complete History of Ancient Greece.* He resides with his wife, Christine, in Massachusetts.

SOCIETY AND PAUPERISM

STUDIES IN SOCIAL HISTORY

edited by

HAROLD PERKIN

Professor of Social History, University of Lancaster

A catalogue of books available in the
Studies in Social History and new books
in preparation for the Library will be
found at the end of this volume

SOCIETY AND PAUPERISM

English Ideas on Poor Relief, 1795–1834

by

J. R. Poynter

Ernest Scott Professor of History
University of Melbourne

LONDON: Routledge & Kegan Paul
TORONTO: University of Toronto Press
1969

First published 1969
in Great Britain by
Routledge & Kegan Paul Limited
and in Canada by
University of Toronto Press
Printed in Great Britain by
C. Tinling & Co. Ltd
Liverpool, London and Prescot

RKP SBN 7100 6316 4
UTP SBN 8020 1611 1

Contents

'A secure provision for the indigent is to the philanthropist what a pineapple is to the epicure.'

Jeremy Bentham, unpublished MS (1796)

Preface

THIS book is a revised version of a thesis submitted in the University of Melbourne in 1961. In the course of the revision, material on the practice of poor relief and on legislation has been omitted or abbreviated, and the work is now primarily a study of the ideas and attitudes expressed in the very extensive literature on poverty, pauperism and relief published in England between the 1790s and the 1830s. Anyone acquainted with this literature will know how rich and various it is, and the difficulties of tracing a pattern of development in a continuing public discussion which had periods of climax but neither beginning nor end. Another explorer of the same intellectual country could produce a very different map; I am conscious that my treatment of the 1820s in particular ignores certain new developments and ideas which others might think both important and characteristic of the period. And I may have lingered overlong in one or two intellectual bye-ways simply because I found the scenery picturesque.

One result of a revision which concentrates attention on ideas rather than practice has been the virtual exclusion of the poor themselves from the story. Their records, if not their writings, are voluminous, hazardous to interpret though they may be. An anonymous pamphleteer opposing James Scarlett's attempt to restrict relief in 1822 complained passionately that 'the Poor, God help them, have no one to defend them', an exaggeration, though a humane one. Certainly the labourers and paupers of the generation of Waterloo and Peterloo have had their champions since, and it is the upper classes of those years who have lacked informed and intelligent defenders for much of the twentieth century. It is not my purpose to defend or justify the attitudes of those who rejected Samuel Whitbread's Minimum Wage Bill in 1796 or sought to abolish public relief in 1817; indeed I do not find them sympathetic, either in their original setting or in transplanted form in colonies beyond the seas. Nevertheless they were important enough to deserve understanding, and recent attempts to rehabilitate the reputation of the old Poor Law in justification of social service payments in the United States may remind us that not all ideas go out of date everywhere at once. I have tried to describe, and to some extent to analyse and explain, the recorded attitudes to poverty as a social phenomenon in a particular period, assuming that in every generation some men deserve respect for their intellect and others for their humanity, and a few rare souls for both.

Most of the work on this book was undertaken in Melbourne and Canberra, though it could hardly have been completed without a period of research in England. I am grateful to the staffs of the National Library of Australia, the State Library of Victoria and the Baillieu Library for their assistance, and to past and present colleagues in the University of Melbourne—and in particular Professor J. A. La Nauze, Dr. F. B. Smith and Dr. P. F. Bourke—for advice and guidance. The award of a Nuffield Dominion Travelling Fellowship enabled me to spend 1959 in England, and my thanks are due to the Nuffield Foundation and to the staffs of the British Museum, the Public Record Office, the Institute of Historical Research, Nuffield College, Oxford, and above all the Goldsmiths' Library in the University of London, a rich mine indeed for students of economic and social literature. During my time in England Dr. R. M. Hartwell gave me much assistance, and I also benefited from the advice of Professor C. W. Everett and Professor Asa Briggs. I acknowledge with gratitude the permission granted me to consult the Bentham Papers in the Library of University College, London, the Whitbread Papers in the Bedfordshire County Record Office, and the Dumont Papers in the Bibliothèque Publique et Universitaire de Genève. My thanks are also due to the Australian National University for its hospitality; the work was begun on a brief visit to Canberra in 1957, and the typescript completed during a longer visit more than a decade later. For the delay, and the shortcomings of the book itself, I am alone responsible. Mrs. L. Dempster, Mrs. M. Richardson, Mrs. B. A. Gallina and my wife have at various stages produced typescript versions of my drafts with commendable accuracy and patience. The further debt which I owe to my wife for her encouragement is known only to her, but it is fitting to make public my gratitude.

Abbreviations in the text and notes are, I think, self-explanatory, but it should be noted that the titles of pamphlets have been shortened in the footnotes to the minimum which will permit identification from the Bibliography, where longer—though by no means full—titles are given.

J. R. Poynter

University of Melbourne

Introduction

THE subject of this study is the debate on poverty and its relief which took place in England in the last decade of the eighteenth century and the first decades of the nineteenth. Its focus is the Poor Law, a network of law and practice which in two hundred years had become entwined in the fabric of society and the economic system. Englishmen exaggerated the uniqueness of their system of public relief, and accepted it as a venerable national institution, though the continual mutterings of criticism show that it was not thought to be perfect; early in the nineteenth century, however, the Poor Law became quite suddenly one of the chief public issues of the day, the object of a vigorous attack, and the centre of a controversy in which new assumptions of social order challenged the old. The debate ranged far and wide and became involved with most of the other disputed issues of that contentious time. The Poor Law survived, but the conflict was not wholly inconclusive; in 1834 the system was subjected to drastic surgery in accordance with a new creed on poverty and its relief which had emerged in the debate and was to continue as social orthodoxy until well into the twentieth century, when both the Poor Law and the 'principles of 1834' were smothered by the institutions and values of the Welfare State. The period examined here formed but an episode in this larger drama, but it was an episode with incident, and with important causes and consequences.

Some historians have seen this crisis in the Poor Law as a reflection of England's changing social structure as she led the world in that specifically modern pilgrimage from an agricultural to an industrial state, with its new tempo of social change and new concept of prosperity. It is true that the new Poor Law, with its uniformity and bureaucracy, was more consistent with large-scale capitalist enterprise in both agriculture and industry than the old Poor Law's local paternalism could ever have been. But England's industrial revolution, if the first, was also one of the slowest, and social institutions adapted themselves to it so gradually that compromise was more usual than the sharp conflict of 1834. In the long run, moreover, the fruit of industrialism was not the workhouse but the Welfare State. The crisis in pauperism could reflect at most a particular stage of the process: the stage (some historians would argue) when the reorganisation of agriculture and industry was imposing hardships on the labouring classes and offering them only a faint promise of future benefit in return. According to this view there was more pauperism in those years because there was more real poverty (thanks to the coincidence of deserted villages and satanic mills), and the Poor Law Amendment Act of 1834 was an act of discipline and not of relief.

Unfortunately for the historian, accidents interrupt processes. In English social history the Napoleonic Wars were (strictly speaking) an accident; but how much of the distress and repression, how much of the economic and political progress of those years, should be attributed to the national crisis which stimulated even as it deprived? Such crises are not mere interruptions, but catalysts of latent change. Trends were accelerated, conflicts revealed, and in the realm of thought debates on public questions were stimulated which were more rich, if more bitter, than is usual in periods of tranquil development. It may be dangerous to generalise from such periods because they are not typical; nevertheless they may be characteristic. Crises leave imprints on men's minds which determine reactions to the future, and the problems of the future are met with the solutions of the past. The crisis in pauperism as it occurred in the early nineteenth century was only in small part a result of England's developing industrialism, but it produced almost all the ideas on poverty and its relief which were to dominate English social policy in the great age of her industrial flowering in the late nineteenth century. It is the emergence of these ideas, and their clash with traditional assumptions, which are examined here.

Much that is relevant is not examined. This is an essay in social thought, and only incidentally in social history. Few subjects in economic history are more hotly disputed than the condition of the lower classes, their suffering or well-being, in the early years of the industrial revolution in England. Something of what contemporaries thought about the situation will be found in the following pages, but no adequate assessment of the accuracy of their insights. And because discussion is focused on existing institutions for the relief of indigence, and on attempts to reform or abolish them, relatively little attention is given to those social radicals who were not really interested in the Poor Law because to them it was merely a part of an old rotten society they intended to supplant with a new. On the other hand some views on private charity were so influential in poor-law matters that they have had to be considered in detail; if the inclusion of the saints and the omission of the radicals gives a conservative and respectable bias to the whole discussion this may nevertheless reflect fairly accurately the balance of articulate opinion at the time. Finally, no real attempt is made to offer an adequate account of the practice of poor relief and the workings of the Poor Law in the period. More work is needed, despite the labours of the Webbs in their great *English Poor Law History*, to provide a firm basis of local studies on which safe generalisations can be built, and in particular to test the assertions made in contemporary sources, including the Report of the Royal Commissioners of 1832–4. Something of contemporary views of the system as it existed will be found below, with remarks on their plausibility but no real test of their truth.

Is poverty inevitable? Answers to questions so basic are usually assumed rather than stated. Poverty is a relative condition, as Jeremy Bentham was careful to point out; even in the crudest physical terms definition is difficult. What is an adequate diet? Certainly one which will maintain life, but life with what expectancy? Men may be fed, clothed and sheltered, but doomed to live and work in such surroundings that all but the exceptional will be poor in spirit. Statisticians can compare what is measurable, provided the data is available, but not all the ingredients of poverty can be counted. That the great mass of eighteenth-century Englishmen were very poor is undeniable by any standards, except those of a society in which the masses are even poorer; the available material on wages, diet and housing leaves no illusions, though it is not sufficient to show conclusively the variations in condition in space and time. Poverty can be conquered only in so-called affluent societies, and they are so modern a development that there is not one in which the conquest is complete. It is an assumption of the mid-twentieth century that poverty is not inevitable, but such a view could be held a century ago only by visionaries or cranks. Even in Victorian England, where the miracle of modern industrial productivity was first manifesting itself, the pessimism of a man like John Stuart Mill on the future prospects of the working classes was not at all implausible. The poor could not be anything but poor for reasons weighty enough to explain the harshness of the more callous among the rich, and to explain also the condescension continually associated with the charity of the merciful. Where self-interest and cogent argument both supported the social structure of rich and poor, it required exceptional benevolence or a degree of eccentricity to deny their logic.

Not that all the arguments supporting the inevitability of poverty in eighteenth-century England were cogent, though some were. The simple fact that there had always been poverty, and that the very best of authorities had said there always would be, was hardly an argument, but it put the onus of proof on the other side. Poverty could be seen as part of Divine providence, if not quite of Divine creation; specifically, as a sign and consequence of God's judgment on the wicked. R. H. Tawney argued that such a view of Divine justice emerged in England after the Puritan revolution, fruit of the Anglican form of marriage between the Protestant ethic and the spirit of capitalism. Earlier religious ethics saw poverty as a natural misfortune and as a challenge to compassion, a view echoed by a recent Italian Prime Minister when he argued that there must always be poor, in order that the rich could practise the virtue of benevolence. Tawney's brilliant essay perhaps condenses and exaggerates a tendency in English religious thought which can be traced even into contemporary discussion, but probably never became typical. It was rarely asserted that vice was the sole cause of poverty, although in practice it might be assumed that any pauper was vicious until he was proved innocent. And there were many who pointed out that if vice and indigence were found together, depravity could be the result of poverty as easily as poverty might issue from depravity.

Divine providence apart, simple arithmetic could prove the inevitability of present, if not of future, poverty. The rich might be ostentatiously rich and the poor very evidently poor, but the luxuries of the one class were statistically insignificant beside the appetites of the other. It was a simple matter of the quantity of wealth and the numbers of the people. This view of poverty was not a Malthusian invention, but was already something of a platitude before he wrote. Bentham (among others) had insisted that the surplus of the 'matter of abundance' over the necessities of the population was small and precarious; and Burke had made this point succinctly in 1795:

The labouring classes are only poor, because they are numerous. Numbers in their nature imply poverty. In a fair distribution among a vast multitude, none can have much. That class of dependent pensioners called the rich, is so extremely small that if all their throats were cut, and a distribution made of all they consume in a year, it would not give a bit of bread and cheese for one night's supper to those who labour, and who in reality feed both the pensioners and themselves.[1]

Further arguments were needed, of course, to justify the rich, with throats uncut, in the enjoyment of their surplus; but Burke, Bentham or almost

[1] Edmund Burke, *Thoughts and Details on Scarcity* etc. (1795), printed in *Works* (1808 ed.), VII. 376.

any other member of the upper classes could provide a variety of these. Not everyone defended the rich. No one suggested that a simple redistribution of the wealth of society would banish poverty, though that eccentric agrarian reformer Thomas Spence came close to it.[2] On the other hand it became a radical commonplace in the early nineteenth century that poverty would be alleviated if not removed if only the parasitical burden of aristocratic luxury and government extravagance were removed from the backs of the labouring classes. However justified their complaints of inequity, there is no doubt that the radicals exaggerated the relief to be expected from a more just distribution. It was more logical, if less realistic politically, to assert with Owen and the social radicals that plenty for all could be achieved not by a mere redistribution of wealth or public burdens but only by 'the getting into a better system' of production as well. They were not, of course, given the chance to test their claims; in the event poverty has been diminished in England by increased productivity under a capitalism modified only slightly by socialist reorganisation or by planned redistribution of social income.

Social radicalism of this sort was not at all strong in the nineteenth century, especially in the early years, and the orthodox view of poverty was Burke's as refined and extended by Malthus. Burke's static balance of wealth and people was developed by Malthus into a theoretical apparatus capable of discounting the future as well as justifying the present. Malthus's message as it was absorbed into nineteenth-century economic thinking was relatively simple: if the prosperity of the masses depended on the ratio of wealth to population, it was unfortunate that people tended to multiply much faster than subsistence could be increased. It was theoretically possible to conquer poverty, but not by redistribution towards equality, which would only stimulate population and at the same time destroy that system of private property which alone could provide a surplus above necessities; the poor could achieve prosperity only by accepting an abstinence from reproduction which (on Malthus's terms) would be practically superhuman. Malthus was naturally pessimistic on the chances of attaining such a degree of virtue in the populace, and also perhaps unduly pessimistic on the possibility of economic expansion, having set his face against reliance on imported foodstuffs bought with the products of industry. When England waxed rich by developing precisely the trading economy

[2] Spence argued. In *The Constitution of a Perfect Commonwealth* etc. (2nd ed. 1798), p. iii, that if land were made common property rents could meet all state taxes and leave £9 per head to be distributed to the population each year. But few Englishmen sang Spencean songs (such as 'The Spencean Plan for a' that') either in English or in Spencean phonetics.

Malthus deplored, his followers could still remain pessimistic by doubting the possibility of checking population growth sufficiently to raise living standards appreciably. Hence J. S. Mill's caution in mid-century; and decades later Marshall would not admit that the Malthusian devil had been exorcised. England's favourable position had enabled her to increase the ratio of wealth to population to heights Malthus could not have dreamed of, but even in England the situation was precarious. Could similar benefits be extended to the whole world? Marshall's question still awaits an answer, in practice if not in theory.

It was not always assumed that poverty, if inevitable, was also undesirable. In the early eighteenth century there were popular economic arguments in favour of low wages, mainly in the interests of foreign trade. But the balance of economic opinion later in the century favoured high wages, and Adam Smith with characteristic humanity made high per capita income the criterion of national wealth. Apart from occasional dissidents, such as John Weyland, economists of the early nineteenth century were in favour of high wages and rising living standards for the poor, though they were generally gloomy over the prospects of attaining them. Only critics who had misread the *Essay on Population* could accuse Malthus of actually defending misery, and if Ricardo sometimes assumed that wages would tend to subsistence level he most certainly wished them to be above it. The alleged harshness of the 'dismal science' in the classical age must be seen in the light of current conditions and of earlier doctrines; at least poverty was no longer thought economically desirable.

Poverty could still, however, be thought necessary for social discipline. In 1771 Arthur Young remarked (echoing Mandeville) that everyone but an idiot knew that the poor must be kept poor, or they would not work. Before the industrial revolution human labour was so obviously the basis of wealth—and of the comforts of the rich, surrounded as they were by personal servants—that idleness in the lower classes was as much to be feared as sedition, which was indeed often regarded as one of its fruits. How but in labour and frugality could the poor perform their social duty, and what but their poverty could spur them from their sloth? Paley might argue that honest manual toil was actually more enjoyable than the care of a fortune, but who believed him? Joseph Townsend's arguments no doubt seemed closer to reality:

It seems to be a law of nature, that the poor should be to a certain degree improvident, that there may always be some to fulfil the most servile, the most sordid, and the most ignoble offices in the community. The stock of human happiness is thereby much increased, whilst the more delicate are not only relieved from drudgery, and freed from those occasional employments which would make them miserable, but are left at liberty, without interruption, to pursue those callings which are suited to their various dispositions, and most useful to the State ... There must be a degree of pressure, and that which is attended with the least violence will be the best. When hunger is either felt or feared, the desire of obtaining bread will quietly dispose the mind to undergo the greatest hardships, and will sweeten the severest labours.[3]

Townsend's views were regarded as extreme by many of his contemporaries, by which they meant that his frankness was unseemly.

It is, of course, quite sensible to maintain that men labour not from choice but to satisfy needs; but why should it be assumed that those needs are limited to the most basic physical necessities? In the eighteenth century the belief that only the grinding pressure of poverty could stimulate labour gained some plausibility from the widespread habit among the poor of riotously consuming any occasional surplus they might obtain, and of taking holidays whenever their earnings permitted it. But more enlightened observers pointed out that labourers gorged themselves at harvest feasts because such opportunities for filling stomachs came so rarely. If the poor did not work harder to better their position, it was either because there was no probability of success, or because poverty had blunted their taste for superior comforts. The notion of discipline through repression died slowly, but the alternative appeal to ambition through suitable incentives became the fashionable policy among the enlightened. If Townsend had complained of the excessive niceness of the southern labourers who insisted that their bread be white, Ricardo believed on the contrary that an increasing taste for the conveniences of life would lead the poor to better their condition. To Malthus restraint from marriage could only come from self-denial and a puritan conscience, but Senior and the second generation of Malthusians hoped that the human passion of ambition would counter-balance the demands of more carnal instincts. In the nineteenth century men looked to the carrot rather than the goad to stimulate labour, but it is not surprising that goads were fashionable while carrots remained in short supply. Only an expanding economy could offer tangible rewards for honest labour in this world as well as in the next; the change of emphasis in upper-class exhortation was gradual, but an assumption that self-help could effectually improve the lot of the labourer was common at least by 1795.[4] Samuel Smiles' persuasive

[3] [J. Townsend], *A Dissertation on the Poor Laws* (1786), pp. 39–40. Townsend's attack on the Poor Law as an unnatural interference with this process is discussed in Chapter II below.
[4] In 1824 the Report of the Select Committee on Labourers' Wages was outspoken on the question: 'There are but two motives by which men are induced to work: the one, the hope of improving the condition of themselves and their families; the other, the fear of punishment. The one is the principle of free labour, the other the principle of slave labour'. (*Parliamentary Papers*, 1824, VI (392), p. 4.)

advocacy of its merits was, when it appeared, a slightly old-fashioned essay on a virtue which had been preached for at least seventy years, as Smiles well knew.

Many currents of thought contributed to the doctrine of self-help and to the discrediting of other forms of relief (especially through the Poor Law) which was its corollary. Constantly in the literature of the period one finds reiterated the pious wish that the poor should be 'independent'. Not everyone agreed. Alcock, Townsend, Weyland and others thought it proper that the poor should be dependent on the rich, and improper that they should ever forget it. In practice many an employer preferred his labourers to be dependent, even pauperised. Farmers frequently complained that labourers became saucy if they had resources such as garden plots to reduce their dependence on wages, and the practice of making up wages from the rates was tolerated by many because it ensured docility, or at least made any assertion of independence short of insurrection impracticable. There were subtle shades in the idealisation of independence: with most it was an equivocal ideal, in which the poor were to be independent of charity and poor relief, but also duly mindful of their place in the social hierarchy. Only exceptionally did independence imply social fluidity, in which a hierarchical social structure would be dissolved by the beneficent force of competition. English conceptions of status and deference were still too deep-rooted for so radical a weed to flourish among them.

The cynica might suggest that the new passion among the rich for the independlence of the poor was kindled merely by the increasing expense of maintaining them on the rates. Certainly this was a factor, but not the only one. There was also a sincere belief that the labourers were excessively improvident, to their own detriment even more than that of the rate-payers. Thomas Ruggles and Sir F. M. Eden were not merely rationalising the interests of the rate-payers when they concluded that the principal cause of indigence was lack of economy among the poor, though their conclusion may have been wrong. Moreover a genuine revulsion against pauperism as a way of life grew rapidly, especially after 1815; in the 1790s assistance from the rates was not thought to be so degrading, except by men like Fox and Whitbread who feared that political servitude might follow from economic dependence. And Malthusianism added great theoretical force to the desire that the poor become independent through self-help by placing the control of destitution in the hands of the poor themselves. The ideal labourer of the eighteenth century had been docile, industrious and sober; the nineteenth century added to these desirable virtues frugality in cooking and domestic management, determination to suffer almost anything rather than become a pauper, restraint from improvident breeding, and (finally) membership of a friendly society and a growing deposit in a savings bank.

To encourage the poor in these virtues was the duty of the rich, and it became another cliché of the period that the best way to help the poor was to help them to help themselves. Opinions differed on how it should be done. A sizeable minority believed that the economic situation of the labourers precluded the exercise of the desirable virtues, and that they could not be provident until they were given economic security and opportunity. The principal remedy urged (for the agricultural labourer at any rate) was access to the land, in the form of garden allotments, with the prospect of becoming independent small-holders as a reward for prodigious frugality. Such schemes made little headway against interests entrenched on the land, despite the propaganda of the Earl of Winchilsea and Arthur Young, and later of the Labourers' Friend Society. It was easier, and hence more popular, to offer medals and prizes for worthy labourers through agricultural and charitable societies. On the whole much more effort was expended in urging the poor to be more economical with what they already possessed than in trying to provide more for them. Count Rumford tried to bring science to the aid of frugality, and the Society for Bettering the Condition of the Poor waged a long campaign to introduce scientific methods and economical recipes into cottage kitchens to make self-help effective.

The poor, however, had already begun to help themselves through one of their own inventions, the friendly society or benefit club. It being, as one contemporary said, an age of insurance, these proletarian institutions were seized on by the rich as the remedy for distress, and perhaps even as an alternative to the Poor Law. Although many features of friendly societies offended them—the meetings at ale-houses, the feasts and processions, the haphazard management, and the potential usefulness for subversive economic or political combination—philanthropists strove hard to make friendly societies both respectable and general, and in 1793 the state gave official encouragement and offered some privileges. For a time most schemes for Poor Law reform included an element of insurance through contributory schemes, as in Pitt's and Whitbread's abortive Bills. Within a few years the savings bank appeared, another institution even more admirably suited to assist virtue into economic independence. After 1815 a brief war flared up between supporters of friendly societies and savings banks (friendly societies were vulgar and seditious, savings banks were based on selfishness and hence anti-social), but a truce ensued with a general recognition that both institutions were more or less admirable and certainly deserved support. Some of the schemes based on the contributory principle foreshadowed modern developments in national insurance, but the practical difficulties were so great that the dream soon faded. Most men recognised that the Poor Law could not be remodelled into a gigantic benefit society through which the poor would be morally elevated (and would also, incidentally, pay for their own relief). The Poor Law and institutions facilitating providence had to develop separately, until modern instrumentalities could combine some elements of both.

The Poor Law thus remained the chief public instrument for the relief of distress, and suffered no major legislative alteration until 1834. It was not a simple instrument, as the survey offered in the first chapter of this book attempts to show; moreover the reasons for its complexity are as important as the fact. The three injunctions of the Elizabethan Poor Law, which bade each parish to relieve the impotent, employ the able-bodied, and 'correct' the wilfully idle, were interpreted, obeyed or neglected in a bewildering variety of local circumstances. In the late eighteenth century England remained in many—perhaps most— important respects a confederation of localities, and local initiative and torpor were alike tolerated by a central government which did not assume uniformity even as an ideal. The responsibility to administer the Poor Law was local, and was jealously restricted by ever more complex interpretations of the Law of Settlement; at the same time a host of special local acts and a few general permissive acts introduced a wide variety of administrative structures, each interpreting its obligations according to its conscience and convenience. There were fashions in poor-law matters, but no national policies, and although a persuasive reformer might occasionally succeed in steering a general act through Parliament its provisions were usually permissive, increasing the range of action which local officials might take within the law. One of the reasons why the pamphlet literature on the subject is so large is simply the fact that change depended on example rather than prescription, and successful innovation had no influence unless publicised. The curse of such localism was of course confusion, and reform and decay could be simultaneous and contiguous; its benefit, however, was flexibility, and by 1795 a whole range of administrative structures and methods of relief had been developed to meet the needs, at least partially and intermittently, of particular local situations.

No doubt the quality of poor-law administration and the adequacy of relief varied as much as their form. Certainly there is evidence of continual if limited dissatisfaction with the system, and a succession of proposals for a general reform appeared in print and occasionally in Parliament in the eighteenth century. Little was achieved, but the failure even of such an able and persistent reformer as Thomas Gilbert, who produced a succession of schemes and bills in the 1770s and 1780s, should not be attributed simply to Parliamentary apathy. The system included its own procedures for reform, but they were typically local even if particular schemes often required the sanction of a Parliament generally tolerant of such endeavours. The gentry in Parliament assumed, in this sphere as in so many others, that it was proper for the natural leaders of society to show initiative in poor-law matters in their own localities, but improper for such local initiative to be stifled by particular schemes imposed on varying situations by legislative fiat. This was not merely obscurantist conservatism, but rather an accurate reflection of the facts of eighteenth-century society and government. How could Parliament impose uniformity on such a variety of circumstances? How could it declare a truce in the perpetual war of parish against parish which the Law of Settlement had long created as a sort of national sport? How could conflicting interests be reconciled, when it was not clear what they were? Gilbert was allowed to sponsor permissive legislation under which parishes could unite into larger units without benefit of a special act; why should Parliament go further, and replace local initiative and consent with central compulsion? Central control and professional administration occurred to so few eighteenth-century minds that we are tempted to see the exceptions, such as Jeremy Bentham, as causes rather than mere prophets of nineteenth-century developments in state administration. And even Bentham, a compulsive proposer of systematic legislation, was thwarted in drafting his great Poor Plan of 1796–7 by lack of 'intelligence', by which he meant information. In the eighteenth century Parliament did not possess or even dream of suitable facilities for collecting information, devising legislation, and (more difficult still) imposing a new general law on recalcitrant local authorities. In the absence of such facilities no individual, not even Pitt at the height of his power, could produce a general bill on poor-law reform which could not be riddled with the grape-shot of plausible local objection.

Against this background the Poor Law Amendment Act of 1834 seems a radical departure indeed, not only in its dogmas on relief and its blue-print for administrative reform but above all in itself, in the challenge it represented to the old order of local discretion under permissive laws. The procedure of Lord Grey's government in appointing a Royal Commission to investigate facts and to produce a bill— a bill moreover which announced a national policy and created an instrument to carry it out—was as modern in concept as Pitt's own attempt at poor-law reform had been typical of his own era. In the first years after Waterloo select committees of the Commons had attempted to find a concensus of opinion on reform and to impose it on

Parliament and country, but their efforts had been almost as ineffectual as the individual endeavours of earlier reformers. The early nineteenth century thus saw a revolution in the accepted methods of reform, as well as a major reform of the Poor Law itself, and with the creation of a professional central administration the old nexus of private local initiative and permissive legislation was broken. This development, and others related to it, indicate that the debate on poor relief was concerned as much with government as it was with poverty. In discussing the Poor Law men were assessing the propriety of an important function of government, and assessing too the correctness of policies pursued, and the suitability of particular administrative instrumentalities. Perhaps only Bentham analysed the question explicitly in this way—which is why his writings on the subject, for all their eccentricity, probe so much more deeply than those of most of his contemporaries—but almost all contributors to the debate implied or expressed views on government as well as on poverty. The notion that the early nineteenth century was an age of *laissez faire* in England, when the functions of government were systematically reduced to a minimum under pressure of class interests and a liberal ideology, has long been questioned; it was rather an age of transition in government, in which the same generations which dismantled ancient devices of legislative and administrative control built the foundations of the modern administrative state even as they wrecked the old. The process of transformation, with its intricate relationship between interest, ideology, and the pressures inherent in administrative procedures themselves, cannot as yet be completely described or explained. This theme is not the subject of this book—if it were the formulation and passing of the Act of 1834 would for example have required much more extended treatment—but points of relevance may emerge from the discussion. Poor relief was not a new function of government, created in the nineteenth century; on the other hand it was not an old function left undisturbed. In 1834 the Poor Law was transformed, even if not as completely as the authors of the Act intended. It was, to a degree, centralised and strengthened, and it is a paradox not uncharacteristic of the period that this strengthening was the outcome of an attempt to abolish rather than to develop. The attack on the old Poor Law, the main subject of this book, was radical, seeking its abolition; the outcome was a new Poor Law which—harsh and restricted though it seemed to many—possessed a stronger administrative structure and a more consistent theoretical basis than the old system had ever enjoyed.

So great a transformation in an ancient national institution is inconceivable except as the result of a considerable crisis in poor-law affairs. Judging by the frequency with which pamphlets on the subject were published it was an intermittent rather than a perpetually deepening crisis: the largest output from the presses on this topic appeared in in the later years of the 1790s, the first years after Waterloo, and the period immediately before 1834. In the intervals between these periods of intellectual productivity important individual works were published, and from time to time proceedings in Parliament provoked a flurry of pamphleteering, but the debate was relatively dormant. The periods of intense discussion were also, on the whole, times of general distress among the labouring classes, and times of high poor rates and perhaps of economic pressure on the ratepayers themselves. No doubt this correlation between distress, expense and dissatisfaction with the system was the mainspring of the pressure for reform, but it did not determine, in any simple way, the types of reform sought. While some wished to change the system because it was inadequate for the poor, and many because it was onerous to the rich, the subject gained a wider significance as men sought to understand these periods of crisis and to seek a remedy. The Poor Law was seen not merely as a device for relieving distress, but as an important element in that economic and social system in which distress so obviously occurred. Was it, perhaps, a crucial causal element, a major producer of that very indigence it seemed so ineffectual in relieving? In the eighteenth century occasional critics had claimed that the Poor Law was fundamentally misguided and a national tragedy rather than a source of pride; indeed almost all the later arguments for the abolition of the system had been put before 1790. The years of scarcity after 1795 strengthened such suspicions, and in 1798 and 1802 Malthus produced a theoretical justification for them. In the crisis which followed the peace the suspect Poor Law became a fashionable object of blame, and for the first time the case for its abolition received wide (though not universal) support among the upper classes, and became the orthodox and respectable opinion.

The argument for abolition was, in brief, that a legal establishment for the relief of poverty created the paupers it set out to relieve. The theoretical explanation of how it did this was relatively simple. Relief by law demoralised the labourer, undermining industry and that reliance on his own labour which alone could provide personal sustenance and national wealth. As the funds for the maintenance of labour were limited, expenditure on idle or unproductive paupers could only be at the expense of independent workmen, worsening their condition and forcing them to become paupers also. Attempts to employ the paupers profitably were merely diversions of capital from its natural and efficient employment to an unnatural and inefficient one, which would either fail to be profitable or if profitable would force free enterprises to fail until the whole national capital would be required to maintain a population which had all become paupers. Finally, the granting of a right to relief from the Poor Law implied that all comers could be guaranteed sustenance, destroying the natural relationship between the demand for labour and the growth of population, encouraging imprudent marriage and excessive breeding. All these baneful tendencies made the system a powerful engine for generating pauperism, making it seem possible that the time might come when all the labourers were paupers, rates had swallowed rents, and the surplus in the hands of the rich had been utterly extinguished by the clamorous demands of an ever-increasing pauperised population.

The theory was crude, but the circumstances of the time made it plausible to some enlightened and benevolent men as well as to rate-payers and landlords clamorous for relief. Many of its propositions are, and probably always were, untestable, but support for the doctrine as a whole never dependeid on rigorous social investigation and analysis. Whether pauperism was n fact increasing, when, and why are questions which are not probed inthis book, and in any case the answers could not alone explain the attitudes of contemporaries. Men alarmed by the present and fearful for the future are easily swayed by isolated indications of impending doom, and a few examples of extreme pauperisation were seen as portents of calamity to come. In particular the practice of making up wages by allowances from the poor rates could easily be seen as the logical outcome of the whole system, and as a procedure which demoralised, tended to absorb all labourers into the pauper body, wasted resources by employing them inefficiently, and perhaps encouraged excessive population growth, though Malthus was less confident on this point than were some of his disciples. How widely, and how continuously, the allowance system actually existed is very uncertain, and its ieconomic and social significance was more complex than contemporar es assumed. But their alarm is understandable, and so is their preoccupation with a phenomenon which was never more than one among the many expedients practised under the old Poor Law.

If the first years of the peace saw the climax of the attack on the old Poor Law, and a widespread acceptance of abolitionism as a correct social doctrine, abolition itself remained impossible. The ruling classes were always aware of the usefulness of the Poor Law as an insurance against rebellion, and insurrection was then sufficiently threatening without provoking the poor by stopping relief. The doom of abolitionism was that it could never achieve powerful support except when rates were high and distress great, the very circumstances in which abolition was least practicable. For all its sound and fury the debate after Waterloo produced little change in the law, though circumstances provoked the usual ferment of local reform and experiment. When, in the next decade, the rates receded and pauperism was reduced—with much publicity and self-satisfaction—in a significant number of parishes, some questioning of the new abolitionist orthodoxy began. Perhaps, after all, the Poor Law was not inherently disastrous; the English system had existed for two centuries without manifesting its monstrous tendencies. A purified system, selective in its operation, efficient and uniform, could perhaps be found. It was the proud claim of the Royal Commission of 1832-4 that it had found such a system, a Poor Law which would not merit the censure of the abolitionists; if the paupers were segregated from the economy and from society, and relieved according to their needs but in circumstances which tempted no man from self-help and independence, public relief could no longer be feared—except by those in need of it. The doctrine that pauperism must be made less eligible as a way of life than independent labour was one towards which many reformers had long been groping; its intellectual ancestry was manifold, though a clear statement of it could be found (and perhaps was found by the Commission) in an essay Jeremy Bentham wrote in 1796 but never published.

The fifty years before 1834 thus saw a revolution in attitudes to poor relief in England—or rather, a revolution and a counter-revolution. The revolution was abolitionism, with its roots in the eighteenth century and its climax in the Select Committee of 1817. It could never be put into practice, but it nevertheless set the terms against which the continuance of the system had to be justified, a continuance which required, in the event, a major administrative revolution. England retained a Poor Law, but almost against its better judgment. The new Union Workhouse, a symbol of harshness and oppression to the lower classes, appeared in a very different light to most upper class opinion, even (or perhaps especially) to the philanthropic. It was a fortress protecting society from two quite different evils, the starvation and insurrection of unrelieved indigence on the one hand and the moral depravity and economic ruin of progressively increasing pauperism on the other. Behind these public defences capitalist progress could continue, while private charity and their own self-help elevated the character, improved the condition, and secured the loyalty of the labouring classes.

It is tempting, but dangerous, to interpret a development in terms of its outcome. In the course of writing this book the material showed an inconvenient reluctance to be marshalled in a coherent relationship to the reform of 1834, which appeared eventually as an epilogue rather than a culmination. An account of public attitudes towards poverty and its relief in this period would be falsified if variety were sacrificed to analytical coherence; the richness of the debate is its most notable feature, apart from the sheer bulk of the material. A large number of the literate inhabitants of England thought themselves qualified to write pamphlets on the subject, and the silly are often as revealing as the profound. In the discussion of the 1790s, in particular, a great diversity of attitudes and actions had to be counted, and the complexity and importance of the contributions of Malthus and Bentham defied condensation. After the war the debate was more sharply focused and can be expounded with more coherence, if only at the expense of divorcing it a little roughly from related issues concerning the condition of England. Generalisation about a debate on such a topic can only be made at a risk, for what may appear ephemeral and eccentric to one reader has pith and moment to another. Great writers have no doubt a timeless significance, but the understanding of a period, and its preoccupations and concerns, can only be gained from the thoughts and actions of those who belonged to it alone. A secondary account can only partially recapture the flavour of contemporary discourse, its insights and banalities, and its peculiar logic.

I

The Poor Law Before 1795

1. *Inherited Diversity*

THE practice of poor relief in England in the eighteenth century defies simple generalisation. The evidence, though copious, is fragmentary and frequently unreliable, being for the most part material left by a host of unskilled local officials careless of statistical accuracy. Parliament rarely called for information, and when it did—in 1750, 1776 and 1783–5—the returns could be no better than the records overseers had kept, and accuracy was inevitably exceptional until government gave notice in advance of the information it required, thus imposing some uniformity on the records themselves. Lack of uniformity was, of course, of the essence of the old Poor Law, and the overseers' haphazard bookkeeping was at least faithful to the facts in this respect. Only by courtesy could poor relief be described as a system before 1834, being rather a multitude of practices within (and sometimes without) the framework of a complicated aggregation of law. Handbooks on the Poor Laws prepared for the use of overseers or justices rarely covered their subjects in a single volume,[1] and no one attempted a really exhaustive examination of the law in practice. If the *Act for the Relief of the Poor* of 1601 remained for nearly two and a half centuries the basis of the system, it did so only in the sense in which the first cluster of polyps form the foundation of a coral reef.

---

[1] See, for example, F. Const, *The Laws relating to the Poor* (1800); M. Nolan, *A Treatise of the Laws for the Relief and Settlement of the Poor* (1805); W. Toone, *A Practical Guide to the Duty and Authority of Overseers* (1815); Sir G. A. Lewin, *A Summary of the Laws* etc. (1828).

The great Elizabethan Act survived because it was adaptable, permitting diversity of practice in time as well as place. Even the massive researches of Sidney and Beatrice Webb produced only the most tentative of attempts to divide the history of the old Poor Law into stages of development, and their account is organised on an analytic rather than a chronological basis. In a larger view they characterised the whole period before 1834 as 'The Relief of the Poor within a Framework of Repression', and as 'Charity in the Grip of Serfdom'.[2] Certainly, in that ferment of legislative experiment of which the Acts of 1597 and 1601 were the culmination, the aim of relief was always closely related to the desire to restrain, since rulers feared vagabonds before they pitied the indigent, and the Poor Law was often confused in practice with the Vagrancy Acts and their harsh provisions for vagabonds of different degrees of roguery. Relief continued to be associated with discipline well into the twentieth century, but practice varied between liberality and harshness. The 'Framework of Repression' was a habit of mind, not a matter of central policy, at least after the collapse of the Privy Council's attempt to impose central supervision on poor relief in the first decades of the seventeenth century. At the height of its power the Council could not even ensure that the administrative structure envisaged in the Acts of 1597 and 1601 was everywhere established, let alone put to use. Important initiatives in the relief of poverty continued to be local, and the process of local experiments was hardly disturbed by either the legislation or the administrative exhortations of central government. The Act of Elizabeth became but gradually the basis for local practice, and if it eventually achieved veneration as a sacred text it was much honoured in the breach.

As a social institution the Poor Law was not an entity existing in a legal and social vacuum; if it had links with the Vagrancy Acts on the one hand it represented on the other the overlapping of the realm of law with the realm of charity. The quantity and quality of private charity is difficult to estimate in any society, and though recent research has thrown new light on the origin and early history of the Poor Law mere mortal historians cannot estimate exactly the power of lights hidden under bushels. A harsh Poor Law, or a failure to administer a Poor Law, is not conclusive evidence that society was altogether neglectful of the claims of the indigent to relief. W. K. Jordan has argued that in the sixteenth and seventeenth centuries private charity was more extensive than public relief, the Poor Law existing mainly as an aid or back-stop to private philanthropy, and that the true indicators of the social values of the age were the liberal aims of the charitable

[2] S. and B. Webb, *English Poor Law History: Part I, The Old Poor Law* (1927), pp. 396–401.

rather than the legislators' more repressive intervention.[3] Certainly a belief that private charity was morally and socially preferable to relief by law persisted, and indeed still persists. The impulse to remedy social ills through voluntary activity was perennial; watered usually by religious teachings it sprouted anew in most generations. The ideals it strove to serve were neither pure nor permanent, but were continually changing under pressure of altered social circumstances. The literature on the subject is, in any age, difficult to assess fairly: while Tawney found in the late seventeenth century a 'new medicine for poverty', harsh in its Puritan identification of poverty with vice, Professor Jordan finds in the same material the culmination of a century of increasing enlightenment, of benevolent activity unprecedented in scale and fired by a new constructive aim of secular utility. Certainly two distinct strands of moral opinion—the one attributing indigence to misfortune which it is Christian charity to relieve, and the other regarding it as the result of vice which it is Christian discipline to correct—can both be found through the eighteenth century and beyond.[4] In any case it is apparent that in the century after 1660 payments under the Poor Law became almost everywhere the ordinary source of relief for indigence, with private charity a supplementary source of varying importance, called on for great efforts only in times of extraordinary distress. If this was in fact a reversal of the situation in the early seventeenth century it is nevertheless not a surprising development. Poor rates may have been opposed at first, and private benevolence preferred, but once rates had been imposed and the machinery of relief set in motion, if only in an emergency the procedure must have tended to become permanent. The evidence gathered by Chalmers and others who, like him, tried to stem the tide of poor-rate assessments which eroded the Scottish voluntary system in the early nineteenth century indicated that assessments, once imposed, soon became normal procedure.

2. Settlement

The Poor Law of the eighteenth century inherited from the preceding century not only the Elizabethan statute and a tradition of local

[3] W. K. Jordan, *Philanthropy in England* 1480–1660 (1959), especially chaps. IV–V. For other accounts of the origins of the Poor Law see E. M. Leonard, *The Early History of English Poor Relief* (1900), and Sir George Nicholls, *History of the English Poor Law* (1898 ed.), I.

[4] R. H. Tawney, *Religion and the Rise of Capitalism* (1926), pp. 253–76; and compare M. James, *Social Problems during the Puritan Revolution* (1930), chap. VI. Dorothy Marshall, in *The English Poor in the Eighteenth Century* (1926), pp. 20–2, describes a hardening of attitudes in the early eighteenth century but not earlier.

initiative, but also the Law of Settlement.[5] If the efforts of the Privy Council made little headway against the entrenched localism of parishes and municipalities, the victory of local independence was consolidated by the use to which the Settlement Acts of 1662 and later were put. Of all the barriers facing later reformers of the Poor Law system, settlement was the greatest, and even the authors of the Poor Law Amendment Act of 1834 could do no more than modify a law which they would have preferred to destroy. The Law of Settlement divided the kingdom into a multitude of little principalities in matters of poor relief, each with its own citizenship and each willing to beggar its neighbour rather than increase its own local financial commitment. Thus reformers faced not only a local variety in problems and methods, but a system inherently inimical to the growth of a common interest in reform.

It was widely assumed in the eighteenth century that the Poor Law provided the indigent with a right to relief. The statute of Elizabeth did so, if at all, only by implication, since it simply imposed an obligation on parishes to relieve. As Jeremy Bentham saw, the Law of Settlement went much further in encouraging the notion of a right or title to relief, though once again by implication. By assuring parishes that they need relieve only the poor possessing some legally demonstrable claim to be settled in them, it created settlement as a legal status; a man possessing a settlement had a right to relief in certain circumstances which was enforceable eventually through appeal to the magistracy. On the other hand, as later critics pointed out, the Law of Settlement virtually repealed the Poor Law, not only for the small group with no ascertainable settlement anywhere, but for any man as long as he was absent from his own parish. It was therefore logical enough for later critics of the whole principle of relief, such as Sydney Smith, to argue for restriction of the grounds for settlement as a form of abolition of the right to relief.

The notion that each man 'belonged' to a certain place, normally a parish, can be traced far back in English society, and the concept of settlement was certainly not created by the Act of 1662. The statutory right to settlement and hence to relief developed as the obverse of the right of parishes to remove; the Act of 1662 required overseers to return the removed man to his place of settlement and not merely to 'pass' him to the next parish as a vagrant. But why should the parish

[5] For accounts of the law and its operation see S. and B. Webb, *The Old Poor Law*, chap. V; D. Marshall, *The English Poor in the Eighteenth Century*, chap. VI; E. Hampson, *The Treatment of Poverty in Cambridgeshire* 1597–1834 (1934), chap. XI; and A. W. Ashby, 'One Hundred Years of Poor Law Administration in a Warwickshire Village', *Oxford Studies in Social and Legal History*, III, chap. V.

alleged as home accept him? Unfortunately neither Parliament nor the courts ever put the matter on a simple and comprehensive basis, but attacked contentious issues piecemeal as they arose. Various acts added hiring for a year, apprenticeship, serving in parish offices or paying parish rates as grounds for gaining a settlement, but failed to recognise a simple period of residence as a qualification; and in the eighteenth century the Court of King's Bench evolved the doctrine of derivative settlement, holding that unless a person specifically gained a settlement on statutory grounds his place of settlement would be that of his father or any other ancestor who had gained a statutory settlement. Thus history had to be questioned as well as present circumstances, and litigation flourished. For lack of a better guide through the jungle of statute law and judicial decision we may accept Eden's generalisation that the greater part of the labouring poor acquired settlements in one of four ways: most illegitimate children by birth; most legitimate children by birth, unless a derivative settlement could be ascertained; women by marriage, provided the man's settlement was known; and any person by possession of any freehold, however small. Eden should probably have added the renting of a tenement worth four shillings a week, an increasingly important method of gaining settlements in large towns as urban rents rose.[6]

The whole question of settlement was fully discussed in the main period of this study, but the principal themes in the debate were clearly stated before 1795. Adam Smith, in the most famous of all attacks on the system, criticized removal as 'an evident violation of natural liberty' and alleged that 'there is scarce a poor man in England, of forty years of age ... who has not, in some part of his life, felt himself most cruelly oppressed by this ill-contrived law of settlement'. It was thus an affront to natural justice as well as a serious interference with the system of natural liberty in economic affairs; his rejection of the law became an orthodox tenet of political economy, and his disciples from Pitt and Crumpe to J. R. McCulloch stressed the evil consequences of restricting the free circulation of labour, some of them even asserting this to be the main cause of indigence. Nevertheless Smith's account was misleading on the facts of the situation: that independent-minded cleric John Howlett effectively denied any widespread interference with the mobility of labour, despite obvious cases of individual injustice:

How seldom do the young and healthy, while single, find any difficulty in changing their residence, and fixing where they please ... Were it otherwise, how has it happened that Sheffield, Birmingham and Manchester have

---

[6] For the full complexity of the law in its maturity see Sir James Barrow, *Decisions in the Court of King's Bench upon Settlement Cases* (1786), and J. Sculthorpe, *A Compendium of the Laws relating to the Settlement and Removal of the Poor* (1827).

increased, from almost mere villages, to populous towns that rival or even surpass in magnitude our largest cities, the capital alone excepted ?[7]

Howlett's general point, that the application of the settlement laws was no more than partial, would seem unanswerable. The Webbs estimated that the 15,000 parishes of England did not enforce more than a few tens of thousands of Removal Orders each year, involving the removal of some fifty or a hundred thousand persons distances averaging forty or fifty miles. Removal was expensive, especially if a family had to be conveyed a great distance, or if their settlement was disputed. In manufacturing towns overseers simply could not afford to remove all men made indigent by a slump in trade; in general, in most parishes, they were careful to prevent people gaining settlements but normally removed only those strangers obviously liable to become chargeable. This principle—that he that hath not shall be taken away—undoubtedly caused great suffering, and the cruellest cases were those involving women and children. Overseers did not need a Malthus to teach them to fear the reproductive capacity of the human animal. But not all parish officers were unkind, and some were more cunning than brutal. Moments of comedy appear in these sorry annals when overseers turned marriage brokers and bribed men settled elsewhere to marry women obviously a source of future expense to the parish, or on the not infrequent occasions when the wiles of the chargeable out-matched those of the parish officers.

The greatest absurdities in settlement matters appeared, naturally enough, in litigation; and the classic example is Henry Crabb Robinson's account of a case in Clerkenwell Sessions where a settlement was disputed because the pauper's home lay across a parish boundary, which passed, indeed, through his bed. 'The Court held the pauper to be settled where his head (being the nobler part) lay, though one of his legs at least, and great part of his body, lay out of that parish'.[8] But litigation on disputed removals was not merely sometimes absurd, and usually inconvenient to the person removed as he was shunted back and forth between disputing parishes: it was also expensive. Expenditure on litigation grew, if official returns of overseers' expenses (including legal costs) are a guide: totals rose from £35,071

---

[7] Adam Smith, *Wealth of Nations* (ed. Cannan, 1904), I. 158; J. Howlett, *The Insufficiency of the Causes* etc. (1788), p. 115; and compare S. Crumpe, *An Essay* etc. (1793), p. 92, and Sir F. M. Eden, *The State of the Poor* etc. (1797), I. 296–8. Eden accepted Howlett's criticism of Smith. Howlett, vicar of Great Dunmow in Essex, was a prolific and pungent writer on economic and social questions. He is remembered chiefly for his refutation of Price's arguments on depopulation; McCulloch described his *Enclosure a Cause* etc. (1787) as unanswerable (*Literature of Political Economy*, chap. IV). Howlett died in 1804 at the age of seventy-three.

[8] Quoted in S. and B. Webb, *The Old Poor Law*, p. 347 n.

in 1776 to £91,996 in 1783–5, more than doubled to £190,072 in 1802–3 and nearly doubled again to £327,585 in 1813–15.[9] These figures may be suspect, but certainly show a rate of increase greater than that of the sums expended in relief. Perhaps parishes found it desirable to remove more paupers, or to dispute more removals, as the pressure on the rates increased in the years of crisis; or perhaps the costs of court actions increased more rapidly. Certainly the lawyers were the only gainers from such expenditure, as the parishes transferred their burdens one to another.

Whether the number of removals increased or not, mounting expenditure lent impetus to reform of the Law of Settlement towards the end of the eighteenth century. In 1793 Thomas Ruggles expressed a common view: to him, settlement was a national burden, clogging the economic and political liberty of the people and reducing wages. It should be reformed, despite the awful example of unrestrained liberty on the other side of the Channel.[10] Nevertheless neither Ruggles nor most of the other critics dared suggest that settlement be swept away, partly from the old fear of vagrancy, but mainly because local financial responsibility implied some limit on local commitments. The alternative to settlement was a truly national poor law, and only the boldest spirits could conceive such a radical departure. Ruggles supported strongly the proposal made in 1788 by Sir William Young to prevent removal until the person concerned was actually chargeable, a reform urged earlier in the century by Hay and others. Preventive removals of soldiers and sailors had been stopped in 1784, and in 1793 Rose's Friendly Societies Act gave the privilege of exemption from removal until chargeable to all members of friendly societies. Finally, in 1795, an Act freed from the fear of removal until chargeable all except women with child.[11] The last exception is to be regretted; single women continued to be the chief object of overseers' suspicions, and oppressive removals undoubtedly increased with the marked increase in bastardy cases in the early nineteenth century. The Act of 1795 achieved something in the cause of humanity but little in that of administrative logic and economy, and dissatisfaction with settlement remained one of the main themes in the debate on poverty and its relief after 1795.

3. *Administrative Structures*

The local officers who waged internecine war over settlements earned

[9] *Parliamentary Papers*, 1818, XIX, *Abridgement of the Abstract of . . . Returns* (82), appendix 2.
[10] T. Ruggles, *The History of the Poor* etc. (1794), pp. ix, 158.
[11] Eden printed the act in *The State of the Poor*, III. cxxx–cxxxi.

themselves little honour, either among their contemporaries or from historians. The shortcomings of the system of local autonomy in poor-law matters are indeed obvious; nevertheless they should not be exaggerated. Eighteenth-century administration exhibits more variety, and (within limits) more flexibility than its critics sometimes allow. The typical pattern in each locality was periodic reform interrupting gradual decay, and the reform was often effective, at least until, in certain areas, the problems became too great for such local self-regeneration. Administration which was limited in technique might remain adequate while the problems were also limited, but by the early nineteenth century many towns were swamped by a surge of population and even the virtual isolation of the self-contained rural parish was breaking down. By 1815 perhaps only London and the largest of provincial cities suffered administrative diseases incurable except by legislative surgery, but local government was becoming a political issue and the new broom of reform swept away not only old abuses but also the old, slow methods of reforming them. The drastic administrative remedies of the Poor Law Amendment Act of 1834 may have been more severe than the state of affairs made absolutely necessary.

The centralisation of 1834 was a rejection not only of eighteenth-century localism, but of the traditional methods of reducing its disadvantages. The usual remedy, when local units were obviously too small, had been the voluntary incorporation of a convenient number of them into a new administrative whole. By 1834 some 125 incorporations had been made under local acts, and another 67 under Gilbert's Act of 1782. But despite this development the total number of units had increased from about 12,000 to 15,000 in the preceding century and a half, as more townships in the North gained autonomy in Poor Law affairs. The great majority of these units remained very small; in 1831 some 6,681 parishes had a population of no more than 300 each, while another 5,353 counted no more than 800 inhabitants each. At the other end of the scale were the crowded urban parishes, many of them faced with rapid increases in population.[12] In this medley of local units, various in size, shape and population, the Poor Law was administered by a host of authorities, equally various in their status, administrative structure and even in the degree of local autonomy they enjoyed. The two main forms of administration were the individual parish and the incorporated area, but there was no uniformity even within these broad classes.

Generalisation about the parishes is particularly hazardous. Ancient usage had produced haphazard parish boundaries, and within them a variety of constitutional structures, from the apparent primitive democracy of the ordinary parish vestry to the closed oligarchy of the

[12] S. and B. Webb, *The Old Poor Law*, pp. 171, 156.

select vestries, but in all cases accidents of local practice and of personal influence determined administrative operation. Moreover on the antique peg of the parish the central government had hung new clothes; as a result the parish became, not a coherent administrative organisation, but a mere 'unit of obligation'.[13] In most parishes the significant fact for the average householder was not the right to speak his mind in the vestry, but his obligation to pay parish rates and to undertake in his turn the unpaid and thankless tasks of a parish office. The Overseers of the Poor were statutory officers appointed by Justices and legally accountable to them. In practice, if not in law, the overseer served one of two masters—the vestry and the Justices—or both, or neither, depending on local circumstances.

Vestry control over overseers was always precarious. The selection of overseers varied with local custom, but by the eighteenth century it was usual for vestries to submit lists to the Justices and for the latter to choose the men at the head of them, though in some parishes conflicts between vestries and Justices were common. But most overseers aimed primarily at avoiding trouble, and hence regarded themselves as accountable to the vestry. In the small parishes (that is, in the majority) effective power lay in a local oligarchy of squire, cleric and principal inhabitants, and tension rarely arose. Even in larger urban parishes affairs were sometimes well handled by small oligarchies careful of public opinion, providing in effect some semblance of government by consent. But in London and in unincorporated mining and manufacturing districts the situation was less happy; parish officers tended to be either uncontrolled, or under the sway of corrupt individuals or groups. The most damning evidence of parish corruption and inefficiency comes from these areas, and most of it is scandalous indeed. In Bethnal Green one Merceren ruled as a parish boss for some fifty years after 1787 by organising the local weavers at vestry meetings; and in Manchester in the 1790s Thomas Battye led a crusade against parochial mismanagement laying bare very serious shortcomings in local affairs.[14] The problem of reforming such large urban parishes was made greater by the prevalence of select or closed vestries in these areas. Although select vestries varied greatly in constitution, they tended to become permanent oligarchies insulated from public opinion; when enlightened, they could provide useful continuity in policy, but when corrupt they were in a position to usurp the functions of Justices as well as of open vestries. In general London select vestries show the best and worst local administration in the eighteenth century, sometimes alternating in the same parish. But in all parishes of any size the same

[13] S. and B. Webb, *The Parish and the County* (1906), p. 37.
[14] For Battye's works on the subject, see the Bibliography.

pattern can be observed, of periodic regeneration followed by years in which new brooms gradually grew old, and zeal departed. The more populous the parish the more difficult to sweep it clean, and by the early nineteenth century some metropolitan parishes at least would seem to have so outgrown their parish machinery that they were as difficult to purify as the fabulous stables.[15]

While vestry enthusiasm waxed and waned, the Justices of the Peace, individually and collectively, interfered spasmodically to reform or to confuse. Individually they were either part of the local oligarchy, or the rival of it; collectively they formed the link between the parish and the county, and beyond the county with that confederacy of local interests, Parliament. They were thus the principal check on the autonomy of local units, a check which apparently increased in the forty years before 1834, the period of the zenith and overthrow of the Justices' power in Poor Law matters.

The most continuous interference by the Justices was in their individual activities in their own parishes. Here everything depended on the character, energy and ability of the men concerned; legal powers were less important. Always supremely confident of his superior social standing, the local Justice was at best the father of his parish, at worst a rural tyrant.[16] In Poor Law matters clerical Justices seem to have been especially active; their education was usually superior, and they were very influential on social questions. The work of Burn, Poulter of Hants, Lowe of Bingham, and Becher of Southwell provides a framework on which the whole debate on the Poor Law could be built. These men, certainly, could not be accused of undue liberality, a fault more common in idle magistrates who would not be troubled with difficult inquiries. Although in the eighteenth century writers generally welcomed and encouraged the interference of Justices in matters of relief, seeing them as the protectors of the poor against cruel overseers, there were occasional complaints that they granted relief too easily. Conflict between Justices on the one hand and overseers and vestries on the other became more frequent after 1815, when the tide was running against the Justices' Poor Law, and the letter of the law was perhaps more frequently invoked against them.

If individual Justices often stepped outside the Law, the County Bench assembled at Quarter Sessions frequently assumed the power to

[15] For examples of periodic local reform see S. A. Peyton (ed.), 'Kettering Vestry Minutes 1797–1853', *Publications Northants. Record Society*, VI (1931); F. G. Emmison, 'The Relief of the Poor at Eaton Socon, 1706–1834'; *Publications Beds. Historical Record Society*, XV (1933); and A. W. Ashby, *op. cit.*

[16] S. and B. Webb, *The Parish and the County*, chap. II, and compare their *Manor and Borough* (1908), pp. 476–7, 667, for the activities of aldermen in towns incorporated.

remake the law itself, as well as to be judges of it. By the end of the eighteenth century an extra-legal constitution had developed: a growing executive of county officials and of committees of Justices, and an 'incohate Provincial Legislature' of the Bench as a whole. In poor-law matters the main activities of the Quarter Sessions (apart from deciding legal cases on disputed settlements and challenged rates) were in making orders on presentments or reports from individual Justices, and in deciding policy on methods and quantity of relief. Such legislative and administrative activity hardly needed a legal basis, for the individual magistrate was the common denominator in Parish, County and Parliament; as a class the magistracy made the decisions, at different levels of generality. The status of Quarter Sessions as a sort of sub-parliament is evident in the fact that most Bills on poor-law matters were circulated to the magistrates for discussion, while the proceedings and orders on local matters reveal their parochial roots.[17]

It might seem that the magistracy interfered less in the affairs of the areas specially incorporated. So they did—as magistrates—but their ubiquitous and capricious administrative endeavours reappear in the work of the Guardians. Incorporation for poor-law affairs could alter the administrative pattern, but not the social structure. Municipal experiment in poor relief bore little relation to the administrative pattern laid down in 1597; from the middle of the seventeenth century special arrangements in urban areas were put increasingly on a statutory basis, in a long series of local acts. The prototype of most eighteenth-century developments was the Corporation of the Poor of the City of Bristol, established by an Act of 1696 on a plan of John Cary's. Almost all urban incorporations aimed at combining administrative reform—especially the amalgamation of inconveniently small urban units into larger wholes—with employing the poor at a profit in Houses of Industry, a favourite dream of eighteenth-century poor-law reformers.

Similar incorporation in rural areas was much more difficult to arrange. Various schemes were urged, especially by John Hay in mid-century, most of them recommending a poor-law authority composed of the justices and freeholders of each country, or alternatively of each hundred. The first rural incorporation was achieved by local act in 1756, in the Suffolk Hundreds of Carlford-Colneis; its early success led to its imitation in other hundreds in East Anglia so that by 1785 the greater part of Suffolk and Norfolk was no longer under the old management. The structures established by these local acts, both in town and country, varied considerably, but the basic pattern was the incorporation

---

[17] S. and B. Webb, *The Parish and the County*, chaps. IV–V. The Pitt Papers in the Public Record Office (P.R.O.) include comments from Quarter Sessions on his Poor Law Bill.

of a large body of 'Guardians of the Poor', usually the Justices, Rectors and Vicars and substantial freeholders or leaseholders. The Guardians appointed a permanent committee of Directors which decided policy, and also chose a group of Acting Guardians who supervised the relief given by overseers. In practice, if not in law, the upper ranks of this administrative hierarchy took over the functions of individual Justices and Quarter Sessions; the overseers retained their local menial duties, but their masters had new titles. In general these administrative ventures achieved early success, but usually lapsed into bad old ways as the initial zeal of Guardians evaporated in the tedious routine of day-to-day administration. It was, after all, the old system of compulsory labour at the bottom of the hierarchy and voluntary supervision at the top, except in so far as salaried officers were included in the plans, which was usually only in the management of Houses of Industry. Failure gave point to Jeremy Bentham's claim that reform through disinterested voluntary activity was a chimera, and to his insistence that the principle of 'farming', or at least of professionalism, had to be built into the administrative system, and not merely called in as an adjunct to it.

Thomas Gilbert's famous Act of 1782 was a poor mutilation of his general plans for poor-law reform, but it did make incorporation possible without special local acts. Here, at last, salaried Guardians were to be appointed, though still under the control of voluntary Visitors. By 1834 some 67 Gilbert Act Unions had been formed, incorporating 924 parishes, mostly in rural areas in eastern England and the Midlands.[18] Unfortunately they were hardly more successful in the long run than earlier ventures, and did not even supersede the old practice of seeking reform by local act.

The results of all these statutory departures from the simple pattern of the parochial overseer and the supervision of the Justice were very complex by the end of the eighteenth century. Most large towns and a significant proportion of rural parishes had established organisations extending beyond mere parochial bounds; at least some elements of professionalism had been introduced alongside the old framework of compulsory service and voluntary endeavour; and some flexibility had been achieved at the expense of greater confusion. Parliament was later shocked to discern how far some of these local modifications of the general Poor Law had gone; investigations into local acts revealed that some parishes had taken the opportunity to smuggle into law clauses giving themselves wide power to punish and oppress the poor, and even wider privileges especially in escaping the granting of settlements.

[18] S. and B. Webb, *The Old Poor Law*, pp. 272–6. On incorporated areas see also their *Statutory Authorities for Special Purposes* (1922), chap. II.

4. *Methods of Relief*

What procedures did this host of authorities adopt for the relief of indigence? Here, once again, we must beware of placing too much reliance on legislation as evidence of actual practice. When the reformers of the 1820s looked back at the history of the Poor Law to find the source of the evils they complained of, they too commonly stopped short at what appeared to them to be legislative mistakes. A mythical division of poor relief into periods determined by legislation developed; 'good' periods being distinguished by the use of the workhouse as the main method of relief and as a test of indigence, 'bad' periods being those in which outdoor relief predominated. Sir Edward Knatchbull's Act of 1722 encouraged workhouses, and was therefore assumed to have introduced a golden age of the old Poor Law, a happy situation undermined by the encouragement allegedly given to outdoor relief in Gilbert's Act of 1782 and in further acts in the 1790s, acts which opened the door to the allowance system itself. Unfortunately, eighteenth-century legislation cannot bear the weight of this interpretation; it consisted for the most part of Acts which were introduced by private members, and which bound only those poor-law authorities which chose to submit to them. It would be too much to say that most general poor-law Acts represented merely the schemes of their individual sponsors, since some general sympathy in the House and country was necessary for their passing, but this support could not be expected unless Acts were either local or were merely permissive. The few clauses which imposed obligations on all parishes were either procedural (like that of 1692 facilitating legal proceedings against overseers for embezzlement) or were treated in the parishes as though they were merely permissive (like the famous Act of 1697 stipulating that paupers be badged). The pattern of eighteenth-century practice was not one of law determining methods of relief, but of fashions in relief receiving the sanction of law, the statutory framework providing an ever-increasing number of alternative procedures which could be adopted. Eighteenth-century writers such as Ruggles or Eden did not fall into the error of exaggerating the importance of legislation, but the same could not be said of nineteenth-century reformers such as Copleston, Nassau Senior or Sir George Nicholls when they surveyed the past.[19]

[19] D. Marshall, 'The Old Poor Law 1662–1795', *Economic History Review*, VIII (1937), 38–47. See E. Copleston, *A Second Letter* etc. (1819), p. 77, for one of the earliest of such attacks on Gilbert's Act; the development of a rosy view of the period 1722–82 can be observed, for example, in McCulloch's writings in the late 1820's, in Senior's (anonymous) *Remarks on the Opposition to the Poor Law Amendment Bill*, by a Guardian (1841), and in H. Fawcett's *Pauperism, its Causes and Remedies* (1871). The belief that the period 1782–1834 saw a major aberration in poor-law policy was an important aspect of the justification for the reform of 1834.

The Act of 1601 had stipulated three main forms of relief: 'sums of money' for the impotent unable to work; employment on 'a convenient stock of flex, hemp, wool, thread, iron, and other necessary ware and stuff' for children and adults without 'means to maintain them'; and apprenticeship for children as an alternative to direct employment. The Select Committee of 1817 insisted that the Act nowhere gave warrant for simple relief (other than employment) for the able-bodied, but two centuries of practice were against this legal quibble. Eighteenth-century overseers assumed that the alternatives open to parish officers were various: to employ or to relieve, to rely on a workhouse or outdoor relief, to manage the poor themselves or by contract. These distinctions cut across each other, for it was not unknown to employ on a parish stock, on the roads, or on a parish farm, although the workhouse was the most common device for employment. Similarly workhouses were used for simple relief as well as for employment; and contract management, though mainly used for workhouses, was sometimes arranged for the whole poor, outdoor as well. At no stage was the mixture quite as before, as changing circumstances and fashions determined parochial practices. But it is clear that in general simple outdoor relief was the easiest and hence the commonest form of relief; that employment inside or outside a workhouse was most difficult to organise, and was certainly rarely profitable; and that institutional relief in all its aspects was generally an administrative and social failure, despite high hopes and brave endeavours. Contract management was also a failure, although in some forms it remained indispensable in populous parishes, especially in London.

The simple dole or pension was ubiquitous, not only because it was the easiest form of relief to provide, but because it was the most logical (and indeed the cheapest) in the large number of cases in which individuals suffered from inadequacy of income through temporary or permanent disability. Most small parishes in the early eighteenth century had relatively simple problems in relief: firstly to care for a small group of permanently distressed persons, and secondly to relieve temporarily the sick, the injured, fathers overburdened with children, and the victims of occasional general economic distress brought by bad harvests, cold winters, or inadequate seasonal employment. It was, indeed, inevitable that much relief in money or kind would be paid to men in partial employment, or to others wholly employed but with special burdens; moreover there was frequently a lack of winter employment and consequently a need for temporary relief even for ordinary labourers. This situation could easily develop quite imperceptibly into a genuine surplus of available labour, a general inadequacy of wages, and that confusion of wages and relief

14

characteristic, it is alleged, of the allowance system. Settlement may have checked natural processes towards greater mobility of labour in these circumstances, but at least as important was the common assumption that the farmers of a parish were morally obliged to employ all the poor. The result was the widespread adoption of procedures variously called the 'Roundsman' system, or the 'billet' or 'stem' system, in which the unemployed were voluntarily or compulsorily allotted to employers and the parish provided part of their wages. Inevitably, the parish contribution tended to rise whenever this device was more than a temporary measure to meet an emergency. But in admitting the evils of later perversions of outdoor relief we must not forget its evident efficacy in innumerable cases in more suitable circumstances.

We may be less confident that eighteenth-century workhouses were ever really satisfactory, either as a means of employment or a method of relief. Leaving out of account the simple parish poorhouses which merely provided accommodation as a sort of relief in kind, there were by 1815 some 4,000 actual workhouses where there was a regular dietary, some control, and authority in the form of a master or matron. They varied greatly, in size and condition as well as in the aims of their founders, but, as the Webbs show, they shared a common tendency to failure.[20]

The most ambitious aim in the establishment of workhouses, and the one pursued with most persistent optimism until the end of the eighteenth century, was the profitable employment of the poor. The most spectacular attempts were the early houses of industry modelled on Cary's Bristol 'Hospital' of 1696, the similar establishments built in mid-century in the newly incorporated rural hundreds, and the later, much publicised Houses of Industry at Shrewsbury and in the Isle of Wight. But large numbers of smaller workhouses made similar attempts to employ inmates, almost always in some of the simpler processes of the textile industry. The reasons for the failure of workhouse employment to make any significant profit are now obvious, and were, indeed, clear to many contemporaries. Workhouse labour was necessarily inefficient—the labourers incapable or at best unwilling, the management inferior—and the only processes of which it was capable were precisely those in which the free market was most competitive, such as spinning and weaving, processes increasingly less profitable as machinery usurped the functions of human hands. Tragically, workhouses succeeded in training children in such occupations at precisely the time when their skills were becoming redundant in the labour market.

The other functions normally expected of workhouses necessarily reduced their efficiency for profitable employment. Thus many workhouses operated also as houses of correction, some local acts providing

[20] S. and B. Webb, *The Old Poor Law*, p. 218.

wide powers to punish and detain not only inmates but also the local poor in general, while the regulations of most workhouses assumed punitive powers with or without the sanction of law. Such harshness was more consistent with the notion of the workhouse as a deterrent than as a place of employment. The experiments of Matthew Marryott between 1714 and 1722 are the first known attempts to use the workhouse as a test of indigence rather than a source of direct profit, and the years before and after the Act of 1722 saw a large number of workhouses established for this purpose.[21] The principles of deterrence and of profitable employment could not but conflict, since only those least able to support themselves would enter the institutions. Critics of the principle of deterrence claimed that it encouraged mendicity and vagrancy by virtually abolishing the Poor Law for those who would not enter, and by establishing a penal system for those who would. But frequently, throughout the rest of the century, the usefulness of 'offering the house' as a device for reducing pension lists and deterring applicants for relief was noted, to appear finally with much trumpeting of principle in the reformed parishes of the 1820s. In general, in the half century before 1820, there was considerable disillusion over workhouses, both for deterrence and as places of employment. All the evidence suggests that workhouse schemes gave only temporary relief to the rates from either employment or deterrence.[22] In existing institutions there was an increasing tendency to use them principally as convenient places for the relief of those who through impotence or delinquency were unsuited to receive outdoor relief. Harshness within workhouses met growing criticism from humanitarian Justices and others, and while here and there attempts to provide efficient employment were made, too many institutions became virtually unsupervised asylums for a mixed population of the impotent and the vicious, and (unfortunately) children. Their chief characteristics would seem to be a liberal diet and a low moral tone. Having abandoned employment and deterrence, they failed on the other hand to become effective places of relief for the impotent, most of whom required more specialised treatment than these institutions could provide.[23]

The largest of the various workhouse institutions were under the

---

[21] The Webbs attribute the useful *Account of Several Workhouses for Employing and Maintaining the Poor* to Marryott and cite editions of 1725 and 1732, overlooking the edition of 1786 (entitled *Account of the Workhouses of Great Britain* etc.) with its interesting and nostalgic preface.

[22] S. and B. Webb, *The Old Poor Law*, especially pp. 233–40, 252–3; E. Hampson, *op. cit.* chaps VII–X.

[23] The best contemporary source on workhouses in the 1770's is *Parliamentary Papers*, First Series, IX, 249–96, Second Report from the Committee . . . respecting the Poor (1776).

16

management of special officials established under local acts or under Gilbert's Act, but elsewhere management by contract was common, at least in the second quarter of the eighteenth century. Contract management was a popular device in many aspects of eighteenth-century administration, from bridge building to street lighting, but in poor-law matters it fairly soon acquired a very bad reputation. Writers of the later eighteenth century, with the notable exception of Bentham, attacked the practice of farming the poor in very vigorous terms indeed. It had been claimed that contract management would avoid parochial jobbery, and that contractors would enforce frugality and industry on the poor, but critics soon pointed out that contractors' profits depended on oppression, and made bitter denunciations which we lack the evidence to check.[24] But in a great many parishes contract management was killed, not so much by humanitarian disfavour, but because contracting became increasingly precarious as a business venture.

5. *The Poor Rate*

For obvious reasons contemporaries were apt to judge the poor-law system by its cost rather than by its efficacy in providing relief or employment. There is no doubt that the trend of rising rates was the mainspring of the growing suspicion that the whole system was radically faulty; it is inconceivable that the Amendment Act of 1834 would have been passed had the ratepayers not been so urgent in their demands for relief. But more than simple greed put the focus of attention on the rates, which were widely regarded as a real indicator of malaise either in the system or in society at large. It was usually assumed that the rates ought not to rise, and that something was wrong since they did rise.

The rate for the relief of the poor did not begin as an ordinary tax: it was rather a form of alms which no one could refuse.[25] The transformation of a voluntary contribution into a compulsory assessment was probably complete in England by the end of the seventeenth century, though Scotland did not pass through a similar stage for another century or more. Early Elizabethan legislation indicates that the rate was intended to be imposed according to ability to pay, but already by 1601 the law was tending rather towards the taxing of the

---

[24] R. Burn, *History of the Poor Laws* (1764); and compare Eden, *The State of the Poor*, I. v. D. Marshall, *The English Poor in the Eighteenth Century*, pp. 135–40, surveys writings on farming.

[25] E. Cannan, *The History of Local Rates in England* (2nd ed. 1912), chaps. III–IV; and compare J. S. Bayldon, *A Treatise on the Valuation of Property for the Poor's Rate* etc. (1828).

'visible assets' of occupiers in each parish. In some parishes a general assessment based on ability, varying with the expenses as well as the property of the payer, did persist into the nineteenth century, but generally speaking the rate became a tax on the occupiers (not the owners) of houses and land assessed according to a conventional or actual rental. Taxing occupiers on the rental rather than the profits of farms did not matter much perhaps, and neither did the omission from rating of salaries, fees and wages, since the rent of a man's home would correspond to his social status and income. Courts gave it as their opinion that the Poor Law would be very oppressive indeed if lawyers were rated on their fees.[26] Failure to rate income from rents was perhaps a more serious omission: judges assumed that because rates were paid according to rents to tax rents themselves—that is, landlords as well as occupiers—was to tax rent twice, a fallacious argument since it was quite possible to tax the income of the landlord (consisting of rent) and the income of the tenant (as indicated by rent) and still be taxing separate incomes. In any case the landlords always claimed that the rate fell on them, as it was allowed for in the leases fixed. Thus, normally, only lands, houses, tithes, coal mines and underwood (the property listed in the Act of 1601) were rated, but in some places tradesmen's stock-in-trade was rated also, though usually under local acts. It was urged that such stock should always be rated, since a tradesman's or manufacturer's rent for buildings was rarely in proportion to his profits or to the number of potential paupers he employed, but the law on the subject was always obscure. Lord Mansfield, whose judgments were at first much against the rating of trading or personal property, later fell back on the easy test of 'the usage of the parish' in such cases. The truth is that the procedure of rating occupiers according to rental, a reasonably satisfactory guide to ability to pay in the seventeenth century, had by the late eighteenth century become so inconsistent with the real distribution of property that only a complete reorganisation of the law could have restored the intention of Tudor legislation. With the growing diversity of sources of wealth nothing less than a true tax on income could serve the purpose, and only Pitt and a great war could lead propertied Englishmen to suffer such an indignity even temporarily. The grievance of the inequitable incidence of poor rates remained; the landed interest continually claimed that trade, manufacturing and 'the funds' should share the burden of relieving pauperism, but although these complaints grew to a crescendo in the period of agricultural depression after the war they generally failed to face the problem squarely and certainly shrank from suggesting a return to the hated Property Tax. What they wanted, quite simply, was

[26] Cannan, *op. cit.* p. 95.

relief. In tracing the attack on the Poor Laws, it is extremely important to remember the inequality of the rate, and the consequent grievance of the landed interest, though Dyer may have been right in insisting that it was the small occupier, rather than the landlord or the tenant of the large farm, who bore the brunt of rising expenditure.

Since the poor rate was local its incidence was unequal geographically as well as socially. The Act of 1601 did allow Justices to impose a rate in aid on neighbouring parishes in order to help an overburdened parish, but this was not often done. Even in many incorporated areas the rate remained on a local parish basis. Purely agricultural parishes did not perhaps suffer greatly under the system of local rates; the real difficulties arose in manufacturing towns (especially decaying ones) and in some East End parishes where large numbers of workmen, employed in richer parishes, resided. Many writers complained bitterly of this geographical inequality, but the opposition to a more equal rate was very strong. None of the more fortunate parishes wished to share the burdens of others, and each sheltered behind the bulwarks of the Law of Settlement. They used another argument also, that only a purely local financial responsibility could enforce economy on parochial officers. This was plausible, since a local, mainly voluntary administrative system was clearly inconsistent with a national rate.

Certainly the rates rose; but to look beyond the nominal increase to assess the real burden, and to discover who bore it, are difficult tasks. For most of England for most of the eighteenth century they are impossible tasks, since returns from parishes were made only for the years 1748–50, 1776 and 1783–5. But even later, when returns were more continuous, it is difficult to allow for changes in food prices, in the value of money generally, in population and pauper numbers, and for the extent to which relief was paid in lieu of wages. Mere totals do not tell us much. Late seventeenth-century estimates by King (£622,000), and Dunning (£819,000) were only guesses, as was Fielding's estimate of £1 million in 1754. The first Parliamentary returns showed an average of £698,971 for the years 1748–50, but were so imperfect that they were put aside behind the Speaker's Chair and not published until found by the assiduous Rickman and the Select Committee of 1817–18. The later returns were probably more accurate, and revealed an expenditure on the poor of £1,521,732 in 1776 and £1,912,241 on the average in 1783–5. Population figures are equally uncertain, but it is possible that poor relief cost about 2s. per head of population in 1700, a few pence more in 1750, between 3s. 6d. and 4s. in 1776, and a little over 5s. per head in 1785. The average price of wheat was 33s. in 1748–50, 48s. in 1776, and 59s. in 1783–5; thus although the increase in normal rates was great between 1776 and 1783–5—perhaps greater, the Webbs suggest, than in any other decade before or after—the increase in terms of wheat per head of population was negligible, compared with the increase between 1750 and 1776.[27] Most contemporaries were content to note the nominal increase and to express some alarm. But not all: Howlett claimed that rates in the years 1783-5 were exceptionally high, and that the returns were quite insufficient as evidence of a rising trend. Writing in 1788 he asserted that 'those alarms on this subject, which have been so zealously spread amongst us, to our no small affright, are mere childish fancies'.[28]

Events in the 1790s were to overtake Howlett's thesis, even in his own mind, and the mild alarm of a minority became a much more widespread conviction of crisis. Hasty generalisation is a human failing, and it could be argued that inadequate statistics are not always to be preferred to no statistics at all. The habit in this period of calling for returns only when some alarm was felt about the situation encouraged undue simplification of the nature of the system of relief and exaggeration of its problems. When Eden and his indefatigable assistant compiled their three large volumes of material on the state of the poor between 1793 and 1796, on the eve of the crisis of scarcity, not even they could encompass the infinite variety of local circumstance and practice which was laid bare. Almost every method of administration or relief could be found, here in a sound improving condition, there in decay, the health of the system fluctuating with a kind of natural local pulse. In the continuing debate on the poor and their relief the views of protagonists would be determined by their personal, usually local knowledge on the one hand and by very general assumptions on the other; no one man knew, or could know, the whole reality of the ancient and complex institution which was called in question.

[27] See *Parliamentary Papers*, 1818, V, Report from the Select Committee on the Poor Laws (107) for extracts from the returns of 1750; First Series, IX, Report from the Committee etc. pp. 297–539 for the 1776 returns, and Report from the Committee on certain Returns etc. pp. 543–735, for those of 1783–5. Wheat prices are taken from T. S. Ashton, *An Economic History of England: The Eighteenth Century* (1955), p. 239.
[28] J. Howlett, *The Insufficiency of the Causes* etc. (1788), p. 63.

II

The Debate Before 1795

1. *Old Assumptions in a Changing Society*

THE complex edifice of the old Poor Law was constructed by practical men reacting to local problems with varying degrees of intelligence, integrity and zeal, and it is therefore pointless to seek in it the explicit application of social theories. Discussion of poverty and poor relief has left a vast literature, but practice showed an extraordinary reluctance to be moulded by general arguments, or to be remodelled on a national, dogmatic basis. In fact, in all the literature, there was scarcely a suggestion of such a basis on which to build. The reform of 1834 required not only an administrative revolution but also the emergence of a doctrine of poverty systematic enough to support a national policy. The 'principles of 1834', like the reform itself, were not quite as systematic as they were later assumed to be, but they were much more coherent and explicit than the assumptions to be found in the eighteenth-century literature; they had, however, roots in these assumptions.

Most of the pamphlets and books on the Poor Law itself were written to urge or oppose specific schemes of reform in administration and methods of relief, and although each writer implied general views on the nature and causes of indigence few offered systematic analysis of the question. It is therefore difficult to reduce the mass of comment—on pauperism, the condition of the labouring classes, social subordination and public morality—to order or coherence, and hazardous to generalise. Even in more formal writings on economic questions there are few coherent views on poverty, since most of these works were also written for specific purposes and did not offer general economic analysis. Literature on moral questions, on public and private virtues and vices, was sometimes more systematic and is certainly relevant, since

21

there was no presumption at that time that social theory could or should be ethically neutral. If the basic assumptions on poverty and the poor have to be inferred from a mass of isolated remarks and opinions they nevertheless existed: in every society it is the most fundamental assumptions which remain unstated, because they are so widely assumed.

We can observe, looking back, the duality of English society in the late eighteenth century, discerning industrial democratic Britain in the womb of the old order. But a preoccupation with the origins of a later social system misleads into anachronism; change was to come soon and rapidly, but by 1795 or even 1815 it had not progressed far, and in any case social consciousness lagged behind social reality. The old, relatively stable rural society had made its terms with an extensive domestic industry feeding an enormous overseas commerce, but the towns of the new machine industry heralded a transformation in which new relations of economic class would overwhelm the old hierarchy of social subordination. Relationships between rich and poor were to become less personal, with a new discipline in working hours and clearer segregation of class from class in other aspects of life. By the late eighteenth century new industry and the new towns were already objects of wonder, but they were still in a sense outside ordinary English society, geographically and in spirit. Their distinctive problems were attacked locally, rather than by appeal to a national legislature or a wider public opinion. Hence it is not surprising that the new industrial order made so little impact on the national debate on society and poverty until (at the earliest) the 1820s.

In economic thought even the new 'system of economic liberty', of unfettered competition and innovation in commerce and industry, assumed an England still firmly based on its own well-cultivated acres. Adam Smith, for all his emphasis on the division of labour, assumed a basically self-sufficient economy. The notion of England as the workshop of the world, dependent on her customers for food, had not yet challenged that of an England enjoying the fruits of industry and commerce as mere adjuncts to her own agricultural self-sufficiency. This issue was not really to be faced until the debate on the Corn Laws, and then for the most part obliquely. Malthus glimpsed a trend towards a manufacturing state dependent on imported food, but feared and deplored it; Ricardo, always more rigorous, produced in his elegant doctrine of comparative advantage a theoretical basis for a world-wide division of labour, a single world economy, but the starting point of classical economics—if not its conclusions—remained the agricultural phenomenon of Rent. When, in 1807, William Spence maintained that 'our riches, prosperity and power are derived from sources inherent in ourselves, and would not be affected, even though our commerce

22

were annihilated', his arguments were quickly refuted by James Mill, Torrens and the *Edinburgh Review*. But what was remarkable was not the vigour of the refutation but the great deference shown for agriculture as the basis of both the economy and society, even by the champions of commerce; the value of commerce and industry was insisted upon, but not yet their primacy.[1]

In the discussion of poverty and indigence it was the rural poor which received most attention. It had always been recognised that towns had a special problem in pauperism, and required special remedies. The problem was seen in the existence of a large group of rootless, near-criminal paupers, such as the casual poor of London, and it was only slowly recognised that the new towns had a new problem in an industrially specialised working class subject to periodic and virtually universal distress. There were plenty of pamphlets written on the special needs of particular urban areas, but very little discussion of the general problem of industrialisation and indigence. This had to wait, in the main, for the great debate on the factory system itself, though in the discussion of pauperism in the eighteenth century some writers from Defoe to Arthur Young and Bentham showed awareness of the problem of 'stoppages in trade'. But industry was more often seen as a remedy for pauperism rather than a cause. Many writers assumed that because wages in manufacturing towns were relatively high they should have no paupers at all; in 1788 Howlett praised Birmingham as one of the happiest and healthiest towns in the kingdom, thanks to the high wages of manufacturers.[2] If indigence appeared, improvidence must be the reason. A few saw that wages in manufacturing were precarious, and that under urban conditions improvidence could be a natural human reaction to uncertainty, but even the insights of sympathetic observers such as the Rev. David Davies were limited. Life in towns and 'associating at publick-houses' made manufacturers improvident, they were liable to want in stoppages of trade, and their 'sedentary occupations and habitual improvidence' caused premature death and the pauperisation of their dependants; but they were also much to be blamed for not sending their wives and children to work in factories, neglecting opportunities that rural labourers lacked. Child labour, anathema to the next generation of philanthropists, was almost a panacea to this.[3]

[1] W. Spence, *Britain Independent of Commerce* etc. (1807) and *Agriculture the Source of the Wealth of Britain* etc. (1808); J. Mill, *Commerce Defended* etc.(1807); R. Torrens, *The Economists Refuted* etc. (1808). The article in the *Edinburgh Review*, XI (1808) may have been written by Malthus, but B. Semmel, *Occasional Papers of T. R. Malthus* (New York, 1963), pp. 14–15, attributes it to Brougham.

[2] J. Howlett, *The Insufficiency of the Causes* etc. p. 54.

[3] D. Davies, *The Case of the Labourers* etc. (1795), pp. 54–5.

If most of the literature on pauperism was preoccupied with rural indigence it assumed also the traditional rural social structure. The notion of economic class emerged slowly in England, and was essentially a nineteenth-century phenomenon, displacing with difficulty the image of society as a pyramid of 'orders', a stratification based only partly on wealth and still influenced by the old mystique of birth and of land, of aristocratic privileges and responsibilities.[4] Most eighteenth-century writers on the poor assumed a three-tiered society: of gentry (active as Justices or Guardians), of farmers and 'substantial householders' (active as parish officers or in vestries), and of agricultural labourers and servants (only too prone to be active as claimants of relief). They assumed, moreover, a pattern of rights and duties, and not simply the economic relationship of landlord, tenant and wage-earner. Even Burke's *Thoughts on Scarcity*, a doctrinaire defence of the free market in the rural economic structure, showed approval of beneficent paternalism provided it was not permitted to cloud economic realities. The paradox in Burke's pamphlet is symptomatic of the eighteenth century; it is that of sophisticated economic doctrines, developed mainly to explain and encourage a highly developed capitalist commerce, becoming orthodox in a society still in many aspects agricultural and aristocratic. Perhaps it is not strange that so much of the economic writing of the eighteenth century was concerned with commerce; it was written largely to justify commerce to a ruling class which itself required no theoretical economic justification, but simply manuals on estate management, such as Curwen's *Hints on the Economy of Feeding Stock . . . and Bettering the Condition of the Poor*. Certainly it should not be assumed too readily that themes common in economic writings were typical of upper-class attitudes.

2. *Labour and its Reward*

At least one historian has found in the economic literature of the eighteenth century a more or less consistent doctrine on the place of the labourer in the economy.[5] It is suggested that there was, first, a stress on the national importance of the labourer, since only with much labour could trade be increased and national wealth augmented; as a corollary, an insistence that employment should be deliberately provided for all available labour; a demand that the poor fulfil their duty to labour, despite their natural indolence; and a belief that only if

[4] Compare A. Briggs, 'The Language of Class in Early Nineteenth-Century England', in *Essays in Labour History*, ed. A. Briggs and J. Saville (1960).
[5] E. S. Furniss, *The Position of the Labourer in a System of Nationalism* etc. (New York, 1920).

labour were cheap, and wages low, could an increase in national wealth be made certain. All these points can be found in eighteenth-century writings, and some were very common assumptions—especially the desire to provide employment for all, and the complaints that the poor were indolent—but it is doubtful whether they should be elevated to the status of a consistent, let alone dominant, doctrine of the Utility of Poverty.

The national importance of the labourer was stressed by almost all writers, and not merely in the context of theories of the balance of trade. It was recognised that the wealth of the nation, and likewise the fortunes of the rich, were produced by the hewers of wood and the drawers of water, as was indeed more obvious in an aristocratic society, with a large leisured class and a greater contrast between rich and poor, than in a modern economy. An eighteenth-century gentleman could normally justify his existence—in economic terms—only as a consumer and circulator of wealth; hence the spirited debate on the morality and utility of luxury, a debate which merged almost imperceptibly into later, more sophisticated argument about general gluts and under-consumption.[6] Gentlemen were generally unwilling to accept so slender a justification for their privileges, and insisted on the social and intellectual functions of a leisured class as well as on traditional notions of aristocratic rights and duties. Their position was buttressed by religious doctrines of redress in the next world for inequalities in this; it remained for Archdeacon Paley, in an hysterical concern for social subordination in the 1790s, to argue that the lot of the poor labourers was in literal fact happier than that of the rich with their 'heavy anxieties'. (For one thing the poor did not have to worry about the French Revolution.)[7] The upper classes were always well aware that the labourer was important, that the wealth of society depended on his exertions and social tranquility on his acceptance of his lot; there remained, however, room for disagreement on how hard that lot need be.

Social and economic considerations were similarly blended in the common detestation of idleness in the poor. Idleness was a vice if voluntary and a national burden if involuntary; in either case it was also a social danger. These beliefs, together with the obvious hope of reducing the poor rate, gave impetus to make-work schemes, and more sophisticated economic doctrines were unnecessary. Common sense suggested that the poor should not be idle and natural optimism fostered hopes that their labour could be productive; if experience proved otherwise then presumably the old bugbear, bad administration,

<hr />

[6] See E. A. J. Johnson, *Predecessors of Adam Smith* (1937), chap. XIV, for a survey of the early debate on luxury.

[7] W. Paley, *Reasons for Contentment* etc. (1795), *passim.*

was the fault. Defoe's theoretical attack on make-work schemes—in essence a defence of existing manufacturing interests against parish competition in circumstances of limited demand—failed to dispel the dream.[8] Supported intermittently by the notion of deterrence to pauperism through the workhouse test, proposals for institutional public employment persisted, and there were influential spokesmen and examples in every generation. If opposition to workhouse employment increased in the late eighteenth century the objections were humanitarian rather than economic.[9] Thomas Gilbert, one of the most persistent if least successful poor-law reformers of the century, showed a gradual disillusion with institutional employment: his scheme of 1764 was fully institutional, but by 1775 he was strongly criticising small workhouses and his proposals in the 1780s all restricted institutional treatment to the impotent. Thomas Ruggles, at first a naïve supporter of make-work schemes, read Defoe's pamphlet and was converted by it, but remained a supporter of houses of industry of the East Anglican type. Isaac Wood and other late champions of workhouse employment had all to argue the exceptional efficiency and humanity of their own particular projects in the face of mounting criticism, Sir William Young being perhaps the most outspoken of the critics. A new emphasis was placed on the educative and reformative effects of employment, and make-work schemes became increasingly humanitarian rather than economic in their justification and were less frequently institutional in form. By 1815 such schemes were effectively divorced from ideas of workhouse employment, workhouses gaining a renewed support only as instruments of deterrence. If idleness continued to be seen as a vice, a misfortune or a waste according to individual opinion there were fluctuating fashions in proposals to provide remedies.[10]

In the discussion of wages in the eighteenth century the aspect of interest is not the theory (such as it was) of what determined wage levels, but the common beliefs on what wages ought to be. Evidence for the existence of a doctrine of the Utility of Poverty consists mainly of statements that low wages were necessary for profitable exports, and that high wages encouraged idleness and extravagance and hence reduced production and increased expenditure on the relief of

[8] D. Defoe, *Giving Alms No Charity* etc. (1704).

[9] J. Howlett, *The Insufficiency of the Causes* etc. pp. 83–107; J. Townsend, *A Dissertation on the Poor Laws* etc. pp. 67–9; W. Young, *Considerations on the Subject of Poor Houses* etc. (1796).

[10] For the relevant works of Thomas Gilbert see the Bibliography. For workhouse schemes see in particular I. Wood, *Some Account of the Shrewsbury House of Industry* (1791); R. Young, *The Undertaking for the Reform of the Poor* etc. (1792); *A Draught of a Bill* etc. (1787); [W. Gilpin], *An Account of a New Poor House* etc. (1796); W. Sabatier, *A Treatise on Poverty* etc. (1797).

indigence.[11] But the evidence is far from simple: individual writers were often inconsistent—Defoe, for example, and Arthur Young later in the century—and their attitude to wage levels varied with the particular problems they were discussing. Occasional arguments in favour of low wages were to persist into the nineteenth century, but there had long been a growing belief that high wages were desirable, both on grounds of humanity and in order to encourage consumption and hence production. This view had almost won the field even before Adam Smith made national and individual welfare synonymous by insisting that 'no society can be flourishing or happy, of which the far greater part of the members are poor and miserable'. If Townsend still wrote in favour of low wages Howlett was more typical of late eighteenth-century opinion when he insisted that 'the poor are neither brutes nor fools' and claimed that high wages 'are to the bulk of the poor the most powerful incitement to diligent and regular industry'.[12] By the 1790s, and especially in the debate of the scarcity years, there was almost universal belief that the labourer should be comfortable, that he was 'worthy of his hire', although suggestions of economic equality were still of course anathema. But of what hire was he worthy? Were his wages in fact adequate? Were they rising or falling? Was indigence increasing, and if so why? This was the level of most of the debate in the late eighteenth century, a debate aimed at facts but continually upset by value judgments and general assumptions too vague and speculative to be regarded as genuine theoretical concepts.

3. *The Condition of the Labourer*

The condition of the labouring classes at the end of the eighteenth and in the early decades of the nineteenth centuries remains one of the great unsettled questions in English economic history, and it would be unreasonable to expect contemporary observers to show unanimity or exceptional insight when historians continue to disagree. Reliable statistics and adequate evidence of measurable components of welfare have never been available for the period. Even if they were, there would remain genuine grounds for disagreement in judging less tangible changes in the quality of life, and the most sophisticated techniques of

[11] E. S. Furniss, *op. cit.* chaps. VI–VII; E. A. J. Johnson, *op. cit.* pp. 287–9.
[12] Adam Smith, *Wealth of Nations*, I. 88; J. Howlett, *The Insufficiency of the Causes* etc. pp. 55–6. For more detailed discussion see A. W. Coats, 'Changing Attitudes to Labour in the mid-Eighteenth Century', *Econ. Hist. Review*, 2nd Series XI (1958), and 'Economic Thought and Poor Law Policy in the Eighteenth Century', *Econ. Hist. Review*, 2nd Series XIII (1960).

modern analysis are unlikely to produce a real consensus of opinion.[13] The circumstances of the economy and society were truly complex, with contradictory trends of growth and decline, trends distorted and interrupted by accidents of war and climate. Attempts to establish a common experience for the labouring classes as a whole have been justly criticised:[14] there was more variation between the condition of particular groups, and more fluctuation from year to year, than any generalisation asserting catastrophe or radical improvement can comprehend. Contemporaries were as prone to generalise as any, and to assert simple explanations of alleged facts, but with so difficult a problem their views, in all their variety, have a claim to be considered, and not merely dismissed as morally or politically unenlightened.

If the modern debate is in many respects a continuation of contemporary discussion[15] it is at once more selective in the issues it explores and more rigorous in its theoretical analysis. Its constant danger is anachronism: J. L. and Barbara Hammond were inclined to make coincidental the debates on enclosure and on industrialisation which were separated by almost a generation, and have not been alone in quoting descriptive evidence outside the context of its original frame of reference. On the other hand it was especially difficult for observers at the time to distinguish between long-term and ephemeral changes in conditions; historians are heirs to all generations, contemporaries restricted to their own. Discussion of conditions was naturally most active in years of crisis, and there was a tendency to see each crisis as a temporary phenomenon with immediate and obvious causes

[13] The recent debate may be traced in T. S. Ashton, 'The Standard of Life of the Workers in England, 1790–1830', *Journal of Economic History*, Supplement IX (1949); E. J. Hobsbawm, 'The British Standard of Living, 1790–1850', *Econ. Hist. Review*, 2nd Series X (1957); A. J. Taylor, 'Progress and Poverty in Britain, 1780–1850', *History*, XLV (1960); R. M. Hartwell, 'The Rising Standard of Living in England, 1800–1850', *Econ. Hist. Review*, 2nd Series XIII (1961); E. J. Hobsbawm and R. M. Hartwell, 'The Standard of Living during the Industrial Revolution: A Discussion', *Econ. Hist. Review*, 2nd Series XVI (1963). Local studies such as R. S. Neale, 'The Standard of Living, 1780–1844: a Regional and Class Study', *Econ. Hist. Review*, 2nd Series XIX (1966) may form the basis for some new generalisations; J. E. Williams, 'The British Standard of Living, 1750–1850', *ibid*, shows however that the process of analysis of national statistics is by no means exhausted.

[14] A recent and persuasive assertion of a common class experience may be found in E. P. Thompson, *The Making of the English Working Class* (1963); for criticism of it, from different points of view, see R. Currie and R. M. Hartwell, 'The Making of the English Working Class?', *Econ. Hist. Review*, 2nd Series XVIII (1965) and G. F. A. Best, 'The Making of the English Working Class', *Historical Journal*, VIII (1965).

[15] Some aspects of this continuation are discussed in R. M. Hartwell, 'Interpretations of the Industrial Revolution in England: A Methodological Inquiry', *Journal Econ. History*, XIX (1959).

and to adopt temporary measures to meet it. Certainly general prejudices and preconceptions coloured and to a degree determined interpretations of each crisis, and immediate experience reacted upon preconceptions; it is precisely this relationship between inherited assumptions and actual experience which gives each generation its unique moral and intellectual tone. The experiences of these times were both exceptional and variegated: hence the variety of reactions and interpretations, and the blend of originality and conservative dogmatism evident in the attitudes of rich and poor alike.

Even before the scarcity of the 1790s provoked discussion a variety of assessments of the standard of life of the labouring classes was evident and a number of different explanations offered. Only the most modest beginnings of the later outcry against the new industry can be found; even Dyer thought urban workers better off than agricultural labourers and demanded only that they be given a greater share of industrial profits. The most heated debate of the time concerned the engrossing of farms—and not simply enclosure as such—and even in this the broader issue of agricultural innovation versus rural conservatism for a long while overshadowed the specific question of the effects on the labourers. Whether real wages in agriculture were rising or declining was also disputed, in arguments which involved assertions about price movements, population growth, war and taxation.[16] The thesis that the agricultural labourers' position was declining because for various reasons prices were rising faster than wages was firmly put, if as firmly disputed.

Two general causes alleged in explanation of a declining condition for labourers need to be stressed because they have largely disappeared from modern debate. There were perennial complaints that the miseries of the poor, and increases in the cost of relieving them, were primarily due to a deterioration in morals, to increasing idleness and extravagance. Defoe's claim that ' 'tis the Men that *won't work*, not the Men that *can get no work*, which makes up the numbers of our Poor' was echoed in every subsequent generation. In 1752 Alcock was but one of many who lamented the 'unnecessary idle expense' of smoking tobacco and drinking tea 'once if not twice a day'. (Tea drinking impoverished the blood, thus encouraging dram-drinking, another extravagance, in search of 'a short delusory relief'.) There was also extravagance in dress, especially 'the wearing of Ribbands, Ruffles, Silks and other

---

[16] Richard Price, Dyer and Davies were prominent critics of engrossing; Howlett and Arthur Young (in his early works) were ardent in the cause of innovation. Howlett thought that an increase in population had forced down wages; Dyer blamed inflated rents and 'impolitic wars', as did Paine. Townsend was one of those who denied that real wages had fallen.

slight foreign things, that come Dear, but do but little service'. Henry Fielding repeated the complaint of wilful idleness, though he also pointed out that 'the *sufferings* of the poor are indeed less known to us than their *misdeeds*, and therefore we are less apt to pity them. They starve, and freeze, and rot among themselves, but they beg and steal, and rob among their betters.'[17] Howlett, in defence of the poor, pointed out that if decades of complaint of declining moral standards were well founded 'human society among the lower orders in this kingdom must now be a picture of the infernal regions'; continual decline in moral standards was inherently implausible. Thomas Day, the author of *Sandford and Merton*, was one of very few who denied completely that the poor were 'profligate and venal' and claimed they were much more decent than the rich; even Howlett admitted that there was 'a greater degree of moral depravity, and a greater frequency of vice . . . among our present Poor than there were formerly. But this I must beg leave to observe has not been the *cause*, but the *consequence* of their Poverty.'[18] This was a noble sentiment, but how could it be proved? The coincidence of shiftlessness and distress among the labouring classes admitted directly opposite interpretations, and very different remedies suggested themselves according to the bias of the observer. Rising poor rates could be explained on the one hand by the moral fault of the poor, requiring discipline and education, and on the other by genuine economic insufficiency, requiring some change in the social system or at least in social custom. But these different explanations and remedies were not mutually exclusive, and most reformers chose some middle ground of emphasis between moral reform and economic assistance.

Two examples may demonstrate the delicate balance of individual judgment. Thomas Ruggles was a country gentleman with sense and sympathy, if no great intellectual power; the apparent distress of his neighbours, as he wintered in the country, led him to undertake an enquiry into facts and explanations, an enquiry which was less a social survey than a course of reading in the subject. His views changed as it progressed. He expected to find that wages were inadequate and the poor innocent victims, but eventually convinced himself that the indolence of the poor and their growing taste for luxuries were the chief causes of distress. He decided that wages had been higher in the

---

[17] D. Defoe, *Giving Alms No Charity* (Shakespeare Head ed. 1927), p. 187; T. Alcock, *Observations on the Defects of the Poor Laws* etc. (1752), pp. 45–50; H. Fielding, *An Enquiry* etc. (1751). Furniss quotes similar material (*op. cit.* chap. VI), but is inclined to accept it uncritically as evidence of progressive demoralisation; compare E. W. Gilboy, *Wages in Eighteenth-Century England* (1934), p. xxv.

[18] T. Day, *A Dialogue* etc. (1785), p. 43; J. Howlett, *The Insufficiency of the Causes* etc. pp. 25–7.

sixteenth century, but that the creation of the Poor Law was a real compensation for their decline; that in any case wages had risen again in the eighteenth century, and there was no lack of employment.[19] He approved of high wages as an encouragement to ambition among the lower orders, but was convinced that indolence reduced the earnings of the poor below what they might be. There was thus no need to increase wages, but rather to encourage industrious habits by such devices as schools of industry, rewards for good husbandry, grants of small farms to the exceptionally industrious and similar measures to develop 'a spirit of industrious emulation' instead of the 'idle thievish disposition, too prevalent at present among the rising generation of the poor.' Moral reform, and discretion in charity, were the national needs, and Ruggles' long researches had confirmed 'an impression, indelibly received by precept and education in early life, that idleness is the root of all evil'.[20]

David Davies' *Case of the Labourers in Husbandry Stated and Considered* was and remains one of the most important works arguing the contrary case, that the distress of the poor was due to economic insufficiencies. As rector of a Buckinghamshire parish he knew the condition of the local labourers, and 'could not impute the wretchedness I saw to either sloth or wastefulness';[21] he collected family budgets, and concluded that all families had a deficit of a shilling or two per week, thanks to the failure of wages to rise with increased prices. For a fifth of the population of the parish, relief had become a substitute for wages. The impact of these arguments was increased by the book's appearing in 1795, a year of scarcity—though the evidence had been collected in an earlier period—and the work was much quoted. Among later historians the Hammonds, in particular, stressed Davies' recommendation that wages should be regulated and raised, and blamed his contemporaries for failing to adopt this policy. But Davies' estimate of the morals of the poor was not consistently at variance with Ruggles': he included improvidence among 'the circumstances directly increasing the number of the poor', and agreed that if wages were raised it would also be necessary to inculcate habits of industry if misery were to be

---

[19] T. Ruggles, *History of the Poor* (1793), especially II. 103–12. McCulloch rightly described this book as inferior to Burn's *History of the Poor Law* (1764), and superseded by Eden's *The State of the Poor* (*Literature of Political Economy*, chap. XVI). Ruggles lived until 1813.

[20] *Ibid.* II. 130, 142.

[21] D. Davies, *The Case of the Labourers* etc. p. 6. For arguments that Davies (and Eden) gave too gloomy a picture of the labourers' condition see E. W. Gilboy, *op. cit.* p. xxiii. Davies' considerable reputation as an authority on the poor rests upon this single study of one locality.

much reduced. Boys and girls should be employed from an early age, a public system of education adopted, and frugality encouraged by facilitating savings and by making land available as rewards. There was even a hint that poor relief itself should be restricted to increase self-reliance.[22] Davies was quick to explain indolence as a result of indigence, but still recognised moral turpitude as a problem to be faced and overcome, and despite the emphasis in the early part of the pamphlet on the economic causes of poverty the remedies did not differ greatly from Ruggles', except in including wage regulation. Contemporary debate, at least before the advent of the social radicals, reveals a difference of emphasis between economic and moral factors in estimating the condition of the poor, but not a violent clash between opposite interpretations.

The other fashionable contemporary explanation of distress which has since fallen out of favour is the attack on the Poor Law itself— the assertion that the system of relief was the prime cause of the distress it purported to relieve. To be more exact, the indictment of the old Poor Law has long been uncritically accepted, but economic historians have done little to include an analysis of the implications of the system among the variables they weigh. The extent of redistribution of income in the form of relief, and its precise effects on demand, prices, wages and population growth have been assessed only in haphazard fashion.[23] The indictment of the old Poor Law in the massive volumes of the Report and Evidence of the Royal Commission of 1832–4 has formed a barrier to more exact research: it has been accepted in the main as a criticism of the system, except in its central implication that the Law was itself a main cause of distress. Only the beginnings of a more exact analysis of these assertions have been made,[24] and if the Principles of 1834 have suffered the curious fate of being at once accepted and rejected but never thoroughly dissected, the several rival theses of the time concerning the social and economic repercussions of the old Poor Law have been largely forgotten.

[22] D. Davies, *The Case of the Labourers* etc. pp. 98–9.

[23] Thus G. T. Griffith's inadequate examination of the relationship between poor relief and population growth, in his *Population Problems of the Age of Malthus* (1926) has not been thoroughly re-examined. It has usually been assumed that relief might be a factor affecting the birth rate; the importance of the existence of the system as a cushion preventing increases in the death rate remains to be assessed. Compare G. Ensor, *The Poor and their Relief* (1823), pp. 163–92.

[24] Some questions have been re-opened in M. Blaug, 'The Myth of the Old Poor Law and the Making of the New', *Journal Econ. History*, XXIII (1963) and 'The Poor Law Report Re-examined', *ibid.* XXIV (1964); but the analysis of the Report needs to be set in a wider context, extending before 1820.

4. *The Poor Law and its Justification*

Among writers of the second half of the eighteenth century who wished to change the Poor Law (and few who did not wish to change it wrote about it) three different aims can be discerned. Some, indeed most, accepted the law in principle, but wished to reform its administration and methods of relief. Others accepted the need to have some public system of relief for indigence, but hoped to replace the existing Poor Law with some form of contributory scheme. This view was more or less ephemeral; writers developed elaborate proposals, but failed to produce a practicable alternative to the Poor Law, though they convinced almost everyone that contributory institutions were desirable adjuncts to public relief. The third view, rare earlier in the century but increasingly important in the generation of Malthus, was that the system of public relief was fundamentally misguided, and that the Poor Law should be abolished if and when abolition could be practicable. All the writers offered or implied general arguments about the social and economic consequences of existing practices, arguments which formed the groundwork for the more spirited debate after 1795.

The critics did not, at this time, face a clearly articulated defence of the principle and practice of public relief. One cannot find, in the literature of the period, a systematic justification of the Poor Law as it existed, or even of its fundamental assumptions. Of course the mere fact that the law existed was to many a sufficient justification; natural conservatism inhibited them from criticism more radical than an occasional grumble. Even quite outspoken critics were prone to say of the Elizabethan Act (as Reformation divines said of the Christian Church) that its primitive foundation was good, but history had corrupted it. A strong feeling of national pride protected the Poor Law as one of the 'good old laws' of England. 'Our general system of Poor Laws is a venerable pile . . . and stands a distinguished monument of the wisdom and humanity of the British nation. Like every other edifice, it is liable, indeed, to the injuries of time and seasons, and must want occasional repairs and occasional improvements; but if pulled entirely down, we might stand a chance of either being buried in its ruins, or, at best, of never raising anything in its stead of equal grandeur, utility or beauty.' So Howlett; Ruggles echoed his view that the principle of the laws was 'replete with humanity', and that remedies for faulty execution must surely be within the wit of Englishmen. Simple humanity was to many a sufficient justification. 'It is manifest', wrote Davies, 'that our laws consider all the inhabitants of a parish as forming one large family, the higher and richer part of which is bound to provide employment and relief for the lower and labouring part'; and William

Frend thought it only 'common justice' that the poor be relieved by those who had been enriched by their labours. Unsophisticated notions of Christian charity, and paternalistic concepts of social structure, suggested that radical criticism of the system of poor relief was inspired by no more than a selfish desire to pass by distress on the other side.[25]

William Paley was one of the very few who developed a more systematic argument in defence of public relief. Paley's eclectic Christian utilitarianism brought together many strands of common eighteenth-century opinion, and may be accepted as characteristic and influential, though his frankness shocked the timid. Charity, he argued, was both a Christian duty and a corollary of the right to property, a subject on which he drew characteristically conservative conclusions from radical premises. In the state of nature a common claim to sustenance was one of the general rights of mankind; natural reason and hence Divine will justified the establishment of private property, paradoxical as it might seem for the many to labour for the riches of the few—a paradox illustrated in the parable of the flock of pigeons which gained Paley his nickname—but the right to sustenance of the propertyless remained. 'And, therefore, when the partition of property is rigidly maintained against the claims of indigence and distress, it is maintained against the intention of those who made it, and to his, who is the Supreme Proprietor of every thing. . . .' Moreover God had planted the instinct or habit of pity in human nature, 'and the final cause for which it is appointed is to afford to the miserable, in the compassion of their fellow-creatures, a remedy for those inequalities and distresses which God foresaw that many must be exposed to, under every general rule for the distribution of property'. Charity, which Paley defined as 'the promoting the happiness of our inferiors' joined prudence towards superiors and politeness towards equals in his trinity of civilised virtues.[26]

These arguments merely established a right to relief and a duty of charity; more were needed to prescribe relief by law. Paley insisted that the existence of the Poor Law did not excuse men from the obligation

---

[25] J. Howlett, *The Insufficiency of the Causes* etc. p. 118; T. Ruggles, *History of the Poor*, I. 163–4; D. Davies, *The Case of the Labourers* etc. p. 28; W. Frend, *Peace and Union* etc. (2nd ed. 1793), p. 29. Frend, Fellow of Jesus College, Cambridge, pupil of Paley and teacher of Malthus, was 'banished from the University' for the political and theological opinions expressed in this book, after a famous trial.

[26] W. Paley, *Principles of Moral and Political Philosophy* (*Works*, 1843 ed.), pp. 555, 551. Paley's *Principles* appeared in 1785; much of the argument on poverty and its relief had been anticipated by R. Woodward, Bishop of Cloyne, in *An Argument in Support of the Right of the Poor in the Kingdom of Ireland* etc. (1768), and can be traced back to Locke. For later statements see T. Ruggles, *History of the Poor*, I. 12 and J. G. Sherer, *Remarks upon the Present State of the Poor* (1797), pp. 8–10.

of private charity; at the same time he denied that relief could be adequate without the assistance of a legal provision:

> The care of the poor ought to be the principal object of all laws; for this plain reason, that the rich are able to take care of themselves. Whoever applies himself to collect observations upon the state and operation of the poor laws, and to contrive remedies for the imperfections and abuses which he observes, and digests these remedies into acts of parliament ... deserves well of a class of the community so numerous, that their happiness forms a principal part of the whole. The study and activity thus employed, is charity in the most meritorious sense of the word.[27]

But what if the imperfections and abuses were ineradicable and sufficiently dangerous to threaten the structure of society itself? Paley's arguments were abstract, and he revealed no close acquaintanceship with the Poor Law itself; others who claimed more expert knowledge could argue that the Law in fact impeded rather than advanced the cause of charity on which Paley so firmly insisted.

5. *Contributory Alternatives*

Men alarmed by what they took to be a coincidence of indigence and vice despite the existence of the Poor Law were naturally attracted by remedies which might combine relief and moral reform. Even if a public responsibility existed, could not a radically different system avoid the evils complained of? How admirable it would be if the poor could preserve themselves from indigence by their own frugality and foresight, and government discharge its obligation simply by providing facilities for them to do so. A contributory scheme might form such a facility: poor rates could be reduced as the poor maintained themselves, and if the rich patronised institutions of self-help the poor would be grateful and 'less likely to be incited to insurrections and disturbances than those who having no communication with any class of men superior to themselves, are easily led on to those riotous proceedings which are a scandal to good government'.[28] Contributory schemes were widely discussed in the late eighteenth century, most of them based on one of three basic procedures: the purchase of annuities, contributions to friendly societies, and the provision of safe places of deposit for saving.

An elaborate annuity scheme for the poor was produced in 1772 by Francis Maseres, assisted by the political arithmetician and divine Richard Price. Maseres thought high poor rates to be due to the

---

[27] W. Paley, *Works*, pp. 553–4.
[28] T. Ruggles, *History of the Poor*, II. 5.

'idleness and extravagance' of the poor while in good health and their failure to save for old age; the rich purchased annuities to avoid the inconvenience of primogeniture and to maintain unmarried female relations, and the poor should be enabled to make similar arrangements for their own more primitive needs. Under the scheme overseers would be empowered to sell to the poor annuities worth up to £20 per year, backed by the poor rate. No payments were to be made to men under forty-five, since annuities were to be an encouragement to youthful frugality and not enticements to premature retirement. The plan aroused much interest, though critics thought overseers incapable of carrying it out and complained that the minimum purchase price of £5 was beyond the means of the lower classes, and a bill based upon it was thrown out by the Lords. Annuity schemes reappeared later in the debate on the Poor Law, notably in Bentham's plans of 1797 and (most ingeniously) in his Annuity Note proposal of 1800–01, but were overshadowed by other contributory schemes based on the example of friendly societies.[29]

Friendly societies seem to have grown rapidly in number in the eighteenth century as genuinely popular forms of self-help, though such primitive forms of mutual insurance were certainly not new. (Eden said of friendly societies that 'though very meanly descended, they come of a very ancient house',[30] and the Manchester Unity of Oddfellows claimed the early patronage of Titus Caesar.) There were, in fact, innumerable varieties, with differing systems of contribution and differing qualifications for membership, from workmen in particular trades to inhabitants of a particular place, or even to the clientele of particular alehouses. Most were true clubs, providing occasions for conviviality as well as insurance against disasters; most were also purely local, though some were soon to develop into giant federations of lodges, and others into insurance companies. In the main they tried to meet the immediate needs of the poor, for small relief in illness or infirmity, for splendid funerals, and even for paying for substitutes if balloted for the militia.

[29] F. Maseres, *A Proposal* etc. (1772); *Jeremy Bentham's Economic Writings* (ed. W. Stark), II. *passim*. Maseres (1731–1824) published works in a wide variety of fields including history, mathematics and reform of church and state. Bentham described him as a 'public spirited constitutionalist and one of the most honest lawyers England ever saw'.

[30] F. M. Eden, *Observations on Friendly Societies* etc. (1801) p. 2. J. M. Baernreither, *English Associations of Working Men* (1891), Part II, remains an excellent source on friendly societies in this period, but see also N. J. Smelser, *Social Change in the Industrial Revolution* (1959), chap. XIII; C. Hardwick, *Friendly Societies* etc. (1851); and W. T. Pratt, *The Law Relating to Friendly Societies* (1854).

In 1786 the Rev. John Acland produced the first of the great plans for poor-law reform based on the principles of the friendly society. His aims were 'to render the Poor, to a great Degree, independent of Public Charity, by erecting them into an associated Insurance Office, as may secure to them a comfortable Provision, against all the Accidents to which their State is liable', and to annihilate 'that enormous Burden, which the nation now labours under', the poor rate. To achieve all this he urged that the principle of the friendly societies, purged of impurities, be established on a national basis.[31]

Acland, like other writers of his class, approved the principle but found it hard to stomach some features of existing clubs. It is amusing to observe the efforts of the rich to raise the vulgar friendly societies of the labourers to a higher moral plane; frequent failures among the clubs show that criticism of their actuarial basis was cogent, but most of Acland's complaints were not at all mathematical. Why should the poor seek such extravagant sums for burials? And why meet at ale-houses, spending good money which could have been saved? And why, above all, allow strike pay in 'mutinous secessions from labour'? It was clear that the poor needed to be supervised in the practice of self-help. Acland included in his plan a scheme for using charity schools to further encourage industry:

I may venture to say, that all Idleness in Children is just so much Vice in the Bud, which will be sure to shoot forth in due season; and that therefore it is a matter of serious Concern to a State to bring up Children in early Habits of Industry, and to prevent as much as possible all those Assemblies of young persons at Chuckfarthing, Pitch and Toss-up, and the like idle Amusements, which, when justly considered, are only so many Nurseries for Idleness, Dissipation, Gambling, and the Gallows.[32]

When the industrious nurselings of the new order reached maturity' their society for mutual insurance should meet, not at the alehouse' but after church on Sunday.

Acland's plan was of impeccable morality, but was it practicable? Membership of the national club was to be compulsory, and non-subscribers were to be badged DRONE in large letters of red cloth—

---

[31] J. Acland, *A Plan for rendering the Poor independent of Public Contributions* etc. (1786), pp. 7, 1. Acland offered his scheme as an alternative to Gilbert's poor-law reforms, and claimed that it would make unnecessary 'the cold hand of enforced charity'. But E. Harries, in the *Annals of Agriculture*, VII (1787), 180, suggested that the two schemes be combined.

[32] J. Acland, *op. cit.* pp. 52–3. Compare T. Ruggles, *History of the Poor*, II. 222–4, and F. M. Eden, *Observations* etc. pp. 12–24, for other criticisms of existing societies.

unless, of course, they were members of the upper classes. But all classes of persons and most sorts of property were to contribute to the fund; benefits were to be restricted to those in need, the affluent gaining only a reduction in the poor rates. Demands for public relief would greatly diminish, a workhouse test could properly be applied to the Drones, and the Poor Law could supply (Acland glibly asserted) employment for all those whose only lack was 'mere want of labour'. Price found the plan admirable; Ruggles also approved, even of the element of compulsion.[33] But without doubt the scheme was too ambitious and too speculative in its claims to win much support from cautiou-legislators, though the principle continued to gain in popularity. There were dissident voices however, Howlett's among them. He disputed the assumption that 'the present earnings of the Poor, if properly managed, are perfectly adequate for their comfortable management'; contributory schemes could not succeed if the poor had too little to contribute. His second objection was less to be expected from him: the scheme would blunt 'the spur to industry' by giving the poor a 'certain provision. ... The great incitements to active execution, and vigilant economy among the lower classes, are the dread of want on the one hand, and the hopes of a comfortable provision against sickness and old age on the other.' This was the language of the abolitionists; Howlett would use it against Acland's plan, but not against the Poor Law itself.[34]

The immediate outcome of the debate was not an elaborate poor-law reform but George Rose's cautious Friendly Societies Act of 1793, which merely encouraged clubs by offering privileges to members—including exemption from removal unless actually chargeable—in return for registration before the magistrates. This was but the first of a long series of acts regulating friendly societies, and although Rose was careful not to impose any compulsion to register it seems that his purpose was at first misunderstood, the lower classes associating registration with inquisition and taxation. Nevertheless some 5,400 societies registered by 1801, and Eden estimated that they, with perhaps another 1,800 unregistered, had some 648,000 members. 'Friendly Societies have now established, on the broad basis of experience, one great and fundamental truth, that, with very few exceptions, the people, under all circumstances, are, with good management, perfectly competent to provide for their own maintenance.' Not that Eden thought

---

[33] J. Acland, *op. cit.* pp. 41, 49, and (for a letter from Price) pp. iii–iv; T. Ruggles, *History of the Poor*, II. 30.

[34] J. Howlett, *The Insufficiency of the Causes* etc. pp. 109–14.

friendly societies ideal institutions; he himself believed the future lay with other and safer methods of insurance.[35] The hope that a contributory scheme could wholly or partially supersede public relief persisted. In 1796 John Vancouver, in an individual and radical book which deserves a place in the history of socialist thought, even argued that a contributory system embracing all classes could regenerate society by restoring harmony between the "society of the rich' and the 'society of the poor'.[36] In 1796 Pitt produced his scheme, to be followed by Whitbread's in 1807. But already, in 1795, there had appeared the first hints of a rival panacea, the savings bank: Canon Edward Wilson of Windsor published at the request of the Berkshire Quarter Sessions a plan for a Provident Parochial Bank, expressing a hope that a reasonable rate of interest might lead the poor to shun poor relief, and perhaps even the ale-house. At about the same time Bentham included savings banks in his elaborate plan for the prevention and relief of pauperism; he was one of those who were attracted by the principle of self-help but dissatisfied with the practice of existing friendly societies. Rose's Act was good 'as far as it goes', but 'good itself is bad in comparison of better'. Bentham was already one of the few champions of uniformity in matters of poor relief. 'In some instances diversity is excellent: here it is, in proportion as it prevails, departure from excellence ... In laws, uniformity of provision, where uniformity of reason admits of it, is one of the first of excellencies.'[37]

6. *The Beginnings of Abolitionism*

Acland and other champions of contributory schemes frequently implied that the Poor Law as it existed was basically misguided. Incidental remarks deploring the existence of the system of public relief can be found throughout the eighteenth century, for example from Defoe in 1704, Roger North in 1753, William Temple in 1770 and even from the philanthropic Romilly in 1791, while others such as Dyer and Crumpe hinted at such views. Passages written by Isaac Wood suggest that he would have been an abolitionist but for his faith in his own scheme for houses of industry, and even Davies and Howlett admitted many abolitionist arguments. But the two most extended attacks on the principle of public relief before Malthus wrote came from the

---

[35] F. M. Eden, *Observations* etc. pp. 7–10. On Rose's Act see his own *Observations* etc. (1794), published anonymously, and G. Nicholls, *History of the English Poor Law*, II, 110.
[36] J. Vancouver, *An Enquiry* etc. (1796).
[37] E. Wilson, *Observations* etc. (1795); *Jeremy Bentham's Economic Writings*, II. 136.

Rev. Thomas Alcock in 1752 and the Rev. Joseph Townsend in 1786.[38]

The basic argument against the Poor Law was that it caused the very indigence it was intended to relieve: 'these laws, so beautiful in theory, promote the evils they mean to remedy, and aggravate the distress'. Alcock asserted that 'the distressed are many times worse provided for now than when there was no law for relieving them. . . . Miserable creatures, sick and destitute, far distant from or without a Settlement, are bandy'd about, and drove from door to door, till at last they are starved in a barn, or found dead in the Street.'[39] His explanation was primarily moral: the Poor Law demoralised both rich and poor, and the true natural moral bond between classes was broken:

> As Force tends to destroy Charity in the Giver, so does it Gratitude in the Receiver . . . where no Will was concerned in the Deed, no Return can be expected. The pauper thanks not me for any thing he receives. He has a right to it, he says, by law, and if I won't give, he'll go to the Justices, and compel me. So that, what is still more provoking to the Contributor, he's forced to pay largely to the Poor, and at the same time sees them ungrateful and saucy, affronting and threatening, and looking upon themselves as equally good, if not better Men than their supporters, without Dependency or Obligation . . . happy that Nation, where the People live in natural Love and Dependence, and the several Ranks of Kings and Subjects, Masters and Servants, Parents and children, High and Low, Rich and Poor, are attached to each other by the reciprocal good offices of Kindness and Gratitude: . . . But as long as Charity is forced, we can never expect to see the Receivers of it either grateful or respectful.[40]

How much more attractive, in point of morality, was voluntary charity: 'God Almighty, indeed, the Helper of the Poor and Friendless, seems to have made a human law for the relief of [the poor] unnecessary, by having implanted a natural law for that Purpose in every man's

---

[38] For Romilly's lament on the evils of a 'certain provision' see *Memoirs of the Life of Sir Samuel Romilly* etc. (1840 ed.), I. 375–6. Alcock (1709–98), vicar of Runcorn, Cheshire, has been justly described as a miscellaneous writer; his works included a ninety-minute sermon ('An Apology for Esau'), an essay on colic, another on the duty on cider, and *The Rise of Mahomet accounted for on Natural and Civil Principles* (1796). McCulloch described him as one of the ablest critics of the Poor Law, but a self-contradictory one (*Literature of Political Economy*, p. 278). Townsend (1739–1816), rector of Pewsey, Wilts, was a more powerful and better-known writer, and equally versatile. A physician and scientist as well as a clergyman, he published books on mineralogy, health, travel, government and Moses. His sermons show a methodist influence, and he occasionally preached at Lady Huntingdon's chapel at Bath. His *Journey Through Spain* is a major work of its kind, and was perhaps even better known than the *Dissertation on the Poor Laws*. Bentham knew and admired Townsend, though he disputed his conclusions on the Poor Law.

[39] J. Townsend, *A Dissertation on the Poor Laws* (1786), p. 2; T. Alcock, *Observations on the Defects of the Poor Laws* etc. (1752), p. 11.

[40] T. Alcock, *op. cit.* pp. 13–14.

own Breast. We have an innate Philanthropy. We carry . . . a Poor Law about with us.' Under the Poor Law 'People are forced to harden their hearts', while labourers 'labour less and spend more; the very law that provides for the Poor, makes Poor'. The only moral argument in favour of a Poor Law Alcock would admit was that 'it forced open the purses of the covetous rich' while a voluntary system would fall upon the merciful, but in his puritanism he bade the covetous keep their riches to eternal damnation.[41]

Attacks on the Poor Law based only on such moral nicety were a little too strict for most members of the upper classes. Ruggles, for example, feared the effects of abolition on both the merciful rich and the deserving poor:

> As to leaving the poor to private contributions, it would, in our present state of civilisation, refinement, and general apathy to religious matters, be a cruel and unjust dereliction: were they to be supported by those alone who are the best members of society; the compassionate . . . would then witness such scenes of distress, as would wring every penny from their pockets . . . while the gay, the joyous, the unfeeling; those who live in crowds and in the bustle of the world; would contribute not a farthing to those scenes of distress from which they are so far removed.[42]

A preference for private charity remained a very strong sentiment indeed, but abolition of the Poor Law as a goal could gain force only when arguments could be found which called all charity, both public and private, in question. Certainly moral repugnance to forced charity remained one of the chief props of Townsend's abolitionism:

> Nothing in nature can be more disgusting than a parish pay table, attendant upon which, in the same objects of misery, are too often found combined, snuff, gin, rags, vermin, insolence, and abusive language; nor in nature can any thing be more beautiful than the mild complacency of benevolence, hastening to the humble cottage to relieve the wants of industry and virtue, to feed the hungry, to cloath the naked, and to sooth the sorrows of the widow with her tender orphans . . . unless it be their sparkling eyes, their bursting tears, their uplifted hands, the artless expressions of unfeigned gratitude for unexpected favours. Such scenes will frequently occur whenever men shall have power to dispose of their own property.[43]

But if Townsend showed a strong moral preference for private benevolence he also offered arguments that all charity, and not merely public relief, might be in some sense (or at least in some circumstances)

---

[41] *Ibid.* pp. 23, 10–11, 51; and compare Arthur Young's early views in *Farmer's Letters* etc. (1767), p. 171.

[42] T. Ruggles, *History of the Poor*, II. 77.

[43] J. Townsend, *A Dissertation* etc. pp. 107–8. Malthus quoted this passage with approval.

unnatural. The poor should not be permitted to rely on any resource other than their own endeavours:

Hope and fear are the springs of industry. It is the part of a good politician to strengthen these: but our laws weaken the one and destroy the other. For what encouragement have the poor to be industrious and frugal, when they know for certain, that should they increase their store it will be devoured by the drones? or what cause have they to fear, when they are assured, that if by their indolence and extravagance, by their drunkenness and vices, they should be reduced to want, they shall be abundantly supplied . . . The poor know little of the motives which stimulate the higher ranks to action—pride, honour, and ambition. In general it is only hunger which can spur and goad them on to labour. . . . The wisest legislature will never be able to devise a more equitable, a more effectual, or in any respect a more suitable punishment, than hunger is for a disobedient servant.[44]

Clearly the poor had to earn relief by moral desert as they had to earn wages by their labour; indiscriminate private charity was as unnatural as the Poor Law. And Townsend went on to add further arguments for the social utility of hunger. But for its force society could never recruit men for the meanest and the most hazardous occupations; and might there not also be too many men?

There is an appetite, which is and ought to be urgent, but which, if left to operate without restraint, would multiply the human species before provision could be made for their support. Some check, some balance is therefore absolutely needful, and hunger is the proper balance; hunger, not as directly felt, or feared by the individual for himself, but as foreseen and feared for his immediate offspring. Were it not for this the equilibrium would not be preserved so near as it is at present in the world, between the numbers of people and the quantity of food.

Nature, red in tooth and claw, was illustrated by the elegant parable of goats and dogs on the island of Juan Fernandes, and the lesson used to ridicule not only the Poor Law but also delusory schemes of economic equality: the demand for labour should be left to regulate population unimpeded. Poor relief encouraged the idle to breed, while the burden of the rates checked the multiplication of the worthy. 'The farmer breeds only from the best cattle; but our laws choose rather to preserve the worst.'[45]

Alcock had been more typical of eighteenth-century attitudes to population when he attacked the Poor Law for checking population growth. Malthus admitted his indebtedness to Townsend, who anticipated some but not all of the Malthusian arguments: he did discuss checks to population increase and some supposed remedies for popula-

44 *Ibid.* pp. 14, 23.
45 *Ibid.* pp. 57, 62.

THE DEBATE BEFORE 1795

tion pressure,[46] but his analysis of the economic effects of public relief was scrappy and inconsistent. The whole pamphlet made a considerable stir when it appeared, though it was too extreme to gain wide support and Ruggles was probably typical in remarking that it contained 'many sensible observations [though] very few of those who are in the practice of experiencing the execution of the system will join in such an unqualified invective.'[47] Nevertheless the case had been put.

Even Townsend, however, hesitated to urge immediate abolition: the Poor Law could be cursed, but not banished. Alcock, fearing that repeal 'might carry an unpopular Appearance, and perhaps endanger an Insurrection', merely looked for a palliative in a new workhouse system. Townsend offered a more drastic proposal to make relief 'limited and precarious' by progressively reducing it one tenth each year for nine years, at the same time introducing a compulsory contributory scheme. Other radical opponents of the English Poor Law cast envious glances at the Scottish system, alleged to be a voluntary one. Davies, in a passage in which he admitted some basic criticisms of the Poor Law, hinted at the exclusion of certain classes from relief, a solution much canvassed after 1815: in order to 'draw a line of separation' between the deserving and the undeserving, refuse relief to able-bodied single persons and to small families. Partial abolition, or at least restriction, by drawing a line somewhere, became an almost universal aim. The problem was where and how to draw it, and on what principle.[48]

In 1792 Thomas Paine offered a very different plan for the abolition of the Poor Law.[49] The attitude of later political radicals to the system was inevitably ambivalent: they deplored increasing pauperism, but were forced to defend the law against the usual abolitionist arguments because abolition without political and social reform seemed to them rank oppression. Paine, writing earlier, could be less inhibited in attacking poor laws as 'instruments of civil torture', oppressive to both ratepayers and the poor themselves. In his view, the Poor Law and indigence itself were the fruit of a corrupt political system, and especially of high taxation; a revenue of £17 million was far greater than good government required, and expenditure could be cut by at least £6 million. He did not propose to reduce taxation greatly (though some taxes were to be replaced by a progressive income tax) but rather to

[46] Including emigration, illustrated by the example of the Scots: 'like a silent dew, they fall upon the richest pastures' (*ibid.* p. 59).
[47] T. Ruggles, *History of the Poor*, II, 33–4.
[48] T. Alcock, *Observations* etc. pp. 4, 55; J. Townsend, *A Dissertation* etc. pp. 94–100; G. S. Keith, *An Impartial and Comprehensive View* etc. (1797), pp. 44–50 (for the Scottish example); D. Davies, *The Case of the Labourers* etc. pp. 99–101.
[49] T. Paine, *Rights of Man* (1791-2), Part II. chap. V.

43

spend the millions saved by retrenchment on a national system of old-age pensions, subsidies for education, allowances for birth, marriage, the maintenance of children and funeral expenses, and on a scheme for public employment in London—the whole costing, at a rough estimate, some £4 million, or twice the existing poor rate. The plan is remarkable as a prophecy of modern welfare legislation, and doubtless inspired many radicals of the 1790s with rosy visions of social improvement, but its significance in contemporary debate on the Poor Law was simply as a protest. It could hardly be acceptable to the ruling classes, since it pre-supposed radical political change; and even those not shocked by Paine's politics need not be persuaded by his political economy. Was taxation in fact the sole cause of indigence? How would the scheme for national pensions and allowances be administered, especially with the whole civil establishment cut back to less than 1,800 salaried officers? Above all, would such pensions and allowances in fact bring benefit to the poor? If poor relief corrupted, so would national pensions. Even before Malthus wrote, relief was suspect in principle as well as in practice.

Thus, by the 1790s, the Poor Law was the object of much criticism, indeed of almost universal criticism. Certainly no one openly desired the progressive pauperisation of the labouring classes, however willing they might have been in practice to allow such a situation to develop. But criticism could not provide a clear-cut movement for reform, for the critics did not agree on the nature of the disease, or on possible remedies. And, of course, the Poor Law system was so chaotic that it was very difficult indeed to reform, except on a local scale, and so deep-rooted that it was virtually impossible to abolish. The problem, though serious, was not widely regarded as urgent. Pauperism was an annoying but not, it seemed, a probably fatal disease; in contemporary medical language, not the bloody flux, but the itch.

III

<hr/>

Lessons of Scarcity

<hr/>

1. *Scarcity and Indigence*

THE debate on the condition of the labourers and the system of poor relief was quickened and transformed in the years of scarcity which began in 1795. The harvest of 1794 was short, and in the autumn wheat prices began to rise. In January the average was 7s. a bushel, the highest since 1790; by August it had almost doubled, and the new harvest was not good enough to remedy the scarcity. Average prices in 1796 were higher than in 1795, and although two years of slight respite followed, grave scarcity returned in 1799 and wheat reached the astronomical price of 19s. 3d. in March 1801. Scarcity so acute and prolonged caused astonishment and dismay, and the sense of crisis was of course heightened by the stresses of war. No one could doubt that the needs of the labouring classes would be urgent in these circumstances; the intellectual air was thick with proposals for their relief, and the overseers and gentry of almost every parish were busy with devices for keeping the poor not only alive but well-affected towards their superiors and the state.

Remedies proposed for relief depended in part on beliefs about the nature and cause of the scarcity. The simplest and most obvious diagnosis—that the high price of grain was due to a genuine scarcity arising from the failure of crops at home and the difficulties of import during war—did not satisfy many. A conspiratorial theory of scarcity prices, the allegation that they were due to the manipulation of the market by speculating middle men, was lustily asserted, and all sorts of punitive measures proposed to the government, from enforcing the

45

laws against forestalling and regrating to price regulation.[1] Others tried to look deeper, and found the explanation in the condition of agriculture: too much enclosure, or too little; too many large farms, or too many small; failure to cultivate waste lands, and general neglect of agriculture to give undue preference to manufacturers. Others blamed the war: simply because it was a war, or because of its interruption to the corn trade, or in more sophisticated terms because of its repercussions on public finance. Thus questions of the corn trade and the currency began a long career which was to culminate in practice in the 1815 Corn Law and the resumption of cash payments and in theory in the extreme subtleties of Ricardo's *Principles*. And just as the analysis of scarcity led to more fundamental inquiries into economic malaise and the way to prosperity, so the search for the best way to relieve distress produced a general consideration of indigence as a social phenomenon.

These years of crisis were seminal in thought concerning the poor, and perhaps also in the practice of relief. The evident inadequacy of existing wage-rates to maintain the usual consumption of the labourers raised the question of wage regulation, though it was soon dismissed with little theoretical analysis. Eden completed and published his great survey of the poor and the Poor Law, drawing from it characteristic if relatively cautious conclusions. Malthus's *Essay on Population* was not inspired by the scarcity, but the full-scale attack on the system of public relief which he developed in the second edition incorporated what he took to be the lessons of those years. While Malthus wrote, philanthropists developed doctrines of 'scientific' charity and self-help, the great corollaries and even rivals of the later, reformed Poor Law. The details of that later reform owed less, perhaps, to this period, though Jeremy Bentham's still-born Pauper Plan of 1796–7 included its central canon of less eligibility and its rejection of outdoor relief and adoption of the workhouse as the primary instrument of relief. New contributory schemes, the most elaborate of them offered by Pitt in his unsuccessful poor-law reform bill, also gained new impetus, and another favourite panacea appeared in proposals to give allotments of land to labourers in place of poor relief; even Arthur Young, long a champion of agricultural innovation, became an enthusiast for the new small-holdings. The analysis of general economic issues in this period was far less brilliant and penetrating than the debate which followed

[1] W. M. Stern, 'The Bread Crisis in Britain 1795–6', *Economica*, 31 (1964), 168–87, discusses the extent of the scarcity and government policy towards the corn trade; see also W. Illingworth, *An Enquiry into the Laws . . . respecting Forestalling, Regrating and Ingrossing* etc. (1800); and, for 'the revolt of the housewives', J. L. and Barbara Hammond, *The Village Labourer* (1948 ed.), I, 116–18. A number of explanations of scarcity popular at the time are expressed in G. Edwards, *Radical Means of Counteracting the Present Scarcity* etc. (1801).

the war, but it did produce ideas of enduring influence on the question of poverty. Even if few of them were entirely new, and there was no sudden revolution in accepted principles, more definite and coherent patterns of thought mirrored the new urgency of the debate.

In the practice of poor relief the significance of these years is more difficult to assess. Little legislation was passed—Whitbread's minimum wage proposal and Pitt's elaborate Poor Bill were both abortive— and if the years of scarcity provided a testing ground where all sorts of devices for relief were attempted on a local scale their permanent importance is far from clear. Two contrary tendencies are apparent: disillusion with attempted schemes of relief, such as subsidising food-stuffs, as the emergency dragged on; and the usual inertia by which temporary expedients became permanently embedded in the poor-law system. The scale of relief produced at the famous meeting of Berkshire magistrates at Speenhamland may or may not have been the most important of the devices adopted at this time, but a great deal more research into local practice, and into what might be called the ecology of the allowance system, is needed before we can be certain how widely such scales and allowances were adopted, and above all how far their use continued after the immediate period of stress.

Early in 1795 Arthur Young published in his *Annals of Agriculture* a questionnaire concerning the scarcity, inviting replies from corres-pondents on a number of topics including 'the most successful methods adopted for the relief of the poor'.[2] The replies revealed a widespread sense of emergency, if also an assumption that scarcity was a temporary phenomenon which would soon pass away. The main form of special relief offered to the poor, almost everywhere, was a subsidy on food-stuffs to enable them to maintain a reasonable consumption. Some of the schemes were quite elaborate, involving the distribution of special food orders, the value varying with the size of families, and in a few cases special shops were opened to sell food at cost. The source of the sub-sidies was most often public subscription, though the rates were also used in many parishes and special contributions from employers were not uncommon. There was as yet very little attempt to find substitutes for wheat as the principal food of the southern labourer, and one assiduous correspondent, G. Warde of Berkshire, even suggested that Parliament should make it compulsory to subsidise corn for the labourers when it reached a certain price. So considerable was the sum raised by private subscription to soften the pressure of scarcity that some correspondents claimed that the poor rate had not risen at all, and here and there it was even said that the poor were better off than they usually were in time of plenty.

[2] *Annals of Agriculture*, XXIV. 42.

Young's letter included questions about wages, and the replies, though not statistically significant in number, certainly showed that the general attitude to wages was not that which economic theory was soon to assume. Employers represented in the correspondence did not regard wage rates as fixed by automatic economic laws, but rather by an arbitrary assessment of what was 'fair' or 'necessary'. Even more important, they did not clearly differentiate between wages and relief; there were reports of a partial reversion to paying wages in kind, farmers providing corn as a direct supplement to the labourers' diet, and even where cash wages were increased it was usually as part of a general scheme to meet the demands of scarcity. Thus a meeting of gentlemen and farmers in Norfolk agreed to raise wages by sixpence in winter and a shilling in summer, and at the same time to sell wheat at 5s. a bushel to the poor; another correspondent spoke of subsidising bread 'instead of advancing the price of agricultural labour'. Others recommended increasing the number of men employed beyond farmers' immediate needs, especially in winter to increase the labourers' annual if not daily wage. Relief in money or kind, from the rates or by private subscription; subsidies on foodstuffs; increased wages or employment: the mingling of such devices might appear untidy or unjust to those who distinguish between economic rights and charity, but must have seemed obviously expedient to meet a crisis expected to be temporary.[3]

The only correspondent to argue strongly for a general increase in wages was Howlett, who took the opportunity to air his conviction that real wages had declined in recent decades quite apart from the scarcity. He drew a vivid picture of rural destitution; Young thought he exaggerated distress, but concluded from his own summary of prevailing wages that there was a case for an increase. Indeed he began to toy with the idea of wage regulation for labourers. 'If their pay could be made to rise and fall with the price of wheat, there would be an obvious benefit in it; but whether there would be evils springing from such a regulation, unseen till the plan was in execution, must be left to deep and attentive consideration.'[4] Some consideration, at least, it was soon to get.

2. *Wage Regulation*

Only the pressure of scarcity can explain the growing interest, in 1795, in the possibility of regulating wages. It was not an idea which came easily to a generation digesting the *Wealth of Nations*, nor could it be easily reconciled with the existing relationship between employers and

[3] Replies to Young's circular are scattered through *Annals*, XXIV.
[4] *Ibid*. XXIV. 154–61, 335–6.

employed. Even those who had earlier urged that wages should be higher had rarely suggested regulation by law; Howlett's early works ignored the idea, and even the more radical Dyer had suggested less direct measures to ensure higher earnings. Ruggles discussed wage regulation, but concluded that it was likely to remain unnecessary unless the state of agriculture should require a maximum to be fixed. He regarded earlier legislation empowering magistrates to rate wages, which remained in the statute book, as an historical curiosity only. Certainly the relevance of that legislation to the situation of 1795 was very doubtful; Davies was one of the few to claim that it gave a power to fix a minimum, most observers following Capel Lofft in concluding that only a maximum was intended and that the Acts were therefore illiberal and harsh.[5]

Whatever the true state of the existing law, discussion of regulation became more widespread as scarcity continued, and in October 1795 Young published a request for comments, 'it having been recommended by various Quarter Sessions that the price of labour should be regulated by that of bread corn'. Young had himself attended a meeting of Suffolk magistrates at Bury earlier in the month where the bench had ordered 'that the members for this county be requested by the chairman to bring a bill into Parliament' to ensure that wages fluctuate with prices.[6] No doubt Young had also read Davies' ardent plea for regulation: *The Case of the Labourers in Husbandry* included two alternative schemes, one for fixing wages from time to time according to the needs of an average family, the other pegging them to the price of corn. Davies claimed that farmers could well afford higher wages when prices were high, but not even he dared suggest a wage sufficient to maintain a family larger than average, urging systematic relief from the rates—financed, if necessary, by a tax on bachelors—for such cases. For once there is some slight evidence of the labourers' own views: an advertisement published in a Norwich newspaper told of a meeting of day labourers which asserted that other forms of relief were inadequate and suggested a petition to Parliament for regulation by law, and the creation of county organisations of the labouring classes. The reprinting

[5] G. Dyer, *The Complaints of the Poor People of England* etc. (1793), part IV, chap. ii; T. Ruggles, *History of the Poor*, p. 335; D. Davies, *The Case of the Labourers* etc. pp. 106–12. Lofft's discussion of the legislation may be found in *Annals*, XXV. 317–20, 518–20, 561–4; and compare G. S. Keith, *An Impartial and Comprehensive View* etc. (1797), p. 17. Paine and Fox were among those who thought the early general legislation repressive in intent; the Spitalfields Acts and others regulating wages in particular trades were thought to be in a different category.
[6] *Annals*, XXV. 345, 316. Lofft was at the Bury meeting, which inspired his investigation into past legislation. For a decision of the Hampshire Bench that regulation was 'not now expedient' see *Annals*, XXV. 396.

of this account in the *Annals* was enough to make at least once correspondent an ardent opponent of regulation; it was one thing for the
upper classes to suggest such measures, but quite another for the
poor to demand them.[7]

The proposal to regulate wages according to the needs of labourers
was not kept distinct, as it should have been, from that to tie wages
to the price of wheat, and the confusion between them led to one of the
more lasting 'lessons of scarcity' absorbed by the public mind. The
policy of linking wages to wheat prices, like that of subsidising wheat,
assumed not only that the labourer was worthy of his hire but also that
it was possible to pay him that hire in his accustomed food, no matter
how scarce it might be. In fact it became apparent in the summer of
1795 that subsidies would merely produce a greater scarcity, as Lord
Sheffield pointed out to the Grand Jury at Lewes Quarter Sessions in
July. A genuine scarcity required a genuine reduction in consumption
of the food concerned.[8] The point was fatal to the proposal to regulate
wages by the price of wheat; if the wheat was not there, wages could
rise to infinity and still not purchase a peck. The argument needed
only to be generalised to produce the key Malthusian argument against
guaranteeing the right to relief: food is not unlimited in supply, and
therefore an unlimited right to it could not be recognised. The point
must have seemed cogent in a time of prolonged scarcity, especially in
a country unnaturally isolated by war, and the experience of these years
inhibited, for at least a generation, unsophisticated assent to propositions that labourers were worthy of their hire or that the poor had as a
matter of course a right to relief.

General wage regulation could have been separated from this
dilemma, but most of its critics in 1795 were able to damn it without
examining it too closely. Few of the men who answered Young's
circular approved the proposal, and most of those who did were vague
in their support. 'I am one of those who recommended that the price of
labour should be regulated by that of bread corn' wrote one correspondent, 'but how it is to be done I leave to better heads than that of
Your Humble Servant, H. Hill.'[9] Howlett was one of the few who
pointed out that corn was only part of the poor's expenditure and
claimed that the high price of wheat was not the only reason for
regulating wages: a maximum had been enforced in earlier periods,
why not fix a minimum now? But he was forced to admit that it would

[7] D. Davies, *Case of the Labourers* etc. pp. 108–18; *Annals*, XXV. 503, 627.
[8] *Annals*, XXV. 29–32. The anonymous *Address to the Plain Sense of the People*
etc. (1800) suggested that labourers be guaranteed a regulated proportion of the
harvest rather than their usual consumption.
[9] *Annals*, XXV. 493.

be absurd to regulate piece-work rates, and his plea, forceful though it was, did not meet all the arguments of the opponents.[10] It has been suggested by J. L. and Barbara Hammond that the main argument against regulation—and indeed against raising wages even voluntarily in time of scarcity—was the fear that they could not be reduced again when food prices fell. The point was certainly made; one writer offered an ingenious scheme for a wage fixed eternally at six shillings per week together with a 'gratuity' fluctuating with the price of wheat in an attempt to avoid the problem.[11] But, in general, concern lest a regulated wage be difficult to reduce in time of plenty was too rare to be cited as the typical reaction to proposals to regulate. A much more common argument was also a more cogent one, given the crude machinery available for wage regulation in 1795 and the actual circumstance of employment. A regulated wage, it was claimed, would be an equal wage, while inequality of wages was inevitable and desirable. The prevalence of piece-work made a standard wage absurd, and many writers defended piece-work as the main stimulus which roused the labourer from indolence. How could rates be fixed for different kinds of work, especially if manufacturers were included as well as agriculture? Even in agriculture, wages varied with the quality of the work and the ability of the labourer: 'no man but the employer,' wrote one correspondent, 'can judge the value of a man's labour.'[12] Even without assenting to this proposition it is proper to admit that the available administrative machinery was scarcely adequate to establish satisfactory differential wage returns.

Even more characteristic of the times was the assertion that wages should vary not only with efficiency but also according to the moral worth of the labourer. The philanthropist Sir Thomas Bernard thought it obvious that the idle should not get as much as the industrious, and that it was 'mischief' for the magistrate to interfere 'as the farmer is the best judge of what different men deserve'. Stress was also laid on the unequal need of labourers: a wage 'not more than equal to the needs of a man with a large family' would be 'so extravagantly high that it would promote idleness and inactivity in the single man'. Other critics pointed out that any attempt to impose equality in wages would lead farmers to reduce the number employed and force the inferior labourer, not worth the full wage, out of work and on to the rates. As Bentham put it, wage regulation might guarantee an adequate maintenance to those in employment at the cost of an increase in those without employment. His argument was more theoretical than most,

---

[10] *Ibid.* XXV. 599–611.
[11] *A Proposal for a Perpetual Equalisation of the Pay of the Labouring Poor* (1795).
[12] *Annals*, XXV. 501.

but even he made his case mainly in practical terms, with little reference to the sanctity of natural economic laws. Regulation was abhorrent to his contemporaries because it would interfere with village paternalism and the 'natural' relation of employer and labourer; correspondents wrote of the 'endless disputation' which would arise from this interference, and of the 'continual jangle and dispute', alleging that the ill-feeling resulting would put an end to the benevolence of the rich to the poor.[13] For this reason even poor relief was to be preferred to regulation: after all the poor-law organisation already existed to relieve distress, with discretion and according to need. No doubt there were limits to the variation of wages according to discretion, though Howlett reported that in his village wages were varied according to the number of children, and one Cumberland village was said to have 'no stated wages, they are paid as deserving'; and men not yet deeply impressed with the idea that pauperism was necessarily degrading might look to the Poor Law as the obvious source of special assistance for extraordinary needs. If magistrates were to interfere at all it should be to supervise relief, not to regulate wages; correspondents suggested that special scales of relief according to family size and bread prices be adopted, though no one mentioned the Speenhamland example. It must be remembered that the emergency was still expected to be temporary; the whole discussion is nevertheless remarkable for the twin assumptions that it was proper for farmers to exercise discretion in wages paid and for magistrates to use similar discretion concerning relief, the determinants being the needs and desert of the lower classes.[14]

3. *Burke's* Thoughts on Scarcity

Edmund Burke was the only writer in this period to examine the proposal to regulate wages in the light of systematic economic doctrine, if an oratorical denunciation can be called an examination. In November 1795 he wrote his *Thoughts and Details on Scarcity*[15] for the enlightenment of Pitt; both men were early converts to the teachings of Adam Smith, and Burke's not very original tract did express the views of a superficial disciple on a topic which Smith had not discussed in this context. Years before, in his *Vindication of Natural Society*, Burke had shown some compassion for the labouring classes, but by 1795 his obsession with social order and hatred of revolution led him to elevate

[13] *Ibid.* XXV. esp. 499, 501, 614; XXVI. 4, 22.
[14] *Ibid.* XXV. 484–5, 499, 603, 634; XXVI. 148.
[15] References are to the 1808 edition of Burke's *Works*. The tract was not published until after Burke's death in 1797; he had intended to recast it as *Letters on Rural Oeconomicks* for Arthur Young.

Smith's system of economic liberty into a dogmatic faith which the author might scarcely have recognised. 'We, the people, ought to be made sensible, that it is not by breaking the laws of commerce, which are the laws of nature, and consequently the laws of God, that we are to place our hope of softening the Divine displeasure to remove any calamity under which we suffer.' When Arthur Young called on Burke at this time he found him raging against 'the absurdity of regulating wages and the mischief of our poor laws'.[16]

Burke admitted the scarcity was real, but claimed it was exaggerated: scarcity was merely 'comparative', since no one had died of famine. The poor might be miserable, but that misery was inevitable and should not be disguised by misguided pity.

Nothing can be so base and so wicked as the political canting language, 'The *Labouring* poor.' Let compassion be shown in action ... but let there be no lamentation of their condition. It is no relief to their miserable circumstances; it is only an insult to their miserable understandings.... Patience, labour, sobriety, frugality, and religion, should be recommended to them; all the rest is downright *fraud*.[17]

The condition of the labourers was determined by economic forces beyond the control of man; specifically by the ratio of population to resources. He anticipated Malthus in this explanation of poverty, if not in the notion of population pressure as a dynamic force; and the motive—to defend the existing order of society and the distribution of property—was the same as that of Malthus's first edition. The surplus in the hands of the rich was too little to improve the situation of the multitude even if distributed among them, and the function of the rich as bankers and circulators of national wealth made them indispensable to society as a whole. Just as a redistribution of property could not improve the condition of the labourer, so any attempt to raise or regulate wages above the 'natural' market rate would also defeat itself. Burke here came close to the doctrine of a rigid wages fund. A rise in total real wages was impossible because the quantity of foodstuffs, the fund for the maintenance of labour, was limited; hence any attempt to raise money wages must either raise the price of provisions or reduce the demand for labour and the number employed. The argument was

[16] *Works*, VII. 404; J. L. and Barbara Hammond, *The Village Labourer*, I. 131.
[17] *Works*, VII. 377. Compare the passage in the *Third Letter on a Regicide Peace* (1797) in which Burke insisted that only the impotent should be called 'poor': 'when we affect to pity as poor, those who must labour or the world cannot exist, we are trifling with the condition of mankind. It is the common doom of man that he must eat his bread by the sweat of his brow. ... This affected pity only tends to dissatisfy them with their condition, and to teach them to seek resources where no resources can be found, in something else than their own industry, and frugality, and sobriety'. (*Works*, VIII. 368–9).

persuasive (if not a truism) provided short-term periods of scarcity alone were considered, and the possibility of importing food ignored.[18]

An attempt to raise real wages would, at the best, fail; at the worst, it could ruin agriculture. To compel the farmer to pay wages higher than the market rate was to tax him. Burke pleaded at length that the fortunes of farmers and traders were precarious, their profits not as high as they might seem, and that in any case the employer's gain was a small sum compared with his outlay in wages. A small increase in wages to labourers 'may amount to an actual partition of his substance among them', bringing equality of property—'equal want, equal wretchedness, equal beggary'. The conclusion of the whole argument was that a wage fixed by free contract—a contract which provided a margin to cover profit on capital and reward for risk—must necessarily be the wage which was in the best interests of the labourer also. Employer and labourer depended on each other, and their interests were therefore identical. Much eloquence was spent on this point; it was false and wicked to suggest that 'the farmer and the labourer have opposite interests—and that a gentleman called a justice of the peace, is the protector of the latter, and a control and restraint on the former'. A contract was a compromise which precluded a conflict of interests.[19]

With unshakeable confidence in the justice of economic liberty, and the conviction that 'no authority on earth' could judge what an employer's profit should be, it is not surprising that Burke insisted that governments could do nothing to relieve the pressure of scarcity. 'To provide for us in our necessities is not in the power of government. It would be a vain presumption in statesmen to think they can do it. The people maintain them, and not they the people.' He disapproved of measures to increase the supply of food as much as he abhorred interference with wages. Tampering with the trade in provisions was 'most dangerous', and worst when most sought after, in time of scarcity. Public granaries would be expensive, would ruin the corn merchant, upset the market, and be open to depredation from 'popular frenzy'. Even the usual scarcity procedure of stopping the distilleries was attacked: their waste supported pigs, and in any case gin was morally and medically a desirable beverage. 'If not food, it greatly alleviates the want of it.'[20]

'Zealots of the sect of regulation' might point out that wages settled by free contract could be insufficient to sustain life when food was scarce, but Burke accused them of generalising too much from special

---

[18] *Ibid.* VII. 376–7, 387. Burke followed Smith in arguing that wages were determined by the demand for labour rather than the price of food.

[19] *Ibid.* VII. 383–7.

[20] *Ibid.* VII. 376, 400–1, 412–13.

cases, of illness, or numerous offspring. 'When a man cannot live and maintain his family by the natural hire of his labour, ought it not to be raised by authority?' Decidedly not; not only because the fund for the maintenance of labour was limited, but also (a more familiar argument) because labour was not a homogeneous commodity, and no single wage rate could suit all varieties of age and ability. 'Interest, habit, and the tacit conventions that arise from a thousand circumstances produce a *tact* that regulates without difficulty, what laws and magistrates cannot regulate at all.' Burke was willing to ignore the contradiction between the idea of wages determined by an impersonal supply and demand for labour, and of wages decided by the discretion and 'tact' of employers, provided regulation was not adopted. But if wages were in fact inadequate, should men be left to starve? Burke's answer to this question was as fatal to the whole notion of a right to relief as it was to the right to a living wage: the only alternative to wages won in a free market was charity. Charity was an obligation on all Christians, 'next in order after the payment of debts', but the duty must be left to be exercised by 'private discretion' and not public organisation.[21]

Argument in this style on scarcity, wages and relief was not common in 1795, and Burke's tract resembles the lesser writings of the generation after Malthus rather than its contemporaries. But it remains interesting as an early example of that economic dogmatism, reinforced with political hysteria, which was to bedevil the debate on the condition of the labourer and the Poor Laws. Unfortunately for the cause of wage regulation, there were sufficient grains of truth in these bushels of rhetoric to convince an increasing number of intelligent and enlightened men that the income of the labourer was not a proper subject for interference.

4. *Whitbread's Wage Regulation Bill*

Although the Suffolk Quarter Sessions had requested their county Members to introduce legislation to regulate wages in the House of Commons, it was Samuel Whitbread, a Foxite Whig from Bedfordshire, who in fact produced a Bill. On 3 November 1795 Pitt moved the appointment of a Select Committee on the high price of corn, while making it clear that the Government was reluctant to interfere in either the corn market or the determination of wages. In that debate Fox made a long speech, agreeing with Pitt that only a real famine could justify interrupting the free play of commercial dealings, but accusing the

[21] *Ibid.* VII. 390.

Prime Minister of ignoring the aggravating effect of the war.[22] He insisted that the fundamental problem was the failure of wages to keep up with prices; nevertheless he questioned 'whether any compulsory measure ought to be adopted' to raise them. Fox looked rather to 'the justice and humanity of the gentlemen in the different counties' to raise wages, and when on 9 December 1795, Whitbread introduced his Bill to enable Justices of the Peace, meeting in Quarter Sessions, to regulate the wages of labour in husbandry, his leader was hardly enthusiastic, though he gave him some support.[23] Fox spoke of the question as one on which 'rational differences of opinion could exist'. He was as much convinced of the impropriety of interfering with the free market as Pitt, or any other follower of Adam Smith, and the reason he was willing to consider wage regulation as an exception was, characteristically, political. If the general price of labour was inadequate to maintain the labourer, then there were only two alternatives: either wages must rise or the mass of the labourers be supported from the poor rates. Fox rebelled against a situation in which the 'great mass' were on relief because there was no room in his brand of whiggery for charity as the bond of social union binding the generous rich and the grateful poor in harmony. The poor should be independent—'it was not fitting in a free country that the great body of the people should depend on the charity of the rich'—and as poor relief usually excluded the receiver from the franchise, a constitutional point was also at issue. All charity, both public and private, was 'pernicious and degrading', but to compel a man on to the rates and then disfranchise him was to reduce him first to dependence and then to servitude. Thus did politics enter the question, and not to the Bill's advantage.

Having made his point, moreover, Fox was not at all vigorous in his support for Whitbread. As an alternative to regulation, he pleaded that the House should form an 'association' to raise wages, making an agreement and a public declaration, providing moral example rather than legislative interference. The very word association had of course whiggish overtones, recalling Yorkshire in the 1780s; nevertheless the proposal appealed to the House. Parliament's inhibitions in legislating to regulate wages rested in part on Members' deep reluctance to interfere in a compulsory manner in local affairs, or rather—since it was largely the same men who were involved in both spheres—on the assumption that what it might be proper to do as men of local influence and as magistrates on the county bench it was not proper to impose on all county benches as Members of Parliament. Thus Fox's proposed association should not be regarded as mere political evasion, but as a

[22] *Parliamentary History*, xxxii, 238–42.
[23] *Ibid.* xxxii. 700–2.

genuine alternative to legislation. Parliament could act as a conference of local interests and declare a policy, rather than impose its will as a national legislature. In the event the House did make such an engagement, but to reduce consumption of bread corn and not to raise wages.[24]

Whitbread's Bill was not debated again until 12 February 1796, when it was defeated on the Second Reading.[25] Some historians have seen this defeat as the sacrifice of the just claims of the labouring classes on the altar of economic doctrine; perhaps it was, but it would be wrong to see the debate as mainly a clash of opposed philosophies, of a traditional paternalism and a new individualism. It must be admitted that the Bill was hardly a precise and practicable plan as it stood, merely empowering Justices to regulate wages without advising them how to do it or how to enforce their decisions. It could be, and was, opposed merely as a badly drafted measure. But in the main it was killed by Pitt, not so much by an attack on its principles as by a promise that the Prime Minister would make such a measure unnecessary by undertaking a major reform of the Poor Law itself.

Pitt and Whitbread differed very little in their general views on political economy. Whitbread began his speech by recognising the validity of the principles of economic liberalism, but pleaded that the facts required that an exception be made in this case. The problem, he claimed, was not merely one of an occasional scarcity, for 'the labourer had long been struggling with increasing misery'. He relied for his evidence on this point mainly on Price, with not very happy results.[26] The Bill was intended 'to rescue the labouring poor from a state of slavish dependence', to prevent their having to flock to the towns or join the army in order to live, and to give to each man the right 'to a part of the produce of his labour'. According to Whitbread, the Bill was not an innovation; he shared the usual view that the acts of Elizabeth had aimed at fixing maximum, not minimum wages, and appealed not to them but to the Spitalfields Acts and to others regulating tailors' wages. But his peroration consisted of an eloquent plea for a new departure, for giving magistrates the power to redress grievances as they already possessed the power to 'oppress'.

Pitt replied with one of his most persuasive and successful speeches. He began by meeting Whitbread on his own ground, disputing the facts he had alleged. The condition of the labourer was not as bad as Whitbread claimed, though the evil existed 'in a certain extent' and 'the

[24] For Howlett's scorn for the proposal see his *Examination of Mr. Pitt's Speech* etc. (1796), p. 32.

[25] *Parliamentary History*, xxxii. 703–14; and compare R. Fulford, *Samuel Whitbread* 1764–1815 (1967), p. 51.

[26] For example in his assertion that there had been no increase in population (*Parliamentary History*, xxxii. 704).

present situation of the labouring poor in this country, is not such as could be wished, upon any principle, either of humanity or policy'. But what should be done? The precedents Whitbread had cited were acts directed against combinations, not towards raising the standard of life. There was a great risk in attempting regulation: if it failed, either 'severe oppression' or 'the most profligate idleness and extravagance' would result.

Was it not wiser to reflect which remedy might be adopted, at once more general in its principles, and more comprehensive in its object, less exceptionable in its example, and less dangerous in its application. They should look to the instances where interferences had shackled industry, and where the best intentions have often produced the most pernicious effects. It was indeed the most absurd bigotry, in asserting the general principle, to exclude the exception; but trade, industry and barter would always find their own level, and be impeded by regulations which violated their natural operation, and deranged their proper effect.[27]

If wages were inadequate, the fault lay not in too much liberty, but in too little. Imperfections impeded the free operation of economic laws. Whitbread's Bill was superficial, an attempt to alleviate symptoms without curing the disease; and Pitt overwhelmed the unlucky proposal by promising to do greater and grander things himself. The infection in the body economic 'originated in a great measure, in the abuses which had crept into the poor laws of this country, and the complicated mode of executing them'. However wise originally, the Poor Laws were now defective, especially as they 'fettered the circulation of labour', reducing wages below their natural level (Pitt was, of course, following Adam Smith in concentrating his attack on the Law of Settlement). 'Radical amendment' was necessary, to relieve both capitalist and labourer, and especially to prevent the removal of mechanics in times of temporary distress, 'a great and striking grievance'. Pitt foreshadowed a return to the 'original purity' of the Poor Laws, apparently to their condition before the Acts of Settlement were passed.

There is no evidence in the speech that he realised how difficult a problem the Acts of Settlement constituted for the poor-law reformer, and indeed little evidence of a close knowledge of other aspects of the system either. The only point developed at length was an effective argument against Whitbread's Bill, though it was the very point which was to ruin his reputation on this subject in the Malthusian era. Large families, Pitt said, had special needs, but Whitbread's scheme would treat them equally: 'were the minimum fixed upon the standard of a large family, it might operate as an encouragement to idleness in one part of the community, and if it were fixed on the standard of a small

[27] *Ibid.* 707.

58

family, those would not enjoy the benefit of it for whose relief it was intended':

What measure then could be found to supply the defect? Let us . . . make relief in cases where there are a number of children, a matter of right and an honour, instead of a ground for opprobrium and contempt. This will make a large family a blessing, and not a curse; and thus will draw a proper line of distinction between those who are able to provide for themselves by their labour, and those who, after having enriched their country with a number of children, have a claim upon its assistance for their support.[28]

The speech was a triumph. Whitbread himself congratulated the House on its quality, though he still pressed his Bill as a matter of urgency. But it was dead, despite Fox's half-hearted support and Lechmere's affirmation that 'he would rather have the labourer enjoy the honest fruits of his industry, than be obliged to receive his due as an eleemosynary gift'. The proposal to regulate wages, never more than a sickly contender, had its quietus made by the promise of a bright, refurbished Poor Law. Not that Pitt swept all before him. Howlett's very critical pamphlet on Pitt's proposals rejected all his arguments against Whitbread's scheme. Industry and ambition would not be destroyed; if bachelors earned a little more than they should the government could relieve them of it by a tax; and differences in skill would still get their reward, as the superior workman would be 'more eagerly employed'. But even Howlett admitted wage regulation to be a 'nice and difficult matter', possibly beyond the abilities of justices; he made a few vague proposals for some other form of tribunal, and hoped that Pitt's investigations might produce something suitable. And perhaps, after all, it might be better to 'influence the course of events, as gradually to produce the much talked of level between wants and wages without legislative interference'. Howlett was optimist enough to suspect that the true remedy for the distress of the poor lay not in dubious regulation now but in the fruits of future economic progress.[29]

Pitt's Poor Bill drew attention away from the question of wage regulation, and few of the numerous pamphleteers of the next few years discussed it. Fewer still favoured it. Sherer insisted that wages should bear a 'just proportion' to wants and thought relief from the rates an 'improper and injurious' mode of augmenting them, but hesitated to recommend regulation for fear of the 'bickering' it would cause.[30] In other writers a hardening of opinion is evident, even to the extent of deploring a rise in wages at all. Ingram, in a very able pamphlet

---

[28] *Ibid.* 709–10. Ricardo quoted this passage as an example of bad old views on the Poor Law.

[29] J. Howlett, *Examination of Mr. Pitt's Speech* etc. p. 50.

[30] J. A. Sherer, *Remarks on the Present State of the Poor* (1797), pp. 20–1,32.

which anticipated certain Malthusian arguments, claimed that 'for the general interest of society' labourers' wages 'should be reduced as nearly as possible to that of a bare subsistence'; he softened the sentiment by urging ample opportunities for the truly industrious labourer to acquire property and rise in the social scale.[31] An anonymous pamphleteer made a similar argument that common labour should earn a bare subsistence, while greater industry should gain property as well. Wages should not be based on need; prevailing rates were mid-way between the needs of a single man and of a married man, leading both to spend their money in haunts of intoxication, 'the one by superfluity, the other by despair'. Wages should find their natural level on the needs of a single man, while a special national provision, by right and not from charity, augmented family incomes.[32] Thus distrust of regulation and fear of the effects of generally high wages made special schemes for the support of children virtually inevitable, as Pitt's Bill itself showed. It remained for Weyland to build the idea into a systematic economic theory.

Whitbread defined prevailing opinion for a time, and in February 1800 he tried once more to revive his proposals in Parliament. He poured scorn on Pitt's already defunct Bill—'all its provisions were regarded as impracticable'—and claimed that his own measure had been well supported until Pitt intervened so ineffectually. He was willing to admit that in some manufacturing towns mechanics earned too much, and 'usually squandered the surplus money away, in ruinous luxuries', but denied that this was a valid argument against assisting agricultural labourers. 'It was his creed with respect to the poor, that no excuse should be left them for doing wrong, and that when they offended, severity should be employed in punishing their offences'—a procedure perhaps more generous than that of keeping them poor, lest they be tempted to excesses. But he certainly sought no more than to provide magistrates with a power which they should use only in very exceptional circumstances, and his mind was already turning away from regulation to the cause of Poor Law reform itself. He expressed 'alarm' at the extent to which the poor were dependent on private charity, and claimed the Poor Laws were good in principle but faulty in execution. Pitt's reply showed some nostalgia for his own Bill, insisting that special

[31] R. A. Ingram, *An Inquiry* etc. (1797), p. 12. Ingram argued that scarcity had forced wages down by driving men formerly independent into the labour market, but he expected a gradual reduction in population to restore a balance between the supply and demand for labour. Ingram was at this time a fellow of Queen's College, Cambridge. In 1800 he published a proposal that political economy be taught in the universities, though combined with theology. By 1808, when he published a book against Malthus, he was rector of Seagrave, Leicestershire; he died in 1809.

[32] *The Connexion between Industry and Property* etc. (1798), p. 10.

relief for children was to be preferred. Only Wilberforce, however, wanted Pitt's Bill revived, though other speakers agreed that poor-law reform was necessary. The Bill was defeated on 21 February, though Whitbread tried to delay debate until Quarter Sessions had time to discuss the proposal.[33] Wage regulation was never to gain a full-scale Parliamentary debate again in this period. Whitbread himself lost faith in the proposal, though it was not until 1809 that he explicitly rejected it as improper when refusing to support a petition for a minimum from the weavers of Perth.[34] Regulation was never again discussed at length by a major political economist or writer on the poor, and was assumed to be beyond the pale of desirable practice. Nevertheless a handful of later writers pleaded for it, if in general and simple terms. In 1801 John Hills, a surgeon, repeated Davies' arguments in support of regulation, alleging that until it was introduced the poor had a 'just complaint'; wages should be fixed for average families, with the larger relieved in kind from a special fund 'for promoting industry, honesty and population'. In the same year Abraham Jobson, a curate from the Isle of Ely, wrote a simple letter to the *Annals* deploring large farms and pleading for land for the poor and wage regulation, though another (anonymous) correspondent showed more awareness of opposition in claiming that a regulated wage could be reduced, if regulation were frequent. The poor must live, from wages or relief, and that, he complained, had its evils. J. N. Brewer shared this view; in 1807 he deplored allowances in aid of wages and sought regulation, to be combined with a strict moral regimen in which 'a contention in moral decency and parental care' would replace the village cudgelling match. William Clarkson, writing in 1816, wished to introduce wage regulation and also a deterrent workhouse scheme, to make indigence both avoidable and uncomfortable. Two later anonymous pamphleteers were even more simple in their demands: the author of *The Oppressed Labourers* etc. (1819) baldly asserted that wages should be raised by law, and the author of *Notices on Political Economy* etc. (1812) admitted that Malthus might be justified in denying the right to relief, but claimed that labourers were entitled to a fair wage, by law if necessary.[35] No doubt others, especially among the recipients of wages, also hoped for

[33] *Parliamentary History*, xxxiv. 1427–30, and compare *Parliamentary Register*, X. 463–9, 554–6.
[34] Whitbread Papers, 3671–5.
[35] J. Hill, *The Means of Reforming the Morals of the Poor* etc. (1801), pp. 67–77; *Annals*, XXXVII (1801), 32–3, 608–11; J. N. Brewer, *Some Thoughts* etc. (1807), p. 5; W. Clarkson, *An Inquiry* etc. (2nd ed. 1816); *The Oppressed Labourers* etc. (1819), p. 16; *Notices on Political Economy* etc. (1821), p. 22. J. Ovington, *A Certain Remedy* etc. (1816) asserted that refusal to regulate wages was a sin.

regulation, but after the 1790s not one writer with any claim to major importance discussed the proposal except as a curiosity so completely irrelevant to contemporary modes of reasoning that it hardly needed to be refuted, let alone opposed or feared. It remained for later historians to discover its obvious virtues.

5. *Pitt's Poor-Law Bill*

Pitt's attempt to reform the Poor Laws won him little credit. Even his political supporters could praise only his benevolent intentions, and not his performance, while his opponents poured scorn on both. Historians have been equally severe: J. Holland Rose, never one to underestimate the great Minister's achievements, had to place the Bill among Pitt's 'improvident legislation'. Most nineteenth-century historians were supporters of the new Poor Law, and judged by its strict canons much of Pitt's scheme was 'decidedly objectionable', as Sir George Nicholls himself pointed out. More recent writers, unsympathetic to the Principles of 1834, found more to praise, but not much more: the Webbs wrote of 'proposals which would have been ruinous in the crude form in which they were stated', and the Hammonds concluded that 'the scheme as a whole was confused and incoherent, and it deserved the treatment it received'.[36] That treatment was summary. Pitt gave out some *Heads of a Bill* soon after the debate on Whitbread's proposal in February 1796, but the dissolution of Parliament and the pressure of foreign affairs prevented him from introducing it to the House until 22 December. The Bill was taken rapidly through the Committee stage and printed (with some amendments) before the holidays in order that it might lie before the public. A storm of criticism broke—in pamphlets, in petitions to the House, in letters to Pitt himself—and when the Bill again appeared before the House, on 28 February 1797, it was withdrawn, apparently with little debate. 'We are thus left,' wrote the Hammonds, 'in the curious and disappointing position of having before us a Bill on the most important subject of the day, introduced and abandoned by the Prime Minister without a word or syllable in its defence.'[37]

[36] J. Holland Rose, *William Pitt and the Great War* (1911), p. 568; Sir George Nicholls, *History of the English Poor Law*, II. 120–1; S. and B. Webb, *The Last Hundred Years*, I. 39; J. L. and Barbara Hammond, *The Village Labourer*, I. 147.

[37] J. L. and Barbara Hammond, *op. cit.* I. 148. (Pitt might well have thought the war a more important subject than poor relief, though it is possible that more was written on distress and its relief than on any other subject in these years.) Pitt's *Heads of a Bill* was printed in *Annals*, XXVI. 260–92, and by Eden. The debate in Committee was not reported; the *House of Commons Journals* record receipt of a number of petitions against the Bill, and the Pitt Papers in the P.R.O. include a number of letters critical of Pitt's proposals.

Pitt's qualifications for the task he set himself were hardly strong. 'Mr. Pitt had certainly looked into political arithmeticians and political oeconomists. But does it follow that he had a well-digested fund of practical information on political arithmetic and oeconomy?'[38] Pitt himself was later to confess that he was inexperienced in such affairs, though he was incensed by Sheridan's sharp comment that it was a pity he had taken the affair out of the hands of Whitbread, 'who would have prosecuted it, if not with an equal ability, yet with equal zeal, and perhaps with a greater degree of industry'.[39] It is doubtful how much the Bill was Pitt's own work; copies of the *Heads* closely annotated in his own hand have been preserved, but the intellectual ancestry of most of the proposals would seem to be obscure. Although it was the Prime Minister's Bill, it should not be regarded as government legislation in the modern sense, but as a private measure, owing more to Pitt's friends than to his official subordinates. It may be assumed that Rose was consulted, and possibly Wilberforce; Ruggles and Abbot were both called in, but only after the main proposals had been drawn up.[40] But there is little point in searching for the origins of a proposal—or rather a conglomeration of proposals—in which there was so little that was original.

When Pitt foreshadowed his proposed legislation in the debate on Whitbread's Minimum Wage Bill he gave few details, but even the broad principles he suggested were hardly consistent. His strongest

[38] T. Beddoes, *Essay on the Public Merits of Mr. Pitt* (1796), p. 95, and compare J. Nasmith's comment that Pitt was 'a stranger to the police of a village' (*The Duties of Overseers* etc. (1799), p. 3). Both these men were formidable critics. James Nasmith (1740–1808), a Cambridge parson, magistrate and antiquary, was chairman of the Cambridge and Ely bench for many years and was outspoken and influential in poor-law matters. Thomas Beddoes (1760–1808), whom Southey and Coleridge thought one of the most remarkable men of his age, was a famous chemist and physician and one of Pitt's most severe critics. When he established his 'Pneumatic Institute' at Clifton for curing disease by inhalation Watt constructed the apparatus and Davy was his assistant. Beddoes also published several lively works on medicine, a moral tale on the reclamation of a drunken labourer and an extraordinary poem attacking British imperialism in India. He married a sister of Maria Edgeworth; the poet Thomas Lovell Beddoes was his son.

[39] See *Parliamentary Register*, X. 465–7 for Pitt's confession, and *Parliamentary History*, xxii. 1405 for Sheridan's remark. J. Holland Rose, in 'Pitt and the Relief of the Poor', *Pitt and Napoleon* (1912), p. 80, claims Pitt instigated the enquiry of 1786, but the Pitt Papers include no supporting evidence. Ruggles thought that reports that Pitt was to act in the matter killed Gilbert's Bill of 1787 (*History of the Poor*, I. vii).

[40] A letter from Ruggles telling of the call is in University College, Bentham Papers, CLI. 44. Abbot was called in at the last moment to improve the drafting, but 'the bill seemed to me bad in the mode as the principles were good' (*Diary and Correspondence of Charles Abbot, Lord Colchester* (1861), I.82). For Ruggles' claim that his *History* inspired Pitt to act see *Annals*, XXXII. 548.

criticism was of the Law of Settlement; he also insisted that relief should be given to large families, a point difficult to reconcile with the next—that relief should be in some sense deterrent, and given in the form of employment to encourage industry. The method suggested was the establishment of Schools of Industry, Pitt speaking lyrically of the advantages of child labour. Other proposals mentioned briefly were a compulsory friendly society scheme to encourage frugality and reduce the poor rates; relief by loan in certain cases; relief to be allowed to owners of small properties; and a system of annual reports or poor-law 'budgets'.[41]

The Bill included all these points and more, though it did not always make them clearer, a situation scarcely remedied by the many amendments in the Committee. A whole new administrative system was proposed, with the new offices of Wardens, Visitors and Guardians of the Poor. The Wardens were to do the work, and were to be chosen from the overseers. The Guardians, who supervised the Wardens, were to be chosen in rotation from the Visitors, a group appointed by an obscure procedure which the Committee did not clarify, though it insisted on a property qualification. Justices of the Peace were given considerable powers (especially in the amended Bill), not only to unite parishes in larger units and to institute the new system, but to act as Visitors and to order relief; while the clergy also were empowered to lodge complaints with the Visitors if the Wardens were negligent or harsh towards the poor. The Bill thus supported the trend towards giving magistrates more power in poor-law affairs; in general, it also formed one more attempt to remodel the system by introducing the gentry into offices in which they could supervise the activities of more plebeian overseers. One clearly admirable point in the new system was the obligation to report fully on expenditure and the general situation of the poor to a central authority.

Perhaps the most onerous of the duties placed on the new Wardens of the Poor was the establishment of Schools of Industry. The original Bill apparently made this compulsory, and also compelled all existing Houses of Industry to come under the new system, but the Committee removed the compulsion, except that all new workhouses must take the form laid down in the Act. Fairly rigorous rules were laid down for the new Schools, but it would not seem that Pitt meant to return to the principles of the Workhouse Test Act, as the Bill clearly stated that the poor could be maintained in the Schools of Industry or at home at the option of the Visitors. Relief could, however, be refused, if the pauper refused to undertake employment in return, either in the School or at home; on the other hand the converse was strongly

[41] *Parliamentary History*, xxxii. 705–11.

insisted upon, that the poor had a right to demand employment from the parish, in return for money wages at rates fixed by the Visitors. Even more than that: if a man were in private employment he could demand that his wage be made up to 'the full rate' if his employer was paying him less. And fathers with more than two children, or widows with more than one, were to be entitled to relief for the extra children, either at home or in a School of Industry; an amendment made 1s. a week per child a minimum in such cases. In fact in many respects the Committee was more generous even than Pitt: where the Bill said that children might be bound apprentice, amendments gave parents the right to demand that they be; and to a clause allowing loans in certain cases of need, another was added permitting (possibly even as a right) that the poor be given the wherewithal to buy and keep a cow. In general the clauses relating to able-bodied poor were lenient, especially in granting them specific rights: to employment, to relief for children, to a 'full wage', and to their cows. This part of the Bill showed a strange muddling of a new system of workhouses with a new profusion of outdoor relief.

The impotent, on the other hand, were to have to pay for their relief. Pitt proposed for each parish a Parochial Fund, to provide unspecified benefits in sickness and age, for unspecified payments. It would seem that all relief in such cases was to be on a contributory basis, until the Committee excluded certain groups from the benefits. The scheme had no real actuarial basis, and would rely on donations and the parish rates as well as on the contributions for its funds. Contribution was also to give some claims to a settlement, a subject the Bill treated much less systematically than Pitt's strong words in the House might have suggested. A clause allowing settlement after five years' residence could have been a long step towards simplifying the whole matter, had not other clauses brought in new complications. There were to be no removals for any relief given under the new act, whether in respect of employment, or children, or temporary illness, or making up wages. All payments to non-settled poor were however to be reimbursed by the home parishes, and the Committee added a clause excluding relief to the non-settled except under this act. The Law of Settlement was complicated enough without adding such confusion to it, and a whole new class of probable law suits over reimbursements to the already endemic litigation over removals. With all this, the Bill included the usual pious recommendation that the idle and disorderly should be sent to a House of Correction.

6. *Pitt's Defeat*

The overwhelmingly critical tone adopted in pamphlets and in private correspondence to Pitt explains why the Parliamentary history of his

Bill was so brief and unlucky. Although one correspondent avowed that the scheme could earn its author 'immortal honour', and some others expressed 'general support', praise was not only meagre but suspiciously vague. Some critics did not even wait until the Bill reached the House of Commons before mauling it. Early in 1796 Howlett published a vigorous attack on Pitt's speech on Whitbread's Bill, defending wage regulation and denying that the Poor Law was to blame for the unhappy situation of the labourer; his criticisms were polite compared with those of Thomas Beddoes, who thought the Prime Minister's philanthropy a sham and his abilities mediocre. 'I have sought in vain for any work achieved by our Premier to which humanity would adjudge a civic wreath ... in him the only class which needs help, found no helper'. Why had Pitt not acted sooner, especially on the problem of Settlement?[42] Most critics made the opposite complaint, that Pitt's scheme was too hastily prepared rather than too long delayed. Eden, writing shortly before the Bill was introduced into Parliament, complained that Pitt should have made some 'preliminary enquiries' on which to build a plan, and neatly quoted against him his own complaint against Whitbread, that 'general principles' must be considered in these matters. The public had expected a complete revision of the Poor Law from Pitt, and had received instead something much less, an expensive experiment which was (Eden claimed) unattractive to both ratepayers and the poor themselves.[43] There is, of course, little evidence that the poor had any opinion at all. A curate from Whitechapel wrote to Pitt thanking him on their behalf, and complaining of the opposition to the Bill from rich parishes; while Roland Hunt, in one of the few pamphlets praising the proposals, pointed out that the petitions of complaint did not come from the poor. Ingram, on the other hand, complained that the Bill might do much for the pauper, but ignored the condition of the free labourer.[44] But most of the critics were more concerned with the interests of the ratepayers, and the expense of the various proposals was their common plaint. The burden of the rates fell not only on the rich, but on 'lower and middling housekeepers', men not far removed from indigence themselves, and it was but reasonable to consider their condition as well as that of the poor. So argued the Vestry of Kensington; Eden, Isaac Wood and numerous

[42] Pitt Papers, 307–8; J. Howlett, *Examination of Mr. Pitt's Speech* etc. (1796); T. Beddoes, *Essay* etc. p. 201.

[43] F. M. Eden, *State of the Poor*, I. 479–84; and see W. Sabatier, *A Treatise on Poverty* etc. (1797), pp. 287–90 for a plea for a Board to enquire into the Poor Law. Sabatier's interesting if uneven book shows some parallels with, or perhaps the influence of, Bentham's unpublished writings.

[44] Letter from E. Robson, Pitt Papers, 308; R. Hunt, *Provision for the Poor* etc. (1797); R. A. Ingram, *An Inquiry* etc. (1797), p. 77.

others agreed. Two correspondents pleaded that Pitt should have put the burden on the rich and especially on the landlords, rather than attempted to relieve the poor at the expense of the almost poor. Some of the strongest criticism of the Bill came from two powerful London parishes, Kensington and Bloomsbury. Both vestries produced pamphlets attacking the proposals in detail and predicting expense and ruin in their own particular areas if they became law, and as their membership included many Members of Parliament their opposition was not to be treated lightly.[45] They made the general point (echoed in numerous specific criticisms of clauses from all over the country) that a general bill could not be suitable to all conditions: 'The ten thousand parishes in England and Wales form a subject of enquiry so extensive, as to tend to confound rather than inform the judgment, and to lead it astray from the safe path of experience into the untried and probably dangerous regions of mere speculation'. The two pamphlets gave detailed accounts of the problems facing large urban parishes, complaining that well-tried procedures would be upset by the Bill and expenses at least doubled. Bloomsbury feared confusion in applying so poorly drafted a measure to the 150–200 applicants its overseers met daily. Kensington complained that it was largely irrelevant to the real problem; most paupers were impotent, yet the Bill dealt mainly with the able-bodied. Both went on to make detailed criticisms, many of them very telling, and these were only the most elaborate of the many attacks on the Bill from alarmed poor-law authorities in a great variety of urban and country parishes.

Inevitably, much criticism came also from men with schemes of their own for reform. Vancouver found much to praise in the Bill, but his own plan was better,[46] and Pitt's correspondence included many letters from other would-be reformers, some sensible, some cranky. W. Davies of Oxford would have abolished the Poor Laws, regulated wages, established a contributory fund, and established self-supporting district workhouses for occasional employment. John Horne sent a platitudinous scheme for Houses of Industry, mainly as a preface to a plea for patronage. An anonymous reformer would have replaced poor rates with a tax on dogs and other luxuries. Mr. John Jones was more coy: he had perfected a plan for the employment of the poor, and offered it to the Prime Minister—for a fee. Henry Palmer's plan was more interesting than most, and in some ways prophetic: five central

---

[45] *Some Observations . . . Prepared for the use of the Trustees of the Poor of the Parish of Kensington* (1797), and *An Abstract . . . Prepared by a Committee of the Joint Vestry of the United Parishes of St. Giles in the Fields and St. George, Bloomsbury* (1797).

[46] J. Vancouver, *An Enquiry* etc. (1796), p. 140.

commissioners should be appointed, at a salary of £500 each, to establish large workhouses in each county, on the model of Rumford's House of Industry at Munich; the rest of the Poor Law, and especially the Law of Settlement, could then be repealed. This scheme had some resemblance to that of the most illustrious of all these purveyors of panaceas (if not the least cranky), Jeremy Bentham. In February 1797 Bentham interrupted his labours on his own Pauper Plan to write his *Observations on the Poor Bill*, the most damaging of all the criticisms of Pitt's proposals. Though not published until 1838, the pamphlet was circulated in manuscript; it was addressed to Pitt, though if he read it he did not preserve a copy among his papers. Bentham's criticism of particular clauses was sharp enough, as will be seen, but the comments on drafting were even more devastating: Pitt's Bill offended Bentham the legal reformer even more than Bentham the author of *Pauper Management Improved.* Laws were the instruments with which all reforms must be made, and neither the Poor Law nor anything else could be improved with bad legislation. Obscurity in laws would work mischief 'so long as Westminster Hall, the great mine of uncertainty, is open to all who have a golden spade to dig in it with'.[47]

Pitt's Poor Law Bill included so many different proposals that it is not surprising that few men gave it general assent. But simply because the Bill was so comprehensive, the discussion of its various clauses revealed the more clearly the number and variety of the difficulties facing any would-be reformer of the system.

The administrative reforms proposed by Pitt were close enough to traditional assumptions to win some support. 'So long as the execution of the Poor Laws is entrusted in the proper hands, too great a discretionary power can hardly be allowed them', wrote Ingram, and others also welcomed attempts to put more power into the hands of magistrates, gentry and clergy as Visitors and Guardians.[48] But there were weighty objections also. Eden feared that justices were already too overburdened with duties to meet the complex new demands, and correspondents from Lancashire and Sussex complained that not enough Visitors or Guardians could be recruited. Even if they were found, would they do good? Significantly the strongest critics of the proposals were the spokesmen of areas which had already reformed their administration. Isaac Wood feared that the zeal of Visitors would wane, and the Vestries of Kensington and Bloomsbury deplored granting wide powers to 'inexperienced' persons; they insisted that areas administered under local acts must be exempted, especially those

[47] J. Bentham, *Observations* etc. (ed. Chadwick, 1838), pp. 38–47.
[48] R. A. Ingram, *An Inquiry* etc. p. 80; compare R. Hunt, *An Inquiry* etc. and a number of letters in Pitt Papers, 308, urging similar administrative reforms.

which already had the 'best possible' system, under the control of the gentry. And the bottom of the new administrative system was as open to criticism as the top, since the new Wardens were simply the old annual overseers under a new name and with more onerous duties. Even the Bishop of Lincoln, a supporter of the Bill, asked that professional Assistant Overseers be added to the hierarchy, and Wood stressed that annual management had already been proved inadequate and it was therefore absurd to expect it to assume so many new functions, including the running of Schools of Industry. Thus Pitt's proposed administrative reforms not only offended existing authorities but could be plausibly attacked as patently insufficient for his own purposes.[49]

Pitt's scheme for establishing Schools of Industry may have been based on the example of existing institutions;[50] nevertheless it won nothing but criticism from their spokesmen. Wood and others pleaded that existing Houses of Industry must be excluded from the system, and complained that Pitt was ignorant of the circumstances essential to success in such ventures, especially the need for permanence in direction and management. If temporary Wardens and interfering magistrates were admitted to control, the Shrewsbury and similar projects would be 'at one stroke overturned' just when 'the fairest prospects were opening before them'. The Shrewsbury House was caring successfully for both able-bodied and impotent poor; the latter would be excluded under the new regulations, and Pitt would do better to abandon his ill-digested scheme and encourage the gradual extension of Houses on the Shrewsbury model. Bentham, for his part, made unfavourable comparisons with his own Panopticon Poor Houses, the virtues of which he was busy enumerating.[51] And if the champions of institutional treatment for paupers were critical, opponents of workhouses showed implacable hostility. Fenwick and the Earl of Winchilsea objected to all 'legal pest houses'; Eden pointed out how much the poor hated them; Ellis complained that workhouse education ruined children for agricultural employment; and Gidley feared that the new Schools would depress the position of existing grammar schools. Eden also thought that the

---

[49] F. M. Eden, *State of the Poor*, I. 480; letters from Masters, Ellis and the Bishop of Lincoln, Pitt Papers, 307; I. Wood, *A Letter to Sir William Pulteney* etc. pp. 7–15; *Some Observations* etc. pp. 33–5; *An Abstract* etc. pp. 7, 36–42.

[50] Sabatier suggested experiments at Westminster as Pitt's inspiration (*A Treatise on Poverty* etc. p. 288, and compare *Annals*, XXVIII. 164); Wood thought the continental examples of Rumford and Voght more likely influences, but his own writings and Ruggles' enthusiasm for the Suffolk houses are other possibilities. The Hammonds' suggestion of Fielding's influence is less plausible (*The Village Labourer*, I. 148).

[51] I. Wood, *A Letter* etc. pp. 26–30; J. Bentham, *Observations, passim.*

Bill might give the government too much control over education.[52] All these arguments, and more, were drawn together in Sir William Young's pamphlet against workhouses in general and Pitt's Plan in particular. Proud of his campaign against the Workhouse Test Act, and against private bills which included workhouses in their provisions, Young complained that his known hostility to 'gaols without guilt' had led to his exclusion from committees on such bills. If workhouses (and in particular contract management) became universal, the result would be the virtual repeal of the Poor Laws as measures for relief. Young could see some value in Schools for Industry, provided they were simply schools and not residential workhouses, all of which were destructive of a true English spirit.

One principle is common to all these establishments . . . that principle is terror. I will admit the propriety of its application to deter from crime, or from vice, or from idleness, or even from remissness in labour . . . but there is no moral relation whatever between the imprisonment and contracts of a workhouse and the conduct of very many who are forced into it.

In filling workhouses, we are manning, as it were, so many disaffected garrisons, the inmates of which, on the first violence of popular commotion that occasions and prejudices may create, will be let loose on the country.[53]

Young's contrast between the workhouse child bred to crime and the cottage child 'drinking the spirit of the golden day' may have been too extreme to be convincing, but he also produced good economic arguments against expecting any profit from pauper labour in institutions; and Eden and the Vestry of Kensington agreed with him. On the whole the opponents of Pitt's Bill did not express the strong objection to providing work for unemployed labourers which was soon to become orthodox; what many did assert was that such employment was unlikely to be profitable, and that it was folly to build expensive institutions on the expectation of good returns.[54]

If the Schools of Industry proposed in the Bill were thought to be impracticable by most, and harsh by some, the new provisions for outdoor relief were criticised for being too prodigal. Granting so much relief as a matter of right, rather than at the discretion of overseers, was particularly undesirable. The Kensington Vestry objected especially to making up wages to the 'full rate'; endless artifice would result

---

[52] F. M. Eden, *State of the Poor*, I. 481; Pitt Papers, 307 for Winchilsea's comments, and 308 for those of Fenwick, Ellis and Gidley.

[53] W. Young, *Considerations on the Subject of Poor Houses* etc. (1796), pp. 19, 22. Young was at this time a political supporter of Pitt's. The son of a governor of Dominica, and himself governor of Tobago from 1807 until his death in 1815, he wrote books on the West Indies and on classical subjects as well as on the Poor Law.

[54] *Ibid.* p. 15; F. M. Eden, *State of the Poor*, I. 480; *Some Observations* etc. p. 22.

as the poor worked as little as possible and claimed their parish pay. And how, they asked, could one decide what the 'full rate' was, especially in towns? Bentham ruthlessly elaborated this point in his discussion of what he called the *supplemental-wages clause*. Should the 'full rate' be the highest wage in the district? Surely not. In that particular employment? If so, why should bad shipwrights and bad instrument makers get different wages? The average wage? There was no data on which to calculate it. The lowest wage paid in the district? Wages varied according to area; once guarantee them, and a man might double his wage by coming to London.[55]

Pitt's proposal for special relief for large families gave his Bill a special notoriety in the generation of Malthus. At the time, however, critics were less concerned by the effect on population of what Bentham called the *extra children clause* than by its probable expense. Wood claimed it would double Birmingham's rates, while Bloomsbury Vestry objected that the Irish would swarm from their tenements and demand vast sums, as the clause promised relief irrespective of settlement. Fears were expressed that parents would no longer send their children to work; to prevent such infantile indolence Kensington Vestry suggested that relief be restricted to children incapable of labour, and Ellis proposed eight as a maximum age for such relief. To Bentham the clause seemed at once too rigid, in removing discretionary power in relief for children, and too loose, in establishing a right which might not coincide with a need. He pointed out that the clause was so badly drafted that parents could claim relief by showing simply that the children could not maintain themselves, whatever the resources of the family as a whole.[56]

The *cow money* clause was easy game, especially to Bentham. It had some supporters, notably among those who championed the cause of giving land to the poor; thus the Bishop of Lincoln and the Earl of Winchilsea approved it. But the Kensington Vestry pointed out how difficult it would be to provide the town poor with cows. Wood thought the clause 'crude speculation', and drew a picture of fearful extravagance if cows were claimed by every citizen, and crude favouritism if they were restricted to a few.[57] To Bentham, the plan was simply benevolent folly; where other clauses threatened income it threatened capital—'the spigot was *there* opened, *here* the bung-hole'.

[55] *Some Observations* etc. p. 15; J. Bentham, *Observations* etc. pp. 9–11.
[56] I. Wood, *A Letter* etc. pp. 18–19; *An Abstract* etc. pp. 21–3; *Some Observations* etc. p. 13; Pitt Papers, 307, for letter from Ellis, and compare that from Clavering suggesting that relief be restricted to legitimate children only; J. Bentham, *Observations* etc. pp. 11–15.
[57] I. Wood, *A Letter* etc. pp. 21–4.

The cow *dies* or is *stolen*, or (what is much more likely) is *supposed* to be stolen, being clandestinely *sold* to an obliging purchaser at a distance. What is to be done? *'Want of relief'* warranted the *first* cow; the same cause will necessitate a *second*—limit who can the succeeding *series* of cows. The disappearance of the *first* cow (it may be said) will incite *suspicion*; the disappearance of a second cow will *strengthen suspicion*; true, but upon a mere suspicion without *proof* will a family be left to starve?

If capital was to be given, why a cow? 'Milk is a wholesome as well as a pleasant beverage; milk is particularly good for children'; and much good had been done by charitable individuals providing the needy and deserving with cows. But as a system it raised problems. A cow was expensive, and she was perishable. Ownership would not encourage industrious habits—'attendance upon a *single* cow is a species of industry, if industry it can be called, which is, of anything that *can* bear that name, the nearest of kin to idleness'. Of the 'other animals in the offscape' Bentham would prefer swine, but for the problem of feeding them. In fact he would prefer manufactures to agricultural aids.

The resource presented by a *loom* is a *permanent* one: it *may* be *rendered* an *unfluctuating* one. A loom eats nothing; is not apt to be sick; does not sink in value by underfeeding; has no legs to be driven away upon, and is not exposed to sudden death. The working of one loom need not hinder the working of another.

A loom is but one example of a machine. But protesting against the donation of capital in any shape, protesting against *principle*, I will not dive further into the mode.

The crucial flaw in the cow-system, Bentham thought, was the question of land. Were the bearers of certificates of good behaviour to be given the necessary three acres? If not, the cow must go on the already crowded common, where both she and the rest of the stock would deteriorate. And if they were given land, 'so far so good for the existing generations of a family. But at the next generation the number of the family is doubled. Are they to have landed estates given them in the way of charity? If not, why not? If they are, where is this to end?' In Jacobinism and an Agrarian law, he thought. The real problem was to keep the means of the poor sufficient for their wants; Bentham claimed to have solved it, in another place, but not by singling out individuals for special benefits:

By donations in any shape you may take a few favoured individuals out of the class of poor, and place them in the class of people of easy circumstances. But this, which is only the system of monastic charity upon a great scale, giving the beef whole instead of dealing it out in broth, is limited in its extent

72

LESSONS OF SCARCITY

as well as pernicious in its effects, and in relieving present indigence sows the seed of future.[58]

The practice of granting relief in the form of loans was suggested to Pitt by Malachi Hitchins of Cornwall in 1795. It was generally approved, though Howlett dismissed it as 'the mere fabric of a vision'. Loans were efficacious if given privately, with discretion. But if the parish granted them without security, funds would be wasted; if they demanded security, they could not make the loan.[59] Bentham had no particular objection, except to the drafting of the clause, and indeed his own plan of reform included the idea of loans. But he certainly objected to what he called the *opulence relief clause*, allowing poor relief to men possessing up to £30 in property. Apart from faults in the drafting, the flaw in Pitt's clause was that it promised what it could not perform, because it offered indiscriminate relief. What group would it entitle to assistance? 'I cannot help vehemently suspecting it would be found to include a vast majority of the good people of England. . . . The system of *home provision*, as thus explained, would be found (I much fear) to amount to a plan for *throwing the parish upon the parish*'.[60]

Bentham was of course a supporter of institutional relief, at least in Benthamite institutions. To him all these clauses on outdoor relief showed a lamentable prodigality, and a desire to elevate the condition of the labourer without consideration of practical possibilities. Even the apprenticeship clause, welcomed by most, seemed to Bentham to promise the mass of the population promotion to the class of tradesmen, a project contradictory in itself. Pitt's Bill was humane in purpose, but true humanity must always exercise itself within the limits of the possible. The poor deserved compassion, 'but compassion is one thing; relief, efficacious and unmischievous relief, a very different thing'. Relief should not be attempted without 'the strictest and most comprehensive enquiry whether the undertaking lies within the sphere of practicality. . . . We commiserate *Darius*, we commiserate *Lear*, but it is not in the power of *parishes* to give kingdoms'.[61]

Bentham wrote, of course, with the confidence (and dogmatism) of a man who believed he himself possessed the true and only answer to the problem of indigence, if not of poverty. It is only fair to quote, alongside his strictures, Hunt's defence of the Bill; writing against Wood, he denied—perhaps wrongly—that Pitt intended to do more than give authorities useful powers to apply at their discretion:

[58] J. Bentham, *Observations* etc. pp. 16–21.
[59] Letter from Hitchins, Pitt Papers, 308; J. Howlett, *Examination* etc. p. 36. Hitchins, a country parson of humble origins, became a mathematician and astronomer of note.
[60] J. Bentham, *Observations* etc. pp. 22–3.
[61] *Ibid.* pp. 25–6.

I will . . . offer to lay my friend a wager, that his multiplication of cows will never take place, under the order of any magistrate in Britain—that no justice of Worcestershire will order a *live cow*, to relieve the poor of a button manufactory at Birmingham—that one of Count Rumford's boiling houses will never be erected at the top of Plinlimmon by a justice of Montgomeryshire; nor that a house of industry, like that of Shrewsbury, will be built in a hurry on an island of the Hebrides, by order of a Scotch justice. I will wager that no such hasty orders will be made; but that each mode of relief will be adapted to its proper situation.[62]

Some of the most cogent criticism of Pitt's Bill was directed against his scheme for Parochial Funds and his treatment of the Law of Settlement. All the critics, except Howlett, thought well of friendly societies and were sympathetic to contributory schemes, but compulsory parish funds were another matter. Eden stated frankly that the poor would prefer their own clubs, and the Bishop of Lincoln insisted that only voluntary charitable organisations could effectively supplement them.[63] Bloomsbury Vestry complained that Pitt's plan was too crude an attempt to generalise the benefits of friendly societies 'without any knowledge of the principles on which these Societies are managed and supported'. Societies exercised some control over membership; only persons in the same rank in life could safely defend themselves against imposition by other members. The Bill's clause against embezzlement was too weak to control the artful poor of Bloomsbury, and the management of the Fund would waste overseers' time in a 'chimerical speculation, for such it will ever prove to be in populous parishes'. What could prevent persons offering one or two subscriptions and then retiring on the Fund?

There is great reason to believe that many hundred of the lower classes of the natives of Ireland would come from that kingdom to establish themselves in the said Parishes, for scarcely any other purpose (for many of them now come thereto from more trifling motives) than to take the benefit of this proposed Fund.

A dozen Beadles and messengers and three or four clerks would be needed to administer the plan and check imposture; surely the Bill should not compel parishes to such courses.[64] All this was cogent criticism. Pitt had in fact made no attempt to calculate the cost on

---

[62] R. Hunt, *Provision for the Poor* etc. p. 12.

[63] J. Howlett, *An Examination* etc. p. 35; F. M. Eden, *State of the Poor*, I. 480. The Pitt Papers do not support the suggestion that John Harriott's scheme for old age pensions was an immediate influence on Pitt's bill; the plan did not reach Pitt until 1797. Bloomsbury Vestry thought Pitt influenced by Townsend's contributory scheme (*An Abstract* etc. p. 36 n.).

[64] *An Abstract* etc. pp. 8, 35–6.

actuarial principles, and did not see the impossibility of establishing contributory schemes financed only from local resources but open to all comers. All such schemes faced the dilemma that if the funds were local they could not be adequate; but if they were national they could hardly be administered, as Whitbread was to be told in 1807.

In his speech against Whitbread, Pitt had made the reform of the Law of Settlement the crux of his plan to improve the condition of the labourer. In the Bill the extension of the right to a settlement (by five years' residence, or payment to the Parochial Fund) was a much less drastic innovation than the obligation on parishes to relieve non-settled poor, with its concomitant right to reclaim the cost from home parishes. It was this new complication which aroused most opposition, for the idea of relieving men without a settlement horrified both rural and urban parishes. The Clergy and Churchwardens of the Parish of Kingsclere, Hampshire, predicted that parishes would entice labourers with promises of high wages, and then throw them on the rates, reclaiming the relief from their places of settlement. To the Vestry of Bloomsbury the clause was the worst in the Bill. There would be more litigation over orders for reimbursement than there had been on orders for removal; and how could one calculate likely expenses and strike a rate if vast sums were outstanding in reimbursements? They calculated that relief to non-settled poor would add 2s. to the rate in wage subsidies and child allowances alone, and judging from the difficulties of reclaiming militia allowances (on a similar principle), little would come back to them. The alternative proposals of Kensington Vestry showed how each parish interpreted the problem in the light of its own condition: make manufacturing towns support their own poor, by restricting settlement to service, and relieve populous parishes by rating owners of speculative tenements.[65] This would suit Kensington, but where else? Pitt's difficulties on this question should not be judged too harshly. After all, even the government which produced the new Poor Law in 1834 was afraid to grasp tightly the nettle of conflicting local interests flourishing in the complexities of the Law of Settlement.

Pitt did not persist in the face of so much criticism. Perhaps he gave in too easily. J. Holland Rose felt obliged to support 'the charge of weakness in not bringing forward an amended measure at a time more favourable than the winter of 1796–7'.[66] In 1800, in the debate on Whitbread's second attempt at a wage regulation bill, Pitt admitted that he had been discouraged, rather than persuaded, by criticism of his Plan. 'He was, as formerly, convinced of its propriety; but many objections had been stated to it by those whose opinions he was bound

[65] Pitt Papers, 308; *An Abstract* etc. p. 25; *Some Observations* etc. pp. 37–40.
[66] J. Holland Rose, *Pitt and Napoleon*, pp. 91–2.

to respect. Inexperienced himself in country affairs, and in the condition of the poor, he was diffident of his own opinion, and would not press the measure upon the attention of the House'.[67] The Hammonds were highly critical of Pitt's persistence in opposing Whitbread; 'he had spent his only idea, and he was now confessedly without any policy at all'. This is not quite fair: Pitt was at least consistent in opposing Whitbread's remedy, and the rejection of his Bill gave him some justification in reverting to a view that questions of relief should be left in the hands of those who traditionally decided them, on a local rather than a national scale. On the other hand the Hammonds' praise of Pitt for having made 'one statesman-like discovery . . . that it is bad policy to refuse to help a man until he is ruined' may not be justified either, at least if Bentham's point is accepted that extending the bounds of relief was not the way to reduce pauperism. 'The grievance is that the industrious *poor* should be so liable to be *indigent*, that the *independent* hand should be so liable to fall into *dependence*. . . . But the keeping them *from* thus falling upon the parish is what the Bill neither does, nor so much as *professes* to do. So far from it, as far as it does anything, it *throws* them there, it throws them in greater *numbers*; it throws them with greater weight.' Bentham's own plan would at least attempt to distinguish between relieving the indigent and ensuring the continued independence of the labourer.[68] Modern notions of state intervention for social justice assume modern instrumentalities, and if many of the forms of relief Pitt attempted now seem to us proper social services, contemporary criticism was surely cogent in complaining that the chief characteristics of Pitt's Bill were confusion in aim, administrative incoherence, and extremely poor drafting.

7. *The Justices' Poor Law*

The failure of Pitt's Bill, following as it did the defeat of Whitbread's, brought to an end major legislative attempts to meet the problems of scarcity. Initiative in policies of relief remained with local authorities, and especially the magistracy, and the Hammond's assert that 'the Justices' Poor Law' was the true outcome of these years in the practice of relief.[69] Many historians join them in accepting the Speenhamland 'Act' and the establishment of the allowance system as the most important development of the time, as the real alternative to legislative

[67] *Parliamentary Register*, X. 465–7.

[68] J. L. and Barbara Hammond, *The Village Labourer*, I. 147; J. Bentham, *Observations* etc. p. 27. J. Holland Rose defended Pitt's proposals against Bentham's: 'the one scheme emanated from an enthusiast, the other embodied the frigid calculations of a doctrinaire' (*Pitt and Napoleon*, p. 91).

[69] J. L. and Barbara Hammond, *The Village Labourer*, I. 158.

76

reform and as the chief or indeed only fruit of magisterial intervention. But how systematic, and how uniform, were local responses in fact in these years? It is not, on the face of it, likely that in the history of poor relief one meeting of magistrates and other 'discreet persons' at the Pelican Inn on 6 May 1795 should gain a fame far greater than any Parliamentary proceedings of the time, while innumerable other meetings of equally important and discreet persons in provincial towns secured only the most ephemeral and local attention. Can Speenhamland's fame be justified, as a true and influential beginning of a new order in policy and practice, or even as a symbol and precursor of things to come? Only a thorough study, beyond the scope of these pages, could answer this question; nevertheless it is important to set alongside the Parliamentary proceedings on Whitbread's and Pitt's Bills some at least of the thoughts and decisions of the magistracy.

The Speenhamland meeting itself occurred early in the scarcity, and arose directly from a speech by Charles Dundas, the Foxite Whig, before the Berkshire Quarter Sessions at Newbury.[70] Dundas called for an increase in wages as the obvious remedy for scarcity, and claimed that the legal power to rate wages already existed; the meeting at the Pelican Inn was called to discuss the question. The motion to rate wages was defeated, for reasons undisclosed. Instead those at the meeting agreed to do two things: to urge farmers to increase wages in accordance with the price of provisions; and to act, in their individual capacities as magistrates, by ordering relief according to a scale under which total income in wages and relief would fluctuate with the price of bread. According to Eden, the scale recommended was the more generous of two considered, and was intended primarily as a guide to relief for the impotent, though its wording specifically envisaged relief to those in employment.[71]

Relief to men in employment was not new, and there were precedents even for the adoption of a scale. There is no clear reason why the Speenhamland meeting should remain more famous than that of the Oxford Quarter Sessions of 13 January 1795, when a scale was drawn up and sent to all overseers in the County.[72] The Berkshire meeting was not at first widely publicised: the report in the *Annals of Agriculture*

[70] The primary source for the Speenhamland meeting is the *Reading Mercury*, 20 April and 11 May 1795; it is quoted at length in J. L. and Barbara Hammond, *The Village Labourer*, I. 158–60, and in S. and B. Webb, *The Old Poor Law*, pp. 177–9.

[71] F. M. Eden, *State of the Poor*, I. 576–7.

[72] J. L. and Barbara Hammond, *The Village Labourer*, I. 160. A Dorset precedent was more obscure (S. and B. Webb, *Parish and County*, pp. 546–7 n.); the Buckinghamshire justices had ordered that wages be made up from the rates in January, but with a fixed sum and not by a sliding scale (S. and B. Webb, *The Old Poor Law*, p. 177).

was brief and inconspicuous, and far more space was given to the Suffolk magistrates' demand for wage regulation. Few of the other bread scales which survive were identical with the Speenhamland model, and scales must indeed have occurred to more than one group of magistrates as obviously useful devices. It may be that Speenhamland (like that paragon of rural virtue, Anne Strudwick) owes its immortality to Eden, who discussed the magistrates' decision at length in *The State of the Poor*, even if only to attack it. The Berkshire meeting then virtually disappeared from the literature on pauperism; indeed writers of the next three decades were extremely vague on the origins of the allowance system, which so many of them—at least after 1815—deplored vehemently. In 1801 a correspondent in the *Annals* wrote that in his parish allowances in aid of wages had existed 'beyond memory'; thereafter there was very little reference at all to the practice before 1817. In that year J. E. Bicheno quoted the Speenhamland table in attacking allowances, but there is evidence that he had read his Eden, and the reference is exceptional in these years. Thus T. P. Courtenay merely wrote that the system was 'said' to have begun when prices increased twenty to thirty years earlier; in 1818 he added that it was generally understood that allowances became 'systematic' and 'extreme' in 1795–9, though many magistrates remembered earlier precedents. In 1817 Lieutenant General Craufurd and the Reverend George Glover, Archdeacon of Sudbury, both saw sudden high prices as the occasion for the practice, though Glover attributed the inflation to increased taxation after the American War. In 1819 Sir Egerton Brydges traced the degeneration of the Poor Law to the beginnings of wage subsidies in the 1790s, but in the same year Richard Blakemore referred only to a 'recent unwise benevolence'. In his *Second Letter* of 1819 Edward Copleston began another historical tradition by linking the origins of allowances with both Gilbert's Act of 1782 and the Act of 1795 which permitted justices and vestries to order outdoor relief in those parishes formally bound by the Workhouse Test Act.[73] Most writers of the 1820s were more interested in the system itself than in its origins, but the foundations had been laid for later historians' dogmatic summaries of the period. Thus Sir George Nicholls saw the 1795 Act as 'a source of great and universal abuse' (though he was well aware that many parishes had anticipated its passing by decades), gave much prominence to the Speenhamland scale,

[73] *Annals*, XXXVII. 98; J. E. Bicheno, *An Enquiry* etc. (1817), pp. 106–8; T. P. Courtenay, *Copy of a Letter* etc. (1817), pp. 16–18, and *A Treatise on the Poor Laws* (1818), p. 101; Lieut. Gen. C. G. Craufurd, *Observations* etc. (1817), p. 46; G. Glover, *Observations* etc. (1817), pp. 18–22; E. Brydges, *The Population and Riches of Nations* etc. (1819), chap. XXI; E. R. Copleston, *A Second Letter* etc. (1819), pp. 76–9.

and clearly attributed the allowance system largely to its example.[74] So much for tradition: the absence of more frequent contemporary references to the Berkshire meeting casts doubt on its importance as either precedent or example.

It is a more important question whether the policy of relief exemplified by Speenhamland was a common one, and even perhaps the usual remedy adopted by magistrates and discreet persons in the years of scarcity. Behind this question lies another and wider issue. Were allowances in aid of wages, even at their most 'systematic', ever much more than haphazard and occasional devices adopted to meet the accidental circumstances of scarcity, or later of post-war distress? Or should the 'system' be regarded as an important new social institution, born of major structural changes in the economy? Karl Polanyi has championed the institutional view, even claiming for Speenhamland a universal significance as a reflection of a particular stage in the development of the market economy and of modern industrial society.[75] To him, as to the Hammonds, the poverty of these years was institutional in origin, and Speenhamland a system erected by a doomed paternalism to prevent the labourer from becoming a mere commodity in a new labour market. Whatever the intention, allowances may well have become a major social calamity, as the reformers of 1832–4 alleged. These assertions cannot be tested until the nature and extent of the 'system' is more thoroughly explored and set in its economic and social context.[76] But it is certain that in the minds of some reformers a general conviction about the system and its effects emerged, at least eventually. They found, or claimed to find, degradation associated with systematic relief, and asserted that careless benevolence itself generated social calamity. To them the crisis in pauperism was less a doom or an accident than a mistake; their view became dominant after 1815, as will be seen, but it was not to be expected in the 1790s.

The Speenhamland meeting has certainly some significance in symbolising the importance of the magistracy in these years, and in revealing the dilemma magistrates faced. Parliament could not, or would not, produce a policy for them; the scarcity which created the problem was unduly severe and unexpectedly protracted; its duration and extent soon exhausted many of the remedies usual in such a situation; and (above all) the powers of the magistrates and the structure of poor-law administration permitted interference only of a quasi-judicial

---

[74] Sir George Nicholls, *History of the English Poor Law*, II. 115–7, 131–4. Nicholls, unlike Copleston and many modern writers, did not link Gilbert's Act of 1782 with the increase in outdoor relief and allowances; for a contrast with Copleston's view see also Lord Sheffield, *Remarks* etc. (1818), p. 14.

[75] K. Polanyi, *The Great Transformation* (New York, 1944).

[76] This question is discussed further in chapter VIII below.

nature except where overseers were willing to accept administrative direction, and vestries allowed them to do so. The Speenhamland meeting was also symbolic in that it spoke the words of compromise: the compromise between simply raising wages (as the Devon Quarter Sessions attempted to do) and merely exhorting the poor to eat less (as Lord Sheffield's Charge suggested). Certainly a decision to lay down scales of relief, even where adopted, was only one of a host of complementary or conflicting remedies which won the favour of the magistracy.

A thorough examination of the problem facing the bench in 1795 was presented in a report drawn up for the Epiphany Sessions in Hampshire by the Rev. Edmund Poulter.[77] Poulter claimed that the immediate problem of a catastrophic rise in food prices concealed a more permanent decline in the real wages of the agricultural labourers; nevertheless he thought it improper to rely on either wages or public relief to meet the immediate crisis and looked to private charity to augment incomes. His whole attitude to the labourer was strongly paternalistic. Wages must be related to labourers' needs, as determined by the upper classes; the Report itself was generous in its estimate, recognising beer and animal foods as necessities. Wages should never be more than adequate, or relief other than parsimonious, lest idleness and degradation spread among the labourers; nevertheless wages should be raised, and the Report even threatened regulation, assuming that legal power to fix wages (but not prices) already existed. But compulsory arrangements, either by wage regulation or in poor relief, were described as a poor second best to voluntary action. Let farmers raise wages, taking care that the increase be not sufficient to tempt single labourers into 'idleness, drunkenness and other vices'; as for the large families, let them be frugal. 'It is far more useful to teach them to spend less, or to save a little, than to give them more'. Paternalistic control should extend to the labourer's expenditure as well as to his earnings: 'one obvious way of masters' promoting this great point of economy in their servants is to lessen the objects of it, by leaving as little as possible to their own management; the more of their maintenance they receive in kind, and the less in money, the better'. Let farmers learn from the army, and be shopkeepers to their servants. To supplement this economic paternalism a principle was suggested for the use of overseers and magistrates: 'determine what is the proper subsistence; what the several parts of the family do or may earn . . . order in relief whatever may be the deficiency of the greatest income under the best employment for the least outgoing under the best management.'[78] Who could blame a busy parish officer for

[77] Printed in *Annals*, XXV. 349–98.
[78] *Annals*, XXV. 361–2, 371.

reducing such calculations to a scale, or at least a rough rule of thumb? As long as pauperism was not thought absolutely deplorable, allowances in aid of wages were always likely to be adopted in conditions of emergency, even if seen as third best to voluntary charity and wage increases. Moreover the prejudice against paying single labourers a wage sufficient for a family implied either differential wages or allowances from the rates. But the value placed on various alternatives could be expected to vary from parish to parish.

The dangers of confusing wages and relief did not go long unnoticed. In 1797 Eden wrote of wage subsidies from the rates as 'a deplorable evil' and chose the Speenhamland example for particular criticism because of the public, systematic and (allegedly) coercive nature of the scales adopted. He admitted that such proceedings were consistent enough with the usual assumptions on public relief, but claimed that many a worthy labourer gave the lie to those assumptions by maintaining himself and his family with far less income than the Speenhamland scale thought necessary. The proper remedy in scarcity was the consumption of substitute foods; and in any case fixed allowances from the rates discouraged exertion, especially in piece-work.[79] Eden thought such measures unnecessary, because he was, unlike many magistrates and farmers, a believer in the sanctity of economic laws, as shall be seen. He also anticipated the views of the Select Committee of 1817–8 in believing relief to able-bodied men illegal.

Other critics of allowances were less influenced by economic dogma. Sir Thomas Bernard noted that 'in some parts of England tables have been printed, by order of the magistrates, fixing the precise amount of parochial relief . . . according to the number of children, and the price of bread'. What he deplored was the impersonal nature of the procedure, and its lack of moral discrimination; he expressed the usual belief that 'a fixed income, independent of personal industry and economy, has a tendency to weaken the energy of the poor, and to diminish their exertions for their own support', but added to it a plea for enlightened charity of a particular sort in place of mechanical relief. Neither wages nor charity could guarantee maintenance without self-help, and for this the poor needed the voluntary and disinterested encouragement of the other classes in society'.[80] Systematic allowances were as inconsistent with 'scientific' charity as they were with economic liberalism.

A closer analysis of allowances in practice was made in 1800 by the Rev. J. North, in an essay on *The State of the Poor in the Parish of Ashdon, Essex*.[81] Rates in the parish had risen steeply; since the sums

[79] F. M. Eden, *State of the Poor*, I. 575–84.
[80] *Reports of the Society for . . . Bettering the Condition of the Poor*, I. 48–9.
[81] *Annals*, XXV. 459–73, and compare XXXVII. 97–111.

paid to impotent paupers had increased little, the fault lay in payments to the able-bodied. All labourers were dependent on the rates for rent, fuel and clothing, and some for the maintenance of children. North dismissed as idle talk the argument that wages found their own level naturally, alleging that farmers combined to prevent increases and the labourers were too dependent on their employers' good-will to protest. He also attacked, as a dangerous delusion, the view that it did not matter how the poor were paid, as long as they had enough. Labourers taught to rely on begging from vestries instead of earning from farmers ceased to save, or to care for the clothing and other goods given them in charity. Hence the total spent on such things was rising, and the rich in the parish had to pay more than if wages had been varied instead; allowances were an expensive form of wage increase, as well as a fraudulent one. And while the poor became improvident their employers became tyrannical, thinking it a kindness to speak in the vestry in favour of an employee when in fact he had become an applicant only through their own injustice. North analysed at length the manner in which the large farmer profited from the system, and its inevitable spread as the burden of rising rates forced small farmers and householders into the pauper class.

It appears . . . that as the little farmer is a loser in proportion to his littleness, the great farmer is by this administration, a gainer in proportion to his greatness; and as the great farmers govern the parish, the increase of the wages of labour will always be opposed by great farmers; and as great farms are daily increasing in number and in size, the hope of seeing the wages of labourers *find their level*, or, in other words, become more adequate to their daily wants, seems to me not to be drawing near; and what is almost of equal importance to establish is this—that it is not the same in any point of view, to pay labour by rate, because the effects of this latter mode are pernicious to labourers, are uneconomical to the parish, unjust to all its inhabitants who are not farmers, oppressive to all small occupiers, and a matter of profit only to the greater farmers, and more so in proportion to their rentals.[82]

Thus a number of objections to making up wages from the rates had been put by 1800, though they were not at all common in the literature before 1815.

The infrequency of criticism of the allowance system before the end of the war has been noticed by the Webbs, who suggest that the prosperity of the agricultural interest before 1815 made farmers willing to pay high rates, if not high wages. But another explanation is possible: that the system itself was not widespread. It is true that outdoor relief in lieu of wages was paid very widely indeed in England by 1834, and not

[82] *Ibid.* XXXV. 472–3.

in agricultural parishes only, but also in manufacturing districts. Almost all the published evidence on allowances comes from the years after 1815, and although the Select Committee on Labourers' Wages of 1824 and the Royal Commission of 1832–4 published material on earlier periods, most of it was mere hearsay about the past.[83] The extent and continuity of the allowance system before (and indeed after) 1820 can only be guessed. If we regard the bread scale as the essential element, few examples are known before 1815; in the Webbs' list only Gloucestershire (1795), Chichester (1804–5), Ongar and Harlow (1801) and the Speenhamland scale itself come from the war years. But the bread scale, while it may have been on the whole the greatest innovation, was not the central element, which was simply the provision of relief to the ordinary labourer in employment. This was undoubtedly much more extensive than the use of scales, and in times of acute distress must have been more or less universal.[84] The crucial question is how often it was a mere temporary expedient, abandoned after the emergency, and how much it became the normal method of maintaining labourers. There are reasons why it tended to become the norm, but the facts for the early period remain obscure.

The effects were not necessarily always disastrous, especially if allowances were only one among other methods of relief. Thus in 1799 the vestry of Shipton Moyne adopted a crude bread scale and ordered 'that every poor person and family who shall prove to the satisfaction of the vestry that they use their utmost exertion to maintain themselves, shall receive such an allowance from the poor's rate, as together with their earnings, shall be equal to the above income', but allowances were combined with an elaborate scheme of incentives to labour, with insistence that women and children work in a house of industry or attend school, and with special arrangements for medical relief. Moreover a salaried assistant overseer was appointed to supervise matters. The whole arrangement, which Arthur Young described as a 'splendid

---

[83] For the Webbs' summary of the evidence see *The Old Poor Law*, pp. 180–2. The paucity of pamphlet comments on allowances between 1800 and 1815 is remarkable, but compare [Thomas Thompson], *Further Observations on . . . the Poor in the Town of Kingston upon Hull* (1801), p. 9 for complaints of a 'conspiracy' to keep down wages and an appeal to benevolent men to destroy it and emancipate the poor; and J. N. Brewer, *Some Thoughts* etc. (1807), p. 15 for a general complaint that farmers aped the standards of the gentry at the expense of the poor, by keeping wages low with the aid of the rates. For other references before 1815 see chapter V below.

[84] As early as 1801, however, Thompson alleged some geographical pattern: 'this pernicious system seems to keep the poor in some of the southern counties, in a state of ignorance and depravity far below those in the north of England' (*Further Observations* etc. p. 9).

example', may not have avoided all the alleged evils of the allowance system, but it probably mitigated most of them.[85]

It is thus too simple to cite the allowance system as 'the remedy adopted' for the problem of scarcity, and is certainly dangerous to attribute to the meeting at Speenhamland an overwhelming influence on the course of events. Among many remedies tried, with success or failure, it is possible to see systematic allowances developing out of old methods of outdoor relief, but only as one new thread in a tangled skein. When, in 1799–1800, Arthur Young called for more reports from correspondents on measures adopted in their parishes, allowances and scales were not prominent in the replies. Howlett complained that 'the farmers in the neighbourhood . . . fearing many inconveniences not unlikely to result from an advance of wages have made additional allowances according to their respective judgments or inclinations', but these were allowances from employers—in effect differential wage rates—and not from the parish. One correspondent in Cornwall said the poor received about one-quarter of their wage from the rates 'in the usual way', and another implied that the situation was the same in his area. But from Berkshire itself George Warde wrote not of the establishment of the allowance system, but of its abandonment.

In the year 1795 a table was established, calculated upon the consumption of families, according to their numbers; and what a man's earnings fell short of supply was made up in money by the rates. The consequence was, the ill-disposed . . . found they could do as well upon half a day's work as a whole one; and not only ceased to exert themselves, by which we calculated a serious loss of labour, but they soon learnt to demand the supply as a right. I believe it was then found most of this money went to the ale-house, instead of the baker. This year the relief is in bread, instead of money, assuming as a fact that the family earn what they ought to do.[86]

In fact the great majority of the correspondents wrote of relief in foodstuffs, especially in substitute foods, rather than in money. Soup and potatoes, and even beer substitutes (made from treacle and ginger), were the common topics, not bread scales or wage subsidies. Indeed the trend of opinion against associating bread and relief together was very strong; when Lord Dunstaville wrote from Bath asking what was wrong with ensuring that the poor could purchase their usual diet, he was quickly enlightened by Young and other correspondents.[87] There were a few hints that private charity was finding the prolonged demand

[85] *Annals*, XXIV. 151–5. In Speenhamland itself the evils of the system were checked by good management, at least by 1820; see the interesting *Comparative Statement of the Accounts of the Parish of Speen* etc. (1820). The copy in the Goldsmiths' Library includes a scale in MS. It should be noted that the deserving poor were paid more than the scale, and the indolent less; thus moral paternalism persisted.

[86] *Annals*, XXXIV. 654.

[87] *Ibid*. XXXIV. 263.

exhausting, and of an increasing reliance on the rates. No doubt this relief was often in the form of wage subsidies, but the lesson of scarcity was clearly against bread scales. Diversity of opinion was as evident in the counties and parishes as it was in Parliament, and the lack of agreement which frustrated Pitt was inherently unlikely to produce a system uniform enough to be called 'The justices' Poor Law'.

8. Scarcity and Charity

While Parliament and the magistracy discussed problems of relief in the years of scarcity, individuals continued to initiate schemes for voluntary action. In many parishes little distinction was made between relief under the law and private charity, magistrates, overseers, philanthropists and employers co-operating in arrangements which called on both public and private financial resources. Nevertheless, wherever private charity was extensive and systematic there was always a potential conflict between its aims and ideals and traditional patterns of public relief, and the charitable were likely to become outspoken critics of the Poor Law. The conclusion that the Poor Law should be partly or wholly superseded could be reached from a variety of premises, but a ground swell of opinion can be discerned moving towards the conviction that the only true solution to the problem of indigence was self-help, with or without the assistance of newly enlightened public policies. The circumstances of scarcity, and new doctrines of charity, reinforced an existing moral preference for self-help. There remained room for disagreement on how much assistance the poor needed in helping themselves, and whether that assistance should be material or moral. Land and cows on the one hand, and education on the other, emerged as powerful supplements or even rivals to relief by law. Count Rumford's science, Sir Thomas Bernard's evangelical morality, and Arthur Young's concern for agrarian reform all tended towards an emphasis on self-help rather than public charity.

It was inevitable, in a scarcity of bread-corn, that charity should be primarily concerned with the food of the poor, and that a programme of diet reform should develop from the search for substitute foodstuffs. The payment of subsidies on flour or bread was a common immediate reaction to the situation, but it was soon realised that such a policy was self-defeating in a real and prolonged scarcity, and much attention was given to the search for alternative foods. Young's circular of January 1795 asked for information concerning substitutes; by June he was deploring the folly of subsidising bread and urging the consumption of barley, oats and rice. A circular from the Board of Agriculture urged subsidies on fish, vegetables and whole meal rather than white bread, in July Lord Sheffield attacked wheat subsidies in his Charge at the Lewes Quarter Sessions, and Lord Waldegrave heralded the most fashionable of all substitutes when he arranged with the Lord Mayor for experiments with soup recipes. Replies to another circular from Young in October showed an increasing use of substitutes throughout the country, though the simple bread subsidy was still common. In November Parliament itself endorsed the cause of substitute foods, despite the protests of Fox and his followers that mixed bread was no diet for a labourer and their demand for drastic measures such as the establishment of public granaries.[88] Throughout the following years, and especially in the extreme scarcity of 1800–01, the drive for economy and substitute foods continued, and virtually all the active philanthropists of the time encouraged soups, rice puddings, potatoes and other varieties in the usual diet of the labourers. Only mixed flour and brown breads fell somewhat from favour, as it became clear that in the forms tried they were apt to disturb the bowels. Parliament, in 1801, made solemn agreements to save corn and to encourage substitutes, but abandoned its advocacy of mixed bread.[89]

The search for substitute foodstuffs soon developed into a general movement to reform the domestic economy of the labouring classes, but it had its critics. Earlier attacks on the extravagance of the poor had aroused men like Davies and Howlett to their defence; and in truth it was not nicety of taste but a desperate conservatism which made southern labourers cling to a diet of white bread as their birth-right. No doubt many members of the upper classes shared Lord Sheffield's stern view that 'if any wretches should be found so lost to all decency, and so blind as to revolt against the dispensations of providence, as to refuse the food proposed for their relief, the parish officers will be justified in refusing other succour'.[90] But many, perhaps most, of the philanthropists active in the cause of diet reform were more sympathetic towards the labourers' position, and realised that the poor must be

[88] Correspondence concerning substitutes may be found in *Annals*, XXIV, *passim*; see also W. M. Stern, 'The Bread Crisis in Britain 1795–6', *Economica*, 31 (1964), pp. 181–6.

[89] After 1796 the *Reports* of the Society for Bettering the Condition of the Poor supplement the *Annals* as a source for attempts at diet reform; see also [J. C. Lettsom], *Hints respecting the Distresses of the Poor* (1795) and *Hints designed to promote Beneficence* etc. (1797). The Royal Proclamation on Economy was printed in *Annals*, XXXVI. 194; and the debates on the high price of corn in *Parliamentary History*, xxxii. 235–42, and the Reports of Select Committees summarised in *Annals*, XXVI. 159, 208, 302. Amid so much economising it is pleasant to find that in 1798 Lord Egremont was still serving 'very fat' beef and pork pies to 328 families at his annual feast in Sussex (*Annals*, XXVIII. 255).

[90] *Annals*, XXV. 678; and compare J. L. and Barbara Hammond, *The Village Labourer*, I. 119–29.

led and not driven into new habits. Certainly this is true of the group which founded the Society for Bettering the Condition of the Poor at the end of 1796, and true also of a man who strongly influenced their views, the American-born Sir Benjamin Thompson, Count Rumford, authority on heat, light and philanthropy.

9. *Count Rumford and the Poor*

There were few important foreign influences on English attitudes to poverty and its relief in this period. Occasionally men looked north to Scotland for examples to support their arguments, and a few accounts of foreign practices were published. In 1832 the Royal Commissioners sought information on foreign systems, but did not wait for the replies before drawing up their Report. In the 1790s interest was shown in the views of Baron von Voght; he spent eighteen months in England, visiting prisons, workhouses and other 'monuments of British sensibility', and his *Account of the Management of the Poor in Hamburgh* was published in England in 1796 and again in 1817. On the whole Voght's work appealed mainly to champions of make-work schemes, though the Hamburg plan did include an elaborate system of district 'visiting' to test claims for relief which interested some English philanthropists and was influential in Scotland.[91] But among occasional foreign influences on thought and practice in these years Rumford's was the most important.

Born in Massachusetts in 1754, Rumford remained a loyalist during the Revolution, went to England, and earned the doubtful honour of an office under Lord George Germain. Peace found him a half-pay colonel with a knighthood; in 1784 he was given employment in Munich by the Elector of Bavaria. In the next ten years Thompson reformed the Bavarian army, established a system of poor relief and gave Munich its English Garden, while continuing the experiments in heat and light which earned him a place in the history of science. In 1791 he was made a count of the Holy Roman Empire, and it was thus a strangely transformed Massachusetts school-master who returned to

[91] Voght's *Account* appeared in *Annals*, XXIV, and was published separately in 1796 and 1817. See also the Bishop of Durham's account in *Reports*, II. 31–41; and on Voght's influence in Scotland Ewing's *Report of the Directors of the Town's Hospital of Glasgow* (1818). Voght's 'principle' of relief—'to reduce ... support lower than what any industrious man or woman ... could earn'—anticipated less eligibility. John Good's *Dissertation* (1798), a prize essay, made some use of Voght and other continental writers; for a later general description of foreign systems see *Collections Relative to the Systematic Relief of the Poor* etc. (1815). Thomas Chalmers was, after 1815, the great champion of Scottish ideas for English imitation; among English references to the Scottish system George Rose's, in his *Observations on the Poor Law* (1805), pp. 15–18, was better informed than most.

London on holiday in 1795, and published his *Experimental Essays* there early in the following year.[92] They, and their author, caused a considerable stir, earning the approval of so searching a critic as Jeremy Bentham and the honour of an indifferent sonnet in Rumford's praise by Coleridge. Between 1795 and 1802 Rumford spent much of his time in England and was prominent in philanthropic circles, though by the end of the period, when he retired to France, he had quarrelled with many of his English friends. Rumford was always something of an adventurer and a dilettante, but his achievements were considerable; certainly the 'scientific' veneer which overlaid much English charity of these years must be attributed largely to him, as must the passionate conviction of many Englishmen that the poor could thrive if only they would eat soup.

Rumford's measures against mendicity in Munich had been simple and dramatic. Having converted a disused factory into a military warehouse, he suddenly announced in 1790 that begging was forbidden, arrested all beggars, and offered them employment making uniforms for the army. Relief was also provided at home under the careful supervision of a new voluntary administrative hierarchy, and the system eventually included a hospital and a school. Children were taught, but were also set to work; indeed it was claimed that they cried until allowed to spin. (Since the only alternative was to sit still watching others work, the tears may have sprung from simple frustration.) The motto 'No Alms received here', emblazoned in gold above the workhouse door, proclaimed the principle of self-help. For the time being, at least, the whole scheme seemed extremely successful.[93]

In Rumford's teachings the Munich system served mainly as an example, a successful experiment. His aim was more comprehensive; he saw himself as a scientist with a mission to apply the discoveries of science to everyday life, and especially to the life of the poor. Thus the fruits of his researches into heat were a long series of designs for better fireplaces, grates, stoves, boilers and kettles, with appropriate recipes for soups, puddings and other economical fare. Brougham was later to ridicule the tiresome detail in which these panaceas were expounded by citing a passage in which Rumford 'gives a receipt for a

[92] References below are to Rumford's *Complete Works* published in Boston in 1874; the edition includes a *Memoir* by G. E. Ellis. See also W. J. Sparrow, *Knight of the White Eagle* (1964); E. Larsen, *An American in Europe* (1953); J. A. Thompson, *Count Rumford* (1935); T. C. Nichols, *Count Rumford, how he banished Beggary from Bavaria* (1873); and K. de Schweinitz, *England's Road to Social Security* (1943). Marx called Rumford 'an American humbug, the baronised Yankee' (*Capital*, III. 601).

[93] Rumford's *Works*, IV, include several accounts of the Munich reforms; for a description of the system when past its best see George Sinclair's essay in *The Philanthropist*, VII (1819), 281.

pudding, and then a page of description how to eat it'. And on economic questions Rumford was certainly not 'scientific' but extremely naïve: the poor should always be employed and never underpaid, but how to ensure a fair wage was never made clear; and he would not admit that the success of his employment scheme at Munich depended on capital from the military chest, and on an assured market from the army, while no less than a third of the running expenses were met from certain tolls and fines. The objections that pauper labour was inherently unprofitable could hardly be met by suggesting simply that its products be 'sent to some good market and sold'. He certainly wished charity to make use of the inventions of the physical sciences, but his basic assumptions concerning relief were not scientific but moral.

Much that Rumford wrote about indigence was commonplace, at least in terms of common English assumptions of the time. He believed that men would not work without fear of penalty or hopes of reward, and insisted that poor relief tended to weaken the spur to industry and to demoralise. Unlike earlier moralists, however, he placed more stress on rewards than on punishments, and showed an unusual consideration for the feelings of the poor:

In endeavouring to make the poor industrious, the utmost caution will be necessary to prevent their being disgusted. Their minds are commonly in a state of great irritation, the natural consequence of their sufferings . . . and their suspicions of everybody about them . . . are so deeply rooted that it is sometimes extremely difficult to soothe and calm the agitation of their minds, and gain their confidence. This can be soonest and most effectually done by kind, gentle usage.

Moreover this delicacy was to be extended even to the vicious:

To make vicious and abandoned people happy, it has generally been supposed necessary, *first*, to make them virtuous. But why not reverse the order! Why not make them first *happy*, and then virtuous! If happiness and virtue be *inseparable*, the end will be as certainly obtained by the one method as by the other.[94]

This was not perhaps the usual order of priority suggested by moralists though some English philanthropists were soon to support it.

Rumford made no detailed criticisms of the English Poor Law; he did, however, offer his Munich plan as a successful example to be followed. He insisted that schemes should be voluntary, and that governments should merely recommend a good plan to the public and repeal any laws which might hinder it. The supervising committee should be of the highest rank, assisted in administration by good

[94] *Works*, IV. 390, 385, 258. Rumford compared the management of the poor with horse-breaking; punishment should only be employed when good usage failed (p. 356).

people of the middle class; funds were to be voluntary and centralised in each city, and all methods of relief made uniform. New institutions, including workrooms and kitchens (serving four kinds of soup) should be built by subscription. It was essentially a plan for urban areas, but Rumford claimed that if overseers everywhere co-operated, a 'perfect system' for the management of the poor would gradually develop, the Poor Law could be superseded, and voluntary subscription replace the rates.[95] The plan was more elaborate than most schemes proposed by the charitable; perhaps for that reason it received little support in London. In 1798 Rumford wrote to Sir Thomas Bernard arguing that 'a well arranged House of Industry is much wanted in London', but Bernard and his friends were not admirers of workhouses. They were attracted rather to another of Rumford's institutional schemes, a proposal for establishing a centre 'for diffusing the knowledge and facilitating the introduction of useful mechanical inventions and improvements, and for teaching, by courses of philosophical lectures and experiments, the application of science to the common purposes of life'. With the support of a powerful committee the Royal Institution was established; Rumford was active in the venture, but by 1802 he had quarrelled with most of his associates in the venture, and he soon departed.[96]

One issue in the quarrel was the chief purpose of the venture. The Royal Institution became primarily a centre for lectures and research, while Rumford wanted it to be also (and perhaps mainly) a repository for his inventions. Two complete Rumford kitchens were to be built there—one suitable for gentlemen, another for farmers—and cottage fireplaces, utensils, stoves, looms and so on were all to be displayed. The Directors were quite eager to make these improvements known, but they had neither the resources nor the desire to build a museum, and were faced also with opposition from manufacturing interests. Rumford found it difficult to persuade tradesmen to adopt his designs, and almost impossible to convert the English to central heating, baths on the Roman model, or methods of making good coffee, though many a Victorian fireplace still holds its Rumford-style grate. His essay *Of Food and Particularly the Food of the Poor* was much more readily assimilated; it was largely responsible for the popularity of soup among the charitable, and if many a customer at a soup kitchen might have thought his section on the 'Pleasure of eating and Means of Increasing It' a joke in poor taste it is only fair to add that Rumford himself protested at the 'thin wash' so often offered to the poor.[97] There is no

[95] *Ibid.* IV. 328–42.
[96] Rumford's proposals and other documents are printed in *Works*, IV.
[97] *Ibid.* IV. 395–472, and compare III. 172.

doubt that Rumford hoped that the application of science to everyday life would make the poor more comfortable as well as more economical; on the other hand he certainly provided ammunition for those who argued that the discomfort of the poor came mainly from their own improvidence.

10. The S.B.C.P.

The Society for Bettering the Condition and Increasing the Comforts of the Poor was influenced by Rumford, but it rested also on a firm native tradition. Its principal founders were a group of evangelical churchmen, friends of William Wilberforce. These men founded societies as if by instinct, each with a specific aim; to reform manners, promote Christian knowledge, encourage good servants, build schools, abolish slavery, or bring experimental charity and evangelical morality to the labouring classes. In each society one or two members of the group took the lead in the management of its affairs. The guiding spirit of the S.B.C.P. was Sir Thomas Bernard, son of a former governor of Massachusetts and a conveyancer by profession until business success and a good marriage enabled him to retire to a life of good works. He was an indefatigable philanthropist, involving himself in the affairs of the Foundling Hospital, the Cancer Institution, a school for the Indigent Blind, the London Fever Hospital, a society for the protection of Climbing Boys and another for the Relief of Poor Neighbours in Distress, as well as the S.B.C.P. In the summer of 1796 Bernard, Wilberforce, the Bishop of Durham and the Hon. E. J. Eliot discussed the possibility of founding an organisation for bettering the condition of the poor. 'Joint labours,' they wrote in a circular letter to friends, 'have produced inventions etc. in other fields; why not in the science of promoting welfare?' They paid tribute to Rumford, and proposed that the new society examine 'everything that concerns the happiness of the poor' adding that one inducement to such an enterprise was the consideration that 'in proportion as we can multiply domestic comforts, in the same degree we may hope to promote the cause of morality and virtue'. At the end of the year the new Society was founded, with the King as patron and an illustrious committee of bishops, lay peers, Members of Parliament and philanthropists such as William Morton Pitt, Patrick Colquhoun and the Earl of Winchilsea. An appeal for public support produced a long list of respectable subscribers; Pitt and Paley each gave his guinea. Matthew Martin, later to be a prominent authority on London mendicity, was appointed paid secretary, but Bernard himself became the editor and principal author of the Society's publications.[98]

[98] *Reports*, I. 262–74.

The infant society acknowledged Rumford as its godfather by appointing him a life member of its Committee, but it had no intention of imitating his reforms at Munich. Propaganda was its aim: 'to collect information respecting the circumstances and situation of the poor, and the more effectual means of ameliorating their condition', so that the best schemes known anywhere in England might be extended to every parish, and the poor rates gradually reduced. The best means to attain these ends was 'the circulation of *useful* and *practical* information, derived from experience, and stated *briefly* and *plainly*'.[99] Thus the Society was not to conduct experiments, but to report on them; its assumptions were empirical, and its methods educational. Its interests were certainly wide, and Bernard showed a willingness to consider and assess the whole range of problems associated with the labourers' condition and both public and private charity. He was later to propose a general reform of the Poor Law, but in the first few years the Society looked rather at specific problems and devices.

Despite his empiricism concerning methods, Bernard had definite preconceptions concerning indigence and its relief. Like Rumford, he deplored compulsion in charity, whether for donors or receivers, and wished to appeal to the ambitions of the poor rather than to impose discipline on them. 'Let us give effect to that master spring of action, on which equally depends the prosperity of individuals and of empires— THE DESIRE IMPLANTED IN THE HUMAN BREAST OF BETTERING ITS CONDITION'. The principle which Adam Smith had revealed as the source of progress in commerce and industry must be allowed to operate among the poor. 'We may be told that we are endeavouring to serve those who *will not* be served', but give the poor useful and practical information, and time to understand it, and they will show 'as much good sense on the subject, as any other class of men in the Kingdom'. Compulsion had proved itself a failure in ensuring industrious habits, but already incentives such as piece-work had reduced idleness and drunkenness. The rich should avoid hypocrisy: 'I see nothing very exemplary in our own conduct, to induce me to doubt but that the poor are as good and as prudent, and as industrious, as we should have been in the same circumstances'.[100]

The poor needed, above all, prospects of advancement. In America Bernard had seen young men stimulated to industry by the opportunity of attaining wealth, and in England children should be enabled to earn their pittance, young persons their marriage portions, and every cottager adequate wages, with assurance of timely relief in adversity (without going to a workhouse: Bernard abhorred them). Bernard had a

[99] *Ibid.* I. 265.
[100] *Ibid.* I. xiii–xvi; II. 12–13.

prejudice against manufactures and trade, preferring 'productive industry at home', and assumed moreover that employment always could and should be created for the poor. Self-help was the ideal: it could attach the lower classes to their country as an asylum of happiness and liberty, and was a true bond of social union. But it must be guided, encouraged, by the upper classes and to a lesser extent by government. Rich men who did not assist the process were but *'paupers*, of an elevated and distinguished class'. Since it was not obvious how best to help self-help, and 'injudicious or misapplied liberality' could positively hinder it, it was essential to make 'the inquiry into all that concerns the POOR ... a SCIENCE', investigating *'practically*, and upon *system'*, as in all other sciences. For centuries projects to assist the poor had been offered, but the good effects had been limited by the fact that their basis was not fact, but speculation. Like many another avowed empiricist Bernard showed a surprising foreknowledge of the conclusions investigation might reach. His Preliminary Addresses to the Public confidently offered a programme of assistance to the poor, and foreshadowed almost all the expedients later to be given publicity by the Society; nevertheless he should be given credit for some flexibility of mind, even if the flexibility was limited by quite definite assumptions.[101]

The *Reports* published by the Society give an invaluable picture of the practice of private philanthropy, and to some extent public relief, in these years. No doubt Bernard printed, for the most part, those reports he approved, and the 'Observations' he appended to each report imposed some unity of view on the whole series, presumably the view shared by Bernard's friends and the most frequent contributors. But certainly the range of topics discussed was wide. Some essays were simple moral homilies addressed to either the rich or the poor; others were accounts of emergency relief in scarcity, though a permanent moral was usually drawn from them; a few dealt with public relief and its problems, though rarely systematically; several dealt with the problems of special groups, such as chimney sweeps or miners; others with devices such as the provision of land and cows for the poor; while some Reports discussed in fairly general terms questions of health, church attendance and education. After 1802 education became, indeed, a major preoccupation of Bernard's, and his interest was reflected in the *Reports;* by that time his views on the Poor Law had also become more definite.

In its moral exhortation to the Poor the Society stressed piety, purity,

---

[101] *Ibid.* II. 27–8; I. xii–xiii. For a contrast with Bernard's practical benevolence, see Adam Sibbit's ornate lament on moral degeneracy in his *Dissertation, Moral and Political* (1800), a work dedicated to Lord Eldon.

industry and of course self-help. It offered 'Twelve Golden Rules', 'for those who like to fare better than they now do, and at the same time to thrive and grow rich', axioms which could be fitted neatly into Weber's thesis on the Protestant Ethic and the Spirit of Capitalism. A ready penny fetches the best bargain; the best bargain is found in the open market; the government taxes us, so why tax ourselves with drunkenness or laziness; time is our most valuable property; industry and frugality are the best masters; marriage is honourable but it is improvident to enter it without savings; idolatry of the gin bottle is most disgraceful; charity begins at home; roasting and broiling waste meat, and the good wife makes stews; stoves should be covered and fires burned in narrow chimneys; 'sinning is a very expensive occupation'; 'let the poor man go to a cheap market on Saturday, to church on Sunday, and to work on Monday, and be twice as happy here and in Heaven'. All this was sincerely offered as the best gift the rich could bestow on the poor, and it should be noted that the Society printed a quite bitter complaint from Howlett on the inadequacies of upper-class treatment of the lower classes.[102]

The Society never doubted that the poor could attain the moral standards desired of them. After all, some had already succeeded: the widow left with fourteen children under fourteen who reared them with no help from the parish, the peasant who built himself a cottage with his own hands, and other similar paragons were presented as the new folk-heroes of the age. But Bernard and his friends recognised that practical encouragement to virtue was needed, and strongly approved the provision of rewards for outstanding sobriety and industry by various charitable societies. Friendly societies were also commended as aids to frugality and foresight, though there was nothing of the mere vulgar drinking club in the examples praised; all were the creation of upper class patrons, and all were on the highest moral plane. A female society gave considerable sums to its members on the birth of each child—provided it was born in wedlock—and a friendly society at Cork was praised for excluding from medical relief 'distemper contracted by lewdness'. Most elevated of all were the Sunday societies encouraged by the Bishop of Durham, in which the aged poor were repaid their contributions with interest provided they attended Church and a Bible meeting on Sundays and refused to countenance (even by watching) games and other improper practices on the Sabbath. Bernard thought this scheme much superior to the ordinary friendly society, with its drunken alehouse meetings.[103]

In all these projects religion was as much the concern of the

[102] *Ibid.* II, appendices vi and xii.
[103] *Ibid.* I, reports i, xxxvi; II, reports lix, lxvi.

philanthropists as was relief, though only one report dealt solely with a religious issue.[104] Certainly the aims of divine and earthly morality were combined in the Society's concern for education, and schools of industry to set infant hands to early labour were warmly praised. Winchilsea's spinning schools in Rutland improved morals; a school in Lewisham, Kent, did much in 'correcting the little pilfering habits of the infant poor'; and Gilpin's schools in the New Forest brought civilisation to an area 'where the children of the poor have too much disposition to partake of the natural wildness of the place'. The Society was in favour of general education, even for the poor, and Bernard deplored the 'absurd prejudices' against teaching the poor and 'the extraordinary supposition that an uneducated and neglected boy will prove an honest and useful man'. He praised Hannah More's Mendip schools, and later became a champion of Dr. Bell's method.[105]

The Society's views were advanced, in terms of the time, not only on education but also on health and medicine. Bernard himself wrote on the campaign against fever in Manchester, and if the Bishop of Durham's admonitions had been heeded every building in his diocese would have dripped perpetually with whitewash. Ladies were urged to take up medical charities. Perhaps the Society's best contribution to this cause was its reprinting of Dr. Haygarth's rules to prevent infection—admirable precepts, if a little primitive (when in doubt, blow the nose and spit on leaving the area)—and Dr. Ferriar's immensely practical and sympathetic advice on health to the poor of Manchester, together with his tract against superstitious practices in treatment of the dying.[106]

Among the evils Ferriar attacked in Manchester was the effect on the health of children of night work in the mills. The leaders of the Society were no great friends of the manufacturing interest, and soon took up the cause of factory regulation in the interests of children, and especially of apprentices. Bernard's favourable report on Dale's mills at New Lanark included a plea for regulation, and the group supported the factory act of 1801. Other causes which were likewise to become the object of philanthropic campaigns in the early nineteenth century also received attention: thus the sorry plight of the chimney-sweeping boys was recognised, though the Society did not seek abolition of the trade. Bernard wanted a society established to protect the boys; while the Bishop of Durham's writings on the problem emphasised the need for the distribution of soap and Testaments.[107] In urging better treatment

---

[104] Bernard's essay on free seating in a church near Bath (*ibid.* II, report lxiii).
[105] *Ibid.* I, reports iv, xxxvii; II, reports lxi, lxiv.
[106] *Ibid.* I, report xiii; II, reports xlv, lii, and appendices ii, iv, vii.
[107] *Ibid.* I, reports xix–xx; II, reports lvi, lxix and appendix xi.

for prisoners and the blind they were less original, though equally worthy. The Bishop of Durham and Thomas Gisborne also gave attention to the special problems of miners, recognising their unique position in society, and their many disabilities. Gisborne's remedies were mainly moral—more chapels, more Sunday Schools, fewer ale-houses, and stricter superintendence to reduce profanity—though he did recommend improved ventilation to make subterranean occupations salubrious, and urged that colliers be given gardens and thus 'habituated to the desire of acquiring permanent property'. He certainly approved the Duke of Bridgewater's benevolent but strict regimentation of his colliers near Manchester.[108]

Inevitably, in the years of scarcity, a large proportion of the early publications of the Society dealt not with the problems of special classes but with relief pure and simple. Most of the advice on relief was addressed to the charitable, or to the poor themselves, but some was aimed at overseers, revealing the Society's views on the Poor Law itself. Moreover the structure and methods of charitable societies set up under the auspices of the Society embodied important lessons for poor-law administration.

From the beginning, the Reports were frequently critical of the Poor Law as it existed. Bernard and his fellows opposed, in particular, the idea and practice of a harsh, deterrent Poor Law, especially one employing a workhouse test; even the great houses of industry were suspect. The workhouse was, to the Society, a crude instrument inimical to proper moral discrimination; and it was likely to be even worse when farmed. Even if workhouses were indispensable in some places, Bernard insisted that on no account should children be sent to them, but should be relieved at home and if possible sent to a parochial school. In general, in these years, Bernard assumed that the Elizabethan Act was a good old law, but that all harsh innovations such as workhouses and badging the poor were unworthy corruptions of it. The Society's creed of self-help and encouragement was basically incompatible with a universally deterrent system; the ideal Poor Law would be liberal, not harsh, though liberal with discrimination. It would give relief at home, to encourage self-sufficiency, relief which would be 'seasonable' and effect a 'permanent improvement' in the pauper's situation. Employment should be provided, rather than money, and the poor should receive 'the whole produce of their labour . . .; the earnings of the poor should be sacred and inviolate, in order to encourage them to work, and to exempt the character of their employers from the imputation of interested motives'. There was as

---

[108] *Ibid.* I, report v (on jails); II, report xliv (on the blind); I, report xxxi and appendix i (on miners).

yet no concern at the economic difficulties of make-work schemes, which were recommended as a moral regimen rather than as a source of profit to the parish. The reverse of this liberal, sympathetic relief to the worthy cottager was of course the scourging of the unworthy. The 'drones of society' must be punished, since 'it is due to the honest exertions of the industrious cottager, that, while he receives aid and encouragement, they should not escape censure'. A few stiff sentences passed on the worst offenders would elevate parochial morals wonderfully.[109]

In 1799 the Society published *Information for Overseers*, a selection of *Reports* in which a spinning school, a parish windmill, stewed ox-head, whitewash, rice puddings, Gilpin's comfortable poor house, cheap whole flour, and parish dinners were all offered to parochial officials as examples to imitate. In place of an introduction, Bernard's Charge at Stoke was reprinted, including the following admonition:

It is *your* duty, Sir, to be the GUARDIAN AND PROTECTOR OF THE POOR;—and as such, to provide employment for those who *can* work, and relief and support for those who *cannot*; to place the *young* in a way of obtaining an honest livelihood by their industry, and to enable the *aged* to close their labours and their life in peace and comfort.

In the execution of this office, it is your duty to consider how you may best *improve the situation of the poor* in your parish, so as to lessen the calls for parochial relief, and thereby to diminish your parish rate.—In this respect, much may be done by occasional aid and encouragement to parishioners with large families; much, by means of regular employment for children, either at home or in schools of industry, so as to fit them to be placed out in service at an early age;—and much, by a judicious management of your poorhouse, if you have one, and by making a proper distribution and separation between the honest and industrious who are driven thither by age, infirmity, or misfortune, and the idle and profligate, whose loose and vicious habits of life have made them a burthen and a disgrace to their parish.[110]

As yet there was no suggestion of a radical reform of the Poor Law. Bernard was later to offer it, but already he had made a significant innovation at Stoke, in the form of a detailed register of the poor, with all relevant points on their situation and relief tabulated. Discrimination in relief required knowledge of the recipients, requiring in turn records. But there was no substitute for personal knowledge, and by the example of Munich and Hamburg the best way to acquire this was through a system of upper-class visiting. The Bishop of Durham praised this element in Voght's Hamburg scheme; and Wilberforce

<hr/>

[109] *Ibid.* I, reports iii, vii and appendix iv (for criticism of workhouses); and xxvii (for advice on desirable practices).
[110] *Ibid.* I. 251–2.

himself noted visiting as an important factor in the success of a charitable society in Hull. Matthew Martin's investigations among London beggars, a work instigated by Bernard and soon to be continued by the Mendicity Society, relied on personal investigation. And in February 1799, at Clapham, in the very citadel of evangelicalism, the Rev. John Venn and his friends established a local society for bettering the condition of the poor, dividing the parish into eight districts, with visitors appointed for each and a general committee supervising relief. This form was urged as the ideal pattern for charitable activity, anticipating the Scottish-bred propaganda of Thomas Chalmers in the 1820s and the practice of the Charity Organisation Society later in the century. For the time being, however, the Society did not offer it as the basis of a comprehensive poor-law reform.[111]

11. *Land, Cows and Arthur Young*

The philanthropists of the Society for Bettering the Condition of the Poor were not alone in suggesting that labourers be given land to increase their permanent resources and thus facilitate self-help. Land for the poor, either for gardens or to graze cows, became a favourite suggestion in certain quarters, though it faced some active and much passive opposition. The idea was not new, and was to continue for another hundred years, but the scarcity of the 1790s gave it impetus; and in 1800 Arthur Young developed it into an elaborate plan which promised security for labourers and for the nation, and perhaps even the complete superseding of the Poor Law. This question of land for the poor was not of course simply a matter of charity, for very general issues of social justice and economic principle were inevitably involved.

Before 1795 the provision of land for the poor had been championed by the enemies of enclosure, and also by those who wished to encourage industrious habits by dangling the carrot of landed independence before the noses of the labourers. As Davies argued, 'hope is a cordial, of which the poor man has especially much need, . . . the fatal consequence of that policy, which deprives labouring people of the expectation of possessing any property in the soil, must be the extinction of every generous principle in their minds'.[112] The argument was strengthened when, quite early in the scarcity, it was pointed out that giving the poor a little land for potato gardens was a useful emergency measure. But

[111] *Ibid.* I, reports xl, xxxviii, xxii; II, report liv. Lettsom also recommended visiting and cited Rumford in support (*Hints* etc. (1797), pp. 9–13).

[112] D. Davies, *Case of the Labourer* etc. pp. 102–4. Davies deplored the repeal in 1775 of the Elizabethan Act forbidding the erection of cottages with less than four acres of land; the Act, however, had rarely been observed.

the real starting point of the movement for allotments was the publication early in 1796, of a letter by the Earl of Winchilsea *On the Advantages of Cottagers Renting Land*.[113] In Rutland, according to the Earl, the poor were allowed cow-gates and gardens, and were able to maintain themselves in comfort and respectability, even in time of scarcity; they lived well, were 'more fit to endure labour', and were 'more contented, and more attached to their situation, and acquired a sort of independence'. Moreover the poor rates in their villages remained as low as fourpence in the pound. The letter, forceful in argument and well illustrated with examples, concluded with an appeal for information on cottages, gardens and cows for the poor in other parts of the country. Correspondents who praised such schemes in the *Annals* included Nathaniel Kent, the expert in farm management, then agent for Lord Egremont. Sir Thomas Bernard threw the weight of the Society in support; he and the Bishop of Durham both visited Rutland and praised Winchilsea's activities.[114]

Not all comment was favourable. Bentham's criticisms of the cow clause in Pitt's Bill have already been noted. Even Bernard admitted a danger that the labourers concerned might cease to be labourers and try to rely on their cows and gardens, 'being transformed into little starving farmers from opulent thriving labourers'.[115] Other critics alleged the opposite fault, that the poor neglected their gardens, and were not worthy of them. Throughout the following century the movement to provide the poor with land had to meet such criticisms, and also the more serious bar of practical difficulties and vested interests. Where land was valuable, allotments could only be provided at the expense of the farmers or the landowner; shopkeepers were reluctant to see the poor in less need of their wares; and employers feared that independence would make them saucy. The strength of this opposition can be gauged in the reaction to Arthur Young's elaborate scheme of 1800–1.

Young was in some ways an unlikely person to put forward a scheme for peasant proprietorship to replace the Poor Law. Throughout his long campaign for the development of agriculture he had been the advocate of enclosure and the champion of the large farm, and had frequently criticised both the cottager and the labourer. He had

---

[113] Winchilsea's letter was also printed in *Annals*, XXVI. 227–45, and in part in *Reports*, I. 93–103. A later tract by Winchilsea may be found in *Reports* III (1802), 147–57. For earlier support for cottage gardens see *Annals*, XXV. 530 (a letter from Thomas Estcourt, a Wilts M.P.), and XXVI. 213.

[114] Comments on the scheme are scattered through the *Annals* and the *Reports* in these years. The Hammonds suggest that the practice of giving land to the poor was virtually restricted to Winchilsea's own estates (*Village Labourer*, I. 151) but argue from the evidence in the *Reports*, ignoring Young's more extensive material.

[115] *Reports*, II. 178.

brushed away complaints that labourers suffered from enclosure and the engrossing of farms, had attacked poor relief as 'pernicious to the good of the state, and detrimental to the poor themselves', and had blamed the indolence and extravagance of the poor, rather than insufficient wages and high prices for the increase of the poor rates.[116] It was the scarcity which changed his views; he remained an advocate of enclosure, of high prices for agriculture produce, and of a corn law, but his attitude to the poor became much more sympathetic.

This conversion sprang from fear as well as sympathy. Young was one of those in whom the French Revolution and the Revolutionary War inspired a political and social hysteria, clearly evident in his *Inquiry into the State of the Public Mind amongst the Lower Classes* (1798). Economic equality, that 'romantic phantom of imagination', was a delusory temptation dangled before the poor by 'those revolutionary spirits who are incessantly plotting the works of darkness' in a 'torrent of atheism, deism, irreligion and contempt of all duties, human and divine, which has pervaded the nation like a pestilence'. Young appealed for an ideological war against French Jacobins and English Radicals, religion leading the van; new churches should be built, shaped like theatres, with seats for the poor and with preachers trained in a simple style suitable for the populace. But he also showed concern lest the depressed condition of the labourers make them too susceptible to radical notions, and sought economic betterment to buttress religion in supporting the social structure.

From the beginnings of the scarcity in 1795, Young expressed the belief that wages should be higher. He spoke strongly against rioting, and preached a sermon on the inevitability of retrenchment in a scarcity, but freely admitted the right of the poor to relief in these circumstances. Although he warmly praised the philanthropy of the rich, he was convinced that more drastic steps were necessary. In 1799 he lamented that so many were forced into workhouses; in the next year he published a blistering essay *On the State of the Poor*. 'Do we merit the blessing of Divine Providence either at home or abroad while we feed our poor in such a manner? ... it is a disgrace to a Christian country.' Young soon revealed his main thesis by deploring the existence of waste lands while the people starved. 'Starving labourers with plenty of waste land, is a satire upon legislation. Give a man with ten children four acres and a half; that is a rood a head: he would contrive, with very little assistance, to hut himself upon it, and soon sow it with potatoes and cabbages, or grass for a cow; and the best interests of the

---

[116] *The Farmer's Letters to the People of England* (1767), p. 162; compare pp. 177–8 for a suggestion that relief be restricted to the impotent. Young also complained of the 'absurdity of the poor laws' in his *Political Arithmetic* (1774), p. 300.

nation would be promoted, while a disgraceful and immoral poverty, immoral in those who have the power to remove it, would be converted into comfort.'[117] Thus by 1800 Young's political fears, his concern at the distress of labourers, and his instinct for the extension of agriculture, had prepared his mind for the production of a great and comprehensive plan, and in March he drew together his views in a pamphlet called *The Question of Scarcity Plainly Stated*. The scarcity, Young claimed, was real, and was not the work of farmers or monopolising traders; hence the poor could be assured that they 'suffer from the hand of God alone'. The chief lesson of such a scarcity was the necessity of encouraging agriculture, especially by a General Enclosure Bill, but Young was no longer an uncritical enthusiast for enclosure. In the past enclosure had been mainly for pasture, producing food for the townsmen but not for the agricultural labourer; henceforth arable enclosure must be encouraged. And the rural poor should be benefited directly, by providing potato gardens of half an acre, and grazing for a cow, for all labourers with more than two children, either from newly enclosed wastes or by renting land. As yet nothing larger than potato gardens and grazing was urged, the aim being to make the poor less dependent on the wheat crop, but Young felt so strongly on the matter that he claimed that each labourer had the right to a certain sum in money relief until given his land. It was still a plan for auxiliary resources, not of peasant holdings; Young announced that he was drawing up a Bill to give the poor gardens, with the support of the Board of Agriculture, and called for comments from correspondents, as was his habit.

Some replies to his circular were enthusiastic, but by no means all. Dr. Hinton of Norfolk stressed the difficulties in giving the poor land: landlords would charge excessive rents, parish officers could not be trusted to distribute such patronage justly, and the poor were generally unworthy of such privileges, except on a probationary basis. Ruggles thought the scheme 'quixotic in the extreme': 'it smacks of an agrarian law'. Others asserted that poor with gardens lived in wretched squalor, or they 'got into an idle habit, and do not make good labourers'. But some, like Harries, were in favour of making the labourer 'comfortable and independent of his employer' and did not object if he took time off to work on his own land if he felt like it. Most of those who favoured the scheme wanted very small gardens only, objecting to anything like peasant holdings. Few calculated the cost; and replies did not suggest that many labourers in fact owned land, though some cited cases where they were 'amazingly better off' with gardens.[118]

Young was not deterred by criticism, or dependent on praise. In

[117] *Annals*, XXXIV. 186–91.
[118] *Ibid.* XXXVI, *passim* for replies to the circular.

1801 he prepared and published, in his *Inquiry into the Propriety of Applying Wastes to the Better Maintenance and Support of the Poor*, an even more elaborate plan.[119] Using his notes from his extensive tour of 1800, he marshalled examples from many counties to show that cottagers with access to land did not become paupers, even in scarcity. Young was not scrupulous in handling evidence, but his account of 48 parishes in Lincolnshire where 753 labourers and their families rented land for cows and made no claims on the rates at all was good prima facie evidence of the benefit of land to labourers. For the converse argument, that labourers without land became paupers, he pointed to newly enclosed parishes, in his new role as critic of enclosure as formerly practised. His indictment of its effects on the labourer has been much quoted, especially the lament of the unfortunate individual who once had a cow, and then had none. But he hastened to add that this suffering was not a necessary result of enclosure, which was still to be desired, and even asserted that loss of land merely offset the benefits of increased employment following enclosure. Enclosure was not to blame for pauperism; if the rates had risen as much in enclosed as in unenclosed parishes, this was shocking because they should have risen much less. Young was never as stern a critic of enclosure as some later historians suggest; it was still desirable, but should be carried out with the interests of the labourer in mind. Young no longer sought mere potato plots, which he referred to scathingly as 'little gardens', admitting that they were usually ill-kept. Instead the labourer should be given what amounted to a peasant holding, the actual size depending on the soil and the number of children in the family: a family of five would probably need seven acres, and so on up to fifteen acres for a family of twenty-one. The cost would be considerable, between £20 and £50 for each farmlet, depending on whether the land was rented or reclaimed from waste.

Young claimed that his scheme would not merely ease the burden of poor rates, but would in part supersede the Poor Law altogether. The poor were to be offered land only on condition that they took it 'in lieu of all future parish assistance'. It was thus a good investment for the parishes, which were to be empowered to borrow on the security of the rates to settle three families for every £100 of rates raised on the average in the years 1798–1800; the cost would be written off in twenty years, whereas it would cost £20 a year to maintain each family from the rates. Young had by this time raised his estimate of pauper numbers to five million (half the population); his plan could rapidly reduce this by half and remove for ever the danger that rates would swallow the whole

[119] Published in *ibid*. XXXVI. 497–652, and also separately.

rental of the land. Returning to practicality from this glorious vision, he begged that each parish at least experiment with one labourer, very fairly suggesting that men of average character be chosen, rather than the most sober and industrious in the village. But he stressed the urgency of the matter; the wastes would inevitably be enclosed, and if the opportunity were not taken to settle the poor on them soon, it would go for ever.

Thus the great advocate of enclosure, agricultural improvements and large farms proposed precisely that sort of peasant holding which was to be the scorn, and indeed the fear, of later political economists and poor-law reformers. His motives, however, were plain. He was genuinely perturbed at the increase in the rates, but also he had a real desire to improve the condition of the poor, and above all to strengthen their political and social loyalties. 'The great engine wherewith the poor may be governed and provided for the most easily and the most cheaply is property.' Peasant proprietors and large farmers could unite in demanding a corn law and high wheat prices, against the protests of mere townsmen. And the evil from which the labourers could be delivered was not simply indigence, but the demoralising effects of the Poor Law itself. The Poor Law encouraged improvidence, by making the poor dependent on the parish rather than on their own efforts; in twenty years their aversion to accepting relief had been quite overcome, and the burden of the rates had forced many of the small ratepayers into the pauper class. Each time high prices forced the rates up, they did not fall to their former level, for pauperism was a progressive social disease, fruit of 'a struggle between the pauper and the parish, the one to do as little and to receive as much as possible, and the other to pay by no rule but the summons and order of the justice', a struggle of which indolence and insubordination were the natural outcome:

Go to an alehouse kitchen of an old enclosed county, and there you will see the origin of poverty and poor rates. For whom are they to be sober? For whom are they to save? (Such are their questions.) For the parish? If I am diligent, shall I have leave to build a cottage? If I am sober, shall I have land for a cow? If I am frugal, will I have half an acre of potatoes? You offer no motives; you have nothing but a parish officer and a workhouse!— Bring me another pot—[120]

If Young really hoped that his scheme would be adopted, his optimism must have been greater than usual. He could not even carry the Board of Agriculture with him, Lord Carrington, the President, insisting that the plan be published simply as a private document.[121]

[120] *Ibid.* XXXVI. 508–9.
[121] In 1801 the Board offered a Gold Medal for the best scheme for giving land to cottagers, but did not award it to Young (*Communications to the Board of Agriculture*, III (1802), xix).

Sinclair, President until 1798, was a convert, publishing a plan of his own for a model village in which each labourer had three acres of arable land and pasture for a cow. But the General Enclosure Act passed in 1801 was not modified in the slightest by Young's plea, though there is evidence that the interests of the poor were considered more carefully in at least some subsequent enclosures. Even Young's propaganda misfired. In 1801 he commissioned Robert Gourlay to carry out an inquiry into the state of the cottagers in the counties of Lincoln and Rutland, and rushed his findings into print as 'a Result and Proof of the Cottage System'.[122] But Thomas Smith soon made a long attack on Gourlay's Report, alleging inaccuracy and elementary mistakes, such as including towns in the parishes chosen for unfavourable comparison. Young defended Gourlay tersely and rudely, but Gourlay's own reply bitterly attacked Young for publishing his reports before they were completed or digested. Young's impatience to have proof had betrayed him.[123]

Nevertheless Young and others continued to urge that the poor be given land, and Estcourt even succeeded in persuading most of his labourers to foreswear poor relief for ever in return for it.[124] The S.B.C.P. did not altogether abandon support, and some of its members later formed the Labourers' Friend Society specifically to campaign for allotments of land for the poor, a campaign which continued with indifferent success long after the passing of the 1834 Poor Law Amendment Act.[125] But the Malthusians had little time for such schemes (and Malthus himself none at all for Young's Plan), and the opposition of village interests persisted. When Cobbett proposed to the vestry of Bishops Waltham that they should 'ask the Bishop to grant an acre of waste land to every married labourer . . . all . . . but the village schoolmaster voted against it, on the ground . . . that it would make the men "too saucy", that they would "breed more children" and "want higher wages".'[126] Indeed the effect of Young's campaign may well have been to aid the abolitionist cause, since many of his readers would note his strictures on the Poor Law while rejecting his alternative. The years of

[122] Annals, XXXVII. 514–49, 577–97.
[123] Ibid. XXXIX. 240–51 for Smith's attack, and 251–69 for Gourlay's reply. Gourlay later became a forceful if eccentric writer on the Poor Law.
[124] Ibid. XLIII. 1–8, 289–99; and compare Estcourt's An Account of the Result etc. (1804). All but four aged labourers accepted the exchange; and 'the farmers of this parish allow they never had their work better done'. For reports of experiments by Sir William Pulteney and Thomas Babington, see Annals, XLIV. 97, 101; and compare J. C. Curwen, Hints etc. (1808), pp. 45–163.
[125] On the Labourers' Friend Society see especially The Labourers' Friend (1835), a selection from publications of earlier years, including a history of the Society.
[126] Quoted by J. L. and Barbara Hammond, The Village Labourer, I. 156.

scarcity undoubtedly brought a considerable extension of relief under the old system, and perhaps even—though this is more doubtful—important new developments in its forms of operation, but they also brought it into increasing dispute. Debates on Whitbread's and Pitt's bills emphasised the need for reform of the Poor Law, but revealed above all the difficulties of achieving it. Distress gave great impetus to private charity and to particular schemes of social and economic change, but most assumed that some new departure must be made from the principles believed to be inherent in the old Poor Law. Radical reform, if not abolition, was the lesson to be drawn by those who gave a general and more theoretical examination of the problem of indigence and its relief.

IV

Eden, Bentham and Malthus

1. *Three Major Writers*

A MONG the host of authors who wrote about indigence and the Poor Law in the years of scarcity three stand out as major contributors to the continuing debate on the subject. Sir Frederick Morton Eden published *The State of the Poor* in 1797; it was for the most part a compilation of fact and comment rather than a treatise, but Eden's cautious general discussion 'Of National Establishments for the Maintenance of the Poor' included arguments of importance, and usefully reveals the views of a moderate and well-informed man on the eve of the Malthusian onslaught on the principles of public relief. The first edition of Malthus's *Essay on the Principle of Population* appeared in the following year. If Eden was a patient collector of facts, diffident in speculation, the first edition of the *Essay* was simply an argument virtually innocent of evidence, indefatigable though Malthus was to be in packing later editions with illustrative material and in elaborating his indictment of the Poor Law. The third major writer active in these years was Jeremy Bentham, the constructor of programmes of utilitarian reform so vast and detailed that they were rarely finished and as rarely read. In subsequent debate on poverty Eden was often cited as a learned authority, of probity and weight. Malthus became the most famous protagonist of all, the acknowledged leader of the attack on the Poor Law, and the object of unbridled praise and criticism. Bentham's influence, in this as in so many other matters, is an enigma, frequently asserted but rarely proved. No one else analysed the problem of indigence with such intellectual rigour, or proposed a solution of such complexity. And yet, paradoxically, Bentham's reputation as an important figure in the history of poor relief exists in spite of his writings on the subject rather than because of them.

106

The reason for this is simple. The Poor Law Amendment Act of 1834 is one of those pieces of nineteenth-century legislation in which historians discern (or deny) the influence of Bentham the great advocate of legal and administrative reform. But Bentham's actual writings on pauperism almost all date from the 1790s, and might seem remote indeed from the proceedings and principles of 1834. They have been dismissed as just another of the numerous workhouse schemes of the eighteenth century, though of more ingenuity than most.[1] And the dismissal is almost justified, if we judge simply by Bentham's published work on the subject. *Pauper Management Improved,* which appeared in 1797, was but the sketch of such a plan, and the discussions of indigence in the *Theory of Legislation* of 1802 and in the *Constitutional Code* of 1830 were brief, though important; the great bulk of Bentham's writings on pauperism remains in manuscript. A considerable bulk it is, including several quite separate works as well as the unpublished parts of *Pauper Management Improved.* Inspired by the scarcity of 1795 to give his attention to the condition of the poor, Bentham produced, in rapid succession, an essay on the *Independent Labourer,* three *Essays on the Poor Laws,* and two massive works, *Pauper Systems Compared* and *Pauper Management Improved,* interrupting their composition in 1797 to produce his *Observations* on Pitt's Bill. The Pauper Plan, as published, was thus but a part of a much more comprehensive study of the whole subject.[2]

Unpublished books can be of interest, but are not usually of historical importance: Leslie Stephen contended that 'Bentham's principles are sufficiently stated in his published works, and the papers which have been reposing in the cellars of University College can have had no influence on the world'.[3] But Bentham had the habit of distributing his work in manuscript among men of influence, and Stephen himself granted historical importance to the unpublished *Observations* on Pitt's Bill. Bentham even claimed that he had converted Pitt and Dundas to

---

[1] For example by S. E. Finer in his *Life and Times of Sir Edwin Chadwick* (1952), pp. 43–4n. Bentham's works on pauperism received summary treatment in L. Stephen, *The English Utilitarians* (1900), I. 203, and in E. Halevy, *The Growth of Philosophic Radicalism* (22nd ed. 1949), pp. 232–4; for a brief but perceptive reference see C. W. Everett, 'The Constitutional Code of Jeremy Bentham', *Jeremy Bentham Bicentenary Celebrations* 1948, p. 14.

[2] *Pauper Management Improved* first appeared in the *Annals of Agriculture,* 1797–8; references below are to the separate publication of 1812. The *Theory of Legislation* was prepared by Bentham's Swiss collaborator Dumont and published in French; references below are to C. K. Ogden's edition of R. Hildreth's translation (1931). The bulk of the relevant MSS are in the Bentham Papers, University College, London, but the Bentham Papers in the British Museum and the Dumont Papers in Geneva include further material.

[3] L. Stephen, *op. cit.* I. 326.

his views, and that only the opposition of George III foiled his great scheme for poor-law reform. In 1830, in his bitter and nostalgic *History of the War between Jeremy Bentham and George III, by one of the Belligerents*, he blamed the monarch for the frustration of both the Pauper Plan and the more famous Panopticon prison. 'But for George the Third, all the prisoners in England would, years ago, have been under my Management. But for George the Third, all the paupers in the country would, long ago, have been under my Management.'[4] This was the exaggeration of dotage; there was never any real hope (or fear) that the Pauper Plan would be adopted. But the evidence of backstairs work justifies some attention to manuscripts as well as published work.

Nevertheless the chief justification for setting out Bentham's views on pauperism at length is their intrinsic interest. There are many surprising things in the enormous mass of material. Bentham was a system builder, and we would expect to find a whole hierarchy of principles expounded, linking the great principle of utility at the top to the most detailed rules of management. Since the systems required a careful definition of terms and the study of causes and effects in the real world, we would expect also much making of fine distinctions and many attempts to explain and predict, with attention to facts. But we might not expect anticipations of later wage theories in the discussion of independent labourers; or a refutation of much of the Malthusian case against the Poor Law before Malthus himself had thought of it; or a final justification of a legal system of relief by that very principle of less eligibility which the Royal Commission of 1832 was later to use for the same purpose. And we can certainly be surprised at the scope of Bentham's investigations, his painstaking analysis of the statistics he wanted (and could not find) and his detailed and systematic consideration of almost every aspect of social and economic life.

The Plan itself is remarkable. Beginning as a simple adaptation of the Panopticon Prison to workhouses, it grew into an elaborate engine for general social improvement. The 250 Houses of Industry, in a network all over England, run by a Joint-Stock Company, were to do much more than merely relieve the 2,000 paupers each would hold. They would be managed, not by the usual regulations, but according to the most elaborate principles of administration. They would employ their paupers, not in the usual pale imitations of free industry, but in the mass production of new inventions (for the creation of a system of national railways, for example). And stretching far beyond management, relief and employment, the system would provide a whole range of social services—national education, a medical service, labour

[4] J. Bentham, *Works* (ed. Bowring), XI. 96–7.

exchanges, savings banks, insurance against unemployment and old age, and a number of other 'collateral benefits', including opportunities for radical social experiments. All this was worked out in very great detail; the ageing bachelor philosopher even wrote a lengthy memorandum on care of children under the age of two.

The Pauper Plan grew into a Utopia, and is not the least interesting of the species. If, in much of his work, Bentham preserved a delicate equilibrium between economic liberalism and public planning, in this scheme the planner ran riot. Enough systematic regimentation was involved to make the plan horrible to modern minds: Bentham the Big Brother was no doubt benevolent in intent, but was as dogmatically authoritarian as most of the kind. Not always, perhaps. Flashes of a third Bentham appear behind the planner and the defender of free capitalist competition, Bentham the patron of co-operation between free individuals. The Pauper Plan became, in the end, a pattern for a new society, to exist within a free capitalist economy; a society which would be planned, but with a productive system based on mutual co-operation; the whole serving to remedy the flaws in the free economy, and to lead it in the search for knowledge and social improvement. The Panopticon Penitentiary may have been the project closest to Bentham's heart, but the Panopticon Poor Plan was the more elaborate and the more original.

Whatever the intrinsic interest or possible influence of Bentham's writings on poverty and indigence, it must be admitted that for every reference to him in later discussion of the Poor Law there were twenty to Malthus. If we judge influence by fame, then Malthus's contribution to shaping opinion on pauperism was incomparable. He did not invent abolitionism, but he gave it form and coherence, while circumstances gave it a powerful appeal. Whether he should also be credited with a creative, as well as a destructive, influence on reform is another matter. Paternity of the new Poor Law is often attributed to him, but his own legislative recommendations did not go beyond gradual abolition, and few inklings of the Principles of 1834 can be found in his writings. Malthus may be regarded as the grandfather of the Amendment Act, since the principles of the reform meant little except in relation to the creed of abolitionism; but its immediate sponsors were Malthusians of the second generation, decidedly heretical if still respectful sons.

It is not always the clearest arguments which are most influential, and there are major difficulties in expounding and assessing Malthus's views. The first might be called his theoretical evasiveness. Malthus could present a general argument with great force, and occasionally revealed flashes of insight into difficult problems, but he seldom maintained consistency throughout a long and complex thesis. The accretions which the *Essay* received in its many editions made it a mine from which various and conflicting propositions can be extracted, though careful reading can reduce the variants within a more or less limited range. But textual analysis can do little to overcome another major difficulty in interpretation, the question of moral tone. Malthus's writings provoke prejudices; even today few can write about him without undue animus or admiration. The extreme vilification by early critics—the allegations that Malthus was a hard-hearted wretch who thought misery desirable as well as inevitable, defended inequality and oppression, and opposed all schemes for human betterment and for present relief—was based on ignorance, or at least on misunderstanding and exaggeration. It can now be agreed that Malthus was no misanthrope, but a kind and benevolent man in his personal relationships, and quite sincere in his protestations that he deplored misery and welcomed such improvement he thought possible. But the same can not be said of all early Malthusians, of the men who welcomed the principle of population as social conservatism pure and simple; and a man gets the disciples he deserves. There was a definite ambivalance in his writings. Malthus the sincere philanthropist was also the author of passages of harsh dogmatism and extraordinary insensitivity to human sufferings. Were such passages lapses, arising from a passion to defend and elaborate principles so great that humanity was forgotten, or were they the revelations of the real man?

The polemical origin of the Malthusian writings was in part responsible for both the theoretical inconsistencies and the moral ambivalence. The *Essay* of 1798 was an unashamed polemic against Godwin and others; that of 1803, while expanded into a treatise, was still 'weakened as a constructive scientific work' by being 'more provocative than necessary'.[5] The search for truth still seemed subordinate to the demands of controversy, and radical critics discerned the cloven hoof of an arch-conservative beneath the academic gown. The whole argument seemed too convenient a defence of the status quo:

It was not an uncomfortable doctrine for statesmen, not one which they would be disposed to visit with much severity of criticism, which represented the happiness of a people as the work of its government, which made their wealth and their comforts to flow from the wisdom of their rulers, but taught that misery and want were the mere inflictions of Providence: evils inevitably inherent in our nature, which could not be relieved, no not even mitigated by any institutions of men.[6]

[5] J. A. Field, 'The Malthusian Controversy in England', in *Essays on Population* etc. (1931), p. 2. Not until the *Principles of Political Economy* (1820) or the *Summary View* etc. (1830) did the Malthusian argument appear shorn of polemical asides.
[6] 'Piercy Ravenstone', *A Few Doubts* etc. (1821), p. 9.

This was a fair comment on some Malthusians, but it certainly exaggerated Malthus's own conservatism. Malthus was no common anti-Jacobin, and no whole-hearted enthusiast for the existing order. He looked like one, because he so consistently opposed all methods of improvement except his own. Against Godwin's prophecy of a virtuous, equal and perfect social state he produced, in 1798, an almost completely negative refutation, but by 1803 he was offering a way to the alleviation of distress, though a strait and narrow one indeed. His fanaticism for his one great idea, and his single remedy, made him seem a very wet blanket in discussion of other more popular avenues to advancement. But his rejection of claims that mere political reform could bring prosperity for all should not be allowed to conceal his own political liberalism, his concern for civil liberty, and his friendship with at least some radicals. Similarly his systematic pricking of so many bubbles among the various plans for the betterment of the poor may seem monotonously gloomy, but he did in fact offer an alternative, though a difficult one. Malthus was a pessimist, but probably not, like some, a believer in the utility of misery.[7] And despite Ravenstone's claim that the upper classes took him to their bosoms with gratitude, initial suspicion of Malthusianism was almost as evident among conservatives as among radicals. Like others among the political economists of his day, Malthus was unpopular with the left because he seemed to defend existing institutions, but unpopular also with the right for defending them for the wrong reasons. Firebrands like Windham and Pulteney might welcome the principle of population as the justification of social order, but they were more outspoken and more fond of paradox than most of their class. Malthus and his principle were too 'speculative' for men who assumed existing society justified by tradition and theology; defending society as a necessary evil was almost as bad as attacking it as an unnecessary evil. In time the conservatives had second thoughts, but it is significant that for a long while the *Quarterly Review* was as hostile as Cobbett's *Political Register*. A man so sniped at from both hedgerows could not have been far from the middle of the road.

2. *Eden and the Poor Law*

Eden is perhaps of minor importance as a theorist, at least in comparison with Bentham or Malthus. Nevertheless, some survey of his views is a necessary preliminary to a more detailed examination of

---

[7] Except, it must be admitted, as a goad to spur men to avoid it by virtue. This is a crucial point in assessing Malthus, and a difficult one; passages can certainly be quoted (especially from the first *Essay*) showing misery to be relatively if not absolutely desirable.

theirs; the originality of thinkers can only be assessed against the accepted assumptions of their times, and Eden, like so many lesser writers, reveals current assumptions the more clearly for his very lack of originality.[8] His general views on political economy and his moral assumptions concerning self-help were very characteristic of his time, although he showed some individuality in their application to particular circumstances.

Eden was a disciple of Adam Smith, and his admiration for the system of economic liberty was fervent and uncritical. All government regulation in economic affairs might be presumed harmful, unless it had positive justification; Elizabethan regulations, of which the Poor Law was a part, were an aspect of that public servitude which it was progress to throw off. Only liberty could bring progress, and if progress imposed occasional suffering on individuals, they must be sacrificed to the good of the majority. On the whole it was not innovation, but the lack of it, which caused indigence, a situation which could only be made worse by misguided attempts to interfere with the free market in land and labour. Wastes and commons should be enclosed and improved: as they stood they were waste indeed. By all means give labourers and cottagers gardens, but peasant proprietorship was not the road to progress. Only large farms could bring increased productivity; and earnings, comfort and civil liberty could all be expected to advance together. The humblest labourer had as great an interest in an 'improving' state of society as the richest farmer or capitalist.[9]

To a man with these assumptions, the element of regulation in the Poor Laws could not be attractive. It was this aspect, and not the burden of the rates, which Eden most deplored. In fact he did not think the burden crushing, denying that it had increased more rapidly than trade or national expenditure. And he could see that there were economic advantages in relieving distress, as well as a moral obligation. Rescuing the infant poor augmented useful population—he assumed an increase in population to be an unmixed blessing—and curing the sick increased the productive powers of the nation. He would readily admit that the aged had a fair right to assistance, and would even recognise a

[8] Marx described Eden as 'the only disciple of Adam Smith during the eighteenth century that produced any work of importance'; he dismissed Malthus's first *Essay* as a 'schoolboyish, superficial plagiary' (*Capital*, I.616). Eden, the second baronet and son of a governor of Maryland, was thirty-one when *The State of the Poor* appeared. He later became chairman of the Globe Insurance Company, and died in 1809.

[9] The benefits of economic liberty are stressed continually in volume I of *The State of the Poor*; whereas Smith saw some social disadvantages in too highly developed a division of labour, Eden thought his criticism 'too highly coloured' (I. 420).

prima facie right to employment for the able-bodied. Perhaps too the idle deserved to be compelled to labour. But were these questions for government, or for private employers and philanthropists? In all civilised countries, he conceded, governments recognised some obligation in the matter. In defence of the Poor Law, it might be said that the poor could not maintain themselves without unremitting labour, and were exposed to unforeseeable calamities which might make labour impossible. The rich were obliged, both by nature and the origin of property, to relieve just claims, and it was not just that the burden should fall only on the benevolent. How, without a Poor Law, could it be guaranteed that man would not perish from want? And how could mendicity and vagrancy be checked, or the clamorous and least deserving poor be prevented from gaining more relief than the modest and deserving?[10]

While admitting some force to these arguments, Eden complained that the Poor Law undertook more than could be justified on these principles. For example there was the attempt to create employment, by 'setting the poor on work', which smacked of the old, bad doctrines of political economy. Eden lucidly expounded the view that parish employment could only be provided in competition with free: even an unprofitable workhouse distorted the market, 'and a poor industrious manufacturer will, perhaps, often have the mortification to reflect, that, in contributing his portion of Poor's Rate, he is helping the parish to undo him'. Moreover the expenditure of capital on make-work schemes diverted it from its natural channels, and ultimately diminished its amount. 'The capital stock of every society, if left to its free course, will be divided among different employments, in the proportion that is most agreeable to the public interest, by the private views of individuals. When it is thus employed, it will accumulate: and it is its accumulation only, which can afford regular and progressive employment to industry.' Thus make-work schemes were a delusion, likely to have effects precisely opposite to those intended.[11] Lacking Malthus's concern for the balance of population and resources, Eden did not add the Malthusian point that the funds for the maintenance of labour were too limited to guarantee relief as well as employment.

Eden did object to relief for the able-bodied, not on Malthusian grounds but because it hindered self-improvement. The right to relief was not one of the true rights of men, which Eden followed Burke in defining as security of property, authority in the family, and 'instruction in life and consolation in death'. True rights assisted the desire to

[10] *Ibid.* I. 411–6. Eden cited Bishop Woodward of Cloyne, and not Paley, in support of the argument from the origin of property.
[11] *Ibid.* I. 467–8.

better oneself, while the spurious right to relief hindered it. Others might deny that the poor were tempted into idleness by the refuge of the rates, but Eden claimed he had proof: parishes which had large charitable bequests also had high poor rates, and thus did ease in obtaining relief increase the demand for it. A legal provision for the poor weakened 'the strongest tie of civil society, the desire of acquiring property; for it declares, that, whether a man is industrious or idle, his most pressing difficulties, the necessity of food, lodging, and cloathing, shall be provided for'.[12] The Poor Law did not even distribute the burden of relief fairly, as its defenders claimed. In practice the rate was a land tax, and an inequitable one because it did not allow for differences in the productivity of the land. A tax on all property, or on consumption, would be more just, but Eden could not see how it could be assessed or collected. In any case the benevolent would still suffer, because the Poor Law did not make private charity unnecessary; charities disbursed some six million pounds over and above the rates, Eden calculated. And public relief did not prevent mendicity: Scotland's beggars were not more numerous than England's—a claim some observers disputed—and if Ireland was more thickly infested with them its 'languid state of industry' and not the absence of a Poor Law was the cause.[13]

Thus, to Eden, the whole system was of very doubtful value. Public employment was quite improper; relief weakened ambition and personal obligation; the rate could only be burthensome and unequal; and one could expect neither efficiency nor honesty in the administration of relief by mere parochial officers. 'Upon the whole, therefore, there seem to be just grounds for concluding that the sum of good to be expected from the establishment of a compulsory maintenance for the Poor, will be far outbalanced by the sum of evil it will inevitably create.' Malthus did not need to add many points to the argument to convert it from moderate disapprobation to a prediction of impending calamity. Eden, lacking that sense of calamity, thought the case conclusive against founding a poor law where none existed, but never suggested that England should abolish the system she was saddled with. 'Faulty and defective as our Poor System may be in its original constitution, and in its modern ramifications, he must be a bold and rash political projector, who should propose to level it to the ground. . . . No temperate political speculatist of the present day, therefore, has ventured to recommend the wholly lopping of this vast member of our system of jurisprudence.'[14]

It was, however, imperative that the Poor Law be reformed, to

[12] *Ibid.* I. 444–50.
[13] *Ibid.* I. 451–66.
[14] *Ibid.* I. 467, 470.

check idleness and immorality and to give the labourer 'full possession of his right to exercise his industry in the situation and manner most agreeable to himself'. Most of the ideas for reform popular earlier in the century had been discredited: 'the public mind is once more afloat, and like some dove sent out from the ark, anxiously solicitous to find, if it be possible, amid the surrounding confusion, some spot of permanent tranquility, on which the nation may rest'. Eden himself could suggest no such refuge, and was content to map the confusion in detail in the thick volume of parochial reports. As a disciple of Adam Smith he might have been expected to seek changes in the Law of Settlement, but Howlett had convinced him that Smith had exaggerated its effects and he offered no suggestions for its further reform; for the rest, his long account of eighteenth-century schemes for reform was critical, but rarely constructive. Pitt's plan was treated as the aberration of a great mind. No general reform could be successful without an investigation even wider than Eden's own, and until it was undertaken he could suggest only a few minor administrative changes. He did set his face against all extensions to the system, such as allowances in aid of wages, and made a proposal to impose a maximum on the rates, an idea later to be quite popular as an alternative to abolition. Like the Charity Organisation Society a century later, Eden hoped for a Poor Law which would provide no more than a back-stop for private charity, with the compulsion of law 'merely confined to the removal of extreme wants, in cases of the most urgent necessity'.[15]

In the debate concerning the adequacy of the labourer's resources to maintain a life of reasonable comfort Eden aligned himself firmly with the optimists, Ruggles and Rumford, against Davies and Howlett. The tables of labourers' income and expenditure he collected showed more deficits than surpluses, but Eden asserted that labourers always understated their earnings, from fear that wages might be reduced. He admitted that his evidence was incomplete, but that did not prevent him preaching a sermon. His theme was the superior economy of the northern labourer compared with the southern: labourers in Cumberland earned less than those of Hertfordshire, but lived much more cheaply and (he alleged) much more comfortably. Wages were fixed by economic laws; the variable factor was the use made of them, and they would certainly be adequate if only labourers would take to heart the good advice presented to them in the long chapter on the 'Diet, Dress, Fuel and Habitations of the Labouring Classes':

It is not probable, that the arguments of philanthropists ever will have much weight in persuading the great mass of employers to increase the wages

[15] *Ibid.* I. v–vi, 297–8, 479–83, 484–90.

of the employed; for it is by imperious circumstances alone . . . that the demands of the one, and the concessions of the other, are regulated. . . . The poor should not be deceived: the best relief they can receive must come from themselves. Were the Rates once limited, the price of labour would necessarily advance. To expend what labour actually produces, in the most beneficial manner for the labourer, depends entirely on good management and economy.[16]

Eden's moral preferences were, of course, as much involved in this argument as his economic theories. The Hammonds make much of the cheerlessness of a moral code which could praise Anne Strudwick, paragon of economy and repository of all the least amiable virtues, as the heroine of frugality. But that particular illustration exaggerated Eden's puritanism; he approved of recreation, even on Sundays, and could even see good coming out of those reprehensible celebrations, friendly societies' annual feasts. (If feasts were not an aid to virtue, why were collections at church smaller than the sums received after charitable dinners at the London Tavern?) As for friendly societies as an aid to self-help, the future chairman of the Globe Insurance Company found them more beneficial to the poor than any act of parliament. Eden took their success as further proof that labourers' resources were adequate for their maintenance; why, then, should they not replace the Poor Law? He discussed the problem of compulsory contributory schemes with much discernment, and decided that compulsion was both impracticable and undesirable, although he unearthed two interesting examples of contributory schemes established by law. On balance, this was a sphere not for governmental intervention but for encouragement by enlightened philanthropists, and even they should realise that 'these institutions do not aim at *perfection*, but *improvement* . . . if they cannot correct the inclination (which is too often caused by hard labour) for conviviality and dissipation, they at least convert a vicious propensity into a useful instrument of economy and industry. . . .'[17] Eden may have been dogmatic in his economic theory, and his optimism may have led him to underestimate the sufferings of some at least of the labourers, but he was more sympathetic to lower-class values than many of his contemporaries.

The State of the Poor was a work of such extraordinary diligence that its influence was bound to be considerable. Historians have used Eden's material to support conclusions very different from his, but contemporaries were impressed by the arguments as well as by the facts. Bentham, for example, absorbed Eden's claim that there was almost unlimited scope for the exercise of frugality. Indeed the book's

[16] *Ibid.* I. 494, 587.
[17] *Ibid.* I. 579, 600–24, 631–2. On Anne Strudwick, compare J. L. and Barbara Hammond, *The Village Labourer*, II. 8–9.

most influential message was probably its insistence that only self-help could bring real benefit to the poor. Eden's deep suspicion of the Poor Law—as a relic of ancient public servitude, as a product of glaring economic heresies, and as a public enticement to indolence—merely brought the doctrine of self-help into bolder relief. A reader could find in the work incitement to careful and discriminating charity, to be combined however with a drastic narrowing of the sphere of public relief. If Eden was not quite an abolitionist, not much needed to be added to his argument to support abolition as the desirable goal. In theory, Malthus was to provide the final arguments; while in the realm of fact the unprecedented distress after the war was to suggest that the system was not merely an unfortunate national aberration, but was also a rapidly growing menace to the structure of society and the prosperity of the country.

3. Bentham: Poverty, Indigence and Law

Jeremy Bentham prided himself on the logic and consistency of his thought, a consistency he claimed to maintain throughout the diversity of subjects to which he gave his attention. It may indeed be conceded that although his views showed development—for example towards an increasing political radicalism—it was his estimate of situations which changed rather than the principles by which he attempted to analyse them. In assessing any particular piece of Benthamite elaboration it is important to note its position in the hierarchy of generalisation: only the basic principles of utility were applicable to all places in all seasons, and the further one descends in the scale of subsidiary rules the more limited their reference. The Poor Plan of 1797 was a project for its own time and place, and only its most general principles had a wider application. Its analysis should begin, therefore, with the larger Benthamite propositions concerning property, poverty and indigence, before following the course of Bentham's application of them to the specific circumstances.

In his *Theory of Legislation* Bentham laid down four aims for the civil law—subsistence, security, abundance and equality—the first two deserving preference above the others. He saw, in particular, continual conflict between the aims of security and equality, and his analysis of this tension was important in his theory of poverty. The closer the distribution of wealth approached equality, the greater the sum of happiness; a poor man would gain more from the transfer than a rich man would lose.[18] Poverty being a relative term, a grievance

---

[18] *The Theory of Legislation*, pp. 102–9. Bentham later applied the notion of the marginal enjoyment of money in an analysis of gaming (*Pannomial Fragments, Works*, IV. 228–30).

existed whenever one man was poorer than another. But complete equality was an improper aim, for two reasons: the matter of abundance in the hands of the rich was not sufficient to provide more than a negligible increase in the happiness of the poor if distributed among them; and attempts to distribute it would undermine security, a superior aim to equality. Equality, even if it could be achieved, could not last more than a day, and in any case it was unjust that the idle should gain the fruits of labour.[19] Security, especially of property, was what distinguished the civilised state from the savage; without it there could be no effective industry, no sure subsistence, no abundance. So fragile was security that no matter how desirable a greater equality might appear, a legislator should not attempt to change the existing distribution of property among the living. 'When security and equality are in conflict, it will not do to hesitate a moment. Equality must yield. ... The establishment of perfect equality is a chimera; all we can do is to diminish inequality.' To this argument Bentham added the more conventional one that inequality and luxury formed a barrier to famine, by ensuring a reserve of wealth.[20] He concluded, after careful consideration, that it was desirable to have property widely distributed in society, with an even gradation from affluence to poverty, rather than a small very rich class and a large number of poor. Fortunately, he claimed, the progress of the arts and of manufactures in a rural society tended to produce such a distribution, and if the legislator wished to hasten it he could regulate inheritance in favour of equality. Death duties were an acceptable device; the dead, and only the dead, had no need for security of property. But if security was a superior aim equality still had its claims, and at several points in the Poor Plan Bentham showed regard for them.[21] On questions concerning subsistence and abundance the legislator must be guided by the relevant science, political economy: Bentham's *Manual of Political Economy* and his *Institute of Political Economy* were both written for the guidance of government. Bentham invented the term *facienda* for the functions it was proper for government to undertake in economic matters, and *non-facienda* for spheres in which it should not interfere. The content of the categories would depend on the state of civilisation existing in a particular country; thus backward societies would require far more government interference than England. In general, and certainly in England, the pursuit of abundance could be left to the spontaneous action of individuals, but Bentham always included questions of subsistence in the facienda of government. Government could not

[19] 'Poor's Cry', University College, Bentham Papers, CLI. 7.
[20] *The Theory of Legislation*, pp. 120, 101.
[21] *Ibid.* pp. 122–3; *Pannomial Fragments, Works*, IV. 230.

usually promote subsistence directly, but it could do so indirectly by affording security to the fruits of labour, that is to property.[22] And a man who could gain no subsistence for himself would always have a claim on the abundance of another. Thus the question of relief for indigence arose.

In the first part of the *Essays on the Poor Laws* of 1796[23] Bentham made an elaborate distinction between poverty and indigence:

> Poverty is the state of everyone who, in order to obtain *subsistence*, is forced to have recourse to *labour*. Indigence is the state of him who, being destitute of property . . . is at the same time, either *unable to labour*, or unable, even *for* labour, to procure the supply of which he happens thus to be in want.[24]

Poverty, thus defined, was 'the natural, the primitive, the general, and the *unchangeable* lot of man'; it could not be remedied, and indeed the spur to labour for necessities was the ultimate source of all wealth. Indigence alone was to be pitied and relieved. All sorts of accidents and calamities could precipitate into indigence those in society whose sole resource was their daily industry:

> This aspect of society is the saddest of all. It presents that long catalogue of evils which end in indigence, and consequently in death, under its most terrible forms. This is the centre to which inertia alone, that force which acts without relaxation, makes the lot of every mortal gravitate. Not to be drawn into the abyss, it is necessary to mount up by continual effort; and we see by our side the most diligent and the most virtuous sometimes slipping by one false step, and sometimes thrown headlong by inevitable reverses.[25]

Bentham was always so confident in argument that it is easy to overlook the fear that lay beneath his certainties; to him prosperity was a fragile plant, only too easily blighted, and progress an uncertain good hedged about with risk.[26] Most men would always be poor, and if governments must prevent and relieve indigence the task required the nicest judgment and the utmost care.

Labour was the only natural source of subsistence; property was an artificial right to the produce of one's own or another's labour. What power to produce subsistence by their labour did men possess? Bentham distinguished between four states of ability to gain subsistence

[22] *The Theory of Legislation*, p. 100.
[23] The manuscript of the *Essays* is in Bentham Papers, CLIIIa. 1–54, and copies in CLIIa.
[24] Bentham Papers, CLIIIa. 21. The argument was later adopted by Patrick Colquhoun, and by the Royal Commissioners of 1832–4.
[25] *The Theory of Legislation*, pp. 127–8.
[26] Compare his *Defence of Usury*, in *Jeremy Bentham's Economic Writings* (ed. W. Stark 1952–4), I, where economic innovation is defended but its risks stressed.

—utter inability, inadequate ability, adequate ability and extra-ability—and pointed out that extra-ability was, fortunately, the ordinary state of man. It was this extra-ability which produced 'the matter of wealth or abundance', the surplus left over after necessaries had been consumed; this surplus, though considerable, was precarious, and depended in particular upon security of property. Because surplus wealth was precarious and limited, relief for indigence must also be limited, extending to necessaries only. 'A Pension is a good thing: and it were a good state of things if all of us could have pensions. But still there remains this difficulty: when everybody is to receive pensions, who will there be to pay for it ?'[27]

The immediate source of relief for indigence was the 'matter of abundance' in the hands of the rich, but its ultimate source must be the independent labourer. This was the basis of Bentham's principle of less eligibility: the independent labourer must not be asked to bear a burden of relief larger than was absolutely necessary, and the Poor Plan included from the beginning direct and indirect assistance to the independent labourer as a primary aim. In a fragment entitled the *Poor's Cry*,[28] which may have been written as early as 1786, Bentham had argued that government could do nothing for labourers beyond removing unnecessary burdens from them, and had attacked the settlement laws in particular. Controversy over the scarcity led him to consider the position more deeply, and Davies' *Case of the Labourers* forced him to admit that the inadequacy of agricultural wages was 'incontestably established'. In May 1796 he set out 'J. B.'s Facienda' on the plight of the labourers; ever since the beginning of the Panopticon project in 1791 he had envisaged panopticon workhouses as well as penitentiaries, but he now approached the question of relief much more systematically and with the position of the independent labourer rather than the pauper as his starting point. A number of short essays and fragments on the subject were written before the Poor Plan itself was drafted.[29]

Bentham thought high wages desirable. A country was rich or poor according to the condition of the mass of its inhabitants, and if Eden later persuaded him that the labourer could be comfortable if only he would be more economical, it remained desirable that he should have more to be economical with. In the *Manual of Political Economy*

[27] Bentham Papers, CLIIIa. 23; CLIVb. 604.
[28] *Ibid.* CLI. 7–8.
[29] 'Independent Poor: Partial Relief', *ibid.* CLIIIa. 214–49. In the preface to *Panopticon* (1791) Bentham included, in his eulogy of the 'simple idea in Architecture', 'Economy seated, as it were upon a rock, the gordian knot of the Poor-Laws not cut, but untied' (*Works*, IV. 37). The original idea was of course not Jeremy's but his brother Samuel's.

Bentham had already discussed the determinants of wages, and had included passages on the relationship between population and subsistence which Dumont claimed as anticipations of Malthusian principles.[30] In 1796, in an essay on the *Independent Husbandman*, he stated more explicitly that wages were determined by the 'multitude of hands' compared with 'the quantity or money's worth in store' to pay for their labour, and argued that a rise in wages would be likely to encourage marriage and thus an increased population which could force wages back to their former level. Declining wages were a sign of a decreasing proportion of capital to labour; Bentham thought this situation existed in agriculture, but not in manufacturing industry.[31] Attempts to raise wages were classified as *competent* or *incompetent*, with the *competent* divided again into *immediate* and *gradual* measures. Chief among the incompetent was the rating of wages, 'a regulation of the prohibitive kind, excluding from employment all such hands the value of whose labour does not rise to a level with that rate'. To this argument he added a claim that it might drive capital out of agriculture and worsen the proportion between capital and labour. Thus he disposed of Whitbread's remedy, as definitely if less colourfully than he had assailed Pitt's.[32]

In his own suggestions for competent measures to raise wages Bentham showed a perhaps surprising sympathy for the agricultural interest, urging the abandonment of policies favouring commerce, colonies or manufactures, and pleading for the cultivation of wastes; he opposed, however, proposals for bounties on agricultural production. Government should encourage capital to enter agriculture, should provide remedies (unspecified) for local disadvantages of supply and demand, and should make easier the movement of labour to areas where there was a demand for it. The proposals were not worked out in detail at this stage, and Bentham seems to have become worried by the difficulties of attracting capital to agriculture without reducing employment elsewhere.[33] To these gradual measures he later added a system of public granaries, a reduction in the number of ale-houses, and the encouragement of 'economic supply', the diet reform urged by Rumford and his followers.[34] These devices might not raise money wages, but they could increase effective earnings; and above all, among immediate measures, there was the adoption of his own Poor Plan

[30] Dumont's note is in *Works*, III. 73.
[31] Bentham Papers, CXXXIII. 93; CLIVb. 598–601; CLIIIa. 237–8.
[32] *Ibid.* CXXXIII. 12; *Observations* etc. (1838 ed.), pp. 6–7.
[33] Bentham Papers, CLIVb. 534–45; CLIIIa. 239–42.
[34] 'Anti-scarcity Magazines', *ibid.* CLIVa. 142–5. Later still his Annuity Note scheme and *Defence of a Maximum* were largely intended as aids to independent labourers.

With its aid the labourers could be relieved of all their 'Standing Burthens'—the support of children and infirm dependants, and child-birth expenses—and also of 'Occasional Burthens' such as funerals and medical expenses.[35] All burdens, that is, except one: in an early note in his *Commonplace Book* Bentham had discussed the problem of 'occasional stagnation' in manufactures, and had suggested employment on public works as a remedy; this was now dropped in favour of a contributory Stagnation Fund. Wages in manufactures were high enough to permit regular contributions to be made without hardship, and the fund might even be sufficiently large to pay superannuation annuities as well as stagnation allowances.[36] Apart from this important exception the problem of the condition of the independent labourer would be solved by the same devices which provided a remedy for indigence, by the Poor Plan with its correct principle of relief and all its ancillary services.

4. *Bentham: Principles of Relief*

The first principle of relief Bentham set out to establish was that indigence should be relieved by law. The notion of a 'natural' right to relief was of course repugnant to him, and he rejected it in his criticism of the French Declaration of Rights.[37] The justification of a Poor Law must be utilitarian, in the broadest sense: it was contrary to the basic principle of utility and the general aim of security that any man should starve to death while food existed. Only a legal provision could make this certain, and only Bentham's legal system could do it well. To establish these arguments he wrote *Pauper Systems Compared*, a work on a very large scale in which the principles of a number of systems, legal or voluntary, were assessed. The first alternative he considered was the *No Provision System*, or absence of a Poor Law; in doing so Bentham justified his proposal against abolitionist arguments in terms which were often remarkably similar to the later justification for the reform of 1834.[38]

Bentham was acquainted with Joseph Townsend, and he respected Townsend's abolitionist views sufficiently to reply to them. As has

---

[35] Bentham Papers, CLIIIa. 214.

[36] *Ibid.* CLI. 219–21. For the earlier proposal, see *Jeremy Bentham's Economic Writings*, I. 13.

[37] *Anarchical Fallacies, Works*, II. 533–4. To infer an 'absolute right' from the 'duty of benevolence' would be 'to give the indigent class the most false and danger-ous ideas' and 'put arms in their hands against all proprietors'.

[38] The justification was stated most fully in the unfinished *Pauper Systems Compared* (Bentham Papers, CLIIb. 411–564), and most succinctly in *Essays on the Poor Laws*. Some arguments were summarised in *The Theory of Legislation*.

EDEN, BENTHAM AND MALTHUS

been seen, Townsend anticipated Malthus in alleging that the Poor
Law upset the natural balance between population and subsistence;
Bentham, on the other hand, rejected what he called 'the forced-
continence preaching, or irregular-satisfaction preaching' argument.
Because on an island with pasture for a thousand goats any surplus
must die, did it follow that on an island inhabited by men some should
be allowed to starve? 'There may be justice in the inference, but I
cannot find it.' Certainly those unable to maintain children should not
have them; 'admitted—for argument's sake, but what then? Because
the parents ought not to have married, ought the children be left to
starve?'³⁹ He dismissed the argument as weak, but later saw that the
question was more complex. Believing that the poor valued easy
marriage even above a good diet, he boasted that his scheme would
allow them to combine matrimony with high wages since children
would cease to be an economic burden. But he soon admitted that this
would encourage population growth, which could in turn force do wn
wages.⁴⁰ At this point the Plan transformed itself from a scheme for
relief into a pattern of economic progress; the large population would
not press upon subsistence because the plan would encourage agriculture until England was cultivated like a garden—presumably mainly
by Benthamite paupers—and when England was fully peopled, the
Plan would still suffice:

This Plan is not a plan for a day—it looks onwards to the very end of
earthly time. . . . Sooner or later the yet vacant lands in the country will have
been filled with culture and population. At that remote but surely not ideal
period the Company will have turned its thoughts to colonisation: and the
rising strength of these its hives, will by art, as in other hives by nature, have
been educated for swarming.⁴¹

Eventually, colonisation would be inevitable, and how much better
if planned and hoped for than if 'performed without appropriate
preparation and only under pressure of distress'. And when the whole
earth was fully peopled, 'then will the policy of the statesman be directed
to the arrestment of population, as now to the increase: and what is
now stigmatised as vice will then receive the treatment, if not the name
of virtue'. No doubt Bentham here referred to birth control, which he
had already mentioned (in a passage written discreetly in Latin) in his
Manual of Political Economy as a means of preventing population
increasing more rapidly than capital.⁴² Later still he was to express a

³⁹ Bentham Papers, CLIIb. 424–7.
⁴⁰ *Ibid*. CLIVb. 534–5.
⁴¹ 'Population and Colonisation', *ibid*. CLI. 108. For arguments in favour of
colonisation at home rather than abroad, see CLIVb. 544–5.
⁴² *Jeremy Bentham's Economic Writings*, I. 272–3.

123

more gloomy view on population increase in the *Pannomial Fragments*,[43] but in the Poor Plan he looked to economic growth as a counterbalance to population increase, with colonisation and birth control as remedies for the future. Arguments about population had in his view no weight against a legal provision of relief, provided always it was the Benthamite provision.

Bentham found it easier to discuss the most common abolitionist argument of all, the moral preference for private charity and self-help. He was very much in favour of frugality, but while it could be made more general it could never be universal unless man himself were made anew. And how could it be proved that private charity would replace public if the Poor Law was repealed?

Shut up the Temple of public charity to promote benevolence!—shut up the law courts then, to promote Justice. If this does with the poor rates, try it upon *tithes*, and call them *offerings*.[44]

Some countries had no public relief, and very little private. Charity could not be distributed with equal justice, or fall with equal justice on the givers; benevolence was capricious, and needed to be educated and aided by the state.[45] Many moderate abolitionists wanted public relief to become a mere supplement to private, but Bentham reversed the preference and offered a place for private charity in his public plan.

There were also, of course, positive arguments for relief by law. Repeal the Poor Law, and beggars must thrive; his scheme would 'extirpate' mendicity. 'At present, when a street Beggar is troublesome, the answer is short—Go to your Parish—Where could a man bid a beggar go, if there was no parish, nor anything to replace it?'[46] Above all, the absence of a legal system undermined security of property, and in England the poor would rather be shot than lose a system they had enjoyed for two hundred years; this point Bentham thought conclusive against the 'no-provision' system.[47] But one argument in the abolitionist case worried him, as it did most of his contemporaries. Surely the certainty of relief reduced the diligence of the labourer, and thus created as much indigence as it relieved? This was in Bentham's view the central difficulty in all public relief, and it was therefore vital to establish a principle of relief which overcame it.[48]

[43] *Works*, IV. 227, and *Jeremy Bentham's Economic Writings*, I. 109–11.
[44] Bentham Papers, CLIIb. 428; *Pauper Management Improved*, p. 30.
[45] Bentham Papers, CLIIb. 425, and compare *The Theory of Legislation*, pp. 427–32.
[46] Bentham Papers, CLIIb. 429.
[47] *Ibid.* and compare *The Theory of Legislation*, p. 386.
[48] Bentham Papers, CLIIb. 426–7.

One device, suggested by Eden, Townsend and others, was the fixing by law of a maximum beyond which poor rates could not rise; this Bentham dismissed, calling it the 'limited provision system'. It was not a principle of relief at all, since it offered no rule for discrimination, and under it 'false indulgence' and 'inexorable inhumanity' could exist side by side. It made no distinction between just and unfounded claims; the rates could properly be limited only by a truly economical system, and not by arbitrary decision. 'If the fabrick of felicity were to be raised by a man's shutting his eyes and drawing a line anywhere, the limited or inadequate provision system might soon raise it: but happiness is not to be purchased, or wisdom displayed at quite so cheap a rate.'[49] Poor rates could be wiped off, but it must not be at the expense of the truly indigent. 'I too have my spunge; but that is a slow one, and not quite so rough a one. Mine goes, I promise you, into the fire, the instant you can show me that a single particle of necessity is deprived by it of relief.'[50]

Bentham's purpose in assessing rival systems was to establish the true requirements of a poor law and to prepare for a statement of the principle which alone could meet them. He summed up the question succinctly in the second *Essay on the Poor Laws*. A fund for the relief of indigence must be certain, permanently adequate and yet capable of meeting a fluctuating demand; only a public fund could meet these conditions. But even a public fund could cause 'destruction of society' if it granted relief on terms which encouraged indolence and thus indigence. Such a calamity was inevitable if the 'condition of persons maintained at the public charge were *in general* rendered *more eligible*, upon the whole, than that of persons maintained at their own charge, those of the latter number not excepted, whose condition is *least eligible*'.

If the condition of persons *maintained* without property *by the labour of others* were rendered more eligible, than that of persons maintained by their *own* labour then, in proportion as the existence of this state of things were ascertained, individuals destitute of property would be continually withdrawing themselves from the class of persons maintained by their own labour, to the class of persons maintained by the labour of others: and the sort of

[49] *Ibid.* 440–4.
[50] *Pauper Management Improved*, p. 31. N. Himes, in 'Jeremy Bentham and the Genesis of English Neo-Malthusianism', *Economic History* (1936), 267–75, interprets this passage as a reference to contraception, to prove Bentham the 'fountainhead' of pre-Malthusian neo-Malthusianism; P. Fryer, in *The Birth Controllers* (1965), pp. 67–9 elaborates the interpretation. But Bentham was clearly referring to his Plan as the 'spunge' wiping out poor rates and rejecting Townsend's proposal to limit them; the passage in Latin in the *Manual of Political Economy* is better evidence for Himes' contention.

idleness, which at present is more or less *confined* to persons of *independent* fortune, would thus extend itself sooner or later to every individual . . . till at last there would be *nobody* left to labour at all for anybody.[51]

This is clearly the less-eligibility principle of 1834; Bentham did not give it a name, but based two working rules upon it—the 'industry-enforcing' or work test, and the 'neighbours' fare' principle. The need to make relief deterrent in this way was argued also in a curious little essay on *Badging the Poor*, in which he defended a device repugnant to the sensibilities of most of his contemporaries. A pauper's badge was not degrading: it merely indicated degradation, or at any rate a particular rank. A coronet on the coach of a baron was not degrading, though 'it shows him to be below a Viscount'. Distinctive dress for paupers rendered 'the condition of the man of industry more eligible than that of the man of non-industry: it consequently tends to dispose men to embrace the former condition in preference to the latter'.

Rank is relative: you cannot raise one of two contiguous ranks but you depress the other; you cannot depress the one but you raise the other. Poverty you have on both sides: poverty you have at any rate. How do you like it best? with or without industry? Take your choice.[52]

Men of resolute humanity, 'determined, in the teeth of possibility, to bring happiness to a level' might deplore the position of the pauper; to grant relief was pleasant, but to be indulgent was to impose a tax on others. Bentham was certainly concerned that his principle of relief seemed harsh, and he insisted that it could be combined with comforts for paupers. Later, in discussing objections to the separation of families in his Houses of Industry, he admitted that a real conflict of principles was involved: from the point of view of free labourers 'it was to be wished that the public provision should appear less eligible to him than the provision resulting from his own labour', but for those who really needed relief it should be and appear to be as eligible as possible. To resolve this conflict he clung to less eligibility but incorporated in his

---

[51] Bentham Papers, CLIIIa. 25–6. S. E. Finer claims that in 1833–4 Chadwick developed the doctrine of less eligibility by analogy from Bentham's work on crime and punishment, implying that Bentham did not apply it to pauperism himself. 'He [Chadwick] wrenched from an obscure context a highly qualified principle and with a questionable genius turned it into the fulcrum of a gigantic social lever'. (*Life and Times of Sir Edwin Chadwick*, p. 75). Finer compares a passage from *Panopticon* with others from the Poor Law *Report* and Chadwick's letter to Althorp; but is it likely that Chadwick did not read the *Essays*, several copies of which were in Bentham's papers? He had access to the papers, and later published Bentham's *Observations*.

[52] Bentham Papers, CLIVb. 602–3, and compare *Pauper Management Improved*, p. 88: 'Soldiers wear uniforms, why not paupers?—Those who save the country, why not those who are saved by it?'

plan a host of 'collateral aids' for independent labourers so that 'the refuse of the country is all that ... will ever fall to the Company's share'.[53]

A great many of Bentham's contemporaries sought to make a clear line of distinction between paupers and independent labourers as a means of checking pauperism; they differed from him in seeking a moral distinction, between the deserving and the undeserving. Bentham also hoped to do this in effect, by ensuring that only the 'refuse' suffered under less-eligibility, but he specifically rejected desert as a ground for relief. Necessity was the only ground, and good or ill desert added nothing to it, though it might as a special service earn a reward. To refuse relief for moral unworthiness was a punishment, and should be bound by the rules of punishment and not of indigence and relief; indeed refusal of relief caused starvation, a worse punishment than any given for crime. If a good man became indigent, despite all the 'collateral aids', he could not expect exceptional treatment. 'A man may be a very worthy good sort of man: but so ought we all to be: and if everyman who is so were to bring in his *bill* for being so, who would there be to pay it?'[54] Instead of drawing a line of moral distinction between pauper and free labourer Bentham sought to establish an objective difference in condition and status, while at the same time taking steps to prevent free labourers being forced into pauperism. Other reformers sought to influence the discretion of poor-law administrators, Bentham to establish rigid and objective principles and an administrative machine which would automatically carry them into effect.

5. *Bentham's Pauper Kingdom: Large Establishments*

Bentham's Plan was based on a series of very large workhouses, and he thought it necessary to argue, in general terms, that only a 'large establishment system' could effectively apply the proper principles of relief. All systems could be classified in terms of the quantum of relief (eligible or ineligible), the place (public or private), and the fund (national or local); and the criteria for judging superiority included economy, universality of application, moral influence and justice. A good system must be capable of introducing the necessary reforms, especially the reduction of relief to a simple sufficiency, the combination of relief with labour and the greatest efficiency in the employment of labour.[55] Outdoor relief (called 'Home Provision' by Bentham),

[53] Bentham Papers, CLIIb. 273.
[54] *Ibid.* CLIIIa. 23.
[55] *Pauper Systems Compared, ibid.* CLIIb. 431, 453; *Essays, ibid.* CLIIIa. 30.

least satisfied these conditions: it could not be universal, since the impotent and homeless required institutional treatment; it could not employ paupers effectively, since what was needed was not a type but a system of employment; it could not be combined with education; and in almost all respects it was less economical than a large-establishment system. Outdoor relief 'may do tolerably well for the strictly virtuous', but too much relief would in fact be wasted on drink or luxuries. An institutional system, publicly run, was perfectible; home provision was out of the public eye, not susceptible to permanent improvement, and hence must always be restricted to a minimum of relief while institutional relief could be copious without ill effect.[56] One of Pitt's major sins was his profusion in outdoor relief; Bentham would have restricted it to superannuation under an annuity scheme, temporary relief from a contributory stagnation fund, and relief in the form of loans in special cases.

A system of 'small establishments'—and Bentham regarded even the largest existing houses of industry as small—was almost as bad as home provision; he was extremely scathing in his criticism not only of parochial administration but also of 'reformed' systems in incorporated areas. His own proposal was for an analytic division of the whole country, not a synthetic combination of parishes. As an ideal he suggested five hundred great Houses, ten and two-thirds miles apart so that no man would live more than half a day's march from one, but he would settle for two hundred and fifty as the initial establishment.[57] He was well aware that institutional relief was in bad repute in the 1790s, and took care to argue that proper management would overcome the physical and moral unhealthiness of existing institutions. His basic argument for very large establishments was simply economy of scale: the larger the unit the greater the economy in building, in management, in the division of labour in employment, and in supply, and the greater too the 'conspicuousness of the theatre of action' compared with 'the narrow and sordid obscurity of an ordinary Poor House'.[58] As for the Law of Settlement, the buttress of small local endeavours, that in the end could disappear when poor rates had diminished to nothing. Bentham shared much of Smith's animus against settlement, but saw some use for it as a unit of rating as long as rates were necessary, until 'the law of universal settlement' replaced 'the law of local settlement'. The only simple ground for settlement was birth, though even it had one disadvantage in that 'the circumstance of birth is not of itself a matter of notoriety at every subsequent period of a man's life: for

[56] *Ibid.* CLIIb, 454–99, 509–15.
[57] *Ibid.* CLIIb. 433–8.
[58] *Ibid.* CLIIb. 517–28.

though every man is present at his own birth, yet he might as well have been absent, for anything that he can say to it from his own memory'. But if all infants were branded, painlessly and indelibly, with name, place and date of birth, identification for settlement and for a host of other useful purposes would be instantaneous. A half-day's march and the baring of the brand could ensure a pauper his due relief at Jeremy Bentham's large establishments.[59]

It was one thing to assert economies of scale, and another to prove them. Bentham's claim that his Houses of Industry could be more economical, on a national scale, than houses of the Shrewsbury type by £16,578,754 per year was implausible in its exactitude.[60] Lack of 'intelligence', of accurate statistics, continually frustrated him in the preparation of his plan. Deductive though many of his generalisations might be, Bentham had a real passion for the systematic collection of information, and insisted that without it both legislation and administration groped in ignorance. A proper system of book-keeping was one of the main elements in the management of his Houses of Industry, and his elaborate analysis of Italian and other systems of accounting is of interest to the specialist.[61] In the *Manual of Political Economy* he had insisted that 'intelligence' was a responsibility of government, and he chafed under its failure to undertake even such basic exercises as a census of population. Forced back on his own enterprise, he prepared in 1796 some very elaborate tables of the information required for the completion of the Poor Plan, later sending them to Young for publication in the *Annals*.[62]

Bentham described his *Table of Cases calling for Relief* as 'a general map of pauper land and all roads to it'. The classification was certainly exhaustive: under the heading 'Personal Causes' he set out all the permutations of infirmity of mind and body, including 'non-age' or infancy; 'External Causes' included twenty-six causes of loss of property. This table formed the basis for an essay called *Classes Mustered*,

---

[59] 'Poor's Cry', *ibid.* CLI. 8; *Essays, ibid.* CLIIIa. 21, CLIVb. 595–7; 'Fragment on Settlement', *ibid.* CLI. 12–19. Bentham's argument against equalisation of the rates was characteristic: the suffering of those whose rates were increased would be greater than the pleasure of those whose rates were reduced, because the latter were accustomed to carrying the burden (*ibid.* CLI. 9, CLIIIb. 481–4). For a humbler scheme for the registration of settlement rights see *The Names of Parishes* etc. by a Justice of the Peace of Westmorland and Lancaster (1802).

[60] *Pauper Management Improved*, pp. 43–7.

[61] On book-keeping see *ibid.* pp. 99–111 and a letter to Young in Bentham Papers, CLIVa. 33–5. Bentham's passion for information is evident in 'Collectanea', *ibid*, CLI. 25–101, and compare British Museum, Correspondence of Arthur Young, Additional MSS 35127–8, II. 338, III. 368.

[62] Bentham Papers, CXXXIII. 4, 66–73; and compare *Pauper Management Improved*, pp. 1–27, and *Annals of Agriculture*, XXIX (1797), 393.

intended as a chapter of the Plan but never printed, in which the appropriateness of a Benthamite House of Industry for the treatment of each class of pauper was argued at length. But if such a classification was essential for planning relief it could not solve 'the grand question— the difficult question—the question to the solution of which individual sagacity is essentially inadequate . . . the number of individuals that are likely to come under each class'.[63] In a forlorn hope that voluntary labour might provide the answer Bentham sent to Young his *Pauper Population Table*, asking parishes to return complete lists of indoor and outdoor paupers with full details of their personal and social circumstances. The response was negligible; even if it had been adequate there would still have remained the question of projecting future numbers, a problem on which Bentham attempted an analysis acute enough to interest a demographer but to little avail.[64] And his statistical ingenuity took him into the realm of fantasy in his *Non-Adult Value Table*; he was confident that his Houses of Industry, being better than the best existing, could employ the able-bodied at a profit, but it remained essential for the economy of the whole scheme to utilise the 'under-ability' hands and thus make the whole body of paupers self-supporting. He needed to know the number and probable net value of the largest group, the infant or 'non-aged'. Was the average child worth more or less than nothing? Children were burdens to their parents; need they be absolute burdens to their country? Child labour was a vital element in Bentham's Plan, and he showed his usual ingenuity in calculating the effect of mortality and other factors on the estimated value at each age.[65] But he became increasingly aware that he was speculating without a solid basis of fact, and it was partly in despair that he decided to send the skeleton of his plan to be printed by Arthur Young. It might appear half-baked, but surely it was plausible;[66] and once the public become aware that Jeremy Bentham had solved the problem of the relief of indigence then surely too he would be given the resources and the opportunity to put it into effect.

6. *Bentham's Pauper Kingdom: its Constitution*

Bentham proposed, as the managing authority for his scheme, a National Charity Company. Its elaborate constitution gave a central

[63] Bentham Papers, CLI. 113. *Classes Mustered* is in *ibid.* CLI. 120–70; and compare CLIIb. 264–73.
[64] 'Pecuniary Estimates', *ibid.* CLIIb. 315–29; 'Numbers: Natural Stock', *ibid.* CLIVb. 407–524; miscellaneous calculations, *ibid.* CXXXIII. 35.
[65] *Pauper Management Improved*, pp. 21—7.
[66] Bentham to Arthur Young, Bentham Papers, CLIVa. 32.

board of directors very wide powers—to raise capital, purchase land and even to apprehend beggars and vagrants—and imposed even wider obligations, extending beyond the relief of all paupers seeking assistance to the whole system of collateral services. The weight of business would be less, he claimed, than that sustained by the directors of the East India Company; and he suggested special restraints to prevent the Company interfering in elections or speculating in 'bubbles'.[67] In a defence of this structure, under the title *Company not Government*, Bentham admitted that a government department would have the necessary unity of authority and universality of extent to run the scheme, but argued that government administration was notoriously bad ('its cardinal weakness is procrastination'), and that a department would have difficulty in maintaining parliamentary confidence, in raising money and in preventing jobbery. Joint-stock management had been bad also, but was improving; capital could be raised from the willing investor in search of profit, and there would be greater political security, since the administration could watch the company and Parliament both. Bentham's attitude towards government administration was clearly ambivalent: he sensed that it could be best of all, but feared that it would be worst. At times in the discussion he approached the concept of the public corporation.[68]

The Directors' first duty was to raise £4–6 million in capital, in small shares of £5–10 in order to spread an interest in the undertaking as widely as possible. Income would include the annual produce of the rates, the product of pauper labour, and voluntary contributions to provide 'extra comforts'; Bentham's estimate of profits was never completed, though he was confident that profit was certain and would be adequate to repay capital in twenty years and to reduce poor rates to nothing. Two-fifths of the profit was to be retained by the Company and the rest distributed among the parishes, with special bonuses to those exceptionally burdened by high rates. In an elaborate argument to forestall objections of 'Profit exaggerated' Bentham tried desperately to prove that earnings would be much higher than maintenance costs, but was forced to appeal mainly to general arguments on economies of scale and good management.[69]

The management of each House was to rest with a Governor,

[67] *Pauper Management Improved*, pp. 3–16.
[68] 'Company Not Government', Bentham Papers, CLIIIb. 266–92; and compare CLI. 312–3, 321–6 and 'Why One Company', CLIIIb. 293–332. Bentham later remarked that management by company would have been impracticable at the time of the South Sea Bubble, and unnecessary in a century's time since government would then be capable of the task (CLIVb. 547).
[69] *Pauper Management Improved*, pp. 6, 12; Bentham Papers, CLI. 252–77, 278–307. Only if subscribed capital proved insufficient should government provide funds,

assisted by a Chaplain, Medical Curator, School Master, Governess, Matron-midwife, Organist-clerk, Husbandry Bailiff and Foremen and Forewomen to supervise employment. Management was to be 'interested', controlled by a system of rewards and penalties, and Bentham found it necessary to defend in detail the discredited system of 'farming' the poor. He admitted he had shared the common prejudice against it. Burn had 'drawn a hobgoblin' under the name of farmer of the poor, and Adam Smith another of a farmer-general; so had Bentham, and 'like Smith's the colours of it were French: Montesquieu could not have done it better, for it was all epigram: consequently all false'. After consideration he had thrown it in the fire. 'Shutting up Burn, Montesquieu and Smith and looking a little more closely into the back of human nature' he decided that the farming principle gave 'the strongest stimulant to what is good in management, and the strongest check to what is bad'.[70]

Every system of management which has disinterestedness, pretended or real, for its foundation, is rotten at the root, susceptible of a momentary prosperity at the outset, but sure to perish in the long run. That principle of action is most to be depended upon, whose influence is most powerful, most constant, most uniform, most lasting, and most general among mankind. Personal interest is that principle: a system of economy built on any other foundation, is built on quicksand.[71]

Even as it existed, farming had its advantages: 'the Farmer of the Poor will always be watched. . . . The Overseer of the Poor will comparatively speaking not be watched at all'. It was a popular delusion that the evil most to be feared in administration was corruption; 'inability and indiscipline' were far more dangerous, and 'interested management' would weed them out. It was in the farmer's interest to employ paupers profitably, and not to injure or kill them. Objections to farming mistook for a vice a characteristic virtue of the system: 'farming is but one of a set of institutions which, with or without design . . . have the effect of rendering the constitution of the pauper in reality or appearance less eligible than that of a self maintaining hand; and thus of deterring men from the act of investing themselves with this condition'.[72] In *Pauper Management Improved* interested management was ensured by the 'Duty and Interest Junction Principle', operating through a system of rewards, and supported by the 'Publicity or Transparent Management Principle'. Houses were to be open to public inspection, and under the 'Life Assurance or Life Warranty Principle' the salaries of governors were to vary with the rate of infant mortality in their houses, while midwives

[70] 'Objection, Farming the Poor', *ibid.* CLIIb. 330–51.
[71] *Pauper Management Improved*, pp. 55–6.
[72] Bentham Papers, CLIIb. 351.

and matrons were to pay head-money for each woman who died in child-birth.[73] At all levels Bentham devised rules to ensure that the plan could be operated by men with no more than average zeal or honesty. Only the chief director needed uncommon ability, and Bentham thought it a happy coincidence that he had discovered the remedy for indigence at a time when another man existed 'beyond all example fitted for the conduct of a business of this nature . . . a man in whose [character?] genius and benevolence contend with each other . . . the man I am speaking of is Count Rumford'. The American-Bavarian scientist had cast his spell over more than the S.B.C.P.; Benthamite Houses of Industry were to have Rumford stoves and Rumford privies, and also, if possible, the Count himself in control over all.[74]

7. The Pauper Panopticon

The internal management, and indeed the design, of each Benthamit. House were determined by the principles of 'Central Inspection' and of the 'Separation and Aggregation' of the various classes of pauperse Health, morals and the prevention of annoyance required separation and Bentham planned it in great detail: the diseased and lunatic must be segregated from the healthy, the morally corrupt from the innocent, sex from sex above a certain age, and those with extra comforts from the rest 'for the prevention of unsatisfiable desires'. All this could be done within one building, given good design:

Next to every class, from which any inconvenience is to be apprehended, station a class unsusceptible of that inconvenience. Examples: 1. Next to raving *lunatics* or persons of *profligate conversation*, place the *deaf and dumb* . . . separated as to sight. 2. Next to *prostitutes*, and other loose *women*, place the aged women. 3. Within view of the abodes of the blind, place melancholy and *silent* lunatics, or the shockingly deformed. 4. Next to each married couple, place at bed-time a set of children, under the age of observation.[75]

Clearly a high degree of regimentation was intended, and although Bentham claimed that there would be compensating advantages in

[73] *Pauper Management Improved*, pp. 51–6.
[74] Bentham Papers, CLI. 393. Bentham hoped to develop Rumford's work in his own search for 'Suitable Fare' under the less-eligibility principle. He recognised that diets in existing workhouses were often generous, and therefore admitted a 'Habit Recognising Principle' so that 'old-stagers' could continue their accustomed fare. Beer, 'not natural to the human frame', was excluded under the 'Non-fermented Liquor Principle' (*Pauper Management Improved*, pp. 68–70, 80–6; Bentham Papers, CLIVa. 105–23).
[75] *Pauper Management Improved*, pp. 21–2; Bentham Papers, CLI. 401–53, CLIVa. 84–104.

suitable 'aggregation'—for example of the sick for treatment, or children for education—he admitted that the poor hated segregation in workhouses, and justified it mainly on the basis of efficiency and less eligibility. Certainly he combined it with specialised treatment, planning 'appropriate establishments' for the insane, the deaf and the blind with considerable benevolence and intelligence.[76]

The principle of Central Inspection was of course the kernel of the original Panopticon design, and Bentham drew up the internal plan of a typical House with almost childish delight. It was to be circular or polygonal, of five stories divided into wards, all visible from the central inspection lodge except when 'circumferential skreens' were drawn to allow periods of privacy. The elaborate system of ventilation, the beds which turned over to become work-tables, the ceiling which came down to form a chapel (complete with pulpit, reading-desk, clerk's desk and communion table), the method of central heating, all these and a host of further details show the mechanical ingenuity of Bentham and his brother Samuel at its most exhaustive. Samuel's sketches reveal a severely functional if not inelegant elevation; it is unfortunate that he did not also illustrate the entrance, with its 'occasional barrier . . . to keep out the promiscuous influx of employment-seeking hands'; or the aged and infirm taking the air along the covered walks, drawn in droshkies by sturdy children. (The brothers Bentham were willing to learn from Imperial Russia, as well as to teach it.) Even the central Board-room in London was planned as a 'panopticon of information', with a round central table surrounded by charts and maps.[77]

Virtually all the inmates of these Panopticon workhouses were to be set to work. Inability to labour was a relative term; even the blind could knit. The Company must push the division of labour to the utmost, recognising however that each pauper's work should be varied for his health and relaxation. Piece-work was to be the rule; all paupers must work off the value of relief received (the 'Self Liberation Principle') and the able-bodied should work before they ate (the 'Earn First Principle'). There should be no relief to children unless they were bound apprentices in the house to the age of twenty-one; their talents were to be cultivated, they were to instruct themselves (on Dr. Bell's Madras system), and could eventually rise to fill salaried positions in the house.[78] Bentham distinguished between the 'permanent stock' of paupers and the 'coming and going' stock of temporarily indigent, and as the plan developed he became more and more interested in the

[76] Bentham Papers, CLI. 223–51; *Pauper Management Improved*, pp. 113–14.
[77] Bentham Papers, CLI. 448–9.
[78] *Pauper Management Improved*, pp. 57–74.

'indigenous' paupers brought up and perhaps bred in the house itself. He saw such opportunities for moulding their bodies and souls that the scheme for relief began to take on the aspect of a blue-print for a new society.

Pauper Management Improved set out only the general principles of employment, and while it insisted that free employment 'is the primary and preferable object' it did not meet in detail the objections to all make-work schemes, that they would compete with free labour or at best divert capital from free employment. It included, however, the principle of 'Self Supply', of a subsistence economy outside the normal market and therefore free of the whole system of 'value in exchange', and free too of gluts, changes in fashions and wars. Self supply became an almost Owenite ideal of co-operative production, in which working for all would be the same as working for oneself:

> Community of interest will enable the willing to spur the lazy, without exposing themselves to the reproach of officiousness or ill-nature—working for sale would, unless laid under restraint by superior authority, expose individual competitors to universal ruin:—self supply injures nobody—affords grounds of complaint to nobody. In the case of an individual, indeed, the principle of self supply is repugnant to good economy, and is the forced resource of a nation little advanced in the career of opulence: for, in that case . . . the benefit of the labour-division principle is foregone. But in this vast populous establishment, affording within itself the means of carrying the division of labour—not only to the ordinary pitch, but beyond it, the two principles act in conjunction, and the operation of each is favoured by the assistance it receives from the other.[79]

Despite the temptation to regard his pauper kingdom as a new social system, Bentham was forced to admit that it would exist within, and to some extent compete with, the old. The obvious field for self supply was agriculture, and here there need be no real competition with free labour since the scarcity had revealed that agricultural production was too low.[80] But despite this emphasis on agriculture both the Benthams were fascinated by the possibilities of using unskilled labour in manufactures, with a division of labour extreme enough to compare with modern mass production. In Russia Samuel had built ships with female labour only; together they planned to build coaches with completely standardised parts.[81] In 1802, when Dumont wrote asking for samples of Benthamite manufactures to show to an interested monarch, Jeremy suggested 'the art of *wheel-making* by Machinery, to the working of which neither *dexterity* in any degree nor *good-will* is necessary':

[79] *Ibid.* pp. 61–2.
[80] Bentham Papers, CLIVb. 295–326; CLI. 171–3, 176, 191.
[81] Bentham to Young, *ibid.* CLIVa. 31.

L

A system of wheels, made by such a system of Machinery, would be particularly commodious for a general and connected system of national *roulage*, upon a plan analogous to that of our Mail-coaches: for the multiples of each of the several component parts, being precisely the same dimensions one as another . . . in case of an accident to any such part it might be replaced by a *spare* part, either kept at the several houses of call, or carried in the carriage itself for that purpose: and if (as with us) it were deemed advisable to prescribe dimensions of wheels by law . . . such a system of machinery would afford the means of conforming to such prescription with peculiar accuracy: especially if *Iron Rail-Roads* were adopted (as grooves for the wheels to run in almost without friction) as they begin to be with us.[82]

With such grandiose plans for pauper manufactures, where was the alleged benefit of the Plan to the free labourer? Bentham admitted some diversion of capital from free employment, but claimed that the release of the poor rates into ordinary commercial channels would stimulate demand in compensation. Public employment should try to avoid direct competition with free, undertaking as far as possible tasks free labour could not attempt, and in training apprentices the Houses should choose those trades in which wages were high. But there remained continual tension between his concern for the free economy and his vision of pauper employment, and he had already admitted that the whole Plan would tend to increase population and thus depress wages. There remained, however, his collateral aids, and especially the provision of lan Employment Exchange at every House and the printing of a nationa Employment Gazette. 'Demand for labour might as well not exist, as not be known to those who have labour to bestow: and as far as under the existing order of things, this demand fails of being known, thus to *cause* it to be known is as much as creating it.' Thus Houses of Industry would be prevented from absorbing more labour than was genuinely redundant; and the Gazettes could become 'pauper-population reports', suitable to be read in churches 'engrafted into the liturgy, with prayers (deprecatory) for the unprosperous, thanksgivings for the prosperous part of the results'.[83]

Bentham did not hesitate to make child labour the core of his employment plan. A child was better off employed in a factory than starving at home, and apprentices were to form the permanent, the replenishing stock of labour; the children would benefit by training, society by their employment, and parents by the removal of an economic burden. Not least among the advantages would be a reduction in infant mortality, for the House of Industry, with its constant medical supervision, its ventilation and its patent cribs, would be far healthier than any cottage.

[82] Bibliothèque Publique et Universitaire, Geneva, Dumont Papers, 33 (1). 101.
[83] *Pauper Management Improved*, pp. 126–39.

Bentham investigated in detail the proper care of children; their condition inside the House was to be made more, not less, eligible than that of children outside, and Bentham even hoped that once the advantages were known parents of the superior classes might abandon private boarding schools and send their children to the new houses.[84] Thus Bentham's *Chrestomathia*, his great plan of education, had its beginnings in the Poor Plan, and a most elaborate programme for the period of non-age was prepared at this time, but not published. In the printed sections of *Pauper Management Improved* only employment was discussed, including such devices as a platform on which infants exercised and at the same time pumped water while it tilted like a see-saw. One of the unpublished pieces is a solemn little essay proposing a National Music Seminary, in which Bentham discussed the charge that music encouraged drunkenness. He concluded that this might be true of vocal music, but that it was evident that instrumental music must cease as the executant became intoxicated; even so, he admitted vocal music to the House of Industry, provided apprentices sang *God Save the King* and not 'the Marseilles song'. As an afterthought he suggested that the assembled paupers might sing a song listing the qualities of a good House of Industry governor, a pleasant recognition of merit if deserved and a suitably ironic reminder if not.[85]

Bentham's concern for learning did not cease with the education of apprentices. 'Observation and experiment compose the basis of all knowledge. . . . The institution of the proposed Company would afford the first opportunity ever presented to mankind, of enriching the treasury of useful knowledge by contributions furnished on a national scale, and on a regular and all-embracing plan, and would thus form an epoch—not only in political economy, but in many and many another branch of science.'[86] With such facilities for experiment science could reach peaks of certainty hitherto undreamed of, and Bentham set out plans of research in medicine, child welfare, technology, meteorology and many other fields. One might even make discoveries in such hitherto unexplored territories as the best age for matrimony, a question of some importance for the apprentices. They should be allowed the 'comforts of matrimony' at 'the earliest period compatible with health', but when was that? If marriage was a desirable state, the longer the duration the greater the happiness; there would be no economic bar to early marriage in the House, but what of the physical danger of early indulgence

---

[84] *Pauper Management Improved*, pp. 229–43. Compare Bentham's essay on the care of infants in Bentham Papers, CXXXIII. 13–16, 98.

[85] Bentham Papers, CXLIX. 54–65, 91; on Sunday sport and relaxation see *ibid.* 83–90.

[86] *Pauper Management Improved*, p. 243.

and the moral danger of entering a state of power and independence before intellectual faculties were fully grown? Let the answer be discovered by experiment:

Nature shows the commencement of the ability—nature shows the commencement of the desire—How long must the ability continue useless? How long must the desire be a source of vexation instead of enjoyment?—Questions, surely, not uninteresting—surely not undeserving of solution! To give the solution, I see but one course:—to take the visible commencement of physical maturity in each individual for the standard and basis of experiment; from this starting point to mark out periods of delay—3 months–6 months—9 months and so on, for a small—it surely need not be a large—number of years—21 in the male ought to be the utmost. From thenceforward observe the condition of the classes—see whether there be any and what perceptible differences in point of health and strength, as between class and class.

Fiat lux were the words of the Almighty:—*Fiat experimentum*, were the words of the brightest genius he ever made. O chemists!—much have your crucibles shown us of dead matter;—but our industry house is a crucible for men![87]

Harsh and repellent though much of Bentham's plan must always appear, the sincere exultation with which he wrote the section on Pauper Comforts is undeniable:

We now stand upon proud ground. Having elsewhere plucked the mask from the visage of *false charity*, the arch enemy no less of comfort than of industry, let us take up *true charity* and seat her upon her throne. *Economy* too shall have her day. But her place is in the second rank. Charity is the *end*, economy but the *means*.[88]

Apprentices would enjoy, as well as the comfort of early matrimony, a scientifically determined diet, 'exemption from intellectual exercises of the most painful kind' (such as learning dead languages), and freedom from a sense of privation and confinement (never having known anything else). Female apprentices would also enjoy 'security against seduction', opportunities for safe discourse with the opposite sex and a complete training for matrimony, including Rumford's cookery. All paupers would enjoy health and longevity, security against want, cleanliness, healthy employment, comfortable nights ('vermin, of course, extirpated') and a 'clear conscience brightened by religious hopes' (aided by 'seclusion from incentives to sin'). There would be 'entertainments of various kinds, a day in a week—psalmody and other suitable music—concourse drawn by music, physico-theological lectures' and other pleasant trifles. All classes would have special benefits, and even the physically handicapped would gain opportunities for marriage. As

[87] *Works*, VIII. 437. This section of *Pauper Management Improved* was printed in the *Annals of Agriculture* but omitted from the edition of 1812.
[88] *Pauper Management Improved*, p. 265.

rewards for the diligent there would be extra comforts, such as pocket money and holidays, a superior diet and even separate cottages. 'Post-Prosperity' or 'Decayed Gentility' hands would be given some extra comforts as a matter of course, as would 'Old Stagers' from existing workhouses.[89] All these superfluities, all relief above necessities, would come from private charity, the Company acting as trustee.

So much for comfort; what of liberty? The restraint, Bentham alleged, would be no greater than in the army, the navy or the diplomatic service. 'If security against everything that savours of tyranny be liberty, liberty, in the instance of this hitherto luckless class of human beings can scarcely ever have yet existed in anything near so perfect a shape. . . . But liberty, in a favourite sense of it, means *lawless power*: in this sense there will not only be no liberty, but in plain truth there will be none.'[90] And the restraints on liberty in the House were nothing compared with the powers given for the Extirpation of Mendicity: rewards were to be offered for the apprehension of beggars, who were to be forced into the House until they had paid off all costs and found employment outside. Mendicity must be destroyed as an attractive profession:

In this country . . . the condition of the common beggar is more eligible' in his own estimate at least, than that of a pauper; for, if it were not, he could become a pauper. . . . If notwithstanding the adoption of the proposed system in other respects, begging were to be tolerated, the nuisance could be much greater than at present.

It was essential to free society from 'a species of extortion to which the tender-hearted, and they only, are exposed. . . . From the digsust excited by a filthy beggar, none by the equally filthy stand exempt'.[91]

The Extirpation of Mendicity was but one of the collateral benefits to society promised by the Plan. Employment secured (by the Gazette), Temporary Indigence Relieved (by loans), Infant Mortality Diminished, Useful Knowledge Disseminated, Voluntary Charity Assisted, National Force Strengthened (by military training), Conveyance Facilitated (by making Houses inns for travelling workmen), Imprisonment Rendered Inexpensive and Reformative (for debtors), Domestic Morality Enforced (by using Houses as reformatories for bad parents and children, and as asylums from 'domestic tyranny')—all these advantages and others were planned in detail. The terms of reference for the directors obliged them to establish Registry Offices, Loan Offices, Frugality Banks, Superannuation-Annuity Banks, Post-obit-benefit

---

[89] *Ibid.* pp. 265–88.
[90] *Works*, VIII. 436.
[91] *Pauper Management Improved*, pp. 140–52; and compare Bentham Papers, CXLIX, 47–53, CLIVa. 168–277.

Banks, Charitable Remittance Offices, Frugality Inns, Dispensaries, Lying-in Hospitals, Midwifery Lecture Schools, Veterinary Lecture Schools, Military Exercise Schools and Marine Schools. The Midwifery Lecture Schools and Medical Dispensaries were mentioned only in passing in *Pauper Management Improved*, but the *Essays* show them as a comprehensive plan for medical relief with much interesting administrative detail and progressive views on treatment.[92] And the proposal for Frugality Banks was the first detailed scheme for savings banks, differing from those fashionable later mainly in holding the funds in the form of annuities rather than simple interest-bearing deposits. The annuities were to be for specific purposes, even including 'ostentatious burials (a phantastic, yet generally prevalent demand)', and thus bore some resemblance to friendly society benefits. Bentham shared the usual upper-class ambivalence towards friendly societies: 'if there were any option in the case, choosing a tippling house for a school of frugality, would be like choosing a brothel for a school of continence'. Labourers could and should save, and the Frugality Banks were designed to meet their needs; ultimately the Banks could also insure the poor, but until it was possible to calculate risks on an actuarial basis it was better to leave that function to the friendly societies, perhaps with the Houses acting as bankers to them.[93]

8. *The Fate of Bentham's Plan*

Such was Bentham's Poor Plan, and he thought the time propitious for its adoption: 'the state of society and the progress made by political intelligence is up to the requisite pitch, and is not got beyond it'. Criticism of the plan as Utopian stung him. 'Utopia is a country in which desirable effects are exhibited as being brought into execution, but without the exhibition of any causes adequate for the production of such effects', whereas Bentham had shown effectual causes based on 'authenticated facts'.[94] All sensible men should be convinced, and all benevolent men overjoyed. 'A secure provision for the indigent is to the philanthropist what a pineapple is to the epicure.'[95]

[92] Bentham Papers, CLIIIa. 46–50; and compare CLIIa. 201–5 on veterinary schools.
[93] *Ibid.* CLIIIa. 32–42; *Pauper Management Improved*, pp. 166–208. Bentham also suggested special marriage deposits. 'A maiden known to have lovers, may come to take pride in the magnitude [of their savings]. . . . Frugality, being thus brought forward by desire, as it were in a hot-bed, in the spring of life, will maintain itself in the maturer seasons' (*ibid.* pp. 178–9). Bentham rejected the argument that this would provide an artificial stimulus to population: the multiplication of the productive was always to be encouraged, but not of the unproductive, be they rich or poor.
[94] Bentham Papers, CLIVb. 547; CLI. 400.
[95] *Ibid.* CLIIb. 539.

He was to be disillusioned. In 1795, when the Poor Plan was begun, the act authorising the establishment of an experimental Panopticon‑Penitentiary was but a year old; by 1798 he had spent much of his fortune on preparations, and was complaining of 'four years of chilling neglect and disturbing silence'. In 1797 a committee on finance reported favourably on the penitentiary, but its advice was disregarded. In the midst of his growing concern about the prison plan, Bentham threw himself into gaining support for the pauper Panopticon, with the assistance of Patrick Colquhoun; Colquhoun had prepared a plan of his own for the poor in 1796 and was later to press his system of police on the public attention, but he assisted Bentham in gathering information and consented to sponsor the Plan. An advertisement was drafted calling on all those interested in investing in the National Charity Company to send donations to a fund (to be administered by Colquhoun and Bentham) for collecting information to complete the plan, and for gaining parliamentary support.[96] Arthur Young was said to have been 'enraptured' with the proposal, and to have provided 250 copies from the *Annals* for distribution.[97] Some lists have survived, and among those appealed to were Abbot, Morton Pitt, Wilberforce, Sir Charles Bunbury, Eden, Romilly, Lansdowne, Fox, Holland, Bernard, Parr, Sinclair, Rumford, and of course Rose, Dundas and Pitt. The appeal for information (to complete the Pauper Population Tables) did not get much response. Some parishes (such as St Giles' and St George's, Bloomsbury) refused to co-operate, and the comment of one correspondent was typical: he would try to complete the table, but the records were imperfect; in any case the plan looked better suited to a charity school than a poor-house. Bentham himself sought the support of various philanthropic societies, without much success.[98]

The crucial question was the reaction of Pitt and Rose. There is no evidence that they seriously considered so daring (and so eccentric) a proposal, except Bentham's own assertion. In 1830 he told a dramatic story: how Rose sent for him, told him that Pitt and Dundas had read the plan and wanted to discuss it with him, only to dash his hopes later with the news that the plan was disapproved, (by George III, Bentham

---

[96] Colquhoun's plan is in *ibid*. CLI. 40; and the advertisement in *ibid*. CLI. 102–5. For Colquhoun's assistance with the later annuity scheme see *Jeremy Bentham's Economic Writings*, II. 73. In 1805 Bentham wrote a petulant letter to Dumont accusing him of unfaithfulness and comparing him with Colquhoun, a true friend (Dumont Papers 33 (1). 124).

[97] *Works*, XI. 102. Young certainly gave space in the *Annals* to the Plan in 1797–8, but there is no evidence that he felt real enthusiasm for it apart from Bentham's claim.

[98] Bentham Papers, CXXXIII. 74–80; CXLIX. 115–17; CLIVa. 53–4, 586; CLIVb. 586–8. 'Silver and gold have I none: but what I have—a project—that I give unto you'.

presumed). Thereafter the Pauper Plan joined the Panopticon Penitentiary in the limbo of government procrastination. Both were eventually presented to a Parliamentary Committee in 1811 and rejected, and Bentham received £23,000 compensation. 'Never', wrote Wilberforce, 'was any one worse used. I have seen the tears run down the cheeks of that strong-minded man through vexation. . . .' Bentham did not suffer in silence, and his friends had frequently to restrain him from provocative action; it is to be supposed that he did not in fact send Pitt the memorandum of 1798 on 'the want of dispatch in public work' which is preserved in his papers.[99] By 1830 the whole episode seemed the great disappointment of his life.

Never does the current of my thoughts alight upon the Panopticon and its fate, but my heart sinks within me: upon the Panopticon in both its branches, —the prison branch and the pauper branch: upon what they are now, and what they ought to have been.[100]

In the early years of the century the disappointment, though just as bitter, undoubtedly contributed to turning his mind from reform by government initiative to the radical reform of government itself.

Two questions remain to be considered. Did Bentham abandon his plan in later years? And did his analysis of the problem have any influence in the later debate on pauperism and the reform of 1834? The latter question will be discussed below, though it should be noted that neither Bentham nor his Plan was much mentioned in the spate of discussion of the years that followed; his influence must be sought through personal discipleship rather than public fame.[101] Surprisingly, perhaps, it is not easy to decide whether Bentham abandoned his plan. Why were his writings on pauperism almost entirely restricted to the years 1795–98? Why did he hold aloof in the great post-war debate on the subject? Why was the Plan not reprinted after 1812? Most puzzling of all, why was it not mentioned in the discussion of indigence in the *Theory of Legislation* of 1802, or the *Constitutional Code* of 1830?

Bentham's nostalgia for the Pauper Plan in 1830 suggests that he had never repudiated it. He is said to have been 'converted' by Malthus in 1802—and certainly he wrote some gloomy passages on the population

[99] For a brief account of the Panopticon negotiations see L. Stephen, *op. cit.* I. 193–206. No copy of Bentham's Plan survives in Pitt's papers. The memorandum of 1798 is in Bentham Papers, CXXXIII. 79.

[100] *Works*, XI. 103; and compare Bentham Papers, CXV. 143–5.

[101] The plan was mentioned in some accounts of workhouse schemes; in 1814 William Allen claimed that *Pauper Management Improved* contained 'on the subject the best ideas we have met in print' (*The Philanthropist*, IV, 18), but such enthusiasm was exceptional.

question after that date—but did the conversion extend to Poor Law matters? It could have been no more than a clarification of ideas Bentham already held, and a critical aside in 1808 on Malthus's 'inflexibility' and 'bitter remedy' suggests that Malthus's practical conclusions were not acceptable to him.[102] All the references to indigence in later works show that Bentham was still in favour of a Poor Law; and if the Malthusian argument could not make him an abolitionist, how could it persuade him to abandon his own Plan, which specifically provided for an increase in population?

Bentham's later silence can be explained in quite other terms. He hated working over old material, and increasingly left even the final drafts of his plans to his assistants. And having published a plan, the onus was on the government to be wise enough to adopt it. With little time and less inclination for propaganda, Bentham moved on to solving the rest of the problems of the world. Before the Pauper Plan was complete he was already immersed in other questions in political economy, in currency reform, his annuity note scheme, and ultimately in his *Defence of a Maximum*.[103] And the omission of the Plan from the sections on indigence in the *Theory of Legislation* and the *Constitutional Code* is only puzzling until it is remembered that Bentham always distinguished carefully between general principles applicable to all states, and particular plans prepared for particular countries and circumstances. Thus Dumont omitted the Pauper Plan from the *Theory of Legislation*, but his papers preserve an attempt to recast it for continental readers in another work.[104] And the *Constitutional Code*,

---

[102] *Works*, V.21. On Bentham's alleged conversion see *Jeremy Bentham's Economic Writings* I. 57n; and *Theory of Legislation*, note to p. 114 and the appendix on sex, pp. 473–97. The gloomy remarks on population in *Pannomial Fragments*, *Works*, IV. 227–9 have already been cited.

[103] In *The True Alarm* Bentham asserted that depreciation of the currency was a more urgent problem than indigence, since it was progressive (*Jeremy Bentham's Economic Writings*, III. 66, and compare 164).

[104] Bentham's letters to Dumont include criticism of his work on *The Theory of Legislation* (for example for making him preach equality among priests, 'who am a Church of England man') but did not object to the omission of the Pauper Plan (Dumont Papers 33 (1). 91, 95). In later correspondence he continued to lament the fate of the Panopticon scheme, referring to all three forms—prison, school and workhouse—in a letter from Ford Abbey in 1817 (*ibid.* 33 (1). 159). The MSS of Dumont's *Examen des maux qui opposent au bonheur public* includes a chapter based on the *Essays*, and also a brief statement of the Malthusian principle of population with a claim that Bentham anticipated it, and that it did not invalidate his Plan (*ibid.* 56. 50–5). In another MS, *Mémoire et observations sur l'administration des Pauvres, d'après un ouvrage de Bentham*, Dumont adapted and generalised *Pauper Management Improved*. There is no evidence that either work was published. See also W. Stark, 'Jeremy Bentham as an Economist', *Ec. Journal* (1946), 583–90, for stress on Bentham's inductive approach to economic problems.

being a work for the world at large, was very properly cautious in its references to particular conditions in any country. Significantly, the chief point insisted upon in the section on indigence was the justice of claims to relief. For a man who did not believe in abstract rights, Bentham came closer than most of his contemporaries to consistently asserting the right of the poor to relief through a legal provision:

In his endeavour to provide a remedy against deficiency, in regard to subsistence, the legislator finds himself all along under the pressure of this dilemma—forbear to provide supply, and death ensues, and it has you for its author; provide supply, you establish a bounty upon idleness, and you give increase to the deficiency which it is your endeavour to exclude.

Under the pressure of this dilemma, how to act is a problem, the solution of which will in a great degree, be dependent upon local circumstances: nor can anything like a complete solution be so much as attempted without continual reference to them. One leading observation applies to all places and all times. So long as any particle of the matter of abundance remains in any one hand, it will rest with those, to whom it appears that they are able to assign a sufficient reason, to show why the requisite supply to any deficiency in the means of subsistence should be refused.[105]

9. *Malthus: the Thesis*

The *Essay on the Principle of Population etc.* which Malthus published in 1798 was an effective piece of pamphleteering, claiming originality only in the application of ideas and not in the ideas themselves. Malthus always professed that the principle of population was simple, and in part self-evident; the lengthy additions which swelled the second and later editions were illustrations of its operation, not proofs of its validity. Of course Malthus exaggerated the simplicity of the question, and the clarity of his own argument. The considerable debate which soon developed concerning both his theory and the conclusions he drew from it was as full of misunderstanding as it was of recrimination. Although it is primarily the application of the principle of population to the question of poverty and its relief which is relevant here, some account of the Malthusian chain of argument must be attempted, if not an assessment of its validity.[106]

---

[105] *Constitutional Code, Works*, IX. 13. Stark surprisingly describes the passage as 'clearly Malthusian' (*Jeremy Bentham's Economic Writings*, I. 57). The Code differed from the Plan in proposing an Indigence Relief Minister rather than a Company, but of course one aim of the whole work was to reform government so that it would be capable of such functions.

[106] References below to *An Essay on the Principle of Population, as it Affects the Future Improvement of Society* etc. (1798) are to the fascimile edition of 1926, cited

Put most briefly, the Malthusian thesis claimed that the natural rate of increase of population was much greater than the highest conceivable rate of increase in subsistence, and population was therefore restrained within the limits of subsistence only by the operation of a number of checks. The argument began with two postulates: 'that food is necessary to the existence of man'; and 'that the passion between the sexes is necessary, and will remain nearly in its present state'. The principle followed:

Assuming, then, my postulata as granted, I say, that the power of population is indefinitely greater than the power in the earth to produce subsistence for man. Population, when unchecked, increases in a geometrical ratio.

Subsistence increases only in an arithmetical ratio. A slight acquaintance with numbers will shew the immensity of the first power in comparison with the second. By that law of nature which makes food necessary to the life of man, the effects of these two unequal powers must be kept equal. This implies a strong and constantly operating check on population from the difficulty of subsistence. This difficulty must fall some where; and must necessarily be severely felt by a large portion of mankind.[107]

Ratios are merely comparative things, unless there are indications of the speed of the process. Malthus cited the United States as an example of an exceptionally favourable situation for population growth, and claimed that its population had doubled within twenty-five years. He was content to accept this as the natural rate of growth, although checks to population did exist even in America. In a long-settled country like England it might be possible to double the output of subsistence within twenty-five years, but inconceivable that it could be doubled again within the next twenty-five. Hence the pressure of population

---

[107] *Essay* (1798), pp. 11, 13–14. Malthus cited Hume, Wallace and Price as the main sources of his views in 1798; by 1803 he had read much more widely. On pre-Malthusian views on population see J. Bonar, *Theories of Population from Raleigh to Arthur Young* (1931). An essay anticipating some Malthusian points may be found in *The Cabinet; by a Society of Gentlemen* (Norwich, 1795) I. 195–212.

---

as *Essay* (1798). References to the later editions entitled *An Essay on the Principle of Population; or a View of its Past and Present Effects on Human Happiness* etc. are cited as *Essay* with the relevant date. Among secondary works on Malthus, J. Bonar, *Malthus and his Work* (1885) and J. A. Field, *Essays on Population* etc. (1931) are still indispensable; G. F. McLeary, *The Malthusian Population Theory* (1953) is clear and sound. K. Smith, *The Malthusian Controversy* (1951) and R. B. Simons, 'T. R. Malthus on British Society', *Journal of the History of Ideas*, XVI (1955) are relevant to this study but sometimes unsympathetic. For typical claims that Malthus was the father of the new Poor Law see Bishop Otter's Memoir in the 1836 edition of the *Principles of Political Economy*, p. xix; Bonar, *op. cit.* pp. 304–5, 317–8; and Smith, *op. cit.* pp. 296, 301.

upon resources in long-settled countries existed in the present, and not merely in the future.[108] Since nowhere except in newly-settled lands did population increase at its natural rate, the existence of checks must be presumed. Malthus classified the checks to population in two quite different ways. He first drew a distinction between positive checks (those bringing premature mortality through pressure of want) and preventive checks (prudential delays in marriage through inability to maintain a family). This distinction was, or could have been, objective and empirical; the second was openly evaluative. In 1798 Malthus described all checks as resolvable into vice or misery, vice as a 'highly probable consequence' of the pressure of population, and misery as an 'absolutely necessary consequence'. In 1803 he added a third pigeon-hole, moral restraint 'that restraint from marriage which was not followed by irregular gratification'.[109] The distinction between preventive and positive checks was the more significant theoretically, but that between vice, misery and moral restraint was vital to his conclusions on practical affairs. Malthus did not introduce moral restraint as a new check in 1803, as is often alleged, since the practice itself was fully described in 1798; all he did was to modify the assertion that all checks were resolvable into vice and misery. Hazlitt, and many others, alleged that this completely destroyed the argument against perfectibility. This is an exaggeration; it merely weakened it sufficiently to allow a loophole for improvement, since Malthus could argue plausibly that moral restraint was unlikely to become universal.

Malthus illustrated the preventive and positive checks in 1798 with English examples.

The preventive check appears to operate in some degree through all the ranks of society in England. There are some men, even in the highest rank, who are prevented from marrying by the idea of the expences they must retrench, and the fancied pleasures that they must deprive themselves of, on the supposition of having a family . . . .

The labourer who earns eighteen pence a day, and lives with some degree of comfort as a single man, will hesitate a little before he divides that pittance

---

[108] *Essay* (1798), pp. 18–26. The figures for the American increase were disputed and eventually disproved.

[109] The 1803 edition listed all the checks in more detail than in 1798, distinguishing in the preventive between chaste delay in marriage (moral restraint) and 'promiscuous intercourse, unnatural passions, violations of the marriage bed, aud improper acts to conceal the consequences of irregular connexions' (p. 11). Malthus reprobated birth control as a vice, and assumed reproduction up to the physiological limit after marriage: compare Field, *op. cit.* pp. 93–4; N. E. Himes' edition of Place's *Illustrations and Proofs* etc. (1930), pp. 283–90; and Himes' own *Medical History of Contraception* (1936). Malthus also mentioned an 'ultimate check' to population—starvation—but claimed it rarely operated.

among four or five. . . . He must feel conscious, if he thinks at all, that, should he have a large family, and any ill luck whatever, no degree of frugality, no possible exertion of his manual strength, could preserve him from the heart rending sensation of seeing his children starve, or forfeiting his independence, and being obliged to the parish for their support.[110]

The positive check, on the other hand, operated mainly among the poor alone, and its symptom was high mortality among the young:

> The sons and daughters of peasants will not be found such rosy cherubs in real life, as they are described to be in romances. It cannot fail to be remarked by those who live much in the country, that the sons of labourers are very apt to be stunted in their growth. . . . The lads who drive plough, which must certainly be a healthy exercise, are very rarely seen with any appearance of calves to their legs; a circumstance, which can only be attributed to a want either of proper, or of sufficient nourishment.[111]

It was the multiplication of such examples, drawn from all the world from Indostan to Van Diemen's Land, which swelled the second edition into so weighty a volume.

The whole argument was summed up in 1803 in three propositions:

1. Population is necessarily limited by the means of subsistence.
2. Population invariably increases, when the means of subsistence increase, unless prevented by some very powerful and obvious checks.
3. These checks, and the checks which repress the superior power of population, and keep its effects on a level with the means of subsistence, are all resolvable into moral restraint, vice and misery.[112]

The argument was simple, but it provoked almost as many questions as it answered. What, for example, is the use and validity of the famous ratios? Although Malthus always kept them at the forefront of his exposition, they proved an embarrassment to later Malthusians such as J. S. Mill. The geometrical ratio could be applied to all living things, but only at so abstract a level that it is completely misleading as a 'law' of increase for any actual population; not until Booth and

[110] *Essay* (1798), pp. 63, 67.
[111] *Ibid.* p. 73. This is one of the few passages in the 1798 edition revealing direct observation of the lower classes. Simons criticises Malthus for not making 'any first-hand study of the life and work of the English poor in a factory town' (*op. cit.* p. 73); on the other hand he is often praised as an 'empirical' or 'historical' political economist in comparison with Ricardo. P. James (ed.), *The Travel Diaries of Thomas Robert Malthus* (1966) shows that Malthus did visit Dale's mill at Lanark in 1810 (pp. 221, 223–4) and that he was always inquisitive about conditions on his Scandinavian visit in 1799. But it would be difficult to argue that his theories were based on systematic empirical observation, voluminous though the practical illustrations of the theories became. And Malthus showed little interest in the actual administration of poor relief, at home or abroad; he was to have dined with 'Mr. Voght' in Hamburg in 1799 but the engagement was cancelled (*ibid.* p. 37).
[112] *Essay* (1803), p. 16.

Ravenstone attempted to estimate the reproductive powers of populations with given age and sex structures did realism enter the demographic calculations.[113] And the arithmetical ratio was not even a co-ordinate of the geometrical, since it was a loose empirical generalisation about things as they are, while the other was a calculation of things as they might be. As an empirical generalisation it was extraordinarily crude, based on no real investigation of the actual conditions under which subsistence could be increased. By the time of J. S. Mill the arithmetical ratio had been replaced in the theory by the doctrine of diminishing returns, a concept Malthus may or may not have hinted at himself.[114] On the whole the ratios were not as vital to the argument as Malthus and many of his critics thought. They gave a misleadingly precise form to a thesis which did not need to be precise at all, the thesis that even a moderate estimate of the power of increase of human population was greater than even an optimistic estimate of the possible increase in subsistence.

The Malthusian law of population had some resemblance to Newtonian mechanics in assuming tendencies which in the real world could never be observed in unchecked operation.[115] Most of the rival 'laws' of population growth, from Weyland to Sadler, denied this distinction between the natural and the observable growth of population, and the hypothesis of pressure and checks. But all the 'historical' laws of population so constructed could be translated into the Malthusian pattern, which had the basic scientific virtue of adaptability to most situations. Nevertheless Malthus was not always careful in applying it, and his theory of wages and attack on the Poor Law in particular rested on questionable assumptions. As Senior and Whately pointed out, it is one thing to assert the potentiality of population to increase faster than subsistence, and another to claim that numbers did press more or less constantly on food supply. The saving clause in the theory was the preventive check, which, if common enough, could permit subsistence to increase without a corresponding increase in population. But Malthus was never willing to abandon his pessimistic view of the precariousness of the balance between population and

[113] In *ibid.* p. 491 Malthus admitted that the fecundity of the human species depended on 'the power of women in bearing children' and not simply on 'the passion between the sexes', but did not develop the point. Field aptly described the ratios as 'a particularly good example of his misrepresentation of what is incontrovertible' (*op. cit.* p. 6).

[114] Compare E. Cannan, *A History of the Theories of Production and Distribution* etc. (1953 ed.), pp. 113–14, 142; and Field, *op. cit.* pp. 15–16.

[115] For an acute analysis of the logic of the Malthusian argument see A. Flew, 'The Structure of Malthus' Population Theory', *Australasian Journal of Philosophy*, 35 (1957) pp. 1–20.

subsistence as a generalisation, although in specific cases he would admit that happier circumstances could exist.

Malthus recognised several possible relationships between population and subsistence in the short run, and cannot be acquitted of adopting the particular hypothesis which best suited his polemical purpose in the discussion of actual examples. Thus in attacking schemes of equality and the Poor Law he usually assumed that every increase in subsistence would be followed automatically by a corresponding increase in population, although (to be fair) he supported this prediction by claiming that such systems were especially unfavourable to the practice of the preventive check.[116] For society as it in fact existed, Malthus offered in 1798 (and retained in later editions) a relatively crude model of population and subsistence increasing alternately in 'a sort of oscillation'. If population and subsistence were balanced, population would increase, forcing down real wages and discouraging marriage; low wages would make labourers work harder and would then encourage farmers to cultivate more land; an increase in produce would restore 'tolerable comfort' to the labourers, and encourage them to multiply again. This model assumed that the power of increase of population was the mainspring of the process, that any increase in subsistence would soon be overtaken, and that the condition of the labourer varied below, and not above, tolerable comfort. It was never repudiated, but in examining English population growth in later editions, and in his only systematic discussion of the determinants of wages (in the *Principles*, in 1820), Malthus recognised happier alternatives. Had his starting point in the whole argument been the explanation of contemporary circumstances, rather than the refutation of future predictions, the whole structure of the argument might well have been very different.[117]

Malthus recognised that 'subsistence' was a relative and not an absolute standard, although he failed to analyse it (for example into necessaries, comforts and luxuries as Senior did later). In discussing English conditions in the *Essay*, and in the chapter on wages in the *Principles*, he admitted that an increase in real wages (that is, in available subsistence per head), might lead not to increased population but to a permanently higher standard of living, provided the labourers chose to exercise a preventive check to preserve it. Since a higher standard of living would reduce the positive checks, a prodigious prudence would

[116] See *Essay* (1798), pp. 184–5, where it is assumed that the preventive check could not operate at all in a system of equality.

[117] *Ibid.* pp. 29–31. Despite common assertions to the contrary, Malthus was not stimulated to write by observation of contemporary English population growth. In 1798 he believed that growth was very slow, though he rejected Price's allegations of depopulation.

be required to restrain population and maintain that high standard of living unless subsistence was increasing extraordinarily rapidly. In the English case he found precisely this situation—an expanding economy, a falling mortality, and a lower birth rate than might have been expected—but he did not think it could last. Alternatively, population could increase faster than the increase in subsistence, if the accepted standard of living were allowed to fall, as in Ireland. Malthus was of course no enemy to population increase as such; what he desired was an increase which was accompanied by fewer positive checks and more preventive, a healthier and more prudent population with a higher standard of living.[118]

It was, however, only in 1820 that the variables in the relation of population to subsistence were discussed at all systematically. Earlier, the successive editions of the *Essay* continued to give the impression that the pressure of population on subsistence was hard and more or less constant. The preventive check, although freely recognised in 1798, was continually presented as the desirable but not the usual limitation on population. It was desirable only in the form of moral restraint, and Malthus's formulation of this virtue was so strict that his pessimism on the future spread of the preventive check followed logically enough. What labourer could be certain, before he married, of being able to support a large family, come what may? Yet this was what Malthus required of him.[119] Even if the majority delayed marriage until the age of thirty, what proportion could be expected to remain virtuous through the lusty years of youth? Malthus undoubtedly exaggerated the need for an increase in the preventive check, by over-estimating the reproductive powers of an actual population. In the English case he also under-estimated the power of increase in subsistence; English population increased vastly in the nineteenth century, with no fall in living standards. But the case was a special one, and in so far as Malthus foresaw the development of an industrial trading economy dependent on food imports, he deplored it. To some extent he also under-estimated the pressures working in favour of the preventive check. To him, moral restraint was born of prudence out of fear; in all the examples he quoted in 1798 the motive for prudential restraint from marriage

---

[118] See, for example, *Essay* (1806), II. 433–4, 441. In the successive versions of the chapter on English population in Book II of the second and later editions of the *Essay* Malthus always stressed that population was increasing from a declining death-rate; G. T. Griffith under-estimated this emphasis in claiming that Malthus 'emphasized the wrong side of the problem' (*Population Problems of the Age of Malthus*, pp. 99–100).

[119] In *Essay* (1803), p. 595, Malthus conceded that a man with more than six children might have some claim to relief since he was burdened beyond rational expectation.

was the fear of falling in the social scale. This coloured his attitude to the Poor Law: men needed misery, or at least insecurity, to prod them into virtue. Malthus did note, once, that extreme misery was an enemy to both virtue and prudence,[120] but refused to admit that the relief of abject distress might encourage prudence, rather than destroy it. Hope could be a stronger incentive to foresight than fear, and a rising standard of living might generate its own safeguards. When Senior stressed ambition as an effective motive for moral restraint he did not refute the Malthusian theory, but he did alter its practical corollaries. Nevertheless Malthus's pessimism on the future practice of moral restraint was not altogether unreasonable, since so many modern societies have thought contraception to be a necessary alternative form of preventive check.

The Malthusian theory soon became an essential part of the classical doctrine on wages, despite the fact that the *Essay* contained little systematic discussion of the question.[121] Malthus was largely responsible for the notion of the Wages Fund, which, in its cruder forms, gained classical wage theory so bad a reputation. When, in 1820, Malthus considered the question of wages in general, his treatment of both the demand and the supply of labour was much more flexible than in the *Essay*. In earlier writings, and especially in the attack on the Poor Law, the implied views on wages were rigid and gloomy in the extreme. The demand for labour was defined solely in terms of 'the funds for the maintenance of labour'—the existing stock of necessities in society—and the supply of labour was assumed to increase not only with every increase in these funds, but with every attempt to raise money incomes. Neither poor relief nor wage increases could therefore raise the real income of the poor, which depended ultimately on their own moral restraint alone. The attack on the Poor Law reveals Malthus at his most dogmatic. Since it is our main concern here, it is as well to stress that Malthus's contribution to social thought was greater than the following pages might suggest; we still, with justice, associate his name with our continuing concern with the balance of population and resources. His great achievement was to suggest that numbers and prosperity, as goals and tendencies, may work not in harmony, but in opposition.

10. *Malthus: the Attack on the Poor Law*

Malthus first attacked the Poor Law in 1798, in asides in the discussion

---

[120] *Ibid.* pp. 513–16.
[121] On the Malthusian contribution to wage theory see Cannan, *op. cit.* pp. 187–90, and F. W. Taussig, *Wages and Capital* (1896), chap. viii.

of preventive and positive checks. Prudence did restrain some labourers from premature marriage, 'though the parish law of England, it must be confessed, is a system of all others the most calculated gradually to weaken this sentiment, and in the end, may eradicate it completely'.[122] And the positive checks of misery and premature mortality operated despite the vast sums spent on the relief of poverty. Why? Because a Poor Law could not in fact relieve misery; its natural tendency was to increase it.

The Malthusian attack on poor relief began with a sweeping claim that no distribution of money could possibly raise the general standard of comfort among the poor. If, by contribution from the rich, all those on eighteen pence a day were given five shillings a day, the only result would be to raise the price of food in that proportion. A monetary contribution to an individual could improve his position, but it would proportionately depress the rest of his class. The redistribution of money from rich to poor might encourage a greater production of foodstuffs (although, unlike manufacturers, food responded slowly to demand) but 'the spur that these fancied riches would give to population, would more than counterbalance it, and the increased produce would have to be distributed among a more than proportionately increased number of people'. Moreover, there would be less work:

> The receipt of five shillings a day, instead of eighteen pence would make every man fancy himself comparatively rich, and able to indulge himself in many hours or days of leisure. This would give a strong and immediate check to productive industry; and in a short time, not only the nation would be poorer, but the lower classes themselves would be much more distressed than when they received only eighteen pence a day . . . no possible contributions or sacrifices of the rich, particularly in money, could for any time prevent the recurrence of distress among the lower members of society whoever they were. Great changes might, indeed, be made. The rich might become poorer, and some of the poor more rich: but a part of the society must necessarily feel a difficulty of living; and this difficulty will naturally fall on the least fortunate members.[123]

This general argument was then applied to the Poor Laws:

> Their first obvious tendency is to increase population without increasing the food or its support. A poor man may marry with little or no prospect of being able to support a family in independence. They may be said therefore in some measure to create the poor which they maintain; and as the provisions of the country must, in consequence of the increased population, be distributed to every man in smaller proportions, it is evident that the labour of

[122] *Essay* (1798), pp. 67–8.
[123] *Ibid.* pp. 75–9.

152

those who are not supported by parish assistance, will purchase a smaller quantity of provisions than before, and consequently, more of them must be driven to ask for support.[124]

Everything given to the undeserving and unproductive paupers was given at the expense of the deserving independent labourers, since it raised the price of food and reduced real wages. And, above all, the very existence of the Poor Law destroyed that prudence which, under the stimulus of fear of want, best protected the comfort of the labourer. 'The labouring poor, to use a vulgar expression, seem always to live from hand to mouth.'

Finally the system as a whole, and the harshness of cruel overseers and the Law of Settlement in particular, formed a collection of 'grating, inconvenient and tyrannical laws, totally inconsistent with the genuine spirit of the constitution'. This very harshness had in some measure limited the natural evil effects of the principle of relief itself:

Fortunately for England, a spirit of independence still remains among the peasantry. The poor-laws are strongly calculated to eradicate this spirit. They have succeeded in part; but had they succeeded as completely as might have been expected, their pernicious tendency would not have been so long concealed.[125]

Two conclusions were drawn from the discussion:

Hard as it may appear in individual instances, dependent poverty ought to be held disgraceful. Such a stimulus seems to be absolutely necessary to promote the happiness of the great mass of mankind; and every general attempt to weaken this stimulus, however benevolent its apparent intention, will always defeat its own purpose. . . .
Every obstacle in the way of marriage must undoubtedly be considered as a species of unhappiness. But as from the laws of our nature some check to population must exist, it is better that it should be checked from a foresight of the difficulties attending a family, and the fear of dependent poverty, than that it should be encouraged, only to be repressed afterwards by want and sickness.[126]

This was vigorous denunciation indeed, but as a thesis it lacked thoroughness. Certainly it did not all follow closely from the principle of population. The allegation that the system was harsh and tyrannical conflicted with the general trend of the argument, as Malthus later saw. More important, the principle of population was not invoked at

[124] *Ibid.* pp. 83–4.
[125] *Ibid.* pp. 86, 92, 84–5. Malthus had criticised the harshness of workhouses and removals in *The Crisis*, an unpublished tract of 1797, extracts from which are quoted in the 1836 edition of the *Principles of Political Economy*, pp. xxxv–xxxvii.
[126] *Essay* (1798), pp. 85, 89–90.

all in the analysis of the immediate effects of a distribution of money from the rich to the poor. The simple assertion that no such distribution could increase consumption in the face of a limited supply of food was merely one of the obvious 'lessons of scarcity', and a truism in an exaggerated form. In anything but the very shortest run it ceased to be a truism at all. Malthus at first admitted that the increased money demand for food would stimulate production, but claimed that increased idleness and the stimulus to population from 'fancied riches' would offset it. The arguments were weak; inflated incomes would hardly seem riches at all since prices would be even more inflated, and the increased food supply would be produced more quickly than the new generation of children. Nevertheless Malthus was so reluctant to admit that distribution of money, even to potential consumers, could be an effective stimulus to production that he ignored the question altogether when arguing that the Poor Law increased population without increasing food for its support. Like so many of his contemporaries, he refused to see poor rates as anything but a waste of resources on unproductive paupers, neglecting the effects of redistribution of money on the demand for food and other commodities. The argument against the Poor Law could only be saved by further assumptions: that the very existence of a system of relief so weakened the spur to industry among free labourers that their labour was less productive than it would otherwise have been, and that they were induced to marry with less care for the future. But how could harsh and tyrannical laws so sap the moral fibre?

The thesis that money distributed as relief could not stimulate production was retained in all subsequent editions of the *Essay*, although some statements of it were deleted at Ricardo's request. And it was retained despite qualifications and admissions which quite undermined it. In his pamphlet on scarcity in 1800 Malthus gave a very different picture of the economic consequences of relief. When scarcity forced up food prices, the justices 'humanely, and I am far from saying improperly, ordered parish relief to make up the difference between wages and the cost of subsistence'. Of course no relief in money could provide them with their usual quantity of food—prices rose, and 'like the water from the mouth of Tantalus, the corn still slipped from the grasp of the poor'.[127] So far the argument was perfectly consistent with the *Essay* of 1798, but what followed? No hint of fancied riches as a spur to population, no hint of the relaxation of labouring effort, but a simple admission that the high price not only encouraged economy but also stimulated both importation and new

---

[127] *An Investigation of the Cause of the Present High Price of Provisions* (1800), pp. 9–10.

cultivation, increasing available food supplies. Moreover the distribution of relief did in fact improve the condition of those who received it—admittedly at the expense of the classes above them—but Malthus defended this as just. He even called the procedure 'the best' method for the relief of scarcity; 'I do not . . . by any means intend to infer . . . that the parish allowances have been prejudicial to the state; or that, as far as the system has been hitherto pursued, or is likely to be pursued, that it is not one of the best modes of relief that the circumstances of the case will admit'. He only protested that any attempt to proportion wages exactly to provisions would soon reduce all fortunes to poor rates and all of the upper classes to paupers.[128]

Perhaps Malthus repented of these admissions, for in the 1803 edition of the *Essay* he not only let the original indictment of relief and redistribution stand, but also criticised scarcity measures for forcing prices to unnatural heights, for encouraging a dangerous reliance on food imports, for enabling the poor to continue consumption at the expense of the classes above them, and for consequently frustrating the proper effect of scarcity on the poor, which was 'that of making the lower classes of people do more work'.[129] Thus Malthus continued to claim that the poor relief was a pure waste of resources, and not a redistribution of them, and that it did not tend to increase production, although it kept men eating who would otherwise have starved to death. But he began to withdraw another argument from his attack, the assertion that relief encouraged population. In view of the harshness of the laws, he decided that 'it may be asserted, without danger of exaggeration, that the poor laws have destroyed many more lives than they have preserved'.[130] What then was left of the attack on the Poor Law? Relief could not improve the condition of the poor, although in fact it had in 1800. Relief encouraged population, although in fact it was offered on such terms that it killed more than it cured. Relief was a fraud, therefore it should be abolished anyway. Astonishingly, Malthus let such contradictory assertions stand with their inconsistencies unresolved. The *Essay* became not a reasoned case against poor relief, but a farrago of all available abolitionist arguments. If the reader were not convinced by an argument on one page, he might well succumb to its rebuttal half a volume later.

11. *The Malthusian Remedy*

What could properly be done for the relief of poverty? In 1798 Malthus

---

[128] *Ibid.* pp. 18–19.
[129] *Essay* (1803), pp. 399–401, 406.
[130] *Ibid.* p. 416; and compare p. 575, where it was admitted that the Poor Laws do not encourage marriage so much as might be expected from theory'.

asserted that 'no human ingenuity' could remove the distress of the lower classes, and palliatives were all that could be hoped for. He suggested three. The first was 'the total abolition of all the present parish laws'. The repeal of the settlement laws would be of particular benefit to the poor, enabling them to obtain higher wages in a free labour market. Secondly, agriculture should be encouraged 'above manufactures' to increase output, and legal restrictions which made the artisan more prosperous than the agricultural labourer should be removed.[131] Finally, Malthus suggested county workhouses 'for cases of extreme distress', supported by a national rate, and open to all without restriction of settlement. They should not be 'comfortable asylums', but places of hard fare and labour; and he suggested, surprisingly enough, that they include workshops 'where any person, native or foreigner, might do a day's work at all times, and receive the market price for it'.[132] Thus, despite the phrasing of the first proposal, Malthus did not in 1798 urge the abolition of the Poor Law altogether, but the establishment of a new national workhouse scheme. Clearly he had not given much thought to the problem.

By 1803 his views had developed much further, and were set in the pattern they were to retain. Workhouses and employment were no longer recommended but condemned. Since 1798 Malthus had read Eden, and, in Eden, Defoe's attack on public employment. All public employment, he repeated, by competing with private, merely maintained a pauper by putting a free labourer out of employ. To this old argument he added the newer one that 'the greatest part' of funds used for employment were not new capital but old, turned into new and unprofitable channels; this aggravated the 'absurdity of supposing that it is in the power of a government to find employment for all its subjects, however fast they may increase'.[133]

With the abandonment of his workhouse scheme came the famous plan for the gradual abolition of the Poor Law altogether. The Law was the 'first grand obstacle' to improvement, an evil far greater than the National Debt, and 'a monstrous deformity in society'. There was a new urgency in the attack, and a new conviction that pauperism was a rapidly progressive canker: 'how melancholy are our future prospects'. Immediate abolition was impossible, since the evil was so deeply seated and so widely extended, but its increase could be checked, and abolition gradually approached. Malthus's proposal was simple:

[131] *Essay* (1798), pp. 95–7. Malthus here assumed that a greater produce would increase real wages rather than encourage population growth.

[132] *Ibid.* pp. 97–8.

[133] *Essay* (1803), pp. 417–18. Malthus did not disapprove of employment schemes on a very limited scale.

I should propose a regulation to be made, declaring, that no child born from any marriage, taking place after the expiration of a year from the date of the law; and no illegitimate child born two years from the same date, should ever be entitled to parish assistance.[134]

The plan seemed extraordinarily harsh to many contemporaries because its first victims would have been children. Malthus insisted with great force that public relief must cease even to illegitimate and deserted children, and that the law of nature which bade a man support his family must on no account be superseded by a legal provision:

> In the moral government of the world, it seems evidently necessary, that the sins of the fathers should be visited upon the children; and if in our overweening vanity we imagine that we can govern a private society better by endeavouring *systematically* to counteract this law, I am inclined to believe that we shall find ourselves very greatly mistaken.[135]

To many this seemed the monstrous fruit of an overweening moral strictness, if not of actual inhumanity. But Malthus was confident that withdrawing relief from children would bring parents to shoulder their moral obligations. Similarly the eventual withdrawal of all relief would lead men, or most of them, to cease needing it:

> When the poor were once taught, by the abolition of the poor laws, and a proper knowledge of their real situation, to depend more upon themselves, we might rest secure, that they would be fruitful enough in resources, and that the evils which were absolutely irremediable, they would bear with the fortitude of men, and the resignation of Christians.[136]

Apparently it was better to starve as a man of God than to fill one's belly as a pauper. But Malthus sincerely believed that no man need starve, since private charity could assist genuine distress; 'the only difficulty would be, to restrain the hand of benevolence from assisting those in distress in so liberal a manner as to encourage indolence and want of foresight in others'. Malthus was often accused of wanting to abolish private as well as public charity. This was unfair; he merely wished to guide it. Charity, like all virtues, must be controlled in practice by considerations of utility. Most large charities were as pernicious as the Poor Law in their lack of discrimination, but private benevolence could and should be free of all the vices of legal relief. Malthus echoed Alcock's denunciation of compulsory charity, and quoted Townsend on the disgusting aspects of the parish pay-table.

---

[134] *Ibid.* pp. 536–8. His suggestion that parsons should read, at every marriage, a homily on the evils of matrimony without adequate means, was much ridiculed by his critics.
[135] *Ibid.* p. 544.
[136] *Ibid.* p. 539.

Under the Poor Law the applicant was a liar or at best evasive, and the dispensation of charity usually partial and oppressive. In the distribution of voluntary charity, all would be sweetness and light. Those given relief would be grateful, and those refused could not complain of injustice, since 'every man has the right to do what he will with his own'. Malthus argued that 'this kind of despotic power' was 'essential to voluntary charity', since it gave full discretion in selecting the worthy and prevented any man depending with confidence on the charitable.[137] The deserving were the only genuine 'objects of charity'; if the idle were also given relief it must be with the greatest care. Malthus hinted at the principle of less eligibility, not as a rule in poor-law administration, but as a guide to moral discrimination in private charity. 'We may perhaps take upon ourselves, with great caution, to mitigate, in some degree, the punishments which they [the unworthy] are suffering from the laws of nature', but 'they should on no account be enabled to command so much of the necessaries of life, as can be obtained by the worst-paid common labour.'[138]

Abolition of the Poor Law, and discriminating private charity, were nevertheless mere palliatives in the relief of distress. The only true remedy to poverty was the encouragement of moral restraint. God had ordained that comfort was solely the fruit of virtue, at least for the poor. Life in this world was a state of trial, with rewards for good conduct here as well as in the after-life.[139] God required that the earth be filled with people, and a strong natural tendency towards population was necessary 'to overcome the acknowledged indolence of man, and make him proceed in the cultivation of the soil'. Since Malthus had so often described misery as the inevitable result of population pressure, this looked very much like a claim that misery was desirable as a spur to industry. But misery was only inevitable in the sense that perfect morality in man was impossible; God left it to man to decide whether population would increase in vice and misery or in virtue and comfort. Individual morality was the only key to the problem of poverty. Wider practice of moral restraint would raise wages, and remove all 'squalid poverty' from society, except of course that arising from inevitable misfortune. It would also purify society, since the passion of love, no longer satiated by early sensuality, would 'burn with

---

[137] *Ibid.* pp. 563–4. This passage is typical of Malthus's unguarded exaggeration. Having asserted an absolute right of disposal of property, he proceeded in the next paragraph to recognise the claims of the poor 'even at the expense of three-fourths of the fortunes of the rich' if only indiscriminate charity did not aggravate distress.
[138] *Ibid.* p. 565.
[139] The *Essay* of 1798 was more pessimistic on earthly rewards; see especially chap. xviii.

a brighter, purer and steadier flame'. Marriages would be happier, because well-considered. More women could ultimately marry, and spinsterhood would no longer be the object of ridicule. Moreover the lower classes would not only be more comfortable, but would be freed from 'irrational discontents' against forms of government or social inequality. Knowing the true causes of poverty, they would be 'on all occasions less disposed to insubordination and turbulence', and grateful for timely assistance.[140]

Malthus thought it necessary to rebut some possible objections to the encouragement of moral restraint. He admitted that an increase in the virtue would lead to 'a market rather understocked with labour', but aptly remarked that anyone who claimed sympathy for the poor and yet opposed high wages could not 'really be in earnest in their professions. . . . Their benevolence to the poor must be either childish play, or hypocrisy; it must be either to amuse themselves, or to pacify the minds of the common people with a mere shew of attention to their wants.' It might be alleged that greater moral restraint would lead to depopulation, but this was not the case. Population might be kept stationary for a time, until subsistence had increased sufficiently to provide a higher standard of living, but could then increase rapidly as the more vigorous industry of virtuous labourers increased the means of subsistence.[141] The only objection which caused Malthus any concern was the claim that delay in marriage would lead to more widespread vice. Against this he launched a long argument that abject misery was the real cause of vice, marshalling much evidence from Colquhoun's *Police of the Metropolis* in support. 'I believe there will be found very few, who pass through the ordeal of squalid and hopeless poverty, or even of long continued embarrassed circumstances, without a considerable moral degradation of character. . . . Squalid poverty, particularly when joined with idleness, is a state the most unfavourable to chastity that can well be conceived.' An admirable argument, but even Malthus felt some embarrassment in combining it with the thesis that the fear of misery was the essential stimulus to virtue. Having just claimed that uncertainty in relief was essential to promote self-reliance, how could he then admit that crime and vice were inevitable among 'miserable individuals of various classes, (who) rise up every morning, without knowing how, or by what means, they are to be supported during the passing day'?[142] He saw the contradiction but evaded it by simply arguing that if only their parents had not married so

---

[140] *Essay* (1803), pp. 495–501, 602.
[141] *Ibid.* pp. 511–12.
[142] *Ibid.* pp. 513–16.

prematurely and the children had not been brought up in vicious workhouses or immoral homes, the misery might have been averted.

Whatever the objections, failure to encourage moral restraint could only be disastrous. Even with no Poor Law, greater misery would inevitably follow, and a continual increase in the undesirable positive checks to population was the necessary consequence of failure to increase the preventive. 'Nature will not, nor cannot be defeated in her purposes.' And the political fruit of greater misery could only be despotism and the decay of civil liberty. Political reform was not a remedy for poverty; on the contrary, only the true remedy for poverty could bring political reform:

> The pressure of distress on the lower classes of people, with the habit of attributing this distress to their rulers, appears to me to be the rock of defence, the castle, the guardian spirit of despotism. It affords to the tyrant the fatal and unanswerable plea of necessity. . . . It is the reason that so many noble efforts in the cause of freedom were foiled, and that almost every revolution, after long and painful sacrifices, has terminated in a military despotism.[143]

The poor, disillusioned when revolution brought no benefit to their condition, turned on the successors to power, 'and so on without end'. Malthus believed mobs to be the instruments of tyranny, and called on country gentlemen to act as bastions of political liberty against corruption and despotic power. His political preferences and assumptions harked back to the days of the Yorkshire Association, not the French Revolution.

Thus the encouragement of the virtue of moral restraint was to Malthus a real panacea, and the true road to all economic, social and political improvement. His proposals for encouraging it were not all as negative as the plan to abolish the Poor Law or as eccentric as his proposed inclusion of sermons against marriage in the wedding service. The poor must be taught, and since all men were at least partly rational, teaching would have some effect. Malthus supported Smith's plan for parochial education, and later welcomed the educational systems of Bell and Lancaster. All opposition to education for the poor was 'illiberal' in sentiment and 'feeble' in argument; let the poor read, even if they would read Thomas Paine.[144] With a national system of education, and the abandonment of all positive encouragement to population by law and precept, the hare of population pressure might be persuaded to sleep and the tortoise of comfortable subsistence have some chance of overtaking her. Until the truth was published misery could not be alleviated, and the poor could not be blamed either for contributing to

---

[143] *Ibid.* p. 526.
[144] *Ibid.* pp. 553–5.

their own distress or for attributing it to the sins of their social and political superiors. Critics attacked Malthus for teaching restraint only to the poor, and for failing to put due weight on the encouragement of increased output to relieve the pressure on subsistence. He believed, however, that the upper classes were already reasonably prudent in marriage, although unjust in their attitude to spinsterhood; and he did urge unrelaxed effort to increase subsistence, although he gave little attention to the means. He assumed, of course, that in the matter of production the pursuit of obvious individual interest was on the whole effective and sufficient; only in the matter of population did native instinct and rational behaviour conflict.[145]

12. Malthus and Rival Remedies

Although Malthus did offer some slight hope for the alleviation of distress, and did propose some measures for social improvement, his reputation as a gloomy prophet was not undeserved. The theme of the first *Essay* was almost entirely negative, and even in 1803 his positive suggestions were less prominent than his exceedingly severe criticisms of all other proposals for relief. Moreover the criticisms were not as logically scrupulous as they should have been, and earned him some just criticism for sophistry.

The initial object of attack was Godwin's concept of human perfectibility in a state of social equality, or rather Godwin's doctrine as Malthus understood it. It can be argued that Godwin was a more subtle and realistic thinker than his detractors (and some of his admirers) assumed, but a reader of Godwin's *Political Justice* could easily find in it the optimistic speculation on human perfectibility to which Malthus made an equally speculative reply. If human society were judged by the highest standards of justice, property had no justification except that of need. Inequality of property could be seen as the root of most social evils; of a 'servile and truckling' sense of dependence; of false values excited by the spectacle of injustice; of the stifling of the intellects of the mass of the people; of the multiplication of vices, and especially of crime among the poor and warlike passions among the privileged; and of depopulation. Since the minds of men were moulded by the circumstances in which they were placed, a system of political and social equality could generate those virtues essential to its maintenance. Godwin offered such a state as a possible culmination of human progress, which might be assisted into being by the promulgation of truth; he offered little as a

---

[145] *Ibid.* pp. 549–53, 505–10.

political programme to hasten its coming, and eschewed revolution.[146] Malthus simplified Godwin's argument and offered a simple reply: a state of perfect equality, attractive as a speculation, was impossible in practice; and hence the speculation itself was a dangerous sin against truth. Assume a state of equality realised, with all its virtues—no misery, no vice, no war, no unwholesome trades, no cities, no marriage ties—and with all men living amicably together growing food for common consumption. In these circumstances population, with no positive checks, and (an important assumption) no preventive, would double itself within fifteen years, and within thirty would press so hard on subsistence that men would be forced to compete with each other for food, self-love would triumph over benevolence, vice and misery would re-appear, and it would prove absolutely necessary to re-establish private property, marriage and trade.[147] As Hazlitt pointed out, it was a little sophistical of Malthus to admit perfectibility in all aspects save one, and then claim that the exception made perfectibility impossible. Having swallowed the camel of perfect amity, why strain at the gnat of perfect prudence? Had Malthus merely asserted that of all human passions the sexual was the least likely to be brought under complete rational control and the most necessary to control for social improvement, the argument would have been more honest if less picturesque.[148]

The Malthusian defence of social inequality was thus mainly a negative one, a denial of the possibility of a happy equality. Some points in favour of inequality were raised incidentally—thus a wealthy and leisured class was held necessary for intellectual advancement, while only a class of rich could maintain a reserve of wealth to meet times of scarcity—but Malthus's assumption that even if misery were more or less inevitable, equality in misery was undesirable, was nevertheless nowhere defended in detail. And since he did not attempt to calculate, as Bentham did, how far society could safely move in the direction of equality, he seemed to imply that the existing distribution of social wealth was acceptable. But in a letter to Godwin, in 1798, he

---

[146] *Enquiry Concerning Political Justice* (1793), especially book VIII. Certainly in *The Enquirer* etc. (1797) Godwin was less speculative: in the essays 'Of Riches and Poverty' and 'Avarice and Profusion' he conceded the inevitability of present poverty, and in 'Of Beggars' he deplored indiscriminate charity. For an admirable analysis of some of Godwin's leading ideas see D. H. Monro, *Godwin's Moral Philosophy* (1953).

[147] *Essay* (1798) pp. 181–93.

[148] The point was made, more or less clearly, when criticising Godwin for exaggerating the rationality of man (*ibid.* pp. 250–5). For Hazlitt's criticism see *A Reply to the Essay on Population* (published anonymously, 1807), especially Letter IV; and compare Southey in the *Quarterly Review*, IX (1812), 321–3.

claimed that in defending existing society he defended only its basic principles, 'the existence of a class of proprietors and a class of labourers, . . . the system of barter and exchange, . . . and the general moving principle of self love'.[149] And in 1803 he suggested that the happiest states seemed to be those with a large middle class, where labourers might hope to improve their station, and 'human society would appear to consist of fewer blanks and more prizes'.[150] Desirable as such a distribution of wealth might be, the only way to approach it was (of course) by encouraging moral restraint among the poor. Thus against Paine's relatively modest proposals for the redistribution of property in society, Malthus flung out his usual reply that all such schemes merely aggravated the problem they attempted to relieve.[151]

Malthus's conviction that the distribution of property inherent in a capitalist economic structure was best for the poor as well as the rich appeared also in his discussion of proposals to provide labourers with land, proposals based, he claimed, on an unwarranted generalisation from particular cases. Fortunate labourers in grazing country could enjoy such benefits, but they would cease to be benefits at all if made general, because population would be much encouraged and there would be neither land nor cows nor even ordinary employment enough for later generations. Hence the absurdity of Arthur Young's plan for superseding the poor rates by giving land to the poor:

> The specific cause of the poverty and misery of the lower classes of people in France and Ireland, is, that, from the extreme subdivision of property of the one country and the facility of obtaining a potatoe ground in the other, a population is brought into existence, which is not demanded by the quantity of capital and employment in the country; and the consequence of which must . . . be . . . to lower in general the price of labour by too great

---

[149] Printed in Bonar's notes in the 1926 edition of the *Essay* of 1798, pp. iii–viii. Note the curious passage in which Malthus refused to support universal prudence as an aim: 'should such a system ever prevail so generally as to remove the constant want of an increasing quantity of food, it is highly probable that cultivation would proceed still more slowly than it does at present. I only approve the present form of society because I cannot . . . see any other form that can, consistently with individual freedom, equally promote cultivation and population' (p. vii). Malthus here seems to value increased cultivation and population above universal moral restraint and to imply that misery and vice were essential to progress.

[150] *Essay* (1803), pp. 594–5.

[151] *Ibid.* p. 530. It was in this context, in criticism of Paine's doctrine of the rights of man, that Malthus included the notorious parable of 'Nature's Feast' to show that 'a man born into a world already possessed . . . has no claim of *right* to the smallest portion of food, and, in fact, has no business to be where he is. At nature's mighty feast there is no cover for him' (pp. 531–2). The passage was deleted from later editions; Bonar (*op. cit.* p. 307, n2) wrongly attributes the deletion to Sumner's influence. It was withdrawn in 1806, long before Sumner's criticism of the *Essay*.

competition; from which must result complete indigence to those who cannot find employment, and an incomplete subsistence even to those who can.[152]

Cheap foods were useful in scarcity, but to encourage the poor to live on their own vegetable productions alone was to make them liable to real famine in poor seasons. Neither their own cows nor their own potatoes would guarantee comfort for the poor. And as an encouragement to population, Young's plan would be far worse than the existing Poor Law, offering 'fascinating visions of land and cows' instead of harsh overseers and uncomfortable workhouses. This particular blend of theoretical and practical arguments against a subsistence peasant economy recurred in the writings of other political economists, and strongly influenced the attitude of the Royal Commission of 1832 on the question of land for the poor.

Contributory schemes, the other popular alternative to existing poor relief, also found no favour with Malthus. He approved of self help through voluntary friendly societies, and foreshadowed the later establishment of savings banks, but strongly opposed all proposals that the poor be compelled to contribute to funds for their relief. This, Malthus complained, would be simply a tax on wages, which would inevitably be passed on to the consumer. 'The landed interest, therefore, would receive no relief from this plan, but would pay the same sum as at present, only in the advanced price of labour and of commodities, instead of in the parish rates. A compulsory subscription of this kind, would have almost all the ill effects of the present system of relief, and, though altered in name, would still possess the essential spirit of the poor laws.'[153]

In 1803 emigration was not the widely-supported solution for the evils of poverty which it was to become after the war. Malthus discussed it, but more because he wished (vainly) to forestall an objection to his theory than because it was much urged as a matter of policy. In the long run, of course, emigration could not prevent the pressure of population on the world's resources, but might it not bring immediate relief to thickly populated territories, since so many parts of the world were but sparsely peopled? Not according to Malthus; even as a present remedy emigration was 'but a very weak palliative'. New countries were not comfortable havens for redundant souls and bodies. All the evidence, from the first settlement of New England to the infant colony of New

---

[152] *Essay* (1803), p. 574; and compare pp. 575–6, 579–80. Malthus later developed the argument that the poor were better off when their habitual food was expensive in his defence of the Corn Law; compare W. D. Grampp, 'Malthus on Money Wages and Welfare', *American Econ. Rev.* xlvi (1956), 924–36.

[153] *Essay* (1803), p. 568; the argument was amplified in the 1817 edition. For proposals for banks for savings, see *ibid.* p. 589.

South Wales, showed the difficulties and hardships of colonisation. Only 'the thirst of gain, the spirit of adventure, and religious enthusiasm' could lead men to triumph over such obstacles. New settlements could not support themselves even in the simplest subsistence until much labour and capital had been invested, and even when they eventually flourished (if they did) the transport of new settlers from the homeland would continue to be expensive. Prospects overseas would have to be very good indeed to justify public expenditure on emigration, especially as only temporary relief from the pressure of population could be expected. Malthus was inclined to leave all to private interest: if colonies really offered an attractive alternative to misery in the homeland, men would go, and the fact that so few did go therefore proved that colonies were no remedy to misery. But he insisted that restraints on emigration were tyrannical and impolitic, and should be removed.[154]

As new proposals for the relief of distress appeared in the years after 1803, Malthus dealt with them in similar fashion in successive editions of the *Essay*. Little of the criticism, and few of the new proposals, dented the armour of his conviction, although he sometimes made admissions which were hardly consistent with his main contention. Consistent in the great, if not in the small, he continued to urge the abolition of the Poor Law and the encouragement of moral restraint as the only effectual mode of improving the condition of the poor.

13. *Malthus: the Beginnings of Controversy*

Although few books in history have provoked as many replies as the *Essay on the Principle of Population*, the controversy began quietly enough. As the *Edinburgh Review* later remarked, the works of Malthus were at first more talked of than read;[155] little criticism of importance was published before the third edition appeared in 1806. The increased flow thereafter may perhaps have been provoked by Malthus's unfortunate manner with critics, and his dismissal of much of what they wrote as 'illiberal declamation . . . so entirely destitute of argument, as to be evidently beneath notice'.[156] He sometimes seemed obtuse as well as abrupt in rebuttal, and the intellectual confrontation between author and critics was fogged by misunderstanding, and too often by ill-feeling. In practical matters, however, and especially on questions of poverty and its relief, the differences of view were more clear-cut than in the realm of theory.

---

[154] *Ibid.* book III, chap. iv.
[155] And 'more generally read than understood', *Edinburgh Review*, XVI (1810), 465.
[156] *Essay* (1806), II. 429. The 1807 edition was identical with that of 1806.

Most early critics of the *Essay* praised it, and Godwin's first reaction was as warm as any. He even took some pride in having 'furnished the incentive to the producing of so valuable a treatise', and admitted the truth of Malthus's principles 'in the fullest extent', apparently thinking it a small matter to disagree utterly with the practical conclusions drawn from them. Godwin under-estimated Malthus's tenacity in clinging to his practical proposals, and still hoped to convince him that the principle of population was no bar to unlimited improvement, since prudence could check procreation. His later fury against all things Malthusian was not evident in 1801; he merely offered a gentle warning that the doctrine could be used by the 'advocates of old establishments and old abuses . . . to cut out reform and improvement for ever'.[157] An extreme case in point appeared in 1806, when the slave trade was defended as a check to population in Africa. Malthus repudiated the argument with bitter eloquence, but the gulf between his views and Godwin's remained wide indeed.[158]

In 1802 Sir Thomas Bernard also quoted the *Essay* with approval. He agreed that population pressed upon subsistence, and was checked by misery and vice; that this 'natural evil [was] necessary to the existence of the most excellent virtues', since 'without distress, there can be no charity'; and that the Poor Law held out a 'false and doubtful' encouragement to population, by promising an 'unqualified support' which it was 'not possible' to supply. But he refused to agree that the Poor Law should be abolished, and warned that charity should not be discouraged by the impossibility of removing distress entirely. The principle of population merely strengthened his own belief that 'whatever encourages and promotes habits of *Industry, Prudence, Forethought, Virtue and Cleanliness* among the poor, is beneficial to them and to the country; whatever removes, or diminishes, the incitement to any of these qualities, is detrimental to the *State* and pernicious to the *Individual*. This is the *Polar Star* of our benevolent affections. . . .'[159]

Malthus's general views were not difficult to reconcile with the principles of the S.B.C.P. It is more surprising to find Arthur Young printing twenty pages of the *Essay* in the *Annals*, since Malthus had been

---

[157] *Thoughts occasioned by the Perusal of Dr Parr's Spital Sermon* etc. (1801), pp. 56, 61. Malthus, in his letter to Godwin in 1798, had insisted that 'the very admission of the necessity of prudence . . . removes the blame from public institutions to the conduct of individuals' (printed in the 1926 reprint of the first *Essay*, notes, pp. iii–viii). In the very first number of the *Edinburgh Review* Sydney Smith mercilessly rebuked Godwin for failing to see the main argument of 'Mr Malthias' (sic). *Edinburgh Review*, I (1802) 26.

[158] Compare *Cobbett's Political Register*, VII (1805), 230–1; IX (1806), 65, 73–6; *Essay* (1806), II. 481–4.

[159] *Reports*, III (1802), 2–10.

so critical of Young's favourite plan. But Young quoted Malthus against the Poor Law to emphasise the superiority of his own scheme for superseding the rates by settling the poor on land, and he rejected Malthus's criticisms. 'Writers who have such confidence in their theoretical reasonings as to give a desultory attention to facts, are too apt to venture their conclusions without due care for the foundation.' Rutland was not Ireland. Small holdings need not be mere potato cabins, and since all who accepted them were to renounce poor relief, the incentive to independence would be great. Moreover the children, brought up in comfort and independence, would delay marriage until they could support a family. But Young admitted that some of the children would have to migrate to towns, and was content to rest his case on the present generation: should they be miserable and vicious paupers, or comfortable and moral cottagers? Malthus's scheme for abolition was harsh, and his ideal of universal moral restraint both visionary and contrary to the heart of man. Deny the right to marry, and profligacy of manners was inevitable. The poor were justified in their complaints against the rich, until they were offered land; Malthus was right in attacking the Poor Laws, but wrong in seeking abolition without full compensation. A cottage and land, and that alone, would make a poor man industrious and frugal.[160] Malthus was unconvinced, and added further criticism of Young's plan to the 1806 edition of the *Essay*. Young had admitted that his scheme could not provide for future generations: why, then, persist with it? Any why object to a declaration against the right to relief, if relief was in fact impossible? Malthus defined his views on land for the poor more carefully. Give land as a 'useful palliative', but be careful 'not to let the division of land be so great, as to interrupt the cottager essentially in his usual labours; and always to stop in the further distribution of land, when the price of labour, independent of any assistance from land, would not at the average price of corn maintain three, or at least two children'. Go further, and the poor would be debased to the Irish level. Malthus thus rejected Young's contention that peasants were necessarily and inevitably more frugal and more prudent than labourers, and discouraged peasant holdings in the interest of the poor themselves.[161]

Among other early critics who found Malthusian principles convincing but the proposal to abolish the Poor Law unacceptable were George Rose, always a cautious man in affairs of state, [162] and Charles Hall, an interesting if minor figure in the history of English socialist thought. Hall argued that colonisation and other preventive measures

---

[160] *Annals*, XLI (1804), 208–31. Malthus was quoted on pp. 52–71.
[161] *Essay* (1806), II. 457–68.
[162] G. Rose, *Observations on the Poor Laws* (1805), pp. 8–12.

would keep population pressure at bay, and in any case the claims of social justice were the primary consideration: 'I suppose a part of the nation, especially a small part of it, to have no right to induce a state of want, disease and mortality, on the other parts of it, exempting itself at the same time from them.' Malthus's remedy was 'inhuman to the last degree'.[163] Nevertheless, Hall wrote of Malthus with some respect; there were few at this time who attacked the man, his principles and his remedy together. Coleridge annotated his copy of the 1803 edition of the *Essay* with marginilia which combined coarse interjections with more sober assessment of Malthus's philosophic assumptions; he then gave the volume to Southey, who added even coarser comments of his own and put the more printable remarks together in a short review. In a letter to his friend John Rickman in 1804 Southey lamented that 'Malthus is as great a favourite with the *British Critic* as with other voiders of menstrual pollution'; in another he summed up his and Coleridge's arguments as they had appeared in the *Monthly Review*:

> The ground I have taken is this—that he supposes lust to be like hunger an appetite of physical necessity when he argues against Godwin, that when he proposes his own damned plan he founds it upon the possibility of moral restraint, and the practical virtue of chastity—ergo the scorpion strikes his tail into his own head—the end of his book confuting the beginning. . . . Mr. Malthus . . . is cast in his action against God Almighty. . . . If he replies to any effect I will gibbet him in a pamphlet, and draw and quarter him, for I have something of the same sense of strength in me in reference to this dog that Milton must have had when he made mincemeat of Salmasius.[164]

Southey never hesitated to purloin other men's ideas and words without acknowledgment; having copied Coleridge's notes in his brief review he looked forward to a more extended attack on 'the mischievous booby' using factual ammunition provided by John Rickman, the sober census-taker. Rickman certainly sympathised with the cause—'if it [that cursed Book of Malthus] be *true*, it contains *truth* so deleterious . . . that a man ought to be rather indicted for it than for a publication of the Grossest Obscenity'[165]—and Southey's later small reputation as an authority on social questions was to rest almost

[163] C. Hall, *The Effects of Civilization on the People* etc. (2nd ed. 1813), pp. 328, 340. The first edition appeared in 1805.

[164] K. Curry, ed., *New Letters of Robert Southey* (1965), I. 357, 350–1. Coleridge's copy of the *Essay* is in the British Museum; extracts from the marginilia are quoted in Bonar, *op. cit.* pp. 371–6, and in A. Cobban, *Edmund Burke and the Revolt against the Eighteenth Century* (1929), p. 205. See also G. Carnall, *Robert Southey and his Age* (1960), pp. 62–6; J. Colmer, *Coleridge, Critic of Society* (1959), esp. pp. 141–6; and other references cited in Curry, *op. cit.*, I. 350 n.2. Southey's review of Malthus is in the *Annual Review*, II (1803), 292–301.

[165] Quoted in Curry, *op. cit.*, I. 350 n.2.

wholly on Rickman's unacknowledged researches, but the second blast of outraged romantic conservatism against Malthus did not appear from Southey's pen until 1812.

A more polite expression of shock appeared in Thomas Jarrold's *Dissertations on Man etc.* of 1806. Jarrold was a cautious and intelligent man, and the first critic to attempt an assessment of the Malthusian theory in any detail; he made some good points, especially against Malthus's vagueness on the question of fertility, but also the metaphysical assertion that it was possible to prevent conception by mere mental effort.[166] No acceptable alternative general theory was offered, and he probably exaggerated his disagreements with Malthus by misreading the Malthusian scale of values. The devout did not find it easy to accept the *Essay* until Sumner elaborated Malthus's view of the principle of population as part of a divine plan of moral trial, and Jarrold was shocked by what he took to be the exclusion of the Deity from the government of the world. He was also a humane optimist reluctant to abandon cheerful hopes for the future: 'I cannot give up the idea that the period is hastening when the condition of mankind will be in a far better state than it now is. . . . Already I fancy I have seen the first dawning of this wished for morning . . .; the human intellect is everywhere maturing; institutions unfriendly to man are ready to fall by the force of reason'. Malthus was wrong about nature and God; on society he was pernicious, for even if population did press upon subsistence Malthus's abolitionism was an incitement to murder, worthy of Nero. Guests might be excluded from Diocesan dinners, but not from nature's feast, where 'none are bishops but all are men . . . and the life of a guest is sacred . . . to possess life is to possess the invitation. . . . Nor is it the prerogative of one guest to dismiss another from the hall'.[167] But Jarrold had nothing positive to offer in the debate on pauperism.

14. *Malthus: the Edition of 1806*

When Malthus prepared a third edition of the *Essay* in 1806 he ignored most of the critics and simply rebutted certain 'common objections' to his views. He objected to being called an enemy of population and of medical improvements such as vaccination, setting out clearly (for the first time) his approval of population increase provided it was 'a

---

[166] For a sympathetic summary of Jarrold's theoretical criticisms see K. Smith, *The Malthusian Controversy*, pp. 56–63. Jarrold, born in 1770, was a physician in Manchester from 1806 until his death in 1853. He wrote several books on medicine and education.

[167] *Dissertations on Man* (1806), pp. 366–7, 21–2.

healthy, virtuous and happy population, not an unhealthy, vicious and miserable one'. The signs of health and virtue were low birth- and death-rates, and high wages; the things to be checked were vice and misery, not population.[168] Of course, as the critics claimed, England could maintain two or three times her existing population, but to Malthus this was a goal which should only be approached gradually, letting subsistence wait upon the existing social order, and population on both. The only objection to his thesis which Malthus admitted as having any considerable force was (significantly) political: surely 'improved government' would increase the 'personal respectability' of the poor and bring 'the diminished proportion of births, which I consider as absolutely necessary to the permanent improvement of the condition of the poor'. Malthus was inclined to admit the point, but not a corollary 'that it is not necessary . . . to risk the promulgation of any new opinions, which may alarm the prejudices of the poor'.[169] By all means seek political improvement, and expect some increase in prudence when it was achieved, but it was no alternative to his plan. Surely political improvement and truth went hand in hand, and why therefore should the great principles of population and poverty be hidden from sight? Malthus would never capitulate to the radical argument that his theory was wrong because misgovernment was the real cause of distress; he had his own notion of political progress, and if it included some genuinely liberal elements it was puritan in refusing to avoid unpalatable social truths.

In the new edition the denial of the right to relief was softened in expression, but defended in essence.[170] Let those who preached the right to relief practise it. 'If the poor had really a claim of *right* to support, I do not think, that any man could justify his wearing broad cloth, or eating as much meat as he likes for dinner; and those who assert this right, and yet are rolling in their carriages, living every day luxuriously, and keeping even their horses on food of which their fellow creatures are in want, must be allowed to act with the greatest inconsistency.' But let the horses be fed and the carriages roll, for the principle of population proved a right to relief impossible in the fulfilment; thus 'our conduct, which denies the right, is more suited to the present state of our being, than our declamations which allow it'.[171] Malthus would have it both ways. Relief was impossible, hence the

---

[168] *Essay* (1806), II. 432-3, 441. For Malthus's preference for high wages rather than too rapid an increase in population see also p. 477 n.

[169] *Ibid.* II. 473-4.

[170] Thus the Nature's Feast passage was omitted, and the expediency and duty of relieving the poor in scarcity affirmed (*ibid.* II. 92-4).

[171] *Ibid.* II. 446.

Poor Law was an error; the Poor Law did not in reality provide relief, and thus relief was proved impossible. In 1806 he rested his case against the Poor Law much more strongly than before on its fraudulent character. An unfulfilled promise was more galling than an outright denial, and thus it was politic as well as honest to tell the poor the truth. In practice the abolition of the Poor Law required caution, but in the expression of principles it was best to be bold. Only when the poor were told that the Laws of Nature (that is, of God) gave no claim of right to support could one expect of them frugality, resignation, gratitude, and prudence.[172] Of course (as Malthus had hinted in 1803) the Poor Laws, being a fraud, were not as pernicious in practice as they might appear; they did not, for instance, encourage population. Their 'obvious tendency' was to encourage marriage, but in practice perhaps they did not, although they discouraged sobriety and economy and 'put virtue and vice more on a level than they otherwise would be'. In 1817 Malthus was to change his mind yet again on this question, but in 1806 he left it with the following passage of quite extraordinary evasiveness:

> The most favourable light, in which the poor laws can possibly be placed, is to say, that under all the circumstances, with which they have been accompanied, they do not encourage marriage; and undoubtedly the returns of the Population Act seem to warrant the assertion. Should this be true, many of the objections which have been urged in the *Essay* against the poor laws will of course be removed; but I wish to press on the attention of the reader, that they will in that case be removed in strict conformity to the general principles of the work, and in a manner to confirm, rather than to invalidate, the main positions which it has attempted to establish.

It is a pity that Malthus himself did not rewrite the chapters on the Poor Law to show how this could be done.[173]

15. *Critics, Radical and Conservative*

In the years between the publication of the third edition in 1806 and the end of the war the main lines of the controversy over the Malthusian case on pauperism emerged quite clearly. It was, for the most part, the critics who wrote; if we believe Whitbread's statements of 1807, they

[172] For Malthus's attempt to put himself 'in the place of a poor man' and his consequent disgust at the fraudulence of the Poor Law see *ibid*. II. 451–2.
[173] *Ibid*. II. 473 n. For an interesting argument that poor relief in fact prevented the demoralisation of extreme indigence, encouraged moral restraint and thus restricted population increase by stimulating desirable preventive checks see the anonymous *A Method of Improving the Condition of the Irish Poor* etc. (1810). This potentially fruitful line of thought was only intermittently developed by Malthus's early critics.

wrote in reaction against 'a revolution in the public mind' on the subject of pauperism, a revolution associated with Malthusian views. But we can find very few staunch and orthodox Malthusians in these years; if they existed, in large numbers, most of them were silent. Many men, like Curwen or Whitbread himself, spoke with respect of Malthusian principles, but were not orthodox on practical matters. The strongest support for Malthus came from the *Edinburgh Review*, and doubtless many of its numerous readers accepted Malthusianism as part of their whiggish and progressive creed. The strongest criticism appeared in the tory *Quarterly* and in Cobbett's radical *Political Register*.

The *Edinburgh Review* quoted Malthus with approval in its very first number, but it was not until 1807 that his views on pauperism were discussed at length. The reviewer accorded Malthus 'the rare commendation of having added to that class of important truths which have only to be explained in order to command our universal assent', and defended him against the 'illiberal antipathy' of the critics. 'It is because the poor laws, instead of "rescuing the trembling limbs of age from cold and wretchedness", are a most fertile source of misery to the poor, that Mr. Malthus wants them gradually abolished.' Indeed the disciple went further than the master, demanding that relief to the able-bodied be banned at once, and refused even in time of scarcity. It was 'safer to fall short than to exceed in relieving distress by public charity. What may be wanting in public, is generally made up by private benevolence. But there is no way of correcting the evil of profuse donations enforced by the authority of law.'[174] Three years later the *Review* published an able and moderate summary of the Malthusian argument, stressing the benevolence of attempts to encourage preventive rather than positive checks to population, and chiding Ingram and Hazlitt for accusing Malthus of raising selfishness into a social principle. It was only when Malthus later appeared as a defender of Corn Laws that the *Edinburgh Review* firmly but regretfully attacked him, using his own principle of population against him.[175]

[174] *Edinburgh Review*, XI (1807), 100–115. The reviewer is not identified in F. W. Fetter, 'The Authorship of Economic Articles in the Edinburgh Review 1802–47', *Journal Pol. Econ.* LXI (1953).

[175] The Malthusian review of Ingram and Hazlitt in *Edinburgh Review*, XVI (1810), 464–73 was said to be 'possibly' by Malthus himself by Bonar (*op. cit.* p. 33 n.); Smith converts the possibility to 'strong probability' with no further evidence (*op. cit.* p. 78). Fetter argues that Malthus would not praise his own work so warmly; it could also be argued that the article puts the Malthusian case more clearly than Malthus was wont to do. Jeffrey is suggested as the author by B. Semmel, in his *Occasional Papers of T. R. Malthus* (New York, 1963), pp. 15–16. Semmel discusses the *Review's* attitude to Malthus; and compare J. Clive, *Scotch Reviewers: The Edinburgh Review* 1802–15 (1957). John Allen's article on the Poor Law (*Edinburgh*

Like the *Edinburgh Review* itself, the Malthusian doctrine was assailed as subversive by conservatives and as too cautiously conservative by radicals. The author of *A Summons of Wakening; or the Evil Tendency and Danger of Speculative Philosophy, exemplified in ... Mr. Malthus's Essay on Population etc.* (1807) dismissed the *Essay* as an 'impious book', full of wicked French principles, and especially blameworthy because it preached a 'general combination' among workmen to raise wages by refraining from breeding. This was the lunatic fringe of criticism; R. A. Ingram's *Disquisitions on Population etc.* (1808) had more substance. Ingram thought the Poor Law faulty in principle and intolerable in administration, but the Malthusian argument had no appeal for him: 'the religious mind revolts'. His moral sense was even more scrupulous than Malthus's. Poverty was a penalty for sin, and not a law of nature, and England was burdened with luxury, not surplus population. Useless manufactures, large towns and great fortunes were all lamentable; in a virtuous state a few domestic industries would meet the needs of a large and frugal population innocent of a taste for fripperies. To preach moral restraint was to mock the poor and to encourage the rich in a selfish preservation of immoral standards of luxury. If all were frugal, and property more widely diffused, there would be no need to fear population growth, just as there was no need to abolish the Poor Law, provided relief was severely restricted; Ingram was one of the few champions of the workhouse test in these years. His contempt for economic progress and his austere ideal of a frugal society make Malthus seem by comparison a thirster after fleshpots. If Malthus defended existing society, he believed nevertheless in a progressive economy; since he was later to be widely attacked as a dupe of landlords, it is refreshing to find him assailed by Ingram as a pander to manufactures.[176]

Ingram was a sober and austere conservative; Southey and his

---

[176] For an early and virulent attack on Malthus as 'an ignorant agriculturist' see *A Clear Fair and Candid Investigation etc.* (1810); and see also W. T. Comber, *An Enquiry etc.* (1808) for a more sober examination of Malthus's preference for agriculture. *A Summons of Wakening* is attributed to Sir J. Leslie in the British Museum Catalogue. Ingram's *Causes of the Increases of Methodism and Dissension, and of the Popularity of what is called Evangelical Preaching, and the Means of obviating them* (1807) included a postscript discussing Whitbread's poor-law Bill of 1807.

Review, XXII (1813), 184–98) was Malthusian in tone, and included an attack on the allowance system as the natural culmination of the Law four years before Malthus made the point himself. The article attacking Malthus's views on the Corn Law (*Edinburgh Review*, XXIV (1815), 491–505) was still respectful; and even when McCulloch was the *Review*'s chief economic writer he was not free to attack Malthus as he wished. He is said to have given up writing for the journal because it published Empson's eulogistic obituary of Malthus in 1837 (Semmel, *op. cit.* p. 13).

friends were altogether more outspoken and romantic in their reaction against what they took to be Malthusian irreligion and sedition. Southey was soon to return to the attack. In December 1910 he wrote to Walter Savage Landor that he was meditating 'a mortal blow at Malthus, who is the especial object of my contempt and abhorrence', and told Sir Walter Scott that he was 'making ready to come upon that precious philosophist, or philosophicide, with a thunder clap'. His article in the *Quarterly Review* of 1812 put that journal firmly among the opponents of Malthus, if not quite as consistently as Southey wished.[177]

Southey did not deny that the 'utterly improvident' character of the poor and the 'frightful proportion of paupers' were scandalous; he was mainly concerned to refute the explanations for the situation offered by political radicals and by Malthus. The birds were of a feather. Malthus's 'discovery' that 'a great error has been committed in the physical constitution of the universe, in as much as men multiply too fast, and therefore the land is over-stocked' was a pernicious reply to the pernicious 'brute materialism, blind necessity, and black atheism' of Godwin and the French Revolution. 'Worthless as Mr Malthus's system is, it stands in the way of an inquiry into the state of the poor, and must be removed.' To remove it, Southey employed much abuse and some argument. Malthus was accused of defending plagues, of pitting his 'science' against God's law, of 'detestable hard-heartedness' (as in the Nature's feast parable, a passage of such 'naked deformity' that none could stomach it but those who 'have an appetite, like the Hottentots, for garbage'). Such was the abuse; for argument Southey produced charges of inconsistency. If the poor were capable of moral restraint, then Godwin was not refuted; if they were not, then how could the Poor Law be abolished?[178] The pressure of population was not the cause of present distress; in fact there should be more Englishmen, not fewer— 'more of that flesh and blood which has carried our name to every part of the habitable globe; more of that intellect which has compassed earth and heaven'. The real cause of distress was man's fault, not God's. In the good old days before the Reformation, when men were still attached to their Church, there was no pauperism. It was the rise of manufactures which had poisoned society. 'The peasant ... can not grow up without receiving some of the natural and softening impressions of religion' (he could always hear church bells, for example), but the townsman was isolated, brutalised, and bred into radicalism, murder,

---

[177] K. Curry, *op. cit.*, I. 546, 551. Murray, one of the founders of the *Quarterly*, had considered using 'Malthus for the department of political economy'; had he done so the journal would have had a different—and perhaps more consistent—attitude on economic questions (Semmel, *op. cit.* p. 23).
[178] *Quarterly Review*, VIII (1812), 319–27.

and the 'fearful spirit of insubordination'.[179] While so much moral evil persisted pauperism was inevitable, and the Poor Law had to be retained and even extended, especially in the provision of employment. Only national education under a national church—'Dr Bell's discovery to vaccinate the next generation against the pestilence which has infected this'—could finally solve the problem. All would be well when every child could and did read its Bible. Southey was above all anti-radical, and Malthus with his radical arguments was abhorrent to him despite his relatively conservative conclusions.[180]

Southey the renegade revolutionary was matched on the other side by Cobbett the renegade anti-revolutionary. On several occasions over the years Cobbett had quoted Malthus with approval, but early in 1807, in his campaign against Whitbread's poor-law Bill, he railed against 'the hard-hearted doctrine of this misanthropic philosopher' in introducing to the *Political Register* a series of anti-Malthusian letters by Hazlitt.[181] Cobbett's new anti-Malthusianism, like his new political radicalism, was emotional rather than intellectual—in 1819 he affirmed that he had in his life detested many men, 'but never any one so much as you'—and he contributed to the debate immense moral fervour, but very little intellectual analysis. He now saw the 'check-population philosophy' as a cloak for injustice and a bar to his own remedies, higher wages, lower taxation and political reform. He was, nevertheless, as alarmed at the increase in pauperism, and as critical of paupers, as most Malthusians: too many labourers were sinking 'quickly and contentedly into that state, from which their grandfathers, and even their fathers, shrunk with horror'. Cobbett lamented, like any abolitionist, that relief never excited gratitude, and that a pauper demanded it 'like a dun'. He pined for the traditional paternalism of the village, where the gentry stood 'as umpires between the farmers and the poor, with a little harmless bias towards the latter'. But not too much; gentry should be firm to the poor, refusing to employ the dissolute, and 'fixing a mark

---

[179] *Ibid.* 354, 338–40.

[180] As usual Southey had relied on Rickman for powder for his blunderbuss; but Rickman's own views were less extreme. He praised 'the abundance of wit' in the article but protested there was no evidence that manufactures increased poor rates; indeed Sussex had much higher rates than Lancashire, thanks to the system 'of equalising wages according to the number of mouths in the family' from the rates. 'I do not approve of this, nor of the poor laws at all; but it is a view of the matter which in your opinion (more perhaps than in mine) may lessen the amount of their mischief.' O. Williams, *Life and Letters of John Rickman* (1911), p. 167.

[181] *Political Register*, XI (1807), 397; and compare pp. 878–81 where a regular reader protested against this new attitude to Malthus. For Cobbett's earlier support for Malthus see *ibid.* VI (1804), 869–74; VII (1805), 230–1; IX (1806), 64–5; and compare H. Ausubel, 'William Cobbett and Malthusianism', *Jnl. of the Hist. of Ideas*, XIII (1952), 250–6.

of disgrace upon pauperism'. Charity, even enlightened scientific charity, was not to his taste. 'I cannot endure the idea of a labourer's receiving regularly, while he and his family are all in good health, a part of his subsistence in the character of a pauper. Nothing does good but that which is *earned*. There are particular cases when acts of charity ... are useful; but I like not the system of *presents* and *rewards*. ... In short, I am for giving the labourer a sufficiency, in the shape of *wages*, to maintain his family, and leaving him to live and manage his affairs entirely in his own way.'[182] These were sound and healthy sentiments indeed. But in what respects would Malthus have disagreed with them, except to deny that they were an answer to the problem he had raised? Cobbett was not really a contributor to the Malthusian debate; he was simply anti-Malthusian.

Hazlitt's criticism of Malthus had greater theoretical pretension. His letters to the *Political Register* were reprinted, with lengthy additions, as *A Reply to the Essay on Population* in 1807, but despite occasional shrewd criticisms of Malthus's principles the work was more important as a protest against his conclusions concerning the poor. Hazlitt accused Malthus of plagiarism, and made a cogent criticism of the ratios, but accepted the basic Malthusian thesis that population would advance more rapidly but for the checks of vice, misery and moral restraint.[183] Nevertheless Malthus had, in his eyes, 'sunk the philosopher and the friend of his species ... in the sophist and party-writer'.[184] He should have seen that human institutions encouraged vice and misery and discouraged moral restraint, and reached the obvious conclusion, political radicalism. Instead he defended the existing order and preached moral restraint 'for the single purpose of torturing the poor under the pretence of reforming their morals'; moreover he urged the abolition of the Poor Law:

> Now I shall not myself be so uncandid as not to confess, that I think the poor laws bad things; and that it would be well, if they could be got rid of, consistently with humanity and justice. ... The reason why I object to

[182] *Political Register*, XIV (1808), 73–6. Cobbett was also bitter against the Saints, with their spelling-books and 'comforts': 'fifty pounds expended in *good cheer in the old fashion*' was much to be preferred (*ibid.* p. 77). He later wrote a stinging account of 'the dictatorship of the Methodists and members of the Suppression of Vice Society' in the parish of Mitcham (*ibid.* p. 384).

[183] *A Reply* etc. *Complete Works* (1930 ed.), I. 231–2. Smith finds the work 'shot with shrewd logic' (*op. cit.* p. 71), but there were as many misses as hits; in 1819 Hazlitt admitted that the work was 'a little exuberant' (*Complete Works*, VII. 350 n.). See also W. P. Albrecht, *William Hazlitt and the Malthusian Controversy* (Albuquerque, 1950).

[184] *Spirit of the Age, Complete Works*, XI. 112. The essay on Malthus in this work gives Hazlitt's views more succinctly than in *A Reply* etc.

Mr. Malthus's plan is that it does not go to the root of the evil, or attack it in its principle, but its effects. . . . The wide spreading tyranny, dependence, indolence, and unhappiness of which Mr. Malthus is so sensible, are not occasioned by the increase of the poor rates, but these are the natural consequence of that increasing tyranny, dependence, indolence, and unhappiness occasioned by other causes.[185]

In two hundred lively but discursive pages Hazlitt argued that Malthus was wrong in his analysis of distress, sophistical in his arguments against equality and against the distribution of money to the poor, repulsive in the callousness of such passages as Nature's feast, and pernicious in his discouragement of political and social improvement and in his acceptance of the rich 'as a sort of Gods upon earth'. 'In his division of the evils of human life, he has allotted to the poor *all* the misery, and to the rich *as much vice as they please.*'[186] Much of this was excellent polemic, if sometimes less than just to Malthus's intentions. But we will look in vain, in Hazlitt's work, for practical suggestions for the reform of an admittedly faulty Poor Law, or for any clear advice on the economics, as distinct from the politics, of social improvement.

16. Weyland's Defence of the Poor Law

The early writers on Malthus thus produced a diverse literature of protest. Their criticisms were frequently pertinent, but they failed to dispose of the Malthusian thesis because they gave no adequate alternative answer to the fundamental problems Malthus had raised. For the most part Malthus did not deem them worthy of lengthy rebuttal; he reserved that honour for John Weyland, a man much less famous than Cobbett, Hazlitt or Southey and noticed in modern scholarship only because of Malthus's treatment of him in a later edition of the *Essay*. Weyland was provoked by the 1803 edition of the *Essay* into a study of the Poor Law, preparing material which was published in part in *A Short Inquiry into the Policy, Humanity and past effects of the Poor Laws* etc. in 1807, the rest appearing in *The Principles of Population and Production* etc. in 1816. He was a political economist of ability, but something of an anachronism in his own generation; since his theory included a positive defence of the Poor Law and a rejection of most of the fashionable arguments against it his views deserve some attention here. It may be that Malthus thought him a redoubtable opponent because his old-fashioned views might well appeal to laymen if not to other theorists; on the other hand Malthus was in some respects a little

---

[185] *A Reply* etc. I. 355.
[186] *Ibid.* I. 300.

177

old-fashioned himself, and may have seen more force in Weyland's arguments, and especially in his defence of the Poor Law, than he was willing to admit in public.[187]

Weyland expressed great respect for Malthus, but denied that his main thesis—that population had a constant tendency to increase faster than food supply—was applicable to any but exceptional societies.[188] In his view the natural tendency of population was to keep within the means of subsistence, exerting only a mild pressure upon it; moreover this pressure was not a cause of vice and misery but a beneficent incitement to economic progress, a progress which would be more rapid if population growth was judiciously encouraged. Weyland argued that the Poor Law provided the best means of encouraging population growth and thus economic progress, and urged systematic wage subsidies from the rates for the purpose. His views thus clashed with those of Malthus on almost every essential point.

Malthus sometimes, but not consistently, asserted that population could not increase without a preceding increase in subsistence; Weyland claimed that on the contrary an increase in food supply could only come from a previous increase in demand, and an expanding population was essential for the expansion of agriculture and later also of commerce and industry. He presented a survey of historical development to illustrate this proposition, and to show that only political or moral vice could upset this providential progression. Pressure of population naturally excited the savage hunter to cultivate crops and domesticate animals; the inconvenience of such pressure was 'a salutary consequence of vice from which a little industry would relieve them' and not 'a dispensation of Providence from which they can only escape by a decrease in the number of the people'.[189] As a stimulus to advancement incipient population pressure was the remedy, not the cause, of the misery of primitive peoples. And the stimulus would continue to operate once agriculture was established, and would eventually bring about a natural rotation between advances in agriculture on the one hand and commerce and manufactures on the other, as the population

[187] Weyland was born in 1774, was admitted to the Bar in 1800, represented Wiltshire in the House of Commons 1830–32, and lived until 1854. His other works included *Observations on Mr Whitbread's Poor Bill* etc. (1807), *A Letter to a Country Gentleman on the Education of the Lower Orders* etc. (1808), *The Principles of the English Poor Laws Illustrated* etc. (1815), and *Thoughts Submitted to the Employers of Labour* etc. (1830). Malthus added a respectful postscript noticing Weyland's *Short Inquiry* to his own *Letter to Samuel Whitbread Esq.* etc. (1807), and criticised his views at length in the 1817 edition of the *Essay*.

[188] *A Short Inquiry*, preface; and compare *Principles of Population*, Book I, chap. ii. Weyland cited Townsend as the originator of the view he was attacking.

[189] *Principles of Population*, p. 36. Ricardo admitted the force of some but not all of these arguments.

employed by commerce made the cultivation of poorer land profitable.[190] Thus in the natural course of things population, agriculture and manufactures stimulated each other by providing demands which called forth increased supplies.

Weyland was not, however, rash enough to suggest that this process could continue indefinitely with unabated force. The increasing population would inevitably press on food supplies as cultivation moved to inferior soils, were it not that certain checks to population would emerge at the same time. Of course he insisted that these checks were natural, and were not vicious or miserable. They arose mainly from the growth of towns: the commercial virtues of traders were largely incompatible with the marriage state, or at least with early marriage and large families. Similarly as civilisation produced a larger upper class with lower fertility, the rate of population growth would fall. More familiar was the argument that towns reduced the birth rate and increased the death rate through their effect on health, and indeed Weyland here quoted Malthus in support. These three factors produced 'an abatement in the progress of population which is voluntary, natural and unavoidable', so that in advanced states population never pressed on absolute subsistence but only on superfluities.[191] A typical population of nine millions might include a third in towns, not reproducing their number; a quarter in agriculture, supplying the deficiency; and the remainder—gentlemen, servants, soldiers, country shopkeepers and so on—on the whole a net drain on population. Eventually the 'Point of Non-Reproduction' would be reached, as the desire for 'artificial necessaries' led more of the population to be voluntarily celibate. These were the 'real facts' of population growth as opposed to Malthus's 'abstract theory', and they made the policy of checking population folly. Theories based on abstract ratios, or on analogies from goats, did not apply to men with foresight. Only the vices of mankind could upset the beneficent plan of providence in the matter.[192]

The obvious rejoinder which Malthus could (and did) make was that Weyland was claiming as the 'natural' rate of population growth the rate as hindered by checks, checks which Malthus had himself noted and insisted on describing as vice, misery, or moral restraint.[193] More damaging to Weyland's position was Malthus's claim that the growth of

[190] *A Short Inquiry*, chap. III. Weyland was in general a supporter of the landed interest, and later of the Corn Law, but he explicitly rejected physiocratic theories on agriculture and was not at first alarmed at the prospect of England becoming dependent on foreign supplies of food (*ibid.* pp. 27–9).
[191] *Principles of Population*, p. 65.
[192] *Ibid.* Book I, chaps. v–vi; *A Short Inquiry*, p. 49.
[193] On the use of the word 'natural' compare Weyland's *Principles of Population*, p. 17, and Malthus's *Essay* (1826), II. 485–6.

towns had not in fact checked the rate of population growth, and that Weyland was quite misguided in refusing to admit that the checks which towns provided were vicious or miserable. Weyland was on weak ground in claiming that the high mortality of towns and 'the weaker spark' in the constitution of townsmen was not to be deplored, and was merely a price to be paid for their more refined enjoyments and civil liberty; but he could well have made more of the assertion that prudential restraint from producing large families was normally to be expected as civilisation and the taste for 'artificial necessities' grew. This was of course the Malthusian moral restraint, but a very different cast would be given to the Malthusian outlook if moral restraint were something which could be expected of the average townsman rather than an ideal which could rarely be lived up to.[194]

The link between Weyland's views on population and on the Poor Law was his theory of wages, and in particular the argument that rapid economic development required a reservoir of surplus labour. A commercial and manufacturing country needed such a reserve if it were to take advantage of new opportunities to produce, to trade, and to colonise, and if it were to defend itself without an undue economic burden.[195] In normal circumstances wages regulated population growth, and for that growth to be rapid wages must be high. But Weyland was opposed to high money wages, repeating against them the old-fashioned arguments that high wages made it impossible to compete in foreign markets and encouraged vice and indolence among the labouring classes. The crux of the matter was that population could not increase rapidly unless wages were high enough to maintain a man with more than two children, but if wages were generally at such a high level the single man would be indolent and trade strangled; moreover even then a reserve of labour would not be provided.[196] Hence a dilemma—high wages were necessary to produce the population required for rapid progress, but at the same time they would prevent it by making impossible secure means of employment—'instead of a population employed at high wages we should presently have a population for whom there would be no wages at all'. Left to itself progress would be slow, with great fluctuations in employment, wages, and the standard of life. 'The supply of labour in the market' could not accommodate itself quickly enough 'to prevent the most extensive misery to the

[194] *A Short Inquiry*, pp. 35–6. By 1816 Weyland was less inclined to deny the possibility of a 'mischievous' increase of population in England.
[195] *Ibid.* pp. 50–1.
[196] *Ibid.* pp. 36–9; and compare *Observations on Mr. Whitbread's Poor Bill* etc. p. 17: 'A peasant or a manufacturer in the vigour of his youth and height of his passions with a superfluity of money and under no control, must necessarily contract vicious habits'.

labouring classes' in times of reduced demand or inordinate profits to the capitalist in times of increased demand. If only wages could be made unequal, so that childless bachelors received less and fathers of families more, 'it seems clear that the breeding stock would be supported without any expense to the public'. Direct attempts to assess wages in terms of need always failed; the only proper solution lay in the Poor Law, and Weyland saw relief paid to assist large families as its most important benefit:

> The money paid ... under the operation of the Poor Laws ... may be considered in a great measure as a premium given in lieu of high wages, at once to encourage population and to enable the manufacturer to work cheap; consequently to find a market for his commodities; thus rendering the country the most commercial, and, by providing a constant supply of active men for any speculations that may open to its views, at the same time the most powerful, in proportion to its natural resources, of the society of nations among which it flourishes.[197]

Was Weyland merely re-stating the old arguments that the labourers must be kept poor, or they would not work and England could not trade? Not quite; he repeatedly claimed that he was in favour of rising real wages for the labouring classes, that they were essential for agricultural expansion, and that a taste for artificial enjoyments among the labourers was required if industry were to flourish. This rise in real wages was the natural process, and attempts to prevent it were 'tyrannical' and 'impolitic'. Under his system, with wages adequate for two children and larger families subsidised from the rates, wages would be more stable. Money wages would not be forced down, but merely prevented from rising too sharply, while real wages would rise as the labourer was stimulated to work harder and the employer enabled to produce more cheaply. 'The general consequence, therefore, is to produce, really and truly, the same rapid progress of commercial and manufacturing prosperity under a regular but moderate rate of wages, as could only be contemplated in theory as possible under the previous operation of very high wages.'[198]

Despite these comforting predictions that the labourers' position would improve if only their money wages were kept down, Weyland also wrote several less benevolent passages. If Henry IV of France had succeeded in giving his peasantry 'a capon in every kettle', France would have been in misery:

> All would have been silence and apathy and phlegm; the peasant would have reclined upon his hearth, as stupid and unmoveable as the sloth upon a

[197] *The Principles of Population*, pp. 173–4; *A Short Inquiry*, pp. 41–2.
[198] *The Principles of Population*, pp. 175–8.

tree; like that disgusting animal, roused only by the calls of appetite, and having gorged to excess, he would have relapsed into his former state of torpor and lain stretched at length and snoring in his den.[199]

It is difficult to reconcile a rising real wage with this insistence that some 'pressure' must be maintained on the poor to make them industrious. Certainly their improvement was to be gradual, and luxury was not for them. Not for them either was the independence which property of their own might give them—among the 'mischievous' encouragements to population Weyland included peasant holdings or 'hovels on small patches of land' which provided their occupants with that 'subsistence compatible with idleness [which] removes the necessity of that mutual dependence between the employer and the employed, so essential to good order in every community'. As 'too scrupulous a delicacy is neither to be expected or encouraged among the lower orders of the people', it was wrong to 'infuse into their imaginations fanciful notions of independence which neither the frame of their minds nor their fixed and necessary habits could enable them to appreciate or enjoy'.[200]

If the Poor Law produced all the advantages of high wages with none of the disadvantages, abolition was simply folly.[201] Paradoxically, however, Weyland's defence of the Poor Law because it encouraged population had by 1807 to be argued in the face of Malthus's growing doubts whether in fact it did so. Weyland attempted an elaborate analysis of the poor returns of 1803 to prove that at least 280,000 children were supported from the rates and would otherwise have perished. Extending his arguments to the past, he found the origin of the Poor Law in the necessity of maintaining a population which had become partly redundant after the alienation of monastic lands had briefly stimulated the demand for labour. Had the Poor Law not been adopted, this surplus labour would have expired; instead it made possible the commercial expansion of the seventeenth century. Thus the Poor Law was the handmaid of the progress not only of population but of prosperity, culminating in the triumphant opposition to Napoleonic predominance. But Weyland did not want to prove too much; the Poor Law must be established as a stimulus to population, but not as an

[199] *Observations on Mr Whitbread's Poor Bill*, p. 63. 'The poor must always undergo a certain degree of privation, or they would not be poor' (p. 62).
[200] *The Principles of Population*, p. 215; *Observations on Mr Whitbread's Poor Bill*, p. 25.
[201] *A Short Inquiry*, pp. 79–80. 'The Poor Laws of England have been accused of depressing the condition of the poor, because they encourage population, without encouraging the growth of food for its support: an accusation that does not appear more reasonable, than if one were made against the bills for lighting the streets of London and Westminster, because they encourage the consumption of oil, without encouraging the catching of whales for its supply' (p. 256).

uncontrollable engine for producing people. There were, he claimed, automatic checks to excess built into the Poor Law, as into population growth itself: labourers remained reluctant to go upon the parish, except in obviously exceptional circumstances such as illness or being burdened with a large family. This natural resistance to becoming paupers would prevent the Poor Law producing a population far beyond the existing demand for labour.[202] This argument implied that the system of relief did not demoralise the labourer, at least when it was properly administered. Relief on account of children was not degrading: it merely gave a man a choice between bachelorhood on wages or family life on the rates. There were not, Weyland claimed, a large number of idlers on the rates. Indeed he went further and asserted that the existence of the system had improved the moral tone of the community.

While others saw the rise in the poor rates as the chief evidence of the evil effects of the Poor Laws, Weyland disagreed. In 1807 he produced an elaborate diagram to show that in real terms the rates had risen by only one-third between 1783 and 1803; if the burden seemed heavy, it was because of its inequitable distribution in the community. Poor rates, as a subsidy on economic progress, should be borne by the community as a whole, and not by land alone, or even by the employers alone. In the existing state of the law, land was unfairly burdened; in 1807 Weyland claimed that only a general tax on profits would be equitable, but hesitated to propose openly an income tax in place of the poor rate.[203] He did suggest an interesting variant of the proposal to freeze the rates; let them be frozen not at a certain total, but at (say) ninepence in the pound, and the total would increase in equilibrium with prosperity and population, and would moreover provide a useful political and economic barometer. Relief in times of scarcity should come not from the poor rates but from general revenue under Parliamentary supervision; Parliament could insist on the consumption of substitute foods, relieving the poor-law administration of the odium of recommending unpopular measures.[204]

The redistribution of the rates was only a part of Weyland's plan to reform the Poor Law. He always stressed the need to employ paupers, in simple manufactures, arguing that it would never drive independent workmen out of employ; at worst it could slow down

[202] *Ibid.* pp. 111–13.
[203] *Ibid.* pp. 224–32, 330–42. Weyland here noticed a problem: if rates were merely a transfer, a different method of paying wages, how could they increase national wealth, or benefit any one except at the expense of another? He decided, sensibly enough, that the productivity of labour was increased, but did not elaborate the point (*ibid.* p. 46).
[204] *Ibid.* pp. 348–60.

expansion in the free section of the economy. Parishes should be united into small districts, each with a salaried 'employment officer', and a general board of men of enlightenment and large fortune established in London to correspond with magistrates and to inform employment officers of areas where labour was in demand. Weyland objected to workhouses: used as deterrents they were inhuman, for employment expensive, and as asylums for children disastrous. He placed great stress on the necessity of educating children, in sound morals and religion, if little else.[205] With efficient employment for the able-bodied and education for the children the moral evils which sometimes accompanied poor relief would be much reduced. Between 1807 and 1816 Weyland apparently became less certain of the beneficial effects of the existing system, however; in his later work he greatly extended his discussion of institutions to encourage self-help, characteristically preferring savings banks to friendly societies, and was prepared to abolish relief to some classes of paupers. He added a chapter defending private charity against allegedly Malthusian objections, but concluded with an attack on 'thoughtless profusion' and a eulogy on self-help which any Malthusian might have written.[206]

This concern to restrict relief in certain cases and to encourage self-help may seem hardly consistent with Weyland's general claim that the Poor Law produced moral as well as economic benefits. The strength of the various strands which made up abolitionist objections to legal systems of relief is shown in the extent to which some of them were supported even by critics of Malthus and defenders of the Poor Law. Weyland became increasingly aware that he was arguing against dominant opinion, and against the apparent facts of the situation; in 1830 he at last admitted that there was a surplus of labour, and could only insist that the circumstances were exceptional and temporary. He maintained his belief that English labourers were not demoralised, and showed 'vigour and alacrity in making themselves free from dependence, if only a fair prospect is afforded them of reaping their just reward in comfort and independence'.[207] This confidence that the moral integrity of the labourer could survive even an unreformed Poor Law, even more than his theory of wages, set him apart from Malthus and the Malthusians. But it must be said also that Weyland's notion of the 'comfort

---

[205] See especially *A Letter to a Country Gentleman* etc. (1808), *passim*.

[206] *A Short Inquiry*, pp. 139–42; *The Principles of Population*, pp. 340, 367–82, 396–99. Compare *Observations on Mr. Whitbread's Poor Bill* etc. p. 17, where Weyland even suggested that the young and able-bodied should be excluded from relief altogether.

[207] *Thoughts submitted to the Employers of Labour* etc. (1830), p. 12.

and independence' proper to the labourer included reliance on the rates if he had more than two children.

If Weyland found that circumstances made his theories increasingly less plausible, Malthus suffered no such disability. His general views on the poor and the Poor Laws seemed persuasive to all those who were not allergic to the tone of his argument, or committed to alternative analyses and remedies; and all the more persuasive for being comprehensive rather than precise. His basic distrust of the Poor Law supported current presumptions and seemed to be supported in turn by the facts of the situation. But his plan for abolition was another matter. It was precise, bold and uncompromising, and hence too much altogether for all but the staunchest of his disciples. The Malthusian influence on attitudes to the problem of pauperism was greatest where it was most vague. Hence the widespread assumption that abolition was desirable, and the equally widespread refusal to countenance it as an immediate proposal.

V

Returns and Reformers

1. *The Debate Subsides*

DESPITE the discussion aroused by successive editions of Malthus's *Essay* the debate on poor relief was hardly vigorous in the years between the end of scarcity and 1815. The problem of pauperism had not been solved, but it lost some of its urgency; the spate of books and pamphlets on the subject abated, and there were few full-scale debates in Parliament. Perhaps the ruling classes were reluctant to tamper with existing institutions while the war lasted, from fear of popular discontent and from a conservatism heightened by the struggle with revolutionary France, but it is more likely that the lull in the discussion arose rather from the relative prosperity of these years. Landlords and farmers, with rents and profits inflated under the protection and stimulus of war, could afford to pay either adequate wages or higher poor rates. Prosperity was not uninterrupted—1812 and 1813 were bad years, especially in manufacturing towns—and some areas remained more or less continuously depressed, but on the whole the pressure of discontent on most of the ranks and orders of society was reduced.[1]

---

[1] W. Smart, *Economic Annals of the Nineteenth Century*, 1801–1820 (1910), conveniently charts fluctuations in conditions and reactions to them. J. Boys, *General View of the Agriculture of the County of Kent* (1805), pp. 206–7, and other surveys published by the Board of Agriculture in this period, remark on the favourable condition of the labourers; J. Willis, *On the Poor Laws of England* (1808), p. 75, was in a minority in complaining that wages were too low. For an example of radical protest in 1811–12 see *The Beggars' Complaint* etc. (1812); and for details of a particular depressed area see William Hale, *Letter to Samuel Whitbread* etc. (1806) on conditions in Spitalfields, and J. Cottingham, *Letter to Samuel Whitbread Esq.* etc. (1807) on neighbouring Mile-End New-Town.

In Parliament Whitbread was the major advocate of poor-law reform in these years; the distress of 1812–13 also brought some general discussion, which was followed by the campaigns of Horner, Romilly and Heron against harsh clauses in local acts in 1813–15, and by Sir Egerton Brydges' attacks on settlement and workhouses in 1814–16. Minor acts, passed with little debate, aimed mainly at humanitarian reform or administrative efficiency: thus the power of badging paupers was withdrawn, farming contracts were restricted to residents, the ill were exempted from immediate removal, and an attempt was made to ensure that the mothers (but not the fathers) of illegitimate children were treated more leniently. Magistrate's powers were widened, in acts increasing their powers to amend rates, to regulate workhouses, and to audit accounts.[2] And if Whitbread's Bill of 1807 was the only Parliamentary attempt at fundamental reform of the system, most of the pamphleteers of the period were content to discuss detailed questions of reform in administration or in methods of relief, rather than to ventilate more basic questions. There were, however, some notable contributions to the debate, especially from Patrick Colquhoun, and the discussion aroused by Whitbread's proposals showed clearly enough that dissatisfaction with the system was widespread and that fundamental issues were likely to be debated with more heat as soon as a new crisis in the condition of the labouring classes arose.

It is perhaps surprising that more debate was not provoked by the official Returns of expenditure on poor relief for the year 1802–3, collected on George Rose's instigation and published in 1804, for they showed that expenditure had doubled since 1783 and trebled since 1776. Close examination might reveal that the Returns were unreliable, especially in exaggerating pauper numbers; that the year they referred to was hardly normal, being influenced by the aftermath of scarcity; and that if allowance were made for movements in prices and population the increase in expenditure was not excessive. A few writers did notice these points, but on the whole the Returns were regarded as proof of a state of affairs which was unsatisfactory but not an urgent problem.[3]

---

[2] On the question of local acts see *Parliamentary Debates*, XXVII (1813), 278–81, (1814), 385–6; XXXIII (1815), 850–3; and *Parliamentary Papers*, 1812–13, III, Report from the Committee on Poor Houses and Poor Rates (113). See also P. Medd, *Romilly* (1968), p. 244.

[3] *Parliamentary Papers*, 1803–4, XIII, Abstract of the Answers and Returns etc. (175). Thomas Poole's 'Observations' at the end of each county's figures contain useful additional material; Poole had been selected for the task of collecting the returns by John Rickman. See also J. Marshall, *Statistics of the British Empire* (1837), pp. 36–9, for useful summaries of these and other returns.

The total raised by the Poor's Rate in 1802–3 was £5,348,204, of which £4,077,891 was spent on the relief of the poor—an increase of 108% in eighteen years—while expenditure on removals, litigation and other overseers' expenses had risen by a similar percentage to £190,072.[4] All counties showed increased expenditure, though by percentages varying from 200 in Hereford to 74 in Gloucester. The greatest increases were on the whole in those areas with lowest expenditure in earlier years, especially in the north and west, and probably reflected increasing population, a greater accuracy in Returns and a wider recourse to the poor-law machinery in those counties in the scarcity, rather than any serious decline in the relative position of labourers there.[5] Much more significant was the expenditure per head of population, which averaged 9s. 7d. for England and Wales as a whole, but was noticeably higher in the Midlands and south-east (apart from London itself). Sussex headed the list, with 23s. 4d., while Lancashire was the lowest, spending only 4s. 11d. per head of population.[6] The high expenditure in the Midlands, south and east perhaps reflected recent enclosures and the growth of the allowance system, but these were also the areas where labourers were most dependent on wheaten bread for food, and the effects of scarcity prices might still have persisted in 1802–3. As Colquhoun and Rickman noted, expenditure was greatest in primarily agricultural counties, though it also appears that most towns reported rates rather higher than the average of their counties. But rates are a treacherous guide, since few were struck on rack rentals, which were increasing rapidly in the wartime boom in agriculture. Even so, the average rate as reported was only 4s. 5d., which was hardly a crushing burden on the property of the country. Poole estimated (or guessed) that on rack rentals the average rate would have been only 3s. 4d., and no more than 2s. 10d. if calculated on Tax Office returns of property. Local variations in rating practice make it pointless to compare county averages, beyond noting that the areas where expenditure had increased most markedly had by no means the highest rates.

[4] The total rate raised can be a misleading indication of pauperism. The parish of Lanvihangel Lantarnam in Monmouthsire struck a rate of 18s. (while its neighbour Lanvihangel Pontymoile made do with 2s. 6d.) not because it was overburdened with poor but in order to buy a new set of church bells.

[5] For a note on the recent introduction of poor rates in some parts of Yorkshire see W. Marshall, *A Review of the Reports to the Board of Agriculture* etc. (1808) p. 440.

[6] Expenditure was more than 14s. per head in Sussex, Berks, Bucks, Essex, Northants, Oxford, Wales and Wilts. These figures are of comparative significance only, since they were calculated from uncorrected population figures from the census of 1801.

If expenditure on relief looked alarmingly high it was the large size of the pauper population which seemed especially shameful. According to the Returns a total of 1,040,716 received relief in 1802–3, about one in nine of the population as estimated in the census of 1801. Since overseers often counted twice over many paupers who were relieved more than once,[7] the figure was undoubtedly inflated, but it was enough to shock many contemporaries. They did not stop to notice that 305,899 were relieved only occasionally, that of the permanent paupers at least 315,150 were children under fourteen, and that 166,829 were aged or impotent. The total of able-bodied men and women permanently on relief could not have been more than 200,000, admittedly a large number, but not surprisingly large in the aftermath of scarcity, especially while poor rates were being used to maintain the families of soldiers and sailors in a protracted war. The distribution of this pauper population followed quite closely the expenditure per head of population; highest in the Midlands and south-east, it was generally low in the north and west.

Finally, the Returns included information on methods of relief. The 14,611 parishes declared that they possessed some 3,765 workhouses between them, and maintained 83,468 paupers indoors. Of course these institutions varied in size and type: the national average, for what it is worth, was only 22 inmates per house. More significantly, only ten counties had more than 2,000 indoor paupers, and seven had fewer than 500. The most noteworthy figures, however, were those indicating workhouse expenses. The small proportion of indoor paupers—less than one-twelfth—absorbed £1,016,446, about one-quarter of total expenditure. The national average expenditure per head on indoor paupers was £12 3s. 7d.; in no county was it less than £8, and in the three counties with most indoor paupers it was over £14. Outdoor paupers, on the other hand, cost only £3 3s. 8d. on the national average, and only in Rutland was the expenditure more than £6 per head. Thus the cheapest county expenditure on indoor relief was one-third more expensive than the dearest county expenditure on outdoor relief, a point quickly grasped by critics of workhouses. What the critics did not notice, however, was the obvious lack of precision in the statements of expenditure per head. One-third of the pauper population was relieved only occasionally, and it is to be presumed that outdoor relief was usual in these cases. Workhouse inmates were probably the hard core of the pauper population, and it was naturally more expensive to maintain them, on the average, than to relieve a larger number only occasionally and also, in all probability, with much less than full

[7] On this inaccuracy see *Parliamentary Papers*, 1822, V, Report from the Select Committee on Poor Rate Returns (556), p. 13.

maintenance. The evidence did not disprove Bentham's contention that outdoor relief was extravagant.

These Returns were not, on the whole, examined critically by contemporaries, though George Rose himself stressed that they should not be quoted without making due allowance for population and price movements. Weyland, as has been seen, alleged that the real burden of the rates was not great; Colquhoun agreed with him, though he in turn inflated pauper numbers.[8] In general, however, the figures were quoted in confirmation of views already formed, such as convictions that pauperism was an increasing burden, or that workhouses were an undesirable method of relief. Far less alarm was inspired by these Returns than by those collected in the next decade, and the very absence of a sense of urgency from the debate gave the lie to the superficially alarming picture of pauperism which the Returns presented.

2. Sundry Reformers

The pamphlet literature on the Poor Law in these years was concerned for the most part with those questions of administration, settlement, rating and methods of relief which for at least a century had been matters of debate. Thus Robert Saunders of Lewisham echoed the old complaint that the administrative system was basically at fault in placing so much responsibility upon ignorant overseers; 'no person of respectability and independence' could accept the office as the law defined it, and consequently the whole Poor Law was made liable to corruption and incompetence. James Nasmith, the scholarly Chairman of the Quarter Sessions of the Island of Ely, retorted that the system was sound enough, or could be if only men would do their duty, inserting in his argument asides against innovation and 'French principles'. Saunders replied in turn that if good advice could solve the problem Nasmith's charge would remove all abuses; if victory in a pamphlet war can be judged by the measure of support a contestant receives Saunders won this brief campaign over the merits of the system of voluntary overseers.[9] Some writers suggested the appointment of

---

[8] G. Rose, *Observations on the Poor Laws* etc. (1805), pp. 1–40; Colquhoun's calculations are discussed below. See also [T. Pemberton], *An Attempt to Estimate the Increase of the Numbers of the Poor* etc. (1811) for another argument that the increase since 1785 had not been inordinate.

[9] R. Saunders, *Observations* etc. (1799), p. 111, and *An Abstract of Observations* etc. (1802); J. Nasmith, *The Duties of the Overseers of the Poor* etc. (1799). See also W. Bleamire, *Remarks on the Poor Laws* etc. (1800), pp. 26–8; T. Thompson, *Considerations* etc. (1800), p. 42; J. Hill, *The Means of Reforming the Morals of the Poor* etc. (1801), p. 115; Rev. H. Bate Dudley, *A Few Observations* etc. (1802), p. 11. Bate Dudley, known as 'the fighting parson' for the duelling of his disreputable youth,

permanent salaried overseers, a device popular after the war; others proposed a system of visitors or inspectors, with functions similar to those of Guardians in incorporated areas.[10] Saunders himself went much further, advocating a national administration for poor relief, a Board of Commissioners entrusted with 'superintendence and controul'. This was but one of several schemes for a national system in these years, Bentham, Colquhoun, Weston and the author of an anonymous *Essay* of 1810 all offering proposals of this sort. The schemes were of two types. Weston, like Bentham, sought a national administration with executive powers; he offered a plan for the division of the country into thirty districts, each divided further into four, sub-divided in turn into ten 'parishes' each, with a hierarchy of Commissioners built up from a base of individual 'resident officers' in each parish. The supreme authority was to be a Board of Industry, with the organisation of employment its chief responsibility. *An Essay on the Poor Laws, as they regard the real interests both of Rich and Poor* (1810) was less bold, suggesting a re-organisation of the magistracy as supervisors, under the direction of a National Board of Commissioners. Neither Saunders nor Colquhoun sought any such national executive power, however. Saunders specifically rejected Weston's Plan, and his own central Commissioners were merely to collect information and disseminate good advice, such as Rumford's recipes. And, as shall be seen, Colquhoun's central Board was to be an instrument of intelligence, not of executive power. A true national poor-law administration was still a bold and visionary suggestion.[11]

The thorny problems of settlement and of the unequal incidence of the rates were, of course, difficult to solve while administration remained local; Weston and the author of the *Essay* of 1810 sought a national system primarily to cut such Gordian knots. Almost all the

[10] On salaried overseers see W. Bleamire, *Remarks* etc. p. 26; and J. Willis, *On the Poor Laws* etc. (1808), p. 53; and compare Howes' proposals of 1796 and Lofft's criticism of them, *Annals* XXVII. 215–21, 313–31. On visiting schemes see T. Thompson, *Considerations* etc. p. 31 and *Further Observations* etc. (1801), p. 1; E. Wakefield, *A Letter to the Landowners* etc. (1802), p. 31; and *The Philanthropist*, II (1812), 173.

[11] *An Essay on the Poor Laws* etc. (1810), chap. IV; R. Saunders, *Observations* etc. pp. 158–67, and *An Abstract* etc. p. 17; C. Weston, *Remarks on the Poor Laws* etc. (1802), pp. 143–57. Weston also suggested 'collateral aids' such as schools and hospitals, and may have been influenced by Bentham.

was a journalist rather than a cleric. An early editor of the *Morning Post*, he was gaoled in 1781 for libelling the Duke of Richmond. Johnson remarked to Boswell: 'Sir, I will not allow this man to have merit. No, sir; what he has is rather the contrary.' Bate Dudley wrote a large number of comic operas, but he took his duties as a magistrate of seven English and four Irish counties quite seriously, at least intermittently. He was made a baronet in 1813, and died in 1824 aged 79.

other writers were highly critical of the Law of Settlement, but most were barren of practical proposals. Bate Dudley alone stood out to defend it, deploring the relaxation of the system in 1795, and complaining that only the law protected society from widespread vagrancy and 'restless ambition'. But, as Whitbread discovered, the real barriers to settlement reform were interests, not arguments. For somewhat different reasons, most pleas for rating reform were just as vain: rates could only be equal geographically if they were national, and they would always fall more heavily on land unless they copied the hated Property Tax. Bate Dudley complained loudly of the burden on the landed interest, but shrank from such drastic innovations, and Bleamire, Willis and Bate Dudley all wished piously for equality in payment without suggesting any means of achieving it. Edward Gardner was more bold, suggesting a Property Tax of 6–7% to provide a national fund for the relief of the poor. Others proposed rating systems of more or less ingenuity and eccentricity, but none offered a practical solution to the problem.[12]

More was written in these years on methods of relief, and the principles which should govern them. The chief butt of the critics was still the workhouse, and not yet the allowance system.[13] Ingram was exceptional in proposing the abolition of outdoor relief, and even he insisted that the institutional relief which should replace it must be in reformed houses of industry. Brydges, the author of the anonymous *Essay* of 1810, and Rigby (a disciple of Dr Ferriar who tried to get the Norwich House put down) were more typical in their strong criticism of all institutional relief. Rose favoured Schools of Industry, but marshalled the evidence of the Returns against common workhouses and sought the repeal of the Workhouse Test Act. Incorporation and large houses still had their defenders (and their critics), but the emphasis was strongly on reform and not on deterrence.[14] There was little in this

[12] Settlement and rating were discussed in all the pamphlets cited above; see also E. Gardner, *Reflections* etc. (1800), pp. 11, 89–94, for a proposed property tax; *Annals* XLV (1808), 289–91, for a proposal to tax bachelors; P. Lovelass, *A Proposed Practicable Plan* etc. (1804) for better use of endowed charities; and R. Walthew, *A Moral and Political Essay* etc. (1814) for complaints that middle-class ratepayers suffered because agricultural land was not rated on rack rentals.

[13] But note T. Thompson's attack on a 'conspiracy' to keep down wages (*Further Observations* etc. p. 9); and the oblique reference to allowances by Rose (*Observations on the Poor Laws* etc. p. 14).

[14] Rose criticised deterrence and argued that the Workhouse Test Act was the first great deviation from the original intent of the Poor Law, an interpretation directly contrary to that usual after 1834 (*Observations on the Poor Laws* etc. pp. 31–7). Bate Dudley, Thompson and Wakefield all criticised ordinary workhouses and approved only reformed houses, but [Jones], *Letters to John Probert Esq.* (1801) attacked large houses and pleaded for local, personal supervision of relief. E. Rigby's *Further Facts*

period to herald the revival of the workhouse test as a major principle of relief in the 1820's; many writers complained of undue prodigality in relief, but sought other modes of limiting it. Most wanted, like Saunders, to 'draw the line strongly' between the deserving and undeserving; some thought that firmness, or closer personal investigation, could achieve such a distinction. Bate Dudley, always conservative, toyed with the idea of reviving badging. The author of the *Essay* of 1810 would have excluded certain classes from relief, if not from public employment, but as he spared large families and all those suffering because of high prices the exclusions would have been negligible. Only Bleamire hinted at less eligibility, in insisting that the diet of the pauper be reduced below that of the independent labourer, while 'the idle, lazy and abandoned, who now, to the shame of our modern governors of parishes, crowd every poor house, were, and still ought to be, objects of punishment.' But the debate as a whole was still dominated by the idea of moral discrimination, and hence discretion and not rules was the aim; moreover, while workhouses and badges remained in such disfavour, 'drawing the line' had to be done in overseers' minds rather than by institutional devices.[15] The minor literature of the period offered few practicable schemes of reform, and fewer hints of the changes which were to come.

Schemes for contributory institutions, either to replace the Poor Law or more modestly to supplement it, continued to win support in this period. Curwen, an active organiser of friendly societies in his own county, expressed a hope that this might eventually make public relief unnecessary, and Whitbread's Bill included an elaborate contributory system. One other plan, produced by John Bone in 1805–6, deserves brief attention, since it included a peculiar combination of institutional relief and the contributory principle.[16]

[15] Thus while Bate Dudley would have badged the undeserving he insisted that 'there is nothing immoral in actual indigence' and gave no guidance on how to decide who should be badged (*A Few Observations* etc. p. 15); compare W. Bleamire, *Remarks* etc. pp. 19, 35; and *An Essay* etc. (1810), chap. V.

[16] J. Curwen, *Hints* etc. (1808), Essay V; J. Bone, *Outline of a Plan* etc. (1805) and *The Principles and Regulations of Tranquillity* etc. (1806). See also a letter of Bone's in the *Political Register*, XI (1807), 447–54, in reply to a critical letter in *ibid.* X (1806), 558–67. For other discussions of contributory schemes see *Annals*, XXXVII (1801), 562–71; W. Bleamire, *Remarks* etc. p. 35; J. Willis, *On the Poor Laws* etc. p. 65; E. Wakefield, *A Letter* etc. p. 5; and *Political Register*, XII (1807), 370 (for a strange plan for compulsory fire insurance to subsidise poor relief).

relating to the Care of the Poor etc. (1812) is a good source on abuses alleged to be common in large workhouses; Rigby, who became Mayor of Norwich in 1805, is credited with introducing both vaccination and the flying shuttle to the city. H. Wansey's *Thoughts on Poor Houses* (1801) is a useful source on some southern institutions.

Bone thought the Poor Law evil and absurd; private charity and in particular self-help were much to be preferred. He attacked the localism inherent in the existing system, and quoted Smith against the Law of Settlement, urging instead the establishment of a national contributory fund, to be augmented by donations from the charitable. Relief should be in proportion to contributions, which would be as large as the contributor chose. Included among his 'principles' of relief were a 'proper distinction' between the worthy and the dissolute, education for children, and the encouragement of cleanliness, almost an obsession with Bone. The fund was to be managed by twenty-five directors elected by the subscribers, and one of their first duties was to be the erection of 'very extensive premises', to be named Tranquillity, near London. The main purpose of the institution seemed to be to provide apartments for aged families in retirement, but it was to include a school, an inn for visiting subscribers, a primitive labour exchange, a trade school (in lieu of public employment, which Bone rejected, quoting Defoe in support), a sort of bank to provide loans for embarrassed subscribers and to safeguard the savings of children, and a large public bath, available to subscribers on demand and to visitors for a small fee. Bone thought that baths would lead vagrants to reform themselves, cleanliness being apparently a stimulus to godliness. The state, he argued, had not protected the interests of the labourer as it had those of the landed and merchant classes; if it supported his plan, the fund and the institution could provide all the facilities needed for self-help and would make both wage regulation and labourers' combinations unnecessary.[17]

It seems that Bone tried hard to arouse public interest in his plan. In April 1806 he founded a Society for the Gradual Abolition of the Poor's Rate; Fox, the Archbishop of Canterbury, the Commander in Chief, the Speaker of the House of Commons, the Lord Mayor, the Chancellor of the Exchequer and the Chairman of the East India Company were all proposed as Directors, but there is no evidence that any of them accepted the honour, or that there were any subscribers to elect them.[18] He also published detailed regulations, with an elaborate classification of subscribers and the benefits they would obtain, ranging from a set of rooms, a £50 annuity, and domestic help for those paying the maximum contribution down to a dwelling in return for labour for those who had not subscribed at all but had been recommended by a contributor as frugal and sober and too poor to save. The building

---

[17] J. Bone, *Outline* etc. esp. pp. 26–52.

[18] Rose later wrote of Bone's plan that 'I believe no progress was made in it, although very respectable Trustees were named' (*Observations on Banks for Savings* (1816), p. 40).

itself was to form a large hollow square, with orchard walks, the office and the school in the courtyard; and to preserve peace and harmony the Governor would appoint one person from each four families as an elder, with power to try before a jury for disorderly behaviour, the punishment being solitary confinement. In point of democracy the plan thus fell somewhere between Bentham's authoritarian Houses and Owen's cooperative village.[19] Bone was eloquent in support of his scheme. The poor were 'extremely wretched'; they must be taught to help themselves, and the worthy among them helped liberally to do so. If despite all efforts to save they yet could not provide for old age 'society is unjust if it does not make up the deficiency, not as a matter of charity, but of right'. Let the rich each pay their guinea to the Society, let the poor pay their subscriptions and receive their benefits, let Parliament exempt subscribers from paying the Poor's Rate, and the whole antique edifice of the Poor Laws would gradually crumble as the new, contributory, institutional system developed. If the adult poor were too depraved to be taught new ways, their children would do better. But there is no evidence that Bone extracted many guineas from the rich, or that the baths of Tranquillity ever filled to wash away the sins of vagrants with their grime.

3. Charity and Education

The principle of self-help, implicit in all contributory schemes, continued also to be a characteristic belief of the champions of private philanthropy. Charitable activity continued after the scarcity subsided, though a change in emphasis can be observed in the views of some of the philanthropists. Thus the Society for Bettering the Condition of the Poor became less concerned with direct material assistance to the lower classes, and more with permanent aid and especially the cultivation of the intellect. In 1802 Bernard warned that 'if ever the mass of the common people of this island look up to the rich for the *daily alms* of food, the energy of the country will be destroyed',[20] and the volume of reports published in that year was concerned with allotments of land, rewards for diligence, friendly societies and the prevention and treatment of disease more than with scarcity measures. A Ladies Committee of the Society was formed in 1805, and was soon very active in good works which gentlemen could not 'decorously' undertake, although

---

[19] J. Bone, *Principles* etc. pp. 4–25. Bone's suggestion of a bank for small savings inspired Henry Duncan's experiments in Scotland (H. O. Horne, *A History of Savings Banks* (1947), p. 43). Little else seems to be known of him.

[20] *Reports*, III (1802), 27–8.

there were critics who thought the Ladies' activities indecorous and morally dangerous. Of course it was not thought to be 'the province of females to legislate', although a woman was said to have been a great success as an overseer at Stoke Poges; charity schools were commended as particularly suitable for their encouragement, and the Committee responded enthusiastically when Bernard called for a survey of all such schools in 1805.[21]

Education loomed large in his own interests by this time. Schools of many types had been described and commended in the *Reports* from the beginning, and the monitorial system of Bell and Lancaster, under which the children largely taught each other, seemed entirely consistent with the Society's ideals of enlightenment, economy and self-help. Bernard had not begun his work for the poor with the assumption that the chief assistance they needed was intellectual and spiritual, but he reached that conclusion in due course: 'in the progress of our investigations', he wrote, 'it became evident that nothing essential or permanent could be done for *bettering the condition of the poor*, without the improvement of their moral and religious character, by an increase of places for worship for their sacred duties, and of schools for the *education* of their children.'[22] When sectarian divisions split the educational reformers the society naturally—if sometimes a little reluctantly— sided with Bell and the established church against Lancaster and dissent; Bernard himself pleaded for peace and unity in the matter, but on the Church's terms. Thus the path of scientific charity led into the tortuous maze of educational controversy.

Despite this new emphasis on education, Bernard still gave some attention to relief and the Poor Law. In 1801, when he discussed the Malthusian attack on the system he rejected abolitionism and called for reform, but offered few suggestions. Workhouses were attacked once more, and care in charity urged as a counter to vice and misery in a population already too much debased by the growth of commerce and

[21] The work of the Ladies Committee is described in *Reports*, IV and V. *passim*. See also Catherine Cappe, *Observations* etc. (1805) and *Thoughts* etc. (1841): Mrs Cappe, widow of a unitarian divine of York, quoted Malthus on the inevitability of spinsterhood, urged unmarried women to be active in charity, and proposed a kind of less-eligibility principle as a deterrent not to pauperism but seduction: 'a modest, prudent young Woman would surely wish that the strongest line of distinction should be drawn ... between herself and the wretched victims of profiligacy and vice' (*Observations*, p. 119). For criticism of ladies joining a committee to rescue fallen women see *An Address to the Guardian Society* (1817), p. 230: 'Not content with endeavouring to bring back lost women across this line [of virtue] themselves, they take virtuous women to the other side of it for this purpose: dangerous experiment!'

[22] T. Bernard, *The Barrington School* etc. (1812), p. 4. The work was first published, in shorter form, in 1809, and republished in 1810, 1812 and 1815.

manufactures.[23] Four years later he produced a more definite plan of reform. The poor had just claims on society and government, not for unrestricted physical relief, but for the prevention of vice and contagion, for the promotion of virtue and industry, and for moral and religious education; seldom can the rights of man have been defined so much in terms of paternalistic duties. Bernard lamented that vice, and not virtue, was so much encouraged, directly by indiscriminate poor relief and indirectly by bad example, by Sabbath breaking, dram drinking, and by 'profane and immoral' stage plays such as *The Beggars' Opera*. Relief should be part of a moral regimen, and it was therefore necessary that 'a marked and distinctive line' be drawn 'between the idle and profligate and the honest and industrious'. The Poor Law should be rebuilt for the purpose, with a new administrative system in which counties would be divided into district Petty Sessions obliged to hold meetings, to receive returns, and to supervise relief, and empowered to appoint salaried Assistant Overseers in parishes which needed them. Each parish should have a Benefit Fund for the impotent, guaranteed by the rates, and thus a 'more secure and unexceptionable form of friendly society'. Subscription to it would earn a settlement, in time and under certain conditions; it would also gain exemption from the rates for labourers' cottages and gardens. These were the immediate measures proposed, to be followed later by a reform of charity schools, the removal of children from workhouses to parish schools, and the establishment of a Fund for the Encouragement of Virtue, especially the virtue of saving in preparation for marriage, since the Poor Law tended to promote 'wasteful youth and thoughtless marriages'. Apart from this sop to Malthusianism the whole plan was conservative, and was obviously based on Pitt's, Bernard being a warm admirer of 'the great Minister'.[24]

In 1808, in a letter to Wilberforce, Bernard defended his plan against more radical alternatives, and amplified his views on methods of relief. The S.B.C.P. was consistently in favour of the creation of employment, though opposed to workhouses and parish manufactures as neither 'just nor politic'. New industries could be introduced into cottages, or the poor settled on waste lands, or employed in fisheries.[25] Problems of relief and employment became urgent in 1812–13, and Bernard had his schemes to offer to the Association for the Relief and Benefit of the Manufacturing and Labouring Poor, founded in May, 1812. The association raised money by voluntary subscription, and distributed it to local

[23] *Reports*, III. 1–42.
[24] Letter to the Rt. Hon. Henry Addington, *Reports*, IV. 4–29; *Outline of Measures* etc. (1805), also published in *Reports*, V. appendix I.
[25] *Reports*, V. 1–60.

charities to be spent on relief in kind or in employment. The encourage-ment of fish as a food, and fishing as an industry, became Bernard's chief suggestion for relief; became indeed almost an obsession with the ageing philanthropist. In 1813 he founded a Fish Association for the Benefit of the Community, commending fish as 'a *moral* Remedy for increasing Population and the vicissitudes of commerce and manufactures'. In 1817 his contribution to the great post-war debate on distress was a plan for promoting employment, primarily by repealing the Salt Duties and thus opening up a vast field for endeavour upon the seas. Salt was a fertiliser, useful for cultivating waste lands, a food for animals, and a necessity in the production of soap; Bernard wrote fifty pages on the precious mineral.[26] By this time the Society no longer possessed the potent influence of its early years; its Fortieth Report, published in 1817, had little new or weighty to offer puzzled philanthropists. Fish, salt, schools, savings banks and a house of recovery were recommended, in familiar terms. Who, in 1817, would gain much enlightenment or stimulus by reading a letter in praise of vaccination from a Brahmin? And was the Malthusian challenge to be met so easily with a kettle of fish and a grain of salt? Bernard died in 1818.

The Association for the Relief and Benefit of the Manufacturing and Labouring Poor was hardly a successor to the Society. Although leading evangelicals were prominent among its sponsors, its principles were less coherent and its aims less precise; it was significant in its cautious liberality, in its suspicion of poor-law machinery, and perhaps above all in the fact that some special organisation for the manufactur-ing poor was thought necessary. The Committee estimated that half the population of industrial districts were paupers in 1812–13, and en-couraged relief in forms which (it hoped) would alleviate evils without impairing the incentive to work, recognising, nevertheless, that 'extreme misery' was as fatal to industry as was reliance on charity and relief. But the Association was primarily a channel for the distribution of funds rather than ideas.[27]

The appearance of Brougham among the Saints on the Association's Committee reminds us that men who were—or were to become—of very different political persuasions collaborated in charitable activities in these years. The united front of philanthropy was split by the post-war political issues, a cleavage which began before the peace with religious differences in the controversy over education. In earlier years

[26] T. Bernard, *Account of a Supply of Fish for the Manufacturing Poor* (1813); *On the Supply of Employment* etc. (1817).
[27] See the Association's *Report* of 1813 for an account of its founding, aims, and early attitudes.

even Bentham had his links, through Colquhoun, with the work of the S.B.C.P.; but the quarrel between Church and Dissent in education turned Bentham against the Establishment, just as the failure of his other plans made him a political radical with an intermittent connection with the later Brougham. Since 1808 Bentham had also been intimate with James Mill, who was in turn a friend of William Allen, Quaker associate of Robert Owen and founder of *The Philanthropist* in 1811. It was Allen who induced Bentham to invest in Owen's mills at New Lanark and who interested Bentham and Mill in Lancaster's schools, thus setting in train that long process of exasperation and composition which ultimately produced Bentham's bitter works on 'Church of Englandism' and his vast educational treatise, *Chrestomathia*. Although Allen had contributed to the Reports of the S.B.C.P., his *Philanthropist* had a decidedly more radical and utilitarian and a less ecclesiastical air than the writings of Bernard and his friends, and much more incisive views on the Poor Law.[28]

There was, nevertheless, much in the early volumes of the new journal which Bernard could have written, for example the essay on benevolence as the cement of social union, the accounts of cottage gardens, penny clubs and schools of industry. He could also have approved the stress on philanthropy overseas, on missions and on the abolition of slavery. But in the frequent references to education it was Lancaster who was praised, while his critics in the Church were berated and Dr. Bell ignored; and in writings on crime and punishment, and on pauperism, a strong and radical Benthamite influence was evident from the first. In 1812 the Poor Laws, as they existed, were attacked as 'a curse and scourge on the poor', oppressing the ratepayers, while ruining the character and impairing the comforts of the poor themselves. This, it was claimed, was admitted by all save 'unintelligent aristocrats' and tyrannical manufacturers who cared only for low wage costs.[29] Bernard himself would willingly have criticised the manufacturers, but would have been much more polite to the aristocracy; and although he might have agreed with the *Philanthropist* that moral degeneracy was the principal cause of increasing pauperism, he would certainly have denied the journal's claim that 'bad government' was the main cause of moral degeneracy, and would not have described Bentham as the man 'who had advanced further in the science of legislation than all the philosophers who have gone before him.'[30] Allen admitted that

[28] On the links between Bentham, Mill, Allen and Owen see E. Halevy, *The Growth of Philosophic Radicalism* (1949 ed.), pp. 285, 301; and A. Bain, *James Mill* (1882), pp. 81–2, 113–14. See also *Reports*, IV. report ci, for a contribution by Allen.

[29] *The Philanthropist*, II (1812), 309–34.

[30] *Ibid.* II. 321; for further praise of Bentham see *ibid.* I. 66–77, 184, 228; II. 129. Comments on Malthus were more ambivalent.

beggary was proportional to its encouragement, and the Poor Laws were themselves a cause of pauperism, but only bad government, by bringing distress and degradation, could undermine independence so thoroughly. The Poor Laws should be repealed, but necessary prerequisites were the reform of government, peace, low taxes and an end to sinecures. Such a combination of abolitionism and political radicalism could never have sullied the pages of the *Reports* of the S.B.C.P. When a correspondent complained that political matters were appearing in the *Philanthropist*, Allen replied that this was inevitable.[31] If the philanthropists of these years were agreed on the need for education and for discrimination in the relief of distress, they were increasingly divided over religious and political issues.

4. *Patrick Colquhoun*

Without doubt the most important work on the question of poverty published between the scarcity and the end of the war was Patrick Colquhoun's *Treatise on Indigence* of 1806. The book was less original than it is sometimes claimed to be, but Colquhoun was nevertheless a prominent figure in the debate; when Jeremy Bentham had enlisted his aid in 1796 it was not as a mere assistant but almost as a patron, for Colquhoun was already much more widely known as an authority on such subjects than was Bentham himself. Like Sir Thomas Bernard, Colquhoun spent his early life making his fortune and his later years in good works. In the 1780s he had been Glasgow's chief magistrate, founder of the city's Chamber of Commerce and a pamphleteer in her economic interests; in 1789 he retired to London at the age of forty-four, and accepted appointment as one of the new Police Magistrates in 1792.[32] His *Treatise on the Police of the Metropolis* (1796) made him the foremost authority on that subject, but he was also an indefatigable philanthropist. He advised, organised and publicised a number of city charities, worked with the Society for Bettering the Condition of the Poor, supported the work of Matthew Martin and helped to found the

[31] *Ibid.* III (1813), 84. *The Philanthropist* continued to be critical of the Poor Law after the war (*ibid.* V (1815), 153) but would not support abolition without full investigation (*ibid.* VII (1819), 224, 313); it continued to support Benthamite law reform (*ibid.* p. 149). Its account of Harmony, Pennsylvania, in 1815 may have been one of Owen's sources for his plan, which Allen printed in *The Philanthropist*, VII (1819), 66–78.

[32] For a brief life of Colquhoun written by his son-in-law see 'Iartos' [G. D. Yeats], *A Biographical Sketch of the Life and Writings of Patrick Colquhoun Esq. LL.D.* (1818); and for a general discussion of his views R. Pieris, 'The Contributions of Patrick Colquhoun to Social Theory and Social Philosophy', *University of Ceylon Review*, XII (1954).

Mendicity Society, pleading its cause to government and eventually before the Select Committee on Mendicity in 1815–6. Pitt consulted Colquhoun on the condition of the labouring classes, and an impressive report on the need for relief in the winter of 1799–1800 is preserved among the Prime Minister's papers.[33] But despite his prestige and influence Colquhoun did not succeed in achieving his principal aim, the prevention of both crime and indigence through the establishment of a general 'system of police', with a central authority investigating the problems and supervising the remedies. No doubt, like Bentham, he prepared the way for future reforms; his own work as a theorist and a statistician was very uneven in quality, but he was one of the most important of those practical reformers who contributed so much to the general movement for legal and administrative improvement which is loosely called Benthamite.

For a time Colquhoun kept his interests in police and in indigence separate, at least in his publications, but in 1799 he published a small tract entitled *The State of Indigence and the Situation of the Casual Poor in the Metropolis Explained* in which he asserted that indigence was a main cause of crime and that the system of relief for the casual poor actually encouraged misdemeanours. This material was then included in the sixth and later editions of his *Treatise on the Police of the Metropolis*, under the heading 'The Origin of Crimes: State of the Poor'. All his main themes were stated briefly: his distinction between poverty and indigence, his defence of the principles of public relief and complaints of mismanagement in practice; his concern to prevent indigence rather than to relieve it; and his belief that this could best be achieved by appointing commissioners to investigate problems and to guide local authorities. These points were supported by practical examples from his own philanthropic experience, but they were not elaborated into a thesis until *A Treatise on Indigence* appeared in 1806.

The *Treatise* began with a distinction between poverty and indigence, the wording following Bentham's unpublished *Essay* of 1796 very closely. Poverty was the necessity of working for a living, and indigence inability to make a living even by working; 'indigence, therefore, and

---

[33] P. R. O. Pitt Papers, 308. On Colquhoun's philanthropic activities in these years see *A Plan for . . . extensive Relief to the Poor* etc. (1795); *Explanation of the Plan* etc. (1795); [Colquhoun?], *An Account of a Meat and Soup Charity* etc. (1797) and *The Economy of an Institution established at Spitalfields* etc. (1799); Colquhoun, *Suggestions* etc. (1799); M. Martin, *Letter to the Rt. Hon. Lord Pelham on the State of Mendicity in the Metropolis* etc. (1803); and *Parliamentary Papers*, 1814–15, III, Report from the Select Committee on the State of Mendicity in the Metropolis (473) and 1816, V, (396). The MS minutes of a special committee set up at Lloyds to administer charities, to which Colquhoun was adviser, are in the National Library in Canberra.

not poverty, is the evil', while poverty is 'a most necessary and indispensable ingredient in society'.[34] (When Laski quoted Colquhoun on the inevitability of poverty as a 'justification which satisfied' middle-class consciences faced with social evils, he missed the point as well as the correct attribution of the idea; most of us are still poor, under Bentham's definition.[35]) Colquhoun then followed Bentham further in distinguishing between inadequate-, adequate,- and extra-ability to produce subsistence, and repeated Bentham's dictum that 'the great desideratum . . . is to prop up poverty by judicious arrangements . . . when it is in danger of descending into indigence'. But his table of causes of indigence was much less exhaustive than Bentham's, and the main distinction made was moral: he listed twenty-six causes of 'culpable indigence' and twenty-nine of 'innocent indigence'. Bentham might well have agreed that only 'improvement in the morals of the vulgar' could prevent culpable indigence but he would not have inserted the point at that stage of the argument, and would certainly not have insisted that a system of relief must distinguish between culpability and innocence: this was the old process of moral discrimination, which he wished to replace with a more objective test of actual condition. Colquhoun made the point because he was as much concerned to prevent crime as to relieve indigence; the virtuous indigent were treated in the same way as the vicious, and consequently they became vicious. Indigence and crime were two sides of the same coin, 'since it is a state of *indigence*, fostered by idleness, which produces a disposition to moral and criminal offences, and they are so linked together that it will be found impracticable to ameliorate the condition of the poor without taking more effectual measures at the same time for the prevention of criminal offences'.[36] Colquhoun's concern with the prevention of crime made him an important and progressive figure in the history of police; his writings on indigence were as admirable in intent, but there were serious shortcomings in his understanding of the problem, and especially its economic aspects.

Colquhoun's limitations are most obvious in his work as a statistician. The large collections of statistics he made on important subjects would be invaluable, if only they could be trusted. Bentham left his Plan unfinished for lack of accurate figures, but Colquhoun was content to

[34] *Treatise on Indigence*, p. 7. The wording of similar passages in *The State of Indigence*, p. 18, the *Treatise on Police* and the *Treatise on the Wealth, Power and Resources of the British Empire* (1814) are less like Bentham's but the sense is the same. For a re-statement of the distinction in an American work see the *Report to the Managers of the Society for the Prevention of Pauperism in New York* (1819), pp. 4–5. Colquoun was acknowledged as the source.

[35] H. J. Laski, *The Rise of European Liberalism* (1936), p. 209.

[36] *Treatise on Indigence*, pp. 8–9, 48–9.

accept any statistics which suited his argument and to guess when he could find no figures at all. He was also a patriot, and it was almost with pride that he claimed that never in the history of the world had so much indigence been supported by so great riches. Pauperism he thought to be increasing faster than population, but he did not predict economic calamity: the resources of the Empire were so vast that all the indigent could be employed given a proper system. To nearly £4½ million raised by the rates he added about £400,000 from endowed charities and an estimated £3,332,035 from private benevolence, this last a mere guess modified to produce a round total of £8 million as the total cost of relief; and if another £4 million were added as the potential worth of the indigent's labour how alarming the total—but how prosperous the country which could afford so much indigence.[37] Colquhoun went on to estimate that one-seventh of the population of the country lived off the labour of the rest, by accepting uncritically the total of 1,040,716 paupers given in the returns of 1802–3 and adding thereto 50,000 mendicants, 20,000 vagrants, 100,000 'lewd and immoral women', 10,000 rogues and vagabonds, 80,000 'highway robbers, foot-pad robbers, burglars, house breakers, pick pockets, horse stealers, sheep stealers, stealers of hogs and cattle, deer stealers, common thieves, petty thieves, occasional thieves who cannot resist temptation': a grand total of 1,320,716.[38] As a police magistrate and philanthropist Colquhoun doubtless knew the varieties of crime and indigence, but he was in no position to count the criminal and the indigent.

On economic questions he was equally naïve. He was orthodox enough to insist that 'the wages of labour ought certainly to find their level in the natural course of things' but assumed that that level would be sufficient to maintain a labourer and an average family, since 'otherwise this useful class could not last beyond a single generation'. Perhaps government should attempt to prevent great fluctuations in wages, though how to do this was not specified; certainly 'free circulation of labour' should be encouraged by relaxing the Law of Settlement, and the rates equalised to remove undue burdens from certain labourers.

[37] *Ibid.* pp. 60–2.
[38] *Ibid.* pp. 38–43. Colquhoun gave special mention to 'foreign vagabonds, who also wander about the country, pretending to sell pictures, but who are also dealers in obscene books and prints, which they introduce into boarding schools, on pretence of selling prints of flowers, whereby the youth of both sexes are corrupted, while at the same time some of these wanderers are suspected of being employed by the enemy as spies.' By 1814 he claimed that paupers and vagrants had increased to 1,828,270 (*Treatise on the Wealth ... of the British Empire*, p. 107). McCulloch described the latter work as a 'tissue of extravagant hypotheses and exaggeration' (*Literature of Political Economy*, chap. VI).

He was also alarmed by rumours of the allowance system: 'if ever (as has been alleged) the parochial funds have been resorted to for the purpose of preventing a rise of wages to their natural level, in proportion to the advance in the price of articles of the first necessity, such a system of collusive fraud upon the community at large deserves the severest reprehension'.[39] Clearly Colquhoun missed the point of objections that relief could lower wages. He also continually insisted that paupers should be employed, claimed their employment could be profitable, and lamented the waste involved in idleness, without making any precise suggestions on ways and means. He was, in fact, a reformer of laws and of morals, not of economic systems; his economic optimism did not waver until 1818, when he at last feared that there might be a genuine redundancy of labour and wrote a pamphlet urging systematic colonisation of the Cape of Good Hope.[40] But this tract was written in retirement, two years before his death, and in his active life he sought rather the reform of the Poor Law as part of the systematic reform of Police.

Colquhoun seems never to have doubted that a Poor Law was necessary. He once admitted that Malthus had 'never been surpassed' as a logical reasoner—a rash claim in itself—but the arguments of the abolitionists could not divert this instinct for magisterial superintendence. The rich must support the indigent somehow; only a Poor Law could do it systematically, and only central supervision could ensure that the Poor Law did it well. The Elizabethan Act was excellent in theory, and all that was lacking was 'a superintendence equal to the direction of so complicated a machine'. Indigence and the rates had increased, not because population had outrun resources, but because the national principle of poor relief had been left in local hands to enforce. Localism, exemplified above all in the Law of Settlement, was the chief cause of expense, indigence and vagabondage. It inhibited employment. It distorted the very purpose of the system, by encouraging deterrent devices such as workhouses—Bentham had not converted Colquhoun to institutional relief—when the chief aim should be the preservation of the virtuously indigent from contamination with vice. Moreover localism made the burden of maintaining indigence unequal; if a Poor Law was a national necessity, its cost should be a national charge.

The national principle established for the maintenance or relief of paupers, was originally lost sight of, in local or parochial provision. Limiting the burden to a mere parochial fund laid the foundation of all the evils that have followed. Hence the intricacy of the machinery introduced; hence the be-

[39] *Treatise on Indigence*, pp. 14–16, 278–9.
[40] *Considerations of the Means of Affording Profitable Employment to the Redundant Population of Great Britain* etc. (1818).

wildering code of laws which grew out of the system; hence, as has already been seen, the warfare between parish and parish and the excessive waste of time and public money on vexatious litigations . . . let the fund be national and parish settlements, removals, appeals, certificates, and all the miserable train of endless litigation, of questions of no earthly importance to the nation or to individuals, will vanish. The poor man's liberty will then cease to be abridged; labour, so necessary in an agricultural, commercial and manufacturing country will have free scope, and will find its true level . . . their country should be their settlement and the legislature their guardian.[41]

If the whole nation should be regarded as one family and one parish, as Colquhoun recommended, some sort of central supervision would be necessary. He had long been urging a 'Board of General and Internal Police' for the prevention of crime, and now proposed that its responsibilities should include indigence as well. The police function was defined in the most general sense: a 'systematic superintending police' included 'all those regulations in a country which apply to the comfort, convenience, and safety of the inhabitants' which were of a preventive nature.[42] The first duty of such a Board of Commissioners would be to collect information, digest it, make annual reports to Parliament, and advise parishes at any time on reforms. Colquhoun thought the information collected should include not only statistics of all paupers relieved, vagrants removed and so on, but also rentals and rates, the wages and expenses of the labouring classes, resources for employment and state of the demand for labour, information about schools, and about morals—'in what degree and proportion . . . the inferior classes are generally sober and industrious or the reverse'. Information should likewise be collected on all crimes, prisoners, licensed premises and second-hand dealers, for the prevention of crime and idleness.

The Board was to be a centre of intelligence rather than an executive authority, except insofar as it collected and disbursed the national rate. Apart from making recommendations to the central government or to the parishes, the Board should disseminate its information widely through a weekly Police Gazette, a bizarre publication as Colquhoun planned it. An abstract of some Act of Parliament (for example on pawnbrokers or combinations) would be followed by short essays in narrative style on various crimes—treason or stealing turnips, rape or murder—and on one of twenty-four moral and religious duties, such as keeping the Sabbath, providence and economy, being a good husband or wife, 'the government of the passions', or the commendable

---

[41] *Treatise on Indigence*, pp. 240–2; see *Treatise on the Wealth . . . of the British Empire* etc. p. 2 n. for Colquhoun's praise of Malthus.

[42] *Treatise on Indigence*, p. 82. Colquhoun was careful to distinguish between the police function, thus defined, and judicial processes and punishments.

pride of rearing a family without parish assistance. Statistics of crime could be included also, with lists of wanted men, accounts of 'the number of convicts sent to New South Wales with proper remarks', and descriptions of executions 'with commentaries suitable to the comprehension of the vulgar'. At the cost of three halfpence each per week, 25,000 copies could be distributed to all central, county and parish authorities and another 50,000 to alehouses, to influence that part of the public most in need of reform.[43] It would be easy to ridicule such a plan, and to point out that the disadvantages of local responsibility could not be overcome by a Board with no authority to do more than advise and harangue; nevertheless Colquhoun deserves credit for insisting that accurate facts were a necessary pre-requisite of reform.

Colquhoun himself made few practical suggestions for changes in parochial practice in relief. He did, however, recommend that the system be supplemented by devices aimed at 'preventing virtuous poverty from descending into indigence', suggesting in particular the creation of a national deposit bank and a system of national education. The 'bank' proposed was in fact a scheme of national insurance, with depositors paying between one and ten shillings each month and collecting benefits according to a schedule established by a quite elaborate administrative structure. Insurance was a feature of the age, but friendly societies were inadequate and too often vicious; creating an adequate instrument of contributory self-help was a 'godlike work', and in due course the labourer would 'look up to the government and the bank as guardian angels'.[44] And since ignorance was also a major cause of indigence a new national system of schools, on the monitorial system, and a radically reformed scheme of apprenticeship, were also urgent needs. But instruction in the schools should be for morality and religion only: 'it is the interest of every nation that the people should be virtuous and well-disposed; but science and learning, if universally diffused, would speedily overturn the best-constituted government on earth'.[45] There was much of the old-fashioned moralist in Colquhoun, despite his instinct in the direction of administrative reform. If indigence was a cause of crime, so too was prosperity, and he urged that the poor be given land to preserve their rural virtue and to keep them away from 'the tempting lure of manufacturers, or the delusive luxuries of large towns'. The increasing wealth of the Empire might be a source of fascination, but Colquhoun was no friend to the new economic forces which produced it. If he borrowed

[43] *Ibid.* pp. 79–109.
[44] *Ibid.* pp. 110–38.
[45] *Ibid.* pp. 148–9.

from Bentham, he nevertheless emasculated Bentham's ruthless administrative logic in restricting the functions of a central authority mainly to admonition rather than action, and did not follow the utilitarian sage in attempting to grapple with the economic problems of employment and relief. Of course half-baked Benthamism was more acceptable to contemporaries than the genuine unpalatable article, and Colquhoun's emphasis on the prevention of indigence through self-help and education was a very common reaction indeed to the circumstances of the time. Despite his own economic optimism and defence of the Poor Law there was much in his work, and especially in his calculation of pauper numbers, to give strength to abolitionist arguments. His contribution to positive reform of the system of relief is more difficult to estimate; the abolition of settlement and the creation of a national rate were vain hopes, though not uncommon, but his insistence on the need for central supervision had some logic in the existing situation. The reform of 1834 was to involve more positive central initiative than Colquhoun envisaged, though very much less than Bentham advocated. But new crises and further abortive attempts at reform were necessary before effective action was eventually taken.

5. *Whitbread's Poor Law Bill*

In 1807 Samuel Whitbread added poor-law reform to the list of lost causes he had made his own. This was the last attempt by a private member to remodel the whole system, and it is not surprising that it failed completely. As a plan 'for the Promoting and Encouraging of Industry amongst the Labouring Classes of the Community, and for the relief and regulation of the necessitous and criminal poor' it was too complicated and unwieldy to gain approval from critical country gentlemen who all regarded themselves as authorities on the subject; moreover Tory squires were not likely to give a Foxite Whig approval which they had withheld from Pitt himself. But quite apart from political prejudice and defects in the plan itself, Whitbread's failure arose from factors which inhibited all major poor-law reform in this period: little could be suggested which did not provoke powerful objections, and opinions on the subject were so confused and indeed contradictory that no measure of more than minor importance could hope to make its way through Parliament. The day of the independent purveyor of general reform was past; Whitbread's bill was not merely a failure, it was almost an anachronism.[46]

---

[46] Whitbread's friend Francis Wrangam claimed the bill failed because it became a party measure (Bedfordshire County Record Office, Whitbread Papers, 3646), but compare *Diary and Correspondence of Charles Abbot, Lord Colchester*, II. 127–9 for a contrary opinion. Whitbread did not consult his friends in the Ministry before

One cannot compare the fortunes of Whitbread's and Pitt's attempts at reform without recognising that a 'great revolution in the public mind' had occurred in the intervening years, as Whitbread himself remarked in his speech introducing the Bill on 19 February.[47] The Act of Elizabeth, he admitted, was no longer generally accepted as good in principle, and he thought it necessary to justify his intention to reform the law rather than repeal it. He had abandoned the cause of wage regulation; why persist with attempts to develop the Poor Law?

It is an assertion now pretty generally made, that the system of our Poor Laws is certain to degrade those whom it was intended to exalt, to destroy the spirit of independence throughout our land; to hold out hopes which cannot be realised; to encourage idleness and vice; and to produce a superfluous population, the offspring of improvidence and the early victim of misery and want. That which in speculation ought to have been our glory has been turned to our reproach.[48]

Whitbread paid tribute to Malthus's part in enlightening the public mind on the matter, in a passage which is often cited as evidence of the impact of Malthusian views; but in fact Whitbread gave Malthus credit only for completing a change of opinion which had already begun, and his own acceptance of Malthus's teachings was far from complete.[49] The general principles expounded in the *Essay* were incontrovertible, and he was no Godwinian 'visionary enthusiast'—'I believe man to be born to labour as the sparks fly upwards: that a certain portion of misery is inseparable from mortality'—but Malthus's practical conclusions were unacceptable. Even if 'the prevailing sentiment' that the Poor Law caused more poverty than it cured was well founded, abolition was the wrong policy. It would cause confusion and cruelty, bring forth a plague of beggars, and incite insurrection by the poor: 'if you deny their right to assistance, your metaphysical oppositions may be unquestionable, but you would collect a set of dangerous enemies'. The Poor Law must be retained, if only as a 'sure and legal refuge' for cases

[47] *Parliamentary Debates*, VIII. 865. References below are to the separate publication *Substance of a Speech on the Poor Laws* etc. (1807).

[48] *Substance of a Speech*, p. 3.

[49] In 1815, speaking in support of the Corn Law, Whitbread included a harshly Malthusian passage on wages, remarking that if agricultural production increased 'some little brat or other would be bound to eat the surplus corn' (R. Fulford, *op. cit.*, pp. 246–7); but in these last months before his suicide not all his statements are to be taken at their face value.

introducing the Bill, rightly remarking to his brother-in-law Grey that they would not be interested: 'I know how flat the subject is'. William Wilshere, Whitbread's adviser on his estates and partner in the brewery, helped him in the preparation of the Bill (R. Fulford, *Samuel Whitbread* 1764–1815, pp. 176–80, 94–6).

of extraordinary need. Indeed Whitbread was abolitionist enough to want no more than that, and to hope that 'by taking proper steps' it might 'hereafter become almost obsolete'.[50] In 1796 he had urged wage regulation against principles he in general accepted; he now sought Poor Law reform although he admitted the cogency of much of the abolitionist case.

Whitbread hoped to meet the objections of the abolitionists by seeking, on the one hand, some restriction in relief, and on the other new means of assisting the labouring classes to free themselves from the need for it. He was groping, like so many others, towards the twin principles of less-eligibility and self-help, principles which would at once deter and entice labourers from pauperism. Loosen restraints on the labourer, and give him hope for reward from his own industry: 'excite him to acquire property that he may taste its sweets'. At the same time reorganise relief to distinguish between the criminally and innocently necessitous, and 'to render dependent poverty, in all cases, degradation in his eyes, and at all times less desirable than independent industry'.[51] Unfortunately for Whitbread's Bill—both for its logical consistency and for its fate—his constant impulse towards humanitarian relief inhibited his search for a deterrent principle of action.

The greatest innovation Whitbread proposed was a national system of education, incorporated in the structure of parish relief. Pitt had sought schools of industry, utilitarian in aim, and Colquhoun wanted only moral instruction for the poor; Whitbread welcomed Lancaster's new general schools, and did not shirk from the prospect of a literate labouring class. Vestries and overseers were to establish such schools in every parish, at the expense of the rates, and schooling was to be free for the children of the labourers. The belief that educating the minds as well as the hands of the poor would improve their morals and reduce pauperism was new enough to be controversial, and Whitbread was careful to marshal evidence in support. Malthus was quoted as an authority, but the chief appeal was to the example of Scotland; it was widely believed that the Scots poor were poorer but more moral and provident than the English, and their superior education seemed a plausible explanation of this phenomenon. 'In the adoption of the system of education', Whitbread explained, 'I see the enlightened peasantry frugal, industrious, sober, orderly and contented because they are acquainted with the true view of frugality, sobriety, industry and order.'[52] These precepts were to be made more attractive by a system of rewards to the deserving poor, paid from the county rates.

[50] *Substance of a Speech*, pp. 7, 10, 19, 21.
[51] *Ibid*. pp. 21–2.
[52] *Ibid*. pp. 24–35, 95.

Large families, which should not have special relief from the parish, as Pitt had so wrongly provided, might be rewarded if they succeeded in surviving without assistance. Whitbread suggested prizes of £20 or more, and badges of merit to wear, and spoke sentimentally enough of 'the honest glow of self-gratification appearing on the rugged countenance of industrious labour at the sight of the unexpected boon; the tear of joy trickling down that furrowed cheek which had been often moistened with the tear of anguish and disappointment'. But what could the poor do with the £20, or any other money they succeeded in accumulating? Whitbread proposed a National Poor's Fund as a suitable place for investment, a central bank accepting deposits of up to £200 and investing them in Bank of England annuities. Associated with it was to be a national Poor's Assurance Office, offering a variety of benefits on actuarial principles. The scheme was Pitt's Parochial Fund writ large—too large, its critics said, to be practicable.[53]

All this was to be added to the existing Poor Law; the reforms proposed in the code itself were more cautious. Whitbread was highly critical of the Law of Settlement, but he proposed only one major amendment: a householder was to gain a settlement by five years' residence, provided he did not become chargeable and was not convicted of any crime in the period.[54] Whitbread was clearly setting his sights low, in the hope that the Bill might prove acceptable, and his approach to administrative reform showed the same caution. Nothing in the Bill was to apply to areas administered under special acts, and the unit of administration elsewhere was to remain unaltered. He did, however, seek a reform in the vestry system; vestries were to meet regularly and to have the power to order relief, an innovation which involved some limiting of the powers of overseers and magistrates. Moreover, as vestry meetings were 'too frequently disorderly and tumultuous' and under the 'influence of popular clamour', voting rights were to be redrawn in favour of large rate payers; no longer would all who paid the rates have equal voices. In order to redistribute the burden of the rates, Whitbread proposed that capital other than land should be rated, that poor householders should be exempted, and that overburdened parishes be relieved from the county rate.[55]

Whitbread was similarly cautious in his reform of methods of relief. The great innovation was to be the revival of the power of parishes to build cottages at the expense of the rates, to be let to the poor at

[53] *Ibid.* pp. 74, 36–42; *Substance of a Bill* etc. (1807), pp. 7–16.
[54] *Substance of a Speech* etc. pp. 46–54; *Substance of a Bill* etc. pp. 17–19. Another clause permitting parishes to ascertain settlement before the person concerned became chargeable was attacked as an incitement to litigation, and was withdrawn.
[55] *Substance of a Speech* etc. pp. 54–68; *Substance of a Bill* etc. pp. 19–21.

whatever rent they could afford. The immediate aim was simply humanitarian: 'the poor are greatly distressed for habitation and large families are compelled to live in single rooms, or in outhouses or places unfit for the inhabitation of men', because of increases in population and in the expense of building.[56] But Whitbread had another motive: he wanted to bring the poor out of workhouses, wherever possible. As a magistrate in Bedfordshire, he had been active in inspecting workhouses and in getting orders for their reform from the Quarter Sessions.[57] The Bill made no attempt to abolish them, but Whitbread argued at length that they were expensive and demoralising, and sought closer regulation of their management and a further relaxation of the Workhouse Test Act 'which goes to drive into the workhouse, oppressively, all persons applying for parochial relief'. He was thus in favour of outdoor relief; and the Hammonds accuse him of being short-sighted on the problem.[58] In fact he was frankly puzzled by it. He saw the objections to subsidising wages (though he did not think the practice worked badly in his own area), but could see no way to abolish it. On the other hand he did wish to introduce an element of deterrence into relief: to all but the aged, the infant and the sick it should be reduced to bare necessaries, and the criminal poor should be punished and badged. But what could be done with the innocent able-bodied poor? Workhouses were unacceptable; so too were all other schemes for public employment. 'We are now sufficiently enlightened to know that individual capitalists alone could employ their capital to advantage in commerce . . . and that all attempts to establish manufactures for the purpose of making the poor support themselves out of their compulsory labour (except in very few cases) have either failed, or been kept alive by extraordinary labour and pecuniary aid . . . National employment would be a losing and indeed impracticable scheme.'[59] But how, then, could relief be made less eligible, if public labour was not to be demanded? The new Poor Law was of course to retain the workhouse, but with no illusions that the employment it provided would be profitable. Whitbread suggested as the only possible combination of outdoor relief and deterrence a complicated regulation, that parish relief (even if in aid of low wages), was on no account to be made up to the full 'usual' wage. But he was well aware that this was no real

---

[56] *Substance of a Bill* etc. pp. 25–6; *Substance of a Speech* etc. pp. 75–7.

[57] *Bedfordshire County Records*, I. 96–7; and compare the numerous reports on workhouses from the years 1801–14 preserved in the Whitbread Papers. In 1801 Whitbread sought legal opinion on magistrates' powers to reform workhouses, as a preliminary to an active campaign against abuses (Whitbread Papers, 762–72).

[58] *Parliamentary Debates*, IX. 490; J. L. and Barbara Hammond, *The Village Labourer*, I. 177.

[59] *Substance of a Speech* etc. p. 89; *Parliamentary Debates*, VIII. 919.

solution to the problem, and could only look to the relaxation of the settlement laws to reduce its scale.[60]

6. Whitbread's second Defeat

The Bill was not well received by the House of Commons. For Ellison, 'the Act of Elizabeth contained the great principles of every good system; and all that was required was to simplify and improve the system established upon those principles'; Whitbread's reforms were too tainted with Malthusianism to be acceptable. For Giddy, however, only abolition would do: 'It might be asked of him, would he abolish the Poor-Laws altogether? He had no hesitation to declare he would; for, although they relieved many persons, who were certainly objects of compassion, they were also abused by contributing to the support of idleness and profligacy; and he could never admit it to be just or reasonable that the labour of the industrious man should be taxed to support the idle vagrant'. To this creed Rose gave a familiar answer: 'With respect to the poor-rates, if they did not now exist, he would propose them, because he thought that the relief of the poor ought not to be left with the generous to the exemption of the miser'.[61] In fact Whitbread's failure arose less from the opposition of extremists than from a lack of support from men like Rose, acknowledged authorities on the poor and men of influence in the House. Rose had, the year before, promised Whitbread general support, but to him the crucial reform was 'to provide employment for the poor and thereby to render their own industry as effective as possible towards their maintenance'.[62] When Whitbread failed to do this, Rose's promise meant so little that he even sought an adjournment of a second reading debate on the grounds that he had been unaware it was down for that day and was not ready for it. Whitbread did, however, heed his advice to divide the Bill; when the House resumed in April he announced that he would present three Bills—on Education, on Settlement and Relief, and on the Poor's Fund. In the event the first was mauled by the Commons and rejected by the Lords, the second abandoned in Committee, and the third not introduced at all. And some clauses of the original Bill had already received such hostile notice from the public that they were omitted altogether.[63]

[60] Substance of a Bill etc. pp. 29–30; compare Substance of a Speech etc. p. 90.
[61] Parliamentary Debates, VIII. 919; IX. 799, 800. Davies Giddy (1767–1839) later changed his name to Gilbert, having married an heiress of that name. He was a very active member of the House of Commons from 1804 until 1831; in 1827 he became President of the Royal Society.
[62] Ibid. VII. 292–3.
[63] The adjudication of settlement before the subject became chargeable, plural voting in vestries, and the rating of personal property.

The debates in the House were imperfectly recorded, but they were preceded by a full discussion of the proposal in the pamphlet literature and the press. Malthus himself contributed to it; his *Letter to Samuel Whitbread Esq. etc* was the only pamphlet he wrote on the Poor Law. It was sympathetic in tone, Malthus even 'putting all idea of the abolition of the Poor Laws out of the question' and asking only that the Bill's object should be 'to elevate as much as possible the general character of the lower classes of the community, and to draw a more marked line between the dependent and the independent labourer.'[64] Whitbread had claimed that 'Mr. Malthus never intended to push his principles to extremes',[65] and it is true that Malthus praised much of the Bill, but his criticism of a number of clauses was as unflinching as it was polite. Whitbread could hardly have foreseen the main line of attack, that he was about to remove the very imperfections in the operation of the Poor Law which had in the past restricted the evil effects one might have expected from its principles. Not all Malthusians were quite as severe as the master; J. B. Monck, in a fervent if rather crude exposition of the new creed, gave the Bill general approval. More approval, in fact, than came from certain prominent critics of Malthus who entered the discussion, and would certainly have dismissed Monck's thesis 'that the poor are such as we find them, swarming, indolent, improvident, discontented, dispirited, oppressed, degraded, vicious, is chiefly owing to the system of the Poor Laws'.[66] Jarrold chided Whitbread for yielding too much to Malthus's 'false, injurious and wicked' principles, 'such as ought not, in any form, to be made the basis of legislation', though his conclusion that Whitbread should attempt chiefly to encourage virtue and providence in the poor could have been heartily supported by Malthus himself.[67] This could not be said of an anonymous *Letter* from Scotland appealing to Whitbread to establish Poor Laws there, and presenting a very able analysis of Malthus's theory of population to show that its author had drawn the wrong conclusion from right principles when he had demanded abolition. Yet more stirring of the Malthusian pool came from Weyland, taking the opportunity to expound again the principles of his recently published *Short Inquiry* against both Whitbread and Malthus.[68]

While the Bill satisfied neither Malthus nor his opponents, criticism

---

[64] *Letter to Samuel Whitbread*, reprinted in D. V. Glass (ed)., *Introduction to Malthus* (1953), p. 191.

[65] *Substance of a Speech etc*. p. 77.

[66] J. B. Monck, *General Reflections etc*. (1807), pp. 14, 23–9.

[67] T. Jarrold, *A Letter to Samuel Whitbread Esq. etc*. (1807), p. 11.

[68] *A Letter on the Nature, Extent and Management of Poor Rates in Scotland etc*. (Edinburgh, 1807); J. Weyland, *Observations on Mr. Whitbread's Poor Bill etc*. (1807).

213

from other quarters was perhaps even more damaging. Bernard produced a detailed attack, chiding Whitbread for not consulting the Society for Bettering the Condition of the Poor, and rather ungraciously concluding with a paean of praise for Pitt.[69] And if the saints were critical, so too were the squires; the anonymous author of *Remarks upon a Bill* complained it 'set at nought, most rashly, . . . the wisdom and experience of centuries', and sacrificed 'old and lawful interests, with unrestrained boldness'. The amendments to the settlement laws, the proposal to relieve certain parishes, and even the new schools were seen as part of a manufacturers' plot to increase the burden on the landowners, with Whitbread as their tool or dupe; the Poor Law was perfectly satisfactory when the right people, the magistrates of England, were allowed to manage matters.[70] And the radicals were even less impressed than the saints and the squires. Cobbett and correspondents in his *Political Register* opened fire on Whitbread, beginning an engagement which continued long after the Bill was defeated (for so long indeed that the original issue of poor relief fell away, the *Edinburgh Review* replaced Whitbread as the opponent, and the point in dispute at the last was whether Scotsmen washed). Within a week of Whitbread' speech Cobbett took his stand:

At present I shall content myself with giving it as my decided opinion, that the scheme, except as far as it goes to do away with the restrictions as to settlements, has in contemplation regulations the most absurd as well as most unjust that ever were conceived by mortal man. If a plan like this were really to be adopted, I, for my part, should not be at all surprised, if someone were to propose the selling of the poor, or the mortgaging of them to the fund-holders—Aye! you may wince; you may cry Jacobin and Leveller as long as you please. I wish to see the poor men of England what the poor men of England were when I was born.[71]

He promised to make his criticisms more specific when he had actually read the Bill; having done so, he insisted that the whole plan was a red-herring to divert attention from the real causes of the misery of the poor, 'taxation and the idleness of the innumerable swarms who live upon the taxes'. Whitbread had recently disappointed the radicals in the matter of the Westminster election; hence Cobbett's added bitterness against the man who would reform the people, even to badging them, rather than reform the Parliament which oppressed them.

Whitbread's proposals inevitably called forth the usual crop of more

[69] T. Bernard, *A Letter to the Rt. Rev. the Lord Bishop of Durham* etc. (1807).
[70] *Remarks upon a Bill . . . for promoting and encouraging of Industry* etc. (1807) p. 5.
[71] *Political Register*, 28 February 1807; and compare G. D. H. Cole, *Life o. William Cobbett* (3rd ed. 1947), pp. 137–41.

or less eccentric schemes from men as eager as Bernard or Weyland to propose their own plans, but with less claim to serious attention.

Daniel Carpenter, a Hertfordshire justice ambitious to be thought 'a man of reflection', surveyed with a patronising air not only the Bill but also the general views of Malthus, Rose, Weyland and Colquhoun, as a prelude to his own scheme for remodelling the Poor Law. Relief would be available only after attendance at church, and Carpenter proposed a neat refinement in Malthusianism in his suggestion that special rewards be paid when labourers married, provided they did not do so below an age fixed by the government with due regard to the current pressure of population. Tipplers, 'old men marrying young women', and those who (after the passing of the Act) seceded from the Established Church were to be excluded from such benefits.[72] Much less eccentric was a correspondent in the *Gentleman's Magazine* who claimed that the poor commonly caught the habit of pauperism in times of illness; more dispensaries and better medical relief would consequently ultimately reduce the burden. And there was some irony in Brewer's attack on Whitbread for neglecting the only true remedy to distress, wage regulation. Hazardous though it might be to interfere between employer and employee, the Poor Law already upset the natural processes determining wages and magistrates should have power to intervene to protect the labourer from greedy farmers.[73]

Of all Whitbread's proposals, only the education scheme had a good run for its money; as a separate Bill it passed the Commons, though in emasculated form. Whitbread tried to disarm criticism, especially from the Established Church, by stressing the benefits religion would reap, and appealing against opposition based on 'bigotry and prejudice', but the plan for parochial schools established by overseers and not by the clergy or private benefactors was a radical one, unlikely to gain favour in Parliament, especially when (as Romilly lamented) 'a much greater portion of the House think it expedient, that the people should be kept in a state of ignorance'.[74] The plan had Malthus's warm approval, and this was enough to convince at least one member of its utility, but Giddy was not alone in fearing that education would lead the poor to 'despise their lot in life, instead of making them good servants in agriculture and in the laborious employments to which their rank in society had destined them; instead of teaching them subordination, it would render them fractious and refractory . . .;

[72] D. Carpenter, *Reflections suggested by Mr Whitbread's Bill* etc. (1807).
[73] *Gentleman's Magazine*, June 1807; J. N. Brewer, *Some Thoughts on the Present State of the English Peasantry* etc. (1807).
[74] *Memoirs of the Life of Sir Samuel Romilly*, II. 213.

would enable them to read seditious pamphlets, vicious books, and publications against Christianity; would render them insolent to their superiors, and would burden the country with a most enormous and incalculable expense'.[75] Carpenter brought this old and respectable argument up to date by blaming education (on the loose principles of Bell and Lancaster) for the whole French Revolution; and even Rose could not approve teaching the poor to write, though reading might be suitable for them. So long as the Bill compelled parishes to establish schools, this suspicion of education had a powerful ally in a widespread apprehension of expense. On the point of compulsion even the supporters of education were cool, partly from a strong preference for private charitable institutions, and partly from the tensions already arising between Church and Dissent; Carpenter and Weyland each proposed, in opposition to Whitbread, schemes in which the containment of dissent was an essential aim of education.[76] In the House John Simeon, elder brother of the evangelical divine Charles Simeon, pleaded the superior merits of Sunday Schools, and Sturges Bourne, Rose and Wilberforce all wanted education left in the hands of charity. The views of the Society for Bettering the Condition of the Poor, as expressed by Bernard, limited government intervention to the establishment of a board of education, to disseminate information and conduct experiments.[77] Against Whitbread's opposition, the critics succeeded in amending the Bill to make it merely permissive, and in that form it was allowed to pass. But the Lords made short work of it; and it is significant that the only aspect they discussed was religion, pauperism being ignored.[78]

Not everyone thought the relation between education and pauperism to be obvious. Windham asserted in the Commons that 'it was impossible that a great quantity of reading in a country could banish poverty entirely out of a nation; we might as well say that we could remove poverty from among a people by teaching them all to play the fiddle'.[79] Cobbett and correspondents in his *Political Register* agreed, from a very different point of view; what could education do to lower taxes, reform paper money or check rapacious landlords? One correspondent, Hazlitt, thought education a positive danger, as the poor might be taught too much religion; C.S., in the same journal, admitted ironically that learning was of use to the Scottish poor as 'it enables them to

[75] *Parliamentary Debates*, IX. 798.
[76] D. Carpenter, *Reflections* etc. pp. 5–7, 35–7; J. Weyland, *A Letter to a Country Gentleman* etc. (1808).
[77] T. Bernard, *A Letter* etc. pp. 21–30, 59.
[78] *Parliamentary Debates*, IX. 1174.
[79] *Ibid.* IX. 548.

understand what is passing in other countries, and they emigrate in pursuit of it as naturally as the sparks fly upwards'.[80] Cobbett himself thought it absurd to suggest that labourers needed book learning, and the appeal to the Scottish example aroused his belligerent Englishness, especially against the 'upstart set' of 'juvenile oeconomists' of the *Edinburgh Review*, 'who know nothing of England but what they have seen from the deck of a smack or through the pane of a stage coach window, and who have the audacity to bid . . . English labourers look for an example to the gardenless, and floorless, and chimneyless cabbins of Scotland, where the master of the mansion nestles in at night in the company of his pig or his cow'. Many issues later, in articles still headed 'Poor Laws', Cobbett had reached the point of arguing that the poor should not be enabled to read the Bible, since it was a dangerous book, and that Scotsmen needed cleaning when they joined the army.[81] The belief of Whitbread and other champions of education that 'book-learning' would ultimately defeat pauperism by amending the morals of the poor certainly did not command general assent until much later in the century.

The other clause which aroused Cobbett's ire was the reform of vestries. In August the *Political Register* defended democracy against plural voting with some heat. Cobbett insisted that everyone, and not merely the large rate-payers, had an interest in vestry business, and only the small men could represent the interests of the poor; even if they usually deferred to the influence of the landowners, they remained a 'dormant' barrier to the tyranny of the rich. The poor rates were not the property of the rich to be controlled by them. It was not 'other people's money' which vestries gave to the poor: 'it is *not* the money of others, any more than the amount of the tithes is the farmer's money. The maintenance of the poor is a charge upon the land, a charge duly considered in every purchase and in every lease'.[82] And Whitbread had once been a true reformer! In fact Whitbread had abandoned this clause four months before, not because of democratic protests but from the general opposition to his aim of giving the vestries more powers at the expense of magistrates. To Bernard vestries were factions responsible for many evils, and the clause was a slight on the magistracy, a view that was echoed in the debate. To the author of the *Remarks*, it was another manufacturers' plot. Weyland however welcomed any increase in the influence of property: 'any measure which tends to bring persons of property and enlightened minds to the vestry room must be attended

---

[80] *Political Register*, XI. 400–401 (Hazlitt); 456 (C.S.).
[81] *Ibid.* XII. 334–8, 481–94, 531–2, 648.
[82] *Ibid.* XII. 328–9.

with beneficial effects'.[83] Although the cause was lost, vestry reform was later to become the one major administrative change left to the old Poor Law; but Sturges Bourne could succeed where Whitbread failed only because the gentlemen of Parliament later became more concerned with the burden of the rates than with their prestige as magistrates.

The settlement clause was not defeated so easily, though men like Monck (who wanted a radical loosening of the system) and Weyland (who thought the poor had too much liberty already) agreed in attacking it. Bernard and the Society for Bettering the Condition of the Poor were in favour of allowing residence as a ground for settlement, but insisted on the need for certain safeguards: only men with fewer than four children, regularly employed in the parish, and contributing to parish funds should qualify. Whitbread refused to abandon the clause, and defended it passionately in the second reading debate, drawing a harrowing picture of the sufferings of an old man, removed to the distant parish of his settlement to die unwanted among strangers. But the critics who eventually succeeded in striking out the clause in committee were not thinking of old men, but of able-bodied labourers in manufactures. As the author of *Remarks* pointed out, such men resided in many rural parishes though they were employed elsewhere; give them a right to settlement and with the next failure of the manufacture the value of land in the parishes would be annihilated. Thus the clause was 'one of the most extraordinary and alarming to the landed interest in the neighbourhood of great towns, ever submitted to Parliament . . . (and) surely manufactured by some great Manufacturer'.[84] Similar objections could be made to the proposal to relieve over-burdened parishes from the county rate. Cottingham, spokesman for an East-end parish, had made a cogent plea for a national rate; what could a parish do, when all its inhabitants were poor and half of them indigent, but sink deeper into debt as the poor tried to relieve each other?[85] But the author of *Remarks* insisted that no attempt be made to equalise the rates without at least fifty years notice, in order not to upset existing land values. 'This clause was, probably, no part of the original Bill, but foisted into it (out of doors) by some bold manufacturer, who fancied the oscitancy of country gentlemen to be much greater in degree than it is. Surely, when the proposed clause shall be duly *proclaimed*, the sound will awaken them from the deepest

[83] T. Bernard, *A Letter* etc. pp. 8–11; *Remarks* etc. p. 18; J. Weyland, *Observations* etc. p. 40.

[84] *Remarks* etc. pp. 15–17.

[85] Rev J. Cottingham, *Letter to Samuel Whitbread Esq.* etc. (1807). Cottingham wrote of Mile-End New-Town, supplementing the alarming picture of Spitalfields given by Rev W. Hale in *Letter to Samuel Whitbread* etc. (1806).

repose that was ever enjoyed, after the hardest fox-chase, and some tankards of the best October.'[86] The proposal to rate personal property was by comparison a matter for warm approval, though the author did not know how it could be done. Neither apparently did Whitbread, as he dropped the clause; though he may have been moved to this by the criticisms of Bernard and Malthus. Bernard feared that rating (for example) the stock of a shop-keeper would merely push up prices, and the consumer would pay. Malthus's analysis was more sophisticated:

If the burden of the poor's rates were really divided equally among all sorts of property, I am afraid it might be shown, from incontrovertible principles of political economy, that it would be a pecuniary advantage to all those who employ labour, and who would according to your Bill have the principal influence in all the determinations of Vestries, to push this encouragement to population to a considerable extent; because, in the employment of their capital, they would gain much more by the cheapness of labour, than they would lose by the payment of their rates.[87]

Pressed to the point, Malthus would accept the extension of the rating, provided the cottage-building clause was abandoned; he predicted disaster from the combination of the two:

You will probably allege that under your Bill both the landlords and the parishes will still have a strong interest not to build fresh tenements unless called for by the increasing demand for labour. But it appears to me that your proposal for making every kind of productive capital rateable, will effect a most important alteration in this interest.

It has been observed by Dr. Adam Smith, that no effects of the legislature had been able to raise the salary of curates to that price which seemed necessary for their decent maintenance; and the reason which he justly assigns is, that the bounties held out to the profession by the scholarships and fellowships of the universities always occasioned a redundant supply. In the same manner if a more than usual supply of labour were encouraged by the premiums of small tenements, nothing could prevent a great and general fall in its price.[88]

Malthus repeated the admission he had made in the latest edition of the *Essay*, that the effect of the Poor Laws in encouraging population was not in fact as great as might be expected from their principles:

The specific cause of this unexpected effect is, I have little doubt, the difficulty of procuring habitations. As the great burden of the poor's rates

[86] *Remarks* etc. pp. 25–6.
[87] *Letter to Samuel Whitbread*, in Glass, *op. cit.* p. 194. The argument was developed fully and persuasively.
[88] *Ibid.* pp. 194–5.

falls upon the land, it is natural that landlords should be fearful of building cottages except where the demand for labour is absolutely urgent; and they will often submit, or at least oblige their tenants to submit, to an occasional scarcity of hands, rather than run the risk of fixing on their estates a permanent increase of rates. Under this difficulty of procuring habitations, which I have reason to think is very considerable, and which indeed I stated in the last edition of my work as the principal reason why the Poor Laws had not been so extensive and prejudicial in their effects as might have been expected, the rates have not only increased during late years with unusual rapidity; but (what is the only just criterion) the number of the dependent poor continually bears a greater proportion to the whole population. And it is highly probable that if this difficulty be removed by any of the regulations in your Bill, we shall soon see the proportion increased in a much greater degree than has ever hitherto been experienced.[89]

Even Weyland, opposed though he was to the Malthusian position, thought that the clause would have a harmful effect on population, or at least on its distribution. Carpenters in vestries would make sure that more cottages were built than the demand for labour justified, and population would be encouraged where it was not needed. Bernard also was alarmed at the prospect of parishes replacing landowners as the cottagers' landlords and blamed the poor themselves for what he agreed was a shortage of cottages. But others were more sympathetic to the proposal, and Brewer even suggested that vestries should be compelled and not merely permitted to build.[90]

Whitbread did not put his proposed Poor's Fund before the House, perhaps discouraged by the failure of his other Bills, perhaps because of the criticism it received. Malthus accepted it as an improvement on his own plan for county banks, though with reservations; but Curwen 'did not think that the poor would fund, and even if they did, it would encourage idleness'.[91] And Bernard presented very damaging and indeed cogent arguments against it. A central office corresponding with up to half a million subscribers (many of them illiterate), scattered over 14,000 parishes, with all the transactions involving trivial sums, was quite simply beyond the capacity of existing postal services. The National Assurance Office would face the same problems, and moreover be particularly liable to fraud. And would the poor be encouraged to providence by such remote (and complicated) benefits? Bernard was however unconvincing in urging instead Pitt's Parochial Funds; he ignored the other side of the dilemma, the difficulty of rendering small contributory schemes secure in their actuarial basis. Whitbread's

[89] *Ibid.* p. 193.
[90] J. Weyland, *Observations* etc. pp. 52–4; T. Bernard, *A Letter* etc. pp. 55–6; J. N. Brewer, *Some Thoughts* etc. pp. 22–4.
[91] Malthus, *op. cit.* p. 203; *Parliamentary Debates*, IX. 491.

system of rewards did not please him either; he was opposed to badging, and the incitements to industry were too insubstantial. Brewer agreed, insisting that land and cows were the only suitable incentives. Weyland as usual had a plan of his own; on existing wages no one could earn Whitbread's premiums, and in any case rewards were unsuitable for towns, where only a degree of terror could discipline the labouring classes.[92]

Compared with other clauses, Whitbread's proposal on the actual administration of relief provoked little discussion. Rose had a few supporters in standing out for public employment, but a great many others seemed sympathetic with Whitbread's attack on workhouses. It was left to Brewer, the champion of wage regulation, to discuss the allowance system at any length. Labourers were becoming 'systematic beggars' with 'long practice [in] the subterfuges of duplicity', because farmers took advantage of the Poor Laws to keep wages low despite the prosperity of agriculture; 'and thus the Poor Laws are converted into a fund for supplying the difference between the earnings of the Peasant and his natural and absolute wants'.[93] The lack of more discussion, particularly of Whitbread's attempt to make relief deterrent without recourse to the workhouse test, is further evidence that the problem of poor relief did not seem in these years the urgent issue it was to become. Dominant opinion might well agree with Whitbread that 'the poor laws of this country had grown into a system so complicated and embarrassing, and were become such a heavy and increasing expense upon the country, that some revision of them was absolutely necessary';[94] and at least a significant minority might agree with Malthus that the whole poor-law system was an unfortunate mistake. But these remained merely opinions, so long as agriculture (and indeed the labourer) remained relatively prosperous. After the war, when adversity was made more dismal by the spectre of poor-rates swallowing the whole produce of the land, this opinion was to become a demand, though no one could see a practicable way to meet it. It was inevitable that the desire to abolish the Poor Laws would only be really strong in circumstances in which abolition would obviously be more than usually difficult and dangerous. Abolition could never be practical politics and, as Whitbread's attempt shows, reform could rarely be either. He himself remained active in local poor-law matters, continuing to investigate conditions and to attack abuses; and also gave much attention to education, and especially to the affairs of the Royal

[92] T. Bernard, *A Letter* etc. pp. 35–53; J. N. Brewer, *Some Thoughts* etc. pp. 5, 27–30; J. Weyland, *Observations* etc. pp. 10–11, 46–8.
[93] J. N. Brewer, *Some Thoughts* etc. pp. 7, 15.
[94] *Parliamentary Debates*, VII. 292–3.

Lancastrian Institution. (Indeed it was as an authority on the education of the poor, rather than on their relief, that he was sought out by Robert Owen in 1815.) But he came to despair of radical plans for reform of the Poor Law, as his speech on Brydges' Removal Bill, delivered a few months before his suicide in July 1815, showed:

As to the great schemes of general revision, which members have talked of ... he considered them as nothing more than plausible pretences. ... It was only by touching small parts at a time that we could hope to amend a branch of the law so complicated, so wide, and involving so many conflicting interests.[95]

[95] *Ibid.* XXXI. 586. See Whitbread Papers, 762–72, 806–21, and 3655–6 for Whitbread's local poor-law activities; 3649–50, and 3664–70 for his advice to the Association for the Relief and Benefit of the Manufacturing and Labouring Poor in 1812; 3692–3748 for his interest in education; and 3684–6 for Owen's approach to him. On his activities in Bedfordshire see also R. Fulford, *op. cit.* pp. 77–8, 211–19. For tributes in Parliament after his suicide see *Parliamentary Debates*, XXXI. 1147–50.

VI

The Climax of Abolitionism

1. *Post-war Debate*

MANY men expected that Waterloo would bring prosperity as well as peace to England. To be sure, the wars of the eighteenth century had proved unpleasant in their aftermath, with some economic disorder made doubly unwelcome by high taxation; but the dislocation which followed the Napleonic Wars proved so severe that the very structure of society seemed threatened with destruction. The agricultural interest, with rents and costs inflated from the war-time boom, met falling prices with an almost hysterical alarm. Landlords and farmers hoped for that impossible combination, bumper crops and scarcity prices, and looked to the Corn Laws for protection from the vagaries of a free market. The slump in industrial demand in 1811–12 proved only a prelude to much more severe distresses after 1815, when the reduction of government expenditure aggravated a cyclical depression, while demobilisation released thousands on to a glutted labour market. Dear bread was inevitably the crux of a conflict so deep that its echoes were to influence elections a century later. England in 1815 paid the penalty for the essentially transitional nature of her economy, and got the worst of both the old world and the new. It is not surprising that such a complexity of problems was but little understood, that a host of contradictory and never more than partially accurate analyses competed for attention, and that remedies adopted were at best bungling, and at worst tyrannical. A sense of frustration dominated the discussion, and cleavages which had been hidden and polite became open and bitter.

The Poor Law was inevitably an important topic in the great debate. The growth of pauperism was a symptom of distress, and therefore a

223

point to be argued for or against the Corn Laws, or the resumption of cash payments, or free trade, or the reform of Parliament or of society. The extent of distress and disagreement over its causes and remedies in turn heightened criticism of the system of relief itself, and it was in these years that fundamental disapproval of a legal provision for the poor (and especially for the able-bodied) became sufficiently widespread to be regarded as orthodox, while defence of the Poor Law became, if not quite heretical, at least old-fashioned. Of course the Poor Law survived, and its critics had to wait more than a decade for any major reform. Despite the spread of abolitionist beliefs, and their adoption by an influential Select Committee of the House of Commons, nothing approaching abolition was ever attempted. This was not primarily because of opposition to abolitionist principles, although the Poor Law found some strong defenders in these years, but because even the strongest critics of the system hesitated to urge its overthrow when distress was so great. But the conviction that the Law was basically wrong in principle weakened, or at least confused, the impulse to search for practical improvements. Major changes were checked also by the usual clash of contradictory interests and opinions in Parliament, and above all by the continued refusal of the government to impose a remedy on so contentious an evil. Relatively cautious in repression, and very cautious in steps for economic reform and improvement, Liverpool's Cabinet was never willing to act at all on poor-law reform.

The legislative outcome of the many hours of Parliamentary debate on pauperism in these years was, therefore, very meagre, though the few Acts passed did show a significant change in trends in poor-law legislation. While acts of 1815 and 1816 strengthened magistrates' powers in poor relief, and showed the old humanitarian concern at harshness in workhouses, the next three years saw attempts to discourage undue liberality in relief. Under the influence of its successive Select Committees the House agreed to permit changes in the vestry system which limited magistrates' powers, the first fruit of that criticism of the Justices which was to become surprisingly strong even among the squires themselves.[1] But the attempt at 'Reform by Committee' was ineffectual and brief, and proved a merely temporary departure from the usual practice of leaving the sponsoring of bills on poor relief to the effort of private members; only when government itself intervened by appointing a Royal Commission in 1832 was the legislative paralysis which checked the cause of poor-law reform overcome.

This legislative paralysis did not, of course, preclude reform of the

[1] For a summary of legislation in this period see Sir George Nicholls, *History of the English Poor Law*, II. 151–98.

system at a local level, and doubtless much was attempted, although most of the evidence for local improvement at present available deals with the period after 1820 rather than before. And since even local reform was influenced by dominant opinion, it was the debate which was important in the first years of peace rather than its immediate outcome. It was a debate in which the wisest showed genuine perplexity at the difficulties of the problem, while most were rash and dogmatic enough to mount their favourite hobby-horses; men with strong views were not deterred from asserting them by the difficulties of proof. Statistics on pauperism for the years 1812–15 were not available until 1818, annual returns did not begin until 1821, and the Select Committee which sought these returns prepared its main report before the material was complete and was highly selective in its search for further evidence. On the whole the case presented by the abolitionists was the more coherent and clear-cut, though it had its inconsistencies; few of their opponents chose to rebut it, but rather to offer a variety of competing diagnoses and remedies, most of them as dogmatic as the abolitionist case itself. Dogmatism is not an uncommon response to crisis, when the urgency of circumstances bends plausibility to radical simplifications. But at least the questions were debated, and if the ruling classes of these years have earned a reputation for being at once harsh and ineffectual in their treatment of distress they cannot be accused of ignoring the problem.

2. *Malthus and Malthusians*

In 1817, when discussion was at its height, two abolitionist classics were reprinted: Townsend's *Dissertation* appeared with a laudatory introduction by Lord Grenville, and Malthus produced the fifth edition of his *Essay*. Much of the new material included in this edition criticised other men's proposals for reform, but in new chapters on the Poor Law and on civil liberty Malthus adapted his message to the post-war situation. The distresses of 1815–17 were real, and in themselves proved the Poor Law a mischievous fraud; parishes were simply unable to maintain the indigent or employ those willing to labour. Since it was unpardonable knowingly to promise an impossibility, the poor must be told why they suffered, and what could not be done for them. Neither high prices, nor taxation, nor the National Debt, were the chief causes of distress; and even if political reform was desirable in itself any suggestion that it could relieve the situation of the labouring classes was a sin against truth and an invitation to clamour and disorder, inimical to liberty. Distress arose from a 'sudden falling off of demand', a reversion from an artificially forced 'progressive state' to a 'stationary or declining state'. The main causes of the increase in pauperism, apart from this immediate crisis in demand, were the growth of the manufacturing system, with its fluctuating demand for labour, and the Poor Law itself, especially 'the practice . . . of paying a considerable proportion of what ought to be the wages of labour out of the parish rates'. Malthus thus for the first time placed considerable emphasis on the allowance system as the 'natural' outcome of the Poor Law, and claimed that it was likely to make the majority of the community paupers by depressing wages and forcing a 'cheaply raised population'. In 1807 he had denied that the Poor Law in fact encouraged population; he let that passage stand in the new edition, but added a new assertion that the Law raised surplus numbers in the country which then flowed into the towns, depressing wages everywhere. 'The poor-laws tend in the most marked manner to make the supply of labour exceed the demand for it.'[2]

What should be done to relieve the crisis? The remedies Malthus proposed for the depression of these years scarcely justify the recent praise he has received for anticipating Keynesian teachings on unemployment. It is true that he rejected the views of Say and Ricardo on 'general gluts', and denied that supply created its own demand, but his arguments on this point were relics of physiocratic preferences for agriculture rather than anticipations of modern doctrines on full employment. Malthus was concerned to defend the landowner and his 'unproductive consumption' against the Ricardian emphasis on savings and rapid capital accumulation, and in particular he objected, on social as well as economic grounds, to a rapid increase in investment in manufactures. In 1820, in the *Principles*, he did recommend government expenditure on public works, but stressed more strongly a suggestion that landlords and men of property hire 'workmen and menial servants' to improve their estates; only unproductive employment was to be created. The Ricardians hoped that economic expansion through new investment might absorb redundant labour, but according to Malthus 'the great object' was 'to support the people through the present distresses' until the 'prodigious stimulation' to population had subsided. Checks to population were to be preferred to stimulants to production.[3] And even the cautious recommendation of public works in the *Principles* of 1820 was scarcely evident in the *Essay* of 1817, where public employment was only approved 'to avoid the bad moral affects of idleness,

---

[2] *Essay* (1826), II. 98, 106–7, 110. The sections added in 1817 are indicated in the 1826 edition.

[3] *Ibid.* II. 101; *Principles of Political Economy* (1820), pp. 472–3, 511. Malthus predicted that the 1821 census would show a check to population growth, and was surprised when it did not.

and of the evil habits which might be generated by depending for a considerable time on mere alms', and to spread distress more evenly in society. There was no suggestion that total demand for goods and services could be beneficially controlled, and the earlier arguments against make-work schemes were amplified and emphasised. Money spent on public employment 'must of course be lost to the various sorts of labour which its expenditure in the usual channel would have supported'. Malthus would argue for the possibility of general gluts when justifying the unproductive consumption of landowners, but not when considering proper modes of relief for the poor. 'When, . . . from deficient demand or deficient capital, labour has a strong tendency to fall, if we keep it up to its usual price by creating an artificial demand . . . we evidently prevent the population of the country from adjusting itself gradually to its diminished resources, and act in much the same manner as those who would prevent the price of corn from rising in a scarcity.'[4] Thus Malthus reached his usual conclusion, that the only real remedy for distress, even for the rather special distress of 1817, lay with the poor themselves; not in 'irrational and ineffectual' combinations to keep up wages, but in restricting population through moral restraint. Teach the poor the truth, and repeal the Poor Laws as a monumental error. The closing pages of the new chapter in the 1817 edition made yet another plea for abolition: without it increasing pauperism was inevitable.

Malthusian echoes in the pamphlet literature of these years were almost innumerable, though much opposition was still evident. The *Essay* severely inhibited the charitable impulses of some simple and benevolent men. Thus one W. Richardson, D.D., conceived the idea of planting his meadows with vegetables for the benefit of the poor, but 'these splendid reveries were soon interrupted by the perusal of Mr. Malthus's *Essay on the Principles of Population*; that able writer at

---

[4] *Essay* (1826), II. 100–101, 406. On Malthus's cautious approval of public employment see P. Sraffa, 'Malthus on Public Works', *Economic Journal*, LXV (1955), 542–3, and B. A. Corry, 'The Theory of the Economic Effects of Government expenditure in English Classical Political Economy', *Economica*, XXV (1958), esp. pp. 38–41. On the limitations of his theory of gluts see M. Blaug, *Ricardian Economics, An Historical Study* (1958), chap. V; but see also M. Paglin, *Malthus and Lauderdale: The Anti-Ricardian Tradition* (New York, 1961), int. and chap. V, for criticism of Blaug's interpretation. Paglin claims that Malthus offered a coherent theory of effective demand in the *Principles*, but never reconciled it with arguments in the *Essay*. For Ricardo's criticism of Malthus on this subject see P. Sraffa (ed.) *The Works and Correspondence of David Ricardo*, II (Notes on Malthus), pp. 429–31, 446, and VI (Correspondence), pp. 132, 148, 225; IX. 10–27. R. A. Slaney followed Malthus in his defence of upper-class unproductive expenditure in his *Essay on the Beneficial Direction of Rural Expenditure* (1824). He also recommended cricket as a bond of social union.

once demonstrated to me the futility of my Utopian speculations, and convinced me that by adding to the stock of the food of men (which I knew would be the result of my discovery) I was only laying the foundation of future evil, aggravating impending calamity, and preparing a wider range for the depredations of *vice* and *misery*'.[5] The disillusioned philanthropist instead published a pamphlet against the Poor Law and began to grow potatoes to feed stock, cunningly foreseeing that they could be fed to men in that really severe emergency which the next scarcity and the progressive depression of labour by the Poor Law would inevitably bring. James Mills feared the wrath of Malthus when humbly suggesting the building of large (but separate) 'receptacles' for unmarried women and men in each county, each with land for growing vegetables: 'Mr Malthus probably would shake his head at this proposition, as furnishing a bounty to population', but should note that he was not suggesting cottages for married people.[6] Among other writers on the Poor Law Charles Jerram, the pious evangelical rector of Chobham, Surrey, addressed to the banker Samuel Thornton a tract which was almost all crude Malthus; John Duthy berated the 1817 Select Committee for not immediately adopting Malthus's plan for abolition in full; S. W. Nicoll, author of a thoughtful pamphlet on practical reforms in 1818, read Malthus's fifth edition and produced a much more doctrinaire work within a year; pamphlets attributed to W. G. Hayter and R. A. Slaney were strongly Malthusian; and another work attributed to the redoubtable Samuel Parr gave thanks for 'the luminous and profound treatise of Mr. Malthus'.[7] In

[5] W. Richardson, *Simple Measures*, etc. (1816), p. 159.

[6] J. Mills, *The Simple Equation of Tithes* etc. (1817), pp.90–1.

[7] C. Jerram, *Considerations* etc. (1818); J. Duthy, *Letters* etc. (1819); S. W. Nicoll, *A Summary View* etc. (York, 1818) and *A View of the Principles* (York, 1819); [Sir W. G. Hayter], *Proposals* etc. (1817); [R. A. Slaney], *Some Facts* etc. (1817); [S. Parr], *Considerations* etc. (1817), p. iv. The attribution of these three pamphlets (in the Goldsmiths' Library catalogue) may be doubtful. Hayter (1792–1878) did not enter Parliament until 1837, and was prominent in the 1850's; the pamphlet, a plea for emigration, was not followed by further contribution to the debate. Slaney (1792–1862) was also a young man in 1817; the works he produced on the Poor Law between 1819 and 1824 are rather more sophisticated than this pamphlet, which might conceivably have been written by his father, also Robert Slaney. The son entered Parliament in 1826, campaigned for the reform of the Poor Law in 1828–30, and was very active in the reformed Parliament on committees and commissions on education, public health and poor relief. Parr (1747–1825), once described as 'the whig Dr Johnson', wrote little on the Poor Law despite his continual involvement in a wide range of political, theological and literary controversies. A friend of Burdett, Priestley, Fellowes, Copleston, Romilly and Bentham (among others), he is said to have supported Bentham's Poor Plan; this pamphlet is Malthusian rather than Benthamite, though it includes a statement resembling less eligibility, as is noted in chapter VIII below. For another abolitionist work probably influenced by Malthus see *Thoughts* etc. (1818) by Charles Turner, prebendary of Lincoln.

1818 Henry Booth, later a prolific writer on free trade and currency reform, paid Malthus the compliment of working out the Malthusian thesis before he read the *Essay*; he admitted his own work was inferior but still published it as *The Question of the Poor Laws Considered* etc. (1818). For the most part such writers merely contributed numbers to the Malthusian cause. A few, however, stood out from the chorus to offer solo variations of their own. Chief among them was probably John Bird Sumner, the man who did most to reconcile God and Malthus in the consciences of the scrupulous.

Sumner was very respectable; he wrote for the *Quarterly Review* and became Archbishop of Canterbury. He was also cautious, moderate and sensible. His *Treatise on the Records of Creation* (1816) provided for his generation what Paley's *Principles* gave to an earlier—a justification of the existing social state and inspiration for its cautious improvement—without Paley's paradoxical, two-edged modes of reasoning. (Paley, after all, was never more than an archdeacon.) According to Sumner, the all-wise Creator had established the world and the Laws of Nature not to provide indolent satiety but a sphere where virtue might be exercised under pressure of adversity. A state of social inequality provided the best conditions for the development of faculties and the trial of virtues; equality would not end vice, and would see the 'great occasions of virtue cut off for ever'. Only in an unequal state could each rank pass through its 'separate probation', performing its own obligations: the rich the 'peculiar duty of judicious expenditure', the middle ranks 'prudential restraint upon the passions', and the lower classes a 'cheerful equanimity under those hardships which no discontent can remove or alleviate'.[8] Sumner had read his Colquhoun, and perceived that poverty was inevitable but indigence deplorable, though he added a moralistic tinge to the distinction: 'poverty is often both honourable and comfortable; but indigence can only be pitiable, and is usually contemptible.... It is one of the moral advantages of society, that every condition has a tendency to sink into the degree immediately below it, unless that tendency is counteracted by prudence and activity'.[9]

To this social creed, readily conformable to religious opinion of the day, Sumner wedded the principle of population. He was no uncritical disciple of Malthus: 'we have not been hasty in adopting Mr Malthus's conclusions; and ... we have condemned the unqualified severity and

---

[8] J. B. Sumner, *Treatise* etc. (2nd ed. 1818), pp. 92–100. Sumner was Bishop of Chester (1828–48) before becoming Archbishop of Canterbury; he was a member of the Royal Commission on the Poor Law of 1832–4. Like his brother, Bishop of Winchester, he was a leading evangelical.

[9] *Ibid.* p. 110.

harshness with which they were originally accompanied and introduced to the public notice'. Useful though the early versions of the *Essay* may have been in refuting the chimerical views of 'sweeping reformers', Sumner was not surprised that their 'unnecessary violence' and continual stress on the 'evil' of the law of population antagonised so many, especially among the religious, though it was 'found a much easier matter to disbelieve Mr. Malthus than to refute him'.[10] Moreover he was critical of parts of the argument itself, rejecting the ratios as mere hypothetical illustrations which should not be stated as 'definite ordinances of the Creator'; but he accepted as empirically proved the three assertions that population was necessarily limited by subsistence, that it normally increased when subsistence increased, and that the checks which kept population to the level of subsistence were moral restraint, vice and misery. Fortunately these truths were emerging more plainly as Malthus moderated the harshness of their earlier expression, and no reader of the *Essay*, Sumner claimed, could assume any longer that Malthus in fact regarded vice and misery as 'benevolent remedies' for the pressure of population. He himself expounded the essential benevolence of the principle of population with less equivocation than appeared in the *Essay*. Thus, the law of increase made an 'imperious necessity' that unequal state of society in which every man was placed in the condition best calculated to improve his faculties and his virtue. Scarcity of subsistence first brought division of property and then division of rank; pressure of population put a premium on economy and individual exertion, and without its stimulus life would be 'a dreary blank'. How inconceivable that Providence did not plan it so. As collateral benefits of the law of population one found universal industry, with each man striving to maintain his family; a quick and easy interchange of products and through it the overflow of European civilisation to raise the rest of the world from barbarism; and as the pivot of civilisation was Christianity, the Divine Revelation was thus taken to every corner of the world. Population pressure was the Great Missionary, 'the mighty engine, which, operating continually and uniformly, keeps our world in that state which is most agreeable to the design of the creator, and renders mankind the spontaneous instruments of the Maker, in filling and converting the habitable globe.'[11]

Had the Poor Law any place in this grand design? Sumner was aware of Malthus's vacillations on the effect of relief on population growth, but himself believed that the Poor Law was a forcing principle, a standing bounty on redundant population, and a bar to the exercise

[10] Sumner's review of the 1817 edition of the *Essay*, *Quarterly Review*, XVII (1817), 373–4, 395–7. Compare *Treatise* etc. p. 123.
[11] For Sumner's exposition, see *Treatise* etc. Part II, chaps. v–vi.

of the virtues proper to the station of the lower classes. The depressed wages of the labourer were proof enough. 'This evil, which we cannot help referring to the existing habit of interference with the wages of labour, and with the ordinary progress of population, can only be remedied by a return to the natural course.'[12] But Sumner, with his usual cautious optimism, hesitated to adopt Malthus's drastic plan. The Poor Law was radically faulty, and should be severely limited, but this should be done not by immediate abolition, but rather by superseding public relief with enlightened charity, education, friendly societies, savings banks and similar devices. Nevertheless his support for Malthusian principles doubtless did much to weaken the defence of the Poor Law among those with old-fashioned consciences and was thus a considerable contribution to the abolitionist cause.

James Ebenezer Bicheno, lawyer, scientist and later Colonial Secretary in Van Diemen's Land, was a man of lesser intellectual stature but more forthright pen. His *Inquiry into the Nature of Benevolence etc.* (1817)[13] expressed a gloomy view of his times: 'idleness, improvidence, prostitution and the want of integrity are alarmingly increased', and with them crime and 'juvenile delinquency'. The middle classes were sound, though the upper were dissolute; the poor were 'an excrescence on the body politic', showing 'a vicious tameness of character'. There were plenty of charity schools, so lack of education was not the reason for increasing depravity. The explanation must be found in the Poor Law, relic of the imperfect purification of moral values at the Reformation, contrary to both moral and natural law, and disastrous in effect.

True benevolence should be guided by reason, and reason taught that it was a far greater good to correct the vices of a fellow creature than to give him medicine or food. There was a duty to relieve suffering, but men were accountable to God for not doing it, not to the poor: 'the language of distress is very properly "asking", "supplicating", "begging"—not "demanding", "insisting" or "threatening".' Bicheno carefully rejected Paley's arguments on this point, and went on to argue that an alleged right to relief was immoral, since 'Labour is the appointment of Deity for good', and impossible in practice, as Malthus had shown with his principle of population. Bicheno's Malthusianism was crude, and was put in terms of a struggle for survival in the animal and vegetable world (minerals being happily exempt); 'the law which declares that an inferior shall give way to a superior' ensured the progress of society from the savage to the civilised state, in which the

---

[12] *Quarterly Review*, XVII (1817), 398–402.
[13] Re-written and re-published as *An Inquiry into the Poor Laws* etc. in 1824.

struggle was transformed into the beneficent clash of interests within a framework of private property and enterprise. But the Poor Law encouraged marriage, removed hunger as the chief stimulus to labour and discouraged the worthy poor, bringing in consequence overpopulation, low wages and nearly universal vice and misery. Bicheno rejected public employment on the usual grounds, adding also the typically moralistic argument that necessity and duty were the only virtuous motives for industry and that therefore to compel a man to labour did nothing for the improvement of his soul. For a similar reason forced benevolence was of no worth in the sight of God. The notion of compulsory, indiscriminate charity was the work of the Devil and the Pope of Rome; Bicheno lamented that the influence of both still persisted in England.[14]

What, then, could be done about the Poor Law? 'We must return to the operation of the natural law from which we have departed; and not reject it because some unhappiness and misery may be the consequence.' Abolition on Malthus's plan was the best suggestion, but even Bicheno hesitated to adopt it immediately. Abolition should be approached through discrimination, giving the authorities power to root out the 'idle, tippling, loose fellows', refusing them relief, or full wages for parish work. Doubtless they would suffer, but a splendid opportunity would be provided for the virtuous to reclaim them to paths of rectitude. In Bicheno's suggested social order the poor would be kept alive, but only just, and would be taught to enter rationally into the struggle for survival and salvation. Then at last the Poor Law could be swept away.

Clearly, to Sumner and Bicheno, and to some extent to Malthus himself, economic arguments against the Poor Law were acceptable mainly because they were consistent with certain moral and social assumptions. Robert Fellowes, the philanthropic former editor of the *Critical Review* and champion of the Princess of Wales, was able to reject the Poor Law as the country's 'greatest evil', and an 'immense millstone', and to recommend 'gradual abolition' over five years, without reference to any theoretical arguments at all;[15] and Edward

[14] Bicheno singled out the allowance system for particular attack, and cited the Speenhamland example (*Inquiry*, pp. 106–8). In 1824, in his *Inquiry into the Poor Laws*, he softened his exposition of Malthusianism in Sumnerian terms. Bicheno was born in 1786, son of a dissenting minister; he wrote many works on botany and natural history, a work on criminal jurisprudence (in which he opposed whipping and questioned transportation) and an influential book on Ireland. On his time in Tasmania (where he died in 1851) see K. E. Fitzpatrick, *Sir John Franklin in Tasmania 1837–1843* (Melbourne, 1949). Another, cruder, argument that the Poor Law was foisted on England by a papal plot may be found in *Two Letters* etc. (1818).

[15] R. Fellowes, *Thoughts on the Present Depressed State of the Agricultural Interest*

Copleston, while praising Malthus as 'the original well-head of political truth', was more interested in the moral aspects of his theory than in the economic analysis it offered. 'It is the high distinction of the *Essay on Population* to have demonstrated that . . . all endeavours to embody benevolence into law, and thus impiously as it were to effect by human laws what the Author of the system of nature has not effected by his laws, must be abortive—that this ignorant struggle against evil really enlarges instead of contracting the kingdom of evil. . . .' He denied, however, that relief necessarily encouraged population, and looked to an improved standard of living to encourage moral restraint; this made him one of the first of the 'revisionist' Malthusians, anticipating Senior.[16] He had, in currency reform, his own panacea for existing distress, but his writings are certainly evidence of the widened acceptance of Malthus as essentially a sound and respectable authority on the poor.

John Davison's *Considerations on the Poor Laws* (1817), a work of much reputation, was more comprehensive and systematic, for the most part in support of the Malthusian case. Davison considered at length possible grounds for a right to relief. Even disability was not, to him, a clear ground, since disability could be foreseen and prepared for; 'if a person has given no proof of a desire to provide at all for himself against such seasons, the fault and the suffering ought to go together'. As for the able-bodied, desirable though it might be to employ them, employment could not (for the usual reasons) be created. Men could be kept busy, but not profitably employed. And how did they become unemployed? Through the fluctuating character of manufactures, (justifying, Davison admitted, some temporary relief), and through the evil effects of the Poor Law itself, which gave 'a carte blanche to population. It creates the labourers. It cannot . . . create the employment for them.' The allowance system, the greatest evil of the law, was no mere aberration but the kernel, the spirit of it:

[16] E. R. Copleston, *A Second Letter* etc. (1819), pp. 22, 27–30; and compare p. 23 for Copleston's admiration for Sumner's brand of Malthusianism. His *Letter to the Rt. Hon. Robert Peel* etc. (1819) was mainly a plea for currency reform, but included an early statement of the view that the Poor Law was not harmful to society until the relaxation of the Workhouse Test Act in the 1790's (p. 34). Copleston (1776–1849) became a Fellow of Oriel in 1795 and its Provost in 1814; he was largely responsible for the College's outstanding reputation in the period, and was a strong influence on Newman and many other Oxford men. A tory of the Canning persuasion and a moderate high churchman, he became Bishop of Llandaff in 1827.

___

etc. (1817), and *The Rights of Property Vindicated against the Claims of Universal Suffrage* etc. (1818), esp. chap. 14. Fellowes (1771–1847) was in many respects an advanced liberal despite his ardent opposition to universal suffrage. Maseres bequeathed him £200,000, and he was notably generous to deserving causes. Fellowes was one of the promoters of London University.

The labourer reckons half with his master, and half with the overseer. Towards his master he has neither the zeal nor the attachment he ought to have to his natural patron and friend, and with his parish he keeps up a dependence which has something in it at once abject and insolent ... To supersede the personal motive is to throw away so much force of labour; and to equalise the compensation is to add a positive discouragement to it.[17]

The Poor Law should be indicted, if this were its fruit. It provided a 'pressing invitation to be idle', and of course relief generated no gratitude in return; how could it, when it was a forced generosity, and when the law perpetually promised more than it could perform? Davison's proposed solution was to abolish all relief to the able-bodied poor within ten years, and to supervise strictly relief to the impotent. The book, although hardly original in any point, was a clear and forceful addition to the abolitionist case, and was frequently quoted and cited in these years.

In the years after Waterloo the *Edinburgh Review* continued to support the Malthusian case on the Poor Law, and when, in 1817, Thomas Chalmers began to contribute to the journal an important new figure joined the attack on the existing system. Although still relatively young, Chalmers was already a force to be reckoned with in the Church of Scotland, and his campaign against pauperism in his own parish of St John's in Glasgow was soon to become famous. A powerful controversialist in the great Presbyterian tradition, his attack on the English Poor Law was eloquent and persuasive; he insisted that it was the defenders of the Poor Law, and not the abolitionists, who were theorists and visionaries, despite popular prejudice to the contrary. A hypothetical reformer of 1601 could, he claimed, have seen the Poor Law as a rash experiment, a departure from nature undermining industry, social relations, charity and morality. If men surrounded by the wreckage of the system in 1817 refused to see the obvious, their blindness could only be due to habit, fear of innovation, and deception by the absurdities spoken by 'merely practical men'. If a Poor Law seemed necessary, it was only because a Poor Law had created the apparent necessity. Pauperism was to Chalmers, as slavery was to Rousseau, a human invention created against nature.[18]

---

[17] J. Davison, *Considerations* etc. pp. 58, 62; and compare 10, 28–9. John Davison (1777–1834) was another Oriel man; a Fellow from 1800 until 1817 when he became vicar of Sutterton in Lincolnshire, he was rather more stern in his teaching and opinions than Copleston. His main writings were theological.

[18] *Edinburgh Review*, XXVIII (1817), 1–31; XXIX (1818), 262–301; and compare *The Christian and Civic Economy of our Large Towns* (1821–6), chap. X. (In later editions this work was entitled *The Christian and Economic Polity of a Nation*; references below are to the edition of 1861.) Chalmers' minor writings on pauperism were brought together in *Tracts on Pauperism* (1833). He also wrote part of the article

Beneficence could not banish poverty; had not God said the poor would be always with us? And did not Malthus say it too? Attempts to remove distress from society had always been frustrated by the impossibility of the enterprise. Chalmers accepted Malthus's assertion that gifts were not additions to wages, but the same funds distributed in a different way; he argued too that relief created a new demand for more relief, at first resting his case on the fact that only the slightest relaxation of effort was necessary to depress the independent labourer into dependence, but later adding the Malthusian point that relief, and especially allowances in aid of wages, encouraged population and forced down wages. Nature provided the only true 'guarantee' against starvation for those able to work—the stimulus to labour of pain and hunger—and provided also charity, the only recourse of those unable to work. Critics argued that Nature, in Chalmers' world, was selective in her guarantees, since she approved the laws of private property but denied the poor a legal right to relief, but Chalmers was content to accept Malthusian political economy into his system of divine and natural law.[19]

Chalmers had no time for the argument that those who wished to abolish the Poor Law should provide some alternative to put in its place. He simply averred that it would have been better for the parishes of England had 'the natural order of human feelings, and human arrangements, not been encroached on'. It was 'preposterous to demand of him who deprecates the inroads of any artificial process . . . that he should substitute another process in place of that which he thinks ought to be simply abandoned'.[20] The mere absence of relief would turn people's minds to industry and neighbourly assistance, the true sources of independence and comfort. For proof he cited the Scottish system, at least as he had remodelled it in his Glasgow parish. Englishmen, in their not infrequent references to Scottish practice, assumed its distinctive quality to be its administration; Chalmers disagreed, insisting that the nature of the fund was the crucial difference. In Scotland the source of relief was neither legal nor certain, thus ensuring the 'withdrawal of that prospective security as to a maintenance from external

[19] Chalmers' political economy relied heavily on Malthus, and he sided with him on the question of general gluts. J. A. Schumpeter called him 'the McCulloch of the Malthusians' (*History of Economic Analysis*, p. 487). For respectful but forthright criticism of Chalmers' Malthusianism see Scrope's article in the *Quarterly Review*, XLVIII (1832), 39–69, and compare the earlier anonymous *Enquiry into the Consequences of the Present Depressed Value of Human Labour* etc. (1819).

[20] *Edinburgh Review*, XXIX (1818), 271.

on the poor in the *Edinburgh Review*, XXIX (1818), 498–501, but was not responsible for the absurd arithmetical error which made 92.5 per cent of the English population paupers.

sources, which must have the effect of tempting many an English labourer to such thriftlessness and improvidence'. Elders of the Church carefully disbursed weekly donations, benefactions, and, in case of need, voluntary gifts from heritors, among the poor known personally to them. The natural virtues of filial obligation and neighbourly assistance were encouraged by education, and all relief was voluntary and secret, free from 'public inquisitorial officials'. Chalmers insisted that the whole procedure was natural and not artificial, comparing its relationship to poverty with that of courts of justice to trade; it provided a framework for the operation of the benign principle of laissez-faire. Scotland should beware, lest the rising tide of the compulsory system, already across the border, destroyed her ancient heritage.[21]

What should be done in England? In 1817 Chalmers rather hastily suggested two separate funds, one from legal assessments and the other from voluntary contributions: all new paupers were to be relieved only from the latter, and as the old died out the former could be spent on education and churches. In 1818, although he retained his enthusiasm for this 'great moral experiment', he admitted that the prevalence of the allowance system and the antiquity of the law made abolition difficult and strengthened the case of its opponents. Simple abolition 'in these circumstances, would carry along with it the grossest cruelty and injustice to the present generation of paupers. They must be seen out— and in as great a sufficiency as they were led to expect under the present arrangement.' The crucial difference between England and Scotland was the character of the poor: the Scots' character had merely to be retained, but the English needed to be restored. Friendly societies and savings banks presupposed good character, and were therefore useless; only education could be relied on to make abolition possible. Later still he was to urge the emigration of surplus population as a pre-requisite for abolition, and in *Christian and Civic Economy* he set out a programme for piecemeal abolition, with each parish choosing (under a permissive Act) to constitute a new voluntary fund beside the old, at the same time stopping the power of justices to order relief to new applicants and abandoning the system of settlement.[22] If Malthus's compulsory abolition seemed harsh, Chalmer's plan was unreasonably optimistic in its expectation of moral regeneration among rich and

---

[21] *Ibid.* XXVIII (1817), 10–13; XXIX (1818), 272–8; and compare *A Speech delivered on 24 May 1822* etc. (1822) and *Statement in regard to Pauperism in Glasgow* (1823) for defence against local critics. Both pamphlets were reprinted in *Tracts on Pauperism* (1833). For arguments that the Scottish poor did have right to relief by law see *A Short Exhibition of the Poor Laws of Scotland* etc. (1816) by Robert Davidson, professor of law in Glasgow.

[22] *Edinburgh Review*, XXIX (1818), 277; *Christian and Civic Economy* etc. chaps. xiv–xvi.

poor alike. But it must be stressed that he was a more perceptive and in some ways more original thinker about society than these early essays on pauperism suggest, and more obviously humane in intent. In 1817 he hinted at the problem of creating, in those harsh impersonal aggregations called cities, the simpler personal relationships common in the country; this was much amplified in his later work, and his insight into the unique social problems of cities was a greater contribution to social thought than any of his forays into traditional political economy or his writings on the Poor Law. He, more than almost any other writer on pauperism of his time, was a man of the modern age in his concern with urban problems, if not in his remedies for them.

3. Mrs Marcet and Ricardo

The Malthusian attack on the Poor Law was thus accepted by some of the most influential moralists and theologians of the period. Its acceptance among political economists was more general, and perhaps more wholehearted; indeed the *Essay* was second in importance only to *The Wealth of Nations* as a formative influence on that school of economics loosely called classical. But classical economics was not of course a rigid and static body of doctrine, even if economists were inclined, like most practitioners of a self-consciously new science, to offer an apparent unanimity in the face of outside criticism while continually disagreeing among themselves. The Malthusian principle of population was absorbed into economic theory with increasing modification but continuing respect, and the same process is evident in views on the Poor Law. The dominant influence on post-war political economy was Ricardo's, though in his case also there were few strictly orthodox disciples and even they soon modified the master's teachings. Ricardo supported Malthus's attack on the Poor Law, both in his writings and in Parliamentary debate, but with theoretical reservations which were less obvious to the public than the general support; political economy was so widely attacked, and with so much misunderstanding, that even the most subtle of its practitioners were apt to welcome the simplifications of Mrs. Marcet in 1816 or of Harriet Marineau in the 1830s as useful contributions in a campaign of public enlightenment, even though what they wrote was rarely altogether true.

Mrs. Marcet's *Conversations on Political Economy*, a popular summary of the subject for the school-room, first appeared in 1816, a year before Ricardo's *Principles*; six further editions were published by 1839.[23] The work took the form of a long and sometimes stilted dis-

[23] Jane Marcet, 1769–1858, daughter of a Swiss merchant and widow of a physician, was virtually the creator of the Victorian fashion for popular works on the sciences.

cussion between a knowledgeable Mrs. B. and a youthful but attentive Caroline, a girl with humane instincts but sadly in need of instruction in economic truths. Mrs. B. proceeded to enlighten her: wages, Caroline was told, could vary between subsistence and some upper limit, depending on the ratio of capital to population, and on conventional notions of necessities; despite the attempts of capitalists to keep wages low, they should normally rise, and profits fall, as national opulence increased ('Oh, that is charming! that is exactly what I wish', exclaimed Caroline). But wages would inevitably fall in time of scarcity, since mere money could not feed men, who 'must bear with patience an unavoidable evil'. And even a rapid increase in capital need not raise wages, unless labourers were sensible and did not marry without a fair prospect of maintaining themselves. 'No amelioration of the condition of the poor can be permanent, unless to industry they add prudence and foresight'. Higher wages would normally stimulate industry, but too often they brought improvidence; Caroline was told to remember the temptations facing the unhappy poor, though left to imagine what they might be. The fruit of improvidence was not, she was assured, starvation, but low wages and high infant mortality.

What could be done for the poor? Caroline suggested that they be settled on the wastes, but Mrs. B. pointed out that capital was limited, and the landlord could best decide whether old or new lands should be cultivated. Caroline, having read her Goldsmith, deplored enclosure, but Mrs. B. enlightened her on the utility of improvements. Emigration might help a little, but should be entirely voluntary. Friendly societies were good; Mrs. B.'s impeccable gardener, a man who had apparently delayed marriage almost to his dotage, was a clubman. The new Scottish savings banks were also good; and so was education in providence, religion and loyalty. As for the poor rate—'a tax which falls so heavily on the middling classes of people, and which is said to give rise to still more poverty than it relieves'—it should be abolished as soon as possible. Caroline could not at first see why, but it was explained to her that certainty of relief weakened the apprehension of indigence, encouraged early marriage, tempted men to drink and dissoluteness, and (worst of all) lowered wages by encouraging population and by wasting capital on the idle. Both teacher and pupil agreed that immediate

---

Her *Conversations on Chemistry* (1806) is said to have sold 160,000 copies in the United States by 1853. Her output was enormous; she was still writing in the 1850's, when she produced *Rich and Poor; Dialogues on a few of the First Principles of Political Economy* (1851). Her friend Harriet Martineau was influenced by the *Conversations on Political Economy*, which as late as 1845 McCulloch could describe as 'the best introduction' to the subject. It is also one of the most interesting and entertaining introductions to the social values of its time.

abolition was impracticable, since men might starve. Education and discrimination in charity could prepare the way for it, and Caroline, at least, would no longer join in 'the ill-judged conduct of the upper classes' which encouraged early marriages among the poor. Doubtless she would wait for a good settlement herself.

Even in Mrs. Marcet's highly unoriginal pages there were some slight modifications of the Malthusian message, not least in her economic optimism and her refusal to admit the special claims of the agricultural interest. She was close to Ricardo on these points, though of course without his subtleties. Ricardo himself did not give more than perfunctory theoretical attention to the question of poor relief; it was not one of the major issues in his debate with Malthus, and his highly intricate theoretical apparatus was constructed to analyse certain other specific problems, in particular the effects of corn laws on economic progress. But there were certainly significant differences between his attitude to the problem of pauperism and Malthus's, despite his strong support for abolitionism in his *Principles of Political Economy:*

> The clear and direct tendency of the poor laws . . . is not, as the legislature benevolently intended, to amend the condition of the poor, but to deteriorate the condition of both poor and rich; instead of making the poor rich, they are calculated to make the rich poor; and whilst the present laws are in force, it is quite in the natural order of things that the fund for the maintenance of the poor should progressively increase, till it has absorbed all the net revenue of the country . . . This pernicious tendency of these laws is no longer a mystery, since it has been fully developed by the able hand of Mr. Malthus; and every friend to the poor must ardently wish for their abolition.[24]

This clear avowal of the Malthusian case did not rest on personal investigation of the problem. In 1816 Ricardo admitted that his knowledge of the *Essay* was neither fresh nor accurate, and in 1821 he told Place that he was no more than an 'ordinary reader' on the subject of population. He read the 1817 edition of the *Essay* and was surprised 'at the little I can discover with the utmost ingenuity to differ from. . . . Time only is wanted to carry conviction to every mind'.[25] But the

[24] *The Works and Correspondence of David Ricardo* (cited hereafter as *Works*), I. 105–6. For discussion of Ricardo's views on poor relief and related topics see M. Blaug, *Ricardian Economics*, esp. pp. 196–202; E. Cannan, *History of Theories of Production and Distribution* etc. esp. pp. 188, 190–202; and L. Robbins, *The Theory of Economic Policy in English Classical Political Economy* (1952), esp. pp. 93–100.

[25] Ricardo to Malthus, 2 February 1816 (*Works*, VII. 2); to Place, 9 September 1821 (*Works*, IX. 49); to Malthus 21 October 1817 (*Works*, VII. 201). Writing to Malthus in 1816 Ricardo revealed his ignorance of the *Essay* by confusing the first and second editions.

friendship of the two economists was in fact marked by chronic and increasing disagreement, and if the Poor Law was not a central issue in the dispute it was involved by implication.

Ricardo accepted Malthus's contention that poor relief encouraged imprudent marriage, that the rates tended to absorb the whole revenue of the country, and that the system was essentially a snare and delusion to the poor. He also accepted, in general terms, the principle of population as the main factor influencing wages from the point of view of the supply of labour; like almost all the political economists of this period he would assent to the proposition that wages depended on the ratio of capital to population, however much he would qualify it in particular cases,[26] and he always stressed that control over the supply of labour rested with the labourers themselves. But it was another matter to put the whole stress for social improvement on such control, and on this point and on others Ricardo wore his Malthusian cloak with a difference. As a man Ricardo differed from Malthus, in temperament and assumptions; he did not share Malthus's pre-occupation with the theological implications of economic theory or with the moral aspects of the Poor Law. As he remarked to Place, the whole question of a 'right' to relief was foreign to his Benthamite presuppositions; did not Bentham claim him as his spiritual grandson?[27] Ricardo was not a man to pen touching passages on the beauties of benevolence in the rich or of gratitude in the poor. His sympathy for distress was deep and sincere, as his correspondence with Mill in the winter of 1816 shows, but his approach to causes and remedies was always secular and strictly rational. He might be misled into excessive theoretical abstraction, but he was singularly free from social prejudices. When Place published a violent attack on the upper class in 1821 Ricardo approved his defence of the labourers, too often 'cruelly calumniated. This part of your work will do much good, if you abate a little of the asperity with which the rich are handled. I find no fault with the severity of the passages, I complain of their injustice'. To Ricardo men were often mistaken but rarely evil in intent; he was scrupulously fair to Owen, despite intellectual contempt for his teachings, and if he attacked Cobbett as a 'mischievous scoundrel' it was because he believed him guilty of duplicity. There were few writers on pauperism in this period as free from cant as Ricardo.[28]

[26] When James Mill stated the thesis crudely in his *Elements* Ricardo remarked that 'I believe I have said the same, and it may perhaps be right to say so in an elementary book, although it is not strictly correct' (*Works*, IX. 127).

[27] Ricardo to Place, 9 September 1821 (*Works*, IX. 52).

[28] See *Works*, VII. 61–2, 87, 90 on the distress of 1816; IX. 54–5 for comments on Place, and compare IX. 59, 61 for similar remarks to Mill and Malthus; VIII. 42–6 for correspondence with Trower about Owen; and IX. 167 for the attack on Cobbett.

Apart from this difference in moral attitudes to the problem of pauperism, Ricardo also made some theoretical criticisms of the Malthusian case. Malthus was prone to argue that poor relief was a pure waste of resources, that money given to the poor simply sent prices chasing after food and did not encourage an increased supply; thus poor relief increased numbers without increasing the means of their support. This Ricardo denied, claiming that the distribution of money would stimulate production: 'I thought you were bound to admit that the poor laws would increase the demand and consequently the supply'. Malthus deleted some of the offending passages, but continued to assert that any attempt to proportion wages to the price of provisions would 'lead to famine', once again mis-applying the short-run lesson of scarcity. Ricardo replied that on the contrary this, like an increase in the poor rates, would encourage greater production.[29] The Poor Law did not increase population above the supply of food; what it did was to divert capital from the production of conveniences and luxuries into the production of food. This he thought undesirable both in its social effects and in its tendency to extend agriculture on to inferior soils and thus to hasten the approach of that stationary state where further progress was impossible. The tendency of the Poor Law was 'to call away the exertions of labour from every object, except that of providing mere subsistence' and 'to busy the mind continually in supplying the body's wants; until at last all classes should be infected with the plague of universal poverty'.[30] Ricardo was aware that by thus modifying Malthus's argument to make relief an unwise diversion of resources rather than a pure waste of them he was undermining one Malthusian objection to equality. When Place repeated Malthus's thesis Ricardo objected that a rapid increase of population supported by a diversion of capital to agriculture was perfectly possible, and that a more equal society would be produced. And to Malthus he insisted that the poor might in fact prefer greater equality even at the expense of fewer luxuries, though he himself joined Malthus in deploring any development in that direction.[31] Malthus insisted that the Poor Law promised the impossible; Ricardo merely lamented that it encouraged the undesirable.

[29] Ricardo to Malthus, 2 January 1816 (*Works*, VII. 2–3) and 21 October 1817 (*Works*, VII. 203). Ricardo thus objected to too rigid a notion of a 'wages fund', admitting in the second letter that combinations could also increase total wages. For discussion of the wages fund and its looseness see F. W. Taussig, *Wages and Capital* (1896), M. Blaug, *Ricardian Economics*, and L. Robbins, *The Theory of Economic Policy*, pp. 110 n. 1.

[30] *Principles, Works*, I. 108.

[31] Ricardo to Place, 9 September 1821 (*Works*, IX. 50); to Malthus, 4 September 1817 (*Works*, VII. 185).

A not dissimilar modification of Malthusian views is evident in Ricardo's discussion of wages in the *Principles*. Malthus had sometimes, but not consistently, admitted the conventional nature of the level of subsistence in relation to population growth; Ricardo went much further in arguing that the 'natural' price of labour depended largely upon labourers' tastes. The 'natural price of labour estimated even in food and necessaries' was not 'absolutely fixed and constant', but depended essentially on 'the habits and customs of the people'. An English labourer would consider his wages too scanty to support a family 'if they enabled him to purchase no other food than potatoes, and to live in no better habitation than a mud cabin'.[32] The so-called 'iron law' by which wages tended to an absolute minimum of subsistence can not be found in this chapter of the *Principles*, though it may be implied in Ricardo's later discussion of taxation. He certainly desired higher wages, and was perhaps a little less gloomy than Malthus on the possibility of gaining them, and he stressed the importance of new tastes for luxuries as a check to excessive breeding, if not quite as definitely as Senior was to do with his emphasis on ambition rather than fear as the motive for prudence. In the controversy over general gluts Ricardo insisted to Malthus that the labourer would be a 'consumer of conveniences' if given a chance; surely if unproductive consumption was to be encouraged it should be consumption by the poor, not the rich?

The friends of humanity cannot but wish that in all countries the labouring classes should have a taste for comforts and enjoyments, and that they should be stimulated by all legal means in their exertions to procure them. There cannot be a better security against a superabundant population.[33]

This difference in emphasis overlay others more fundamental. Malthus, despite his admission that standards of life could improve, always encouraged the view that the balance of population and subsistence was precarious, that the 'pressure' was more or less constant; and he always placed more stress on checks to population than on stimulants to production. Moreover he was constantly suspicious of expansion anywhere but in agriculture, largely for social reasons. In the 1830s the recognition that subsistence had in fact increased faster than population was to discredit much of the Malthusian analysis. Ricardo

[32] *Principles, Works,* I. 95–7. For an anticipation of Ricardo's argument on this point see D. Boileau, *Introduction to the Study of Political Economy* (1811), book II, chap. 8, where the Marquis de Chastelux, *Agriculture and Population* (1772, English ed. 1792) was cited.

[33] *Principles, Works,* I. 100. Compare Ricardo to Malthus, 9 July 1821 (*Works*, IX. 16); Malthus to Ricardo, 16 July 1821 (*Works*, IX. 18); and Ricardo to Trower, 3 October 1820(*Works*, VII. 271–5).

noted Weyland's qualification of the Malthusian case on primitive societies, and Barton's more optimistic view of improvement in modern England, though he did not use this, as his followers did, to make major revisions in the argument on population. But he was much more concerned than Malthus with economic progress, and much more confident that capital accumulation could improve the condition of the poor, even if (or particularly if) the new investment was not in English agriculture. Most economists after 1815 committed themselves to economic progress through industrialisation and a trading economy dependent on food imports, leaving Malthus behind as a reactionary defender of the landed interest and the Corn Laws. Rapid accumulation depended on high profits; if these were not to be gained at the expense of low wages, then the effects of diminishing returns on home agriculture had to be offset by comparative advantage in trade, and (Ricardo's followers stressed) by increasing productivity of labour. Malthus feared that poor rates would swallow rent; Ricardo deplored rather their effects on profits, but did not think it need become really disastrous before the stationary state was reached. To delay that state, repeal the Corn Laws.

Ricardo thus made certain specific criticisms of Malthus's attack on the Poor Law, and his general views on political economy reveal the beginnings of that greater divergence from the Malthusian view of the problem which was to become evident after 1820. But he should still be numbered among the abolitionists, and was an important spokesman of their views:

No scheme for the amendment of the poor laws merits the least attention, which has not their abolition for its ultimate object; and he is the best friend to the poor, and to the cause of humanity, who can point out how this end can be attained with the most security, and at the same time with the least violence.[34]

Ricardo had no ambition to win the palm for himself, and had little to suggest as a procedure for reform. In all discussions of distress he stressed the difficulties of improving the situation, either by changes in the Poor Law or by more general measures. He was no panacea-pedlar; even the repeal of the Corn Laws would bring severe, if temporary, difficulties.[35] His most daring proposal for the alleviation of distress was for paying off the National Debt by a tax on property; 'a wild sort of notion', it was said to have ruined his reputation among the squires in Parliament, who had hitherto thought him a sound man, clever enough to explain to them difficult questions of finance. Most of

[34] *Principles, Works*, I. 107.
[35] Ricardo to Brown, 13 October 1819 (*Works*, VIII. 103).

his remarks on proposals for relief were criticisms of schemes he thought fundamentally erroneous. Wage regulation was rejected on the grounds that labour should be free, in the interests of both employer and labourer.[36] Owen's plan was a particularly mischievous proposal because it added an undue stimulus to population to the common fallacies of all make-work schemes: employment could be re-directed, but it could not be created except by new investment.[37] By a parallel argument, Ricardo concluded that if poor relief were stopped the money formerly raised by the rates would automatically be spent on wages, which would inevitably rise. Abolition was to be sought principally in the interests of the labourer, as he insisted to Place: 'Mr. Malthus be it remembered does not propose the abolition of the poor laws as a measure of relief to the rich, but as one of relief to the poor themselves'.[38]

But how was abolition to be approached? Ricardo did not adopt Malthus's specific proposals. In 1817 he suggested to his friend Trower, as a preliminary to abolition, the refusal of relief to all but 'those whose necessities absolutely require it', and even to them it should be given 'in the most sparing manner'. He noted with approval the claim of the Select Committee of 1817 that the system had been twisted from its original purpose:

I would gladly compound for such a change in the Poor Laws as should restore them to what appears to have been the original intention in framing them; namely, the relieving only the aged and infirm and under some circumstances, children.[39]

But he took little part in the debates on the Committee's proposals, and opposed a bill to remove and educate the children of the poor as 'the plan of Mr. Owen, in a worse shape, and carried to a greater extent'. Sturges Bourne's Settlement Bill he thought unfair to towns. On the whole he lamented the failure to produce effective proposals, and blamed party spirit and the fear of unpopularity for it.[40] In fact Ricardo was well aware that abolition was difficult and would cause distress. The Laws had been so long established, 'and the habits of the poor have been so formed upon their operation', that repeal required caution and skilful management and 'should be effected by the most gradual steps':

[36] *Principles, Works,* I. 105; V. 292, 295–6, 307. On the proposal to pay off the National Debt see *Works,* VIII. 143–57.

[37] Ricardo to Malthus, 3 January 1817 (*Works,* VII. 116); to McCulloch, 28 February 1820 (*Works,* VIII. 159); and correspondence with Trower, VIII. 42–6. Ricardo's involvement with Owen is discussed in the following chapter.

[38] Ricardo to Place, 9 September 1821 (*Works,* IX. 53).

[39] Ricardo to Trower, 27 January 1817 (*Works,* VII. 124) and 26 January 1818 (*Works,* VII. 248).

[40] *Works,* V. 1, 7; Ricardo to Trower, 28 May 1819 (*Works,* VIII. 32); and compare *Works,* VIII. 25. On Sturges Bourne's bills see chapter VIII below.

It is a painful reflection but not less true on that account that we can never get into a good system, after so long persevering in a bad one, but by much previous suffering of the poor. . . . No man in his sober senses would wish for any sudden alteration of the present plan.[41]

Perhaps Ricardo's sober sense left him in 1821, when he supported in Parliament Scarlett's crude measure for the immediate abolition of payments in aid of wages, arguing dogmatically enough that 'the end peculiarly desired' was 'to regulate the price of labour by the demand' and implying that this ultimate good could be achieved without immediate hardship.[42] Ricardo was certainly an abolitionist, but this occasional dogmatism was not the whole man. His practice as an employer of labour were heretical by his own canons. In 1820, when Trower asked him if wages in Gloucestershire had been reduced, as they had in Surrey, with the fall in the price of provisions, Ricardo replied: 'I believe they have lowered the price of labour here, but I, as a gentleman, I suppose, always pay the same'.[43]

4. *The Report of 1817*

The baldest and most dogmatic summary of the abolitionist case published in this period came not from the pen of any political economist but from a Select Committee of the House of Commons. All the common moral and economic arguments against the Poor Law were drawn together and stated without any qualification save the vital proviso that abolition, the obvious remedy, was impracticable, and that the system had consequently to be patched until it could be discarded. The report was more bold than might have been expected from a large committee which included men of various opinions among its forty members; Owen alleged that it had been 'managed' by a small cabal of 'political economists' hostile to his own plan, but there is no evidence to support him, though some of increasing dissension among members as their frustration in finding practicable solutions to the problem grew. The original initiator of the Committee was Curwen, much to Rickman's disgust: 'such an ignorant long-tongued man' would be, he feared, 'the ruin of any poor law improvement' since better men would not work with him. Fortunately Sturges Bourne and other men of more weight in the House than Curwen joined the

---

[41] *Principles, Works*, I. 106; Ricardo to Trower 27 January 1817 (*Works*, VII. 125) and 26 January 1818 (*Works*, VII. 248).

[42] *Works*, V. 113–4.

[43] Ricardo to Trower, 26 November 1820 (*Works*, VIII. 307).

Committee; the report itself is said to have been mainly the work of Frankland Lewis, later a Poor Law Commissioner.[44]

The report accepted in full the argument that relief demoralised the labourer. The 'happiness and welfare of mankind' depended on his exertions, but the Poor Law diminished 'the natural impulse by which men are instigated to industry and good conduct' and thus created 'an unlimited demand on funds which it cannot augment'. The system was devoid of either benevolence or gratitude, and 'not unfrequently engenders dispositions and habits calculated to separate rather than unite the interests of the higher and lower orders of the community'.[45] These were the usual moral objections to legal relief: in objecting also to public employment the report offered a doctrine of a wages fund more rigid than most political economists ever propounded, except in unguarded moments:

> What number of persons can be employed in labour, must depend absolutely upon the amount of the funds which alone are applicable to the maintenance of labour ... whoever ... is maintained by the law as a labouring pauper, is maintained only instead of some other individual, who would otherwise have earned, by his own industry, the money bestowed on the pauper.[46]

But pauper employment was of course a bad substitute for free, because it was unprofitable and hence checked the increase of funds for the maintenance of labour. Moreover the provision of it deceived the poor by suggesting that the availability of employment, and the wages for it, did not depend primarily on their own control of the supply of labour:

> By holding out to the labouring classes that they shall at all time be provided with adequate employment, they are led to believe they have nothing to dread while they are willing to labour. The supply of labour, therefore,

[44] J. C. Curwen was a busy but generally ineffectual spokesman for the agricultural interest. William Sturges Bourne (1769–1845) was a close friend of Canning from their school days. He entered Parliament in 1798; added Bourne to his original name of Sturges in 1803 in order to accept a large legacy; held minor offices in 1801, 1804–6 and 1807–9; was a commissioner for Indian affairs 1814–22; and was Home Secretary for a few months in 1827. He retired from Parliament in 1831. Sir Thomas Frankland Lewis (1780–1855), father of the more famous G. C. Lewis, was another Canningite. Active on Parliamentary committees in his long period in the House of Commons (1812–34 and 1847–55), he became the first Chairman of the Poor Law Commission in 1834. He was described as 'a careful and accomplished man, but formal, verbose and dull'; the 1817 Report is more vivid in style than might be expected from such a man. For evidence of increasing dissension on the Committee see Sir E. Brydges, *Arguments in Favour* etc. (1817), pp. 7–8, and T. P. Courtenay, *Copy of a Letter* etc. (1817), *passim*.

[45] *Parliamentary Papers*, 1817, VI, Report from the Select Committee on the Poor Laws (462), p. 4.

[46] *Ibid*. pp. 16–17.

which they alone have the power to regulate, is left constantly to increase, without reference to the demand, or to the funds on which it depends. Under these circumstances, if the demand for labour suddenly decreases, the provisions of the poor law alone are looked to, to supply the place of all those circumstances which result only from vigilance and caution; the powers of the law, while they profess to compel both labour and wages to be provided, under these circumstances, in reality effect nothing but a more wasteful application of the diminished capital than would otherwise take place; they tend thereby materially to reduce the real wages of free labour, and thus essentially to injure the labouring classes. . . . The smaller capitalists themselves are gradually reduced, by the burthen of the assessments, to take refuge in the same resource [assistance from the rates]. The effect of these compulsory distributions is to pull down what is above, not to raise what is low; and they depress high and low together, beneath the level of what was originally lowest.[47]

The thesis of inevitably progressing pauperism was illustrated by a single example, the wretched parish of Wombridge, Salop. Wombridge was much distressed, and had petitioned Parliament for aid; of its 1,900 inhabitants, 620 received relief and only 33 were both liable to pay rates and capable of doing so. With the rate at 33s. on the pound rental, rents could not be paid and the parish was nearly insolvent. A frightening example, but was it a fair one? How many of the parishes of England were small mining towns in which the mines had recently failed? The report was written before the Committee had progressed far in its rather haphazard empirical investigations.

The report confidently predicted that restriction of relief would restore the funds expended to their 'natural channel' and would bring increased wages, 'for it is the obvious interest of the farmer that his work should be done with effect and celerity, which can hardly take place unless the labourer is provided according to his habits, with such necessaries of life as may keep his body in full vigour, and his mind gay and cheerful'.[48] After such optimism on the beneficence of a free market for labour, it is a little surprising to find, in the recommendations for reform, the pure milk of abolitionism watered down to a pale mess of miscellaneous palliatives. Their reception in Parliament will be examined below, but we may note here that the unequivocal indictment of the Poor Law in the Report had important repercussions 'in another place'. The Prime Minister himself rose in the House of Lords to move the appointment of a rival Select Committee, politely but clearly disapproving of abolitionist agitation and pleading for a

[47] *Ibid*. pp. 17–18.
[48] *Ibid*. pp. 18–19. On Wombridge, see p. 10 and Minutes of Evidence, appendix D, pp. 158–9.

search for sensible and practicable remedies for admitted evils.[49] Two months later the Lords Committee presented a brief report which was innocent of theoretical speculation, moderate in its estimate of rising expenditure, critical of abuses in the system, and very cautious in its recommendations:

> The Committee are . . . decidedly of the opinion, that the general system of these laws, interwoven as it is with the habits of the people, ought, in the consideration of any measure to be adopted for their melioration and improvement, to be essentially maintained . . . The subject is in its nature so extensive and difficult, that little more can be expected . . . from any exertions that can be made by individuals, or perhaps from the collective wisdom of Parliament, than such alleviation of the burdens as may be derived from an improved system of management, and from rendering the laws more simple in execution.[50]

The Prime Minister praised the 'candour and liberality 'of the Committee, and expressed the opinion that much more labour was necessary before the report of either House could be a basis for action.[51] Clearly the Government was not to be stampeded by a dogmatic report; in the event it could not be goaded into any action at all on the question. The growth of abolitionist opinion after 1815 may have been spectacular, but it did not sweep all before it.

[49] *Parliamentary Debates*, XXXVI. 297–300 (9 May 1817). Lord Holland made a strong speech against the Poor Law, as befitted a great Whig patron of progressive thought.
[50] *Parliamentary Papers*, 1818, V, Report of the Lords Committee on the Poor Laws (400), pp. 7, 10.
[51] *Parliamentary Debates*, XXXVI, 365.

248

VII

Contrary Opinions

1. *Conservative anti-Malthusians*

No one in this period defended the Poor Law unconditionally, for all admitted at least some obvious imperfections. Malthusian influence was strongest on the main stream of moderate progressive opinion, though there remained room for disagreement on ways and means of reducing the evil effects of the system. The most vehement defence of the principle of relief came from the radicals, even if they had little to offer for the constructive reform of the system; they were for parliamentary reform and prosperity, not for pauperism, but defended the right of the poor to relief because labourers had, in their view, lost so many other rights already. The attitude of conservative critics of Malthus to the Poor Law was more ambivalent. Some thought that the obvious remedy for the post-war distress was more government activity, not less, and make-work schemes and plans for land settlement were vigorously advocated, though workhouses continued in disfavour; but it is noticeable that some of those shocked by what they thought to be Malthus's unnatural and blasphemous theses became increasingly reconciled to his views on the Poor Law and suggested changes almost as drastic as his own. Thus opposition to abolitionism as a social doctrine persisted, but objections to a severe curtailment of relief came only from a few sturdy independents, and from those who hoped to reduce the necessity for relief by means of their own favourite panaceas.

Many writers were content, of course, to reject abolition as a remedy with little or no argument against it. To William Clarkson relief was a simple moral obligation; the Rev Richard Vivian of Bushey thought it better than beggary; William Hanning, a Somerset magistrate, and J. Ashdowne insisted that the principle of relief, if not its practice, was

249

perfectly sound; Samuel Roberts observed that whatever the rich thought about the Poor Law, the poor were grateful for it; and James MacPhail and the author of an anonymous pamphlet of 1820 thought scriptural quotation sufficient to refute merely mortal arguments for abolition. As Chalmers had observed, habit and fear of innovation were powerful props of conservatism in this matter.[1]

The conservatism of Southey and Coleridge was altogether more sophisticated. As has been seen, their defence of the Poor Law and their contempt for Malthusian arguments did not rest on satisfaction with the existing state of society. Hating innovation, they yet sought change; reactionary in the strict sense of the term, they abhorred 'progress' and wished for a restoration of what they claimed to be the principles of an altogether more desirable past. They have gained some reputation for enlightenment as critics of fashionable opinions, especially on the question of poverty and its relief. Did they deserve it? The case seems plausible only if particular points they made are examined in isolation.[2]

Coleridge's *Lay Sermon, addressed to the High and Middle Classes on the existing Distresses and Discontents* (1817) certainly included criticism of some common economic notions which have since been shown to be erroneous.[3] But the views were rejected, not refuted. Moral denunciation took the place of sober analysis, denunciation against 'political empirics', such as Malthus, and radicals who dared suggest that pensions and sinecures had anything to do with distress. Coleridge did notice, as an immediate cause of depression, the sudden retrenchment after the war, and urged increased expenditure as a remedy, but he was even further from Keynesian views on this subject

---

[1] W. Clarkson, *An Inquiry* etc. (1816), pp. 7, 33; R. Vivian, *Thoughts* etc. (1817), pp. 4–5; W. Hanning, *A Letter* etc. (1818), pp. 4, 8; J. Ashdowne, *An Essay* etc. (1817), pp. 5–6; S. Roberts, *A Defence of the Poor Laws* etc. (1819), pp. 27–34; J. MacPhail, *Observations* etc. (1819), p. 5; *The Oppressed Labourers* etc. (1819), chap. i. Samuel Roberts (1763–1848), a silver-plate manufacturer in Sheffield, was a prolific writer of pamphlets and edifying tales. He refused to publish for profit, or to write contrary to morality or religion; he became known as 'the pauper's friend'.

[2] H. and H. C. Shine claim that they 'perhaps suggest even some of the twentieth century's efforts to deal with poverty and unemployment' (*The Quarterly Review under Gifford* (1949), p. xiv); F. W. Fetter, on the other hand, contends that their arguments were 'but special pleading for a privileged few' and that 'it is not hard to understand why, in such a setting, amoral political economy triumphed over noble philosophy' ('The Economic Articles in the *Quarterly Review*, and their Authors', *Jnl. Pol. Economy*, LXVI (1958), 48). J. Colmer, *Coleridge, Critic of Society* (1959), is brief in its treatment of economic questions; W. F. Kennedy, *Humanist versus Economist, The Economic Thought of Samuel Taylor Coleridge* (Berkeley, 1958), argues for Coleridge's views on society against Ricardo's and Bentham's.

[3] References are to R. J. White (ed.), *Political Tracts of Wordsworth, Coleridge and Shelley* (1953).

than was Malthus.[4] In any case the real burden of the *Sermon* was contempt for the 'overbalance of the capitalist spirit', and reverence for rank, ancestry and religion. The low moral principles of 'storekeepers', and above all the growth of the manufacturing system, were the true sources of increasing pauperism. The Poor Law was defended only as part of the ancient order, against new criticisms. 'As the best remedies for this calamity, we propose that we should pay less to our landlords, less to our labourers, nothing to our clergymen, and either nothing or very little to the maintenance of the government or of the poor. ... In almost every page we find deprecations of the poor laws. .....' We find them in Coleridge's pages also: 'I hold it impossible to exaggerate their pernicious tendency and consequences. ... But the Poor Laws form a subject, which I should not undertake without trembling, had I the space of a whole volume to allott to it. Suffice, that this enormous mischief is undeniably the offspring of the commercial system.'[5] Coleridge might have been an abolitionist, if it would not have brought him into such repugnant company. He was against abolition, not for the Poor Law; he was also against every other reform of Church or State except a return to morality as he preached it. It is not surprising that many genuinely benevolent men could not discern the undoubted insights concealed among his passionate reactions against what seemed obvious improvements.

Southey's voluminous contributions to the *Quarterly* on the subject of the poor perhaps constitute the book which Coleridge did not write; between 1815 and 1818 he continued to pour scorn on Malthus and the abolitionists, while gradually abandoning the defence of the Poor Law as it existed.[6] 'As for political economists, no words can express the thorough contempt which I feel for them', not even, it seems, words like 'foul philosophy' and 'diarrhoea of the intellect'. Southey continued to assert that the relation of population to subsistence should be left to God, and that 'we cannot deny the [poor's] claim to a maintenance from the public'. He admitted that distress was real, and, like Coleridge, blamed retrenchment as the immediate cause and the growth

---

[4] Thus the trade cycle was pictured as essentially a moral fluctuation (*ibid.* pp. 77–80, 101–3).

[5] *Ibid.* pp. 112–13. Significantly, Weyland's defence of the Poor Law attracted Coleridge.

[6] See in particular his reviews of Colquhoun (*Quarterly Review*, XII (1815), 398–428); of works on charity (XV (1816), 187–235); and on parliamentary reform (XVI (1816), 263–78). The review of the 1817 *Report* in XVIII (1818), 259–96, was mainly by Rickman, with additions by Southey. The article on the poor in XII (1814), 146–57, was almost certainly not by Southey; see H. and H. C. Shine, *The Quarterly Review under Gifford*, pp. 44–5 and compare K. Curry, *New Letters of Robert Southey*, II. 178–9, 317–8.

of capitalist manufactures and the decline of the yeomanry as the underlying social ills. His ideal society would be a pyramid with a chivalrous apex and a dutiful base; his attitude to the existing social structure was necessarily ambivalent, since too sweeping an attack gave fuel to radicals, while too vigorous a defence would betray his own ideals. Thus he insisted that there had been progress, but that much of it was false and 'cancerous'. The principal remedy he prescribed for distress was moral reform: education (Bell's, not Lancaster's), friendly societies, savings banks, and the suppression of alehouses were the first steps to be taken. He also recommended high government expenditure and public employment as a 'partial and temporary remedy' for unemployment caused by 'stagnant manufactures, languishing agriculture' and demobilisation, thereby winning himself a reputation for economic sagacity, though not for more than a century. Contemporaries saw rather the defence of sinecures, the resistance to economic innovation and the obsessive fear of revolution.[7]

Nevertheless despite all these protestations against abolitionist principles Southey became increasingly critical of the Poor Law. In 1815 he deplored undue liberality in relief; in 1816 he admitted the 'crying necessity' for reform; and in 1818 he presented as his own an article almost entirely written by Rickman which was quite scathing in its attack on the system. As early as 1810 Rickman had decided that 'the poor rate is a great evil, more in the trouble it gives than in the expense—and I much doubt whether it does any good at all'. In May 1817 he wrote to Southey that 'a rule of reasonable duress must be general . . . you must steel your soul for a short time for future good. Bread and water and straw for all who have not character to elicit, or industry to acquire, better maintenance'. And in October he wrote of the 'abolition' of the Poor Law, insisting that 'human civilisation is founded on the sacredness of private property', that the system authorised the poor to plunder the rich; 'never was so unjust an agrarian law'. He offered his own version of less eligibility, and a harsh accompaniment for it:

The poor then have no *right* to relief, they must be made *to ask* and not to *demand* it; and in the case of bad character, the overseer, if confirmed by the decision of the magistrate, shall be entitled to refuse it, and send the poor man of lazy habits to the workhouse; there to be fed on the lowest species of fare

[7] See especially *Quarterly Review*, XV (1816), 208–20; XVI (1816), 277. For criticism of romantic conservatism by an equally romantic progressive, see Macaulay's review of Southey's *Colloquies* in the *Edinburgh Review*, L (1830), 97–118; Macaulay claimed that Southey preferred 'rose-bushes and poor-rates' to 'steam engines and independence'. Southey, incidentally, was one of the last Englishmen to lament tea-drinking as demoralising and effeminate (*Quarterly Review*, XV (1816), 196–7).

that any working man in Great Britain eats. . . . Volunteer cavalry must be maintained in such proportion to check all Jacquery. . . .[8]

Rickman was busy at this time assisting the Commons Select Committee on the Poor Law, and in the article he prepared for Southey he welcomed its 1817 Report as an admirable example of British sagacity. Both men still detested Malthus, but the article admitted that the Poor Law encouraged population, endangered property, and had brought England to 'the very brink of ruin'; the country was becoming a 'paupers' farm', a worse fate even than Spencean communism. 'What are the causes of pauperism?—misfortune in one instance, misconduct in fifty. . . .' A strict moral regimen, under an enlightened aristocracy, was necessary to restore the situation. Southey may have added this moralistic message, and the wistful references to medieval virtues; Rickman would not have disagreed with them, but the detailed discussion of the system, the proposals to ensure 'that the mode of subsisting of those who prey on the substance of others be not better than that which is the lot of any who subsist on their own resources', and the suggested special militia to suppress 'jacquerie and insurrection' provoked by reform of the Poor Law, were all his.[9] In 1831 Rickman hoped that Sir Robert Peel might introduce a Tory reform of the system, and claimed that he himself could 'fit up the apparatus readily, having not only *arguments* but *clauses* ready drawn in store'.[10] It might not have differed as radically from the 1834 reform as Rickman's continued animosity to Malthus and other political economists would suggest—unless of course it included a repressive special militia.

The *Quarterly* had been weakening in defence of the Poor Law even before Southey adopted Rickman's arguments. An article in 1814 had complained that the law interfered with the 'natural' economic system, though it did not recommend abolition; and in 1816 the *Quarterly* published Sumner's defence of Malthus, earning thereby warm praise

[8] O. Williams, *Life and Letters of John Rickman*, pp. 151-2, 193-4, 196-7. For Southey's earlier criticism of relief see *Quarterly Review*, XII (1815), 327, and XVI (1816), 278.
[9] *Quarterly Review*, XVIII (1818), 261, 209, 306, XIX (1818), 85. Rickman attacked workhouses, and incidentally argued that Gilbert's Act was intended to extend their use, a view soon to become unfashionable (pp. 271-3). He claimed that agreement on poor-law reform was in sight: 'When a similarity of opinions is found between men whose views upon fundamental principles . . . are as opposite as light and darkness, it may be presumed that the point upon which they are agreed has very much the force and character of a general truth' (p. 260).
[10] O. Williams, *Life and Letters of John Rickman*, pp. 306-7. When the government was under pressure to act for the relief of distress in November 1830 Peel replied to critics in the Commons that 'he really thought that this subject would be much better dealt with by individual members of the House than by the Government' (*Parliamentary Debates*, 3rd Series, I. 336).

from Ricardo.[11] In 1821, when G. Taylor defended Malthus against Godwin, the right to relief was explicitly denied; thereafter the journal's attitude was hardly consistent, though rarely sympathetic to the general arguments of the political economists. Its contributors were inclined, like Sir Egerton Brydges, to object to all systematic social theorising on such subjects:

> I hate abstract modes of judging! I cannot endure a mere result of figures as the ground of legislation. . . . Oh those abstract, calculating matter of fact fellows, who call themselves men of business. . . .

With Brydges, as with so many other conservative opponents of Malthus, it was the manner of the argument rather than its matter which repelled him; by 1819, when Brydges had overcome his contempt for political economy enough to learn a little of it, he was very nearly a Malthusian abolitionist himself.[12]

2. Make-work Men

Coleridge and Southey were by no means alone in urging that employment be created as an antidote for distress. The abolitionist argument that the system of relief was inevitably a cause of distress was frequently denied, or circumvented, on the grounds that the real fault lay in the failure to 'set the poor on work'. Employment seemed such an obvious remedy for idleness, and for the mischief Satan found for idle hands to do, that the arguments of Malthus and other political economists were of little more avail than Defoe's had been a century earlier. Since workhouses were still in general disfavour, the make-work schemes of the time usually aimed at public employment on roads and bridges, though a significant minority were proposals for agricultural settlement, or for the encouragement of new industries. The device of the labour-rate also made its appearance as a compromise between

[11] *Works*, VII. 247–8: 'I am glad to see that so popular a Review is at length employed in advocating the cause of truth. The reveries of Southey on the question of Political Economy will I hope no longer be admitted in any respectable Journal.' Ricardo regretted that Sumner's intention to pursue theology rather than political economy would 'no doubt' reduce his opportunity to benefit mankind.

[12] E. Brydges, *Letters on the Poor Laws* etc. (1813), pp. 3, 18; *Arguments* etc. (1817); *The Population and Riches of Nations* etc. (1819), esp. chap. xix. Sir Samuel Egerton Brydges (1762–1837) imagined himself a man of literary genius; his pretensions did not endear him to the 'book-hating squires' who were his neighbours in Kent, or to his fellow-Members after he entered Parliament in 1812. His attempts to gain recognition of his brother's claim to be Lord Chandos also aroused opposition. In poor-law matters Brydges was generally a warm-hearted enthusiast. In 1818 he retired from Parliament to live abroad.

refusing relief and recognising the responsibility of a parish to maintain all its inhabitants.[13] Supporters of make-work schemes differed in their awareness of the arguments against them. Some, like Clark and the author of *Justice to the Poor*, virtually ignored all objections. Others admitted the need to avoid competing with free labour; Craig, Jerram and Brydges all specified employment on public works to avoid this danger, and Samuel Hill's new machine for treating flax was offered as a means of creating a new industry without competing with an old. And even among those who agreed that it was in fact impossible to create employment, since capital was limited, some approved of setting the poor to work for disciplinary reasons, or for necessary public works. Malthus himself shared this view.[14]

The creation of employment by setting the poor to work on the land was quite strongly supported. Some spokesmen for the landed interest simply appealed for more effective protection and encouragement for agriculture as the true remedy for unemployment, but defence of the landed interest became blended with the old panacea of allotments for the poor, as distress and political tension over the Corn Law led country-men to defend their social values against mere tradesmen and manu-facturers.[15] The Select Committee of 1817 cautiously approved of

[13] For Malthus's complaint of the prevalence of make-work arguments see *Essay* (1826), II. 405–7. Criticism of workhouses may be found in E. Brydges, *The Population and Riches of Nations* etc. pp. 108–10; R. Fellowes, *Thoughts* etc. (1817), p. 38; [S. Parr], *Considerations* etc. (1817), p. 63; *A Letter . . . to . . . Castlereagh* etc. (1818), p. 9, and J. Cull, *A Letter* etc. (1820). W. H. Chamberlin, *A Plan* etc. (1819); *Hints towards an Attempt* etc. (1819); and R. Stephenson, *A Plan* etc. (1820), describe versions of the labour rate. Brydges, in *Arguments* etc. pp. 16–17, recommended an allowance system in reverse: paupers were to be allotted to farmers and employed at a full wage, but one-seventh of their earnings was to be taken by the parish to pay for relief to the impotent.

[14] W. Clark, *Thoughts* etc. (1815), p. 64 (Clark also sought to ban 'the obscene and prurient exhibitions of the Italian operas' as an aid to reducing pauperism); J. Craig, *Elements of Political Science* (1814), p. 319; C. Jerram, *Considerations* etc. (1818), pp. 78–80; S. Hill, *A Plan* etc. (2nd ed. 1817); and see H. B. Gascoigne, *Pauperism* etc. (1818), p. 31, W. Salisbury, *A Treatise* etc. (1820) and *Justice to the Poor* etc. pp. 50–1 for support for Hill's plan. S. W. Nicoll, *A Summary View* etc. (1818), chap. V, and R. A. Slaney's *Essay on the Employment of the Poor* etc. (1819) were particularly persuasive in objecting to make-work schemes, and compare *Cursory Hints* etc. (1817), attributed to Copleston. On John Craig's general views on political economy see T. W. Bruce, 'The Economic Views of John Craig', *Quarterly Jnl. Economics*, LII (1938), 697–707, and E. R. A. Seligman, 'Some Neglected British Economists', *Economic Jnl.* XIII (1903), 347–50.

[15] See, for example, the works of Brydges, R. Preston, *Further Observations* etc. (1816), esp. p. 21, and *A Review* etc. (1816); Lord Sheffield, *Observations* etc. (1818), pp. 41–3; *An Inquiry . . . by a Gentleman of Norfolk* (1817). The title of Thomas Myer's pamphlet of 1814 is revealing: *An Essay on Improving the Condition of the*

parish farms, but the proposal had a mixed reception. Allotments were widely recommended, and the propaganda of the Labourers' Friend Society in their favour was forceful and persuasive, though men like Southey, Fellowes and Lord Sheffield repeated the old objections that small gardens produced indolence and the brutish habits of the Irish.[16] There were also more elaborate plans for settling the poor on the wastes, some of them echoing Arthur Young's unlucky scheme. Most came from philanthropists of the upper classes, but in one case a self-appointed spokesman for the poor themselves took up the cause. Robert Gourlay, the man Arthur Young had employed to investigate the cow system, carried on a slightly ludicrous vendetta with Somerset farmers and with the Duke of Somerset, his landlord, to restore the independence of the poor by giving them land and by returning the commons to public use. In this cause he organised petitions to Parliament, wrote letters inciting insubordination, and published pamphlets exposing the tyrannies of farmers and overseers. Gourlay soon gave up the struggle and emigrated to Canada, returning to agitate for emigration as a means of relieving distress in the 1820s. He has been credited with anticipating the ideas of Wilmot Horton and perhaps Wakefield on systematic colonisation.[17]

Much less inflammatory was the agitation of Henry Barnet Gascoigne for a national institution to set the poor to work in agriculture, mostly in spade cultivation, with special institutions for training the young, and with small holdings made available for worthy graduates of such schools of 'self-support'. Gascoigne justified his plan against the usual objections to make-work schemes with a crude anticipation of the Keynesian multiplier: employment provided would stimulate effective demand and hence further employment, but the initial stimulus, he

[16] C. Jerram, *Considerations* etc. pp. 121–7; Lieut. Gen. Craufurd, *Observations* etc. (1817), pp. 37–8; W. D. Bayly, *The State of the Poor* etc. (1820), pp. 73–100; and J. Cull, *A Letter* etc. *passim*, all sympathised with the aims of the Labourers' Friend Society. (Craufurd was presumably Lieut. Gen. Sir Charles Gregan Craufurd, Member for East Retford and husband of the dowager Duchess of Newcastle, though he was not well known for his interest in any but military matters.) For criticism of allotments see Lord Sheffield, *Observations* etc. p. 47; R. Fellowes, *Thoughts* etc. p. 40; and Southey-Rickman, *Quarterly Review*, XVIII (1818), 278–9.

[17] Gourlay's *Tyranny of the Poor Laws Exemplified* (1815), *Right to Church Property Secured* (1815), and *The Village System* (1817) are forthright and entertaining works; for his later views on colonisation see R. C. Mills, *The Colonisation of Australia* (1915), pp. 136–40. Gourlay is said to have done what many men wished to do, horse-whipped Lord Brougham (p. 136).

Poor: including an Attempt to answer the important Question, how Men of Landed Property may most effectually contribute towards the general Improvement of the Lower Classes of Society on their Estates, without diminishing the Value of their own Property?

insisted, should be given to agriculture, lest the good effects sneak away overseas. Despite the pious dedication of one of his pamphlets to the more responsible of the Royal Dukes, Gascoigne's scheme gained little support, perhaps because he proposed to finance it with a revival of the hated property tax.[18]

The element in these schemes of deliberate opposition to abolitionism and to the new-fangled doctrines of Malthus and the political economists was made clear in 1820 by Earl Stanhope when he introduced proposals in the House of Lords. Stanhope blamed manufactures and undue preference to commerce for distress, and complained that the landed interest was the innocent victim, as poor rates threatened to swallow rents. God forbid, however, that the harsh doctrines of those denying the rights of the poor should triumph. Let the waste lands be cultivated by self-supporting peasants, in spade cultivation, and let agriculture return to its proper place in national life. The Prime Minister quashed the scheme with a bland denial that there was any divergence of interest between agriculture and manufactures.[19] But support for make-work schemes persisted, and critics of manufactures and of abolitionism continued to assert that the existence of waste lands in England provided not only a means of relieving distress but also a refutation of the Malthusian thesis of population pressure as a cause of misery. Even when over-population was admitted, colonisation at home was championed by the landed interest as a more desirable expedient than colonisation abroad.

3. *Robert Owen's Plan*

Robert Owen's famous Plan of 1817 was perhaps the greatest of the make-work schemes of these years. It grew, of course, into something altogether more ambitious, into a blueprint for a new society, but its later elaborations and ramifications in the new world and the old are hardly relevant here. For a few months in 1817 Owen's long pilgrimage in search of the principles of a new society brought him into the company of poor-law reformers; he entered the debate with the brilliance of a meteor, and left it with a meteor's rapidity.

Most of the principles which made Owen a social radical—his contempt for religion, his criticism of a society based on competition, and

---

[18] 'Farmer Meanwell' [H. B. Gasgoigne], *The Antidote to Distress* (1817); H. B. Gascoigne, *Suggestions* etc. (1817); *Pauperism* etc.; *The Old Views of Society* etc. (1820); *Society for promoting the Employment of the Poor* etc. (1827).

[19] *Parliamentary Debates*, New Series I. 396–417. For other plans for agricultural settlement see J. Ashdowne, *An Essay* etc. (1817); *A Plan* etc. (1817); and *The Oppressed Labourers* etc. (1819). Simon Gray's claim that the existence of waste lands 'refuted' Malthus is discussed below.

his questioning of accepted ideas of human nature—can be discerned in his writings before 1817, and it may seem strange that his plan of that year gained so much very respectable support. Royal Dukes, the Saints, eminent champions of the landed interest, and even members of the Cabinet were captivated by the man and the scheme. Their support was brief, not because Owen's social radicalism became evident, but because he very tactlessly criticised established religion in a public speech. Until that unlucky night at the London Tavern he could plausibly be regarded as a sound and conservative man, and a staunch ally against new-fangled doctrines of political economy. Though a manufacturer, he was an outspoken critic of his colleagues, and an agitator for factory regulation; and his analysis of the causes of distress blamed the manufacturing system, not the Corn Laws. His politics were irreproachably anti-radical, and his remedy for distress seemed, on the surface at least, to be based on principles which the S.B.C.P., and even Coleridge and Southey, could approve.[20]

Owen's *New View of Society* (1812–16) was widely praised as a work on education by men who did not notice that its social and psychological assumptions were in fact very different from Bell's and Lancaster's. The comments on indigence in the final chapter of the work were similarly acceptable. The Poor Law was crtised as injurious to both rich and poor, and 'decisive and effectual' reform was demanded, but abolition was rejected as a remedy. Instead 'these laws should be progressively undermined by a system of an opposite nature, and ultimately rendered altogether nugatory'. But the alternative system was, as yet, nothing more radical than national education; and with it Owen would combine a system of public employment, to put down idleness and to remedy fluctuations in the demand for labour. At first he envisaged only employment on public works, but by 1816 he had in mind the establishment of new communities where the employment of the poor could be combined with moral regeneration through education.[21]

---

[20] The S.B.C.P. published accounts of the New Lanark mills, and Owen's educational experiments interested Bernard and the Bishop of Durham. For an excellent brief analysis of the development of Owen's ideas up to 1817 see J. F. C. Harrison, "'The Steam Engine of the New Moral World": Owenism and Education, 1817–1829', *Journal of British Studies*, VI (1967), 76–88. The unreliable *Life of Robert Owen by Himself* (ed. Beer, 1920), pp. 143, 266, 291–2, lists his friends and patrons of 1817. For a favourable remark on his conservatism see the *Gentleman's Magazine*, LXXVII (1817), 195–7, and compare 272, 519; for a later attempt to insist on his respectability see H. G. MacNab, *The New Views of Mr. Owen* etc. (1819), and compare the anonymous *Remarks on the Practicability of Mr. Robert Owen's Plan* (1819), a work addressed to Wilberforce. J. Beatson's *Examination of Mr. Owen's Plan* (1823) forcefully expressed conservative disillusion.

[21] *A New View of Society* etc. (Everyman ed. 1927), pp. 69–70, 85–7; *Address* . . .

CONTRARY OPINIONS

All this was perfectly acceptable to those who opposed Malthusian abolitionism from sentiments of traditional paternalism. The plan for village settlements which Owen offered to the Committee for the Relief of the Manufacturing and Labouring Poor in 1817 seemed to them a positive remedy for distress, unencumbered with theoretical prohibitions. And it was accompanied by a soothing balm for the landed interest in Owen's explanation of distress as the result of 'the depreciation of human labour' by machinery; he calculated (to Colquhoun's astonishment) that mechanical power in England had grown to equivalence with the labour of a hundred million men. Peace had brought a collapse in demand, and it was the men and not the machines which had been dispensed with. Owen did not suggest that mechanical power could be abandoned, but he demanded that it be made subservient to men, and that the labourers it had displaced be set to work. The Poor Law did maintain them, but only in idleness and demoralisation. They should be made to maintain themselves, 'under such circumstances as would obviously unite their real interest and duty and remove them from unnecessary temptation'. This could be done in his famous 'Parallelograms', self-contained villages in each of which 1200 persons would be employed, mainly in agriculture, and educated to 'unite . . . in the pursuit of common objects for their mutual benefit'. The plan as it first appeared was rough-hewn, but it had considerable appeal to men alarmed at the spread of pauperism but antagonistic to the arguments of the abolitionists. Owen became, for a time, the darling of the anti-Malthusians.[22]

The Committee for Relief referred Owen and his Plan to the Select Committee on the Poor Laws. After two days of deliberation it refused to examine either, seduced, Owen always maintained, by the machinations of Malthusian political economists.[23] But Owen now had patrons, and with their help and at the expense of his own fortune the Plan was given much publicity, in the press and at public meetings. But the speech against religion pricked the bubble, Owen was left with only a rump of the staunchest supporters, and he turned into ways that would lead him ultimately to seek support from men of a lower class and of different politics. At the same time the Plan itself was changing as it was elaborated in the campaign. At first evasive on methods of employment,

[22] *Report to the Committee* etc. (1817), same edition, esp. pp. 160, 168. On the reception and development of the plan see F. Podmore, *Robert Owen, A Biography* (1906), I. chaps. x–xii.
[23] *Life* etc. pp. 180–4, 214–5.

at New Lanark (1816), same edition, p. 114. The first essay in *A New View of Society* was dedicated, significantly enough, to Wilberforce.

Owen came to champion spade-cultivation as the most productive labour known to man; certainly the emphasis was on agriculture, with manufactures only as subordinate employments. The great principle of 'united labour' was stressed increasingly; it would remove all dissension over property, and would form the basis of a new society of 'Unity and Mutual Co-operation'. A general invitation was issued to all classes to quit the old rotten order and to enter the new. Utopia for all, and not simply relief for the poor, became the object.

When, in 1819, Sir William de Crespigny moved in Parliament for a Select Committee to examine Owen's Plan the cause was no longer fashionable. Significantly, de Crespigny omitted to mention its radical implications, and was content to appeal to humanity against 'political reasoning', to the fear of revolution, to support for education, and to the landed interest against the manufacturers. The abolitionists rose to attack Owen. Brougham dismissed the Plan as 'wholly erroneous', and deplored the 'melancholy malpractices of the low part of the press' in opposing the principle of population, the truth which was fatal to Owen's error. Ricardo confessed himself 'completely at war with the system of Mr. Owen, which was built upon a theory inconsistent with the principles of political economy', but very fairly offered to join a committee if only to investigate the claims made for spade cultivation. He warned against the dangers of make-work schemes, stressing that diminishing returns at home were already tempting capital to flee abroad. But the speech which ruined the motion came from the Chancellor of the Exchequer, who quoted Owen's speech against religion; Wilberforce himself then admitted that this was the issue which had turned him from a supporter of Owen into an opponent. The motion was lost by 141 votes to 16, the minority consisting mainly of fanatics for the cultivation of wastes, such as Alderman Wood. Ricardo's name stood in the list in tribute to his fair-mindedness, and not as an indication of support. A similar motion in 1821 was as soundly defeated.[24]

Debate outside Parliament was more extensive. Malthus himself attacked Owen's Plan both as a system of equality and as an improper scheme for the relief of the poor. Even if the plan succeeded initially, it would soon be overwhelmed by the increased population it would stimulate; but it would not succeed, because it denied the principle of individual reward for individual exertion, a principle essential even in

[24] *Parliamentary Debates*, XLI. 1189–1216; New Series, V. 1316–25. Brougham was an ardent Malthusian abolitionist; for Ricardo's unwilling involvement in Owen's plans see his *Works*, VIII. 42–6, and compare L. Robbins, *The Theory of Economic Policy* etc. pp. 126–34. It was in the 1819 debate that Ricardo made his proposal for paying off the National Debt (*Parliamentary Debates*, XLI. 1209).

Owen's own mills at New Lanark. Owen, who was an acquaintance and even to some extent an admirer of Malthus, had long before tried to anticipate and rebut such objections.

Mr. Malthus is . . . correct, when he says that the population of the world is ever adapting itself to the quantity of food raised for its support; but he has not told us how much more food an intelligent and industrious people will create from the same soil, than will be produced by one ignorant and ill-governed. It is, however, as one to infinity.

Later Owen added the argument that it was the 'artificial' law of supply and demand which limited production, and even asserted that population could never rise in more than an arithmetical ratio, since 'each individual brings into the world with him the means . . . sufficient to enable him to produce food equal to more than ten times his consumption'.[25] Malthus's perfunctory criticism and Owen's unsystematic reply were both eclipsed by a brilliant essay which Robert Torrens published in the *Edinburgh Review* in 1819. Owen was praised for his benevolence, but the whole analytical apparatus of political economy was elegantly employed to demolish his hopes. Torrens explained distress as the result of fluctuations in trade, determined by rates of profit. Profit in turn was influenced by the quality of the soil, by the productivity of labour, and by the amount of wages (since wages and profits were drawn from the same fund). Since the principle of population kept wages more or less constant, the progress or decline of countries depended in the main on the fertility of the soil and the productivity of labour, an increase in the latter being necessary to offset diminishing returns as agriculture was forced on to poorer land. Unwise commercial regulation and high taxation could check progress and precipitate decline, and England's troubles thus arose from the great extension of tillage, the Corn Laws, and excessive taxation. Which of these evils would be remedied by Owen's scheme? 'So long as he is incapable of accomplishing any one of these things, so long must we continue to regard him as an amiable but mistaken enthusiast, who, had he the means of executing his plans, would aggravate the evils he dreams he could remove'.[26] True, Owen did claim that he would vastly increase the productivity of labour, by spade cultivation. But if the spade were so productive an implement, why had ploughs been invented? The new villages might provide subsistence for themselves, but who would pay taxes, buy

---

[25] Malthus, *Essay* (1826), II. 40–8, 395–9; Owen, *A New View* etc. pp. 85–6, *Letters on Poor Relief*, same edition pp. 181–2. Owen may later have become sympathetic to Place's remedy for population pressure; certainly his son was a propagandist for neo-Malthusianism.
[26] *Edinburgh Review*, XXXII (1819), p. 464. Ricardo admired the article, though he disagreed with some of its assertions (*Works*, VIII. 163–4, 227).

manufactures, or accumulate capital? If villages manufactured goods only for their own consumption, they would lose all the benefits of a highly developed division of labour. The villages must either remain at a much lower level of civilisation, or be raised from it at the expense of the rest of the community. Were the system universal, then trade must cease, canals run dry, and roads decay, with the return of a primitive subsistence economy. And Owen could propose such a plan in the country of Adam Smith, of Malthus and Ricardo, of (even) Mrs. Marcet? The article concluded with a passionate defence of manufactures and of innovation in general, a denial that depression could be brought by underconsumption, and a plea for the removal of unnatural burdens such as the Corn Laws and high taxation. All this may have been refutable, but against it Owen had no direct argument, but only a tremendous optimism that a new society, with different principles of human co-operation, would burst free from the bonds of such depressing laws. He fell back on moral denunciation: 'The political economists, . . . knowing little of human nature, and less of the powers of society when rightly directed, had hardened their hearts against the natural feelings of humanity, and were determined, aided by their disciples the Whigs, to starve out the poor from the land.'[27] The make-work men who shared Owen's belief in employment but not his wish for a new society had even less to offer in rebuttal.

4. *Radical Protests*

The spread of abolitionist sentiment after the war provoked much opposition from political radicals. There were some, especially among the Benthamites, who wanted radical political change and yet accepted the main tenets of Malthus, but to most radicals Malthusianism was a false and wicked doctrine which (they believed) was expounded only to obscure the true causes of social ills. Pauperism was deplorable, but to abolish relief without curing the causes of distress was to deprive the people of yet another of their rights. Shelley put the view succinctly in the following propositions:

That the majority of the people of England are destitute and miserable, ill-clothed, ill-fed, ill-educated. . . .
That the cause of this misery is the unequal distribution which, under the form of the national debt, has been surreptitiously made of the products of their labour and the products of the labour of their ancestors; for all property is the produce of labour.
That the cause of that cause is a defect in the government.

[27] *Life*, etc. p. 177.

He went on to vilify Malthus and all his works ('a priest of course, for his doctrines are those of a eunuch and of a tyrant').[28] Cobbett's animus against Malthus did not diminish with the years. His *Letter to Parson Malthus* of 1819 accused him of 'cool and unrelenting cruelty', and defended the right to relief against him. In his sermon against *The Sin of Forbidding Marriage*, he classified Malthus among the 'sons of Belial', and asked why he did not seek to check the increase of idlers and tyrants. Cobbett would himself preach frugality to the poor, would deplore improvident marriages, and would even admit the inevitability of poverty and its necessity as a spur to labour, but any suggestion that abolition of poor relief was a remedy, while political reform was not, aroused his intemperate fury. As always, it was denunciation he offered, and he made no contribution at all to the debate on the reform, as distinct from the abolition, of the Poor Law.[29]

A strong radical influence was also evident in many of the writers who attempted to refute Malthus's principle of population. Thus George Ensor attacked Malthus not only for his 'want of science' and 'infinite contradiction', but also for 'his inhumanities, his loud abuse of the people; his silence concerning the hard-heartedness of the opulent; his general indemnity for kings and ministers'. Bad government and the burden of idle and luxurious classes, and not the pressure of population, were the causes of distress; 'where property is equitably divided and labour free, there will be no tendency but to supply what is wanting'. Reform and retrenchment were the remedies. As for the plan to abolish the Poor Law, the denial of the right to relief implied that 'a portion of this man's property is more sacred than that man's life'.[30] Much the same tone permeated Godwin's gargantuan *Of Population* etc. (1820), the book Leslie Stephen called 'the longest answer to the shortest argument in modern times'. There was theoretical meat in Godwin's reply to Malthus, but it was well concealed by his prolixity and by his enormous personal resentment against the work he had once been proud to have provoked. He seriously misrepresented Malthus's views

[28] P. B. Shelley, *A Philosophical View of Reform* (1819, printed in R. J. White, *Political Tracts of Wordsworth, Coleridge and Shelley*), pp. 238–9. For evidence that in 1817 radicals were as critical of Owen as they were of Malthus, see Podmore, *Robert Owen*, I. 240.

[29] *Political Register*, 8 May 1819; *Twelve Sermons* (1823); *Cottage Economy* (1823); 'Surplus Population: a Comedy in Three Acts', in *Twopenny Trash* (1831). A review of *Cottage Economy* in the *Edinburgh Review*, XXXVIII (1823), 105–25, by Jeffrey and/or Brougham, argued that much of Cobbett's argument was consistent with Malthusianism.

[30] G. Ensor, *An Inquiry concerning the Population of Nations* (1818), esp. pp. 79, 110, 81. George Ensor (1769–1843), a prolific writer, especially on Ireland, had liberal opinions but was not active in politics. Bentham thought him clever but 'impracticable'.

on charity (as Malthus himself was quick to point out anonymously in the *Edinburgh Review*), and continually protested against the denial of the right to relief. Malthus 'would starve the present generation, that he may kill the next'; he taught 'a doctrine of quietism', to set the minds of the rich at rest; his refusal of relief extended the old adage that 'he who won't work won't eat' to include the innocent impotent and 'those who being both able and willing to work, are yet, by the ill constitution of society ... unable to secure employment'. The parable of the feast was monstrous, the sermons against matrimony absurd. Against Malthus's abolitionism Godwin pleaded the right to relief and the efficacy of political reform to relieve distress. But even he would have preferred to see the Poor Law go: 'I should prefer being the citizen of a country, where the deserted and the helpless should be *sufficiently taken care of* without the intervention of the state. But in England at least we are not yet ripe for this'. What should be done with an admittedly imperfect Poor Law in the meanwhile was not made clear.[31]

5. *Ravenstone and Place*

Two radical writers of the early 1820's made significant advances from this old-fashioned beating of the anti-Malthusian drum. *A Few Doubts as to the Correctness of Some Opinions generally entertained on the Subjects of Population and Political Economy*, which appeared in 1821 over the pseudonym Piercy Ravenstone, made a step from simple political radicalism towards that social radicalism which is loosely called Ricardian Socialism. A work of much originality, if also of many imperfections, it deserves however to stand in its own right rather than as the precursor to any 'school'.[32] After some incisive criticism of Malthusian assumptions of human fertility, Ravenstone reached the

[31] *Of Population* etc. pp. 502, 538, 542, 559–60. By far the most important theoretical contribution in Godwin's volume was an appendix, 'Dissertation on the Ratios etc.' by David Booth, a very damaging criticism of Malthus's crude statistical techniques. Malthus refused to consider Godwin's book at length in the 1826 edition of the *Essay*, but reviewed it anonymously in the *Edinburgh Review*, XXXV (1821), 362–77; Booth replied in *A Letter to the Rev. T. R. Malthus* etc. (1823), incidentally ridiculing abolition as 'mad-brained'. The anonymous *Remarks on Mr. Godwin's Enquiry concerning Population* (1821) was racy and effective in criticism of Godwin and discriminating in defence of Malthus.

[32] M. Blaug, *Ricardian Economics*, pp. 140–1, includes Ravenstone among the Ricardian socialists, but E. Lowenthal, *The Ricardian Socialists* (New York, 1911), does not; Beer describes him as 'a Tory Democrat ... Cobbett édition de luxe (*History of British Socialism* (1940 ed.), pp. 251–2). Ricardo praised the author as 'a strenuous and an able advocate for Reform' but found 'the greatest error' as well as 'good things' in the book (*Works*, IX. 45).

dubious conclusion that the natural rate of increase of population was uniform and not excessive, though it could be, and was, checked by misery brought by bad government. Population increase itself stimulated an increase in subsistence and comfort, since a more productive division of labour was possible in large populations. Whenever population increased faster than subsistence, and misery resulted, the cause must lie in faulty economic and social organisation; specifically, in England's case, in the misdirection of labour resulting from the development of rent, excessive profits and high taxation, all factors which stimulated population but checked production. Labour was the sole source of all incomes, and while some 'unproductive' classes were desirable for supervisory and distributive functions, the superstructure of idleness must not be allowed to press too heavily upon the foundation of labour. Moreover the distribution of property in society determined the form of government, and a wide diffusion of property, supporting a representative system, was to be aimed at. England thus required not only a reformed government but a radical change in her social-economic structure, to remove distress and to ensure progress. Ravenstone still emphasised lower taxation as a remedy, but it was not quite the simple panacea it appeared to be to many political radicals. The door was open to further changes in a direction we might call socialist. With such views, Ravenstone was naturally very hostile to the arguments of the abolitionists. Abolition of poor relief was 'the project of a madman or a knave', since life was inevitably uncertain, and 'the claim to relief . . . is the right of the poor, to grant it with alacrity is the duty of the rich'.

It has been the fashion of late years in this country to reprobate the laws for the relief of the poor, and to ascribe to them the increase of that wretchedness which they are indeed hopeless to relieve. The misconduct of the poor will always be a favourite theme with the rich: it wants less to abuse them than to relieve their wants. . . . With all their defects the poor laws are wholesome, and, in the present state of our society they are absolutely necessary. If they cannot extinguish misery, neither do they create it. . . . Those who know nothing of labour but the toil and fatigues of pleasure, may contend that the certainty of relief has produced habits of idleness among the poor. Such an assertion only shews the ignorance of those who make it. . . . The unceasing labour of the poor has saved from the consequences of their own folly, the rents of those who reproach them with their own idleness. But for the increased exertions of the labourer the estates of the land owners must have long since passed to the stockholders, must have long since proved inadequate to the mortgage.[33]

[33] *A Few Doubts* etc. pp. 458–61; the author's views are summarised on pp. 427–34.

The other radical who made a significant contribution to the debate at this time was Francis Place. It was largely thanks to him that the teachings of Malthus gradually made inroads into the beliefs of reformers more radical than the Benthamites, although only in a form which Malthus detested. He brought into public discussion the recommendation of birth control as a means of improving the condition of the poor, a 'solution' to the Malthusian dilemma previously only hinted at, by Bentham and others. By energetic propaganda, and the conversion of the Mills and of other radicals such as Richard Carlile, Place gave life to proposals which were eventually to emerge into wider public notice in the late nineteenth century.

Place was provoked to write by Godwin's book, and most of his work was a refutation of it and a staunch defence of the essential truth and importance, even to the poor, of the basic principles of political economy. But he had no time for Malthus's practical proposals, much as he might defend his general principles. Place the plebeian radical could not stomach the passages in which Malthus too glibly defended the rich against the complaints of the poor, though he did not accuse Malthus of insincerity. To redress the balance he wrote an equally eloquent (and perhaps equally partial) defence of the poor, and in particular defended their right to relief against Malthus's arguments for abolition. This right was no less natural (and no more) than the right to property; to repeal the one was to make the other morally untenable. Malthus's plan was 'mischievous' and murderous. Fortunately it was also impracticable.[34]

Place's defence of the Poor Law was vigorous, but not unqualified. The system did not greatly encourage population, as Malthus himself had admitted; rates were not ruining the landed interest, and relief had not ruined the character of the labourers. Malthus was ignorant of the real state of mind of the poor, of their firm desire for independence and of their deep resentment at what seemed obvious repression and exploitation. But pauperism was in fact degrading; it did not succeed in demoralising the poor, but it was a state in which they should not be compelled to live. Malthus was quite right in blaming much of the distress on the poor's ignorance of political economy, but how could the poor be expected to listen to the truth on population and wages while more obvious oppressions existed? Let the rich remove the grievances which were within their control—restrictions on emigration and combination, the Corn Laws, and high taxation—and the poor,

[34] F. Place, *Illustrations and Proofs of the Principle of Population* etc. (1822). References are to the reprint of 1930 ed. by N. E. Himes; see chaps. ix and x for the defence of political economy, pp. 167–70 for the attack on the rich, and chap. vi for criticism of abolitionism.

convinced of their benevolence, might listen to instruction. But Place's instruction was not Malthus's. He would tell the poor that their wages were determined by the ratio of capital to population, and that a preventive check to their increase was the only road to considerable improvement in their condition. He was himself burdened with a large family. But he believed that youthful chastity could never be universal, that early marriage was necessary to both moral and physical health, and that the prevention of conception after marriage was therefore the sole effective remedy for population pressure and distress. Early marriage and birth control would bring both moral and physical improvement in the condition of the poor; that, and not the abolition of the Poor Law, was the valid conclusion to be drawn from the Malthusian argument. It was in these terms that Place sought to convince his fellow radicals that in attacking abolitionism they should not neglect to learn some truths from the abolitionist case.[35]

6. *Emigration and the Poor*

A much more respectable alternative to Malthusian abolitionism was urged by the advocates of emigration as a remedy for distress. Thus James Grahame asserted that the whole Malthusian thesis rested on a false assumption; he admitted 'a tendency to exuberance in numbers in a society', but claimed this was both natural and desirable. Prolific breeding among the lower classes enabled the upper classes to be replenished by the most able and worthy, and colonisation extended these benefits to the whole world. Emigration was the 'natural vent' of surplus population, and would remain so until the earth was filled, when Providence would doubtless provide another. Unfortunately emigration was checked, and misery caused, by bad government and by the disproportionate growth of commerce and manufactures. Charity, enforced by law, could relieve incidental distress; Malthus was cruel and unnatural in seeking to abolish the Poor Law, since it was proper to encourage marriage and charity, especially in its most effective form, emigration.[36] Malthus replied to Grahame in the 1817 edition of the

[35] *Ibid.* pp. 171–9. For his campaign to persuade radicals (and London maid-servants) of the truth of his views, see appendix B of the 1930 reprint; and N. E. Himes, *Medical History of Contraception* (1936), pp. 212–20, and the articles cited there. Place may have been anticipated in his criticism of Malthus for opposing birth control by the author of *A Letter on the Nature, Extent and Management of Poor Rates in Scotland* etc. (Edinburgh, 1807). Note the following passage: 'I cannot help observing, that there is one check to population, and worth all the rest, which Mr Malthus has totally neglected, the omission of which, in my mind, brings more discredit upon his work than any man would willingly ascribe to design' (p. 37).
[36] J. Grahame, *An Inquiry into the Principle of Population* etc. (1816). Grahame

Essay, but only to defend himself, quite plausibly, against misrepresentation. He would concede that emigration could remove a special and temporary redundancy of population, but continued to argue that it usually involved distress and was a mere palliative; even in 1827 the Select Committee on Emigration could not induce him to admit any great enthusiam on the subject. Nevertheless some quite orthodox Malthusians, such as Hayter and Sumner, placed more stress on colonisation than he did, and already in 1817 Torrens anticipated later more systematic views on the subject. Malthus claimed that labour in new colonies was unproductive. Torrens argued that on the contrary new settlers could soon repay the cost of their transportation; instead of abolishing the Poor Law, offer all those chargeable grants of colonial land, on condition that they repay the expense of emigration by a period of labour in their new land. Thus colonisation and relief could support each other.[37] In an earlier pamphlet Torrens had made some important and original points in defence of the Poor Law, having noticed that the redistribution of funds in periods of reduced demand could stimulate recovery; in later years, however, colonisation became of more interest to him than the analysis of the existing system.[38]

Another man who was later to be an advocate of emigration for the relief of distress was, before 1820, more concerned to dispute what he thought to be errors in Malthus's analysis of the state of the labourers. In 1817 and in 1820 John Barton produced closely reasoned pamphlets on the condition of the poor which earned the admiration of Ricardo. His aim, at first, was to deny that pauperism was a rapidly growing evil, and to refute the Malthusian notions on wages and relief which the Select Committee on the Poor Laws of 1817 had adopted. His optimism was soon shaken, however, and he became another suppliant for emigration as the means of relief from the pressure of population. Shorn of distinctive practical conclusions, his undoubtedly original analysis became much less influential than it deserved to be.

[37] R. Torrens, *Paper on the Means of reducing the Poor's Rate* etc. (1817), p. 521; and compare L. Robbins, *Robert Torrens and the Evolution of Classical Economics* (1958), chap. VI. Wilmot Horton wrote a pamphlet against Malthus in 1813, but it is lost. For minor schemes for emigration in these years see R. Heathfield, *Further Observations* etc. (1820) and *Thoughts* etc. (N.D.); [Sir W. G. Hayter], *Proposals* etc. (1817); J. Pinsent, *Conversations on Political Economy* (1821); and two articles in the *Quarterly Review*, XXII (1819), 203, and XXIII (1820), 373–90, probably written by Whateley. The Select Committee of 1817 approved emigration from large towns.

[38] For the counter-cyclical argument see his *The Economists Refuted* (1808), pp. 58–9; and compare a not dissimilar argument in Courtenay's *Treatise on the Poor Laws*, pp. 68–71.

defended the principle of the Poor Law, but not its existing administration, the unequal incidence of the rates, or the allowance system (p. 222). But he also approved of higher infant mortality among the lower classes than the upper (p. 168).

In 1817 Barton argued that the condition of the labourer had improved and that pauperism had considerably declined since 1803. He admitted some fall in real wages, which he claimed had been offset by improvements in habits. Malthus was wrong in assuming that high wages brought population increase; it was low wages and a greater availability of employment which stimulated population. Wages were determined by the relative returns from investment in machinery and from expenditure on wages, and it was low wages which had greatly increased the demand for labour and had thus caused recent population growth. At this time he denied absolutely that poor relief encouraged marriage; stopping relief would not check marriage 'unless a certain number of families were allowed to starve, by way of example'. The Poor Law did in fact increase the comforts of the lower classes: money spent on relief might well have been spent on fixed capital, such as horses, if left in the hands of the ratepayers, despite assertions to the contrary by the 1817 Committee. When the demand for labour suddenly diminished, as in 1817, poor relief was an unmixed good.[39] By 1820, however, Barton would admit that the fall in real wages was too great and prolonged for complacency. He conceded at last that the Poor Law was forcing population, not by tempting men into improvidence through too easy a provision, but because the inadequacy of the support it offered caused despair and destroyed all 'delicacy and refinement of affections'. Abolition would thus be fatal to all prudence, and would reverse the relatively happy position in which population was increasing largely through a low mortality. At this time Barton merely hinted at emigration as a palliative; ten years later he, like many others, thought systematic colonisation an essential pre-requisite to all social improvement.[40]

7. Contributory Schemes

Simon Gray, alias George Purves, a very prolific author of books against Malthus, had a simpler and more old-fashioned remedy for pauperism. His criticism of the principle of population had little merit, but he was quite persuasive in arguing that the Poor Law was part of 'the greatest glory of England'. It was imperfect, especially in its

[39] J. Barton, *Observations* etc. (1817); see also B. A. Corry, 'The Theory of the Economic Effects of Government Expenditure in English Classical Political Economy', *Economica* 25 (1958), 46–8, for Barton's analysis of the distress of 1815–6, from his unpublished notebooks; and G. Sotiroff, 'John Barton, 1789–1852', *Econ. Journal*, LXII (1952), 87–102.

[40] J. Barton, *An Inquiry* etc. (1820), and *A Statement of the Consequences* etc. (1830). A similar view of the relation between distress and population increase was stated—with some irony—in the anonymous *On the Means of Retaining the Population within any required Limits* (1820).

tendency to discourage frugality; hence Gray's plan for an elaborate contributory scheme to supplement it. The scheme was to be organised on a county basis, with everyone compelled to contribute and with benefits calculated on sound actuarial principles. Unfortunately, the difficulties of establishing such a system were not explored, and Gray's peculiar theory of money led him to argue that all this relief would not in fact cost anyone anything. The plan has been praised as an anticipation of modern social insurance and as a practicable alternative to Malthus's abolitionism; perhaps it was, but there is no reason to single it out as more praiseworthy than other contributory schemes. And if passages in Gray make him seem more sympathetic towards the poor than Malthus, others—such as his disapproval of high wages—certainly do not.[41]

There were other apologists of the contributory principle in these years;[42] Thomas Peregrine Courtenay was one of them, but his general criticism of the abolitionist case is of more interest. Courtenay was an independent-minded man, as he revealed when a member of the Select Committee of 1817. At first he was inclined to admit that Malthus was right, that mere tinkering with the Poor Law was futile, and that abolition was the only remedy; even if Malthus was wrong there were still strong moral arguments against the system, and especially against allowances in aid of wages[43] But he soon decided that the Report of the Committee was much too strong. Had law and practice departed from the principles of the Elizabethan Act? They might be none the worse for that. Did the Poor Law put an unlimited demand on limited funds? No, since relief was a mere transfer, and in any case rents and incomes were increasing faster than the rates. Had the system demoralised the poor? A little, but abject misery would have demoralised them

---

[41] For a full list of Gray's works see *Historical Catalogue of the Writings . . . of Simon Gray* etc. (1840); those most relevant to this study are listed in the Bibliography. See K. Smith, *The Malthusian Debate*, pp. 86–91, 301–5, for a sympathetic summary of Gray's views and a suggestion that his scheme was 'the alternative' to Malthusian abolitionism. For Gray's defence of low wages see *The Happiness of States* (1815) p. 113.

[42] See, for example, Count Jerome de Salis, *A Proposal* etc. 1814; [M. Burgoyne], *A Statistical Account* etc. (1817); S. Roberts, *A Defence of the Poor Laws* etc. (1819); P. Bayley, *Observations* etc. (1819); and *Justice to the Poor* etc. (1820). Curwen's scheme is mentioned in the next chapter.

[43] T. P. Courtenay, *Copy of a Letter* etc. (1817), pp. 3–19. For his plan for parochial friendly societies see *ibid.* pp. 21–37; *A Treatise on the Poor Laws* (1818); and *Parliamentary Debates*, XXXIX. 1159–60, 1478. Courtenay (1782–1841) was the son of a bishop of Exeter. Member for Totnes from 1811 until 1831, he held minor offices 1807–11, was secretary to the commissioners for Indian affairs 1812–28, and Vice-President of the Board of Trade 1828–30. He was an able and sensible writer on poor-law matters.

more. Had relief encouraged population growth? Population was increasing with low birth and death rates, 'a proof of the efficiency of the system of which the poor laws are a part, if not of those laws themselves, in preserving human life and preventing or alleviating human suffering', and not, therefore, to be deplored. Perhaps the class just a little above the poor suffered under the system, but it could be defended in general as a bar to excessive inequality. Could any abolitionist be certain that without a Poor Law every case of want 'will either be prudently avoided, privately relieved, necessarily abandoned, or worthily punished'? Malthus could be right about population, but wrong about poor relief. And how severe and dangerous was his remedy! Successful abolition would divide society, but an unsuccessful attempt to abolish would destroy it.[44]

Courtenay recommended cautious improvement and investigation instead of hasty denunciation. 'By such a course, we may preserve that honourable distinction of the Laws of England, by which *Starvation is illegal*, while we free them from the reproach of encouraging idleness and profligacy.' Since abolitionists hesitated to abolish, all could agree on immediate aims. 'Our difference then in truth affects very little the general direction of our course. Neither party is ready for abolition, both are desirous of reform, and both are content to acknowledge abolition as the ultimate and desirable object.'[45] But it was one thing to desire reform, and another to find proposals on which Parliament would agree.

[44] *Treatise on the Poor Laws*, pp. 15, 20.
[45] *Ibid.* pp. 161, 18.

271

VIII

Reform by Committee

1. *Parliament and the Poor Law*

In May 1816 Curwen announced in the House of Commons that he would move the appointment of a Select Committee to consider the Poor Law. His action interrupted, and in the event killed, a campaign for the humanitarian reform of workhouses and settlement which Sir Egerton Brydges had waged with a succession of bills since 1814.[1] The support of Whitbread, Romilly and others had brought Brydges close to success, but even before Curwen rose there were signs in the House that a more severe attack on the system was likely to come. In 1815 a debate on the Mendicity Committee's Report saw Lockhart castigating the Law as a perversion of nature and a cause of distress to the poor and of ruin to society. In the great debate on Agricultural Distress in February 1816 speaker after speaker included the Poor Law among the burdens depressing the agricultural interest; no one defended the system, and Brougham in his great speech described public relief as a 'cancer in the state' and demanded a process of abolition more sudden than Malthus's own. But Brougham was too busy or too indolent to proceed in the matter himself, and it was Curwen who sought the appointment of a Select Committee, having first discovered from Castlereagh that the government would not act.[2] Thus began an attempt within Parliament to overcome the usual clash of individual opinion

[1] On Brydges' campaign see *Parliamentary Debates*, XXVII, 562–3; XXVIII 95–7, 678–82 and appendix clxxvii–cxciv; XXXI, 221, 581–6; XXXIV, 587. For his unsuccessful attempt to revive it in 1817 see XXXV, 759–61.

[2] *Ibid.*, XXXIII, 1177; and see XXXI, 686, 1145–9 (on mendicity); XXXIII, *passim* (debate on distress); XXVII, 701 (references to Poor Law in debate on the Corn Law). The Reports from the Select Committees on Mendicity in the Metropolis (*Parliamentary Papers*, 1814–5, III (473) and 1816, V (396)) showed so much evidence

by the device of the committee, an attempt doomed to almost complete failure despite three years of intermittent effort.

Curwen's speech was notable for vehemence rather than lucidity. He agreed with Malthus that 'nothing less than a total change of system can cure the evil', but seemed less concerned to establish the point than to anticipate the Committee's work by recommending his own plan for a contributory National Benefit Society, to be run by some 14,000 local committees, a scheme which did not commend itself to anyone but its author. After an outspoken attack on the Poor Law from Lockhart, and an indignant defence by Brydges, the Committee was appointed; the session was nearly at its end, and the Committee could do no more than order the collection of returns for the years 1813–15.[3] When Curwen rose again in the next session to move its re-appointment he showed an almost hysterical alarm as he pleaded with 'the noble Lord in the blue ribbon' to win a greater victory than Waterloo by solving the problem of pauperism and saving the landed interest. But Castlereagh, the Lord in question, crushed hopes of government action: 'any notion of precipitate measures directed against the system could not be entertained', and the landed gentlemen should not delude themselves 'that in one day they could escape' from their burdens. The government would assist the Committee to find ways of improving the Poor Law— Castlereagh himself thought that professional assistant overseers and insistence on labour in return for relief would check abuses—but more drastic changes would not be supported.[4] In May the Prime Minister confirmed the government's attitude when he moved for the appointment of a Committee of the Lords, going out of his way to deplore abolitionist agitation as he did so.[5] The Cabinet would not be stampeded into extraordinary measures of relief, whether for rich or poor. With similar caution it had already rejected demands for loans to aid agriculturalists, and had produced instead only the modest Poor Employment Act of 1817, which appointed commissioners authorised to advance £1,750,000 in Exchequer Bills to parishes and other bodies

---

[3] *Parliamentary Debates*, XXXIV, 878–900. For Curwen's scheme see also *Sketch of a Plan by J. C. Curwen Esq.* (1817). R. Fellowes, *Thoughts* etc. (1817), pp. 32–3, thought it suitable only for small colliery towns; Malthus objected to its universality and compulsion in *Essay* (1826), II, 399–407.

[4] *Parliamentary Debates*, XXXV, 506–29; and compare 907–12 for Castlereagh's criticism of allowances but not of the whole Poor Law in a debate on petitions from Dorset.

[5] *Ibid.* XXXVI, 297–300, 1365.

---

of the duplicity of professional beggars that they probably strengthened abolitionist views; see Sir John Barrow's article in *Quarterly Review*, XIV (1815), 120–45. Smart, *Economic Annals of the Nineteenth Century*, 1801–20, pp. 512–34, summarizes the debate on agricultural distress.

for approved public works. In the debate on this Bill Charles Western, promoter of the 1815 Corn Law, complained that it gave agriculture no relief and Brougham fulminated against make-work schemes; Rose's comment that 'it might do good, and could not be prejudicial' was probably typical of moderate opinion towards so modest a measure.[6]

The Committee of 1817 produced a report but no bills, and in 181 Curwen complained that the Speech from the Throne included no reference to poor-law reform. Castlereagh, always glib, claimed that it would be 'improper' for the government to interfere while committees of the legislature were active. The Committee was then re-appointed, despite a long speech from Sir Francis Burdett in which the radical veteran predicted its labour would be in vain; he deplored attacks on the character of the labourers, claiming that they were still as independent in spirit as they had been 'when he was a boy, before the last war, . . . playing with the labourers before his father's house'. In the course of the debate Castlereagh openly rebuked Curwen for alleging internal dissension on the Committee, though John Calcraft supported Curwen in criticism of both government and Committee for inaction. By March, when the Poor Rate Returns were laid before the House, more members were displaying annoyance at delay in reform; Davies Gilbert called for a 'radical attack', and Sir Charles Monck claimed 'the country would not be satisfied unless the government came forward, and took under its charge some radical measures for the relief of the country from the intolerable evil of the poor laws'. But Frankland Lewis himself, the author of the abolitionist Report of 1817, replied that 'it was utterly impossible that any man in his senses could entertain such a wish as to get rid of the poor rates altogether'; the most that members could do was to 'set themselves against the system of the poor laws' by seeking checks against its expansion.[7] The die was cast. The government would not act, and the Commons Committee saw itself only as a source of suggestions for amendment, even though some of its members remained abolitionist in principle. Of course its piecemeal tinkering was despised by more ardent spirits; in May Brougham threatened to bring in a radical bill of his own, but when challenged to do so merely

[6] *Ibid.* XXXVI, 27–43, 569–71, 818–19; and see M. W. Flinn, 'The Poor Employment Act of 1817', *Econ. Hist. Review*, 2nd Series, XIV (1961), 82–92, for a general discussion of its significance. For an earlier plea for a loan of six million pounds, mainly to the middle classes, see A. Becket, *Public Prosperity* etc. (1813). The scheme had first been submitted to Pitt in 1792.

[7] *Parliamentary Debates*, XXXVII, 66, 151–5, 735–8. Davies Gilbert (under his former name of Giddy), had opposed Whitbread's Bill in 1807. John Calcraft (1765–1831) was a whig who became Wellington's paymaster-general, then resumed his whiggery in 1831 and committed suicide within a year, allegedly under the pressure of tory reproaches.

attacked 'the power which resisted, or the artifice which thwarted' the original purposes of the Committee. The object could be attained, he insisted, 'in spite of timid panic-struck alarmists, in spite of sceptical, speculative legislators, in spite of quibbling, subtle lawyers—in spite of those whom he was unwilling to name (Hear Hear!)'. Brougham's attack might have been more telling had it not appeared that 'the variety of his avocations' had prevented him attending recent meetings of the Committee.[8] Curwen had perhaps better grounds for resentment; by 1819 he was so thoroughly disillusioned that he opposed the re-appointment of the Committee and demanded some other relief for the landed interest, since poor-law reform was continually checked. He later insisted that the government was the villain in the tragedy:

> It may be more convenient for a weak, divided and unpopular administration to devolve their duties to a committee, and thereby screen themselves from the odium attending a total failure of their plans for relieving the country from the burthens that press so heavily on the community. . . . I think the blame has fallen unjustly on the Committee. Those to whom it is fairly attributable are the ministers of the crown.[9]

The fact that no ministers were present to hear his indictment no doubt increased his resentment.

By 1820 the episode of reform by committee was over, and the ineffective round of private parliamentary efforts began again. Certainly passions had been aroused in the House; it is more difficult to say whether party or factional divisions had helped to inhibit effective action. In 1822 Londonderry complimented the House on the absence of party alignments in debates on the Poor Law: 'it was a subject which had never been discussed with anything like party feeling'.[10] His observation was probably accurate, though we know too little of the composition and rationale of parties in that confused period to be certain. There were certainly political cross-currents muddying the pool—especially, perhaps, whenever Brougham raised his argumentative voice—but it is difficult to identify ideas and interests evident in the debate with even the vaguest party groupings. Dr. Johnson once alleged that Whigs were harsh towards the poor, but he himself liked Tories and pitied the indigent. The abolitionism of the *Edinburgh Review*, and of Brougham, Ricardo and the Benthamites, was by no means universal among Whigs or Radicals, while the paternalist Toryism of the *Quarterly*

[8] *Ibid.* XXXVIII, 894, 1001–2.
[9] *Ibid.* XXXIX, 402–8; XL, 465–6.
[10] *Ibid.* New Series, VII, 777. But compare Ricardo to Trower, 28 May 1819 (*Works*, VIII, 32): 'Why is not a more efficient measure proposed? The fact I believe is that no party in the House dare take upon themselves to propose or support any plan which may make them unpopular. This is one of the ill effects of party; public interest is neglected.'

Review cut little ice with abolitionist but undoubtedly Tory squires. It was only after 1834, when a government had committed itself on the question, that attitudes to the Poor Law became useful criteria in defining party. Before 1834 the debate on poor relief in Parliament has to be chronicled primarily in terms of individuals and their interests, prejudices and intellectual convictions.

2. *Facts and Findings*

The successive Committees of the House of Commons of 1816–19 laboured at three tasks: the collection of information on the system as it existed, the formulation of general principles for its reform, and the framing of concrete proposals to be brought before Parliament. The forceful but almost entirely negative Report of 1817 stands out as an isolated peak of achievement; it was not repudiated by later Committees (and was indeed reprinted in 1819) but its assertions were never fully substantiated, no coherent and comprehensive principles of relief were developed from them, and the Bills eventually brought to the House were a miscellaneous collection of mere palliatives together with one or two radical proposals. Only the least contentious of the clauses survived Parliamentary debate, and the legislative success of the Committees was therefore minimal. In April 1818 Rickman remarked that 'the Poor Law Commn. [sic] have proposed feeble Bills, and if I mistake not the symptoms, the leading members are annoyed and tired by the incessant applications of all possible parish officers and amateur magistrates; and besides much dissatisfied to find that in their own heads they can only find that they have found nothing effectual'.[11] The Bills were not quite as feeble as Rickman claimed—they would, for example, have abolished the allowance system—but the remnants which reached the statute book certainly were; and by 1819, if not earlier, the leading members of the Committee were ready to admit defeat. On all issues of importance Commons, Lords and the Committee itself had been too deeply divided to achieve more than minor, if not entirely negligible, reforms.

The fact-finding activities of the Commons Committees were desultory. An elaborate report on the Scottish system was obtained from the Church of Scotland, but left to speak for itself. The examination of thirty witnesses was reported in 1817, but only three thereafter. The statistics for 1813–15 were printed in 1818, together with those for 1748–50 (recently found behind the Speaker's chair), but no attempt was made to analyse them in detail. Thus the assertions of the 1817 Report were supported only by examples—inevitably at the time, since the

[11] O. Williams, *Life and Letters of John Rickman*, p. 204.

returns were not then available—and moreover by examples which could be thought representative only by those with abolitionist preconceptions. Spitalfields had long been a depressed area; five other metropolitan parishes mentioned had an unusual number of casual poor; Hindon's rates of fifty shillings were claimed by some to be caused by a liberal Parliamentary franchise; Birmingham and Coventry were suffering from industrial depression; Halstead, Essex, had a defunct woollen mill; Wombridge's mines had failed; eleven petitioning parishes in Leicestershire all seemed curiously overburdened with young children; and the area in West Wiltshire cited as a bad example of the allowance system seemed limited and exceptional.[12] S. W. Nicoll justly complained that 'the Committee, formed on a sudden, and meeting without a preconceived plan, has examined such witnesses as were offered to its attention, with little of a systematic or regulated course of proceedings', and pointed out that only an examination of average agricultural parishes and of the state of large towns before the peace could provide a proper basis for conclusions. T. P. Courtenay, himself a member of the Committee, remarked that all the extreme cases cited in the evidence could be 'traced to peculiar circumstances connected with war, commerce, or manufactures'.[13] The Committee certainly did not offer proof that the Poor Law in fact demoralised the poor, encouraged population and depressed wages, or that it inevitably culminated in the allowance system as a progressive social canker.

In questioning its witnesses the Committee frequently asked for confirmation that the system demoralised the poor. It did not always get it, and most witnesses stressed maladministration or special factors such as the failure of manufactures or the influx of the Irish as the chief problems; indeed the strongest criticism of the poor as 'saucy fellows' came from a witness who admitted that in his area wages were adequate, there was no unemployment, and the rates were not a great burden. The Lords Committee, asking different questions, received on the whole more satisfying answers; it certainly attempted a wider survey, calling prominent magistrates and Members of Parliament to give accounts of whole areas rather than isolated parishes.[14] These witnesses certainly produced evidence of distress and high expenditure, but often stressed the failure of manufactures, either urban or rural, as the main cause;

[12] The evidence is clearly set out in *Parliamentary Papers*, 1817, VI, Report of the Select Committee on the Poor Laws (462), pp. 31–168.
[13] S. W. Nicoll, *A Summary View* etc. (1818), p. 17; T. P. Courtenay, *A Treatise* etc. (1818), p. 10. J. H. Moggridge, a Monmouthshire magistrate, attacked the Committee's assumptions as well as its evidence in his *Remarks on the Report* etc. (1818).
[14] For evidence before the Lords Committee see *Parliamentary Papers*, 1818, V, Report of the Lords Committee on the Poor Laws (400), pp. 71–207.

rates were described as 'moderate' for whole counties, at least in view of prevailing economic conditions. Many of the Lords' questions were obviously intended to defend the principle of public relief from abolitionist criticism: a Coventry witness was asked to confirm that restriction of relief would incite a 'march on London', a Scotsman was found who was not enthusiastic about his country's voluntary system, and an abolitionist would have been hard pressed to answer a question asking for suggestions for improvements which 'might be made in the poor laws without infringing upon the spirit of the 43rd of Elizabeth'. Of course not all questions had such general overtones; in both committees some members persistently sought (and usually gained) support for practical proposals to appoint assistant overseers, to establish savings banks, or to amend the Law of Settlement. What to do with the Irish was clearly a pressing problem in London and the North, the Beadle of St. Giles even claiming that nineteen out of twenty of the parish's paupers were Irishmen. But whatever the preconceptions of the witnesses, remarkably few drastic reforms were suggested: one witness recommended a workhouse test, another hinted at less eligibility, and Vivian's reforms at Bushey were reported, but little was offered to either Committee as a clear-cut programme for radical improvement.

Witnesses before the Committees, pamphleteers and Members of Parliament were almost unanimous on one point, that allowances in aid of wages were common in both urban and agricultural areas. Most witnesses from towns regarded allowances as a temporary expedient in bad times, and regretted the necessity rather than the practice; the more severe criticism came from the country, for example in a strong *Memorial from the Magistrates of the County of Suffolk* printed as an appendix to the Commons Report. In pamphlets Bicheno attacked 'the Speenhamland system'; Burgoyne called it a 'perversion' of the Elizabethan Law; Davison complained that 'the invisible corporation of the parish buys its pensioners' ill-will'; Mills saw it as 'wretched and mischievous folly'; Vivian as 'ruinous' in practice, if worthy in intention; Ravenstone and the author of *The Oppressed Labourer* (1819) called it slavery, pure if not simple. The Rev. H. Wake, rector of Over Wallop, Herts, complained of victimisation by malicious farmers who forced down parish wages, drove up the poor rate, and impoverished the incumbent.[15] Such widespread lamentation suggests that allowances were indeed common and pernicious; nevertheless puzzles remain. In an argument which amounts to a vindication of the old Poor Law

[15] J. E. Bicheno, *An Inquiry* etc. (1817), p. 106; [M. Burgoyne], *A Statistical Account* etc. (1817), p. 4; J. Davison, *Considerations* etc. (1817), pp. 57–8; J. Mills, *The Simple Equation of Tithes* etc. (1817), p. 88; R. Vivian, *Thoughts* etc. (1817), p. 10; 'P. Ravenstone', *A Few Doubts* etc. (1821), p. 470; *The Oppressed Labourers* etc. (1819), pp. 1–8; H. Wake, *A Brief Statement* etc. (1818), *passim.* Further criticism

Mark Blaug has concluded that the allowance system did not depress wages, but merely subsidised earnings made inadequate by disguised unemployment in agricultural areas; that if it encouraged population it did so through decreasing mortality; that it did not adversely affect the productivity of labour; and that it is 'not obvious' that the system reduced rents. 'The Old Poor Law, with its use of outdoor relief to assist the underpaid and to relieve the unemployed was, in essence, a device for dealing with the problem of surplus labour in the lagging rural sector of a rapidly expanding but still underdeveloped economy. And considering the quality of social administration in the day, it was by no means an unenlightened policy.'[16] Thus 'the relatively higher level of relief per head in the so-called Speenhamland counties was due, not to the "snowball effect" of the Old Poor Law, but to the chronic unemployment and substandard wages typical of areas specialising in the production of wheat and lacking alternative opportunities in industry'; and Blaug has also argued that 'the Speenhamland system as such had generally disappeared by 1832, even in the South'. All that remained was a practice of paying 'modest' allowances to families with many children.[17] These conclusions are based on an analysis of evidence collected after 1820, and in particular on the findings of the Select Committee on Labourers' Wages of 1824 and of the Royal Commission of 1832–4; some at least of them would probably be confirmed by the little-known work of the Select Committee on Relief to the Able Bodied Poor of 1829.[18] This evidence is limited by a lack of precision in the

[16] M. Blaug, 'The Myth of the Old Poor Law and the Making of the New', Jnl. Econ. History, XXIII (1963), 176–7.

[17] M. Blaug, 'The Poor Law Report Re-examined', Jnl. Econ. History, XXIV (1964), 241–2, 231. The widespread practice of paying allowances in manufacturing areas in times of special distress, and more regular allowances in aid of wages in declining trades, must not be overlooked. The Webbs themselves remarked that 'it is not easy to discover, among the voluminous reports of the Assistant Commissioners, to what extent the Allowance System actually prevailed in 1833' (The Last Hundred Years, I. 61 n. 1).

[18] Parliamentary Papers, 1824, VI, Report of the Select Committee on the Wages of Labourers in Agriculture (392), and 1825, XIX, Abstract of Returns etc. (299); for analysis of the evidence see J. H. Clapham, The Early Railway Age, pp. 123–6, and M. Blaug, 'The Myth of the Old Poor Law etc.', Jnl. Econ. History, XXIII (1963), 59–60. Slaney's committee of 1828 decided that there was a real redundancy of labour but blamed the Poor Law for creating it; returns were received from only 38 parishes, but they were widely distributed. See Parliamentary Papers, 1828, IV, Report from the Select Committee on . . . the Employment or Relief of Able-bodied Persons etc. (494); 1829, XXI, Abstract of Returns etc. (52).

of allowances may be found (for example) in the works of Craufurd, Gourlay, Glover, Jerram, Nicoll, Sheffield, Copleston, Gray and Grahame; see also Parliamentary Debates, XXXV, 907–12, for remarks by Brydges, Castlereagh and Cochrane, and XXXIX, 402–6 for Curwen's strong indictment of allowances.

questions asked and in the answers given, but it is probably sufficient to establish that the practice of granting allowances in aid of wages diminished rather than expanded after 1820, and that relief on account of children was its central core. But it remains to be asked whether the 'system' was ever much more than that, even before 1820, and why it was so widely deplored and reprobated.

The first question may never be answered. Evidence offered by individuals in the first years of the peace suggests that allowances in aid of wages were almost universal in times of special distress, and that in some areas—mostly agricultural—they did become, or threaten to become, a permanent part of the local economic system. But these areas were relatively few, and fewer still show the system continuously in operation since the 1790s.[19] The question of scale is also important. In 1829 Bampton (Westmorland) and Whaddon (Bucks) were of about the same size, and both paid allowances to large families, but Bampton had only eleven able-bodied paupers and Whaddon forty-six, representing 1.8% and 8.4% of their respective populations; the economic and social significance of the same practice in the two parishes was doubtless very different. Perhaps allowances were common, systematic and continuous in the decades before 1820, but the case is not proven; it is perhaps more likely that post-war distress brought a drastic but temporary extension of a practice which had been limited and intermittent. Certainly contemporary alarm at the prospect of a permanent and progressive confusion of wages and relief is understandable in either case. If contemporary economic analysis was more inclined to see allowances as a cause rather than as a result of inadequate wages—though by no means with unanimity—Malthusian dogmatism was by no means the only conditioning influence. To modern minds allowances might seem an acceptable social service, but contemporaries could not see them in that light. The desire to see the labourer independent of public relief was a common point of agreement, the more deep-rooted because it seemed consistent with even violently opposed social and political philosophies. Old-fashioned paternalists, and many coldly rational employers, wanted the labourer to be dependent only on his social superiors; political economists sought his independence in a free economic system which alone could improve his situation in the long

[19] Thus the Select Committee of 1824 was told that expenditure on unemployed or partially employed labourers in the Hundred of Blything in Suffolk was never more than £6 per year between 1811 and 1815, but rose to £1,384 in 1816 and £3,536 in 1823 (*Parliamentary Papers*, 1824, VI (392), p. 58). For evidence on the recent (and temporary) adoption of allowances in Notts see J. D. Marshall, 'The Nottinghamshire Reformers etc.', *Econ. Hist. Review*, 2nd Series, XIII (1961), esp. pp. 386–92. But the Select Committee of 1824 certainly supported the increasingly fashionable view that the practice of paying allowances stemmed from the 1790's (*Report*, p. 5).

run; moralists wished him to be the guardian of his own virtue; and radicals deplored that he be dependent on any man, or any institution. One did not need to be an abolitionist to deplore allowances; indeed to defend them as anything but an unfortunate necessity a contemporary could find little but the illiberal economic authoritarianism of a Weyland, a doctrine as antipathetic to Cobbett as to Bishop Sumner. The existence of only a few examples of the allowance system in highly developed form was enough to excite an apprehension perhaps unwarranted by the facts; in 1817 men were alarmed by what might happen as much as by what in fact was happening.

When the returns of 1813–15 were published in 1818 the figures neither proved the abolitionist case nor obviously undermined it, and the annual series which began in 1821 was also more useful in illustrating assumptions than in testing them.[20] True, even a superficial glance at national averages might cast doubt on allegations of progressive pauperisation: total expenditure on relief in 1812–13 was £6,676,844, half as much again as in 1803, but by 1814–15 it had fallen to £5,418,846. (It then rose again to a peak of almost eight million in 1818, fell to below seven million by 1823, and did not begin to rise again until 1827.) Returns of pauper numbers in 1803 and 1813–15 were not strictly comparable, but as a proportion of total population there was no very great increase. Relief in terms of wheat was in fact less in 1812–13 than in 1803, and if it rose again in 1814–16 it began to fall in 1817.[21]

It was, however, local or regional experience of the Poor Law which influenced attitudes, and thus John Barton's carefully argued attempt to minimise the national problem was largely beside the point.[22] In 1813–15 the average rate in the pound may have been less than 3s. 3d. on property assessed for the Property Tax, but the Sussex rate was 7s. and Northumberland's only 1s. 7d. Expenditure on the poor averaged 12s. per head of population for the whole country in those three years, but in Sussex, Berkshire, Essex and Oxfordshire it was at least twice as great. The areas with high rates and high expenditure per head were, on the whole, those counties in the Midlands, South and East in which allowances in some form were found to be common by the Select Committee on Labourers' Wages of 1824. And there is no doubt that

[20] For a list of Parliamentary Papers containing Returns see the Bibliography. Especially useful are the Comparative Summary in 1818, XIX, Abridgement of the ... Returns (82), pp. 627–9, and 1830–31, XI, Returns on local Taxation 1748–1829 (52).

[21] Wheat prices from J. Marshall, *Statistics of the British Empire*, pp. 36–7, and compare p. 11 for an attempt to calculate pauper numbers.

[22] For Barton's quite searching analysis see his *Observations* etc. (1817), esp. pp. 56–9; for later analysis compare G. R. Porter, *The Progress of the Nation* etc. (1836 ed.) II. 356–64, and J. H. Clapham, *The Early Railway Age*, pp. 363–5.

281

the number of outdoor paupers had increased much more than workhouse inmates; if that implies an expansion of the allowance system, it should also be noted that by far the largest increase was in those relieved 'occasionally', suggesting that allowances had been extended as a temporary expedient rather than as a permanent system. In Berkshire itself there were few more 'permanent' than 'occasional' paupers.[23]

Evidence on the local incidence of heavy expenditure suggests that lamentations of ruin through progressing pauperism were inspired by severe pressure in certain primarily agricultural counties rather than by the national problem as a whole. In these areas the burden was relatively constant, with expenditure rising or falling more or less with the national average, though consistently above it; urban trends were usually very different, reflecting above all the state of local and national trade. Thus in Leeds £29,000 was spent on relief in 1813 and in 1820, but never as much in any other year before 1830, although the population doubled between 1811 and 1831. The panics of 1816 and 1825 temporarily forced Manchester's expenditure up 140 per cent and 70 per cent respectively, but there was no general trend of rising rates, and in fifteen years Nottingham's expenditure fluctuated wildly between seven and twenty-three thousand pounds, but the average of three relatively normal years, 1827–9, was lower than the comparable years 1814–16 despite a population increase of at least 50 per cent.[24] Whenever, in great trading and manufacturing towns, demand for relief suddenly swelled, there was always an obvious explanation in the state of trade, and an obvious remedy in its recovery, a remedy clearly in the interests of both rich and poor. There could be discontent over corruption and inefficiency in the administration of poor relief, but it was difficult to see the system itself as a major cause of distress. But in those rural areas in which high expenditure persisted it was always tempting to blame the Poor Law for creating the distress it was intended to relieve, and to see allowances in aid of wages as its essence.

3. *Principles and Bills*

Alarm at the apparent growth of the allowance system no doubt contributed to the generally favourable reception won by the abolitionist report of the Commons Committee of 1817, though it is more likely that its principles gained the support of committed abolitionists while its caution in practical proposals reassured the wary. Since almost everyone agreed that the Poor Law was imperfect, most could find at

[23] Calculated from the Observations printed in the 1818 Returns. Blaug prints a map of the so-called 'Speenhamland Counties'.

[24] J. Marshall, *Statistics of the British Empire*, pp. 40–41, prints a useful collection of urban statistics.

least one paragraph in the report to praise, although there was plenty of criticism of proposals included or omitted. But the Committee did not offer a clear principle of relief for a reformed Poor Law—mainly, no doubt, because it was intent on attacking the justification of the law itself—and critics were left to suggest their own. A surprising number of them offered quite explicit statements of a doctrine of less eligibility. In 1815 Clark insisted that 'parish relief should *never* place its objects in a better situation than those who support themselves without such relief'; Craig asked that overseers 'be sworn to admit only such relief as . . . would, in their opinion, maintain him [the pauper] in less affluence than a common labourer'; and Copleston asserted that 'by the nature of things [the pauper's] is a lower condition than any employment however menial—and it is an inversion of the order of things to make it the title to privileges of any kind'. It is perhaps surprising that the Committee did not adopt such a principle, since one of its members, Courtenay, suggested that overseers should 'endeavour to place the pauper in a condition, both as to income and comfort, always beneath that of other peasants and artisans, maintaining their own families; so that pauperism would always be a *descent* in the scale of Society', and Nicoll repeated the point even more succinctly: 'The parochial poor of any country, should subsist just so much worse than the industrious labouring poor, as to give no encouragement to pauperism'.[25] Such statements, extracted from their contexts, certainly appear to anticipate the principles of 1834. But no one, apart from Bentham, grasped the theoretical significance of the principle in relation to the abolitionist case; moreover it remained a merely abstract exhortation until embodied in some method of application, and the workhouse test was still unfashionable. Above all it was still stated mainly as an adjunct to moral discrimination, to assist the separation of sheep from goats. Thus Fellowes insisted on a moral 'distinction', Davison on a 'test of worth', Hanning on the exclusion of the wilfully idle, Bicheno on refusal of relief to the 'immoral', and Jerram would relieve only 'unavoidable' indigence.[26] The author of *A Letter to . . . Castlereagh* would relieve

[25] W. Clark, *Thoughts* etc. (1815), p. 19; J. Craig, *Elements* etc. (1814), p. 297; E. Copleston, *A Second Letter* etc. (1819), p. 99; T. P. Courtenay, *Copy of a Letter* etc. (1817), p. 20; S. W. Nicoll, *A Summary View* etc. (1818), p. 89. Compare also [S. Parr], *Considerations* etc. (1817), p. 51: 'none ought, by parochial relief, to be placed, in the scale of comforts, upon an equality with the frugal and industrious poor.' Bentham had approached Parr for support in 1797, and may have influenced this statement.

[26] R. Fellowes, *Thoughts* etc. p. 34; J. Davison, *Considerations* etc. (1817), p. 24; W. Hanning, *A Letter* etc. (1818), pp. 24–5; J. E. Bicheno, *An Inquiry* etc. pp. 138–41; C. Jerram, *Considerations* etc. (1818), p. 56. The 1817 *Report* itself insisted on moral discrimination, quoting Townsend in support (p. 21); for reiteration of the point see the 1819 *Report*, p. 4. For one isolated suggestion that less eligibility be

only church-goers; the stricter author of *A Letter to ... Curwen* went further and demanded a positive recommendation from the clergyman as a qualification for relief. The desire to exclude the unworthy from relief was strong; the notion of providing relief only on such terms that none but the truly necessitous would seek it—the essence of less eligibility—was usually confused with it. The failure of the Commons Committee to produce a clear principle as the basis for its proposals is therefore understandable.

The aim of most reformers in these post-war years was nevertheless the restriction of relief. They sought it not by an apparently simple administrative rule, such as less eligibility, but by the exclusion of certain classes from relief, or the prohibition of certain types of aid by immediate partial abolition as distinct from Malthus's plan for gradual total abolition. Davison, and many others, would simply have banned relief to the able-bodied, while the author of *Hints* etc. (1819) would have refused it to all under the age of thirty, to discourage marriage. On Castlereagh's suggestion the House of Commons tried to be quite systematic in its approach, distinguishing between various classes of paupers and recommending the relief proper to each class. For the aged and infirm, the Report rather surprisingly suggested that reformed work-houses might be the most suitable device, but left the decision to the discretion of parishes.[27] But what should be done with the able-bodied? According to the Committee, relief in money was illegal, and only employment was authorised by the Elizabethan acts. But employment, even if legal, was of course anathema to influential members of the Committee, who urged that it be abandoned as soon as the existing distress eased; according to Brydges the Committee was unanimous in deploring relief in money to idle men, but his plea for public employment won only a grudging approval of parish farms and work on roads. (He, of course, would never recommend employment in work-houses.)[28] But even if relief to the able-bodied was restricted to employment—and that discouraged—there remained one great problem relief in aid of children. To modern minds this might seem the most easily justified of all public assistance; to early Malthusians, however, it was the most alarming, and it is arguable that it was always the kernel of the allowance system since even depressed wages were usually sufficient for single men. The Report asserted that allowances in aid of

[27] *Report*, pp. 20–21.
[28] E. Brydges, *Arguments* etc. (1817), p. 7.

combined with a workhouse test see Lord Sheffield's *Remarks* etc. (1819), p. 43, and compare his *Observations* etc. (1818). Carlyle's famous remark that less eligibility was a principle known to all rat-catchers was a (perhaps pardonable) exaggeration.

children were unjust to ratepayers, and to the industrious poor by giving the idle equal benefits; and that such relief 'familiarised the labourer to a dependence on the parish' and 'swelled the amount of the assessment to a degree that makes it impossible to ascertain how much should be considered as relief, properly speaking, and how much as wages'. According to Courtenay, the Committee's views on alternatives were divided.

Curwen urged his contributory scheme, and Colonel Thomas Wood and William Smith suggested relief in food rather than money, but Sturges Bourne and Brand successfully imposed their view that money relief to children was as illegal as that to able-bodied adults, and that therefore children were only entitled to maintenance and education in institutions, and not at home.[29]

There was, of course, much criticism of the administrative structure of the Poor Law in these years. Some writers demanded quite drastic reforms, such as the establishment of a county administration, control by 'government officials', or elaborate visiting schemes, though the traditional remedies of incorporation or increased powers for magistrates still won support.[30] Members of the Commons Committee agreed that voluntary overseers were too often inefficient, and most followed Huskisson in also deploring the generosity of magistrates' orders; they shared the common desire to interest the gentry in administration, but wanted them to act as part of the system and not as a quasi-judicial irritant to it. It is clear that the Committee did not think radical change necessary or feasible, and its proposals were modest: the appointment of salaried permanent 'assistant overseers', and the reform of vestries to make them more amenable to gentle influence. In March 1818 a Parish Vestries Bill making voting power in vestries depend on the amount of rates paid was introduced into the Commons and was passed quite promptly, although Calcraft opposed it as an infringement of the rights of the poor and Curwen thought it unnecessary, since the plebs would defer to upper-class vestrymen if only the upper classes would attend vestry meetings. Sturges Bourne defended the reform as an approach to the Scottish system, and claimed that more gentlemen would go to

[29] T. P. Courtenay, *Copy of a Letter* etc. pp. 4–6, and compare his *Treatise* etc. (1818), pp. 49–57.

[30] C. G. Craufurd, *Observations* etc. p. 49, proposed a provincial administration, but compare his *A Supplementary Section* etc. (1817), p. 24, where only county supervision of parishes was sought. Visiting was urged by W. Clarkson, *An Inquiry* etc. (1816), p. 63; and government officers to supervise overseers were proposed in 'A Countryman', *A Letter* etc. (1820), p. 19. [M. Burgoyne], *A Statistical Account* etc. (1817) was more traditional in seeking greater powers for magistrates (p. 6), but also suggested salaried assistant overseers (p. 7), as did several other writers; for opposition to them see however *Hints* etc. (1819), p. 9, and *A Letter to . . . Castlereagh* etc. (1818), p. 17.

vestry meetings if they were no longer in danger of being clamorously voted down. The Bill was scarcely controversial, at least among gentlemen; it had lasting importance in the history of local government, but hardly amounted to a major change in the Poor Law.[31]

Sturges Bourne's Poor Laws Amendment Bill, introduced on the same day, was more elaborate and ambitious, and had a very stormy passage. Its principal clauses permitted the appointment of salaried assistant overseers; allowed large parishes to appoint committees—'select vestries'—to supervise relief, limiting magistrates' powers; empowered parishes to rent allotments to labourers, to relieve the vicious with loans rather than gifts, to rate owners rather than occupiers of urban tenements, and to remove Irish to the seaport nearest their homes; and—most controversial of all—forbade allowances in aid of children, compelling parishes to employ children rather than relieve their parents. The Bill was thus a farrago of major and minor changes in administration and methods of relief, and Sturges Bourne was to suffer much frustration as clause after clause was assailed from different points of view.

The clause most bitterly criticised was that concerning relief for children. With the support of Courtenay and Colonel Wood it passed the Commons, despite protests from Curwen and Calcraft that it assumed low wages would continue and did nothing to raise them, and a Malthusian objection from Lamb that it would encourage births since it obliged parishes and not parents to maintain children. But the Lords, scrupulous to preserve the sanctity of family bonds, rejected it.[32] Bourne was most indignant, even alleging a constitutional impropriety; the 1819 Report of the Commons Committee was almost entirely a defence of the principle involved, and in March 1819 a new Poor Rates Misapplication Bill re-introduced the offending clause and added a simple affirmation that all relief to able-bodied men in employment was illegal. This Bill probably represented the high point of abolitionism: all allowances of money in aid of inadequate wages or large families were to be swept away, and poor-law authorities could henceforth offer money only to the impotent, or employment to the able-bodied. Such a measure was, inevitably, too liberal for some critics and too harsh for others. Mansfield, Primrose, Lord Milton, Moore and (above all) Curwen attacked it as intolerably unjust to the virtuous poor; to Philips, Shepherd and other abolitionists the clause guaranteeing maintenance to all present and future children of the

---

[31] *Parliamentary Debates*, XXXVII, 1055–7; XXXVIII, 573–5. Lord Sheffield thought the Bill too mild in its proposals; for an account of his long struggle with the 'low ignorant persons' running the Fletching vestry see his *Observations* etc. pp. 8–19.

[32] *Parliamentary Debates*, XXXVII, 1055–7; XXXVIII, 575–7, 915–16.

poor—even if not the maintenance they desired—was a sin against economic truth. Sir James Mackintosh complained that the Bill would 'create foundling hospitals in every parish'. Ricardo predicted ruinous expense when pauper children grew to manhood, asserted that if 'parents felt assured that an asylum would be provided for their children . . . there would then be no check to that increase of population which was so apt to take place among the labouring classes', and claimed that even if cessation of cash allowances raised wages 'they would still be no more than the wages of a single man'. Courtenay, on the other hand, thought the Bill a fair compromise between refusing relief to children altogether and paying it in allowances, and enough Members shared his views for the Bill to be passed by 69 votes to 46.[33] But again the Lords quashed it, the Prime Minister having the last fatal word in a heated debate. The measure was of 'doubtful utility'; it was 'very problematical'; and he was suspicious of schemes which would cost more initially and merely promised future economy. It would be expensive to rear and employ children away from their parents: 'Let economy be the first result, and he should be disposed to pay more attention to it'.[34] Virtually all speakers, in Commons and Lords, concentrated their attention on relief for children rather than adults, perhaps with good reason. The attempt to destroy allowances by removing the children on whose behalf they were paid—a scheme as drastic as any adopted in 1834—failed to reach the statute book, and Sturges Bourne had to be satisfied with the remnants of his Poor Laws Amendment Bill, the select vestries and assistant overseers; they were left to administer the Poor Law with no major new injunctions concerning principles of relief.

If the Commons Committee hesitated to attack directly the localism inherent in the administration of relief it nevertheless sought reforms in the Law of Settlement and the system of rating. There continued to be some demand for a national rate, and also for a drastic relaxation of settlement restrictions, even if few faced the logical conclusion of such arguments, a national administration. The Committee admitted that a national rate would equalise the burden geographically, but insisted (like Malthus) that only local financial responsibility could prevent undue extravagance. It rejected a suggestion that employers be rated in proportion to their labourers, and rejected also the rating of personal incomes, since it would involve 'inquisitions' tolerable only in a great war. For a time the Committee approved the proposal to set a limit to the total rate raised, the old scheme Bentham had rejected as the

[33] *Parliamentary Papers*, 1819, II, Report from the Committee on the Poor Laws (529); *Parliamentary Debates*, XXXIX, 400–414, 1157–9; XL, 455–72, 1125–9.
[34] *Parliamentary Debates*, XL. 1514–15.

Limited Provision Plan and which Nicoll ridiculed with a question: 'Are the poor to starve in January, that they may feast in December?' The scheme was not brought before Parliament, and the only rating reform achieved was the assessment of owners rather than occupiers of tenements, a change sought earlier in a local bill from Birmingham.[35]

A Bill on Settlement was, however, brought forward. Criticism of the Law of Settlement was almost universal, and only a handful of writers—such as Fellowes, Lord Sheffield and Sydney Smith—defended the principle and deplored relaxation of the law. Many thought the law harsh; most agreed it was obscure, inconvenient and expensive in its encouragement to litigation. Adam Smith and all his followers were ready to offer good theoretical support for Craufurd's simple principle, that 'where the tree falls, there should it lie'. But how could settlement be abolished while local financial responsibility remained? Craig had suggested an answer—'if perfect equality were established all over the kingdom; if the poor received everywhere a maintenance inferior to that of the common labourer, and no where anything more, there could be no inducement . . . to prefer one place of residence to another, and the Law of Settlement might be safely repealed'—but this would have required uniform national administration.[36] The Committee could see no middle way, and satisfied itself that simplification was the only practicable aim, attractive though abolition might be. It proposed, therefore, that settlement by tenancy, by serving an office, by hiring and service and by apprenticeship should be abolished, and settlement by three years residence established. Settlement by residence was a popular proposal in the country, but anathema to the towns. Most towns would welcome the end of settlement by renting a tenement, but what use was its repeal if residence became a ground? Defenders of the manufacturing interest were not slow to complain. More disinterested criticism came from Nicoll, who questioned the common assumption that residence was a simple ground, preventing litigation. If the period specified were short, it could easily be ascertained but the temptation

[35] S. W. Nicoll, *A Summary View* etc. p. 51; and compare T. P. Courtenay, *Treatise* etc. pp. 21–30. Clarkson, Burgoyne and the author of *A Letter addressed to . . . Curwen* (1817) asked for a national rate; Fellowes, Nicoll, and the 1817 *Report* argued against. Craufurd, Mills, Parr, Slaney, Preston, 'A Countryman' and the author of *Observations upon the Report* etc. (1818) called for various forms of property tax (the last offering a geometrical demonstration of the law of gravity applied to progressive taxation); for Burrell's argument that fundholders should not be taxed see *Parliamentary Debates*, XXXV, 910. Curwen and Hanning proposed rates in proportion to pay-roll. An upper limit to the rates was urged by Curwen, Sheffield and Malthus but opposed by Jerram as well as by Nicoll and Courtenay.
[36] J. Craig, *Elements* etc. p. 300.

to short hiring and a war against cottages would be great; if the period were longer, it could not be easily ascertained.[37]

Sturges Bourne introduced his Settlement Bill in April 1818 with an eloquent attack on settlement in general and a carefully reasoned plea for residence as the most effectual reform; Romilly was equally eloquent in support, stressing the inhumanity of the existing Law, but Monck feared an increase in litigation—if residence became the only ground of settlement who would relieve a man who had never lived in any parish for three years at a time?[38] The Bill lapsed with the end of the session, and when Sturges Bourne re-introduced it in March 1819 opposition had increased. Curwen, Frankland Lewis, Huskisson, Canning and Lord Milton all supported him, but Atkyns, General Gascoyne, Lamb and Mildmay predicted a great increase in litigation, and Phillips spoke out for the manufacturing towns. If a manufacture failed, it was surely cruelty to tie the workmen to the town for ever. Such sophistical arguments for retaining the power to remove coincided in effect with the economic argument for total abolition of settlement. Let labour be free altogether, proclaimed Western and Colonel Wood. Why, asked Western, could labourers not move freely? Because of parochial relief? Then abolish the Poor Law altogether, instead of merely tinkering with settlement. The Bill was lost, killed by the general fear of innovation in such matters rather than by the force of any specific arguments against it.[39] And the Commons Committee was, by this time, a spent force. Asked, in 1819, what further proposals it had in mind, Frankland Lewis replied that 'such a division of sentiment at present prevailed, that it seemed hopeless to begin; and those who had most devoted their time to the subject, were, perhaps, least disposed to act with precipitation'.[40]

4. *George Rose's Bank Bubble*

The unhappy legislative ventures of the Committee were not the only occasions for debate on the relief of poverty in Parliament in these

[37] S. W. Nicoll, *A Summary View* etc. pp. 73–81; and compare H. Philpotts, *A Letter to . . . Sturges Bourne* etc. (1819), *passim*. Davison, Jerram and many witnesses before both Lords and Commons Committees urged residence as grounds for settlement; J. H. Moggridge, *Remarks* etc. (1818), pp. 21–3 expressed urban opposition. Brydges failed to persuade the Committee to forbid removals before settlement was adjudicated, though his proposal was supported by Blakemore and others.
[38] *Parliamentary Debates*, XXXVIII, 420–6.
[39] *Ibid.*, XXXIX, 1153–6, 1416–7; XL, 284–6. See also the 1819 *Report* for insistence that settlement was a vital question. A minor act passed later in the year extended the period of renting a tenement as grounds for settlement from forty days to twelve months, a small triumph for urban interests.
[40] *Parliamentary Debates*, XXXIX, 1417.

years, and George Rose's successful campaign for an act to encourage banks for savings should certainly be included in an account of Parliamentary proceedings on the subject. Savings banks aroused expectations comparable with the earlier passion for contributory schemes as an alternative to the Poor Law; if not quite capable of replacing the existing system they might, according to their champions, effectively check the spread of pauperism and perhaps even prepare the way for abolition of the Poor Law. But savings banks had their critics as well as apologists, and Rose's proposals of 1816 and 1817 aroused a wideranging debate on relief and self-help, especially as his Bills included a clause granting depositors certain privileges in poor relief.[41]

There had been, in earlier decades, many schemes for the provision of safe places of deposit for the pittances of the poor, but the post-war discussion was inspired mainly by Scottish experiments, especially Duncan's parish bank founded at Ruthwell in 1810 and the savings bank established in Edinburgh in 1814. Duncan's bank resembled a friendly society in its self-government and its system of special rewards for frugality; the Edinburgh bankers—with whom Duncan waged a long verbal battle—merely provided facilities for deposit as an exercise in philanthropy.[42] By 1817 many banks of various types had been founded in both Scotland and England, though not without dispute on the best methods of organisation. Rose, Bernard, Colquhoun, Malthus, Ricardo, Wilberforce and Vansittart were all trustees of a bank founded in London in 1816, and others had equally eminent sponsors.[43] It was easy to see the savings bank as an almost ideal aid to self-help. Duncan stressed that the rich could by this means assist the poor 'without running the risk of aiding them to their ruin'; Bowles claimed also an educational significance, since 'every walk to such a Bank will confirm Resolution and invigorate Virtue'.[44] It is no coincidence that many champions were outspoken critics of the Poor Law, anxious to escape

[41] H. O. Horne, *A History of Savings Banks* (1947) discusses this period; see also A. Scratchley, *A Practical Treatise on Savings Banks* (1860); W. Lewins, *A History of Banks for Savings* (1866); and (on the earliest ventures) Barber Beaumont, *An Essay on Provident or Parish Banks* (1816).

[42] On Duncan's banks see S. Hall, *Dr. Duncan of Ruthwell* (1910), and Duncan's own *Essay* etc. (1815, 1816), *A Letter* etc. (1819), and his evidence before the 1819 Committee, pp. 11–21.

[43] Ricardo discussed savings banks at length in his correspondence with Trower (*Works*, VII. *passim*). On the London bank and others of the time see J. Hume, *An Account* etc. (1816); C. Taylor, *A Summary Account* etc. (1816); J. Haygarth, *An Explanation* etc. (1816); H. Twiss, *A Tract on Savings Banks* (1816); J. Bowles, *Reasons* etc. (1817); and Rose's own *Observations on Banks for Savings* (1816). *Hints towards the Formation of a Society* etc. (1812–16) showed a strong Malthusian influence on the founders of a bank at Bristol.

[44] J. Duncan, *An Essay* etc. (1816), p. 9; J. Bowles, *Reasons* etc., p. 9.

the abolitionist dilemma by finding a totally unexceptionable form of philanthropy. Nicoll even hoped that a new path to abolition had been found:

> In every new disciple of the Savings Bank I see at least two apostates from the Poor Rate, and in fifteen or twenty years there is no reason to doubt that the inherent and progressive principle of the Savings Bank will have not only stopped the progress but will have entirely routed the influence of its antagonist, the Parish Rate. Next to the Church, I would teach the young the road to the Savings Bank.[45]

Malthus was, as usual, less optimistic: savings banks were 'the best' of the aids proposed for the poor, and could work wonders in a 'natural' state of society, but with the poor already dependent on the rates 'savings banks cannot be considered in the light of substitutes'. Of course if the gradual abolition of the Poor Law could only begin, then the savings bank could assist the process and 'receive a most powerful aid in return'. Others, including Rose himself, thought that Malthus quite under-estimated the reformative powers of the banks, and lauded them as an instrument for the prevention of pauperism, an altogether higher aim than mere relief. Rose claimed that a habit of saving would prevent improvident marriage, 'an attainment that every man who has the good of his country at heart must certainly wish for, without going the length of Mr. Malthus'. Professor Christian added ambition to the list of wholesome fruits: he had seen, in Leeds and Manchester, mansions with 'large plate glass windows and mahogany doors' owned by men who had begun life as mere clerks. 'Happy the country where such instances of talents and industry abound', and it would be happier still if saving and enterprise could be made universal. Saving was the way to honest riches, as well as the barrier against culpable indigence, as countless earnest tracts assured the poor in the following decades.[46]

How feeble in comparison seemed those darlings of yester-year, the humble friendly societies; their aim was simply security, not the just reward of worthy ambition. As Davis put it, they were not in fact consistent with the general design of encouraging saving. 'Our desire is, that every man, by timely saving, may enjoy the fruits of his *own* industry, when his wants shall require; but clubs are a sort of benevolent lottery.' Davison linked this preference for complete economic individualism with abolitionist theory by offering two principles, '*that*

[45] S. W. Nicoll, *A Summary View* etc. p. 102.
[46] Malthus, *Essay* (1826), II. 407–10; G. Rose, *Observations* etc. p. 23; E. Christian, *A Plan* etc. (1816), pp. iii–iv. For examples of later exhortation see [S. Hobson], *Pray, which is the way to the Savings Bank?* (1836), and S. G. Osborne, *The Savings Bank: some particulars of the life and death of 'Old Rainy Day', a lover of funerals* etc. (1836?).

every man should work for himself, which has been rudely discountenanced by the practice of the Poor Laws; and . . . *that every man should save for himself*, an axiom which benefit clubs, contributed parochial funds, and some other plans, trample underfoot'. Individual reward should be exactly proportional to individual virtue, a principle not to be compromised by attempts at co-operative insurance. To these arguments the enthusiasts for banks added all the old objections to friendly societies: their uncertainty, their conviviality, their democracy and—most alarming of all in years of political tension—their potentialities for subversion.[47]

Despite the plausibility of the onslaught, the humble benefit club retained some champions. The Rev. Richard Vivian, benevolent dictator to the poor of his parish of Bushey, noted that 'almost all the rank and fortune of the country were forming into committees, for the purpose of bringing forward savings banks', but warned them that their hopes might be disappointed. Savings brought no real security, since a long illness could exhaust them; they brought temptation to later extravagance in 'unfounded projects' and 'wanton expenses'; and even if men did delay marriage until they had saved, this did not mean that they would not sire bastards in the meantime. 'The number of illegitimate children is in proportion to the number of bachelors', Vivian confidently if sadly asserted. Above all, savings banks were of no use to the really poor. 'The truth is, savings banks are not calculated for the lowest and most numerous bulk of the community'; at best they could' lift a little higher them who were not already very low'. By all means encourage them as a superstructure raised on a firm base of security by insurance, but, first establish that base by improving and extending friendly societies.[48]

In the long run the balance of opinion among the philanthropic was in favour of encouraging both institutions, enabling them to fulfil, side by side, their rather different functions.[49] It was also in favour of

[47] W. Davis, *Friendly Advice* etc. (4th ed. 1817), p. 19; J. Davison, *Considerations* etc. (1817), pp. 18–19. Christian, Bayley, Fellowes, Jerram and Copleston all made comparisons unfavourable to friendly societies, which were also criticised in *The Philanthropist*, IV (1814), pp. 1–17, and very strongly by Rickman in the *Quarterly Review*, XVIII (1818), pp. 277–8. Compare Rickman's remark on Peterloo: 'It is singular that the most likely to be questioned part of the poor law review, the reprobation of friendly societies, should so soon have found ample justification at Manchester, where the lower order of human society is rotten to the core' (O. Williams, *Life and Letters of John Rickman* p. 206). Davis' book is an extreme example of the moralism of savings bank propaganda; by his standards Eden's heroine Anne Strudwick was an extravagant idler.

[48] R. Vivian, *A Letter* etc. (1816), pp. 7, 17, 13–14; and compare J. Barton, *Observations* etc. pp. 72–9, and J. W. Cunningham, *A Few Observations* etc. (1817).

[49] Thus Taylor, Twiss, Ashdowne, Sheffield, Nicoll and Sumner approved both, though with varying emphases; for an ingenious plan to combine their virtues in one institution see J. Woodrow, *Remarks* etc. (1818).

leaving both institutions in private hands, despite plans from Slaney, Nicoll and others for government or parish banks. The gentlemen of Edinburgh were very averse to any government regulation, let alone competition, claiming that an act on the matter could not fail to insult and therefore deter the philanthropists involved. But Rose was convinced that some protection and control were essential, and in April 1816 he sought leave to introduce a bill.[50] The House warmed to his praise of savings banks and his predictions for a rosy future for the labourers as they benefited from the new institutions, but when the Bill itself appeared this mood of benevolent optimism was quickly tempered. Rose sought to require all Trustees to enrol themselves and to deposit the rules of their banks with the Quarter Sessions; all officers handling money would be required to give security. Moreover funds were to be deposited with the Bank of England on account of the Commissioners for the reduction of the National Debt, the banks receiving in return interest of £4 11s. 3d. per cent, a yield appreciably above that of consols. Deposits of up to £30 in a savings bank would not debar a man from receiving parish relief, despite the law and usage refusing relief to men of property. The last two clauses were the cause of contention; Curwen might attack the whole Bill as 'not a feather in the scale of our difficulties', and Monck claim that the requirement to register was 'degrading' to philanthropic gentlemen, but others who approved of savings banks yet jibbed at subsidising them at public expense, and at extending the sphere of relief beyond the completely indigent. Thus Western 'objected to the innovation to be introduced by giving parish relief to persons not absolutely incapable of supporting themselves', and Philips predicted that relief would be regarded as 'less degrading than ever'. General Thornton led the attack against the high rate of interest; Hume was to campaign against it throughout the 1820's. But Huskisson defended the Bill, claiming that 'if the poor man thought that his small savings were to be swallowed up by the first fit of sickness, he would be entirely disheartened from saving at all. The case might be different if the Poor Laws had never existed; but after having given a bounty on improvidence . . . in order to produce good effects it was necessary to incur a present charge by way of encouragement'. Rose did not succeed in passing his Bill until 1817, when Wilberforce and the Government helped him to overcome opposition. It required frequent amendment in the following years.[51]

---

[50] *Parliamentary Debates*, XXXIII, 841–4. On the passing of the Act see H. O. Horne, *A History of Savings Banks*, chap. V.
[51] *Parliamentary Debates*, XXXIV, 515–6; XXXV, 222–6, 348, 1265; XXXVI, 680–3, 833, 1278.

Rose's Act, and savings banks in general, were much criticised by political radicals and by those who thought that drastic measures were required to remove burdens from the poor and to relieve their distress. Cobbett was outspoken on the subject, making great play with Rose's enjoyment of a government pension. The Act, claimed the radicals, was an artful device for getting the poor to pay off the national debt, or an even more artful one for making them fundholders and thereby ensuring their allegiance to the existing system. This was the truth, according to Cobbett, about 'Old George Rose's Savings Bank Bubble'.[52]

Despite such criticism, the cause flourished. Between 1817 and 1820 some 209 new banks were founded, and by 1830 a total of 480 banks held funds of £14,616,936 in the names of 427,830 depositors. This was indeed evidence of prodigious thrift, but critics were proved right in one thing at least: the ordinary labourer was not the man with a surplus to invest. The evidence we have of the social class of depositors in these years suggests strongly that domestic servants were in a majority, that artisans were well represented, and that many accounts were in the names of children; but labourers were not even a significant minority.[53] This was as Vivian predicted, and his claim that savings banks could be the top of a useful pyramid of which friendly societies were the base was also vindicated. The labourers as a class remained true to their clubs, and it is club membership, and not savings bank deposits, which provide most evidence of the activities of the poor to help themselves. Although accurate estimates are lacking, it is likely that membership of friendly societies of one sort or another totalled nearly a million by 1818.[54] Prophets of progressive pauperisation might have noted—but did not— that there were as many clubmen in the land as paupers.

[52] H. O. Horne, *A History of Savings Banks*, pp. 75–6, quotes Cobbett's remarks, and compare R. Gourlay, *The Village System*, p. 19.

[53] On deposits and depositors compare H. O. Horne, *A History of Savings Banks*, appendix II; J. H. Clapham, *The Early Railway Age*, p. 592; N. J. Smelser, *Social Change in the Industrial Revolution* (1959); A. Fishlow, 'The Trustee Savings Banks 1817–1861', *Jnl. Econ. History*, XXI (1961), 26–40; and J. Tidd Pratt, *A Summary of Savings Banks* etc. (1846).

[54] J. H. Clapham, *The Early Railway Age*, pp. 296–7. C. Ansell, *A Treatise on Friendly Societies* (1835), p. 136 estimated one million members in 1835; P. H. J. H. Gosden, in *The Friendly Societies in England 1815–75* (1961), p. 16, accepts the estimate of 925,429 in 1818.

IX

<><><><><><><><><><><><><><><><><><><><><><><><><><><><><><><><><><><><><><><><><><><><><><>

From Abolition to Amendment

<><><><><><><><><><><><><><><><><><><><><><><><><><><><><><><><><><><><><><><><><><><><><><>

1. Legislative Impotence Continues

THE fears expressed in 1817 that pauperism was a social cancer threatening rents, wealth and society itself with extinction were allayed if not dispelled after 1820. Economic conditions continued to be unsettled, with periods of progress interrupted by sudden depressions, and the landed interest remained convinced that its straits were dire; but the extreme and universal distress of 1816–18 did not return. Expenditure on poor relief fluctuated, showing a steady rise only in the last years of the decade, and never returning to the peak total of 1818. Since population increased by more than two million between 1821 and 1831, expenditure per head was lower than before, and the argument that pauperism was rapidly and inevitably progressive hardly remained convincing. But it could still be asserted that expenditure on relief was shamefully high, and its effects crushing as a burden on the landed interest and scandalous in relation to the poor themselves.[1] If the sense of impending doom became less evident in the debate, it was replaced by an increasing exasperation at the continued failure to remodel the system. It was largely an impotent exasperation, at least at the national level. The Government did not act before 1832, the few Select Committees appointed on aspects of the Poor Law did little more than repeat complaints already commonplace, and private reformers failed to achieve more than minor alterations in the law.

---

[1] For recognition that the burden of relief was not increasing rapidly see G. Ensor, *The Poor and their Relief* (1823), pp. 192–200; W. Playfair, *A Letter on Agricultural Distress* (1822); and J. Lowe, *The Present State of England* etc. (1822), pp. 193–7. In 1827 Hume argued forcefully that the landed interest did not suffer unduly from the rates (*Parliamentary Debates*, New Series, XVII. 98).

Decisive action came only with the 'labourers' revolt' of 1830 and the accession to power of a government committed to undertake some settlement of national problems. There were, nevertheless, important developments in this decade, in the debate and in practice. The centre of the post-war discussion had been abolitionism and the Malthusian onslaught on the Poor Law; after 1820 wholesale rejection of the system ceased to be so fashionable. There was more questioning of abolitionist assumptions, not only by the anti-Malthusians but also by disciples who were becoming selective in their acceptance of Malthus's teachings. And, in local experiments, a small but ultimately influential band of local reformers sought a system of relief which would not be open to the objections abolitionists made against the Poor Law as a whole. Their efforts were successful enough to gain endorsement by the Royal Commission of 1832–4, and the new Poor Law was in part these purely local systems writ large. It would be crude but not altogether inaccurate to attribute to the 1820's a movement from the ideal of abolition to the ideal of reform, provided it is remembered that the Act of 1834 was a new beginning as well as the culmination of a search.

The conflict between these two ideals can be seen in 1821–2 in the Parliamentary debate on two important schemes. In 1821 James Scarlett (later Lord Abinger) introduced a bill clearly intended to approach abolition as closely as possible; he sought a maximum on the rates, an immediate end to relief for the able-bodied, and the prohibition of all removals. The bill was a blunt legislative instrument indeed, and a poorly drafted one to come from so eminent a lawyer. The Government greeted it coldly, as did Sturges Bourne, and Scarlett met defeat; in 1822 he returned to the attack with a simpler measure directed only against relief for the able-bodied, and his attack on settlement restrictions was as able and forceful as any made in the House. He appealed equally to economic theory and to humanitarian sentiment in rejecting the whole system as a curse to both the rich and the poor, and left no doubt at all about his sincerity. But few other Members could accept such a clear-cut and simple analysis of the problem; the first bill divided the abolitionists and aroused the ire of most humanitarians, while the second appealed to humanitarians but was certainly not supported by all abolitionists. Men like Monck spoke in favour of drastic restrictions in relief, deploring the Poor Law as a system of 'Spencean justice', but a year later they would have nothing to do with a measure which would abolish settlement without restricting relief. On this point town and country agreed, driven by contrary fears. As Sydney Smith argued very forcefully in the *Edinburgh Review*, stringent settlement requirements were virtually a substitute for partial

296

abolition, since they 'invest fewer residents with the fatal privilege of turning beggars, exempt a greater number of labourers from the corruption of the Poor Laws, and stimulate them to exertion and economy, by the fear of removal'.[2] But humanitarians like Courtenay, Calcraft and General Sir R. Wilson were quite willing to prohibit removals, let parishes complain as they might, but would suffer no limitation of the right to relief, which was to them 'a fair and reasonable claim before God and Men'. This Benett and Frankland Lewis hastened to deny, but they still hesitated to support Scarlett's first bill, thinking it too crude to be practical. Poor Scarlett thus found himself perpetually in a minority amid conflicting opinions and interests; his allies of 1821 were his enemies of 1822. It was no comfort that Londonderry used Scarlett's difficulties as an excuse to show how unfair it was to ask the Government to act in the matter.[3]

In the course of the debate on Scarlett's second bill Courtenay pleaded for a more general discussion in which 'the issue of abolition versus modification [of the Poor Law] could be squarely met'. No single debate of this nature took place, but little remained to be said on the question after Scarlett's abolitionist scheme had been followed by a bill from Nolan which was based on reformist assumptions. Nolan agreed that pauperism was an urgent problem, but rejected abolition as undesirable as well as impossible; it 'would give to popular

[2] *The Works of the Rev. Sydney Smith* (1859), p. 296. Smith's defence of settlement was exceptional, but compare *A Letter to the Rt. Hon. George Canning . . . by a Select Vestryman of Putney* (1823), p. 45. Other attempts to relax settlement were made by Wood in 1823, Althorp and Sturges Bourne in 1824, MacQueen in 1828, and by Weyland in 1830. A Select Committee appointed on settlement in 1828 produced only a brief report on the grounds that the Select Committee of 1817 had exposed the evils (*Parliamentary Papers*, 1828, V (406), 201); for an exceptionally persuasive criticism of the law see *Parish Settlements and Pauperism* (1828). Sydney Smith's general views on pauperism—or at least his expression of them—were fresh and entertaining; he sought gradual abolition of the Poor Law over 200 years. 'Not to attempt the cure of this evil would be criminal indolence, not to cure it gradually and compassionately would be very wicked.' (*Works*, p. 353).

[3] *Parliamentary Debates*, New Series, V. 572–88, 987–99, 1228–30, 1479–83; VII. 761–79. James Scarlett (1769–1844) was an extremely successful barrister when he entered Parliament in 1819, but was never very effective in the House. He became Lord Chief Baron of the Exchequer in 1834. For pamphlet criticism of Scarlett's Bills see G. Long, *Observations* etc. (1821); *A Letter to Jas. Scarlett . . . by a Surrey Magistrate* (1821); and 'Unus Populi', *A Letter to Mr. Scarlett* etc. (1822). 'Unus Populi' offered a radical solution to the Malthusian problem: 'Let the government import a certain number of Turkish operators that are usually attached to the Seraglio . . . and let all those sturdy Radicals, who are suspected of that foul and abominable sin of propagating their kind, be immediately sentenced to deprivation.' The operators would need to be guarded against 'vengeful women' (pp. 11–12). On Scarlett's suggestion Slaney republished his *Essay on the Employment of the Poor* in support of the Bill; the 1822 edition includes an able letter from Scarlett.

commotion the colour of necessary resistance against wanton oppression'. The Poor Law had helped to raise the English labourer above the rest of Europe in skill and comfort, and the evident evils in the existing situation arose not from the principle of relief, but from its administration. Nolan hinted at less eligibility as the key to a good system. A right to relief was valid, but it did not imply that 'a poor man, without work, was to live with his family a co-rival in comfort and respectability with the honest provident labourer who derived his support from his personal industry'. But he provided little (beyond a few administrative reforms) towards the application of this principle; his bill failed, partly from abolitionist opposition, but largely under the weight of its own obscurities.[4]

These two attempts at major reforms, the one by an abolitionist, the other by a defender of the principle of relief, revealed the deep divisions in opinion in Parliament on the question of the Poor Law. This disagreement over principles continued to be evident, although after 1822 Parliamentary discussion was concerned with more limited proposals for the removal of particular abuses rather than the re-modelling of the whole system. Little was offered on the reform of the method of rating, most speakers and writers being reconciled to the necessity of local financial responsibility, and these years were noticeably barren of schemes for administrative reform.[5] Apart from minor tampering with the Law of Settlement, the main efforts of parliamentary reformers were directed first against the allowance system, and later in favour of various methods of providing employment instead of money relief. Russell's Select Committee on Labourers' Wages collected much evidence on allowances, condemned them forcefully and lucidly, demanded a 'separation' of pauper labour from free, and found no practicable means of achieving this aim. In 1825 Monck made a futile attempt to declare allowances illegal. Between 1828 and 1830 Slaney, an able and persistent reformer, fought for a bill to stop the payment of relief to men in private employment. He was frustrated by the pressure of local interests, and by the pessimism of men like Peel who believed that 'there was a necessity in the present condition of the poor, that

---

[4] *Parliamentary Debates*, New Series, VII. 1561–96; VIII. 367; X. 450. Michael Nolan was a noted authority on the law of relief and author of the *Treatise* of 1805. He entered Parliament in 1820, and died in 1827.

[5] Note Lowe's rejection of a national rate (*The Present State of England*, pp. 197–8), and demands for equality in G. Forwood, *The Equity and Necessity of Equalizing Parochial Assessments* (1828). J. S. Bayldon, *A Treatise on the Valuation of Property for the Poor's Rate* (1828) is a useful statement of existing practice. Among the few proposals for radical administrative reform in these years note those in *A Letter to the Rt. Hon. The Speaker* etc. (1820), and *An Apology for the Poor* etc. (1823).

would paralyse any Act of Parliament'.[6] These attacks on the allowance system were of course acceptable to abolitionists, though supported by men of other persuasions as well. But few abolitionists could be sympathetic to demands to provide land and employment for the poor, demands which reached a crescendo after 1830 and became, indeed, the chief rivals of the proposals of the Royal Commission. Nugent, Teynham, Kenyon, the Duke of Richmond and the Earl of Winchilsea were among those who bombarded Parliament with bills to provide allotments, to encourage spade husbandry, to extend the system of allotting labourers to employers known as the labour rate, or with proposals for full-scale 'colonisation at home'.[7] The labour rate seemed an especially attractive device, and Sturges Bourne was to champion it on the Royal Commission with apparently significant examples of successful local reforms achieved through it; and in general proposals for the provision of employment gained increasing support in these

[6] See *Parliamentary Debates*, New Series, X. 1413–14 (appointment of Russell's Committee); XIII. 571–3 (Monck's Bill); XVIII. 1521–46, XX. 538–42, XXI. 1049–53, 1392 and XXIV. 38–52 (Slaney's campaign). Almost all the pamphlets of this decade attacked the allowance system, but see W. Copland, *A Letter* etc. (1824), pp. 53, 75 for a limited defence. Russell's Committee asserted that allowances were unjust to ratepayers, demoralised the labourers, made them inefficient, and created surplus population; but it was not prepared to forbid relief in aid of children, was not unsympathetic to labour-rate schemes and limited employment projects, and hoped above all for better administration: 'it must never be forgotten . . . that the evils produced by the poor laws are different in different places; that all the good effects hitherto produced have been accomplished by improved management; and that, if these effects have not been more general, it is because the management of the poor has in the greater part of the country improved very little' (*Report*, p. 8). It thus looked for local regeneration, not legislative interference.

[7] *Parliamentary Debates*, New Series, XXXIII. 1406–10, 3rd series, I. 596–601 (Nugent's Labour Rate Bill, 1830); I. 1316–27 (debate on allotments and spade husbandry, 1830); I. 371–81, IV. 261–7, 284–5, 358, 930–41 (Winchilsea's Labour Rate Bills 1830–31); IV. 1031, 1035, VI. 451 (Teynham's Bill, 1831); VI. 379 (Richmond's Bill for employment on wastes, 1831); X. 1156–7, XI. 126–8 (Kenyon's Bill for enclosure and allotments, 1832); XI. 286–90 (Weyland's allotments Bill, 1832); XIV. 898–900 (Richmond's temporary Labour Rate Bill, 1832); XVII. 751–2, XVIII. 664–79, XIX. 66–8, XX. 357–9 (renewal of Richmond's Act passed by Lords, defeated in Commons). For labour rate proposals see also R. Stephenson, *A Plan* etc. (1820) and A. Collett, *A Letter* etc. (1824). Sir George Nugent, member for Aylesbury 1819–32, had been Lieut. Governor of Jamaica 1801–6 and C. in C. in India 1811–13; he was made a Field Marshal in 1846. The ninth Earl of Winchilsea succeeded his philanthropic cousin in 1826; a violent opponent of liberal measures he fought a duel with the Duke of Wellington over Catholic Emancipation. Nugent and Winchilsea were strongly paternalist in their attitude to the poor, as was the fifth Duke of Richmond, whom Greville described as 'prejudiced, narrow-minded, illiterate, and ignorant, good-looking, good humoured and unaffected, tedious, prolix, unassuming and a duke'. He entered Grey's cabinet as a dissident tory, but resigned in 1834. In 1830 he confronted and pacified 200 rioting labourers in Sussex.

years, especially in the House of Lords. The champions of colonisation at home were, however, as often inspired by concern to promote the agricultural interest as by simple humanitarianism, and they inevitably aroused the antagonism of those who looked to trade and manufactures as the instruments of economic progress.[8] What prospect of civilising improvement could peasant holdings offer? Should Englishmen ape the Irish, digging potatoes with spades? Colonisation abroad could be more easily reconciled with current doctrines of political economy, and the movement for systematic colonisation certainly gained impetus in these years, but even its advocates were a little unorthodox in being more Malthusian than Malthus in their emphasis on over-population as a cause of distress.[9] It was inevitable, in the political and intellectual climate of the day, that schemes for employment, and for colonisation at home or abroad, would not be debated solely on their practical merits. They competed for approval, but in the event this ferment of Parliamentary debate on particular plans was cut off by the sweeping proposals of the Royal Commission, proposals which were an interruption rather than a culmination, of the efforts of Parliamentarians.[10] The main roots of the Commission's Amendment Bill must be sought outside Parliament. Major reforms required new thought on principles, a new impetus from local experiments in relief, and the novel and forceful procedures adopted by a new Government.

2. New Thoughts on Abolition

While there is evidence of some reconsideration of abolitionist views in the 1820s, it would be wrong to suggest that the belief that England would be better off without a Poor Law ceased to be widely held. As in earlier years, Malthus was the recognised leader of the attack on the system, and he himself certainly did not become reconciled to its continuance. The *Summary View of the Principle of Population*, written

[8] For make-work schemes and proposals for home colonisation see, for example, *Justice to the Poor* etc. (1820); W. Salisbury, *A Treatise* etc. (1820); W. D. Bayley, *The State of the Poor* etc. (1820); W. H. Saunders, *An Address* etc. (1821); J. Hall, *A Plan* etc. (1824); J. Pole, *A Few Observations* etc. (1828); S. Banfill, *Third Letter* etc. (1828); and the *Quarterly Review*, XLI (1829), 240–283, 512–50 (articles by Edwards) and XLIII (1830), 242–76 (article perhaps by Lord Elgin).

[9] Among the many writings on emigration as a remedy for distress in these years see esp. the Reports from the Select Committees of 1826 and 1827 (*Parliamentary Papers*, 1826, IV (404) and 1826–7, V (88, 237, 550); R. Heathfield, *Further Observations* etc. (2nd ed. 1820); R. Wilmot Horton, *The Causes and Remedies of Pauperism* etc. (1830); and (for the debate on Howick's Bill), *Parliamentary Debates*, 3rd Series, II. 875–904.

[10] Thus the Royal Commissioners worked hard to frustrate the renewal of the Labour Rate Act in 1833.

in 1821–2, included an attack on the right to relief as 'absolutely incompatible' with a system of private property, the 1826 edition of the *Essay* retained all the earlier criticism of relief, and in his evidence before the Select Committee on Emigration of 1827 he rejected any merely partial abolition and insisted that total repeal was 'absolutely necessary' to the success of emigration or of any other device for the improvement of the condition of the poor.[11] Moreover, since Malthusianism was never quite synonymous with abolitionism, many men continued to attack the Poor Law without reference to the principle of population; relief was criticised as a cause of vice and an intolerable burden as fiercely, if not perhaps as widely, after 1820 as before. Bayly and Saunders lamented its propagation of vice, crime and indolence; Lowe denied that it encouraged marriage but dismissed it as a degrading fraud; Lord Suffield complained of the 'intolerable' burden of the rates, and John Hall burst out in denunciatory expletives: 'Parochial relief! A system which held out a premium for deception!—degrading falsehood!—sordid wretchedness!—filth!—and vice of all description!' In 1824 Cockburn could write of abolitionism that 'there is perhaps no political truth supported by so unequivocal a course of general experience, or confirmed, on the whole, by so general assent'.[12] But in fact even the 'Scotch feelosophers' of the *Edinburgh Review* were soon to stray from the path of orthodoxy in this matter, led by J. R. McCulloch; and within the ranks of the Malthusians themselves the abolitionist creed was to be modified in several important respects.

These modifications owed little to the assaults of the anti-Malthusians —though such writers as J. C. Ross and the urbane American A. H. Everett kept the population controversy alive—and even less to writers such as Page who defended the Poor Law on lines similar to

[11] The *Summary View* was written for the *Encyclopaedia Britannica*, and published separately in 1830; it is reprinted in D. V. Glass (ed.), *Introduction to Malthus*. It is perhaps Malthus's best and clearest exposition of his views; for an argument that in it Malthus attempted to reconcile the doctrines of the *Essay* with the later viewpoint of the *Principles*, but failed to amend his practical recommendations accordingly, see M. Paglin, *Malthus and Lauderdale*, pp. 147–50. For other statements of orthodox Malthusian abolitionism in these years see *A Letter to the Speaker* etc. (1820); *A Letter to the Hon. J. F. Campbell* etc. (1821); J. Davis, *Common Sense on Agricultural Distress* (1822); and compare *Remarks on Mr. Godwin's Inquiry* etc. (1821) for a very able and perceptive defence of Malthusian views.

[12] W. D. Bayly, *The State of the Poor* etc. esp. pp. 56–7; W. H. Saunders, *An Address* etc. (1821); J. Lowe, *The Present State of England* etc. pp. 201–3; Lord Suffield, *A Charge . . . at the Quarter Sessions for the County of Norfolk* etc. (1830); J. Hale, *A Plan* etc. (1824), p. 3; Cockburn in *Edinburgh Review*, XLI (1824), 229. Compare also T. Single, *Hints to Parliament* etc. (1824); J. Halcomb, *A Practical Measure* etc. (1826); and Edwards' abolitionist remarks in the *Quarterly Review*, XXXVI (1827), 484–94.

Paley's; and if radical criticism of abolitionism persisted its most original protagonists were by this time drifting towards that form of 'socialism' loosely dubbed Ricardian, and offered nothing new on the reform of the system.[13] Much more important was the fact that political economy itself was developing beyond a simple uncritical acceptance of the Malthusian thesis. Ricardo might welcome Malthus's attack on the Poor Law, though with some reservations, but most of the new generation of economists made a wider distinction between Malthus's acceptable theoretical discoveries and his unacceptable practical conclusions. They remained critical of the Poor Law, but abolition was no longer so obviously the remedy.

Among Ricardo's disciples, James Mill did not move far from the abolitionist position, at least until persuaded by the Royal Commission of 1832–4; but the tone of the discussion in his *Elements of Political Economy* was hardly that of the Haileybury professor. He stressed that wages depended on the ratio of capital to population, emphasised the desirability of frugality and deplored stimulants to the birth-rate, but did not include the Poor Law among undesirable influences and was no great advocate of moral restraint. His article on 'Colony' in the *Encyclopaedia Britannica*, and other evidence, makes it clear that Mill accepted Place's arguments for birth control as a more realistic and desirable check to population than moral restraint. Nevertheless he did not defend the Poor Law, although he denied the landlords' claim that it imposed an especially grievous burden on them.[14] And the

[13] J. C. Ross published his large and curious *Principles* etc. (1825) under the pseudonym 'John McIniscon, A Fisherman', and *An Examination* etc. (1827); he, too, could be called a Ricardian Socialist. *An Address to the Members of Trade Societies* etc. (1827) by 'A Fellow Labourer' showed a similar point of view. On the Ricardian Socialists see E. Lowenthal, *The Ricardian Socialists*; M. Blaug, *Ricardian Economics*, pp. 140–50; and E. Halevy, *Thomas Hodgskin* (ed. Taylor, 1956). G. Ensor, *The Poor and their Relief* (1823) offered a more orthodox radical defence of the Poor Law; for defence on traditional grounds see *Observations* etc. (1822); F. Page, *The Principles of the English Poor Laws illustrated and defended* (1822); W. Copland, *A Letter* etc. (1824); *Justice to the Poor* etc. (1820); *A Letter to the Rt. Hon. George Canning* etc. (1823); and *Notices on Political Economy* etc. (1821). A. H. Everett's *New Ideas of Population* etc. (1823) is of theoretical importance but added little to the poor-law debate, though he defended public relief (chap. 10). Frederick Page (1769–1834) had decades of experience in poor-law administration; in the 1790s he had provided Eden with material for *The State of the Poor*.

[14] For Mill's claim that the rates were in part borne by the consumer see his *Elements* (1821 ed.), pp. 217–18, and (1824 ed.), pp. 281–2. In 1864 John Stuart Mill recalled that his father had been converted by John Black's defence of the principle of public relief in the *Morning Chronicle* in 1828, but if so this conversion was not reflected in his writings at the time; see R. D. Collison Black, *Economic Thought and the Irish Question* (1960), p. 104, H. Elliott (ed.), *Letters of J. S. Mill*, II. 14, and A. Bain, *James Mill*, p. 372.

Westminster Review, the Benthamite journal founded in 1824, criticised unenlightened charity in terms harsh and Malthusian enough. In fact the Mills and members of their circle gave little attention to the system of relief, being too intent on publicising progressive doctrines in general, including the great truths of political economy in its teachings on poverty. But three deviations from pure Malthusianism may be noted: a stress on the encouragement of economic innovation, let landlords complain as they would; an impatience with merely teaching prudence as the remedy for distress; and a belief that the economy and society had improved, was improving, and could improve further. Thus an article on emigration in the *Westminster* included a note that 'it may be right to say, that prudence is the only remedy for an excessive population. . . . Yet it is a pardonable, perhaps a laudable, impatience to desire to see some considerable advance made in our own day.' Benthamites clearly found the Malthusian curb to active reforming uncomfortable, and none more than Chadwick. In his important article on life insurance in 1828 he stressed that diminished mortality was a proof of social improvement; if the Poor Law was deplorable, it was as a check to progress, and not (as with Malthus) as an instrument of early ruin.[15]

In 1828 Chadwick was but a minor figure in Bentham's entourage, while Nassau Senior, later to be his colleague on the Royal Commission, was already a political economist of repute. His *Two Lectures on Population* delivered at Oxford in that year were, he believed, fully in accord with Malthusian teaching. But Malthus thought otherwise, and the correspondence which followed reveals the increasing gap between the aged professor and his younger followers.[16] To Senior's surprise, Malthus would not admit that subsistence had in fact generally increased faster than population, and that ambition was as strong a human motive as the passion between the sexes; he clung to his gloomy stress on the precariousness of any surplus, of any 'comforts' for the masses. Moreover Senior wished to place much more emphasis on the encouragement of economic growth, on increase in subsistence, than Malthus thought proper. Malthus would admit that he had overstated his case ('having found the bow bent too much one way, I was induced

---

[15] *Westminster Review*, IX (1828), 112–37 (article on emigration), and 384–422 (Chadwick's article). See also II (1824), 289–311 (review of Mill's *Elements*); IV (1825), 88–92 (review of McCulloch's *Discourse*); VIII (1827), 182–9 (review of Senior's *Lectures*). On the *Review* in general, see G. L. Nesbitt, *Benthamite Reviewing* (New York, 1934).

[16] The correspondence is printed as an appendix to Senior's *Two Lectures on Population* etc. (1829). On Senior see M. Bowley, *Nassau Senior and Classical Economics* (1937); S. Leon Levy, *Nassau W. Senior, the Prophet of Modern Capitalism* (Boston, 1943) includes useful material.

to bend it too much the other, in order to make it straight'),[17] but nevertheless found Senior's criticism of the excesses of vulgar Malthusians too strong. Senior, having found the principle of population 'made the stalking horse of negligence and injustice, the favourite objection to every project for rendering the resources of the country more productive', discovered that Malthus would not follow him in purifying the doctrine.

It is notable that in his lectures Senior attacked 'parts' (but not the whole) of the Poor Law, the offending portion being the allowance system. When, in 1830, he deplored assertions of the 'right' to subsistence, he had in mind not benevolent relief of distress but an evil system of servitude. Pauperism was a form of slavery, and free contract in wages the only way to emancipate labourers from it. 'The instant the labourer is paid, not according to his *value*, but according to his *wants*, he ceases to be a free man.'[18] Senior retained a deep suspicion of poor laws in general, and, when considering the plight of the Irish poor, strongly rejected proposals for public relief for the able-bodied or the aged, much as he deplored the 'revolting' indifference of Irish landlords to their social inferiors. But he proposed other forms of public assistance—government investment in public works and medical services for the impotent, for example—and was in general sufficiently critical of abolitionism to be ready, when the time came, to accept the view that a reformed Poor Law could avoid the evils of the allowance system.[19]

The fullest recantation of abolitionist views was made by an economist with a reputation for being orthodox to the point of aridity, J. R. McCulloch. For years the main writer on economic affairs for the *Edinburgh Review*, his early contributions were Malthusian enough on wages and relief, with much stress on the need for moral restraint and on the futility of attempting to assist the poor by monetary contributions.[20] The first edition of his *Principles of Political Economy* (1825) attacked the Poor Law as a direct cause of low wages: 'no institution can ... be so pernicious to the poor, as that which tends to increase

[17] *Essay* (1826) II. 497.

[18] N. Senior, *Three Lectures on the Rate of Wages* etc. (1830), p.x.

[19] 'Senior did not ever really believe that abolition of all relief to the able bodied was desirable if its abuse could be prevented' (M. Bowley, *Nassau Senior and Classical Economics*, p. 295).

[20] See esp. *Edinburgh Review*, XXXIX (1824), 315–41; XL (1824), 1–26. McCulloch always placed more stress than Malthus on emigration, however. For an account of McCulloch's Ricardian discipleship see S. G. Checkland, 'The Propagation of Ricardian Economics in England', *Economica*, New Series XVI (1949); but compare McCulloch's criticism of Mill's *Elements:* 'the science is far from having arrived at the perfection Mr. Mill supposed'.

the supply of labour beyond the demand'.[21] In 1828, however, he changed his mind. He had already noted that settlement and other restrictions on relief had checked the evils of the system to some extent; going further, he admitted that 'it is no easy matter to reconcile' the abolitionist case against the principle of relief with 'what has actually taken place'. Howlett, Barton and others had denied that the effects of relief were disastrous, and 'however inexplicable it may appear, it is impossible to deny that [their claims] are founded in fact'. The Poor Law had existed for two centuries before pauperism became a serious social problem, and even then there were stimulants other than the system itself. Abolitionist principles remained theoretically valid: 'the establishment of a compulsory provision for the support of the poor would, *unless it were accompanied by some very powerful counteracting circumstances*, have the effects usually ascribed to it'. But it had been in the interests of the ratepayers, both landlords and tenants, to create these circumstances, and they had done so by restricting the building of cottages and by adopting the workhouse test. 'The real use of a workhouse is to be an asylum for the able-bodied poor: . . . But it should be such an asylum as will not be resorted to except by those who have no other resource. . . . The able-bodied tenant of a workhouse should be made to feel that his situation is decidedly less comfortable than that of the industrious labourer who supports himself.' Restore this system (which McCulloch alleged existed until 1795) and the Poor Law would be a social asset, and indeed a better check to population than mere moral restraint, since the poor lacked the 'natural sagacity' and the knowledge to make restraint effective and widespread. Abolish allowances, limit magistrates' powers, rate the owners of cottages, make the Irish emigrate, and all would be well.[22] In 1830 McCulloch added a definite plea for relief: humanity prescribed relief for the impotent, and the vicissitudes of manufactures and the inadequacy of private charity made relief for the able-bodied a social necessity. He was so convinced of the efficacy of a return to traditional practice that he opposed the administrative revolution undertaken in 1834.[23]

[21] *Principles*, 356. A review in *Edinburgh Review*, XLIII (1825), possibly by Jeffrey, cited 'true notions on the Poor Law' as one of the great achievements of modern political economy.

[22] *Edinburgh Review*, XLVII (1828), 303–29. McCulloch acknowledged that his change of view owed much to two articles in the *Morning Chronicle* by John Black, its editor, one of the strongest advocates of a Poor Law for Ireland.

[23] *Principles* (1830 ed.), part III. chap. iii, for the defence of the Poor Law; and note Coulson's review (*Edinburgh Review*, LII (1831), 337–56) with its acknowledgment that Malthus's attack on the Poor Law was 'one-sided' and misleading. In 1831 McCulloch deplored demands for drastic reform of the Poor Law (*Edinburgh Review*, LIII (1831), 53, 43–61); his criticism of the new Poor Law may be found in later

This revolution in the attitude of Edinburgh reviewers to the Poor Law did not escape the *Quarterly's* attention. The rival journal had already repented of its earlier conversion to abolitionist views, and an article by Sir Francis Palgrave in 1826 anticipated most of McCulloch's defence of the Poor Law as it had existed before 1795.[24] In 1831 Scrope reviewed McCulloch's *Principles*, noting his change of heart with a little malice; he quoted Samuel Read on

the late sudden and ample recantations from Mr. Malthus's disciples on the subject of the poor laws, very coolly given by them, after having been engaged all the previous part of their lives in dogmatising on the contrary side. After having for years cried down this institution as the great sore in England's side, urging repeatedly in Parliament its entire abolition, as the only means of saving the country from overwhelming pauperism, after treating with ineffable contempt the opinions of those who, from a practical knowledge of these laws, ventured to support them, these same writers quietly turn round, and, with equal effrontery, triumph forth their tardily acquired convictions on the blessings of the poor laws as a most important discovery of their own.[25]

The acerbity of this criticism may or may not have been deserved, but Read certainly exaggerated the change in view of most of the Malthusians; McCulloch was exceptional in the extent of his conversion, and for the Mills and probably for Senior a complete rejection of abolitionism did not come until after 1832. Certainly the abolitionist cause was weakening, and it was becoming possible to defend the principle of relief without grave danger of being declared a heretic to the canons of political economy, as the important works of Lloyd and Longfield of the early 1830's show.

These changes in attitudes to the English Poor Law were influenced by the agitation which developed in the late 1820s for a system of public relief in Ireland. In this debate, as in others in political economy, Irish questions clarified some issues while confusing others; all intelligent observers were aware that whatever the problems of wealth and

[24] *Quarterly Review*, XXXII (1826), 429–54. Compare the able defence of the Poor Law by Croker and G. R. Gleig in XXVIII (1823), 349–65, including this note: 'A considerable reaction has taken place in the public opinion, on the subject of the poor laws: and by that moderate course of thinking, into which the people of this country gradually subside, even upon the most inflammatory topic, hazardous schemes for their *abolition* have given way to proposals of a more sober kind, for their strict and severe *administration*.' (p. 349).

[25] *Ibid*. XLIV (1831), 50. Read had criticised Malthus in his able *General Statement* etc. (1821); Scrope quoted Read's *An Inquiry* etc. (1829), p. 347. This work included a powerful defence of the right to relief.

---

editions of the *Principles*, and in *A Descriptive and Statistical Account of the British Empire* (4th ed. 1854), part V, chap. viii. His later views are also made explicit in comments on other writers in the *Literature of Political Economy*, esp. in chap. xvi.

welfare in England, Ireland's situation was much more difficult, and while political economists applied the same theoretical concepts to the more backward island most recognised that policies proper in one part of the realm were anomalous in the other. A favourable ratio of capital to population was as desirable in Ireland as in England, and the best means of achieving it remained a free capitalist progress, but the Irish cottier system seemed a barrier inimical to growth which was, happily, absent in England. Overseers in English parishes infested with indigent Irish immigrants might assume that the establishment of a Poor Law in Ireland would help to solve their problems; Irish landlords protested, just as simply, that their rentals would be extinguished by a compulsory rate. At first most economists agreed with the landlords. If a poor law was harmful in England, surely it would be disastrous in Ireland, though there might well be a case for more active government intervention to stimulate economic reform and growth in Ireland than in England. Thus Ricardo subscribed to the Report of the Select Committee on the State of the Irish Poor in 1823 which rejected public relief—equated, on the whole, with the allowance system—but approved some forms of public employment. In 1827 Malthus told the Select Committee on Emigration that a poor law would 'aggravate' distress in Ireland, and other abolitionists such as Chalmers and Bicheno persisted in a strict Malthusianism on this point. But by 1831 Senior approved of relief for disabled Irish, if not for the able-bodied and aged, and if he, Torrens and others continued even after 1834 to oppose the introduction of the reformed Poor Law into Ireland their objections were no longer crude and indiscriminate.[26] The most able of the new advocates of an Irish Poor Law in the 1820s—and in particular Black and Scrope—produced arguments weighty enough to cause some refinement in accepted attitudes to the general question of public relief. By stressing that absolute destitution bred extreme improvidence, and by distinguishing between beneficial and baneful practices in English relief, these publicists raised the question whether the evils of the allowance system were inherent in the Poor Law or merely accidental. Serious consideration of Ireland's needs provoked a more careful examination of English practice, an essential preliminary to the acceptance of the reform of 1834. And there were converts; in 1833, when the Political

[26] This subject is admirably discussed in R. D. Collison Black, *Economic Thought and the Irish Question*, chap. IV. For Senior's view in 1831 see his *A Letter to Lord Howick, on a Legal Provision for the Irish Poor* etc. (1831); and compare G. Strickland, *A Discourse on the Poor Laws* etc. (1827) for a relatively early plea for a reformed system in both countries. Bishop Doyle's *Letters on the State of Ireland* (1825) was perhaps the seminal work in this debate, with Black's articles in the *Morning Chronicle* and Scrope's in the *Quarterly Review* also extremely influential. See also W. Parker, *A Plan* etc. (1816) for an early argument against an Irish poor law.

Economy Club debated the effects of introducing public relief in Ireland a majority of those present proved to be in favour of its establishment. Senior and others who persisted in their opposition rested their case on particular Irish conditions, and not on universal principle. England might have found a satisfactory form of public relief, but how could Irish paupers be made less eligible than Irish peasants, even in work-houses? Thus the discussion of Ireland widened the whole abolitionist debate, and by introducing consideration of a different economic system produced, in some minds at least, a new assessment of the theory and practice of the English Poor Law.[27]

Nevertheless, if some abolitionists modified their views in these years few capitulated to the arguments of their traditional adversaries. T. R. Edmonds, writing in 1832, claimed that support for abolition waned in the 1820s but revived about 1830; certainly demands for radical reform increased under the stress of rural disorder, and old arguments were refurbished in the debate on Ireland.[28] And although McCulloch might plead his new defence of the Poor Law before the Select Committee on the State of the Poor in Ireland in 1830, his conversion could not bring him close in spirit to such protagonists of an Irish Poor Law as M. T. Sadler. Faced with Sadler's rival 'law' of population—that 'the fecundity of human beings, under equal circumstances, varies inversely with the number in a given space'—political economists closed their ranks; revision was one thing, heresy another. The conflict was largely political, for behind Sadler's 'landlordism' lurked the crucial issue of the Corn Law. Thomas Spring Rice offered 'to stake Malthus against Sadler (more fearful odds than any offered at Tattersall's) that all the efforts of party will never produce one placard in favour of high prices or dear bread'; it was this conflict of principle and faction which made Harriet Martineau's relatively crude propaganda on political economy and pauperism acceptable to men like Senior, as Mrs. Marcet's simplifications had been accepted by Ricardo.[29] Free trade and a progressive economy and society were the

---

[27] W. F. Lloyd's *Lectures* etc. (1837), and M. Longfield's *Four Lectures on the Poor Laws* (1834) were much more systematic, and far removed in tone, from most pamphlets on the Poor Law a decade earlier.

[28] [T. R. Edmonds], *An Enquiry into the Principles of Population* (1832), p. 123. Edmonds had his own objections to the Poor Law, and his own scheme of reform; his *Life Tables, founded upon the Discovery of a Numerical Law regulating the Existence of every Human Being* etc. (1832) reveals a certain eccentricity of mind.

[29] Sadler's theory was foreshadowed in *Ireland, its Evils and their Remedies* (1828) and expounded with great prolixity in *The Law of Population* etc. (1830). Macaulay attacked Sadler in two articles in the *Edinburgh Review*, LI (1830); Sadler replied with *A Refutation* etc. (1830), to which Macaulay replied in the *Review* in 1831. For Spring Rice's comment see *Edinburgh Review*, L (1830), 352; and compare Empson's quite critical review of Martineau's *Illustrations* in *ibid.* LVII (1833).

true desiderata, to be defended against extreme political radicals on the one hand and against the Southeys, the Sadlers, and other defenders of the special privileges of a paternalistic land-owning aristocracy on the other.

Under these circumstances it is not surprising that Senior and other economists remained suspicious of the Poor Law, seeking a free economy as the answer to its demoralising serfdom. Since, by this time, almost everyone deplored the allowance system the crucial point at issue—in England, if not in Ireland—was the provision of employment and land, as has been seen. But if political pressures encouraged dogmatic simplification on both sides, some men retained a sturdy independence of view. George Poulett Scrope was that rarest of all intellectual phenomena, an able economist who wrote for the *Quarterly Review;* a bitter critic of the allowance system, and to some extent an admirer of Malthus and Chalmers, he nevertheless rejected abolitionism as wicked and class-biased, and sought instead assisted emigration and a Poor Law based on employment instead of money relief, for both England and Ireland. He was later to be by far the most interesting critic of the 1834 reform, but he created no school of thought just as he refused to join one. Unlike him, most political economists instinctively abhorred paternalistic interference with the natural distribution of capital, at least when proposed by their opponents, and assumed with little argument that the labour rate was as improper as the rate in aid of wages.[30]

Thus the relative weakening of abolitionist attitudes to the Poor Law did not bring agreement, or even narrow the range of disagreement, over what should be done. Rival solutions still competed for approval, with public employment, political reform, retrenchment, emigration, colonisation at home, education and free trade all urged with an instransigence as great as ever.[31] The principles of 1834 did not emerge

[30] Scrope's contributions to the *Quarterly* were numerous and persuasive; see esp. XLIV (1831), 511–50 (Poor Law for Ireland); XLVI (1831), 46–55 (review of Whately); 390–408 (Senior on Ireland); XLVIII (1832), 39–69 (review of Chalmers); 320–44 (Poor Laws). *A Letter to the Agriculturalists of England* etc. (1830) argued for an Irish Poor Law; on English conditions see his *A Letter to the Magistrates* etc. (1828); *Plea for the Abolition of Slavery in England* (1829); *The Common Cause* etc. (1830); *A Second Letter* etc. (1831). See also Redvers Opie, 'A Neglected British Economist: George Poulett Scrope', *Quarterly Jnl. Economics*, XLIV (1929), 101–37, and J. A. Schumpeter, *History of Economic Analysis*, p. 489. Scrope was born George Julius Poulett Thomson in 1797, but changed his name on marriage to an heiress in 1821. He was a geologist of note, author of a book on volcanoes and an associate of Lyell's. Scrope became interested in the Poor Law as a magistrate in Wiltshire; he was so prolific an author that he was known in Parliament as 'Pamphlet Scrope'. He lived until 1876.

[31] Contributory schemes had fewer advocates than earlier, but see J. Cleghorn, *Thoughts* etc. (1824); G. West, *A Plan* etc. (1827); and the *Reports* of the Select

as the culmination of a debate producing an essential concensus; rather the battle-axe of the Royal Commission cut the Gordian knot of intellectual confusion. Some at least of the Royal Commissioners knew what they wanted, and had the strength of will to pursue it. The weakening of abolitionist opinion after 1820 was an important preliminary to the acceptance of their work, and to some extent to that work itself; but their strongest support came not from any substantial body of accepted opinion but from the example of a number of local reforms which seemed to confirm the logic of their revisionist principles in the situation they faced.

3. Local Reforms and Reformers

Despite the failure to achieve any major amendment in the Poor Law there is evidence that the system was changing in practice, in many parishes if not in all. In the 1820s, as in earlier decades, local innovation was the harbinger of national legislation, though the outcome in this case was to be much more drastic than the merely permissive enactments of the eighteenth century. Some, perhaps most, of the Royal Commissioners of 1832–4 were deeply influenced by examples of successful local experiment, and George Nicholls, the dominant figure on the Poor Law Commission established in 1834, always claimed that the origin of the new system lay in local reforms rather than in abstract doctrine, an exaggeration perhaps made pardonable by the fact that he had been a local reformer himself. In the debate on the 1834 Bill Althorp explained that the government's intention was to discover how some parishes had succeeded in reforming the system and to make their practices universal, and this assumption of legislative pragmatism was probably vital in the acceptance of the reform by both Cabinet and Parliament. Nevertheless the empirical element in the proposals of 1834 should not be exaggerated, since the Royal Commissioners were selective in their approach, and local experiments were more varied than the Commission's conclusions suggested. Dogmatism, not empiricism, is evident in the unqualified acceptance of the workhouse test and the neglect of other expedients which, it could be argued, had proved equally useful in checking pauperism. It is the coincidence of selected local expedients with general theoretical assumptions which gives the Royal Commission's findings their peculiar blend of the empirical and the dogmatic.

Committees on Friendly Societies of 1825 and 1827 (*Parliamentary Papers*, 1825, IV (522) and 1826–7 III (558)). For a plan for relief offered for sale at a guinea for six copies see *Bread for All* etc. by an English Gentleman (1824?).

Only a handful of local reforms—notably those of Becher, Lowe, Nicholls, Whately and Baker—received much publicity before 1832, though the Assistant Commissioners discovered many other parishes where the system of relief seemed to have been cured of its worst disorders. The extent and variety of local efforts at reform are revealed in the returns made to the Select Committees on Poor Rate Returns of 1822–6, since many parishes offered brief comments on their situation and problems.[32] Even the most cursory survey of their remarks is a salutary reminder that despite national controversy the system of relief remained obstinately local in execution, with parochial boundaries imposing horizons on both understanding and action. The storms of debate had obviously passed by unnoticed in a parish which in 1826 had just heard of the allowance system and wrote to deplore it. From Trough, Cumberland, to Parliament in 1824 came solemn word that the inhabitants 'having observed the good effect of some of your late Acts . . . and hoping [to] send you some information concerning the poor, which has hitherto been to you unknown' wished to point out that many men begat bastards and left them on the parish 'and often boast how well they have managed'. Complaints about the cost of maintaining bastards were surprisingly frequent in the returns, though few parishes made general assertions that poor relief encouraged population increase, legitimate or otherwise. Local difficulties were attributed to a vast range of causes, from general agricultural depression and a surplus of agricultural labour to the game laws, smuggling, and the introduction of threshing machines, though it is noticeable that many of the worst-hit parishes had specifically local problems, such as the failure of the fishing at Roseland, Cornwall, in 1822. It is difficult to sympathise with a complaint from Staffordshire that the local coroner was extravagant in insisting on inquests into all mining fatalities; the overseers obviously thought accidents inevitable and inquests a waste of ratepayers' money. A great many parishes complained about aspects of settlement or the rating system, but suggested conflicting remedies. All this evidence of local preoccupations would be difficult to reduce to statistical order; what does emerge is the extent to which these preoccupations were local, and how much they varied.

It is perhaps surprising that so many parishes reported attempts at reform, though not unlikely that the somnolent or satisfied made no comment at all. The attempts were often vigorous, and success—at least in the sense of reducing the rates—by no means uncommon. By

---

[32] *Parliamentary Papers* 1822, V (556); 1823, V (520); 1824, IV (420); 1825, IV (534); 1826, III (330). After 1826 simple accounts of expenditure replaced the Reports. In 1834 Althorp estimated the number of reformed parishes at about one hundred (*Parliamentary Debates*, 3rd series, XXII. 879).

far the most popular device was the select vestry authorised by Sturges Bourne's Act, and some scores of parishes reported its effectiveness, though Ilkeston, Derby, abandoned such vestries 'because they did not serve', some failed through poor attendance and a few parishes claimed that full vestries were more efficient in checking imposition. The appointment of assistant overseers was a little less common, but reports on their worth were all favourable.[33] In general, difficulties seem to have arisen from opposition to these administrative devices rather than from their innate inadequacy. Sometimes reform was sabotaged by the ratepayers, or by the paupers themselves, but the usual complaint was against the meddling of magistrates; while most county benches seem to have tried to check allowances in the 1820s, individual justices were often blamed for refusing to ratify the appointment of select vestries or for hindering their work. Thus in 1824 Anderby Steeple in Yorkshire complained that the magistrates were still suspicious of the select vestry, although it had reduced rates by half in four years; Washingley, Hants, asserted that 'the less magistrates interfere with parishes, the better the poor would be provided for'; and a Lincolnshire parish complained of their 'folly and erroneous conduct'. A few correspondents put the whole blame for allowances and surplus population on the magistracy, but such exaggerations were relatively rare in this decade, if not in the next. Unfortunately the methods by which select vestries and assistant overseers reduced expenditure were seldom made clear, though abolition of relief to the able-bodied, insistence on outdoor or workhouse labour as a test, and primitive forms of labour rate were reported, if in statistically insignificant numbers and no coherent geographical pattern. Many parishes seem to have found that more careful administration and new safeguards against imposition sufficed to keep expenditure in check; how the poor fared under the reformed administration was not discussed.

Even in the pamphlet literature the models of reform later emphasised by the Royal Commission were by no means the only successful innovations described. J. Johnson, Deputy Governor of the Corporation of the Poor in Bristol, published an account of the reform of that venerable but worn institution, achieved not by a stricter workhouse test but by the introduction of a system of visiting. Thomas Walker wrote of reforms at Stratford, Manchester, where rates had been reduced from £812 to £368 in 1821 with the help of a select vestry and with a deliberate abandonment of indoor relief. Samuel Banfill achieved success near Exeter with a workhouse used not to deter, but to employ; he demanded universal indoor employment under a national

---

[33] The number of select vestries and assistant overseers in each county in 1824–5 is given in *Parliamentary Papers*, 1826, III (330), 74–5.

board of industry.[34] It is clear that there persisted, even among reformers very antagonistic to the allowance system, much hostility to workhouses, and especially to their use for deterrence. Thus C. D. Brereton, of Little Massingham, Norfolk, undertook a vigorous campaign against both allowances and workhouses, and sought a return to a simple parochial system in which magistrates would no longer interfere with overseers, a programme of reform in some respects not unlike McCulloch's.[35]

Brereton's campaign against workhouses was opposed by the champions of the new 'Anti-Pauper System' of the Rev. J. T. Becher, chairman of the Quarter Sessions of the Newark Division of Notts for thirty years. Becher was an influential figure in the reforms of the 1820s, though he was later bitterly disappointed at what he thought to be the failure of the Royal Commission to recognise his worth.[36] While he thought professional assistant overseers vital for improvement, and select vestries usually desirable, his chief emphasis was on methods of relief. Each parish should have a 'system', a moral regimen of Encouragement, Restraint and Coercion (as one of his disciples classified the various measures).[37] Let parish authorities provide schools, allotments, savings banks and friendly societies to encourage independence, and offer suitable relief for the impotent; to restrain the idle and extravagant, insist on a work test for all able-bodied paupers, preferably in a workhouse, and absolutely refuse relief in aid of wages; to coerce the vicious, enforce the vagrancy law and punish the immoral, for example by sending the mothers of two bastards to the house of correction. To Becher's chagrin, the Commissioners accepted from his teachings only the labour test (and only the workhouse labour test at that) and ignored the rest of his moral regimen, with its stress on

[34] J. Johnson, *An Address* etc. (1820), and *Transactions of the Corporation* etc. (1826); T. Walker, *Observations* etc. (1826, and 2nd ed. 1831); S. Banfill, *Third Letter* etc. (1828).

[35] C. D. Brereton, *Observations* etc. (1824), *An Inquiry* etc. (1825?) *A Practical Inquiry* etc. (3rd ed. 1826), and *The Subordinate Magistracy* etc. (1827). For other criticisms of workhouses see J. Lowe, *The Present State of England* etc. pp. 189–90, and J. Halcomb, *A Practical Measure* etc. (1826).

[36] Becher had been interested in questions of relief since the 1790s, and had published works on the Southwell House of Correction in 1806 and 1808 and several works on friendly societies and savings banks; his *Anti-Pauper System* etc. did not appear until 1828. See J. D. Marshall, 'The Nottinghamshire Reformers and their Contribution to the New Poor Law', *Econ. Hist. Review*, 2nd series, XIII (1961), 382–96. Becher's work was praised in the Report from the Select Committee on Agriculture (*Parliamentary Papers*, 1833, V (612), vi).

[37] J. Bosworth, *The Practical Means* etc. (1824), *The Necessity of the Anti-Pauper System* etc. (1829), and *Misery in the Midst of Plenty* etc. (1833). It is notable that by 1829 Bosworth, like Scrope, made an explicit distinction between the allowance system and the Poor Law as a whole.

encouragement and coercion. And they gave most of the credit to two men whom Becher regarded as his disciples, Nicholls of Southwell and the Rev. Robert Lowe of Bingham.[38]

Unlike most of his fellow-reformers, Nicholls was not a clergyman but a retired sea captain. At Becher's request he became an overseer at Southwell, and although he held office for only two years, he achieved significant improvements which he published to the world in *Eight Letters* addressed to Scarlett in 1822.[39] Against Scarlett's abolitionist proposals he pleaded for local reform as a preparation for general legislation. He attacked pauperism as a way of life as vigorously as any abolitionist, singling out the allowance system as the chief instrument of demoralisation; 'we must *all* retrace our steps'. How? By adopting as a general slogan: 'Reduce the Poor Rates!' Insist that all pay their share, even the paupers; never pay to men without settlements, but rather remove them; prune all pension lists vigorously; insist on work in return for relief, and work for the parish, not for other employers. At first Nicholls thought of workhouses as institutions for the relief of the impotent rather than the able-bodied, but he nevertheless insisted that they should be made unattractive by their 'repulsive rules'. 'I wish to see the Poor House looked to with dread by our labouring class, and the reproach for being an inmate of it extend downwards from Father to Son ... for without this, where is the needful stimulus to industry?' Indoor relief should be not only less eligible, but also a mark of shame. 'It cannot be too often repeated that Vice and Misery are the inseparable attendants of a state of pauperism'; it was necessary to eliminate both by making relief an expression of discipline.[40] As examples of successful reform, Nicholls described at length the changes at Bingham and Southwell, stressing the improvement in morals (no bastards at Bingham) and the very great reduction in the rates in both parishes (from £1,206 to £400 between 1818 and 1822 at Bingham). Nicholls himself claimed that the poor were as grateful for the change as were the ratepayers, labourers stopping him

[38] Becher attacked Assistant Commissioner Cowell, for under-estimating his work, in the second edition of his *Anti-Pauper System* (1834), pp. i–xxxii. Cowell replied in *A Letter to Rev. J. T. Becher* etc. (1834), explicitly rejecting all but the workhouse test in Becher's teachings as misleading complications. He claimed that Lowe's stress on the workhouse test (which was relatively crude) was the essence of reform. Lowe was a cousin of Becher's and father of Robert Lowe the Adullamite. Becher's work was however defended by Assistant Commissioner Wylde, himself a Southwell man.

[39] *Eight Letters on the Management of the Poor ... by an Overseer* (1822), and compare his *History of the English Poor Law;* the 1898 edition included a memoir of Nicholls by his grandson H. G. Willinck. On the limitations of Nicholls' work in Notts see J. D. Marshall, *op. cit.*, pp. 390–4.

[40] *Eight Letters* etc. pp. 19, 61.

in the street to thank him for delivering them from the scourge of pauperism. By 1832 the Assistant Commissioners found similar reforms, some modelled on these examples, in many parishes, including Uley in Gloucestershire, St Werburgh (Derby), and Penzance. Whately's reformed administration at Cookham in Berkshire was also much praised by the Commission, though it differed in some respects from the Bingham model.[41]

The importance of these local examples to the reform of 1834 is obvious, but should not be exaggerated. Without the workhouse test as a practical instrument the principle of less eligibility might have remained a mere abstraction; on the other hand it was probably the plausible theoretical simplicity of less eligibility which led to concentration on the workhouse test at the expense of other apparently successful expedients for reform. The much more comprehensive regimen of Becher and his disciples was essentially local and personal, and Nicholls himself admitted that the incorporation of the area as a Gilbert Union added little to its effectiveness. There was much in Becher's system which smacked of an old-fashioned moralistic paternalism, and there was sense as well as dogmatism in the Commissioners' rejection of it as a basis for a uniform national system. And if it might be assumed that Nicholls was essentially a local reformer translated to the national stage, it should be remembered that his local experience was brief and that it was exceptionally fortunate in its economic circumstances. There is some evidence that longer service as an overseer, or experience in manufacturing areas, might have modified his simple insistence on the workhouse test as a panacea.[42] Nicholls was no rural paternalist; he had from the beginning that strong instinct for administrative coherence and simplicity which was later to make him so effective as a Commissioner. He believed he had learned the efficacy of the workhouse test from practical experience, when in fact he had merely discovered an intellectually satisfying rule:

In all our views and reasonings on the subject, we contemplated the workhouse as little more than an instrument of economy. . . . It was not until these results began to be developed, at Bingham and at Southwell, that the full consequences of the *mitigated kind of necessity* imposed on the working classes, by a well regulated workhouse, were understood and appreciated. We then saw that it compelled them, *bred* them, to be industrious, sober, provident, careful of themselves, of their parents and children. . . . The workhouse thus acted instead of . . . that law of *necessity* wisely imposed by

[41] On Baker's reforms at Uley, the example which Senior stressed above all others to Cabinet, see J. H. L. Baker, *A Letter* etc. (1830).
[42] J. D. Marshall, *op. cit.*, pp. 391–2.

Providence upon mankind, and a neglect of which is ever followed by punishment in some shape....[43]

Here was an answer to the abolitionist dilemma, a form of relief which could be justified in the face of the usual arguments against relief. The extraordinary fanaticism associated with the doctrine of the workhouse test in the nineteenth century—a fanaticism which grew with the years, and was by no means at its strongest among the Royal Commissioners—sprang from the resolution it offered of the conflict between the necessity and the undesirability of a Poor Law. Some form of deterrent Poor Law was almost certain to emerge from the debate of the early nineteenth century, and it is perhaps surprising that the revival of the workhouse test was so belated; until the 1820s most of those who deplored the system of relief accepted the common arguments that workhouses were uneconomic, tyrannical and demoralising, while schemes for reformed workhouses had until recently included unacceptable make-work assumptions. It was the local reformers of these years who set a new example by adopting the workhouse as an instrument of discipline, an example which was isolated from its context and exaggerated into a national principle. If the workhouse test became a dogma, it did so because thirty years of debate and doubt had created a need for one.

4. *Reform by Royal Commission*

It is possible that successful local reform might have spread more widely through the poor-law system in the 1830s, aided by the favourable economic circumstances which were at first of such assistance to the Poor Law Commissioners in their more drastic endeavours. (It could certainly be argued that the reformers of the 1820s succeeded only in areas and periods of economic recovery, and some critics also alleged that they reduced parochial rates only at the expense of neighbouring parishes.) Nevertheless it is likely that many areas were, for various reasons, beyond merely local regeneration, and that 'a Whately in every parish' was an ideal beyond reasonable hope; it is certain that the evils inherent in excessive localism could not be overcome without reorganisation from the centre. Whatever the possibilities, the Amendment Act of 1834 transformed them. Local variety persisted, since the new central authority never attained its goal of national uniformity, but it was variety within a framework exerting strong pressure for uniformity. For the first time, at least since the early seventeenth century, a national policy in matters of relief existed, and the initiative for innovation passed in large measure from the periphery to the centre.

[43] Quoted by Willinck in Nicholls' *History of the English Poor Law*, I. xiii–xiv.

Despite the work of the Webbs and others a full-scale study of the reform of the Poor Law in 1834 is still needed; only an outline can be attempted here.[44] Why, at long last, did a Government act? The rise in the rates after 1828, the jacquerie of 1830, and the obvious fact of widespread distress produced much pressure in Parliament for a new attack on the old annoying problem of reform. The Lords reacted in the traditional way by appointing a Select Committee which collected much interesting (and unduly neglected) evidence, but which made no proposals except to seek a clarification of the legality of relief to the able-bodied and of magistrates' powers.[45] In both Houses there were the usual demands that the Government act, and for once it did. It was of course a new Government, committed in fact if not in words to the settlement of some outstanding national grievances, but even so it hesitated to tackle so difficult and thankless a task as poor-law reform. Senior credited Hyde Villiers, a junior member of the administration, with pricking his leaders into action, but it seems that Brougham, always outspoken on poor relief, publicly committed his colleagues before they had made up their minds.[46]

Brougham promised not only a drastic measure, but also an early one. The Cabinet was more circumspect, and adopted Villiers' suggestion of a Royal Commission, accepting his arguments that only an independent body could bring reform without involving the Government in great Parliamentary unpopularity. Brougham at first opposed the idea, but is credited with suggesting the appointment of itinerant Assistant Commissioners, a distinctive and important feature of the investigation.[47] Villiers had suggested Senior, James Mill and Hodges as Commissioners but in 1832 the Government appointed a larger group, consisting of Senior, Sumner, Charles Blomfield (Bishop of London since 1828), the Rev. H. Bishop, Sturges Bourne, Walter Coulson and Henry Gawler, adding James Traill and Chadwick in 1833. Nassau Senior directed the investigation, negotiated with Cabinet, and became the recognised leader of the work, though it is possible that Chadwick made

[44] The passing of the Act is described in detail in S. and B. Webb, *The Last Hundred Years*, I, and *English Poor Law Policy* (1910); G. Nicholls, *History of the English Poor Law*, II; and T. Mackay, *History of the English Poor Law* (1904). A copy of Senior's MS *History of the Passing of the Poor Law Amendment Act 1834* is in the Goldsmiths' Library.

[45] Its First and Third Reports are printed in *Parliamentary Papers*, 1831, VIII (227); the Second was not printed. Evidence was given by a large number of prominent reformers, and examples of local reform were stressed. See also *Parliamentary Debates*, 3rd Series, III, 10–12.

[46] On Villiers' letter see T. Mackay, *History of the English Poor Law*, pp. 25–7; for Brougham's promise and Melbourne's consequent embarrassment see *Parliamentary Debates*, 3rd Series, IV. 261–7, 284–5, and compare IX. 130.

[47] On Brougham's early scepticism see *Parliamentary Debates*, 3rd Series, IX. 1144.

the most original contribution to the Report and the Act which followed it.[48]

The work of the Royal Commission has been criticised as hasty and partial; certainly a case against the Commissioners' conclusions could be made out from the material they themselves gathered, and especially from the replies to their circulated queries.[49] Their Report was prepared before all the evidence was collected and sifted, and the *Extracts from the Information Received*, published in 1833 to allay criticism of delay, reveals a propagandist aim. The *Instructions* to Assistant Commissioners and the *Queries* circulated to the parishes, documents drawn up mainly by Senior, appeared to be comprehensive but did in fact emphasise precisely those factors later stressed in the Report. The Commissioners found the evils they expected to find, and documented them at great length. They were concerned above all to make a case against the allowance system as a form of relief for the able-bodied, and were themselves surprised and shocked to find allowances so widespread, even in manufacturing districts, but they failed to analyse in any depth the nature or significance of the practices they deplored. They did not believe that overpopulation was the basic cause of distress, and underestimated it as a local, if not as a national problem. They also found grounds for rejecting the remedies they hoped to reject, such as the labour rate and the systematic provision of allotments of land.

No doubt the Commission's Report was, in large part, a dogmatic document, unhistorical and unstatistical as its critics allege. But an emphasis on the allowance system and on the 'de-pauperisation' of the labourer was certainly to be expected, though this preoccupation need not have precluded more consideration of such special problems as periodic unemployment in large towns. The labour rate had its champions, but the Commissioners were not alone in believing that paying wages in lieu of relief was as serious a distortion of the labour market as paying relief in lieu of wages; and to men of Senior's persuasion in economic matters the dreadful example of Ireland's debased peasantry loomed behind apparently inncoent proposals for allotments

[48] S. and B. Webb, *The Last Hundred Years*, I. 47–50, discuss the composition of the Commission. On the rival claims of Senior and Chadwick to be the dominating influence see M. Bowley, *Nassau Senior and Classical Economics* and S. E. Finer, *The Life and Times of Sir Edwin Chadwick*.

[49] S. E. Finer, *op. cit.*, pp. 81–8; M. Blaug, 'The Poor Law Report Re-examined', *Jnl. Econ. History*, XXIV (1964), 229–45; and compare H. L. Beales, 'The New Poor Law', *History*, New Series, XV (1930–31), 308–19. The Report was printed in *Parliamentary Papers*, 1834, XXVII (44); Appendix A (Assistant Commissioner's Reports) filled vols. XXVIII–XXIX, Appendix B (Answers to Queries) vols. XXX–XXXVI, and Appendices C–F (Communications, Reports on Labour Rate and Vagrancy) vols. XXXVII–XXXIX.

for the poor. The Report's dogmatism was not merely wilful. And if the investigation appeared to be—perhaps purported to be—systematic and comprehensive, it is not clear that its authors really believed that they were undertaking a thorough analysis of all the causes of indigence and the whole system of relief. They were required to produce a practicable bill in a hurry, and to support it before Cabinet, Parliament and the public; some simplification in the analysis of the problem, and some crudity in the remedies proposed, may be excused in men who realised that their efforts would be fruitless unless their proposals were simple and economical. It must be stressed, moreover, that the Commissioners were not proposing a final clear-cut solution to the problem, like Scarlett's abolitionist bill of 1822, but were merely laying down a general policy and planning an authority to carry it out. The proof of the pudding would be in the eating, and they were but writing the recipe. This was certainly Chadwick's assumption, and he was so confident that he would be appointed chef that he left unspecified some of his favourite ingredients: like Bentham, he planned 'collateral aids' to buttress a deterrent Poor Law.[50] Later in the century 'the principles of 1834' became widely accepted as the final word on pauperism, but the men who drew them up assumed rather that they were the most important words to say at the time.

If the Commissioners echoed current opinion in their analysis of the situation, their conclusions were nevertheless confident and bold. Their Report described at length the evils arising from existing practices in relief for the able-bodied, but explicitly rejected both abolition and reliance on paternalistic 'discretion':

If we believed the evils stated in the previous part of the Report, or evils resembling, or even approaching them, to be necessarily incidental to the compulsory relief of the able-bodied, we should not hesitate in recommending its entire abolition. But we do not believe these evils to be its necessary consequences. We believe that, under strict regulations, adequately enforced, such relief may be afforded safely, and even beneficially.

All 'extensive civilised communities' provided some relief to the necessitous, either by voluntary alms-giving or by some form of compulsory system; only England, however, went so far as to relieve the ordinary labourer, thus blurring the important distinction which Bentham had made and Colquhoun repeated:

... in no part of Europe except England has it been thought fit that the provision, whether compulsory or voluntary, should be applied to more than the relief of *indigence*, the state of a person unable to labour, or unable to

---

[50] Finer, *op. cit.*, pp. 69–70, mentions Chadwick's collateral aids; the term is of course Bentham's.

obtain, in return for his labour, the means of subsistence. It has never been deemed expedient that the provision should extend to the relief of *poverty*; that is the state of one, who, in order to obtain a mere subsistence, is forced to have recourse to labour.

What was needed, then, was a sound principle for the relief of indigence, and of that alone. The Commissioners offered the same middle way between prodigality and starvation which Bentham had propounded four decades earlier: establish the principle of less eligibility and the Poor Law could at last be justified:

> The first and most essential of all conditions, a principle which we find universally admitted, even by those whose practice is at variance with it, is, that his situation, on the whole, should not be made really or apparently so eligible as the situation of the independent labourer of the lowest class . . . in proportion as the condition of any pauper class is elevated above the condition of the independent labourers, the condition of the independent class is depressed; their industry is impaired, their employment becomes unsteady, and its remuneration in wages is diminished. Such persons, therefore, are under the strongest inducements to quit the less eligible class of labourers and enter the more eligible class of paupers. The converse is the effect when the pauper class is placed in its proper position, below the condition of the independent labourer. Every penny bestowed, that tends to render the condition of the pauper more eligible than that of the independent labourer, is a bounty on indolence and vice. We have found, that as the poor's rates are at present administered, they operate as bounties of this description, to the amount of several millions annually.[51]

Less eligibility was to apply only to the able-bodied, not to the impotent, according to the Report—which had little to say on relief to the impotent in any case—but relief to children was to be deemed relief to their parents, a clause fatal to most allowances. Since the Commissioners believed that it was, as a general rule, impossible to ensure that outdoor relief would be less eligible, all relief to the able-bodied should be in a well-regulated workhouse. Outdoor relief to the able-bodied was to be prohibited, an idea which it proved impossible to attain everywhere at all times. The Commissioners' vision of a well-regulated workhouse was utopian (almost as utopian as Bentham's); they expected a proper classification of paupers and specialised

---

[51] *Report*, pp. 227–8. The resemblance between these passages and Bentham's first *Essay* of 1796 is striking. Thus although the Commissioners could have found the distinction between poverty and indigence in Colquhoun, the wording is closer to Bentham's, and in the case of poverty virtually identical ('Poverty is the state of everyone who, in order to obtain subsistence, is forced to have recourse to labour', Bentham Papers, CLIIIa, 21). Bentham's version of less eligibility is quoted in Chapter IV above. The Report also resembles Bentham's *Essay* in its references to the necessity of a Poor Law to prevent widespread mendicity.

treatment of the various classes. This ideal Nicholls and his colleagues abandoned for the simpler and sadder Union Workhouse, whose indiscriminate discipline became the object of so much legitimate, if sometimes exaggerated, criticism. But the Royal Commission, like Oliver Twist, asked for more, and if they are to be blamed for the harshness of the outcome it can only be on the grounds that their demands were not realistic. Not even the new national administration could work such wonders.[52]

The administrative recommendations were the most revolutionary part of the *Report*, and the most original. National uniformity in relief required central supervision, to be provided by a Board of Commissioners and their assistants, with power to unite parishes into unions, to build workhouses, to control the appointment of permanent officers, and to make 'general orders' on methods of relief.[53] The scheme was Chadwick's, and certainly reflected his own administrative preconceptions, but it also arose logically enough from the situation in which reformers found themselves. The Royal Commission and the Government were well aware that they could not reform every parish simply by legislation, and the only alternative was to establish a central authority. These were certainly the terms on which Althorp justified the proposals to the House; the aim was to make the practices of the reformed parishes universal, and since this could not be achieved everywhere at once, an 'anomalous' course was necessary, 'one which went to establish a new and great power in the country'. In the debate only Grote argued that centralised administration was desirable in principle as well as necessary in the circumstances; Chadwick would of course have agreed with him, but not perhaps Senior. The new authority was given the form of an independent Commission in a vain attempt to keep the Poor Law administration out of politics, rather than in a belief that such a system was theoretically superior.[54]

[52] On the Royal Commissioners' expectations see M. Bowley, *op. cit.*, pp. 331–4, and S. and B. Webb, *The Last Hundred Years*, I. 122–30. On the failure to abolish allowances after 1834 see M. E. Rose, 'The Allowance System under the New Poor Law', *Econ. Hist. Review*, 2nd Series, XIX (1966), 607–20; and for a re-assessment of the Union Workhouse see D. Roberts, 'How Cruel was the Victorian Poor Laws', *Hist. Journal*, VI (1963), 97–107.

[53] The main recommendations on the powers of the Commissioners are conveniently quoted in S. and B. Webb, *The Last Hundred Years*, I. 58–61. Among the very few contemporary pamphlets suggesting administrative centralisation note S. Miller, *Pauper Police* etc. (1831); Miller was an admirer of Colquhoun. The Royal Commissioners hesitated to recommend radical amendment of the Law of Settlement, and achieved only the abolition of settlement by hiring and service and by serving an office.

[54] *Parliamentary Debates*, 3rd Series, XXII, 874–89; XXIII. 812–15; and compare S. and B. Webb, *The Last Hundred Years*, I. 76–82.

5. *The Reform of 1834*

The first barrier to be overcome in converting proposals into law was the Cabinet. The Duke of Richmond, in particular, was very opposed to the substitution of indoor for outdoor relief, alleging that workhouses were expensive and demoralising, that a rural rebellion would be incited, and that provided magistrates' powers were curtailed and unions formed, local regeneration would remove abuses: 'a Whately would arise in every parish'. Against these arguments Senior and Sturges Bourne fought hard, stressing the examples of Bingham, Southwell and Uley, and blaming vestries rather than magistrates for the continuance of abuses. Too many farmers and shop-keepers had vested interests in pauperism for local improvement to be universal. Senior claimed later that the decisive point in the debate was Lord Lansdowne's conversion to the view that only the Commissioners' proposals would suffice, and Cabinet should therefore do its duty whatever the risks might be. But Senior was forced to make some concessions, especially on the powers of the new Commission.[55]

More concessions had to be made when the Bill came before Parliament, but on the whole the Government had remarkable success in avoiding major amendments. Stiffened by Senior's continual exhortation, the Ministers stood firm, and with the forbearance of Peel and Wellington were able to take advantage of Parliament's willingness to risk bold experiments in the hope of attaining early relief. Althorp handled matters skilfully in the Commons, drawing the fangs of criticism by minimising the extent of the changes; sometimes, for example on the abolition of outdoor relief, he almost misrepresented the intentions of the Bill in the interests of conciliation. Brougham was much less tactful in the Lords, and Senior was horrified when he introduced the Bill with a remarkably irrelevant abolitionist diatribe. But by giving a little ground here and there the Government succeeded in passing the Bill in four months with surprisingly large majorities in both Houses. Opposition outside Parliament was more widespread, led by Walter and *The Times*.[56]

Inside Parliament the opposition was interesting, if ineffectual. Members rose, of course, to offer all their own favourite ideas on distress and its relief, and labour-rates, allotments, migration, currency reform, reduced taxation, control of machinery, repeal of the Corn

[55] For accounts of Cabinet discussions, based mainly on Senior's MS, see T. Mackay, *History of the English Poor Law*, chap. V, and S. and B. Webb, *The Last Hundred Years*, I. 90–103.

[56] Brougham was inordinately proud of his speech; see *Memoirs of the Life and Times of Lord Brougham* (1871 ed.), III. 411. On Walter's breach with the government over the Bill see *The History of the Times*, I (1935), pp. 288–98.

Laws and radical political reform were all paraded as more desirable alternatives to the Bill. There was also widespread suspicion that the new Commissioners' powers would be dangerously great, and much complaint that the workhouse test was not the panacea the Bill suggested; what use was it in a manufacturing town? The majority would not push their doubts too hard, but an outspoken if heterogeneous minority fought the Bill clause by clause. Old-fashioned radicals such as Burdett and Cobbett pleaded the right to relief, and attacked the new Commission as a dangerous constitutional innovation, opening immense and frightful opportunities for jobbery and tyranny. On a very different line of argument, but to the same conclusion, Sir Samuel Whalley and other defenders of local interests vehemently opposed central interference. Marylebone was a well-run parish, and be damned to any meddling 'Bashaws'. But Cobbett's tactics were eccentric—he opposed improvements to the Bill lest they make it workable, and thanked God for a House of Lords in the mistaken hope that their Lordships would throw it out—and Whalley weakened his plea for a traditional localism with irrelevant abolitionist asides. The great speech in opposition came not from this temporary alliance of radicals and traditionalists but from that dissident economist, Poulett Scrope, who argued eloquently that the Royal Commission had exaggerated the evils of the Poor Law and that its remedy was unnecessarily severe. Outdoor relief could be made less eligible, and 'costly and cruel workhouse schemes' could therefore not be justified. And while a new central authority might be necessary, there was a danger that the deserving poor might be made to suffer with the undeserving unless some more efficient check to 'flinthearted vestries' was retained. The right to relief was England's glory, and its essence the right to appeal against overseers' judgments. The pauper could not appeal to the Commissioners: 'he might as well be told to apply to the great Mogul'. Retain, therefore, some powers for magistrates, in order to prevent too harsh an enforcement of the workhouse test. Scarlett supported Scrope, but the majority stayed with the Government. The Bill went to the Lords, where, after a somewhat unseemly squabble between two bishops on the subject of bastardy, it was passed with only minor amendments. The elusive goal of a major reform of the Poor Law had been attained at last.

6. *Men and Measures*

It was one thing to amend the Poor Law and another to transform the practice of relief in the country at large. How the Poor Law Commissioners undertook this task, how they modified the intentions of the Royal Commissioners with whose policy they were entrusted, and how they became the centre of political storms, and the objects of intemperate abuse and praise cannot concern us here. The clear-cut provisions of the Amendment Act should not blind us to important continuities in both thought and practice before and after 1834. Debate continued, though its setting was transformed. The existence of a national policy, if not of national uniformity in practice, gave the debate a focus it had previously lacked; the old interplay of local and individual opinion gave way to attempts to influence central policy of a kind much more familiar in modern political systems. And, as in so many spheres of government activity in the nineteenth century, the creation of a permanent, professional central administration injected a new element into debate as well as into practice. Like the factory inspectors, the staff of the Commission formed an influential source of ideas and suggestions, and the system became an organisation capable of growing and changing even without the injection of new life from external public opinion. In time the organism became less adventurous, and the heroic age when the principles of 1834 were an inspiration for reform was succeeded by another in which they were merely the sacred text of a rigid conservatism. The Amendment Act killed abolitionism as an effective force, but the main ingredients of the abolitionist creed— a preference for private charity and a dogmatic defence of a free economy—remained a check on what might have been a natural tendency of central administration to grow more flexible and more comprehensive in its treatment of poverty. The system did expand and become more flexible, but remained sufficiently confined in what might be called the minimal dogmas of 1834 for it to appear a bar to innovation by the end of the century. The reformers of 1908 therefore sought the break-up, and not the extension, of the Poor Law.

The Amendment Act of 1834 has been described, loosely enough, as a Malthusian or a benthamite measure. Of course neither man played any part in the preparation or passing of the Act—Bentham died in 1832 and Malthus in 1834—and such descriptions therefore imply influence rather than participation in the legislative process. In recent years there have been attempts to find a common pattern in the process of administrative and social reform in nineteenth-century England, and it has become fashionable to discount intellectual influences on legislation. Professor Oliver Macdonagh has constructed a plausible 'model' of the growth of government action on social problems, a model in which organised opinion and the impetus for change inherent in administrative instruments react upon each other in specific social situations.[57] There is little room in this process for general social

[57] O. MacDonagh, 'The Nineteenth-century Revolution in Government: A reappraisal', *Hist. Journal*, I (1958), 52–67.

doctrines, and other writers have also questioned old assumptions of a pervasive Benthamite influence on nineteenth-century legislation and administration, assumptions which go back at least as far as Dicey's *Law and Opinion in England* of 1904. The administrators are the new heroes of reform in social matters, and it is usual to insist on the collective influence of innumerable minor figures who, innocent of utilitarian theory, built the coral reef of efficient government action out of the ocean of eighteenth-century jobbery.[58] More recently these new assumptions have been attacked as a 'Tory interpretation of history' in which 'progressive' thought, and especially Benthamism, has too little place.[59] Certainly there has been some exaggeration, on both sides, but also a new realism in the analysis of the relationship between opinion, legislation and administration. The relationship was truly complex, and it would be unfortunate if premature generalisation impeded further research.

The Poor Law was not of course a new sphere of government action, like factory regulation or the control of emigrant shipping. It was certainly the subject of a public campaign in the early nineteenth century, but a campaign for its abolition and not its extension. If the outcome, the Act of 1834, was nevertheless the most important single extension of central government activity in these decades, this should be seen as a paradox rather than as a precedent. Central control was sought less for its own sake than because continued localism was thought intolerable, and the more drastic solution of abolition was politically and socially impracticable. In this sphere, and perhaps in others, the interaction of local and central initiative added an important dimension to the pattern of change.[60] And on the national as well as the local scene the new deterrent policy in relief could be explained by the logic of the situation rather than by major intellectual influences. But would not such an explanation remain a partial one?

The case for describing the Amendment Act as Malthusian is weak.

[58] See, for example, D. Roberts, 'Jeremy Bentham and the Victorian Administrative State', *Victorian Studies*, II (1959), 193–210, and compare his *Victorian Origins of the British Welfare State* (New Haven, 1960); on the difficulties of distinguishing between publicist and administrator in the nineteenth century see G. Kitson Clark, 'Statesmen in Disguise', *Hist. Journal*, II (1959), 19–39.

[59] J. Hart, 'Nineteenth-century Social Reform: a Tory Interpretation of History', *Past and Present*, 31 (1965), 39–61. H. Parris, 'The Nineteenth-Century Revolution in Government: a Re-appraisal re-appraised', *Hist. Journal*, III (1960), 17–37, offered a more moderate criticism of MacDonagh's thesis. The best brief account of the development of government activity in nineteenth-century England may be found in G. Kitson Clark, *An Expanding Society, Britain 1830-1900* (Melbourne, 1967), pp. 126–83.

[60] Compare R. M. Gutchen, 'Local Improvements and Centralisation in Nineteenth-century England', *Historical Journal*, IV (1961), 85–96.

The fact that the Royal Commissioners did not find, or expect to find, over-population as a prime cause of distress would not in itself disprove their Malthusianism, since Malthus himself was equivocal on this point. But Malthus was consistent in his abolitionism, and the Commission's explicit rejection of abolition both as an ideal and in practice makes them at most revisionist Malthusians, heretical by the master's strict canons. Less eligibility was an answer to Malthus's objections to the Poor Law rather than a development of them, though admittedly it had little point except as an answer; it assumed that abolitionist arguments had force, if not complete cogency. Malthus must be admitted relevance as the doyen of the abolitionists, if not as the originator of the doctrine, but the Amendment Act was a new departure and not merely the culmination of the abolitionist attack on the system.

Bentham's case is very different. His name was not bandied about in debate, and it would be difficult to argue that his views on poverty or even on administration were popular, or even widely known. His main influence was on and through disciples, difficult though it might be to determine what distinguished a Benthamite. To attempt a simple definition of Benthamism would be beside the point; the utilitarian sage was a more protean figure than (for example) Malthus, and if no one in his right senses would seriously consider applying in the real world of the 1830s Bentham's blueprint for poor-law reform in the 1790s it is by no means certain that Bentham expected them to do so. The Webbs claim that Chadwick, Coulson and some of the Assistant Commissioners exerted a strong 'Benthamite' influence on the Royal Commission: Finer, on the other hand, stresses that Chadwick was a creative reformer in his own right, and not a mere Benthamite parrot. The point is apposite, but must not be exaggerated. Bentham, with his insistence on investigation of fact and the adaptation of general rules to particular circumstances, assumed that reformers must be creative, or they would not be truly Benthamite reformers. Chadwick was too ambitious and self-confident a man to rest content with the inherited armoury of Benthamite schemes, but we must assume that he was well acquainted with them. He had worked on the chapter on indigence in Bentham's *Constitutional Code*, and in all probability read most if not all of Bentham's published and unpublished writings on the subject. If we knew precisely which of Bentham's manuscripts he thought fit to show to Senior—he certainly showed some of them—we might estimate more exactly Bentham's direct contribution to the principles of 1834. The fact that Chadwick published the *Observations on Pitt's Bill* in 1838 suggests that he wished to emphasise Bentham's attack on outdoor relief, though the work did discuss other matters also. Profitable employment, one of the central themes of *Pauper Management*

Improved, was implicitly rejected by Chadwick and the Royal Commission; of course it did not appear in the *Constitutional Code* either. But the Commission, and Chadwick, shared Bentham's insistence on the distinction between poverty and indigence, on the classification of paupers, on institutional rather than outdoor relief, and on systematic professional management under definite rules as the basis of a reformed Poor Law. And it remains at the least a remarkable coincidence that Bentham, and Bentham alone among his contemporaries, had expounded the principle of less eligibility in its full theoretical significance as a justification for relief, and had concluded, after a systematic examination of the alternatives, that outdoor relief was not consistent with the principle. By 1830 no one was Benthamite enough to look to the Poor Plan as a complete and detailed model of reform, much as the old man himself might regret the lost battles of the 1790s; but the general principles on which it was based bear so many resemblances to the princples of 1834 that the onus of proof is surely on those who would deny Bentham's influence on the Act which created the new Poor Law.[61]

Even if this influence is admitted, however, the differences in style and circumstance between the Bentham of the 1790s and the Benthamites of the 1830s must be recognised. The younger Bentham was a philosopher in search of enlightened despots willing to introduce his systematic reforms, and although he came to despair of despots and developed a utilitarian political radicalism he never quite came to terms with popular opinion as an instrument of political change and reform. Neither, perhaps, did most of his disciples, as they fought to impose a logical coherence on the complex tide of legislative and administrative improvement in the nineteenth century. There was always in Bentham's own work a peculiar tension between empiricism and strict deductive argument as he searched for tidy solutions to the complicated problems of the real world; he recognised that each solution was valid only for its own time and place, and claimed only that the general principles were eternal. Thus his precise schemes and proposals, such as the Poor Plan, receded into history, and Benthamites had to struggle anew in each new situation to achieve the proper blend of general principle and adaptation to circumstance. A bold questioning of traditional assumptions, a systematic analysis of problems, and an empirical search for utilitarian solutions remained hall-marks of the Benthamite, though in many

[61] S. and B. Webb, *The Last Hundred Years*, I. 48–50; S. E. Finer, *The Life and Times of Sir Edwin Chadwick*, esp. pp. 12–27, 44–9, 74–5. For a perceptive comment on Malthusian and Benthamite aspects of 1834 see Professor Asa Briggs' review of D. V. Glass, *Introduction to Malthus*, in the *British Journal of Sociology*, IV (1953), 367.

specimens they wore faint in time.[62] Much work remains to be done before the relationship between Bentham and his followers can be delineated, and the role of the Benthamites in nineteenth-century reform movements unravelled. While important, it was not perhaps very extensive, and success often rested on coincidence with the efforts of others less interested in general social principles. In most spheres of argument and activity, men with a radical utilitarian cast of mind were rare, and practical conclusions which we might regard as Benthamite could be reached by very different processes of thought. Chadwick might take advantage of the situation of 1832–4 to make the Report of the Royal Commission a Benthamite document, but men like Althorp neither saw it as such nor supported it in the same intellectual terms of reference. And if the centralised administration of the new Poor Law came closer to Benthamite ideals than any other administrative reform of the period, Parliament tolerated the innovation for quite other reasons. This victory of Benthamism was not quite coincidental, since in one sense Parliament confirmed Bentham's hypothesis that central control was the only empirically valid solution to the problem. It was also pyrrhic; the storm which arose around the new Poor Law seemed to confirm the rashness of the innovation, imperative though its logic had seemed in 1834.

Certainly the Act of 1834, whether Benthamite or Malthusian or neither, was not passed as an intellectual exercise. On the other hand neither was it a mindless reaction to a specific social-economic situation; it emerged from a debate, and not merely from a conflict of interests. But the debate was complex and many-sided, and if, in any rational distribution of a man's time, only great books are worth reading, a concentration of interest in intellectual history on the truly original minds exaggerates their influence and isolates them from their context. There were few dominating figures in the discussion of pauperism; so many of the minor writers and speakers were groping, in their tedious and limited arguments, to the conclusions we might glibly ascribe to Malthusian and Benthamite influence. But even if we discount the influence of major thinkers in the history of social policy, the true significance of general ideas remains to be estimated and understood. Such ideas, explicit or assumed, are the intellectual spectacles through which men saw their world, judged circumstances, and framed courses of action. And men were often misled by an intellectual astigmatism,

[62] It is nevertheless desirable to reserve the word 'Benthamite' for men or doctrines with an explicit relationship with Bentham himself; Steven Marcus adds little to his analysis of William Acton's social attitude by describing his position as 'generally realistic, liberal and Benthamite' (*The Other Victorians: a Study of Sexuality and Pornography in Mid-Nineteenth-Century England* (1966), p. 5).

mistaking even their own interests almost as often as they failed to estimate fairly the claims of others. Even the Royal Commission, while not without originality, was still obsessed with notions which were no longer entirely relevant, or were at least insufficiently comprehensive to embrace newly emerging circumstances as well as old. The kernel of the intellectual debate on pauperism in the years between 1790 and 1830 was the rise of abolitionism, by no means a new argument but the one which seemed most relevant and cogent at the time. It did not require originality to see in the Poor Law itself a major cause of pauperism; it required either considerable perspicuity or deeply held prejudices in favour of some other explanation to realise that this was a grave simplification of a complicated truth.

The ideas on poverty and its relief which grew to dominate opinion in the early nineteenth century have since gained a bad reputation. The workhouse test was not a generous principle, and it will always be difficult to admire the attitude of those who admitted the existence of widespread distress yet sought to curb or even abolish the most obvious methods of relieving it. We do not blame Count Rumford for being wrong about heat and light, but we may be inclined to think some of his attitudes to poverty detestable. In the debate on distress it is the literature of protest which is immediately attractive, and it is Cobbett— or perhaps Southey, according to taste—who wins our easy admiration. But were Cobbett's arguments more cogent than Malthus's in the circumstances of the day? The historian must strive above all to understand how men viewed their world, partial though those views must be. The allowance system on the one hand, and the Union Workhouse on the other, can all too easily provide the themes for myths of oppression with which to indict whole generations. Attitudes and institutions which could be justly deplored in an age of affluence may be more easily justified in an age of poverty, provided no one claims for them eternal truth. But not completely justified, for it was possible for a few men of exceptional moral and intellectual insight to reject the half-truths of debate and to seek a better solution. But exceptional insight remains exceptional, in our own age as much as in theirs.

Bibliography

'A pamphlet on the Poor Laws generally contains some little piece of favourite nonsense, by which we are told this enormous evil may be perfectly cured. The first gentleman recommends little gardens; the second cows; the third village shops; the fourth a spade; the fifth Dr. Bell, and so forth. Every man rushes to the press with his small morsel of imbecility; and is not easy till he sees his impertinence stitched in blue covers.'

Sydney Smith, *Edinburgh Review*, 1820.

1. Manuscript Collections

Bentham MSS, University College London and British Museum.

The bulk of Bentham's MSS on pauperism is in the University College Library, in Boxes CXV, CXXXIII, CXLIX, and CLI-CLIV. The papers are in a state of confusion, but *The Poor's Cry* and other early material is in Box CLI; copies of the *Essays* of 1796 in Boxes CLIIa and CLIIIa; *Pauper Systems Compared*, almost complete, in Box CLIIb; the *Observations* in Box CLIIIb; and essays on Settlement, on the Independent Husbandman and on Badging in Box CLIVb. The other boxes contain drafts of *Pauper Management Improved*; correspondence on the Plan, and 'marginal outlines' of parts of it, are scattered through the boxes.

Dumont MSS, Bibliothèque Publique et Universitaire de Genève.

Box 33 (i) contains letters from Bentham and others; the incomplete MS of *Examen des Maux qui s'opposent au bonheur publique*, which includes a Benthamite chapter on indigence, is in Box 56, while *Mémoire et observations sur l'administration des Pauvres, d'après un ouvrage de Bentham* is in Box 63.

Pitt MSS, Chatham Papers, P.R.O.

Corresqondence and other papers on the Poor Law and Pitt's Bill

are in folders 307 and 308, the latter containing also an able report from Colquhoun on the distresses of 1799–1800.
Whitbread MSS, Bedfordshire C.R.O.
Papers 3642–3676 consist mainly of correspondence on the poor and the Poor Law, 1806–1812, while papers 762–772 and 806–820 include much material on paupers and relief in Bedfordshire.
Correspondence of Arthur Young, British Museum Add. MSS 35127–8

2. Parliamentary Debates
Parliamentary History of England (1792–1801).
Parliamentary Register (1795–1800).
Cobbett's Parliamentary Debates (1803–1812).
Hansard's Parliamentary Debates (1812–1834).

3. Parliamentary Papers
1775 First Series IX, Report on the Laws which concern the Relief and Settlement of the Poor.
1777, First Series IX, Report from the Committee . . . to consider the Returns made by the Overseers of the Poor.
1787, First Series IX, Report from the Committee on Certain Returns relative to the State of the Poor.
1803–4, XIII, Abstract of the Answers and Returns relative to the Expense and Maintenance of the Poor.
1812–13, III, Report from the Committee on Poor Houses and Poor Rates.
1815–16, III, S.C. on the State of Mendicity in the Metropolis.
1816, IV, S.C. on the Poor Laws of this Kingdom.
1817, VI, S.C. on the Poor Laws.
1818, V, S.C. of H. of L. on the Poor Laws.
1818, V, S.C. on the Poor Laws.
1818, V, Second Report from S.C. on the Poor Laws.
1818, V, Third Report from S.C. on the Poor Laws, with an appendix containing returns from the General Assembly of the Church of Scotland.
1818, XIX, Abstract of the Answers and Returns . . . relative to the Maintenance of the Poor in England 1813–15.
1819, II, S.C. on the Poor Laws.
1820, VII, Supplementary Report . . . on the Management of the Poor in Scotland.
1821, IV, S.C. on Poor Rate Returns (1750–1820).
1822, V, S.C. on Poor Rate Returns.
1823, V, S.C. on Poor Rate Returns.

1824, IV, S.C. on Poor Rate Returns.
1824, XIX, S.C. on Labourers' Wages.
1825, IV, S.C. on Poor Rate Returns.
1825, IV, S.C. on the Laws respecting Friendly Societies.
1825, XIX, Abstract of Returns prepared by order of the S.C. on Labourers' Wages.
1826, III, S.C. on Poor Rate Returns.
1826, IV, S.C. on Emigration from the United Kingdom.
1827, III, S.C. on the Laws relating to Friendly Societies.
1827, V, Three Reports from S.C. on Emigration.
1828, IV, S.C. on the Law of Parochial Settlements.
1828, IV, S.C. on . . . the Employment or Relief of Able-bodied Persons from the Poor Rate.
1829, XXI, Abstract of Returns . . . on Relief to Able-bodied Labourers.
1830, VII, Three Reports from S.C. on the State of the Poor in Ireland.
1830–31, XI, Local Taxation: Account of the money expended for the maintenance of the Poor in every Parish, 1825–9.
1831, VIII, S.C. of H. of L. on the Poor Laws.
1834, XXVII, Report from the Commissioners for inquiry into the Administration and Practical Operation of the Poor Laws.
1834, XXVIII–XXIX, Appendix A, Reports of Assistant Commissioners.
1834, XXX–XXXIV, Appendix B_1, Answers to Rural Questions.
1834, XXXV–XXXVI, Appendix B_2, Answers to Town Questions.
1834, XXXVII, Appendix C, Communications.
1834, XXXVIII, Appendix D, Labour Rate; Appendix E, Vagrancy; Appendix F, Foreign Communications.
1835, XLVII, Poor Rate Returns, 1830–34.

4. *Newspapers and Periodicals*

Annals of Agriculture and other Useful Arts (1784–1808).
Cobbett's Weekly Political Register (1804–19).
Gentleman's Magazine (1790–1817).
Edinburgh Review (1802–35).
Labourers' Friend and Handicrafts Chronicle (1820–25).
The Philanthropist: or Repository of Hints and Suggestions calculated to promote the Comfort and Happiness of Man (1811–19).
Quarterly Review (1809–35).
Reports of the Society for Bettering the Condition and Increasing the Comforts of the Poor (1798–1817).
The Times
Westminster Review (1824–36).

5. *Contemporary Books and Pamphlets*

An Abstract of some important parts of a Bill, now depending in Parliament . . . with some practical observations. . . . Prepared by a Committee of the Joint Vestry of the United Parishes of St Giles in the Fields and St George, Bloomsbury etc. (1797).

An Account of the Work-Houses in Great Britain in the Year 1732. . . . *With many other Curious and Useful Remarks upon the State of the Poor* (3rd ed. 1786).

J. Acland, *A Plan for rendering the Poor independent of Public Contributions, founded on the Basis of the Friendly Societies* etc. (1786).

An Address to the Plain Sense of the People, on the present high price of bread (1800).

T. Alcock, *Observations on the Defects of the Poor Laws and on the Causes and Consequences of the Great Increase and Burden of the Poor* (1752).

An Apology for the Poor etc. (2nd ed. 1823).

J. Ashdowne, *An Essay on the Existing Poor Laws and Present State of the Labouring Poor* etc. (1817).

J. H. L. Baker, *A Letter to the Rev George Cooke, D.D., Chairman of the Quarter Sessions for the County of Gloucester* (1830).

S. Banfill, *First Letter to Sir T. D. Acland, Bart. M.P. on the Means of improving the Condition of the Labouring Classes and Reducing Parochial Assessments* etc. (Exeter, 1817).

——, *Second Letter* etc. (1818).

——, *Third Letter* etc. (1828).

Sir James Barrow, *Decisions in the Court of King's Bench upon Settlement Cases* (1786).

J. Barton, *Observations on the Circumstances which influence the Condition of the Labouring Classes of Society* (1817).

——, *An Inquiry into the Causes of the Progressive Depreciation of Agricultural Labour in Modern Times; with suggestions for its remedy* (1820).

——, *A Statement of the Consequences likely to ensure from our growing Population if not remedied by Colonisation* (1830).

[T. Battye], *A Report of the Committee of the Associated Ley Payers in the Township of Manchester* etc. (1794).

T. Battye, *A Disclosure of Parochial Abuse, Artifice and Peculation in the Town of Manchester* etc. (2nd ed. 1796).

——, *Strictures upon the Churchwardens and Overseers of Manchester . . . also Observations extracted from the most eminent modern writers on the subject of the Poor Laws* (1801).

——, *An Address to the Ley Payers in the Town of Manchester* (1807).

——, *A Reply to Mr Unite's Address to Ley Payers of Manchester* (N.D.).

J. S. Bayldon, *A Treatise on the Valuation of Property for the Poor's Rate; showing the method of rating* etc. (1828).

P. Bayley, *Observations on the Plan of an Institution for the Promotion of Industry and Provident Economy among the Manufacturing and Labouring Classes* etc. (1819).

W. D. Bayly, *The State of the Poor and Working Classes considered, with practical plans for improving their condition in society, and superseding the present system of compulsory assessment* (1820).

J. Beatson, *An Examination of Mr Owen's Plans, for relieving Distress, removing Discontent, and 'Recreating the Character of Men'* etc. (1823).

B. Beaumont, *An Essay on Provident or Parish Banks* etc. (1816).

[J. T. Becher], *Rules, Orders and Regulations . . . for the Government of the House of Correction Provided and Established at Southwell* etc. (1808).

J. T. Becher, *The Friendly Institution established at Southwell* (1823).

——, *The Constitution of Friendly Societies upon Legal and Scientific Principles* etc. (3rd ed. 1824).

——, *Observations upon the Report from the Select Committee of the House of Commons on the Laws respecting Friendly Societies* etc. (1826).

——, *The Anti Pauper System, exemplifying the positive and practical good, realised by the relievers and the relieved under the frugal, beneficial and lawful administration of the Poor Laws prevailing at Southwell* etc. (1828).

A. Becket, *Public Prosperity: or Arguments in support of a Plan for raising six millions sterling and for employing that sum in loans to necessitous and industrious persons* (2nd ed. 1813).

T. Beddoes, *Essay on the Public Merits of Mr. Pitt* (1796).

The Beggar's Complaint, against Rack Rent Landlords, Corn Factors, Great Farmers, Monopolisers, Paper Money Makers, and War, and many other Oppressors and Oppressions etc. *By one who pities the oppressed* (2nd ed. 1812).

J. Bentham, *Works* (ed. J. Bowring, 1833–43):
History of the War between Jeremy Bentham and George III, by one of the Belligerents.
Pannomial Fragments.
Anarchical Fallacies etc.
Constitutional Code etc.
Life of Bentham.

——, *Economic Writings* (ed. W. Stark, 1952–4):
Manual of Political Economy.
Institute of Political Economy.
Defence of a Maximum.

——, *Observations on the Poor Bill introduced by the Rt. Hon. William Pitt* (ed. E. Chadwick, 1838).

——, *Pauper Management Improved: Particularly by Means of an Application of the Panopticon Principle of Construction* (1812).

——, *Theory of Legislation* (ed. C. K. Ogden, 1950).

Sir Thomas Bernard, *The Barrington School* etc. (1812).

——, *An Account of a Supply of Fish for the Manufacturing Poor, with Observations* (1813).

——, *On the Supply of Employment and Subsistence for the Labouring Classes* etc. (1817).

——, *A Letter to the Rt. Rev. the Lord Bishop of Durham . . . on the Principle and Detail of the Measures now under the consideration of Parliament* etc. (1807).

J. E. Bicheno, *An Inquiry into the Nature of Benevolence, chiefly with a view to elucidate the Principles of the Poor Law* etc. (1817).

——, *An Inquiry into the Poor Laws, chiefly with a view to examine them as a scheme of National Benevolence* etc. (1824).

R. Blakemore, *A Letter to the Rt. Hon. C. B. Bathurst, M.P., on the Subject of the Poor Laws* (1819).

W. Bleamire, *Remarks on the Poor Laws, and the Maintenance of the Poor* (1800).

D. Boileau, *An Introduction to the Study of Political Economy* etc. (1811).

J. Bone, *Outline of a Plan for Reducing the Poor's Rate, and amending the condition of the aged and unfortunate* etc. (1805).

——, *The Principles and Regulations of Tranquility; an institution commenced in the metropolis* etc. (1806).

D. Booth, *Dissertation on the Ratios of Increase in Population and in the means of Subsistence* (printed in Godwin, *Of Population* etc. 1820, pp. 243–94).

——, *A Letter to the Rev. T. R. Malthus, M.A., F.R.S., being an answer to the Criticism on Mr. Godwin's Work on Population* etc. (1823).

H. Booth, *The Question of the Poor Laws considered, and the causes and character of Pauperism, in connection with the laws and principle of Population, briefly explained and illustrated* (Liverpool, 1818).

J. Bosworth, *The Practical Means of Reducing the Poor's Rate, encouraging Virtue, and increasing the comforts of the aged, afflicted and deserving Poor* etc. (1824).

——, *The Necessity of the Anti Pauper System, shown by an example of the Oppression and Misery produced by the Allowance System* etc. (1829).

——, *Misery in the Midst of Plenty, or the Perversion of the Poor Laws* (1833).

J. Bowles, *Reasons for the Establishment of Provident Institutions called*

Savings Banks; with a word of caution respecting their formation etc. (3rd ed. 1817).

J. Boys, *General View of the Agriculture of the County of Kent* etc. (2nd ed. 1805).

Bread for All. A Plan for doing away with the Poor's Rates etc., by an English Gentleman (1824?).

C. D. Brereton, *Observations on the Administration of the Poor Laws in Agricultural Districts* (Norwich, 1824).

——, *An Inquiry into the Work-House System and the Law of Maintenance in Agricultural Districts* (Norwich, 1825).

——, *A Practical Inquiry into the Number, Means of Employment and Wages of Agricultural Labourers* (Norwich, 1824, 1826).

——, *The Subordinate Magistracy and Parish System Considered, in their Connection with the Causes and Remedies of Modern Pauperism* etc. (Norwich, 1827).

J. N. Brewer, *Some Thoughts on the Present State of the English Peasantry. Written in consequence of Mr. Whitbread's motion in the House of Commons* etc. (1807).

S. Brookes, *Thoughts on the Poor Laws; with a Plan for Reducing the Poor's Rates Preparatory to their Abolition* (1822).

H. Brougham, *Memoirs of the Life and Times of Lord Brougham, written by Himself* (1871 ed.).

F. Burdett, *Annals of Banks for Savings* (1818).

[M. Burgoyne], *A Statistical Account of the Hundreds of Harlow, Ongar, and the half Hundred of Waltham* etc. (1817).

Sir Egerton Brydges, *Letters on the Poor Laws* etc. (1813).

——, *Arguments in favour of the Practicability of Relieving the Able-bodied Poor, by finding Employment for them* etc. (1817).

——, *The Population and Riches of Nations Considered together* etc. (1819).

——, *What are Riches? or an Examination of the Definitions of this Subject given by Modern Economists* (Geneva, 1821).

E. Burke, *Thoughts and Details on Scarcity, originally presented to the Right Hon. William Pitt in the month of November, 1795.*

——, *A Vindication of Natural Society* (1756).

——, *Third Letter on a Regicide Peace* (1797).

R. Burn, *History of the Poor Laws* (1764).

The Cabinet: by a Society of Gentlemen (Norwich, 1795).

Catherine Cappe, *Observations on Charity Schools, Female Friendly Societies, and other subjects connected with the views of the Ladies Committee* (York, 1805).

——, *Thoughts on Various Charitable and other Important Institutions and on the best mode of conducting them* etc. (York, 1814).

D. Carpenter, *Reflections suggested by Mr. Whitbread's Bill and by several publications, lately circulated, on the subject of the Poor Laws* etc. (1807).

T. Chalmers, *Tracts on Pauperism* (1833).

——, *The Christian and Civic Economy of our Large Towns* (1821–6).

W. H. Chamberlin, *A Plan for the Employment of Labourers* (1819).

Marquis de Chastelux, *Agriculture and Population* etc. (English ed. 1792).

E. Christian, *A Plan for a County Provident Bank, with Observations upon Provident Institutions already established* (1816).

W. Clark, *Thoughts on the Management and Relief of the Poor* etc. (1815).

W. Clarkson, *An Inquiry into the Cause of the Increase of Pauperism and Poor Rates* etc. (2nd ed. 1816).

A Clear, Fair and Candid Investigation of the population, commerce and agriculture of this Kingdom; with a full refutation of all Mr. Malthus's principles etc. (1810).

J. Cleghorn, *Thoughts on the Expediency of a General Provident Institution for the Benefit of the Working Classes* etc. (1824).

W. Cobbett, *Twelve Sermons* (1823).

——, *Cottage Economy* (1823).

S. T. Coleridge, *A Lay Sermon addressed to the Higher and Middle Classes on the Existing Distresses and Discontents* (1817).

Collections relative to systematic Relief of the Poor, at different Periods and in different Countries, etc. (1815).

A. Collett, *A Letter to T. S. Gooch, Esq., M.P. upon the present Ruinous System of relieving unemployed men with money* etc. (2nd ed. 1824).

[P. Colquhoun], *A Plan for the Purpose of affording extensive Relief to the Poor* etc. (1795).

——, *Explanation of the Plan proposed for the Relief of Industrious Artizans . . . and other meritorious Poor* etc. (1795).

——, *An Account of a Meat and Soup Charity* etc. (1797).

——, *Suggestions offered to the Consideration of the Public . . . for the purpose of reducing the consumption of bread corn* etc. (1799).

——, *The Economy of an Institution established in Spitalfields, London, for the purpose of supplying the Poor with a Good Meat Soup* etc. (1799).

——, *A Treatise on the Police of the Metropolis . . . by a Magistrate* (2nd ed. 1796, 6th ed. 1800, 7th ed. 1806).

P. Colquhoun, *A General View of the National Police System, Recommended by the Select Committee of Finance to the House of Commons* etc. (1799).

——, *The State of Indigence, and the Situation of the Casual Poor in the Metropolis, Explained* etc. (1799).

——, *A Treatise on Indigence* etc. (1806).

——, *A Treatise on the Wealth, Power and Resources of the British Empire* etc. (1814).

——, *Considerations on the Means of affording Profitable Employment to the Redundant Population of Great Britain and Ireland* etc. (1818).

W. T. Comber, *An Enquiry into the State of National Subsistence, as connected with the Progress of Wealth and Population* (1808).

Communications to the Board of Agriculture, on subjects relative to the Husbandry and Internal Improvement of the Country (1797–1802).

Comparative Statement of the Accounts of the Parish of Speen, Berks, for the Years ending Easter 1819 and Easter 1820, with some prefatory Observations.

The Connexion between Industry and Property; or a Proposal to make a fixed and permanent Allowance to Labourers etc. (Exeter, 1798).

F. Const, *The Laws relating to the Poor* (1800).

W. Copland, *A Letter to the Rev C. D. Brereton in Reply to his Observations on the Administration of the Poor Laws in Agricultural Districts* etc. (Norwich, 1824).

[E. Copleston], *Cursory Hints on the Application of Public Subscriptions in providing Employment and Relief for the Labouring Class* etc. (Oxford, 1817).

E. Copleston, *A Letter to the Rt. Hon. Robert Peel, M.P. for the University of Oxford on the Pernicious Effect of a Variable Standard of Value* etc. (Oxford, 1819).

——, *A Second Letter to the Rt. Hon. Robert Peel, M.P. for the University of Oxford, on the Causes of the Increase of Pauperism, and on the Poor Laws* etc. (Oxford, 1819).

J. Cottingham, *Letter to Samuel Whitbread Esq., M.P. containing some remarks on the Poor Laws leading to a description of the Peculiar Poor Situation of the Hamlet of Mile-End New-Town, Stepney* (1807).

T. P. Courtenay, *Copy of a Letter to the Rt. Hon. William Sturges Bourne, Chairman of the Select Committee of the House of Commons appointed for the Consideration of the Poor Laws* etc. (1817).

——, *A Treatise upon the Poor Laws* (1818).

J. W. Cowell, *A Letter to the Rev. J. T. Becher of Southwell in reply to certain charges and assertions made* etc. (1834).

J. Craig, *Elements of Political Science* (Edinburgh, 1814).

Lieut. Gen. C. G. Craufurd, *Observations on the State of the Country since the Peace* etc. (1817).

——, *A Supplementary Section on the Poor Laws* etc. (1817).

S. Crumpe, *An Essay on the best means of providing Employment for the People* etc. (Dublin, 1793).

J. Cull, *A Letter addressed to the Rt. Hon. William Sturges Bourne, M.P. on the Subject of the Poor Laws* (1820).

J. W. Cunningham, *A Few Observations on Friendly Societies and their Influence on Public Morals* (1817).

J. C. Curwen, *Hints on the Economy of Feeding Stock . . . and Bettering the Condition of the Poor* (1808).

——, *Sketch of a Plan by J. C. Curwen Esq. M.P. for Bettering the Condition of the Labouring Classes of the Community* etc. (1817).

R. Davenport, *A Practicable, easy and safe Plan for checking the Increase of Pauperism and the Evils resulting from the Poor Laws* (1823).

R. Davidson, *A Short Exhibition of the Poor Laws of Scotland* etc. (1816).

D. Davies, *The Case of the Labourers in Husbandry stated and considered* etc. (1795).

J. Davis, *Common Sense on Agricultural Distress; its Reality, its Causes and its Remedies* (1822).

W. Davis, *Friendly advice to industrious and frugal persons, recommending Provident Institutions, or Savings Banks* (4th ed. 1817).

J. Davison, *Considerations on the Poor Laws* (1817).

T. Day, *A Dialogue between a Justice of the Peace and a Farmer* (1785).

D. Defoe, *Giving Alms No Charity* (1704).

A Draught of a Bill for the Relief and Employment of the Poor etc. (1787).

H. Bate Dudley, *A Few Observations respecting the Present State of the Poor, and the Defects of the Poor Laws* etc. (1802).

H. Duncan, *An Essay on the Nature and Advantages of Parish Banks for the Savings of the Industrious* (Edinburgh, 2nd ed. 1816).

——, *A Letter to W. R. K. Douglas Esq., M.P. on the expedience of the Bill brought by him into Parliament for the protection and encouragement of banks for savings in Scotland* etc. (Dumfries, 1819).

J. Duthy, *Letters on the Agricultural Petition and on the Poor Laws* etc. (1819).

G. Dyer, *The Complaints of the Poor People of England* etc. (1793).

——, *A Dissertation on the Theory and Practice of Benevolence* (1795).

Sir F. M. Eden, *The State of the Poor: or an History of the Labouring Classes in England* etc. (1797).

——, *Observations on Friendly Societies, for the Maintenance of the Industrious Classes, during Sickness, Infirmity, Old Age and other exigencies* (1801).

[T. R. Edmonds], *An Enquiry into the Principles of Population, Exhibiting a system of Regulations for the Poor* etc. (1832).

G. Edwards, *Radical Means of counteracting the present Scarcity, and preventing Famine in the Future* etc. (1801).

Enquiry into the Consequences of the Present Diminished Value of Human Labour . . . in Letters to T. F. Buxton, Esq., M.A. (1819).

G. Ensor, *An Inquiry concerning the Population of Nations, containing a refutation of Mr. Malthus's Essay on Population* (1818).

——, *The Poor and their Relief* (1823).

An Essay on the Poor Laws, as they regard the real interests both of Rich and Poor (1810).

T. Estcourt, *An Account of the Result of an Effort to Better the Condition of the Poor in a Country Village* etc. (1804).

A. H. Everett, *New Ideas on Population with Remarks on the Theories o Malthus and Godwin* (1823).

Extracts from the Information Received by His Majesty's Commissioners as to the Administration and Operation of the Poor Laws (1833).

R. Fellowes, *Thoughts on the Present depressed State of the Agricultural Interests of this Kingdom and on the rapid increase of the Poor Rates* etc. (1817).

——, *The Rights of Property Vindicated, against the claims of universal suffrage* etc. (1818).

J. H. Forbes, *A Short Account of the Edinburgh Savings Bank, containing directions for establishing similar Banks* etc. (Edinburgh, 1815).

——, *Observations on Banks for Savings* etc. (Edinburgh, 1817).

G. Forwood, *The Equity and Necessity of equalising Parochial Assessments and of regulating Parish Accounts* etc. (Liverpool, 1828).

W. Frend, *Peace and Union, recommended to the associated bodies of Republicans and anti-Republicans* (2nd ed. Cambridge, 1793).

E. Gardner, *Reflections upon the Evil Effects of an Increasing Population* etc. (1800).

[H. B. Gascoigne], 'Farmer Meanwell', *The Antidote to Distress: containing Observations and Suggestions calculated to promote the Employment of the Poor* etc. (1817).

H. B. Gascoigne, *Suggestions for the Employment of the Poor of the Metropolis, and the Direction of their Labours to the Benefit of the Inhabitants* etc. (1817).

——, *Pauperism; its evils and burden reduced by calling into action the labours of the Poor* etc. (1818).

——, *The Old Views of Society Revived* etc. (1820).

——, *Society for Promoting the Employment of the Poor* etc. (1827).

T. Gilbert, *A Scheme for the Better Relief and Employment of the Poor* etc. (1764, 1765).

——, *A Bill intended to be offered to Parliament, for the Better Relief and Employment of the Poor within that Part of Great Britain called England* (1775).

——, *Observations upon the Orders and Resolutions of the House of Commons with respect to the Poor, Vagrants and Houses of Correction* (1775).

——, *Heads of a Plan of Police: shewing the causes of the increase of the Poor, and a mode for their better Relief and Support* (1777).

——, *Plan for the Better Relief and Employment of the Poor; for enforcing and amending the Laws respecting Houses of Correction, and Vagrants* etc. (1781).

——, *Heads of a Bill for the better relief and employment of the Poor* etc. (1786).

——, *Considerations on the Bills for the better relief and employment of the Poor* etc. (1787).

[W. Gilpin], *An Account of a New Poor House erected in the Parish of Boldre in New Forest, near Lymington* (1796 and 1803).

G. Glover, *Observations on the Present State of Pauperism in England, particularly as it affects the Morals and Character of the Labouring Poor* etc. (1817).

W. Godwin, *An Enquiry concerning Political Justice, and its Influence on General Virtue and Happiness* (1793).

——, *The Enquirer. Reflections on Education, Manners, and Literature* (1797).

——, *Thoughts occasioned by the Perusal of Dr. Parr's Spital Sermon* etc. (1801).

——, *Of Population, an Enquiry concerning the power of increase in the numbers of Mankind, being an answer to Mr. Malthus's Essay on that Subject* (1820).

J. M. Good, *Dissertation on the Best Means of Maintaining and Employing the Poor in Parish Workhouses* etc. (1798).

R. Gourlay, *Tyranny of Poor Laws, exemplified* (Bath, 1815).

——, *The Right to Church Property secured, and commutation of tythes vindicated* etc. (1815).

——, *The Village System, being a Scheme for the Gradual Abolition of Pauperism and immediate employment and provisioning of the People* (Bath, 1817).

J. Grahame, *An Inquiry into the Principle of Population: including an exposition of the causes and the advantages of a tendency to exuberance of numbers in society, a defence of Poor-Laws* etc. (1816).

S. Gray, *The Happiness of States, or An Inquiry concerning Population* etc. (1815).

——, *Remarks on the Production of Wealth . . . in a letter to the Rev. T. R. Malthus* etc. (1820).

——, *Historical Catalogue of the Writings, published and unpublished, of Simon Gray of Dunse, Berwickshire* (1840).

——, 'G. Purves', *All Classes Productive of National Wealth* etc. (1817).

——, 'G. Purves', *Gray v. Malthus. The Principles of Population and Production investigated* etc. (1818).

J. Halcomb, *A Practical Measure of Relief from the Present System of the Poor Laws* etc. (1826).

W. Hale, *A Letter to Samuel Whitbread, Esq., M.P. containing Observations on the Distress peculiar to the Poor of Spitalfields* etc. (1806).

C. Hall, *The Effects of Civilisation on the people, with an Appendix containing observations on the principal conclusions in Mr. Malthus's essay on population* (1805, 1813).

J. Hall, *A Plan for the Abolition of the Present Poor Rates; and for affecting a general Moral Improvement in the lower classes of Society* etc. (1824).

W. Hanning, *A Letter to the Members of the Select Committees of the two Houses of Parliament, appointed to examine and report on the Poor Laws* (Taunton, 1818).

J. Haygarth, *An Explanation of the Principles and Proceedings of the Provident Institution at Bath for Savings* etc. (1816).

[Sir W. G. Hayter ?], *Proposals for the Redemption of the Poor's Rates, by means of Emigration* (1817).

W. Hazlitt, *A Reply to the Essay on Population* etc. (1807–10).

——, *Political Essays* (1819).

——, *The Spirit of the Age* (1825).

R. Heathfield, *Further Observations on the practicability and expediency of liquidating the Public Debt* etc. (2nd ed. 1820).

J. Hill, *The Means of Reforming the Morals of the Poor, by the Prevention of Poverty* etc. (1801).

S. Hill, *A Plan for Reducing the Poor's Rate, by giving permanent employment to the labouring classes* etc. (2nd ed. 1817).

Hints towards an Attempt to Reduce the Poor Rate; or, at least to Prevent its further Increase (1819).

Hints towards the Formation of a Society for Promoting a Spirit of Independence among the Poor, (1812–16).

[S. Hobson], *Pray, which is the way to the Savings Bank? Addressed to the Labouring Classes. By a Norfolk Clergyman* (1836).

R. Wilmot Horton, *The Causes and Remedies of Pauperism in the United Kingdom considered* etc. (1830).

J. Howlett, *The Insufficiency of the Causes to which the Increase of the Poor and of the Poor's Rates have been commonly ascribed . . . and a slight general view of Mr. Acland's Plan for rendering the poor independent* (1788).

——, *Examination of Mr. Pitt's Speech, in the House of Commons. . . . Relative to the Condition of the Poor* (1796).

J. Hume, *An Account of the Provident Institution for Savings established in the Western Part of the Metropolis* etc. (1816).

R. Hunt, *Provision for the Poor, by the Union of Houses of Industry with Country Parishes* etc. (1797).

W. Illingworth, *An Enquiry into the Laws Ancient and Modern, respecting Forestalling, Regrating and Ingrossing* etc. (1800).

R. A. Ingram, *An Inquiry into the Present Condition of the Lower Classes, and the Means of Improving it* etc. (1797).

——, *Disquisitions on Population, in which the Principles of the Essay on Population, by the Rev. T. R. Malthus, are examined and refuted* (1808).

An Inquiry into the Causes of the Increased Amount of the Poor's Rates, and Suggestions for Reducing the Expenditure and Equalising the Assessments, by a Gentleman of Norfolk (1817).

T. Jarrold, *Dissertations on Man: Philosophical, Physiological and Political: in answer to Mr. Malthus's Essay on the Principle of Population* (1806).

——, *A Letter to Samuel Whitbread, Esq., M.P. on the Subject of the Poor Laws* (1807).

C. Jerram, *Considerations on the Impolicy and Perniciouls Tendency of the Poor Laws; with remarks on the report of the Seect Committee of the House of Commons upon them* etc. (1818).

J. Johnson, *An Address to the Inhabitants of Bristol on the Subject of the Poor Rates* etc. (Bristol, 1820).

——, *Transactions of the Corporation of the Poor in the City of Bristol during a period of 126 years* etc. (Bristol, 1826).

[?Jones], *Letters to John Probert Esq., . . . upon the Advantages and Defects of the Montgomery and Pool House of Industry* (1801).

Justice to the Poor; and Justice to Every Other Class of the People as Respects the Situation of the Poor etc. (Northampton, 1820).

G. S. Keith, *An Impartial and Comprehensive View of the Present State of Great Britain* (1797).

[Sir J. Leslie?], *A Summons of Wakening; or the Evil Tendency and Danger of Speculative Philosophy* etc. (1807).

A Letter addressed to J. C. Curwen, Esq., M.P. on the Poor Laws, containing a Safe, Easy and Economical Substitute for the Present System (1817).

A Letter addressed to the Hon. J. F. Campbell, M.P. on the Poor Laws and the Practical Effect to be produced by the . . . Select Vestries Act (1821).

A Letter addressed to the Rt. Hon. Lord Viscount Castlereagh, on the subject of the proposed alterations in the Poor Laws etc. (1818).

A Letter on the Nature, Extent and Management of Poor Rates in Scotland: with a Review of the Controversy respecting the Abolition of Poor Laws (Edinburgh, 1807).

A Letter to Jas. Scarlett, Esq., M.P. on His Bill relating to the Poor Laws, By a Surrey Magistrate (1821).

A Letter to the Rt. Hon. Geo. Canning on the Principle and Administration of the English Poor Laws, by a Select Vestryman of the Parish of Putney (1823).

A Letter to the Rt. Hon. the Speaker of the House of Commons on the Subject of the Poor Laws etc., by 'A Countryman' (1820).

[J. C. Lettsom], *Hints Respecting the Distresses of the Poor* (1795).

——, *Hints designed to promote Beneficence, Temperance, and Medical Science* (1797).

G. A. Lewin, *A Summary of the Law of Settlement* etc. (1827).

——, *A Summary of the Laws relating to the Government and Maintenance of the Poor* etc. (1828).

W. F. Lloyd, *Lectures on Population, Value, Poor Laws, and Rent. Delivered in the University of Oxford during the Years* 1832–36 (1837).

G. Long, *Observations on a Bill to amend the laws relating to the Relief of the Poor in England* (1821).

M. Longfield, *Four Lectures on the Poor Laws* (1834).

P. Lovelass, *A Proposed Practicable Plan, for . . . a speedy easement of the Poor Rates throughout England* etc. (1804).

J. Lowe, *The Present State of England in Regard to Agriculture, Trade and Finance* etc. (1822).

J. R. McCulloch, *The Principles of Political Economy, with a Sketch of the Rise and Progress of the Science* (1825, 1830).

——, *The Literature of Political Economy: a Classified Catalogue* etc. (1845).

H. G. Macnab, *The New Views of Mr. Owen of Lanark Impartially Examined* etc. (1819).

J. MacPhail, *Observations, exhibiting the Propriety and Advantageous Tendency of the Poor Laws, their policy vindicated against the aspersions cast upon them by numerous Authors* etc. (1819).

T. R. Malthus, *An Essay on the Principle of Population, as it affects the future improvement of Society* etc. (1798).

——, *An Essay on the Principle of Population; or, a View of its Past and Present Effects on Human Happiness* etc. (eds. of 1803, 1806, 1807, 1817, 1826).

——, *An Investigation of the Cause of the Present High Price of Provisions* (1800).

——, *Letter to Samuel Whitbread, Esq., on the Subject of the Poor Laws* (1807).

——, *Principles of Political Economy considered with a view to their practical application* (1820).

——, *A Summary View of the Principle of Population* (1830).

[Jane Marcet], *Conversations on Political Economy; in which the Elements of that Science are Familiarly Explained* (1816).

344

J. Marshall, *Statistics of the British Empire. An analysis and compendium of all the returns made to Parliament* etc. (1837).

W. Marshall, *A Review of the Reports to the Board of Agriculture, from the Northern Department of England* etc. (York, 1808).

M. Martin, *Letter to the Rt. Hon. Lord Pelham on the State of Mendicity in the Metropolis* (1803).

Harriet Martineau, *Poor Laws and Paupers Illustrated* (1833–4).

F. Maseres, *A Proposal for Establishing Life-Annuities in Parishes for the benefit of the industrious poor* (1772).

A Method of Improving the Condition of the Irish Poor, suggested in a letter to Samuel Whitbread, Esq., M.P. (Dublin, 1810).

J. Mill, *Commerce Defended* etc. (1808).

——, *Elements of Political Economy* (eds. of 1821, 1824, 1826).

S. Miller, *Pauper Police: Letters addressed through* The Times ... *showing the necessity and advantages of a Pauper Police* etc. (1831).

J. Mills, *The Simple Equation of Tithes, prepared for the consideration of the Members of Both Houses of Parliament* etc. (1817).

J. H. Moggridge, *Remarks on the Report of the Select Committee of the House of Commons on the Poor Laws* etc. (Bristol, 1818).

J. B. Monck, *General Reflections on the System of the Poor Laws, with a Short View of Mr. Whitbread's Bill, and a Comment on it* (1807).

T. Myers, *An Essay on Improving the Condition of the Poor* etc. (1814).

The Names of Parishes and other Divisions maintaining their own Poor in the County of Westmorland etc. (Kendal, 1802).

J. Nasmith, *The Duties of Overseers of the Poor, and the Sufficiency of the Present System of Poor Laws considered in A Charge delivered to the Grand Jury . . . for the Isle of Ely* etc. (1799).

[Sir G. Nicholls], *Eight Letters on the Management of our Poor, and the General Administration of the Poor Laws* etc., by an Overseer (1822).

Sir G. Nicholls, *A History of the English Poor Law in Connection with the State of the Country and the Condition of the People* (1898 ed.).

S. W. Nicoll, *A Summary View of the Report and Evidence relative to the Poor Laws, published by order of the House of Commons, with Observations and Suggestions* (York, 1818).

——, *A View of the Principles on which the Wellbeing of the Labouring Classes depends* etc. (York, 1819).

M. Nolan, *A Treatise of the Laws for the Relief and Settlement of the Poor* (1805).

Notices on Political Economy; or an Inquiry concerning the effects of Debts and Taxes etc. (1821).

Observations on Banks for Savings; shewing the Expedience of making the Principle on which they are founded applicable to Clerks in Public Offices etc. (1818).

345

Observations on the Poor Laws, and Pauperism, shewing the effects resulting from compulsory parish rates etc. (1822).

Observations upon the Report from the Select Committee of the House of Commons on the Poor Laws; with a demonstration of the injustice of the present laws of taxation and the remedy suggested (Birmingham, 1818).

On the Means of Retaining the Population within any required limits (1820).

The Oppressed Labourers, and the Means for their Relief, as well as for the Reduction of their Number, and of the Poor Rates etc. (1819).

S. G. Osborne, *The Savings Bank. Some particulars of the Life and Death of "Old Rainy Day", a lover of funerals and a well known character in the Parish of* – etc. (3rd ed. 1837?).

J. Ovington, *A Certain Remedy for Existing Distresses, or the Labouring Man's Advocate* etc. (1816?).

R. Owen, *A New View of Society and other Writings* (ed. G. D. H. Cole, 1927).

—, *The Life of Robert Owen* (1857 ed.).

F. Page, *The Principle of the English Poor Laws illustrated and defended* etc. (1822, 1829, 1830).

T. Paine, *The Rights of Man: being an answer to Mr Burke's attack on the French Revolution* (1791–2).

W. Paley, *The Principles of Moral and Political Philosophy* (1785).

—, *Reasons for Contentment, addressed to the Labouring Part of the British Public* (1795).

Parish Settlements and Pauperism (1828).

W. Parker, *A Plan for the General Improvement of the Situation of the Poor of Ireland* (Cork, 1816).

[S. Parr?], *Considerations on the Poor Laws and suggestions for making the public annuitants contributory to their support* (1817).

[T. Pemberton], *An attempt to Estimate the Increase of the Number of Poor during the Interval of* 1785 *and* 1803 *and to Point out the Causes of it* etc. (1811).

W. Peter, *Thoughts on the Present Crisis* etc. (2nd ed. 1816).

S. A. Peyton, ed., *Kettering Vestry Minutes* 1797–1853.

H. Phillpotts, *A Letter to the Rt. Hon. Sturges Bourne, M.P. on a Bill introduced by him into Parliament* etc. (Durham, 1819).

J. Pinsent, *Conversations on Political Economy, or a Series of Dialogues* etc. (1821).

F. Place, *Illustrations and Proofs of the Principle of Population: including an examination of the proposed remedies of Mr. Malthus and a reply to the objections of Mr. Godwin and others* (1822).

A Plan suggested for Mature Consideration, for Superseding the Necessity of the Poor Rates, By means of Cottage Acres, and Farms etc. (1817).

W. Playfair, *A Letter on Agricultural Distresses, their Causes and Remedies* etc. (1822).

J. Pole, *A Few Observations on the Present State of the Poor Laws and a Remedy for the Evils respecting them* (1828).

The Poor Laws England's Ruin, By a Country Overseer (1817).

G. R. Porter, *The Progress of the Nation, in its various social and economical relations* etc. (1836–43).

R. Preston, *A Review of the present ruined condition of the Landed and Agricultural Interests* etc. (1816).

——, *Further Observations on the State of the Nation*, etc. (1816).

A Proposal for a perpetual equalisation of the pay of the labouring poor (1795).

'Piercy Ravenstone', *A Few Doubts as to the Correctness of some Opinions Generally Entertained on the Subjects of Population and Political Economy* (1821).

S. Read, *General Statement of an Argument on the Subject of Population in answer to Mr. Malthus's Theory* (1821).

——, *An Inquiry into the Natural grounds of Right to vendible Property, or Wealth* (1829).

Remarks on Mr. Godwin's Enquiry concerning Population (1821).

Remarks on the Practicability of Mr. Robert Owen's Plan to Improve the Condition of the Lower Classes (1819).

Remarks upon a Bill . . . "for promoting and encouraging of Industry" . . ., By one of His Majesty's Justices of the Peace for the County of Lincoln (1807).

D. Ricardo, *Works and Correspondence* (ed. P. Sraffa and M. H. Dobb).

W. Richardson, *Simple Measures, by which the Recurrence of Famines may be prevented* etc. (1816).

E. Rigby, *Further Facts relating to the Care of the Poor, and the Management of the Work-House in the city of Norwich* etc. (1812).

S. Roberts, *A Defence of the Poor Laws, with a plan for the Suppression of Mendicity and for the Establishment of Universal Parochial Benefit Societies* (Sheffield, 1819).

S. Romilly, *Memoirs of the Life of Sir Samuel Romilly*, written by himself etc. (1840 ed.).

[G. Rose], *Observations on the Act for the Relief and Encouragement of Friendly Societies* etc. (1794).

G. Rose, *Observations on the Poor Laws, and on the Management of the Poor in Great Britain* etc. (1805).

——, *Observations on Banks for Savings* (1816).

[J. C. Ross], 'John McIniscon', *Principles of Political Economy and of*

Population: including an examination of Mr. Malthus's Essay on these subjects (1825).

J. C. Ross, *An Examination of Opinions Maintained in the Essay on the Principles of Population by Malthus* etc. (1827).

T. Ruggles, *The History of the Poor; their Rights, Duties, and the Laws respecting them* etc. (1793).

Count Rumford (Benjamin Thompson), *Complete Works* (Boston, 1874), vol. IV:
An Account of an Establishment for the Poor at Munich.
Of the Fundamental Principles on which General Establishments for the Relief of the Poor may be founded in all countries.
Of Food, and particularly of feeding the Poor.

W. Sabatier, *A Treatise on Poverty, its Consequences, and the Remedy* (1797).

M. T. Sadler, *Ireland, its evils and their remedies* etc. (1828).

——, *The Law of Population: A Treatise, in Six Books, in disproof of the superfecundity of Human Beings* etc. (1830).

——, *A Refutation of an Article in the Edinburgh Review* (1830).

J. de Salis, *A Proposal for improving the system of Friendly Societies or of Poor Assurance Offices* etc. (1814).

W. Salisbury, *A Treatise on the Practical Means of Employing the Poor in Cultivating and Manufacturing Articles of British Growth* etc. (1820).

R. Saunders, *Observations on the Present State and Influence of the Poor Laws . . . and a Plan Proposed for the Consideration of Parliament* etc. (1799).

——, *An Abstract of Observations on the Poor Laws; with a reply to the Remarks of the Rev. Jas. Nasmith, D.D.* (1802).

W. H. Saunders, *An Address to the Imperial Parliament, upon the practical means of gradually abolishing the Poor Laws* etc. (3rd ed. 1821).

[G. P. Scrope], *A Letter to the Magistrates of the South and West of England on the Expediency and Facility of Correcting Certain Abuses of the Poor Laws*, by one of their Number (1828).

G. P. Scrope, *Plea for the Abolition of Slavery in England, as produced by an illegal abuse of the Poor Law, common in the Southern Counties* (1829).

——, *The Common Cause of the Landlord, Tenant and Labourer, and the Common Cure of their Complaint in a Letter to the Agriculturists of the South of England* (1830).

——, *A Letter to the Magistrates of the South of England on the Urgent Necessity of Putting a Stop to the Illegal Practice of Making up Wages out of Rates* etc. (1831).

——, *A Second Letter to the Magistrates of the South of England, on the Propriety of discontinuing the allowance system* etc. (1831).

J. Sculthorpe, *A Compendium of the Laws relating to the Settlement and Removal of the Poor* (1827).

N. W. Senior, *Two Lectures on Population . . . to which is added a Correspondence between the Author and the Rev. T. R. Malthus* (1829).

——, *Three Lectures on the Rate of Wages . . . with a Preface on the Causes and Remedies of the Present Disturbances* (1830).

——, *Letter to Lord Howick on a Legal Provision for the Irish Poor* etc. (1831).

John, Earl of Sheffield, *Observations on the Impolicy, Abuses, and False Interpretation of the Poor Laws; and on the Reports of the Two Houses of Parliament* (1818).

——, *Remarks on the Bill of the Last Parliament for the Amendment of the Poor Laws* etc. (1819).

J. G. Sherer, *Remarks on the Present State of the Poor* (1797).

A. Sibbit, *A Dissertation, Moral and Political on the influence of luxury and refinement on nations* etc. (1800).

T. Single, *Hints to Parliament for a General Act to Prevent Parochial Squabbles* etc. (1824).

Sketch of a Simple, Original and Practical Plan for suppressing Mendicity etc. (1823).

[R. A. Slaney?], *Some Facts shewing the Vast Burthen of the Poor's Rate in a Particular District; and a view of the very unequal mode in which different kinds of property contribute to the support of paupers* etc. (1817).

R. A. Slaney, *An Essay on the Employment of the Poor* etc. (1819, 1822).

——, *Essay on the Beneficial Direction of Rural Expenditure* (1824).

Some Observations on the Bill now Pending in Parliament, for the Better Support and Maintenance of the Poo r. Prepared for the use of the Trustees of the Poor of the Parish of Kensington etc. (1797).

T. Spence, *The End of Oppression* etc. (2nd ed. 1795).

——, *The Constitution of a Perfect Commonwealth* etc. (2nd ed. 1798).

W. Spence, *Britain Independent of Commerce* etc. (4th ed. 1808).

——, *Agriculture the Source of the Wealth of Britain* etc. (1808).

R. Stephenson, *A Plan for the Diminution of Poor Rates in Country Parishes* etc. (1820).

G. Strickland, *A Discourse on the Poor Laws of England and Scotland, on the State of the Poor in Ireland and on Emigration* (1827).

Lord Edward Suffield, *A Charge, Delivered at the Quarter Sessions for the County of Norfolk* etc. (1830).

J. B. Sumner, *A Treatise on the Records of Creation, and on the Moral Attributes of the Creator* etc. (2nd ed. 1818).

C. Taylor, *A Summary Account of the London Savings Bank* etc. (1816).

[T. Thompson], *Further Observations on the Improvements in the*

Maintenance of the Poor, in the town of Kingston upon Hull (Hull, 1801).

T. Thompson, *Considerations on the Increase of the Poor Rates and on the State of the Work House in Kingston upon Hull* etc. (Hull, 1800).

W. Toone, *A Practical Guide to the Duty and Authority of Overseers of the Poor* etc. (1815).

R. Torrens, *The Economists Refuted; or an Inquiry into the Nature and Extent of the Advantages derived from Trade* etc. (1808).

——, *A Paper on the Means of Reducing the Poor's Rate and of affording Effectual and Permanent Relief to the Labouring Classes* (1817).

J. Townsend, *A Dissertation on the Poor Laws* (2nd ed. 1787).

C. Turnor, *Thoughts on the Present State of the Poor, with Hints for the Improvement of their Condition* etc. (1818).

H. Twiss, *A Tract on Savings Banks* etc. (1816).

Two Letters on the Contested Origin, Nature and Effects of the Poor Laws, By a Student at Law (1818).

'Unus Populi', *A Letter to Mr. Scarlett on the Poor Laws* etc. (1822).

J. Vancouver, *An Enquiry into the Causes and Production of Poverty, and the State of the Poor* etc. (1796).

R. Vivian, *A Letter on Friendly Societies and Savings Banks ... occasioned by Mr. Rose's Letter* (1816).

——, *Thoughts on the Causes and Cure of Excessive Poor Rates* etc. (1817).

Baron von Voght, *Account of the Management of the Poor in Hamburgh, between the years 1788 and 1794, in A Letter to some friends of the Poor in Great Britain* (1796, 1817).

H. Wake, *A Brief Statement of Facts, submitted to the Candid and Unprejudiced* (Andover, 1818).

E. Wakefield, *A Letter to the Landowners and other Contributors to the Poor's Rate in the Hundred of Dangye, in Essex* (1802).

T. Walker, *Observations on the Nature, Extent and Effects of Pauperism and on the Means of Reducing it* (1826, 1831).

R. Walthew, *A Moral and Political Essay on the English Poor Laws* etc. (1814).

H. Wansey, *Thoughts on Poor-Houses, with a View to their General Reform* etc. (1801).

G. West, *A Plan for Bettering the Condition of the Working Classes by the Establishment of Friendly Societies upon Legal and Scientific Principles* etc. (1827).

C. Weston, *Remarks on the Poor Laws and on the State of the Poor* (1802).

[J. Weyland], *A Short Enquiry into the Policy, Humanity and past effects of the Poor Laws* etc. (1807).

J. Weyland, *Observations on Mr. Whitbread's Poor Bill and on the Population of England* etc. (1807).

——, *A Letter to a Country Gentleman on the Education of the Lower Orders* etc. (1808).

——, *The Principle of the English Poor Laws Illustrated from the Evidence given by Scottish Proprietors* etc. (1815).

——, *The Principles of Population and Production, as they are affected by the Progress of Society; with a view to Moral and Political Consequences* (1816).

——, *Thoughts submitted to the Employers of Labour, in the County of Norfolk, with a few words to the employed* etc. (1830).

S. Whitbread, *Substance of a Bill for Promoting and Encouraging of Industry among the Labouring Classes of the Community, and for the Relief and Regulation of the Necessitous and Criminal Poor* (1807).

——, *Substance of a Speech on the Poor Laws: delivered in the House of Commons on Thursday February 19th 1807. With an appendix* (1807).

J. Willis, *On the Poor Laws of England* etc. (1808).

E. Wilson, *Observations on the Present State of the Poor and Measures Proposed for its Improvement* (Reading, 1795).

I. Wood, *Some Account of the Shrewsbury House of Industry, its establishment and regulations; . . . to which is added the second edition of the Byelaws, Rules and Ordinances of the said House* (Shrewsbury, 1791).

——, *A Letter to Sir W. Pulteney, Bart., . . . containing some Observations on the Bill for the better Support and Maintenance of the Poor* etc. (1797).

J. Woodrow, *Remarks on Banks for Savings and Friendly Societies, with an Original Plan combining the Principles of Both Institutions* etc. (1818).

J. C. Yeatman, *Remarks on the Medical Care of Parochial Poor, with a few Observations on the Improvement of Poor-Houses* etc. (1818).

[G. D. Yeats], *A Biographical Sketch of the Life and Writings of Patrick Colquhoun, Esq., LL.D.* (1818).

A. Young, *The Farmer's Letters to the People of England* etc. (1767).

——, *Political Arithmetic* etc. (1774).

——, *An Enquiry into the State of the Public Mind amongst the Lower Classes* etc. (1798).

——, *The Question of Scarcity plainly stated and Remedies Considered* etc. (1800).

R. Young, *The Undertaking for the Reform of the Poor of which a principal Branch is the Asylum for industry* etc. (1792).

Sir William Young, *Considerations on the Subject of Poor-Houses and Work-Houses . . . in a letter to the Rt. Hon. W. Pitt* (1796).

6. *Other Works*

W. P. Albrecht, *William Hazlitt and the Malthusian Controversy* (Albuquerque, 1950).

A. W. Ashby, 'One Hundred Years of Poor-Law Administration in a Warwickshire Village', *Oxford Studies in Social and Legal History*, III.

T. S. Ashton, *An Economic History of England: the Eighteenth Century* (1955).

——, 'The Standard of Life of the Workers in England, 1790–1830', *Jnl. Econ. History*, suppl. IX (1949).

H. Ausubel, 'William Cobbett and Malthusianism', *Jnl. Hist. of Ideas*, XIII (1952).

J. M. Baernreither, *English Associations of Working Men* (1891).

A. Bain, *James Mill: A Biography* (1882).

H. L. Beales, 'The New Poor Law', *History*, N.S. XV (1930–31).

G. F. A. Best, 'The Making of the English Working Class', *Hist. Journal*, VIII (1965).

R. D. Collison Black, *Economic Thought and the Irish Question* (1960).

M. Blaug, *Ricardian Economics, an Historical Study* (New Haven, 1958).

——, 'The Myth of the Old Poor Law and the Making of the New', *Journal Econ. History*, XXIII (1963).

——, 'The Poor Law Report Re-examined', *Journal Econ. History*, XXIV (1964).

J. Bonar, *Malthus and his Work* (1885).

——, *Theories of Population from Raleigh to Arthur Young* (1931).

M. Bowley, *Nassau Senior and Classical Economics* (1937).

A. Briggs, 'The Language of Class in early Nineteenth-CenturyEngland', in *Essays on Labour History* (ed. A. Briggs and J. Saville, 1960).

T. W. Bruce, 'The Economic Theories of John Craig, a forgotten English Economist', *Quart. Jnl. Economics*, LII (1938).

E. Cannan, *The History of Local Rates in England* (2nd ed. 1912).

——, *History of the Theories of Production and Distribution in English Political Economy from 1776 to 1848* (1953 ed.).

G. Carnall, *Robert Southey and his Age* (1960).

S. Checkland, 'The Propagation of Ricardian Economics in England', *Economica*, N.S. XVI (1949).

G. Kitson Clark, *An Expanding Society. Britain 1830–1930* (Melbourne, 1967).

——, 'Statesmen in Disguise', *Hist. Journal*, II (1959).

J. Clive, *Scotch Reviewers: the Edinburgh Review 1802–15* (1957).

A. W. Coats, 'Changing Attitudes to Labour in the mid-Eighteenth Century', *Econ. Hist. Review*, 2nd ser. XI (1958).

——' 'Economic Thought and Poor Law Policy in the Eighteenth Century', *Econ. Hist. Review*, 2nd ser. XIII (1960).

A. Cobban, *Edmund Burke and the Revolt against the Eighteenth Century* (1929).

G. D. H. Cole, *Life of William Cobbett* (1924).

——, *Robert Owen* (1925).

J. Colmer, *Coleridge, Critic of Society* (1959).

B. A. Corry, 'The Theory of the Economic Effects of Government Expenditure in English Classical Political Economy', *Economica*, XXV (1958).

R. Currie and R. M. Hartwell, 'The Making of the English Working Class?', *Econ. Hist. Review*, 2nd ser. XVIII (1965).

K. Curry, ed., *New Letters of Robert Southey* (1965).

F. G. Emmison, 'The Relief of the Poor at Eaton Socon, 1796–1834', *Publ. Beds. Hist. Record Society*, XV (1933).

H. Fawcett, *Pauperism: its Causes and Remedies* (1871).

F. W. Fetter, 'The Authorship of Economic Articles in the *Edinburgh Review*, 1802–47', *Journal Pol. Economy*, LXI (1953).

——, 'The Economic Articles in the *Quarterly Review* and their Authors', *Journal Pol. Economy*, LXVI (1958).

J. A. Field, *Essays on Population and other Papers* (1931).

S. E. Finer, *The Life and Times of Sir Edwin Chadwick* (1952).

A. Fishlow, 'The Trustee Savings Banks, 1817–1861', *Jnl. Econ. History*, XXI (1961).

A. Flew, 'The Structure of Malthus' Population Theory', *Australasian Jnl. Philosophy*, 35 (1957).

M. W. Flinn, 'The Poor Employment Act of 1817', *Econ. Hist. Review*, 2nd ser. XIV (1961).

R. Fulford, *Samuel Whitbread 1764–1815* (1967).

E. S. Furniss, *The Position of the Labourer in a System of Nationalism* (1920).

E. W. Gilboy, *Wages in Eighteenth Century England* (1934).

D. V. Glass, ed., *Introduction to Malthus* (1953).

P. H. J. H. Gosden, *The Friendly Societies in England 1815–75* (Manchester, 1961).

W. D. Grampp, 'Malthus on Money Wages and Welfare' *Am. Econ. Review*, XLVI (1956).

——, 'Politics of the Classical Economists', *Quart. Jnl. Economics*, LXII (1947).

G. Talbot Griffith, *Population Problems in the Age of Malthus* (1926).

R. M. Gutchen, 'Local Improvements and Centralisation in Nineteenth-Century England', *Hist. Journal*, IV (1961).

E. Halevy, *The Growth of Philosophic Radicalism* (1934).

S. Hall, *Dr. Duncan of Ruthwell* (1910).

J. L. and B. Hammond, *The Town Labourer*, 1760–1832 (1917).

——, *The Village Labourer*, 1760–1832 (1927).

——, *The Skilled Labourer*, 1760–1832 (1919).

E. M. Hampson, *The Treatment of Poverty in Cambridgeshire*, 1597–1834 (1934).

C. Hardwick, *Friendly Societies, their History, Progress, Prospects and Utility* (1851).

J. F. C. Harrison, ' "The Steam Engine of the New Moral World": Owenism and Education 1817–1829', *Jnl. of British Studies*, VI (1967).

J. Hart, 'Nineteenth-Century Social Reform: a Tory Interpretation of History', *Past and Present*, 31 (1965).

R. M. Hartwell, 'Interpretations of the Industrial Revolution in England: A Methodological Inquiry', *Journal Econ. History*, XIX (1959).

——, 'The Rising Standard of Living in England, 1800–1850', *Econ. Hist. Review*, 2nd ser. XIII (1961).

N. Himes, *Medical History of Contraception* (1936).

——, 'Jeremy Bentham and the Genesis of English Neo-Malthusianism', *Econ. History*, III (1936).

The History of The Times, vol. I (1935).

E. J. Hobsbawn, 'The British Standard of Living, 1780–1850', *Econ. Hist. Review*, 2nd ser. X (1957).

——, and R. M. Hartwell, 'The Standard of Living during the Industrial Revolution: a Discussion', *Econ. Hist. Review*, 2nd ser. XVI (1963).

H. O. Horne, *A History of Savings Banks* (1947).

M. James, *Social Problems During the Puritan Revolution* (1930).

P. James, ed., *The Travel Diaries of Thomas Robert Malthus* (1966).

W. K. Jordan, *Philanthropy in England*, 1480–1660 (1959).

W. F. Kennedy, *Humanist versus Economist. The Economic Thought of Samuel Taylor Coleridge* (Berkeley, 1958).

E. Larsen, *An American in Europe: The Life of Benjamin Thompson, Count Rumford* (1953).

H. J. Laski, *The Rise of European Liberalism* (1936).

E. M. Leonard, *Early History of English Poor Relief* (1900).

S. L. Levy, *Nassau W. Senior, The Prophet of Modern Capitalism* (1943).

W. Lewins, *A History of Banks for Savings* etc. (1866).

E. Lowenthal, *The Ricardian Socialists* (1911).

G. F. McCleary, *The Malthusian Population Theory* (1953).

O. MacDonagh, 'The Ninteenth-Century Revolution in Government: a Reappraisal', *Hist. Journal*, I (1958).

T. Mackay, *History of the English Poor Law* (1904).

Dorothy Marshall, *The English Poor in the Eighteenth Century* (1926).

——, 'The Old Poor Law', *Econ. Hist. Review*, VIII (1937).

J. D. Marshall, 'The Nottinghamshire Reformers and their Contribution to the New Poor Law', *Econ. Hist. Review*, 2nd ser. XIII (1961).

P. Medd, *Romilly* (1968).

D. H. Monro, *Godwin's Moral Philosophy* (1955).

R. S. Neale, 'The Standard of Living, 1780–1844: a Regional and Class Study', *Econ. Hist. Review*, 2nd ser. XIX (1966).

G. L. Nesbitt, *Benthamite Reviewing* (New York, 1934).

T. C. Nichols, *Count Rumford: how he Banished Beggary from Bavaria* (1873).

R. Opie, 'A Neglected British Economist: George Poulett Scrope', *Quart. Jnl. Economics*, XLIV (1929).

M. Paglin, *Malthus and Lauderdale. The Anti-Ricardian Tradition* (New York, 1961).

H. Parris, 'The Ninteenth-Century Revolution in Government: a Re-appraisal Re-appraised', *Hist. Journal*, III (1960).

S. A. Peyton, ed., 'Kettering Vestry Minutes 1797–1853', *Publ. Northants Records Soc.* VI (1931).

R. Pieris, 'The Contributions of Patrick Colquhoun to Social Theory and Social Philosophy', *Univ. of Ceylon Review*, XII (1954).

F. Podmore, *Robert Owen, a Biography* (1906).

K. Polanyi, *The Great Transformation* (New York, 1944).

J. Tidd Pratt, *The Law Relating to Friendly Societies* etc. (1829, 1834, 1838).

——, *The History of Savings Banks in England, Wales and Ireland* (1830).

——, *A Summary of Savings Banks in England, Scotland, Wales and Ireland* etc. (1846).

L. C. Robbins, *The Theory of Economic Policy in English Classical Political Economy* (1953).

——, *Robert Torrens and the Evolution of Classical Economics* (1958).

D. Roberts, *Victorian Origins of the British Welfare State* (New Haven, 1960).

——, 'Jeremy Bentham and the Victorian Administrative State', *Victorian Studies*, II (1959).

——, 'How Cruel was the Victorian Poor Law?', *Hist. Journal*, VI (1963).

J. Holland Rose, *William Pitt and the Great War.* (1911)

——, *Pitt and Napoleon, Essays and Letters* (1912).

M. E. Rose, 'The Allowance System under the New Poor Law', *Econ. Hist. Review*, 2nd ser. XIX (1966).

W. W. Rostow, 'Adjustment and Maladjustments after the Napoleonic Wars', *Am. Econ. Rev.*, XXXII (1942).

J. A. Schumpeter, *History of Economic Analysis* (1954).

K. de Schweinitz, *England's Road to Social Security* (1943).

A. Scratchley, *A Practical Treatise on Savings Banks* (1860).

E. R. A. Seligman, 'Some Neglected British Economists', *Econ. Journal*, XIII (1903).

B. Semmel, *Occasional Papers of T. R. Malthus* (New York, 1963).

H. and H. C. Shine, *The Quarterly Review under Gifford* (1949).

R. B. Simons, 'T. R. Malthus on British Society', *Jnl. Hist. of Ideas*, XVI (1955).

W. Smart, *Economic Annals of the Nineteenth Century* (1910, 1917).

N. J. Smelser, *Social Change in the Industrial Revolution* (1959).

K. Smith, *The Malthusian Controversy* (1951).

G. Sotiroff, 'John Barton, 1789–1852', *Econ. Journal*, LXII (1952).

W. J. Sparrow, *Knight of the White Eagle* (1964).

P. Sraffa, 'Malthus on Public Works', *Econ. Journal*, LXV (1955).

W. Stark, 'Jeremy Bentham as an Economist', *Econ. Journal*, LVI (1946).

L. Stephen, *The English Utilitarians* (1900).

W. M. Stern, 'The Bread Crisis in Britain 1795–6', *Economica*, 31 (1964).

F. W. Taussig, *Wages and Capital: An examination of the Wages Fund Doctrine* (1896).

R. H. Tawney, *Religion and the Rise of Capitalism* (1926).

A. J. Taylor, 'Progress and Poverty in Britain, 1780–1850: a Reappraisal', *History*, N.S. XLV (1960).

E. P. Thompson, *The Making of the English Working Class* (1963).

J. A. Thompson, *Count Rumford* (1935).

G. Wallas, *The Life of Francis Place* (4th ed. 1925).

S. and B. Webb, *English Local Government:*
   The Parish and the County (1906).
   The Manor and the Borough (1908).
   Statutory Authorities for Special Purposes (1922).
   English Poor Law History: The Old Poor Law (1927).
   English Poor Law History: The Last Hundred Years (1929).
   ——, *English Poor Law Policy* (1910).

R. J. White, *Political Tracts of Wordsworth, Coleridge and Shelley* (1953).

J. E. Williams, 'The British Standard of Living, 1750–1850', *Econ. Hist Review*, 2nd ser. XIX (1966).

O. Williams, *Life and Letters of John Rickman* (1911).

Index

Abbot, Charles (Lord Colchester),
63, 141, 207n.
Abinger, Lord, *see* Scarlett, James
Acland, John, 37–8, 39
Albrecht, W. P., 176n.
Alcock, Thomas, xviii, 29–30,
40–1, 42, 43, 157
Allen, John, 172n.
Allen, William, 142n., 199–200
Allotments of land to the poor: xix,
46, 197; Pitt's Bill, 65, 71–2;
Young's schemes, 98–104;
Malthus on allotments, 163–4,
167; post-war discussion of,
255–7, 299–300, 318
Allowance system: xxiv, 14–15;
Speenhamland meeting, 76–9;
question of extent of, 79, 82–5,
188, 278–282; criticisms of, 78,
81–2, 84, 172n., 175n., 192, 204,
211, 221, 226, 233–4, 284–5,
286–7, 298–9, 309, 318, 320, 329
Althorp, Lord, 297n., 310, 311n.,
321, 322, 328
Annuity schemes: 35–6, 139–140,
143
Ansell, C., 294n.
Ashby, A. W., 4n.
Ashdowne, J., 249–250, 257n.,
292n.
Ashton, T. S., 20n., 28n.
Ausubel, H., 175n.

Baernreither, J. M., 36n.
Bain, A., 199n., 302n.
Baker, J. H. L., 311, 315n.

Banfill, Samuel, 300n., 312–3
Barrington, Shute (Bishop of
Durham), 87n., 91, 94, 95–6, 97,
99, 258n.
Barrow, Sir James, 5n.
Barrow, Sir John, 272n.
Barton, John, 243, 268–9, 281,
292n., 305
Battye, Thomas, 9
Bayldon, J. S., 17n., 298n.
Bayley, P., 270n., 292n.
Bayly, W. D., 256n., 300n., 301
Beales, H. L., 318n.
Beatson, J., 258n.
Beaumont, J. T. Barber, 290n.
Becher, John Thomas, 10, 311,
313–4, 315
Becket, A., 274n.
Beddoes, Thomas, 63n., 66
Bell, Andrew, 95, 134, 160, 175,
196, 199, 216, 252, 258
Bentham, Jeremy: on wage
regulation, 51–2; on Pitt's Bill,
68, 69, 71–3, 76; on poverty,
indigence and law, xiii, xiv–xv,
xxii, 117–9, 143–4, 319–320;
on equality, 117–8, 162; on
liberty, 139; his rejection of
abolitionism, 122–7, 142–4;
on less eligibility, xxv, 46, 108,
125–7, 139, 283, 320, 327;
his Plan of 1796–1797, 46,
106–109, 117–144, 327; on
intelligence, xxi, 129–130; on
settlement, 4, 128–9; on administration, 12, 17, 108–9,

250; on Poor Law for Ireland, 307

Chamberlin, W. H., 255n.

Charity, private: and self-help, xviii–xx, 85, 93–4; and early Poor Law, 2–3; Paley on duty of, 34–5; abolitionist preference for, 39–43, 55, 324; in 1795, 47; Fox on, 56; Bentham on, 124; Malthus' principles for, 157–8; and education, 195–200; Association for the Relief and Benefit of the Manufacturing and Labouring Poor, 197–8; see also S.B.C.P.; Bernard, Sir Thomas

Checkland, S. G., 304n.

Christian, Edward, 291, 292n.

Clapham, J. H., 279n., 281n., 294n.

Clark, G. Kitson, 325n.

Clark, W., 255, 283

Clarkson, William, 61, 249, 250n., 285n., 288n.

Cleghorn, J., 309n.

Clive, J., 172n.

Coats, A. W., 27n.

Cobban, A., 168n.

Cobbett, William, 104, 240, 281, 294, 329; on Malthus, 111, 172, 175–6, 263; on Whitbread, education and Scotsmen, 214, 216–7; on savings banks, 294; on 1834 Bill, 323

Cole, G. D. H., 214n.

Coleridge, S. T.: on Rumford, 88; on Malthus and abolitionism, 168, 250–1; on public employment, 254, 258

Collett, A., 299n.

Colmer, J., 168n., 250n.

Colquhoun, Patrick, 91, 159, 229, 259, 290; and Bentham, 141, 199, 201–2, 319–320; on pauperism and relief, 187, 188, 190, 319–320; proposals for reform, 191, 200–7, 209, 215

Comber, W. T., 173n.

Const, Francis, 1n.

Contraception: Bentham on, 123–4, 125n.; Malthus and, 146n.; Place on, 267; Owen and, 261n.

Contributory schemes: xix–xx, 7, 35–9, 46, 164, 193–5, 210, 220–1, 269–71, 291

Copland, W., 299n., 302n.

Copleston, Edward, 13, 78, 232–3, 255n., 278n., 283, 292n.

Corn Laws: 22, 46, 223, 224, 255, 261, 262, 266

Corry, B. A., 227n., 269n.

Cottingham, J., 186n., 218

Coulson, Walter, 305n., 317, 326

Courtenay, Thomas Peregrine, 78, 246n., 268n., 270–1, 277, 283, 285, 286, 287, 288n., 297

Cowell, J. W., 314n.

Craig, J., 255, 283, 288

Craufurd, Lieutenant General C. G., 78, 256n., 278n., 285n., 288

Crumpe, S., 5, 6n., 39

Cull, J., 255n., 256n.

Cunningham, J. W., 292n.

Currie, R., 28n.

Curwen, J. C., 24, 104n., 172, 193, 220, 245, 246n., 272–3, 274–5, 278n., 285, 286, 288n., 289, 293

Davidson, Robert, 236n.

Davies, David, 23, 29n., 31–2, 33, 39, 43, 49, 61, 86, 98, 115, 120

Davies, W., 67

Davis, J., 301n.

Davis, W., 291, 292n.

Davison, John, 233–4, 278, 283, 284, 289n., 291–2

Day, Thomas, 30

Defoe, Daniel, 23, 26, 27, 29, 39, 156, 194, 254

Dicey, A. V., 325

Doyle, Bishop, 307n.

Dudley, H. Bate, 190n., 192, 193

Dumont, E., 121, 135, 143

Duncan, Henry, 195n., 290

Dundas, Charles (Lord Ainesbury), 77

INDEX

Owen, 260–1; Ensor, 263; Booth, 264n.; Ravenstone, 264–5; Place, 266–7; Grahame, 267; Barton, 268–9; Gray, 269–270; Ross, 301; Everett, 301; James Mill, 302–3; Senior, 303–4; McCulloch, 305; Sadler, 308; Royal Commission of 1832–1834, 318; see also Malthus, Thomas R.
Porter, G. R., 281n.
Poulter, Edmund, 10, 80
Pratt, J. Tidd, 294n.
Preston, R., 255n., 288n.
Prettyman, George (Bishop of Lincoln), 69, 71, 74
Price, Richard, 29n., 35, 38, 57, 145n., 149n.
'Purves, George', see Gray, Simon

Quarterly Review: 111, 172, 174, 251, 253–4, 275–6, 306

'Ravenstone, Piercy', 110n., 111, 148, 264–5, 278
Read, Samuel, 306
Ricardo, David, xvi, xvii, 22, 46, 59n., 178n., 268, 302; and Malthusian abolitionism, 154, 226, 237, 239–45; on Scarlett's bills, 245; on Sturges Bourne's bills, 244, 275n., 287; on Owen, 240, 260; on Sumner, 253–4; on Ravenstone, 264n.; on Place, 240; on Ireland, 307; and savings banks, 290
Richardson, W., 227
Richmond, Duke of, 299, 322
Rickman, John, 19, 168, 175n., 187n., 188, 245, 251–3, 276, 292n.
Rigby, E., 192
Robbins, Lord, 239n., 241n., 260n., 268n.
Roberts, David, 321n., 325n.
Roberts, Samuel, 250, 270n.
Robinson, Henry Crabb, 6
Romilly, Sir Samuel, 39, 40n., 141, 187, 215, 272, 289

Rose, George, 87n., 141, 187, 190, 192, 274; and friendly societies, 7, 38–9; and Pitt's Bill, 63; on Malthus, 167; on Whitbread's Bill, 212, 216, 221; and savings banks, 194n., 289–294
Rose, J. Holland, 62–3, 75–6
Rose, M. E., 321n.
Ross, J. C., 301, 302n.
Royal Commission of 1832–1834: xiii, xxi, xxv, 32, 83, 87, 108, 164, 224, 279, 296, 299–300, 310, 316–323
Ruggles, Thomas, xviii, 7, 13, 26, 30–1, 32, 33, 34n., 35n., 37n., 38, 41, 43, 49, 63, 101, 115
Rumford, Count (Benjamin Thompson), xix, 68, 74, 85, 98n., 115, 191, 329; his teachings on relief, 87–91; and S.B.C.P., 92; Bentham's admiration for, 88, 121, 133, 138, 141
Russell, Lord John, 298, 299n.

Sabatier, W., 26n., 66n., 69n.
Sadler, Michael Thomas, 148, 308, 309
Salisbury, W., 255n., 300n.
Saunders, Robert, 190–1, 193
Saunders, W. H., 300n., 301
Savings banks: xix, 39, 109, 139–40, 195n., 289–94
Scarlett, James (Lord Abinger), 245, 296–7, 314, 319, 323
de Schweinitz, K., 88n.
Schumpeter, J. A., 235n., 309n.
Scott, Sir Walter, 174
Scratchley, A., 290n.
Scrope, George Julius Poulett, 235n., 306, 307, 309, 313n., 323
Sculthorpe, J., 5n.
Seligman, E. R. A., 255n.
Semmel, B., 23n., 172n., 174n.
Senior, Nassau William, xvii, 13, 148, 149, 151, 233, 242, 306, 309; and Malthus, 303–4; on Ireland, 307, 308; and reform of 1834, 315n., 317–323, 326

365

THE OUTLAWS OF MEDIEVAL LEGEND   Maurice Keen

RELIGIOUS TOLERATION IN ENGLAND, 1787–1833
                                        Ursula Henriques

LEARNING AND LIVING, 1790–1960: A Study in the History
  of the English Adult Education Movement   J. F. C. Harrison

HEAVENS BELOW: Utopian Experiments in England,
  1560–1960   W. H. G. Armytage

FROM CHARITY TO SOCIAL WORK in England and the
  United States   Kathleen Woodroofe

ENGLISH LANDED SOCIETY
  in the Eighteenth Century   G. E. Mingay

ENGLISH LANDED SOCIETY
  in the Nineteenth Century   F. M. L. Thompson

A SOCIAL HISTORY OF THE FRENCH REVOLUTION
                                        Norman Hampson

CHURCHES AND THE WORKING CLASSES IN
  VICTORIAN ENGLAND   K. S. Inglis

A SOCIAL HISTORY OF ENGLISH MUSIC   E. D. Mackerness

THE PROFESSION OF ENGLISH LETTERS   J. W. Saunders

EDUCATION IN RENAISSANCE ENGLAND   Kenneth Charlton

A HISTORY OF SHOPPING   Dorothy Davis

THE RISE OF THE TECHNOCRATS: A Social History
                                        W. H. G. Armytage

ANCIENT CRETE: A Social History from Early Times until the
  Roman Occupation   R. F. Willetts

PACKHORSE, WAGGON AND POST: Land Carriage and
  Communications under the Tudors and Stuarts   J. Crofts